Introduction to Critical Theory

Introduction to Critical Theory

Horkheimer to Habermas

David Held

University of California Press

Berkeley and Los Angeles

University of California Press

Berkeley and Los Angeles

Library of Congress Cataloging in Publication Data
Held, David.
  Introduction to critical theory.

  Bibliography: p.
  Includes index.
  1. Frankfurt school of sociology.   2. Criticism
(Philosophy)   3. Social institutions.   4. Habermas,
Jürgen.   5. Horkheimer, Max, 1895-1973.   I. Title.
HM24.H457   301'.01   80-10535
ISBN 0-520-04121-6 (cloth)
       0-520-04175-5 (paper)

Printed in the United States of America

2   3   4   5   6   7   8   9

For Peter Held

Contents

10 *Contents*

Acknowledgements

For the planning and writing of this book I am deeply indebted to Anthony Giddens. Without his generous help and criticism the quality of my work would have suffered greatly.

I would also like to express my debt to Jürgen Habermas for both the inspiration I have gained from his ideas and the time he took to answer questions.

I have, in addition, been enormously assisted by the thought and friendship of Lesley Bower, James Bradley, Paul Breines, John Forrester, Jeffrey Herf, Joel Krieger, Charles Lewis, Thomas McCarthy, Gillian Rose, James Schmidt, Larry Simon, John Thompson and Judy Wajcman. I am very grateful to Martin Albrow for his continuous concern and aid. Thanks are also due to the University of Wales, which gave me financial support while I was a Fellow of Politics and Sociology at University College, Cardiff.

Finally, my special thanks to Michelle Stanworth for her continuous help and encouragement.

Note about translation

I have quoted frequently from existing English translations. When the English translation is poor I have either amended it, indicating this in brackets, or re-translated it, indicating this by reference to the German text. The German text is also indicated when quotations are made from hitherto untranslated works. The initial reference to a German work is followed by a translation of its title in brackets.

Introduction

The writings of what one may loosely refer to as a 'school' of Western Marxism – critical theory – caught the imagination of students and intellectuals in the 1960s and early 1970s. In Germany thousands of copies of the 'school's' work were sold, frequently in cheap pirate editions. Members of the New Left in other European countries as well as in North America were often inspired by the same sources. In other parts of the world, for example in Allende's Chile, the influence of these texts could also be detected. In the streets of Santiago, Marcuse's name often took a place alongside Marx and Mao in the political slogans of the day. Critical theory became a key element in the formation and self-understanding of the New Left. Many of those committed to new radical protest movements – to the struggles against imperialism, the private appropriation of scarce resources and the many constraints on personal initiative – found in the works of this 'school' an intriguing interpretation of Marxist theory and an emphasis on issues and problems (mass culture, for instance, or the family and sexuality) which had rarely been explored by more orthodox approaches to Marxism.

Despite the break-up and repression of the movements of the sixties, the writings of critical theorists have been the subject of continuing controversy – controversy which has centred on their theoretical and political merits. Partly because of their rise to prominence during the political turmoil of the 1960s, and partly because they draw on traditions which are rarely studied in the Anglo-American world, the works of these authors are frequently misunderstood. Yet, in their writings, they opposed various schools of thought now being brought into disrepute (positivism, for example) and did so more cogently than many critics today. The critical theorists directed attention to areas such as the state and mass culture, areas which are only just beginning to receive the study they require. Their engagement with orthodox Marxism on the one hand, and with conventional approaches to social science on the other, provided a major challenge to writers from both perspectives. Critical of both capitalism and Soviet socialism, their writings pointed to the possibility – a possibility often sought after today – of an alternative path for social development.

In this book I hope to explicate and assess central aspects of critical theory. My intentions are threefold: first, to sketch the background and some of the main influences on critical theory's development; second, to expound, around a number of themes, its main theoretical and empirical concerns; third, to demonstrate and assess the assumptions and implications of the work of its key exponents. I have not written an intellectual history: this has, in part, been accomplished.[1]* Nor have I provided an account of critical theory which examines its development year by year. Clearly, one cannot entirely escape intellectual history or chronological documentation. But my emphasis is on an interpretation and elaboration of the ideas which were at the centre of the 'school' and I have, accordingly, focused on *themes* – the themes which gave the work its distinct character. With the exceptions of the introductory chapters to Parts 1 and 2, I have concentrated in each chapter on a key area of concern to the critical theorists.

Critical theory, it should be emphasized, does *not* form a unity; it does not mean the same thing to all its adherents. The tradition of thinking which can be loosely referred to by this label is divided into at least two branches – the first centred around the Institute of Social Research, established in Frankfurt in 1923, and the second around the more recent work of Jürgen Habermas. The Institute's key figures were Max Horkheimer (philosopher, sociologist and social psychologist), Friedrich Pollock (economist and specialist on problems of national planning), Theodor Adorno (philosopher, sociologist, musicologist), Erich Fromm (psychoanalyst, social psychologist), Herbert Marcuse (philosopher), Franz Neumann (political scientist, with particular expertise in law), Otto Kirchheimer (political scientist, with expertise in law), Leo Lowenthal (student of popular culture and literature), Henryk Grossmann (political economist), Arkadij Gurland (economist, sociologist), and, as a member of the 'outer circle' of the Institute, Walter Benjamin (essayist and literary critic). The Institute's

---

*Notes and references appear in a section beginning on page 409.

membership is often referred to as the Frankfurt school. But the label is a misleading one; for the work of the Institute's members did not always form a series of tightly woven, complementary projects. To the extent that one can legitimately talk of a school, it is only with reference to Horkheimer, Adorno, Marcuse, Lowenthal and Pollock[2] – and it is for these five men that I have reserved the term 'Frankfurt school'.[3] When referring to the Institute of Social Research, however, I include all those affiliated to the Institute.

Jürgen Habermas's recent work in philosophy and sociology recasts the notion of critical theory. Others who have contributed to this enterprise include Albrecht Wellmer (philosopher), Claus Offe (political scientist and sociologist) and Klaus Eder (anthropologist).

Despite a certain unity of purpose, there are major differences between the members of the Institute of Social Research and Habermas and his associates, as there are between most of the individuals within each camp. My main concern is with the thought of the Frankfurt school – with Horkheimer, Adorno and Marcuse in particular – and with Habermas. These four men are the central figures of critical theory. I refer to them when writing about the 'critical theorists'.

At a general level it may be said that the founders of critical theory preserved many of the concerns of German idealist thought – concerns, for example, with the nature of reason, truth and beauty – but reformulated the way in which these had been previously understood. They placed history at the centre of their approach to philosophy and society. Yet the issues they addressed went beyond a focus on the past and embraced future possibilities. Following Marx, they were preoccupied, especially in their early work, with the forces which moved (and might be guided to move) society towards rational institutions – institutions which would ensure a true, free and just life. But they were aware of the many obstacles to radical change and sought to analyse and expose these. They were thus concerned both with interpretation and transformation.

Each of the critical theorists maintained that although all knowledge is historically conditioned, truth claims can be rationally adjudicated independently of immediate social (e.g. class) interests. They defended the possibility of an independent moment of criticism. They also all attempted to justify critical theory on a non-objectivistic and materialistic foundation.[4] The extension and development of the notion of critique, from a concern with the conditions and limits of reason and knowledge (Kant), to a reflection on the emergence of spirit (Hegel), and then to a focus on specific historical forms – capitalism, the exchange process (Marx) – was furthered in the work of the Frankfurt theorists and Habermas. They sought to develop a critical perspective in the discussion of all social practices.

The work of the critical theorists revolves around a series of critical dialogues with important past and contemporary philosophers, social thinkers and social scientists. The main figures of the Frankfurt school sought to learn from and synthesize aspects of the work of, among others, Kant, Hegel, Marx, Weber, Lukács and Freud. For Habermas certain traditions of Anglo-American thought are also important, especially linguistic philosophy and the recent philosophies of science. He has sought to mediate between and integrate a variety of seemingly quite different approaches. The motivation for this enterprise appears similar for each of the theorists – the aim being to lay the foundation for an exploration, in an interdisciplinary research context, of questions concerning the conditions which make possible the reproduction and transformation of society, the meaning of culture, and the relation between the individual, society and nature. While there are differences in the way they formulate questions, the critical theorists believe that through an examination of contemporary social and political issues they could contribute to a critique of ideology and to the development of a non-authoritarian and non-bureaucratic politics.

The historical context

In order to grasp the axes around which critical theory developed it is essential to understand the turbulent events which were at the root of its founders' historical and political experience. These events affected critical theory both directly and indirectly. In particular, it is worth tracing the main occurrences of the inter-war years which had a profound impact on the Frankfurt school and Habermas.

In the century up to the first world war class conflict was successfully contained by the German nation-state and by the world's other major industrial and capitalist nations. But it is clear that what was contained was also only temporarily staved off. In the next twenty years there was an explosion of events which shook to the core many of Europe's oldest political systems. February 1917 saw the fall of Tsarism in Russia. Nine months later the Bolshevik Party seized power. The success and excitement of the revolution reverberated far beyond the boundaries of Russia. The unity of theory and revolutionary practice, central to the Marxist programme, seemed within reach.

The two years following the end of the first world war, in 1918, testified to the strength and spontaneity of the forces of change. Ten days after the naval mutinies began in Kiel and Wilhelmshaven the foundations of the German imperial system were undermined. On November 9 a republic was declared in Berlin; a coalition of Majority Social Democrats and Independent Social Democrats took office. The Majority Social Democrats were determined to follow a constitutional course toward parliamentary government and a negotiated peace settlement. A large proportion of the war-weary masses, however, shared goals which went beyond a 'republic, democracy and peace'.[5] A large network of workers' and soldiers' councils quickly developed, demanding far-reaching changes in the economy and the military (including socialization of a vast proportion of the means of production and the abolition of military rank). In Austria, Hungary and Italy, meanwhile, a parallel set of events was taking place. In Hungary a Soviet Republic was created after the abdication of the bourgeois government. Workers' councils were quickly formed as they were in Austria and Italy. Large-scale protests and strikes were frequent in Austria. In Italy they culminated in a general strike and extensive factory occupations (centred in and around Turin).[6]

The more immediate triumphs of the Russian revolutionaries were in marked contrast to the fate of the radical and revolutionary movements of central and southern Europe. Despite the devastation of the war, the strategies of revolutionary socialist movements proved inadequate against the resources and organization of the dominant classes. By the end of 1920 they had been checked. The momentum of the Russian revolution – weakened by foreign interventions, blockades and civil war – had been halted. The revolution was isolated. In the context of the fragmentation and repression of European socialist movements, the pressures of encirclement by Western and Eastern powers, the lack of resources as a result of the war, economic blockade and general economic underdevelopment, the Russian revolution itself began to deviate from the path Lenin had hoped to maintain. Lenin died in 1924. Three years later Stalin's victory was complete.

As the process of 'Stalinization' advanced in Russia, with the expansion of centralized control and censorship, the process of subjugating many European Communist parties to Moscow leadership was completed. (The 'Bolshevization' of the Communist International had already laid the foundation for the hegemony of Moscow in the Third International.)[7] Within Germany, the Communist Party, the KPD, while steadily growing in membership throughout the 1920s, became increasingly ineffective. The party's very existence constituted a continuous threat to those who sought to undermine the constitution from the right. But its adherence to the 'International–Bolshevik line', along with frequent changes of strategy and tactics, the dogmatic application of a crude theory to rapidly changing circumstances and the virulent attacks on other parties of the left and on the leadership of the trade union movement, all contributed to its failure to win and organize a majority of the working class. The revolutionary slogans of the KPD often appeared empty in the context of the social divisions of the Weimar republic.

The divisions within the German working class were the product of a long and complex history. An indication of their origin can be found in the history of the Second International and the German Social Democratic Party. Marxists of the Second International had frequently presented socialism as a historically necessary outcome of the development of capitalism. The revolution was held to be on its way. But as one commentator put it, 'a revolutionary party which is content to wait for the Revolution gradually ceases to be a revolutionary party'. This was precisely what the German Social Democratic Party ceased to be. Throughout the last three decades of the pre-war years it had constantly grown in size, commanding a massive vote in the immediate post-war elections. Its rhetoric was Marxist but its programme increasingly reformist. 'If in the future', Eduard Bernstein had written in 1898, 'some event were to place the power in the hands of Social Democracy, the gaping difference between the presuppositions of our theory and reality would appear in all its full dimensions.'[8] In 1914, the Social Democrats – formally committed to an international struggle against capitalism – voted for the war credits requested by the Emperor. In the next

six years the party's fate was established. In 1917 the left wing of
the party formed an independent group. During the two years
following the war the Social Democratic leadership supervised the
crushing of the radical and revolutionary movements. They now
placed complete reliance on 'formalistic legality'.[9] They not only
failed to take advantage of the opportunities to further the democratization and socialization of production in Germany but also, in
the years to come, 'unwittingly', as Franz Neumann has shown,
'strengthened the monopolistic trends in German Industry' and
failed 'to root out the reactionary elements in the judiciary and civil
service or limit the army to its proper constitutional role'.[10]

In the next decade conflict in Germany did not, of course, diminish. The loyalties of the working class were split between the
socialist, communist and national socialist parties. The experience
of the lost war, a frustrating peace settlement, massive inflation,
steadily rising unemployment (with well over six million registered
as unemployed in 1931), and the appearance in 1929 of the worst
international capitalist crisis, intensified and complicated all forms
of social and class struggle. There were only brief periods of
economic recovery and political stability.

The assaults on Weimar democracy came from many sides.
Counter-revolutionary forces were growing in resources and skills.
From 1924 to 1933 European history was engulfed by the rapid
emergence of Nazism and fascism. The liberal and democratic
parties proved ineffective against the organization and determination of these forces. The Communists, although often courageous,
fought mistimed battles with too small and fragmented forces.
Hitler exploited his chances as did Mussolini in Italy and Franco in
Spain. In January 1933 the Nazis seized power. Across central and
southern Europe coalitions between capital, 'big agrarians',
bureaucracy and the military were victorious. All independent
socialist and liberal organizations were suppressed. On 22 August
1939 the Hitler–Stalin pact was signed. It was the end of an era
and, for all those committed to the struggle against capitalism, a
desperate irony.

The character of critical theory

For those inspired by Marxism, but shaken by events of the 1920s
and 1930s, there were fundamental questions to answer. It was
clear that Marxists who had maintained either that socialism was

an inevitable part of 'history's plan', or that correct social action would follow merely from the promulgation of the correct party line, had espoused positions which were misleading and far too simple. While adherents to various forms of determinism had failed to grasp the way 'men make their own history', adherents to the doctrine of the centrality of 'the party' underestimated the way the making of history was affected by circumstances 'directly encountered, given and transmitted from the past'. Political events and revolutionary practice had not coincided with the expectations derived from the Marxist theory of the day. The following questions became urgent: How could the relationship between theory and practice now be conceived? Could theory preserve hope for the future? In changing historical circumstances how could the revolutionary ideal be justified? In order to understand the response of the Frankfurt school and Habermas to these issues, it is useful to look briefly at the thought of two men – Georg Lukács and Karl Korsch – whose own attempts to address these problems opened up new perspectives in Marxism. Although what follows in this book will make evident that Lukács and Korsch are by no means the only significant influences on critical theory, their writings set an important precedent for the critical theorists.

In the early 1920s Lukács and Korsch, active members of the Hungarian and German Communist parties respectively, wrote major works calling into question the dominant Marxist orthodoxies – the established doctrines of the Communist and Social Democratic parties.[11] The publication of Lukács's *History and Class Consciousness* and Korsch's *Marxism and Philosophy* met with a number of bitter polemical attacks. Some of the harshest criticism came from leading spokesmen of the Communist International itself.[12] In the years that followed neither Lukács nor Korsch found it easy to continue his efforts to reappraise Marxism. Korsch was eventually expelled from the KPD in 1926 for his 'deviations', while Lukács, threatened with similar treatment, wrote works to appease his critics. Lukács gradually capitulated to orthodoxy and moved to the Soviet Union. Korsch, after trying to maintain an independent political group, was driven by the Nazi victory into exile and isolation in Scandinavia and the United States.

These two men, however, by challenging orthodoxy and by rethinking Marxism in relation to contemporary events, created a basis for a re-examination of Marxist theory and practice. Both men believed that Marx's writings contain concepts, theories and principles which are violated by orthodox Marxism; and both sought to elaborate and develop this dimension of Marx's enterprise. Furthermore, both believed that this process of elaboration and development requires an examination of the origins and nature of Marx's thought and an engagement with those thinkers, whether they be Marxists or non-Marxists, who can aid the process of reconstruction.

The early work of Lukács and Korsch took issue, specifically, with the 'determinist' and 'positivist' interpretation of historical materialism – with its emphasis on unalterable stages of historical development (driven by a seemingly autonomous economic 'base') and on the suitability of the methodological model of the natural sciences for understanding these stages.[13] The latter interpretation of Marx corresponds, they argued, to a form of thought which Marx himself had rejected – 'contemplative materialism', a materialism which neglected the central importance of human subjectivity. The traditional standpoint of orthodox Marxism, they maintained, fails to grasp the significance of examining both the objective conditions of action and the ways in which these conditions are understood and interpreted. By underplaying human subjectivity and consciousness Marxists missed the very factors which were so central in preventing the emergence of a revolutionary agent. Since Lukács's work was extremely influential on the critical theorists the way in which he developed these themes is of special interest.[14]

Historical materialism, on Lukács's account, has no meaning outside the struggle of the proletariat. There is no objective reality which social theorists can passively reflect upon; for at every moment they are part of the societal process as well as 'its potential critical self-awareness'. The theorist is seen as a participant in a continuous class conflict, explicating objective possibilities immanent in the dynamic of class relations.[15] Accordingly, Marxism's claim to objectivity and truth, like that of all methods, cannot be separated from the practices of a particular social class. But, Lukács argued, 'the standpoint of the proletariat' and consequently Marxism transcends the 'one-sidedness' and distortions of other social theories and class ideologies. For the proletariat is the class on whose genesis capitalist society rests. The process of its own *Bildung* (formation, cultivation) is the key to the constitution of capitalism. As the pivot in the capitalist totality it has the capacity to see and comprehend the essential social relations and processes.[16] In Lukács's opinion, an opinion he buttressed with Hegelian categories, the 'standpoint of the proletariat', society's 'subject-object', is the only basis from which the totality can be grasped.

Lukács's position is predicated on the existence of a class whose social postion is said to be unique – unique because it has the capacity both to understand and change society radically. Even if (mass) revolutionary working-class practice does not exist, one is still able to talk of its objective possibility; for it is, on Lukács's assessment, contained within the dynamic of the historical process. The purpose of theory, therefore, is to analyse and expose the hiatus between the actual and the possible, between the existing order of contradictions and a potential future state. Theory must be oriented, in short, to the development of consciousness and the promotion of active political involvement.[17]

One of the chief barriers to revolutionary consciousness is, Lukács contended, 'reification' – the appearance of people's productive activity as something strange and alien to them. Drawing on Marx's analysis of the structure of commodities in *Capital*, Simmel's account of the commodification of culture, and Weber's work on rationalization, Lukács attempted to show how reification permeates all spheres of life. Although reification involves a process whereby social phenomena take on the appearance of things, it is not, he stressed, simply a subjective phenomenon; rather it arises from the productive process which reduces social relations themselves to thing-like relations – reduces, that is, the worker and his or her product to commodities. Reification is a socially necessary illusion – both accurately reflecting the reality of the capitalist exchange process and hindering its cognitive penetration. Lukács's analysis sought to assess and criticize this. The problem of commodities, of reification, he argued, was 'the central structural problem of capitalist society in all its aspects'.[18] It determined the objective and subjective forms of bourgeois society.[19]

It will become evident in the course of what follows that critical theorists retained many of Lukács's concerns: the interplay between history and theory, the importance of theory as a 'promotive factor in the development of the masses', the relation of production and culture, the effects of reification and the way each aspect of society contains within itself 'the possibility of unravelling the social whole or totality'. The terms in which Lukács cast many of his interests were, however, often regarded unsympathetically by the critical theorists. For instance, they were extremely hostile (with the exception perhaps of Horkheimer in the middle 1930s) to the 'standpoint of the proletariat' as the criterion of truth.[20] They rejected the Hegelian language in which Lukács couched much of his argument and recast the concept of reification. But despite these differences, the impetus Lukács gave to the interrogation of orthodox Marxism and to the reworking of Marx's ideas was built upon by each of the critical theorists.[21] Although Lukács recanted, they continued the project of examining the origins of Marx's thought, exploring Marx's works for dimensions that had been previously neglected and assessing the relevance of the Marxist tradition in light of contemporary events.

In furthering these general aims the critical theorists drew upon a variety of intellectual currents. For example, they looked (as Lukács had done before them) to German idealism, and to Kant and Hegel in particular, to retrieve the philosophical dimensions of the Marxist tradition. Criticisms of German idealism – those of Marxists as well as of non-Marxists like Schopenhauer and Nietzsche – were explored in order to come to grips with idealist views. Marx's early works, especially the *1844 Manuscripts* (which were unavailable to Lukács), were examined both to assess Hegel's impact on his thought and to help uncover the critical basis of Marx's ideas. The contributions of, among others, Heidegger and Husserl were assessed as part of a general engagement with contemporary philosophy. For the reinvestigation of human subjectivity Freud's works were regarded as of paramount importance. Weber's writings, especially in the processes of rationalization and bureaucratization, were thought to be key contributions to contemporary sociology – especially in light of the absence of serious discussion of these and related issues in the Marxist tradition. There was also an extraordinary cross-fertilization of ideas among the members of the Institute of Social Research and among the critical theorists themselves. Horkheimer and Adorno, for example, had a major impact on each other. Benjamin's ideas had a strong influence on Adorno. Marcuse and Adorno had a lasting effect on Habermas.

A negative definition of critical theory

It has often been said that because the critical theorists frequently criticized the works of others, it is easier to say what critical theory is not rather than what it is. There is enough truth in this comment to allow us to begin by defining critical theory negatively. Indeed, this may help to dispel a number of common misunderstandings. Although the thought of Horkheimer, Adorno, Marcuse and Habermas is steeped in the traditions of Kant and Hegel, only selected aspects of their ideas were employed. The critical theorists rejected Kant's transcendental method and many aspects of Hegel's philosophy. For example, against Hegel's claim that history is the process of reason (*Vernunft*) coming to be in self-consciousness – that reason unfolds in practice reconciling thought and object, freedom and necessity – they sought to show the extent to which human reason is still 'unreasonable': that is, tied to material conditions and practices often only dimly reflected in human consciousness.

They all rejected a philosophy of identity. Such a philosophy implies an actual or potential unity between subject and object. They attacked what they saw as Hegel's commitment to an idealist identity theory; the historical process could not be reduced to the manifestations of an absolute subject, a World Spirit, 'developing through individual acts' towards a given or potential unity of the Idea and the world, a state in which the subject fully appropriates its other – the object. They were also critical of what one might call a materialist identity theory propagated by orthodox Marxists; history could not be read as the manifestation of economic laws inexorably moving its carriers towards socialism or communism, a state in which the subject is enveloped by the 'objective workings' of history. They all rejected dialectical materialism. They were also critical of Marxist humanism.[22] They did not maintain, as Göran Therborn has suggested, that society is simply 'reducible to its creator-subject, and history is the continuous unfolding of this subject'.[23] As Horkheimer wrote,

There can be no formula which lays down once and for all the relationship between the individual, society and nature. Though history cannot be seen as a uniform unfolding of human nature, the opposite fatalistic formula that the course of events is dominated by necessity independent of Man is equally naive.[24]

Hence one can find in their work numerous objections to the

abstract humanism of Feuerbach and to the positions established by philosophical anthropologists, existentialists and phenomenologists. They were united in a rejection of the positivist understanding of science and a correspondence theory of truth.

It is, moreover, wrong to characterize their work as simply replacing Marxist political economy with general concerns about social philosophy, culture and social psychology.[25] Neumann, Pollock and, more recently, Habermas have all written extensively on the economy, the polity and their relations. It is also an error to imply that they pursued these issues without regard for empirical research. They have contributed extensively to empirical inquiry. It is, furthermore, mistaken to suggest that the Frankfurt school's work merely comprises a series of fragments – a motley collection of writings. Horkheimer and Adorno frequently chose to express themselves through aphorisms and essays, but I shall argue that the Frankfurt school as a whole developed a systematic account of the nature of capitalist society.

Critics on the left have charged critical theory with a failure to come to terms with practical political questions. This is a complex issue and one that will be discussed later. Here it is simply important to note that for the early Horkheimer, as for Lukács, the practical role of the theorist was to articulate and help develop a latent class consciousness. In Horkheimer's later work the task of the critical theorist was often conceived as that of 'remembering', 'recollecting' or capturing a past in danger of being forgotten – the struggle for emancipation, the reasons for this struggle, the nature of critical thinking itself. But the critical theorists were not just concerned with explicating what was latent or remembering the past; they contributed new emphases and ideas in their conception of theory and practice. Marcuse's defence, for instance, of personal gratification (against those revolutionaries who maintained an ascetic and puritanical outlook); individual self-emancipation (against those who would simply argue that liberation follows from changes in the relations and forces of production); fundamental alternatives to the existing relationship between humanity and nature (against those who would accelerate the development of existing forms of technology) – all constitute a significant departure from traditional Marxist doctrines. Horkheimer, Adorno and Marcuse never advanced, however, a rigid set of political demands. For it is a central tenet of their thought, as of Habermas's also, that the process of liberation entails a process of *self*-emancipation and

self-creation. Nor did they conceive the relation of theory and practice as a given and unchanging one. Time entered into their conception of this relation as a crucial dimension; it is a historical
relation – a relation determined, like all others, by a world in
development and flux.

The following eight chapters, which comprise Part One of the
book, provide an account of the Frankfurt school. Chapter 1 is a
brief history of the Institute of Social Research. Chapters 2–5
expound critical theory's relation to political economy, aesthetics,
psychoanalysis and the philosophy of history. The subsequent
three chapters focus on the conceptions of critical theory of Horkheimer, Adorno and Marcuse. Part Two begins with a summary of
Habermas's work and a discussion of its relation to the Frankfurt
school. Chapter 10 concentrates on Habermas's social theory,
while Chapters 11 and 12 explicate his approach to epistemology
and methodology. In Part Three, Chapters 13 and 14 offer an
assessment of the contributions and limitations of the various
branches of critical theory. They also include an appraisal of some
of the major objections that have been raised against the work of
the critical theorists.

Part One
The Frankfurt School

1 The formation of the Institute of Social Research

The Institut für Sozialforschung (Institute of Social Research), founded in Germany in 1923, was the home of the Frankfurt school. The Institute was established as a result of an initiative by the son of a wealthy grain merchant, Felix Weil, who procured the means to ensure that the Institute could develop with minimum external pressures and constraints; and, in fact, though formally attached to the University of Frankfurt, its private funds did give it considerable autonomy.[1]

When Horkheimer assumed the directorship of the Institute in 1930 most of the figures who later became famous as members of the Frankfurt school began to contribute to the Institute's activities. Although the orientation of the Institute changed markedly under Horkheimer's influence, the experience and concerns of its first director – Carl Grünberg, a figure relatively unknown today – were important to the overall development of the Institute.

The Institute under Grünberg, 1923–9

Grünberg is considered by many to be one of the founders of the Austro-Marxist tradition. After a professorship in law and political science at the University of Vienna, he became, on appointment to Frankfurt, the first 'avowed Marxist to hold a chair at a German University'.[2] He was responsible for establishing and editing the first major European journal of labour and socialist history – *Archiv für die Geschichte des Sozialismus und der Arbeiterbewegung* [Archive for the History of Socialism and the Workers' Movement] or *Grünbergs Archiv*, as it was often called – which transferred, with Grünberg, to Frankfurt.[3]

Marxism was made the inspiration and theoretical basis of the Institute's programme. The regular contacts and exchanges with the Marx–Engels Institute in Moscow (then under the directorship of David Ryazanov), symbolized the close ties between the Institute of Social Research and the traditions of classical Marxism. The two institutes jointly sponsored the publication of the first volume of the *Marx–Engels Gesamtausgabe* [Marx–Engels Complete Edition].

Many of the scholars Grünberg brought together were deeply committed to political involvement. Among his assistants were members of the Communist Party – Karl August Wittfogel, Franz Borkenau and Julian Gumperz – as well as members of the Social Democratic Party. Karl Korsch was also active in the Institute's affairs in its early years, participating in seminars and contributing to the *Archiv*. But the Institute remained officially independent of party affiliations and was a centre for scholars of many political persuasions. As one of its members, Henryk Grossmann, wrote:

It is a *neutral* institution at the university, which is accessible to everyone. Its significance lies in the fact that for the first time everything concerning the workers movement in the most important countries of the world is gathered. Above all, sources (congress minutes, party programs, statutes, newspapers and periodicals). . . . Whoever in Western Europe wishes to write on the currents of the workers movement *must* come to us, for we are the only gathering point for it.[4]

However, the distinctiveness of the brand of Marxism initiated by Institute of Social Research can best be detected in Grünberg's 1924 inaugural address. In this paper Grünberg emphasized his opposition to the trend in German universities toward teaching at the expense of research and toward the production of 'mandarins' only capable of serving the existing balance of power and resources. Marxism, Grünberg argued, as a method of scientific research and as a philosophical system, must be used to counter these tendencies.[5]

On Grünberg's account, the object domain of historical materialism is real social events: 'social life in its ceaseless and ever-recurring transformations'. The goal of research is to grasp 'the ultimate causes of these processes of transformation and the laws according to which they evolve'. The method of research is 'eminently inductive'. But its results claim 'no absolute validity in time and space . . . only relative, historically conditioned meaning'.[6] In contradistinction to positions held by some members of the Second International, Grünberg's Marxism is not a straightforward monistic materialism, maintaining a simple correspondence theory of truth and claiming to reveal transhistorical laws. The categories of materialism, Grünberg maintained, do not grasp universal, unchanging truths; they reflect and describe a dynamic and developing society the future of which is not guaranteed. Social life, he believed, could be understood by uncovering the laws operative in a given economy. Marxism could only develop as a theory of production – as a theory of the *changing forms* of economic life.

Grünberg's Institute sought to combine concrete historical studies with theoretical analysis. His journal published articles on a multitude of topics in the history of capitalist and socialist economies and workers movements. Historians, economists, philosophers, among others, were represented in the journal and at Institute seminars. Works by as diverse figures as Ryazanov, Grossmann, Wittfogel, Korsch and Lukács were printed in the *Archiv*.

The prescription for social explanation offered by Grünberg was not, however, adhered to by the central figures of critical theory; they rejected the idea that all social phenomena were in essence a mere 'reflex' of the economic. Likewise a certain optimistic determinism which often found expression in his work, suggesting a progression in the development of social institutions from 'the less perfect to the more perfect', was not shared by most of those who later became critical theorists. But the strong emphasis Grünberg placed on historically oriented empirical research, carried out in the context of Marx's insights into political economy, was to become a crucial part of their frame of reference.

In 1929, at the age of 68, Grünberg retired. The following year Max Horkheimer was installed as the Institute's director. Within a short period of time he had a major impact on the type of work executed by the Institute's members.

The Institute and its programme under Max Horkheimer

Horkheimer gathered around him a diverse group with an extraordinary array of talents. Within a few years the new entrants to the Institute included Fromm, Marcuse and Neumann, while Pollock and Lowenthal, both of whom had been members since the 1920s, took on more prominent positions. The composition of the Institute under Horkheimer corroborates Benjamin's assertion that 'one cannot say that the group . . . was founded on a specific field. . . . [Rather] . . . it was based on the idea that the teaching about society can only be developed in the most tightly integrated connection of disciplines; above all, economics, psychology, history and philosophy'.[7] In 1935 Benjamin himself became a research associate of the Institute's Paris branch and received a stipend.[8]

Horkheimer's inaugural address, 'The present situation of social philosophy and the tasks of an Institute of Social Research', delivered in 1931, expressed both continuities and breaks with Grünberg's programme.[9] Horkheimer believed, as Grünberg had done before him, in the 'dictatorship of the director': the director of the Institute should take a central role in all Institute activities. Grünberg's concern for both theoretical analysis and empirical investigations was also at the heart of Horkheimer's interests. However, Horkheimer sought to discuss the role of theory and social research in a more radically historical and theoretical mode. The main theme of his address was the relation between social philosophy and science. Horkheimer characterized social philosophy as an attempt to interpret the fate of human beings 'insofar as they are parts of a community, and not mere individuals'.[10] While he accepted the significance of the traditional questions of social philosophy such as the relationship between the individual and society, the meaning of culture and the basis of societal life, he rejected a purely philosophical approach to these issues.[11] Philosophers, he argued, have all too often treated these questions in the abstract, divorced from history and social context; the major schools naively posited either 'an abstract, isolated individual' (e.g. *Lebensphilosophie*, existentialism) or a 'hypostatized social totality' (e.g. Hegelian idealism) as the fount of life and proper object of social inquiry. Horkheimer rejected these approaches and, instead, called for 'a dialectical penetration and development of philosophical theory and the praxis of individual scientific disciplines'.[12] He held that it was necessary to reintegrate disciplines because the division of labour in the humanities and social sciences was so far advanced and their results so fragmented.[13] Neither philosophy nor any of the individual sciences could defend the claim that it alone could uncover 'the essentials' or 'the facts'.[14] I will return to the precise nature of the relationship between philosophy and science recommended by Horkheimer in Chapter 5. But it is crucial to note that he was not demanding, as has been suggested by one critic, 'the development of "social philosophy" supplemented by empirical investigations'.[15] Rather Horkheimer stressed the necessity of a programme of *interdisciplinary study* in which 'philosophers, sociologists, economists, historians and psychologists must unite in a lasting working partnership . . . to do what all genuine researchers have always done: namely to pursue the great philosophical questions with the most refined methods'. In the course of working on particular problems and objects researchers must, he contended, reformulate the philosophical questions, make them more precise, and devise new methods for handling specific issues while, at the same time, 'not losing sight of the universal'.[16]

Horkheimer also rejected the emphasis of those who, as he put it, 'did not understand Marx'. Social phenomena cannot be deduced from material being, that is, from the economy. The Institute's members, he insisted, must explore the question of 'the interconnection between the economic life of society, the psychic development of the individual and transformations in the realm of culture . . . including not only the so-called spiritual contents of science, art and religion, but also law, ethics, fashion, public opinion, sport, amusement, life style etc.'.[17] More specifically they should ask: what interconnections exist in definite social groups, in definite periods of time and in definite countries, between the position of the group in the economy, changes in the psychic structures of its membership and other relevant factors which condition and affect the group's thoughts and practices.[18]

Three themes dominate all others in Horkheimer's address. The first, already described, suggests the necessity of re-specifying 'the great philosophical questions' in an interdisciplinary research programme. The second theme, more implicit but made clearer in later essays, is a call for a rejection of orthodox Marxism and its substitution by a reconstructed understanding of Marx's project. The third emphasizes the necessity for social theory to explicate the set of interconnections (mediations) that make possible the reproduction and transformation of society, economy, culture and consciousness. In his early writings as an Institute member Horkheimer added a note on methodology to the themes of his inaugural address.[19] No one method could, in his opinion, produce definitive results about any given object of inquiry. To take one type of approach is always to risk a distorted perspective on reality. Several methods, drawing on both qualitative and quantitative techniques, have to be supplemented with one another in any systematic investigation. But empirical work, Horkheimer emphasized, is not a substitute for theoretical analysis. For concepts like society, culture and class, indispensable to all inquiry, cannot be simply transcribed into empirical terms. They require theoretical elucidation and appraisal.[20]

During the 1930s and early 1940s, despite the transfer of the Institute – an outcome, of course, of the Nazis' rise to power – to Geneva (February 1933) and then to Columbia University in New York (1935), members of the Institute continued to work in political-economy, philosophy, sociology, psychology, literature, music and other disciplines. The variety of approaches were reflected in the Institute's new journal, the *Zeitschrift für Sozialforschung* [Journal of Social Research], first published in 1932, and in *Studies in Philosophy and Social Science* as the journal was later called on its publication in English, between 1939 and 1941. The term 'critical theory', the label under which so much of the Frankfurt school's work has become famous, does not reflect adequately the different disciplines represented in the journal or at the Institute. Although it is a label which Horkheimer, Adorno and Marcuse seemed happy to employ as a description of their own enterprises from the mid 1930s onward, 'critical theory' does not describe the approach or method of individuals such as Grossmann, Fromm and Neumann (who had a more traditional attitude to their disciplines). Nor does it identify satisfactorily all the stages in the development of Horkheimer's, Adorno's and Marcuse's own thought – the transformations, for example, in Horkheimer's theoretical perspective from an early commitment to materialism and critique to a later interest in 'quasi-religious' phenomena. Moreover, the label conceals a host of differences between Horkheimer, Adorno and Marcuse. When employing the term it is important to bear in mind that there are several models of critical theory. While the term 'critical theory' will be applied here, its different connotations will also be expounded.

The character of the Institute's projects

The most active years of the Institute, 1930–44, coincided with the prominence of Nazism and fascism. Horkheimer had been in his new appointment for less than three years before he and the others were forced to leave Germany. The opportunities to 'promote the development of the masses' rapidly dwindled. But although there were marked differences in the way Horkheimer and the others conceived the political implications of their work, most of the Institute's members hoped that their cumulative efforts would contribute to the making of history with will and consciousness. They intended their findings to become a material force in the struggle against domination in all its forms. The conditions they observed, and the questions which became central for the Institute members, included:

The European labour movements did not develop into a unified struggle of all workers. What blocked these developments?

Capitalism was in a series of acute crises. How could these better be understood? What was the relation between the political and the economic? Was the relation changing?

Authoritarianism and the development of bureaucracy seemed increasingly the order of the day. How could these phenomena be comprehended?

Nazism and fascism rose to dominate central and southern Europe. How was this possible? How did these movements attain large-scale support?

Social relationships, for example those created by the family, appeared to be undergoing radical social change. In what directions? How were these affecting individual development?

Areas of culture appeared open to direct manipulation. Was a new type of ideology being formed? If so, how was this affecting everyday life?

Given the fate of Marxism in Russia and Western Europe, was Marxism itself nothing other than a stale orthodoxy? Was there a social agent capable of progressive change? What possibilities were there for effective socialist practice?

Needless to say not all members of the Institute studied and addressed each issue. Horkheimer, Adorno and Marcuse did, however, comment upon most, if not all, of these questions. It is from their work that one can most directly reconstruct the relation between themes. But there are also important connections, often not explicitly made, between most of the projects conducted at one time or another under the Institute's auspices on the one hand, and the independent work of most of the Institute's members on the other.

Emigration

In the late 1930s and 1940s the activities at the Institute in the United States suffered disruption and a certain fragmentation. A hiatus emerged between works in philosophy and social theory (such as Horkheimer and Adorno's *Dialectic of Enlightenment*) and empirical studies undertaken by the Institute (for instance, *The Authoritarian Personality*). There was also an ever greater gap between theory and practice. Reflecting perhaps on fascist Germany and exile, Marcuse wrote, 'the divorce of thought from action, of theory from practice, is itself part of the unfree world. No thought and no theory (alone) can undo it'.[21]

The programme of research Horkheimer had defended in his inaugural address and in his earliest *Zeitschrift* essays could not be carried out under the changed circumstances. Emigration to New York in 1935, and to California in 1941, dislocated a number of projects. Distress and disarray followed Hitler's ascent to power, the loss of relatives and friends, and the shock of discovering a very alien culture.[22] A sense of disorientation was also created by a change in the audience for whom Horkheimer and the others were writing. Despite the fact that they remained relatively isolated from American social science, the longer they stayed in the United States the more their audience consisted of American social scientists (as opposed to fellow German scholars and émigrés).[23] Horkheimer and Adorno continued to publish most of their writings in German; the *Zeitschrift* itself was issued in German until 1939. But the change in audience eventually forced a reconsideration of the form and content of at least some of their work.

The differences between the intellectual traditions which informed German and American scholarship reinforced the feeling of dislocation. Neumann sought to express this difference when he wrote:

on the whole, the German exile, bred in the veneration of theory and history, and contempt for empiricism and pragmatism, entered a diametrically opposed intellectual climate: optimistic, empirically oriented, a-historical, but also self-righteous.[24]

The Institute's members often found Anglo-American philosophy lacking in depth and insight. According to Adorno and Neumann, American scholars were uncritical and overenthusiastic about the benefits of empirical research.[25] But the clash of traditions and approaches led to a heightening of awareness of the 'prejudices of tradition'. As Adorno put it, he learnt 'not to take things for granted', from general concepts to methods of inquiry.[26] This also seems to have been the experience of Horkheimer and Neumann.

Financial problems, particularly in the early 1940s, also caused difficulties.[27] A number of investments had been unsuccessful. Foundation sponsorship was extremely hard to obtain. As a result, a projected study of aspects of German culture was abandoned and *Studies in Philosophy and Social Science* was discontinued (1941). It is probably fair to say that many of the projects the Institute might have wanted to carry out became impractical and even unwise at this time. Martin Jay has pointed out that there was a conscious toning down of radicalism in the Institute's publications due to fear of political harassment and deportation.[28] But the type of research that could be realized was also constrained by the concepts of 'problems', 'issues' and 'research' held by potential sponsors. The Institute's *Studies of Prejudice* (of which the *The Authoritarian Personality* is but one volume) was financed by the American Jewish Committee.

Emigration, the change in audience and financial circumstances were not the only factors to affect the Institute's activities. I have already outlined the major events which helped to shape the historical and political experience of the Institute's members. The importance of these in the development of the Frankfurt school cannot be underestimated. Horkheimer, for example, frequently acknowledged the inadequacy of the conceptual tools he employed in the 1930s for analysis of major events in the 1940s. The optimism which he had felt during the pre-war years faded away. Critical theorists could hardly think of becoming a stimulating influence on the masses. Marcuse has expressed this view forcefully and noted some of its implications.

If the proletariat no longer acts as the revolutionary class . . . it no longer furnishes the 'material weapons' for philosophy. The situation thus reverts: repelled by reality, Reason and Freedom become again the concern of philosophy. The 'essence of man', his 'total liberation' is again experienced [only] in thought [*in Gedanken erlebt*]. Theory . . . again not only anticipates political practice, runs ahead of it, but also upholds the objectives of liberation in the face of a failing practice. In this function, theory becomes again ideology – not as false consciousness, but as conscious distance and dissociation from, even opposition to, the repressive reality. And by the same token, it becomes a political factor of utmost significance.[29]

The themes covered by the Frankfurt school during this time are extensive. They include discussions of theories of capitalism, of the structure of the state, and of the rise of instrumental reason; analyses of developments in science, technology and technique, of the culture industry and mass culture, of family structure and individual development, and of the susceptibility of people to ideology; as well as considerations of the dialectic of enlightenment and of positivism as the dominant mode of cognition. As always it was the hope of Horkheimer and the others that their work would help establish a critical social consciousness able to penetrate existing ideology, sustain independent judgement and be capable, as Adorno put it, 'of maintaining its freedom to think things might be different'.

The post-war years

Horkheimer, Adorno and Pollock had resettled in West Germany by the early 1950s. Marcuse, Lowenthal, Kirchheimer and others stayed in the United States. By 1953 the Institute was re-established in Frankfurt, Horkheimer had been appointed rector of the University and Adorno had received a professorship. In 1955 Adorno became co-director of the Institute. The *Zeitschrift* was not re-established, but the Institute soon began to publish a series of *Frankfurter Beiträge zur Soziologie* [Frankfurt Contributions to Sociology]. Horkheimer and Pollock retired in 1958. In 1969 Adorno died. Pollock's death followed a year later and Horkheimer's in 1973. Although the Institute of Social Research survived their deaths, the Frankfurt school itself, so dependent on the energy and ideas of these individuals, did not.

Horkheimer and Adorno dominated the Institute in the post-war years. Equally critical (for the most part) of developmental tendencies in capitalist and socialist societies, they maintained staunchly independent intellectual and political positions. They continued to stress an interdisciplinary theoretical approach and the use of a variety of methodological techniques in their teaching and written work. Research techniques developed in America were promulgated and employed in a number of studies, although neither Horkheimer nor Adorno ever defended their use in isolation from theoretical and critical perspectives.

In the atmosphere of post-war reconstruction and the cold war, many key intellectuals from Germany's past were subject to attack in the press and in academia; direct lines were traced, for example, from Hegel, Schopenhauer and Nietzsche to fascist ideology and from Marx to Stalinism. Horkheimer and Adorno resisted this fashion and helped to restore serious discussion of these and other thinkers. Their position, however, was not without tensions. In defending the importance of Marx and critical thinking while criticizing in an increasingly virulent manner Soviet Marxists and others who sought to actualize Marx's ideals, they risked pleasing neither conservative authorities nor radical thinkers, including many of their own students. Their independent positions on political questions led, in fact, to challenges from all these parties. It is ironic that they were attacked in the 1960s for their political pessimism and lack of practical involvement, but, after their deaths, for their supposed encouragement of 'terrorism' and political irresponsibility.

Marcuse's popularity with the New Left in the 1960s and early 1970s, especially in the United States, was in marked contrast to the fate of his ex-colleagues. Although many of his ideas were similar to those they elaborated, his unambiguous commitment to politics and social struggle meant that he became one of the most prominent (if not the most prominent) spokesmen and theoreticians of the left. It was through Marcuse's work that the Frankfurt school's criticisms of contemporary culture, authoritarianism and bureaucratism became well known. The school's concern to expand the terms of reference of the political, by drawing attention to issues such as the division of labour, ecological problems and sexism (as well as the traditional question of ownership and control), was actualized, in part, through Marcuse's influence. But considerable differences between Marcuse, Horkheimer and Adorno remained. The next seven chapters seek to clarify their respective positions on political and other issues.

2 Class, class conflict and the development of capitalism: critical theory and political economy

In the last ten years the work of the best-known representatives of the Frankfurt school has come to be associated with two basic concerns: social philosophy and social psychology. The theoretical innovations for which they are most often recognized are their analyses of the structure of reason and technique, and of the entanglement of enlightenment, myth, domination and nature; while their best-known empirical studies relate to authoritarianism and the authoritarian personality. The texts most often cited are *Dialectic of Enlightenment*, *Eclipse of Reason*, *Minima Moralia*, *One Dimensional Man* and *The Authoritarian Personality*.

Sympathetic interpreters of the Institute's work have come to see these writings as amounting to a 'radical and sustained critique of bourgeois society', although developed and presented in a fragmented way. Critics have charged that these works represent a pessimistic cultural critique which does less to integrate Marxist political economy with socio-cultural and psychological dimensions than to replace the former with the latter.[1] The concerns of the school, still others have argued, collapsed into a 'perennial spiritualistic reaction – romantic, in the last instance – against technique and modern social organization'.[2] In this chapter I want to show that classic Marxist themes are not simply replaced in the critical theorists' work; that class and class conflict remain important categories in their understanding of the formation of capitalism; and that it is insufficient to label their writings as just 'pessimistic' or 'romantic'. Their work contains a fairly systematic theory of the development of capitalism.

Marx's political economy as the foundation for critical social theory

Despite major differences between members of the Institute in their assessment of the development of capitalism, it may be noted from the outset that their respective analyses were informed by familiar Marxian tenets:

1   We live in a society dominated by the capitalist mode of production. It is a society based on exchange, a commodity society. Products are manufactured *primarily* for their realization as value and profit, and not for their capacity to satisfy human wants and desires.

2   The commodity character of products is not simply determined by their exchange, but by their being abstractly exchanged. Exchange, based on abstract labour time, affects the objective form as well as the subjective side of the productive process. It affects the former through its determination of the form of products and labour (labour power) and the latter through its debasement of human relationships.

3   The particular constellation of social relations which ensures the unity of the capitalist social process also ensures its fetishization and reification. The products of human labour are viewed as independent, 'having a life of their own', a 'natural' value. The social and material relations which result from exchange, distribution and consumption are not immediately comprehensible. They are veiled by necessary illusion – the fetishism of commodities.

4   Capitalism is not a harmonious social whole. Both in the realm of the production of commodities and in the sphere of illusion it is based on contradictions. The dominant relations of production 'fetter' the developed forces of production and produce a series of antagonisms. Further, the mass of workers' separation from the means of production produces direct conflict with those that possess capital. Antagonisms arise in the cultural sphere as well as in the economic. Contradictions between socially generated illusions (ideology) and actuality (performance, effects) lead to crisis. For the principles which govern production are often not those which govern wants and needs, and their multifarious expression.

5   A general tendency exists towards capital-intensive industries and increased concentration of capital. The free market is progressively replaced by the oligopolistic and monopolistic mass production of standardized goods.

6   The progressive rise in the organic composition of capital – the amount of fixed capital per worker – exacerbates the inherently unstable accumulation process. In order to sustain this process,

its protagonists utilize all means available – including imperialist expansion and war.

Of all the members of the Institute only Grossmann maintained that a breakdown of capitalism was 'objectively necessary' and 'exactly calculable'. In a number of essays published during 1928–9 and in his major work, *Das Akkumulations–und Zusammenbruchsgesetz des kapitalistischen Systems* [The Law of Accumulation and Breakdown of the Capitalist System], he argued that crisis and the eventual collapse of capitalism could be predicted from an analysis of the long-run tendency of capital to increase its organic composition. Starting from a series of assumptions about population growth, the rate and quantity of surplus value, the relation of fixed to variable capital, which even sympathetic critics have called unrealistic, Grossmann calculated that the production of surplus value would eventually be inadequate to expand capital. Although a number of counter-tendencies were analysed, Grossmann was convinced about the inevitability of economic collapse.[3] This did not mean, however, that there would be an automatic transition to socialism. Grossmann's thinking combined both evolutionary and revolutionary elements. As he wrote,

no economic system, no matter how weakened, collapses by itself in automatic fashion. It must be 'overthrown'. The theoretical analysis of objective trends leading to a paralysis of the system serves to discover the 'weak links' and to fix them in time as a sort of barometer indicating when the system becomes ripe for change. Even when that point is reached, change will come about only through active operation of the subjective factors.[4]

Economic collapse does not guarantee revolution. In Grossmann's opinion, revolution has to be made through the active intervention of the working class and by those who struggle on its behalf.

In age and spirit Grossmann was closer to Grünberg than any of those who later became prominent as members of the Frankfurt school. The two men had become acquainted well before Grossmann joined the Institute in the mid 1920s. They shared a strong interest in the theory and practice of classical Marxism. Further, Grossman's commitment to orthodox Marxist economics, to the Soviet Union – even in the 1940s – and to settlement in East Germany (where he was offered a chair in 1949) distinguished his interests from those of Horkheimer and other members of the Institute who challenged his views. Certainly his stress on the necessity of active, self-conscious intervention was shared by Horkheimer, Adorno, Pollock and others. But his view that break-down is unavoidable was regarded with a great deal of scepticism.

Horkheimer's and Adorno's assessment of the developmental course of capitalism was, as will be shown below, much more ambivalent. Although this assessment relied in a number of respects on Pollock's engagement with economic analysis, the significance of Marx's contribution to the study of capitalism is continually acknowledged. This is especially clear in Horkheimer's work. In an essay published in 1937, he registered agreement with Marx's analysis of the general course of the commodity economy. Critical theory is, on this account,

in its totality, the unfolding of a single existential judgement. Crudely formulated, it states that the fundamental form of the historically given commodity economy on which [more recent] history rests, contains in itself the internal and external contradictions of [its] epoch, which it gen-erates in an increasingly intensified form. . . .[5]

Throughout his early *Zeitschrift* essays, Horkheimer appears to accept most of the tenets of *Capital*. Following Marx, he also argued that it is only through the abolition of the 'economic struc-ture which underlies all contemporary social change', that is, the dominant relations of production, that a 'self-fulfilling praxis' can be established.

Unemployment, economic crises, militarization, terrorist regimes – in a word, the whole condition of the masses – are not due to limited tech-nological possibilities, as might have been the case in earlier periods, but to the circumstances of production. . . .
Production is not geared to the life of the whole community [to the com-mon interest] while heeding also the claims of individuals; it is geared to the power-backed claims of individuals while being hardly concerned with the life of the community. This is the inevitable result, under the present property order, of the principle that it is sufficient for individuals to look out for themselves.[6]

The political task is, therefore, to 'set free' the individual from these material conditions.

In these early essays Horkheimer also defended his political aspirations by drawing upon Freud's libido theory. Freud's early formulation of the theory of human instincts implies, Horkheimer contended, that human beings share a striving for pleasure and self-preservation. Thus, there is a stratum of human existence which is 'an ever flowing source of stimuli'.[7] But the 'struggle for existence' compels the repression of these instincts. Following Freud, Horkheimer held that a crucial condition of civilization is the renunciation of activities leading to immediate pleasure and the satisfaction of needs. The sublimation of libido renders possible the development of society. It ensures sufficient 'energy' for human beings to revolutionize production and, therefore, to escape the contingencies of a hostile environment. The institutionalization of economic growth under capitalism, with its rapid development of technology and labour-saving devices, furthers this process. Horkheimer maintained against Freud that as capitalism facilitates an enormous expansion of production and the ever greater control of nature, it also undermines the necessity for the perpetual postponement of gratification. Yet it tends 'to reduce individuals to the status of mere functionaries of economic mechanisms' and enforces suffering on a massive scale. Although in his early writings Horkheimer defended the view that the proletariat could potentially undo this state of affairs, he argued that the repression experienced by its individual members could bring about feelings of guilt and/or inadequacy and increased aggression towards self and others. This process, he thought, could hinder progressive political change and contribute to a new barbarism.

Horkheimer's position entails the defence of central elements of Marxist political economy as well as of some of Freud's ideas. He sought thereby to sustain the claim that needs were emerging which represented potentially a critical and progressive political standpoint. With Marx and Lukács he suggested that it was possible for the proletariat to transcend this situation and realize a more enriching life. But as the 1930s developed the validity of this analysis was called into question.

Adorno's early views were similar to Horkheimer's. Although he did not draw on Freud's libido theory in a comparable fashion, Adorno placed certain traditional Marxian axioms at the centre of his writings and expressed throughout the pre-war and war years a growing ambivalence about the role of the proletariat.[8] For both men, Marx's social theory was crucial and the axioms outlined above were to remain of lasting importance in their work. However, the significance they were granted changed in time. The same can be said of the role of Marx's political economy in the thought of Pollock, Neumann, Kirchheimer and most of the other members of the Institute.

Reflections on early twentieth-century history

The uncertainty of the epoch which began with the Russian revolu
tion and the council communist movement and ended with fascism
and Stalinism is reflected in the earliest writings of the Institute's
members. Their experience and interpretation of these events
helped create the motivation to develop a non-dogmatic critical
theory of society. An analysis of these views provides a great deal
of insight into their project and ambitions.

In one of Horkheimer's earliest and most remarkable works – a
collection of aphorisms and short essays written between 1926 and
1931 – the ambivalence of the era is succinctly expressed. The
collection's title is *Dämmerung*, which signifies both dusk and
dawn.[9] The first aphorism, entitled *Dämmerung*, captures the tone
of the book.

The more threadbare ideologies are, the crueller the means by which they
are protected. The degree of effort and terror with which swaying gods are
defended, shows the extent to which dusk [*Dämmerung*] has set in. In
Europe the understanding of the masses has increased with big industry,
so that the sacred goods have to be protected. . . . Whoever defends [these
goods] has already [thereby] made his career: in addition to . . . systematically induced stupification, the threat of economic ruin, social disgrace,
prison and death prevent this [newly established] understanding from
violating the highest conceptual means of domination. The imperialism of
big European states does not have to envy the stakes of the Middle Ages;
its symbols are protected by more subtle apparatuses and more terrible
armed guards than the Saints of the Church of the Middle Ages. The
opponents of the inquisition made that twilight [*Dämmerung*] into the
dawn of a new day, nor does the dusk [*Dämmerung*] of capitalism necessarily herald the night of humanity, though this seems to be threatening
today.[10]

Four points appear of immediate interest. First, Horkheimer notes
the demise of competitive, liberal capitalism and the rise of big,
organized industry. Second, he suggests that with the development
of capitalism and imperialism there has been an increase in class
consciousness and understanding among the masses. Third, he
stresses a certain potentiality for the transcendence of class-
dominated institutions. Fourth, he strongly qualifies any optimistic
view that might claim socialism to be imminent. There are a multitude of 'subtle apparatuses' (education, mass media, for example) and direct institutions of force (for instance, the police and
military) which are working to annihilate such hopes. The 'night of

humanity' is threatening. (There are only a few who might hold that the 1930s and early 1940s were not a realization of this insight.) Each of these themes is elaborated in *Dämmerung*.

Reflecting some forty years later on this period, Horkheimer restated his belief that

In the first half of the century proletarian revolts could plausibly be expected in European countries, passing as they were through inflation and crisis. The idea that in the early thirties a united movement of workers and intellectuals could bar the way to National Socialism was not mere wishful thinking.[11]

In *Dämmerung*, the pre- and post-first-world-war attempts to establish a radical democracy, based on workers' councils, appear as a major source of inspiration for his thinking. Horkheimer's conception of socialism implies a collectively controlled society which would provide the condition for the possibility of 'unfolding all individual talents and differences'. In 1940 he made clear that in his view the 'theoretical conception which, following its first trailblazers, will show the new society its way – the system of workers' councils – grows out of praxis. The roots of the council system go back to 1871, 1905, and other events. Revolutionary transformation has a tradition that must continue'.[12] Throughout the collection of aphorisms and essays, Horkheimer often alluded to the intensive struggles which might continue this tradition. He envisaged a society based on the socialization of the means of production, planned management and, importantly, the participation of all. But, as he later put it, the precise nature of such a society cannot and must not be stipulated in advance.

Contemporary reflection in the service of a transformed society should not disregard the fact that in a classless democracy plans cannot be forced on others through power or through routine, but must be arrived at through free agreement.[13]

What then did Horkheimer think of the struggle for socialism in Russia?

Although he wrote little on this topic, his early writings suggest, as do those of Pollock and Marcuse, both feelings of support and a critical concern. As he put it in 1930,

The state of affairs [in Russia] . . . is most problematic. I do not claim to know in which direction the country is going; undoubtedly there is a great deal of suffering. But whoever amongst the intelligentsia is unaware of the breadth of exertion there or who boasts recklessly of it ... is indeed a pathetic comrade, whose company brings no gain. Those who have an eye to the senseless injustice of the imperialistic world which cannot be explained by technical powerlessness, will regard events in Russia as the continued, painful attempt to overcome ... terrible social injustice, or he will at least ask with a beating heart, if this attempt is still continuing. If appearances speak against it, he clings to the hope in the way in which a cancer victim does to the questionable news that a cure for cancer has in all likelihood been found.[14]

However, by the mid 1930s the ambivalence in attitude gave way to disappointment, disenchantment and hostility. Stalin's 'authoritarian bureaucracy' was criticized: its elitist, technocratic and destructive elements were rejected. Horkheimer's position appears thoroughly opposed to those elements of Lenin's thought, extrapolated by Stalin, which sought to defend and legitimate the exclusive role of the party as the true and only representative of the working class (and, therefore, of the future of humanity). As such, his position was close to Kirchheimer's.

In a number of essays published in the early 1930s in *Die Gesellschaft* (the theoretical organ of the SPD), Kirchheimer, while defending the need for organization and an activist, interventionist stance, criticized Lenin's notion of the party and the state.[15] Unlike Horkheimer, he developed a more detailed appraisal of Lenin's (and by implication Stalin's) theory and practice. In his 'Marxism, dictatorship and the organization of the proletariat' (1933), Kirchheimer pointed to a tension between Lenin's doctrine of the state (as expounded in *State and Revolution*) and his theory of the party (articulated in *What is to be Done?*). The former, he argued, is concerned with 'primitive democracy' – altering the structure of society, electing officials, dismantling the regular army, etc. – while the latter defends hierarchy, professionalism and planning. Clearly, the form of the Soviet state progressively approximated that of the party. The powers of the soviets were not developed: discipline was maintained in the face of existing mass consciousness.[16] Kirchheimer recognized that many factors contributed to this state of affairs, but felt that it was (at least in part) a result of 'the natural unfolding of the party structure' and its imposition upon the structure of the state. He shared Rosa Luxemburg's critique of all attempts to impose the 'principle of capitalist factory discipline' on the 'autonomous discipline of the working class'. Although he did not accept her emphasis on the 'supreme importance of spontaneity', he did agree that to crush spontaneity was disastrous. He was extremely critical of the 'primitive purity' and 'autocratic structure' of the Soviet party and state which had 'jeopardized all chances of the development of democratic institutions' within and outside of the party.[17]

By the early 1940s the ironies of the Hitler-Stalin pact led Horkheimer and Adorno, working together during the war years, to subject Stalinism and fascism to many similar criticisms. While they concentrated their analysis on the latter, some of their writings stress a comparable perversion of freedom and democracy in each social system.[18] Marcuse's *Soviet Marxism,* written in the late 1950s, is an immanent critique of the Marxism dominating Soviet society. His views have much in common with those described above. For example, Marcuse writes of Lenin,

His struggle against 'economism' and the doctrine of spontaneous mass action, his dictum that class consciousness has to be brought upon the proletariat 'from without', anticipate the later factual transformation of the proletariat from the subject to an object of the revolutionary process.[19]

Soviet Marxism, with its dictatorship of the 'political, economic and military bureaucracy', is not equated with a programme for genuine socialist development.

In *Dämmerung* Horkheimer also offered an assessment of the situation of those who constitute a crucial element in determining 'the future of mankind'. This is developed in a short essay called 'The powerlessness of the German working class'.[20] In this paper Horkheimer argued that there is a schism among the workers which undermines their capacity to act effectively.

There is today a gulf between those regularly employed and those working only by exception [occasional, part-time work] or rather those totally unemployed ... as formerly between the whole working classes and the Lumpenproletariat. ... Work and destitution [*Elend*] become separated ... and are distributed amongst different carriers. ... This does not mean that all goes well for those working ... the misery of those working remains ... as the condition and foundation of this society ... but the type of active worker is no longer characteristic of those who are most in need of change. Rather [the need for change] unites a certain lower strata of the working class, a part of the Proletariat. ... Those who have a most immediate and urgent interest in revolution, the unemployed, do not possess, as did the Proletariat of pre-war days, the capability for training and organization, class consciousness and reliability of those who are habitually incorporated into the capitalist process.'[21]

Horkheimer explained the growing division in the ranks of the working class in terms of developments within the capitalist economy. The dynamic process of economic concentration and centralization, generating continuous investment in labour-saving technology, is held to have produced mass unemployment. The lives of the employed – who at least have jobs, a basic income and a little security – are contrasted sharply with those who directly face the 'horrors' of unemployment. The effect of this is a fragmentation of the interests of the labour movement. Those who have jobs come to fear the miseries of the unemployed, the loss of a home and perhaps worse. Given the current conditions of their lives, the struggle for socialism appears full of very uncertain risks, dangers and possibly even death. For the unemployed all is already lost. They are more willing to join the revolutionary movement. However, they lack adequate theories and organization. 'It is in the "nature" of the capitalist process of production to separate interest in socialism from the necessary human qualities to bring it about.'[22]

This division, Horkheimer maintained, created the basic constituencies for the SPD and the KPD; it was reflected in each party's organization and programme. The SPD supported policies that sought to stabilize the status quo. Its strategy was defensive, because it was preoccupied with security and the protection of the jobs of the employed.

The reformist wing of the workers movement has lost in contrast to Communism the knowledge of the impossibility of an effective improvement of human affairs on a capitalist base. It has lost all elements of theory, its leadership is the exact replica of its most opinionated [*sichersten*] members: many attempt by any means to maintain themselves in their positions by sacrificing their most elementary loyalties; the fear of losing their jobs becomes progressively the only criterion of their action.[23]

The theoretical framework of the SPD leadership was underpinned by both pragmatism and positivism. The former shaped their day-to-day attitude. Their criterion of success, Horkheimer contended, was what works in the here and now. The latter shaped their understanding of the limits of knowledge and theory. They fetishized the 'facts' immediately given in observation. Their realm

of operation was the existing state of affairs. Their programme had
little relation to Marxism.

The KPD was not criticized as harshly. But Horkheimer saw in
'the party' an ever increasing tendency towards dogmatism and
inflexible responses to political circumstances.

In the mental [*geistigem*] sphere the impatience of the unemployed is
expressed in the mere repetition of the slogans of the Communist Party.
The principles . . . are seized undialectically. Political praxis thus lacks the
exploitation of all given possibilities and frequently exhausts itself in
unsuccessful commands and moral exhortation [*Zurechtweisung*] of the
disobedient and disloyal.[24]

Given the 'Stalinization' of the KPD and Horkheimer's conception
of socialism, it is clear that he could not support its endeavours as a
member. His dilemma – a dilemma shared by many left-wing intellectuals of the time – was almost complete. Even Grossmann, whose
general political sympathies were different from Horkheimer's,
was critical of the KPD. In a letter to Paul Mattick (1933), he
castigated the party's growing subservience to Moscow, the
incapacity of its leadership to take initiatives and its general rigidity; it had become 'a bureaucracy . . . slavishly subject to Moscow'.[25]

The transcendence of the gap and the tension between parties,
and the superseding of the theoretical limitations of both,
depended, Horkheimer argued, on the overcoming of the conditions that divided the working class. What could be done to aid this
process? How could a theorist intervene? Until the late 1930s
Horkheimer still felt that the thought of critical intellectuals could
be a stimulating, active factor in the development of political
struggles. Critical theory could help to promote a 'self-conscious
and organized working class' by fostering a debate between
theoreticians, the advanced elements of the class, and those in
need of greater awareness about social contradictions. This
debate, he held, must unfold as a process of interaction in which
growing consciousness develops into a liberating and practical
force.[26] However, already in *Dämmerung*, his writings reflected a
pessimism about the success of any such intervention. The 'night of
humanity' was threatening.

Adorno was in general agreement with Horkheimer's analysis.
In a letter to Lowenthal written in 1934, he wrote,

I have read the book *Dämmerung* several times with the utmost attention and have an extraordinary impression of it. I already knew most of the pieces; nonetheless, in this form everything appears entirely different. . . . As far as my position is concerned, I believe I can almost completely identify with it – so completely that it is difficult for me to point to differences. . . .[27]

In an essay published in 1932 Adorno spoke of the scars left by alienation on the class consciousness of the proletariat.[28] Like Horkheimer, he was deeply concerned with what hinders people 'coming to consciousness of themselves as subjects', capable of spontaneity and positive action. He was, moreover, antagonistic to aspects of the programmes of both the SPD and KPD. In particular, he was critical of all those in the SPD who thought socialism to be inevitable. He was scathing of all fatalistic thinking. He found the KPD's version of such thinking, incorporated in its doctrine of social fascism, even more pernicious.

Cured of the Social-Democratic belief in cultural progress and confronted with growing barbarism, they [the orthodox party members] are under constant temptation to advocate the latter in the interests of the 'objective tendency', and, in an act of desperation, to await salvation from their mortal enemy who, as the 'antithesis', is supposed in blind and mysterious fashion to help prepare the good end.[29]

The 'good life', Adorno was convinced, was not born of such politics. A reading of Erich Fromm's early works suggest a similar perspective.

Marcuse's views of the SPD often appear as critical as Horkheimer's. In early essays, for example 'The affirmative character of culture' (1937), he accused Kautsky of a politics of culture which 'can mean nothing other than winning the masses to the social order that is affirmed by the "entire culture" '.[30] Marcuse's participation in a soldiers' council in Berlin after the first world war would have also made him sympathetic to a conception of socialism radically different from that propagated by the SPD, which he left after brief membership in 1919. It would have also made him critical of the centralism and bureaucratism of the KPD and Comintern. His work is, of course, famous for his defence of a socialism that is radically democratic and libertarian.[31] Concerned to recapture the 'seminal achievements of the . . . "councils" (soviets, *Räte*) as organizations of self-determination, self-government (or rather preparation for self-government)', Marcuse has defended throughout his life the call for direct democracy in the polity, work-place and in the cultural sphere. However, a qualification is added: 'the theory and strategy of the councils . . . must not succumb to the fetishism of "below"'.[32] The expression of the will of the people need not always be progressive. A radically democratic society requires independent critical thinking. Auschwitz and Siberia were a warning against any naive belief in human capabilities and progress.

Capitalism and the authoritarian state

From the early 1930s, but particularly after emigration, several of the Institute's members sought to understand in much greater detail the causes of the major events of the inter-war years. Their early reflections and opinions were often altered in the light of research and debate. One of their central foci was the changing relation between technique, the economy and the state in Germany, and in other Western capitalist societies.

Writing in 1939, Horkheimer argued that 'he who does not wish to speak of capitalism should be silent about fascism'.[33] Most of the members of the Institute agreed that 'the turn from the liberalist to the total-authoritarian state occurs within the framework of a single social order'.[34] The breakdown of liberal capitalism was thought to have produced the conditions that made this possible. The causes of authoritarianism were closely connected to the inner dynamics of capitalist development. But how exactly they were connected was a source of major controversy in the Institute. The debate turned, to a large extent, on different analyses of the development of capitalism and capitalism's changing relation to the polity.

Those who participated in the discussions divided into two camps. On the one side there were those who maintained that authoritarianism and the fascist state represented a political form suitable to, compatible with and necessary for the conditions created by advanced oligopolistic and monopolistic capitalism.*

* The concept of 'monopoly' or 'monopoly capitalism' refers to a market situation which is open to manipulation by either a small number of companies (national and/or international) or, at the system's limit, by one or two companies. It marks the tendency towards the progressive elimination of the market and of competition. The concept refers less to the market shares, sales, profit, return on capital, etc. a given company or companies can acquire. Rather, it denotes the capacity of these enterprises to control and manipulate prices. No matter how many companies operate in a particular market, a monopoly exists if they are able to fix prices.

Neumann, Marcuse, Gurland and Kirchheimer supported this view in theoretical and empirical analyses of past and contemporary political, legal and economic institutions. Neumann's classic study, *Behemoth*, provided the most important and most detailed defence of this position.

On the other side were Horkheimer, Adorno and Pollock. Their views, some of which Kirchheimer accepted, implied that while the development of competitive into monopoly capitalism was a crucial condition for the advancement of the authoritarian state, the social order that resulted could not simply be referred to as monopoly capitalism (although occasionally Horkheimer and Adorno continued to use the term). It had qualities which were new and distinct. Adorno frequently referred to a 'post-competitive capitalism' or 'post-market' society.[35] He wrote of capitalism's increasingly 'integrative trend' and of the domination of the political apparatus in the interest of planned capital accumulation.[36] Horkheimer asserted the importance of similar concepts.[37] He contended that 'the leaders of industry, administration, propaganda, and the military have become identical with the state in that they lay down the plan of the national economy as the entrepreneur before them laid down policy for his factory'.[38] But neither Horkheimer nor Adorno developed these concepts in any detail. The views they expressed were often derived from Pollock who characterized the developing order as a form of 'state-capitalism'. While Pollock's account did not exhaust the views of the other two men, his analysis was influential. In many respects, it was left to him to develop this second position. The differences between the two sides are worth examining at some length.

On Neumann's account, the process of economic concentration and centralization, to which every capitalist economy is subject, created an increasingly interdependent, interconnected and interlocked economic system.[39] In a joint study Gurland, Kirchheimer and Neumann argued that this process had advanced in Germany more than in any other country.

What has distinguished Germany's economy from that of all other countries is the depth and breadth of the integration of her industrial combinations. Vertical combines very early began to dominate the heavy industries. . . . Horizontal associations of manufacturers . . . crisscrossed the territories of the German Empire of the later Republic with a network of organizations for the control of the domestic and, increasingly, of the foreign markets.[40]

Through a number of case studies, for example of the mining industry, they sought to demonstrate the way in which these combines and associations (especially cartels) furthered the interests of monopolies. They described, again and again, an economic situation characterized by a very high degree of concentration and centralized control. 'In no other country', Gurland wrote, 'was there such an intimate intertwining of production units both within the individual industries and across the boundaries of the individual trades.'[41] As a result, every capitalist enterprise became dependent upon other enterprises; while the economic fortunes of every industry became interlocked with the changes and fates of all other industries.

This economic order had little flexibility and was vulnerable to economic fluctuations. The network of interdependencies among economic units ensured, at best, a delicate economic equilibrium. Any disturbance or disruption to economic life could potentially ramify throughout the system. 'There is no bankruptcy', as Gurland put it, 'that would not implicate numerous apparently sound enterprises. . . . To prevent social disturbances from generating under this hyper-sensitivity of the economic apparatus, state interventionism is called for at an early stage.'[42] The economic and political stability of the monopolistic order required quick responses to potentially threatening situations. The expansion of the 'interventionist machinery' was, therefore, necessary and unavoidable. The increasingly radical effects of endogenous changes within the system (for example higher rates of unemployment and inflation at the troughs and peaks of the political–business cycle) and/or the impact of exogenous factors (the creation of shortages of raw materials as a result of international political events, for instance) had to be carefully managed. The situation was compounded by the involvement of finance capital. As the level of industrialization rises, invested money becomes increasingly fixed capital. Technological change (and rearmament) involved new construction costs on an ever larger scale. Huge investments multiplied risks and demands for the state to safeguard these, both in production and in the market.

The Neumann–Gurland analysis adhered to Marx's view that the accumulation process is inherently unstable and generates concentration and centralization. Anticipating the work of Paul Baran and Paul Sweezy, they contended that the replacement of competitive by monopoly capitalism was inevitable and would exacerbate a tendency to stagnation.[43] The great capitalist post-first-world-war crisis had left many economies in disarray. Germany, following defeat, had been particularly hard hit. More than any other capitalist country, it had failed to sustain an economic recovery. As Gurland argued,

The capitalist automatism [its automatic adjustment mechanisms, for example the business cycle] no longer operated to overcome stagnation and unemployment. Too many commodities were facing too small a buying capacity. Monopolistic price-pegging prevented the aggregate value of commodities from being expressed in less money-units. Creation of additional buying capacity (through investments, more employment, higher wages and increasing productive demand) encountered the resistance of 'vested interests' as expressed in invested capital's claim to at least 'normal' return on capital outlay. Either the investors', the creditors', or the commodity-owners' claim for just return was to be turned aside, or the crisis was to go on and on.[44]

The crisis went on: 'the monopolies paralysed the automatism of capitalist development'.

In *Behemoth*, Neumann sought to pursue the implications of this position and to demonstrate that

in a monopolistic system profits cannot be made and retained without totalitarian political power, and that [this] is the distinctive feature of National Socialism. If totalitarian political power had not abolished freedom of contract, the cartel system would have broken down. If the labour market were not controlled by authoritarian means, the monopolistic system would be endangered; if raw material supply, price control, and rationalization agencies, if credit and exchange-control offices were in the hands of forces hostile to monopolies, the profit system would break down. The system has become so fully monopolized that it must by nature be hypersensitive to cyclical changes, and such disturbances must be avoided. . . . In short, democracy would endanger the fully monopolized system. It is the essence of totalitarianism to stabilize and fortify it.[45]

Neumann, Gurland and Kirchheimer agreed with Marcuse when he wrote, 'the total-authoritarian state brings with it the organization and theory of society that correspond to the monopolistic stage of capitalism'.[46] National Socialism and monopoly capital forged, they contended, a new structure of political compromise.[47] Similar interests ensured the interdependence of the Nazi party and big business. 'National Socialism pursues glory and the stabilization of its rule, and industry, the full utilization of its capacity and the conquests of foreign markets.'[48]

The interests of the Nazi party (articulated in the name of the 'national interest') coincided with capitalist monopolies' interest in expansion. The 'government' was interested in maximum efficiency and maximum production: it was concerned to secure and regulate a continuous supply of the necessary resources to reproduce and solidify its control. Capitalist enterprise was also interested, of course, in its reproduction and security. The vertical and/or horizontal expansion of the enterprise, whether at home or abroad, was the condition for the improvement of its economic position. In general, capitalist competition favours the most efficient: it conditions mechanization and rationalization. The enterprises with the lowest costs of production, *ceteris paribus*, can force a less effective firm out of business. Increased efficiency, through increased technological power, tends to ever larger units of production and to the concentration of ownership and economic control. In a monopolistic system concern with efficiency diminishes as concern for the protection of the existing order increases. The improvement of a company's economic position – its profitability – in this situation, depends on further exploitation of existing markets and, more importantly, on the development of new markets. Expansion guarantees the realization of profit and profit stimulates expansion.[49]

Apart from supporting the interests of monopolies, the Nazi party also represented the traditional claim for economic security shared by many different groups – including small businessmen. The average businessman and shopkeeper resented and often protested against monopolies profiting, as they did, from prosperity as well as from crisis. But in opposing big business they 'did not mean to vindicate prohibition of trusts, combines and cartels; but merely loathed becoming their victim instead of participating in their rise'.[50] Along with monopoly capitalists, they feared the discontent of the masses. Communism and socialism were always a threat to their 'hard-won' gains. The state, in these circumstances and in the hands of the Nazi party, had a choice: should it reform or abolish the monopolies for the sake of the small businessman and others with similar interests, or strengthen them and aid the organization of all business activities?[51] The Nazis' position was clear. They appear to have had little difficulty in making a 'choice'.

In a capitalist economy, economic security can only be maintained with growth. Through expansion severe crises can be avoided. The party, therefore, came to stand for expansion first. This did not mean, Neumann and Gurland stressed, that National Socialism was the sole creation, and a subservient tool, of big business.[52] Both authors talked about the formation of fascism from a conjuncture of the interests of big business (including big agrarians), the party, the bureaucracy and the military. Industrial capitalists did not crave totalitarian militarism. But, as Neumann put it, 'with regard to imperialistic expansion, industry and party have identical aims'. With rearmament the common interests of the monopolies and the party were clarified and reinforced.[53] Once rearmament began, there was no question of curtailing it, for it stabilized the economy. The aggressive and expansionist spirit of German industry became the motivating force of the system. The best name Neumann could find to describe this situation was 'totalitarian monopoly capitalism'. For the German economy had two broad and striking characteristics: it was a monopolistic economy and a command economy. It was 'a private capitalist economy, regimented by the totalitarian state'.[54]

In agreement with Neumann and Gurland, Pollock explained the genesis of monopoly capitalism in terms of the economy's inherent tendency toward concentration and centralization.[55] Like the others, he maintained that the crisis growth pattern of liberal capitalism had not been destroyed under the system of monopolies. Increasing inflation and unemployment, unco-ordinated policies of nation-states – the result of unevenness and disproportionality in national and international economic systems – produced economic problems and political unrest of ever greater severity. These necessitated, and could only be resolved by, massive state intervention. In a number of his earliest essays Pollock sought to document this state of affairs.[56]

But the initial patterns of state intervention, he argued, only exacerbated these trends. State support and subsidization of a highly interlocked economy increased the capacity of large enterprises to resist pressures for price decreases and take advantage of price increases: massive enterprises could rely on state support should it be needed and government manipulation of demand.

Today, many enterprises in industry and banking have grown so gigantically, that no state power, no matter how liberally it behaves [that is within the terms of reference of *laissez-faire* economics], can stand by and witness their downfall. Above a certain size of capital, the enterprise may continue to claim the profit(s) for itself, but the risk is unrolled [passed on] to the mass of tax-payers, since its collapse would bring about the most severe consequences - both for the body economic and political situation.[57]

While Pollock recognized that throughout past decades and centuries the state had intervened to support enterprises, he contended that the scale of such intervention was now quite different. For example, he argued, 'every endangered large bank has to be upheld by means of state aid . . . while in former times measures of this kind were an exception'. The state increasingly guaranteed capitalism. In his view, monopolies took full advantage of this situation.[58]

Pollock analysed German capitalism in terms which appear to be similar to Neumann *et al*. They agreed that

Concentration of economic activity in giant enterprises, with its consequences of rigid prices, self-financing and ever growing concentration, government control of the credit system and foreign trade, quasi-monopoly positions of trade unions with ensuing rigidity of the labour market, large-scale unemployment of labour and capital and enormous government expenses to care for the unemployed, are as many symptoms of the decline of the market system.[59]

They all recognized also that monopolistic organizations no longer operated as 'disturbing intruders'. The growing intervention of the state in the economy, and of monopolies in the state, provided more and more legal backing for restricted competition and control of the market.[60] (Gradually, more or less voluntary entrepreneurial associations, like the cartels, became compulsory.)[61] But Pollock, contrary to Neumann and co., called the developing order 'state-capitalism'. State-capitalism, he argued, was better than any other term to describe four properties of the new system:

1   That the new order is the successor of private capitalism,
2   that the state assumes important functions of the private capitalist,
3   that capitalist institutions like the sale of labour, or profits, still play a significant role, and
4   that it is not socialism.[62]

He distinguished between two ideal-types of state-capitalism: the 'totalitarian' and the 'democratic'. Although his studies were concentrated on the former, he thought many of his findings and conclusions to be relevant to the latter.

Under the impact of National Socialism there had been a qualitative shift in the nature of political and economic organization. In pre-Nazi Germany interference with the market made it more and more unworkable but no provisions were foreseen to eliminate disturbances. In Nazi Germany, on the other hand, there had been, in Pollock's view, a fundamental attempt to eradicate economic disruption and crisis. All the basic principles of organization changed. The basic institutions of capitalism were transformed: 'interference of the state with the structure of the old economic order has by its sheer totality and intensity "turned quantity into quality", transformed monopoly capitalism into state-capitalism'.[63] Above all, Pollock noted the following trends. First, the market, as an indirect control of demand and supply, is superseded by direct state planning. A goal is set for all economic activities and a system of priorities and quotas established to guarantee its execution. Second, prices, as the medium for the management of scarcity, lose their function. They become a 'closely controlled tool'. Third, there is a subordination of the individual's interest in profit to the general plan. Profit still plays a role as an incentive (for efficient investment and management) and as an instrument for social control. The capitalist is increasingly reduced to a rentier (although most of capital remains in private ownership). Fourth, the 'occult entrepreneurial art of guessing what the future market demand will be' is replaced by a comprehensive technical rationality (through the introduction of, for example, modern statistical methods, regular reports of changes in stocks, production and plant, rationalization of technical and administrative processes, systematic training of workers, etc.). Fifth, the whole system is co-ordinated by a powerful bureaucracy and the senior management of the largest enterprises. All these developments were thought to be operative in democratic forms of state-capitalism; but Pollock did not know what political forms they would eventually generate. He was sure, however, about the nature of the regimes under fascist control:

Under a totalitarian form of state capitalism the state is the power instrument of a new ruling group, which has resulted from the merger of the most powerful vested interests, the top ranking personnel in industrial and business management, the higher strata of the state bureaucracy (including the military) and the leading figures of the victorious party's bureaucracy. Everybody who does not belong to this group is a mere object of domination.[64]

The success of the totalitarian state was predicated on the destruction of national and international working-class movements, through internal repression, brutal discipline and war. Writing in the early 1940s, Pollock seemed in no doubt that National Socialism had accomplished this. The new system was, in his view, a new order. He claimed to be describing a new stage of economic and political development, and not just a wartime economy. Such a system, 'could solve the major economic problems that had forced the collapse of liberal capitalism'. There was no logically necessary reason why state-capitalism, whether it be totalitarian or democratic, would fail. In short, it could contain contradictions and conflict. 'The primacy of politics over economics, so much disputed under democracy, is clearly established.'[65]

Pollock's work implied that the contradictions of capitalism could be resolved by political forms other than socialism. Hitherto most Marxists, including Horkheimer and Adorno, had not believed it was possible for capitalism in any form to sustain a rise in social product, to maintain fairly full employment, co-ordinate productive units, expand plant and plant capacity, and reproduce management and labour on a level commensurate with technical progress. With the advance of economic concentration and centralization, the growth of centralized administration, etc., this now seemed possible. State-capitalism could not be expected to break down as a result of internal contradictions.[66] This did not mean, however, that there were no limitations to the system's development. Pollock posited a number of natural and non-economic constraints. These included an adequate supply of raw material, plant and labour at all skill levels, struggles within and between the country's elites, and conflicting interests within the ruling class inhibiting the creation and execution of a general plan. But for all those who had expectations about economic breakdown and/or the necessity of socialism, these constraints did not militate against the thrust of Pollock's main conclusion. It was taken seriously by Horkheimer and Adorno, and became a contributing factor to their post-1940 political pessimism.

These views were strongly contested by Neumann in *Behemoth*. He rejected Pollock's conclusion. 'The present writer does not accept this profoundly pessimistic view. He believes that the antagonisms of capitalism are operating [even] in Germany on a higher and, therefore, a more dangerous level.'[67] On Neumann's account the state did not have complete control over the economy.

Nor was control ever the objective of the state (in any capitalist society), or of the Nazi leadership, in particular. Consequently, the economy's highly rigid structure ensured its continued susceptibility to severe crisis produced by unevenness in growth, disproportionality between sectors and fluctuations in the world market. German capitalism had not ceased to exist. Neumann's position did not imply a belief in the inevitable collapse of monopoly capitalism. 'The flaws and breaks in the system and even the military defeat of Germany will not lead to an automatic collapse of the regime. It can only be overthrown by conscious political action of the oppressed masses, which will utilize the breaks in the system.'[68] Although he maintained that 'there exists objectively a profound antagonism between the two classes' he was quick to add, 'whether and when it will explode we do not know'.[69]

The cracks in the system leading to conflict arose, Neumann argued, from the antagonism between the magical character of propaganda (with its promise of 'strength through joy') and the labourers' actual status and experience. Workers live in a world which is highly rationalized and depersonalized, and where they are often reduced to being mere adjuncts to the means of production.[70] These conditions pervade working-class life. The gap between

pseudo-socialist ideology and the naked facts of authoritarian monopoly capitalism must deepen. The anti-capitalist [and anti-state] propagandas contain inner dynamics, which for a time can be halted by various devices but which cannot be permanently stopped.... [thereby] the regime unwittingly furthers genuine socialist trends.[71]

The gap between promise and actuality was further highlighted by the extensive dislocation and suffering produced by the clashes between the shock troops and the masses in industry and in the army. National socialism *required* complete authoritarianism for the maintenance of a stable disequilibrium. The contradictions of the system were also manifested, with particular acuteness, in the relationship between the engineer – by whom Neumann understood all technicians, foremen and skilled workers – and the requirements of totalitarian monopoly capitalism. 'The engineer exercises the most rational vocation and he knows what beneficent powers the productive machinery can wield. Every day sees how this machinery becomes an instrument of destruction rather than of welfare. The conflict between potentiality and actuality is . . .

taking place before his very eyes.'[72] These circumstances will mould, Neumann contended, the consciousness of the working class and, within it, especially the skilled worker.

He strongly disagreed, moreover, with the concept of state-capitalism. The very term is a '*contradictio in adjecto*'. Following (and quoting) Hilferding, he argued,

'The concept of state-capitalism cannot bear analysis from the economic point of view. Once the state has become the sole owner of the means of production it makes it impossible for a capitalist economy to function, it destroys that mechanism which keeps the very processes of economic circulation in active existence.' Such a state is therefore no longer capitalistic.[73]

Although Pollock recognized that the state was not the sole owner of the means of production, his key concept was not, Neumann asserted, a useful one. Increased state-ownership, planning, centralization and rationalization were important constituent features of the present order. But, like Gurland, Neumann argued that these developments were not incompatible with private capitalism, and owed their very rapid rate of expansion to capitalist production itself. The concept of state-capitalism was misleading on two accounts – the degree to which capitalism was 'alive and well', and the extent to which there was a state. For Neumann, 'National Socialism is – or [is] tending to become – a non-state, a chaos, a rule of lawlessness and anarchy.'[74] The state no longer existed in any traditional sense. (On this score Kirchheimer was in close agreement. He pointed to the inconsistencies and apparent incoherence of the legal structure of the Nazi regime despite its capacity for smooth functioning technical operations. The 'state' was born of political compromise – a compromise which reflected through all its structures.)[75]

Furthermore, there was a basic flaw, Neumann argued, in the methodological basis of the works of state-capitalist theorists. These theorists spoke in terms of ideal-types, or models, which tried to grasp a reality that was as yet unrealized. They admitted that Germany still had remnants of markets and price systems, but maintained that these were unimportant in light of imminent developments. Such an approach, he insisted, was illegitimate: one cannot derive, from an analysis of prevailing trends within one system, the boundaries of another social order.[76] Pollock's empirical work only pointed to trends within German capitalist development. He had produced insufficient evidence to derive a new system of 'politics without economics'.[77]

Pollock retorted that to demonstrate the maintenance of the legal institution of private property and of markets and prices was not to have shown very much. The functions of these institutions, he reasserted, had changed radically.[78] It was the controlling group who decided on the scope and direction of production; the expansion of the enterprise had to fit the general plan.

The disagreements between the two sides were never resolved. They were compounded by personal and political differences, and by Horkheimer's and Adorno's view that Neumann's Marxism was too orthodox and mechanistic.[79] But while Horkheimer and Adorno clearly sided with Pollock, a detailed reading of some of their writings suggests that they had more ambivalent views about the future development of capitalism. This is particularly clear in Horkheimer's work. A tension exists, especially in some of his most radical writings, between a belief in eventual economic collapse and progressive political change, and a more pessimistic view. For example, in '*Die Juden und Europa*' [The Jews in Europe] (1939), he maintained that 'economic collapse is deducible', although he did not see it occurring in the near future.[80] The breakdown of the totalitarian economy is seen as much less likely, as is revolution itself. In 'The authoritarian state', written in 1940, Horkheimer employed many of Pollock's concepts directly, yet an ambivalence in his assessment of capitalist development persisted. On the one hand he wrote, 'state-capitalism is, to be sure, an antagonistic, transient phenomenon. The law of its collapse is already visible: it is based on the limitation of productivity due to the existence of the bureaucracies'.[81] The fascist version of state-capitalism is 'determined by the same economic tendencies which have already destroyed the market system. . . . The eternal system of the authoritarian state . . . is no more real than the eternal harmony of the market system'.[82] The present order, he stated, in its totalitarian or democratic guise, cannot endure; changing material conditions make possible a 'leap to a classless society' – the possibility of active resistance and revolutionary praxis lives on.[83] On the other hand, these remarks are offset by comments like, 'for every conclusion stemming from the belief that history will follow a progressing line . . . there is a counter-argument which is no less valid'. The antagonisms today are 'not only more capable of producing freedom, but also less capable. Not only freedom, but also future forms of oppression are possible. . . . With state-capitalism those in power can strengthen their position even more'.[84] In Horkheimer's later works, this tension was resolved in favour of these more pessimistic views.

I think a similar formulation can be found in Adorno's writings, although it is not always so explicit. Though the main principles which underpin his view of capitalism are compatible with Pollock's position, a reading of essays like '*Gesellschaft*' [Society] (1966) and '*Spätkapitalismus oder Industriegesellschaft?*' [Late capitalism or industrial society?] (1968) suggest, as will be shown later, that while Adorno thought that class conflict and crisis can potentially be managed, he did not think they would necessarily be managed successfully.

Further differences between Horkheimer, Adorno and Pollock can be pointed to by an examination of their general approaches. While Horkheimer and Adorno agreed that fascism arose when the overall economic situation required planned organization, they sought to locate these developments themselves within a philosophy of history developed as a critique of the progressive technical rationalization of everyday life (see Chapter 5 below).

But despite these disagreements, the analysis of those on both sides shared some common ground. All agreed, for instance, that in totalitarian *and* democratic countries there had been a progressive rise in the importance of the polity. They all recognized an increase in

central control over individual decision-making;

bureaucratic deliberation over local initiative;

planning of resources over the market allocation of resources (that is, a shift in the state's pattern of intervention from market complementing to market replacing activity);

technical considerations of general efficiency and rationality over traditional single-minded concern for an individual unit's profitability.

Ideas and themes such as these are, of course, common in the history of social theory. They were often discussed in the nineteenth century. But it is in Weber's work that they were given the most prominence. It is not surprising, therefore, to find in the writings of many members of the Frankfurt school in the late 1930s and 1940s frequent references to Weber. Horkheimer and Marcuse were particularly concerned to come to terms with

Weber's contributions to social thought.[85] It has been said that the history of Frankfurt social theory from the 1930s to the 1950s and 1960s is marked by a shift in theoretical orientation away from Marx to Weber. There is some truth in this. There are both continuities and discontinuities. It is worth clarifying a number of aspects of Weber's work and the Frankfurt school's relation to it.

Rationalization: the rise of instrumental reason

Weber's concept of rationalization is extremely complex. First, it refers to the growth in mathematization of 'experience and knowledge': the shaping of all scientific practice according to the model of the natural sciences and the extension of (scientific) rationality to 'the conduct of life itself'. This in turn must be seen as part of a specific feature of the secularization of the modern world which Weber often terms the intellectualization and/or the disenchantment of the world. Secondly, the secularization of life leads to a growth of means-end rationality, whereby there is 'the methodological attainment of a definitely given and practical end by the use of an increasingly precise calculation of . . . means'.[86] The expansion of capitalism presides over the transformation of social relations to the form which approximates *Zweckrationalität*. Third, there is a growth of rationality in terms of the development of 'ethics that are systematically and unambiguously oriented to fixed goals'.[87]

The notion of rationalization used by members of the Institute mainly encompassed the first two of these aspects. Their analysis of the spread of rationalization, which adhered to a number of Weber's major tenets, was most often focused on the extension of means–end rationality, or as they most often called it, instrumental reason, or subjective reason. Horkheimer, Adorno and Marcuse, for example, agreed with Weber that the emergence of instrumental reason must be traced to ideas and modes of life which existed prior to the development of industrial capitalism; the advance of instrumental reason led to disenchantment (particularly after the Enlightenment) and to the progressive undermining of traditional world views; the Reformation and Protestantism were important for the formation of conditions necessary for capitalist development; and capitalism provided a major impetus to the further development of instrumental reason.[88] They shared Weber's view as to the probability of the continuing expansion of rationalization and bureaucratization. They also shared his pessimism as to the dangers and risks involved which Weber called the 'iron cage' of a highly bureaucratized division of labour. The extension of formal, means–end rationality to 'the conduct of life' becomes a concern as a form of domination: means becoming ends, social rules becoming reified objectifications commanding directions.

But this is where the agreement ends. Weber, on Marcuse's account, acquiesced and capitulated to the rationalized world as it appeared. In Weber's opinion this was a world which *also* made possible the development of social institutions tending toward law and justice that would free the arbitration of civil society from collective and individual substantive interests – a world regulated by technically trained officials that becomes the 'absolutely inescapable condition of our existence'. But the conception of rationalization as a process which is 'inescapable', involving inevitable expansion, masks, Marcuse wrote, a 'concept of fate' which 'generalizes the blindness of a society which reproduces itself behind the back of individuals, of a society in which the law of domination appears as objective technological law'.[89]

For the Frankfurt school theorists, the rise of instrumental reason, the rationalization of the world, is not *per se* to blame for the 'chaotic, frightening and evil aspects of technological civilization'. Rather, it is the mode in which the process of rationalization is itself organized that accounts for the 'irrationality of this rationalization'. In advanced capitalist societies, economic anarchy is interwoven with rationalization and technology. It is the organization of production as capitalist production which, as the members of the Institute wrote in 1956, 'threatens the spirit and today even the material survival of mankind, and not technological progress itself'.[90]

Some of the arguments employed to sustain this view are developed most succinctly by Marcuse in his essay, 'Some social implications of modern technology' (1941). Horkheimer and Adorno developed a parallel position in *Dialectic of Enlightenment*. Within these works the present order is conceptualized in terms of what one might call the 'rule of equivalence'. This is understood in two ways. First, it is explicated within the framework of Marx's analysis of capitalist commodity production – which makes 'the dissimilar comparable'. Second, it is comprehended by examining the ways in which the 'rise' of formal, means–end rationality undermines the status of critical, substantive rationality – the rationality of values, ends and possible attitudes towards life. Critical reason and autonomous thinking are being eroded as a result of both the 'bracketing of human beings within commodity production' and 'the fall of a technological veil'. Following Marcuse, the explanation for these developments can be summarized as follows.[91]

Sixteenth and seventeenth century thought nurtured the principle of individualism, the pursuit of rational self-interest. The philosophies which articulated the principle were committed to the view that the individual is rational, capable of independent thinking. The fulfilment of this individuality was held to be dependent upon certain social and economic conditions; conditions in which the individual would be free to work and think in a setting of his or her choice. Free competition in the market and liberalism in the polity were thought to be sufficient guarantees of the individual's rights. Over time, however, the course of commodity production undermined the economic basis on which freedom of the individual was built. Competitiveness and the autonomy of the individual economic subject was revealed as a facade of capitalist society. Under the impact of 'the institutions, devices and organizations of industry', the notion of individual achievement was transformed into labour productivity figures. The individual's performance became 'motivated, guided and measured by standards external to him, standards pertaining to predetermined tasks and functions'.[92] Conditioned by the necessities and exigencies of capital accumulation, the spheres governed by instrumental reason or, as Marcuse called it, technological rationality, expanded, creating a common framework of experience for all occupations. Compliance and the subordination of thought to pre-given goals and standards was now required of 'all those who wish to survive'. Furthermore, as standardized techniques advanced and the laws and mechanisms of technological rationality expanded over the whole of society, they developed, as Marcuse put it, 'a set of truth values which hold good for the functioning of the apparatus – and for that alone'.[93] Propositions concerning production, effective organization, the rules of the game, business methods, use of science and technique, are judged true or false according to whether or not the 'means' to which they refer are suitable or applicable (for an end which remains, of course, unquestioned).

These developments tend to one general pattern:

the rationalization and standardization of production and consumption;
the mechanization of labour;
the development of mass transportation and communication;
the extension of training; and
the dissemination of knowledge about the execution of jobs.[94]

All these factors appear to facilitate the 'exchangeability of function'. But the private organization of technology counteracts this trend. Under these circumstances, specialization atomizes the masses. The continued extension of divisions within the division of labour leads to the fragmentation of tasks. As tasks become increasingly mechanized, there are fewer and fewer chances for mental and reflective labour. Work experiences are increasingly distinctive and set apart from each other. Knowledge of the total work process is, as a consequence, hard to come by and rarely available, particularly for those on the shop floor. The majority of occupations, despite the possibility of a greater exchange of functions, tend to become atomized, isolated units, which *seem* to require for their cohesion 'co-ordination and management from above'. With the development of the *capitalist* division of labour, knowledge of the whole work process, control and executive functions are ever more absent from daily work situations. Centralized control mechanisms and private and public bureaucracies then appear as agencies which are necessary for, and guarantee, 'a rational course and order'.

The private and public bureaucracy thus emerges on an apparently objective and impersonal ground, provided by the rational specialization of functions. . . . For, the more the individual functions are divided, fixated and synchronized according to objective and impersonal patterns, the less reasonable it is for the individual to withdraw or withstand. 'The material fate of the masses becomes increasingly dependent upon the continuous and correct functioning of the increasingly bureaucratic order of private capitalist organizations.' The objective and impersonal character of technological rationality bestows upon the bureaucratic groups the universal dignity of reason. The rationality embodied in the giant enterprises makes it appear as if men, in obeying them, obey the dictum of an objective rationality. The private bureaucracy fosters a delusive harmony between the special and the common interest. Private power relationships appear not only as relationships between objective things but also as the rule of rationality itself.[95]

As a result, the conditions are created for a decline in the susceptibility of society to critical thinking.[96]

The individual has to adapt, follow orders, pull levers and 'be ready to perform ever different things which are ever the same'. The term 'reason' becomes synonymous with the process of co-ordinating means to given ends, or else it appears as a meaningless word. In societies like the present, where instrumental reason is dominant, 'thinking objectifies itself', Horkheimer and Adorno wrote, 'to become an automatic, self-activating process; an impersonation of the machine that it produces itself so that ultimately the machine can replace it'.[97] The values of instrumental reason are accorded a privileged status since they are embodied in the concept of rationality itself. The confounding of calculatory with rational thinking implies that whatever cannot be reduced to numbers is illusion or metaphysics.[98] The dissimilar is recognized and evaluated only as a difference in quantity or efficiency. The individual changes from a 'unit of resistance and autonomy' to one of 'ductility and adjustment'. But the individual's lack of freedom is not usually experienced as a lack of freedom. It is not experienced as the work of some outside hostile force. Rather, liberty is relinquished to the 'dictum of reason itself'. Subjective reason is pursued and put to 'profitable' use.

A number of factors have, however, conjoined to bring about the present general impotency of critical thought. The expansion of capitalism and technological rationality, while massively increasing coercive power, has, at one and the same time, 'transformed numerous modes of external compulsion and authority into modes of self-discipline and self-control'. All men and women who seek the maintenance of their own lives have to act rationally; that is, they have to act 'according to the standards which insure the functioning of the apparatus'.[99] This introversion of authority reinforces and sustains modes of behaviour that are adaptive, passive and acquiescent. Needless to say, the mechanisms of social control are strengthened.

The decline of critical thought is also furthered by the incorporation of opposition. Opposition has been rendered increasingly ineffective because the representatives of the 'forces of negativity' – although they have not lost the 'title of opposition' – have all too often become mimics of the dominant apparatus. This has been the fate of the labour movement in many countries. Its organizations have all too often been transformed into mass organizations and mass parties with a highly bureaucratized leadership structure.[100]

The process of the incorporation of opposition was analysed in much greater detail by Kirchheimer in terms of the decline of 'issue parties' and 'oppositions of principle'. In a number of essays published in the 1950s and 1960s, he was particularly concerned to show how many former class-oriented Marxist parties in Europe were being transformed into 'catch-all parties' with a concomitant dilution of their political concerns.[101] This change, he found, involves five factors: an interest in short-term political gains and a decline in ideological struggle; a strengthening of leadership, and of the leadership's identification with the entire social system (leaders speak more and more about the national interest and less and less about particular party goals); a decrease in importance of the individual party member; an increase in concern with the general voter and a decline in concern with a specific social class or denominational clientele; a gain in access to financial groups which enhance the party's chances of access to the media etc.[102] These changes follow, Kirchheimer argued, from the weakening of the antagonism between the possessor and executor classes (the latter comprise all those who 'occupy positions, whether blue collar or white collar, where a job is narrowly circumscribed by strict hierarchical subordination and/or restriction to a single phase of a larger project'). This itself, he maintained, was a consequence of the general process of rationalization, the spread of mass culture and consumer orientations – which sustain an illusion of freedom and choice – and the withdrawal of citizens into 'private' life.[103]

Images of society and the prospects of revolutionary change

Many of the themes discussed above were reiterated by Adorno, Horkheimer and Marcuse in their writings from the 1950s onwards. During this period only Marcuse produced a lengthy analysis of the capitalist economy and of its changing relation to the polity. While Adorno and Horkheimer wrote a number of essays on this topic, they did not produce detailed studies.

Unlike many orthodox Marxists who argue that class antagonisms and crises lead to breakdown and revolutionary transformation, Adorno continued to maintain, in his late writings, that crises can potentially be contained and the effects of class conflict managed. While the notion of relations of production still demarcates relations of domination, constraint and inequity, it reflects, less and less, active, self-conscious relations of struggle. In an essay written in 1942, Adorno argued that, at best, the unity of classes can be stipulated negatively; that is, their unity is constituted by virtue of their formal relation to one another and their respective oppositional functions. While in liberal capitalism social classes had a certain real, positive unity – they expressed particular inter- ests and objectives – in advanced capitalism no such unity exists.[104] As a result of the continued extension of the division of labour and the decline in the role of the market – although political and man- ipulative processes become more visible – 'the essence of class society' becomes less obvious.[105] The experience of class diminishes as tasks and knowledge are fragmented. Domination becomes ever more impersonal. People become means to the fulfilment of purposes which appear to have an existence of their own. Increasingly, they become mere functionaries of planned cap- ital accumulation, as society is co-ordinated by powerful organiza- tions and administrations which are ever more self-sufficient but oriented single-mindedly towards production. The particular pat- tern of social relations which conditions these processes – the capitalist relations of production – is fetishized. Social relations become less comprehensible: conflict centres increasingly on mar- ginal issues which do not test the foundation of society. Thus, the general dominates the particular – the capitalist mode of produc- tion overwhelms the individual. Men and women are 'reduced to agents and bearers of exchange value'.[106]

But behind this process, Adorno constantly emphasized, lies 'the domination of men over men. This remains the basic fact'. In 'Society' (1966), he insisted that despite the extraordinary pres- sures on the individual, many of which are outlined in the following chapters, class struggle persists. In this essay he stressed – in con- tradistinction to some of his other writings of the 1960s – that 'in the institution of exchange there is created and reproduced that antagonism which could at any time bring organized society to ultimate catastrophe and destroy it'.[107] Adorno noted that the most recent empirical sociological investigations reveal that how- ever weak class consciousness is, it nonetheless exists. Further- more, he added, if one brackets class consciousness, the objective differences between classes continue to grow. With the increase in the concentration of capital there is increasing impoverishment of the working class.[108] The integration of the masses into society is incomplete and the objective basis for change ever larger.

Yet in the same essay Adorno also wrote that the

adaption of men to social relationships and processes which constitutes history . . . has left its mark on them such that the very possibility of breaking free without terrible instinctual conflicts – even breaking free mentally – has come to seem a fable and a distant one. Men have come to be – triumph of integration! – identified in their innermost behaviour patterns with their fate in modern society.[109]

The possibility of transcending the existing order is, he thought 'threatened with suffocation' – for these are not the conditions on which revolutions are made. Adorno's analysis of these phenomena sought to expose the particular social basis of seemingly anonymous domination. Through his work he hoped to contribute to the development of self-consciousness. 'Such awareness, without any preconceptions as to where it might lead, would', he hoped, 'be the first condition for an ultimate break in society's omnipotence.'[110] But it would only be a first condition. What the other conditions are, however, he did not say.

It should be noted that Adorno did not believe he had an adequate theory of advanced capitalist society. Because of the growing influence of the polity on economic life, the weakening of the market and the massive increase in productive power – the result of technical and industrial progress – he regarded Marx's work, in particular the theory of value, the theory of class consciousness, and the general theory of capitalist development, as inadequate.[111] Although he drew on aspects of the thought of Marx, Weber and Pollock in an attempt to offer an alternative account, he did not offer, he readily admitted, a systematic new theory.

Horkheimer was in a similar position, though the influence of Pollock seems more marked on his writings. He continued to maintain that today the productive process – a process oriented toward profit and growth – 'serves itself instead of men'.[112] He stressed, as he had done earlier, that the fault does not lie in machines and technique. Like Adorno, he held that while the teachings of Marx and Engels 'are still indispensable for understanding the dynamics of society', they can 'no longer explain the domestic development and foreign relations of nations'.[113] The growth of large-scale technology, the spread of commerce, the advance of communication, the expansion of population, the struggle between power-blocks all contribute, he argued, to the growth of organization and central control. The trends point to 'a rationalized, automated, totally managed world'.[114] Fearful of those 'who control the main economic and political levers of social power' and the past and future perversion of socialism in Eastern Europe, Horkheimer saw fewer and fewer reasons for hope, and even fewer for radical political change. In an age which tends 'to eliminate every vestige of even a relative autonomy for the individual', all that was left was 'the yearning for the wholly other' (*die Sehnsucht nach dem ganz Anderen*).[115] For Horkheimer, writing in 1968, the urgent task was 'to protect, preserve, and where possible, extend the limited and ephemeral freedom of the individual'. For it was here that the hope for the 'wholly other' could be preserved.[116]

Of all the members of the Frankfurt school, Marcuse's lifelong relation to his early work and political ambitions is perhaps the most consistent. There are stronger continuities in his political thinking than there are in the political thought of Horkheimer and Adorno. Marcuse was one of the few who sought to create anew a relation between theory and practice in the post-war years. It was his direct concern with developing a critique of capitalism and with the theory and politics of transition that made him a central intellectual figure in the 1960s and early 1970s. His political tract, *One Dimensional Man*, vacillated, on his own account, between two contradictory hypotheses: '(1) that advanced industrial society is capable of containing qualitative change for the foreseeable future; (2) that forces and tendencies exist which may break this containment and explode the society.'[117] In agreement with Horkheimer and Adorno, he saw the first tendency as dominant. But he sought to explore, particularly in texts like *Five Lectures* and *Counterrevolution and Revolt*, the second in greater detail than the other two men did.

Marcuse's analysis began by pointing to a multiplicity of forces which arc combining to render possible the management and control of the capitalist economy. First, he noted the spectacular development of the productive forces – itself the result of the growing concentration of capital and financial control, radical changes in science and technology, the trend toward mechanization and automation, increased productivity and rate of surplus value, and the progressive transformation of management into administration and ever larger private bureaucracies. Second, he emphasized the increasing regulation of free competition – a consequence of state intervention which both stimulates and supports the economy (through waste expenditure in unproductive investment like armaments, for example), the linking of the nation-state's economy to a world-wide network of military and monetary alliances and the expansion of public bureaucracy. Third, he pointed to changes in social structure – for instance, the gradual assimilation of blue-collar and white-collar populations, of business and labour leaders, in terms of occupational structure and consumption patterns. Fourth, he described a curtailment of national prerogatives by international events and the permanent threat of war – created by the cold war, the 'threat of communism', the enemy 'within and without' and the ever present possibility of nuclear war.[118] In short, Marcuse felt that the prevailing trends in society were leading to the establishment of a technical apparatus which threatened to engulf public and private existence.

The system . . . tends towards both total administration and total dependence on administration by ruling public and private managements, strengthening the pre-established harmony between the interest of the big public and private corporations and that of their customers and servants.[119]

For the Marcuse of *One Dimensional Man*, there has been a supersession of capitalist antagonisms by industrial and technological rationality.

Confronted with an 'effective capitalism', revolutionary theory assumes an abstract character and becomes the concern of minorities.[120] But there are forces at work, Marcuse believes, which serve to counteract this trend. The possibilities for revolutionary transformation are not exhausted. The growing productivity of labour, the continued automation of the means of production, and a growing contradiction between the enormous productive capacity and social wealth of advanced capitalist (and communist) societies and their destructive utilization ensures the creation not only of the material prerequisites of freedom but also of the conditions for the struggle against domination. The dramatic increase in productive forces, with its emphasis on the desirability of large-scale consumption, has created the image of a 'world of ease, enjoyment, fulfilment, and comfort' – expectations and needs for a better life, which the established mode of production cannot fulfil.[121] The gap between promise and delivery grows, as does the base of exploitation, the number of people who (in capitalist countries) can potentially experience this gap. Marcuse is convinced that certain objective conditions for revolution exist. These he lists as:

a social wealth sufficient to abolish poverty; the technical know-how to develop the available resources systematically toward this goal; a ruling class which wastes, arrests, and annihilates the productive forces; the growth of anti-capitalist forces in the Third World which reduce the reservoir of exploitation; and a vast working class which, separated from the control of the means of production, confronts a small, parasitic ruling class.[122]

But because of the effect of phenomena such as privatization, consumption orientations, the mass media and the continued domination of instrumental reason, 'the subjective factor is lagging behind'. Revolutionary perspectives are only shared by a relatively small number of people. Marcuse detects, however, significant changes here too: needs are being created which transcend capitalism (and for that matter state socialism). The contradictions between that 'which is and which is possible and ought to be' penetrates everyday consciousness. The satisfaction of basic needs creates demands for a range of other needs, from self-determination to greater self-realization. Marcuse sees in, for example, the spreading of wildcat strikes, factory occupations, absenteeism, the demands and attitudes of young workers, genuine expression of these needs. He recognizes that there is only a small minority of people that articulates these issues in a consistent theoretical framework. Nonetheless, the issues are raised – no matter how diffusely – and represent a protest against the existing form of society. [123] The potential for mass social change exists.

But the unorganized character of much contemporary protest can also support, Marcuse stresses, anti-socialist movements (for example various populist and right-wing movements) and can give rise to a proto-fascist potential. 'The only counterforce', he argues,

is the development of an effectively organized radical Left, assuming the vast task of *political education*, dispelling the false and mutilated consciousness of the people so that they themselves experience their condition, and its abolition, as vital need, and apprehend the ways and means of their liberation.[124]

An important basis for such a development is located in social forces which are, in the first instance, outside the established system. These include two general groups. First, there are those who remain 'underprivileged' in advanced capitalism – those whose very basic needs remain unsatisfied (minorities and the poor, for instance). Outside the capitalist nation-states the 'under-privileged', those struggling for survival, constitute the mass of people and the mass basis of national liberation movements. Their fight against imperialism and neo-colonialism is one of the most important threats to capitalism's capacity to reproduce itself. Second, there are some among the privileged 'whose consciousness and instincts, break through or escape social control' (for example, students, intellectuals).[125] These forces together, Marcuse believes, do contribute to the crisis development of the system. But they do not constitute an effective revolutionary threat against the whole of society. They are catalyst groups; they cannot transform society alone. Whether or not they will trigger a crisis that eventually radicalizes the mass of working people, who could overthrow the system, is an open question. But it seems, for Marcuse, less rather than more of an open question. Given the continuing presence of acute contradictions, the main question appears to be when. Marcuse does not answer this question and readily admits that no straightforward answer to it can be given.

Marcuse desires a social movement which would refuse to participate in the reproduction of capitalism. His advocacy of a 'great refusal' seeks a world that would negate capitalism, reduce overdevelopment in the 'developed' countries, and pursue a 'pacified existence' – a non-instrumental relation between people and between people and nature.[126]

3 The culture industry: critical theory and aesthetics

According to most members of the Frankfurt school, the individual is enmeshed in a world where capital is highly concentrated and where the economy and polity are increasingly interlocked; it is a *verwaltete Welt*, a world 'caught up in administration'. As a consequence, the importance of political economy in the critical project diminished, for it did not provide a sufficient basis to understand the penetration of market and bureaucratic organizations into more and more areas of life. The change in what the critical theorists took to be their object of study demanded the development of concepts and categories. Increasingly, attention was focused on an assessment of the mode in which ideas and beliefs are transmitted by 'popular culture' – the way in which the personal, private realm is undermined by the external (extra-familial) socialization of the ego and the management and control of leisure time.[1] As individual consciousness and unconsciousness were encroached upon by agencies which organize free time – for example the radio, television, film and professional sport industries – the Frankfurt theorists stressed the urgency of developing a sociology of 'mass culture'.

For Horkheimer, Adorno and Marcuse, in particular, sociology and critique are inseparable: to analyse a work of art, or a particular cultural artefact, is to analyse and assess the way it is interpreted. This entails an inquiry into its formation and reception. Such an inquiry seeks to understand given works in terms of their social origins, form, content and function – in terms of the social totality. The conditions of labour, production and distribution must be examined, for society expresses itself through its cultural life and cultural phenomena contain within themselves reference to the socio-economic whole. But a sociology of culture cannot rest with an analysis of the general relations between types of cultural products (for example Western music or, more specifically, opera, chamber music, etc.), and social life.[2] It must also explore in detail the internal structure of cultural forms (the way in which the organization of society is crystallized in cultural phenomena) and the mechanisms which determine their reception. Generally, a theory of culture should include, on Horkheimer's and Adorno's account, reference to the processes of production, reproduction, distribution, exchange and consumption. Needless to say, such a theory was never completed (nor was it ever thought that such a theory could be 'finished'). But a large number of contributions was made to the theory of culture and cultural forms.

Before and during their association with the Institute, Adorno, Horkheimer, Marcuse, Lowenthal and Benjamin were all concerned with aesthetic theory and the critique of culture.[3] An emphasis on studies of 'mass culture' came, however, in the late 1930s and 1940s. The emergence of an entertainment industry, the growth of the mass media, the blatant manipulation of culture by the Nazis and other totalitarian regimes, the shock of immigration to the US, the inevitable discovery of the glamour and glitter of the film and record industries: together all made imperative the task of assessing the changing patterns of culture. In this chapter I intend to focus attention on the critical theorists' views about these changing patterns. I will also try and locate their studies within some of their general perspectives on aesthetics and culture. It should be stressed, however, that my remarks on their writings in this sphere will be of a schematic nature. Adorno and Benjamin particularly wrote at length on aesthetics and on artistic and literary form. Almost half of Adorno's publications were on music. He analysed the works of several composers, including Beethoven, Mahler, Wagner, Schoenberg, Berg and Stravinski.[4] He discussed the nature of different types of musical instruments, for example the violin and saxophone.[5] He also wrote on a number of cultural critics, for example Otto Spengler and Thorstein Veblen;[6] on literary figures such as Franz Kafka and Beckett;[7] on literary critics such as Lukács;[8] and he published a large volume on aesthetic theory.[9] Benjamin's writings are less voluminous but his breadth of reference was also extraordinary.[10] His essays include discussions of Baudelaire, Brecht, Kafka, Nikolai Leskov and Proust.[11] His books include two major volumes on German literature, two books of general reflections presented as short essays and aphorisms[12] and a great number of reviews, commentaries and critical essays.[13] To assess properly the contributions of either of these writers is beyond the scope of this work.[14]

The works I have listed, however, exclude some of their more general studies on the development of cultural forms in the nineteenth and twentieth centuries. It is these that this chapter seeks to concentrate upon. Even here the range of material they covered is impressive. It includes Adorno's and Horkheimer's major assessment of the 'culture industry' in *Dialectic of Enlightenment*,[15] which Adorno thought of as the basis of the two writers' 'common philosophy'. (He also regarded his major work on modern music as an 'extended appendix' to this text.)[16] The range of relevant writings also embraces a number of articles by Adorno on 'high', 'avant-garde' and popular culture; a most important essay by Benjamin investigating 'The work of art in the age of mechanical reproduction';[17] essays by Horkheimer on mass culture;[18] studies by Lowenthal on the history of literature and popular literary materials;[19] and, of course, Marcuse's work on the character of art and particular cultural phenomena (for instance painting, street theatre and rock). If the subject matter covered suggests diversity, so do the techniques of inquiry employed. Adorno and Lowenthal, for instance, often utilized content analysis and carried out detailed investigations into the structure of particular cultural products. Horkheimer's approach, like Marcuse's, was more exclusively philosophical and theoretical. Benjamin's approach was unique. He utilized many different styles of writing and drew upon many different modes of thinking (from the Cabbala to Marx and various schools of Marxism). Benjamin often dissented from the opinions expressed by the other Frankfurt theorists. When general statements are made below about a Frankfurt school position I will be referring to the works of the other four writers. The sections on Benjamin later in the chapter highlight why it is necessary to treat his work separately; they are offered here by way of a contrast – essentially, as a point from which the particularity of the other four men's writings can be appreciated.

The concepts of culture and art

Unlike many orthodox Marxists who relegated culture to the superstructure of society and derived an analysis of the form and content of the superstructure from the 'base', the Frankfurt theorists insisted that cultural phenomena could not be analysed within the simple base–superstructure model.[20] They also insisted on the inadmissibility of treating culture in the manner of conventional cultural criticism, in isolation from its position in the social totality. Any conception of culture which saw it as an independent realm apart from society was to be rejected. Culture could not be understood, as Adorno put it, 'in terms of itself'. To suppose 'anything like an independent logic of culture', he added, 'is to collaborate in the hypostatis of culture, the ideological *proton pseudos*'.[21] In fact, the notion of culture employed by Horkheimer and the others was closer to Freud's than to classical Marxist and non-Marxist understandings of the term.[22] For Horkheimer *et al.* culture emerges from the organizational basis of society as the bundle of ideas, mores, norms and artistic expressions – the heritage and practices of intelligence and art.[23] Within these broad terms of rererence, Marcuse, while discussing bourgeois culture, makes the useful further analytic distinction between the spheres of *material* culture and *intellectual* (artistic, 'higher') culture. Material culture comprises 'the actual patterns of behaviour in "earning a living", the system of operational values', and includes the social, psychological and moral dimensions of family life, leisure time, education and work. Intellectual culture refers to 'the "higher values", science and the "humanities", art, religion'.[24] Although several more distinctions will be introduced throughout the chapter, it should be noted that it is easier to discern the notions of culture Frankfurt writers rejected than the ones they accepted. Their own general concept of culture remains underdeveloped. As a consequence I shall employ Marcuse's distinction throughout the chapter as a shorthand for delineating different realms of cultural phenomena (though it should be remembered that this is not necessarily a distinction each writer would have accepted).

Institute members were, however, agreed that the products of intellectual, artistic culture could be regarded as neither simply the reflection of specific class interests nor the output of a wholly autonomous sphere. They were intent on exploring the modes in which cultural phenomena interacted with, and sometimes determined, other social dimensions. Furthermore, they sought to examine in particular detail the fate of 'art', understood in the broadest possible sense, in the contemporary era. For them, art was to be interpreted as 'a code language for processes taking place in society'.[25] Yet, because of its *form*, as I explain below, it was often thought to be 'relatively autonomous'. Art was unavoidably enmeshed in reality. And just as this reality contained objective contradictions, so art was caught up in and expressed contradictions. But a contrast was frequently drawn between those works which resist assimilation to existing modes of production and exchange and those which do not. In many 'genuine' works of art, they believed, there are both moments of affirmation and negation.[26] In these works society both confirmed itself and maintained a critical image. As Adorno wrote, 'culture, in the true sense, did not simply accommodate itself to human beings; but it always simultaneously raised a protest against petrified relations under which they lived'.[27] Artistic culture represents the 'perennial protest' of the 'particular against the universal', as long as the latter remains unreconciled to the former.[28] The aesthetic may contain a moment of transcendence or it may be integrated into existing conditions of domination.

Affirmation and negation in 'autonomous' art

The meaning and function of art changes historically. But there is a certain unity that underpins authentic or, as Adorno most often put it, autonomous art. The great artists of the bourgeois era, as well as those of the Christian Middle Ages and the Renaissance, had the capacity to transform a particular, individual experience, through the language of music, painting or words, into a universal statement. The work of art has a structure with a signifying function. It presents, or rather represents, the particular in such a way as to illuminate its meaning. Through its *form* or *style* (Horkheimer, Adorno and Marcuse), or *aura* and *new* technique (Benjamin), art can create images of beauty and order or contradiction and dissonance – an aesthetic realm which at once leaves and highlights reality. Art's object world is derived from the established order, but it portrays this order in a non-conventional manner. 'Sensibility, imagination and understanding' give 'new sounds, images and words to the taken-for-granted'. The structure of art forms *enacts* an alternative vision. As such art has a cognitive and subversive character. Although this character was analysed differently by various Institute members, there was general agreement that the 'partisan', emancipatory effects of art are generated by its rejection of the dominant forms of world order; that is, through its very mode of expression it 'opens the established reality' and 'negates reified consciousness'. Art has the capacity to transcend its class origins, while preserving certain conventional images of reality. It has multiple layers of meaning and the ability to embody and promote truth.

For Horkheimer and Adorno in *Dialectic of Enlightenment* the elements in an artistic product which enable it to transcend reality are found in those features which ensure 'non-identity thinking' – the truth-promoting function of art lies in its capacity to undermine the doubtful unity of concept (*Begriff*) and object, idea and material world. (The notion of non-identity thinking is elaborated on page 215.) Bourgeois art strives for identity – an identity between its image of the real and the existent. It presents itself as social reality. For example, some of Beethoven's music, according to Adorno, expresses reconciliation between the subjective and objective, between part and whole. It represents the idea of an integrated community, the promise of the French revolution. The individual part, the note or phrase, exists as a separate entity, but each part is only fully meaningful in the context of the whole, namely in the structure of the sonata or symphony. Beethoven's music is faithful to his period, to the awakening consciousness of individualistic society. But the image it presents contradicts bourgeois reality: 'it transfigures the existing conditions, presenting them in the . . . moment of the musical performance as though the community of human beings were already realized'.[29] The promise held out by such a work of art is, as Adorno and Horkheimer wrote, 'that it will create truth by lending new shape to conventional forms'.[30] The promise is both necessary and hypocritical. It is necessary, first, because of its social origins. The patrons of art, whether aristocrats or wealthy buyers in the market, demand new forms to lend dignity and fresh (often conformist) images to the world around them. More important, it is necessary because in its very commitment to style, art 'hardens itself' against the 'chaotic expression' of the existing order and presents individual experiences in new, and truly general, forms. In the enactment of art, objective trends are played through. The promise, however, is also hypocritical: 'the claim of art is always ideology too'. Art legitimates prevailing patterns of life by suggesting that 'fulfilment lies in their aesthetic derivatives'.[31] Nonetheless, in its very failure to establish identity, art preserves – unlike many forms of conventional expression – a critical perspective. The truth-value of art lies in its capacity to sustain a discrepancy between its projected images (concepts) of nature and humankind, and its objects' actuality.

In his own writings Adorno always insisted that art loses its significance if it tries to create specific political or didactic effects; art should compel rather than demand a change in attitude.[32] Hence he was critical of Brecht's emphasis on the 'primacy of lesson over . . . form'. In so far as art has a true social function it is its 'functionlessness'.[33] Art is most critical, in the contemporary epoch, when it is autonomous; that is, when it negates the empirical reality from which it originates. Autonomous works of art dismantle appearances; they 'explode from within that which committed proclamation subjugates from without'.[34] Social criticism flows from a work's form – not its content. Committed work, such as Brecht's, risks assimilating itself with the existent reality[35] – in order to be fully comprehended, it must speak in the language of that order.[36] For Adorno, 'every commitment to the world must be abandoned to satisfy the ideal of the committed work'.[37] Art 'must intervene actively in consciousness through its own forms and not take instructions from the passive, one-sided position of the consciousness of the user – including the proletariat'. Adorno's emphasis on form, however, should not be mistaken for a simple insistence on the primacy of style and technique. Rather, form refers to the whole 'internal organization' of art – to the capacity of art to restructure conventional patterns of meaning. Under the present conditions of society, the most 'genuine' forms of art are those that resist pressure, created by the 'rule of equivalence', to identity thinking. The 'truth content' of art derives from its ability to reformulate existent relations between subjectivity and objectivity, and to maintain non-identity. 'Closed aesthetic images', on Adorno's account, preserve a gap between subject and object, individual and society. They make no compromise with a society increasingly dominated by modes of 'thought that collapse into subjectivism (the false view that the subjects' concepts produce the world) or objectivism (the false view that the world is a realm of pure objects given independently of the subject).[38] They also challenge, in their very structure, a world of purely pragmatic affairs.

Authentic works of art . . . have always stood in relation to the actual life-process of society from which they distinguished themselves. Their very rejection of the guilt of a life which blindly and callously reproduces itself, their insistence on independence and autonomy, on separation from the prevailing realm of purposes, implies, at least as an unconscious element, the promise of a condition in which freedom were realised.[39]

The truth-value of art resides in its capacity to create awareness of, and thematize, social contradictions and antinomies.[40] 'A successful work . . . is not one which resolves objective contradictions in a spurious harmony, but one which expresses the idea of harmony negatively by embodying the contradictions, pure and uncompromised, in its innermost structure.'[41] As such, art is less and more than praxis. It is less because it retreats in the face of practical tasks which need to be accomplished (perhaps even hindering them). It is more for 'turning its back even on praxis, it denounces at the same time the limited untruth [*die bornierte Unwahrheit*] of the practical world. For so long as the practical rearrangement of the world has not yet succeeded, praxis can have no direct cognizance of that fact'.[42]

Horkheimer argued, as did Adorno, that art only became fully autonomous when it was separated from the pre-capitalist patronage system which ensured its restricted religious and/or private usage.[43] Horkheimer's emphasis on the critical character of art is, however, somewhat different from Adorno's. Horkheimer maintained that classical bourgeois art 'preserved the utopia that evaporated from religion'.[44] Through art one can conceive a world different from life dominated by commodity production. The beautiful and often harmonious images it projected promised a utopia – a vision of an ideal life – that could motivate thought and a critique of reality. Art provided a medium for critical thinking by upholding images of life which contradicted the existent. But art's affirmative vision inevitably assumed an 'escapist character'. Men and women 'had fled into a private conceptual world' and arranged their thoughts in anticipation of a time in which the aesthetic could be systematically incorporated into reality.[45] Art anticipates the good life. It preserves an ideal in danger of being forgotten. But this is all it can do. To the extent that it suggests utopia can be realized in the aesthetic realm, or that its images are the avenue to an ideal community, it is idealist and false. Bourgeois art often advances one of these ideas.[46]

Marcuse's work examines some of these notions in greater detail. On his account, bourgeois culture led in the course of its development to the establishment of a 'mental and spiritual world as an independent realm of value'; a realm of 'authentic values and self-contained ends' claiming autonomy and superiority from civilization (material culture). The essential characteristic of this world, which Marcuse called 'affirmative culture', is the assertion of a universally obligatory, eternally better and more valuable world that must be unconditionally affirmed: a world essentially different from the factual world of the daily struggle for existence, yet realizable by every individual for himself 'from within', without any transformation of the state of fact.[47]

Bourgeois artistic culture serves both to project unrealized possibilities and maintain 'harmonizing illusions'. It stands as a record of the revolutionary aspirations of the bourgeoisie – with its demands for new social freedoms commensurate with the universality of human reason – and of the failure of these aspirations to be realized in practice. Bourgeois dreams remain ideals; ideals relegated, in seeming acknowledgement of the reality of commodity production, to the 'inner world' of humanity. In this 'inner world' the individual is exalted and ennobled. 'Freedom, goodness and beauty become spiritual qualities.' Culture speaks of the dignity of humans and preserves beauty *for the soul*.[48]

The idealism embodied in bourgeois artistic culture is not simply ideology; for it contains remembrance of what might have been and what could be. While 'idealism surrenders the earth to bourgeois society', it preserves, Marcuse contends, the historical demand for general liberation. 'The culture of souls absorbed in a false form those forces and wants which could find no place in everyday life.'[49] It is not that art represents in any clear fashion an ideal reality, but that it presents the existent as a beautiful reality. For Marcuse beauty is *'une promesse de bonheur'*. For what is beautiful is first and foremost sensuous. Its sensuousness occupies a position 'halfway between sublimated and unsublimated objectives'. Beauty is representative of both the pleasurable – the realm of immediate gratification and desire (objects of unsublimated drives) – and the forces of fine arrangement and order.[50] Its meaning converges with the notion of 'aesthetic form'. Through aesthetic form (the style and qualities of a work) aspects of the human condition are revealed. In 'music, verse and image' an object world is created which is derived from and yet is other than the existing one.[51] This transformation does not, Marcuse argues, 'do violence to the objects (man and things) – it rather speaks for them, gives word and tone and image to that which is silent, distorted, suppressed in the established reality'.[52] The 'subversive truth of art' resides in its capacity to create a world which has no actuality.

In this universe, every word, every colour, every sound is 'new', different –

breaking the familiar context of perception and understanding ... in which men and nature are enclosed. By becoming components of the aesthetic form, words, sounds, shapes and colours are insulated against their familiar, ordinary use and function; thus they are freed for a new dimension of existence. This is the achievement of *style*.... The style, embodiment of the aesthetic form, in subjecting reality to another order, subjects it to the 'laws of beauty'.[53]

To be sure, cruelty, ugliness and pain are not thereby cancelled. But they are cast in a different framework. The horror portrayed by, for example, Goya's etchings, 'remains horror', but it is also eternalized as 'the horror of horror'.[54]

The artistic transformation of objects aids insight into the conditions under which objects exist. For art, through the power of negation, releases the object from its contingent surroundings.[55] Images are created which are unreconcilable with the established 'reality principle'. Following Hegel, Marcuse maintains that through art, objects take on the form and quality of freedom. Aesthetic transformation releases objects from constraints that prevent their free realization.[56] As such art, and artistic culture generally, is on the side of the forces which dissociate themselves from contemporary material culture. Artistic culture 'withdraws and rejects' the 'rule of equivalence', the world of commodities and the domination of instrumental reason.[57]

The world which art creates, however, remains, despite its objective content and truth, an illusion (*Schein*). But the images which art projects are not straightforward illusions. For art is itself alienated from an alienated social order. Artistic alienation, as Marcuse put it, 'is the conscious transcendence of ... alienated existence – "higher level" or mediated alienation'.[58] It is only through illusion that art opens the established reality to alternative visions and possibilities: it is in this transfiguration that art transcends its class origins and content.[59] Art must, therefore, 'remain alienation'. Marcuse appears to support Adorno's view that art can only preserve its subversive character by remaining autonomous, although he does stress, more than Adorno did, the direct power of art as negation. Art must obey its own laws and maintain its freedom. In so doing it unites, on Marcuse's account, with all those forces engaged in the critique of ideology and with the revolutionary goal of 'changing the world'. But it 'cannot represent the revolution, it can only invoke it in another medium'.[60]

Benjamin's views on the development of art were often at odds with those of other members of the Institute.[61] His analysis of 'autonomous' art in terms of its possession of 'aura', exemplifies some of these differences. Tracing the beginning of artistic production to ceremonial objects designed to serve in a cult, Benjamin argued that what mattered then was art's 'existence', not its 'being on view'.[62] Embedded in ritual and tradition, these works had an 'aura'; that is, a 'unique phenomenon of a distance however close it may be' conditioned by a magical authority and authenticity. 'The authenticity of a thing is the essence of all that is transmissible from its beginning, ranging from its substantive duration to its testimony to the history which it has experienced.'[63] With the separation of art from ritual, art became more and more a product for exhibition and inspection. It gained a 'semblance of autonomy'.[64] But as long as artists produced works with a 'unique existence', aura was preserved; art objects remained embedded in tradition. The age of mechanical reproduction, the age of photography, cinema and other mass cultural apparatuses, detached artistic artefacts from the domain of custom.[65] Through the substitution of a 'plurality of copies for a unique existence', enabling the 'beholder or listener' to apperceive the work in private, aura and tradition were shattered. Art's appearance of autonomy disappeared. A sense of art's images and objects as unique and permanent was replaced by a feeling of their 'transitoriness and reproducibility'. This shift in perception reflects, for Benjamin, an important change in the masses' actual and potential consciousness. An understanding of the 'universal equality of things' is increased as the authority of fixed or set perceptions, reified notions of historical continuity, is exploded. The function of art radically alters. 'The instant the criterion of authenticity ceases to be applicable to artistic production, the total function of art is reversed. Instead of being based on ritual, it begins to be based on another practice – politics.'[66]

Benjamin's assessment of this situation was not without ambivalence. The end of auratic art (like the threatened end of autonomous art for other members of the Institute), was greeted with 'a sense of loss'.[67] On the other hand, for Benjamin, 'the decay of aura' was related to the growing desire of the masses 'to bring things "closer" spatially and humanly' and to control the reproduction of objects.[68] The age of mechanical reproduction ushered in new techniques and technologies which offered possibilities for progressive political change. 'To an ever greater degree', he believed, 'the work of art reproduced becomes the work of art designed for reproducibility'. Following Brecht's lead, Benjamin pointed to film as a medium, the production and reception of which could coincide with revolutionary objectives. He was well aware that the film industry, conditioned by the requirements of capital accumulation, could promote 'the spell of the personality', 'the phony spell of a commodity'. But film, through its technical structure, could produce 'shock effects' and burst everyday perceptions of the world, leading to a 'heightened presence of mind'.[69] Furthermore, Benjamin stressed that film provided new forms of collective experience.

Mechanical reproduction of art changes the reaction of the masses toward art. The reactionary attitude toward a Picasso painting changes into the progressive reaction toward a Chaplin movie. The progressive reaction is characterized by the direct, intimate fusion of visual and emotional enjoyment with the orientation of the expert. . . . With regard to the screen the critical and the receptive attitudes of the public coincide.[70]

The new mode of perception offered by film and similar media can turn art toward the interest of the masses and contribute to their mobilization.[71]

The other members of the Institute were not as optimistic as Benjamin about the effects of new techniques and cultural media. Adorno, for instance, argued that collective experiences in the cinema were 'anything but good and revolutionary'. The laughter of an audience reminded him of some of the 'worst aspects of bourgeois sadism'. He also accused Benjamin of 'the anarchistic romanticism of blind confidence in the spontaneous power of the proletariat'.[72] It was much too simple to think that mechanical reproduction would bring about dramatic changes in perception and consciousness. For Adorno, Horkheimer, Marcuse and Lowenthal, the new techniques of cultural production and reception had to be understood in the context of the decline of autonomous art and the rise of what Horkheimer and Adorno called the 'culture industry'. For them, the new products of 'mass culture' served to enhance political control and to 'cement' mass audiences to the *status quo*. In the contemporary world, the moments of affirmation and criticism contained in 'autonomous art' are being split apart. In an epoch in which the individual has 'lost his power to conceive a world different from that in which he lives', negation only survives in works of art which, as Horkheimer commented, 'uncompromisingly express the gulf between the monadic individual and his barbarous surroundings — prose like Joyce's and paintings like Picasso's Guernica'.[73] These works are becoming rarer and cannot be found in 'mass culture'. Lowenthal shared this view.[74] On Adorno's account, most art and music in the twentieth century has become 'functional' for a world of commodity production (or socialist bureaucratic elitism). It is manufactured for its 'selling chances' and offers little more than entertainment and distraction. Autonomous and critical art still survives in works which consciously or unconciously reject and react against market requirements and which abandon nineteenth-century naturalism, realism and romanticism. Artistic truth is still conserved by works which express the dissonant character of modern life. Adorno emphasized that Schoenberg's early works, his atonal music, are an important example of this genre. Works like this are 'relentlessly negative'.[75] But they are perhaps too negative. The mode in which the critical function is sustained is remote from general popular taste and, as a result, its effectivity is severely reduced. The negative function of art is, he thought, increasingly on the decline. Marcuse was of a similar opinion. Advanced monopoly capitalism is incompatible with the progressive aspects of affirmative culture. Artistic alienation is continually threatened and tends to disappear (with many other forms of negation) in the process of technological expansion and capital accumulation.[76] The gap between art and reality, so important for the transcendent qualities of art, is closing in ever more realms of artistic culture.

A number of questions arise at this point. How and why have these changes occurred? In what ways has art's style, or form, or aura, been modified by the development of, and developments in, 'mass culture'? What meaning do these changes have?

The rise of mass culture and the culture industry

Irrespective of whether they characterized contemporary society as state-capitalism or monopoly capitalism, the Institute's members thought that developments had taken place which created the conditions for the commodification of major sectors of artistic culture.[77] In their discussion of 'mass culture', the Frankfurt theorists agreed on a number of basic axioms. They maintained that:

1   the more severe the difficulties of reproduction encountered by

contemporary society – they are great, indeed – the stronger becomes the general tendency to sustain the existent 'by all means available';

2 the protagonists of the present distribution of power and property, harnessing the endogenous forces which centralize ownership and control, employ economic, political and cultural means to defend the *status quo*. As a result, most areas of cultural life become co-opted and transformed into modes of controlling individual consciousness. Simultaneously, culture becomes an 'industry'. The profit motive is transferred on to cultural forms; more and more artistic products are turned into a 'species of commodity . . . marketable and interchangeable like an industrial product';[78]

3 ever since artists sold their (life and) work to make a living, art possessed aspects of this form. But trade in art did not prevent 'the pursuit of the inherent logic of each work' – art was *also* a commodity. Today 'cultural entities . . . are commodities through and through'.[79] The process is exacerbated by increased interlocking between different economic spheres and by the dependence of 'cultural monopolies' on industrial and finance capital. Advertising and banking lay down new aesthetic standards. Even where the culture industry does not directly produce for profit its products are determined by this new aesthetic. The economic necessity for a quick and high rate of return on investment demands the production of attractive packages designed either to sell directly or to create an atmosphere for selling – a feeling of insecurity, or want and need. The culture industry either has to sell particular objects or it 'turns into public relations, the manufacturing of "good will" per se.'[80]

What is the culture industry?

The expression 'culture industry' was used, and used for the first time, by Horkheimer and Adorno in *Dialectic of Enlightenment.*[81] The term's early usage was ambiguous but its meaning was subsequently clarified by Adorno in an essay published in 1967.[82] The ideas suggested by the notion are compatible with Marcuse's views. The term 'culture industry' replaced the concept of mass culture which Horkheimer and Adorno had employed in drafts of the *Dialectic*. They felt it was necessary to dispense with the concept of mass, or popular, culture because, as Adorno put it, 'we wished to exclude from the outset the interpretation agreeable to its advocates: that it is a matter of something like a culture that arises spontaneously from the masses themselves'.[83] Such notions are false.[84] Culture today is not the product of genuine demands; rather, it is the result of demands which are 'evoked and manipulated'.[85] However, they occasionally continued to use the term 'mass culture', but always then with the connotation of 'culture industry'.

The phrase 'culture industry', Adorno emphasized, 'is not to be taken literally'. In the main, the sectors of production of the cultural media do not resemble conventional patterns of industrial production. With some notable exceptions, such as the film industry, individual forms of production (namely, creation and composition) are maintained. The term, therefore, does not refer to production in itself but to the 'standardization', the 'pseudo-individualization' (marginal differentiation) of cultural entities themselves – the '*Crimie*', the Western – and to the rationalization of promotion and distribution techniques.[86] The development of the culture industry undermines the intelligibility and validity of autonomous art as the distance between classical and standard advertising aesthetics grows. The seriousness and the challenge of autonomous art is further weakened through incessant 'speculation about its efficacy'. The meaning of local and folk culture is also often destroyed, because pride and rebelliousness embedded within it are taken out of context, repeated in special programmes, and often integrated into the latest fashions. Its songs and melodies are recorded; released as discs, they might enter the charts as another new sound – but the sense and feeling they convey radically alter. Most types of folk music, Marcuse notes, are now heard as *performances* where they once were lived. The 'crying and shouting, the jumping and playing' of black music, for example, now takes place 'in an artificial, organized space'. It is directed to an audience, whether it is in an auditorium or a semi-detached.[87] The culture industry produces for mass consumption and significantly contributes to the determination of that consumption. For people are now being treated as objects, machines, 'outside as well as inside of the workshop'.[88] The consumer, as the producer, has no sovereignty. The culture industry, integrated into capitalism, in turn integrates consumers from above. Its goal is the production of goods that are profitable and consumable. It operates to ensure its own reproduction. The cultural forms it propagates must, therefore, be compatible with this aim. The 'popular culture' it claims to produce masks special interests. But the ideological effects of the culture industry need not be the result of conscious decision or manipulation (although they sometimes are).[89] As a result of the exchange of cultural artefacts, fetishism is reinforced as ideology, more generally, is sustained. The modes in which this occurs are analysed by Institute members in a number of different ways.

The produce of the culture industry: advertising aesthetics

In the classical epoch of bourgeois art a contradiction existed, the Frankfurt theorists claimed, between the human resources and techniques employed in the formation/composition of a work and the organization and processes of social and economic life which served as the conditions for the creation of that work and, more generally, of exchange value. The contradiction between the forces and relations of production manifested itself in the cultural sphere. The production of autonomous art, according to standards which derive from the laws of form and artistic technique, contradicted audiences' expectations and, in particular, their 'norms of thought' or 'standards of intelligibility' (Adorno). The exchange of cultural products led to familiar difficulties of comprehension. The meaning of artistic production remained obscure. But the persistence of a contradiction between autonomous artistic composition and the prevailing level of consciousness always meant that art might contribute to a crisis of values and attitudes. While genuine (autonomous) art is still created today, the bulk of cultural production serves to mitigate a crisis of this kind. The culture industry gears itself almost entirely to the development of cultural forms which are compatible with the preservation of capitalism. The effects of capitalist contradictions on consciousness, Horkheimer and Adorno suggest, can be managed.

The essay on the 'culture industry' in *Dialectic of Enlightenment* summarizes some of the major themes of Horkheimer's and Adorno's separate and joint reflections on the nature of mass culture. Their views expressed in this text by no means exhaust their work on the topic. This is especially true of Adorno. In expounding their views I will draw on a number of their individual writings where I think these clarify and develop ideas contained in the *Dialectic*. Their central concern is to show how the products of the culture industry fall short of claims made on their behalf even by the 'industry' itself. Without regard for the integrity of art, the culture industry leads to the 'predominance of the effect'. Deriving its life and form from extra-artistic technique (techniques of mechanical reproduction), it creates diversions, distractions, amusements – entertainment. Whereas once art had sought to fulfil the idealist dictum – 'purposiveness without purpose' (Kant) – it was now bound by purposes set by the market – 'purposelessness for purposes'.

The fate of culture is a 'symptom' of tendencies in society as well as of institutionalized wants and typical trends in individual identity formation. The desire for distraction reflects needs to escape from the responsibilities and drudgery of everyday life. The lack of meaning and control people experience registers accurately a truth about their lives – they are not masters of their own destiny. They are 'caught' within the present mode of production, with its rationalized and mechanized labour process and all its hierarchies. The pattern of recurring crises of the mode of production, its continuous expansions, recessions and depressions, engenders strains, fears and anxieties about one's capacity to earn a living, employment prospects, the security of family life, health, old age, etc. Capitalism creates conditions of dependence on the powerful, who can give or withhold things greatly wanted. It also creates dependency needs.[90] Situations continually arise in which people cannot cope. They are often beset by ego weakness and narcissistic defenses which aid them to compensate for their feelings of inadequacy and inferiority. More often than not these feelings are expressions of objective conditions in reality; that is, a reality that is inadequate and quite inferior when measured against its promise. 'Personal problems' are frequently internalized 'public issues' (C. W. Mills). But in the face of the system's pressures many individuals seek to 'hide'.[91] One can 'take flight' and escape into the world of entertainment. It offers fun, relaxation and relief from demands and effort. Temporarily, boredom can also be overcome without labour and concentration (both of which are necessary for the enjoyment of autonomous art).[92] Irrational susceptibilities and neurotic symptoms, ever present within most human beings, are open, as a consequence, to exploitation by the mass media. The 'natural' corollary of capitalist industrial production is the culture industry.

The attempt to escape both tedium and concentrated effort is, however, contradictory.[93] New experiences cannot be won through resignation to managed leisure time. Only thought and effort can lead one out of a life of *ennui* and exhaustion; for the media through which escape is sought reinforce the very psychological attitudes to which we are accustomed. As Adorno wrote, 'the modern mass media tend particularly to fortify reaction formations [reaction formations utilize the energy of a repressed wish to constitute a habit and/or set of attitudes in reaction against it] and defenses concomitant with actual social dependence'.[94] Its messages appear to offer escape; they suggest pleasure, spontaneity and 'something metaphysically meaningful'.[95] In fact, their form duplicates an 'opaque and reified' world. They do not shatter existing images of reality – they reproduce them. The culture industry stands for adjustment to existing social organizations. Under its auspices 'free-time' experiences all too often serve to sustain capacities for wage labour. How does this situation come about? How are the 'effects' of the culture industry achieved?

The main characteristics of the culture industry reflect the difficult problems it faces. It must at once both sustain interest and ensure that the attention it attracts is insufficient to bring its produce into disrepute. Thus, commercial entertainment aims at an attentive but passive, relaxed and uncritical reception, which it induces through the production of 'patterned and pre-digested' cultural entities.[96] Horkheimer and Adorno analyse these entities in terms of their negation of style; they present little, if any, new shape to conventional forms. The produce of artistic culture is, less and less, divorced from reality. It is art's 'second alienation' (Marcuse) – alienation from alienation – that is disappearing today.[97] The 'end of art' is threatened. The culture industry's style kills style. Its products fail to come to terms with reality's essence; they have no genuine content; they are essentially mimetic.[98] The culture industry becomes an extension of the 'outside world'. Furthermore, its product reproduces, reinforces and strengthens dominant interpretations of reality; it schematizes, classifies and catalogues for its customers and often represents a spurious reconciliation between society and the individual, identifying the latter with the former. The 'plots', the 'goodies', the 'heroes' rarely suggest anything other than identification with the existing form of social relations. There is passion in movies, radio broadcasts, popular music and magazines, but it is usually passion for identity (between whole and part, form and content, subject and object). The products of the culture industry can be characterized by standardization and pseudo-individualization. It is these qualities which distinguish them from autonomous art.

Standardization refers to a process that affects the general features as well as the details of a work. Structural similarities arise in cultural forms as a result of the technique of the culture industry – distribution and mechanical reproduction. Popular works, or a successful new work, are imitated under the behest of big business agencies anxious to cash in on their appeal. The material's style is 'plugged' (ceaselessly repeated) and 'frozen' (rigidly reinforced).[99] Yet newly released works of the old style, or new fashions based upon them, must maintain the appearance of novelty and originality: hence pseudo-individualization – 'endowing cultural mass production with the halo of free choice or open market on the basis of standardization itself'.[100] Each product 'affects an individual *air*'; its actual differences from other cultural entities are trivial.

> Not only are the hit songs, stars and soap operas cyclically recurrent and rigid invariable types, but the specific content of the entertainment itself . . . only appears to change. The details are interchangeable. The short interval sequence which was effective in a hit song, the hero's momentary fall from grace (which he accepts as good sport), the rough treatment which the beloved gets from the male star, the latter's rugged defiance of the spoilt heiress, are, like all the other details, ready made clichés to be slotted in anywhere; they never do anything more than fulfill the purpose alloted to them in the overall plan.[101]

Within moments of most films starting we can predict quite accurately how they will end, who will win out, lose or be forgotten. The structure of a popular song is well known before the song is actually heard. The first few notes, or phrases, of a hit are enough to tell us what the rest will be like. The surrounding framework of events can automatically be supplied to a detail known about a television show. Magazines and newspapers usually present little news and certainly no surprises. Even special effects, tricks and jokes are all allocated particular places in the design of programmes by experts in offices. The result of standardization and pseudo-individualization 'for the physiognomy of the culture industry is essentially', as Adorno summarizes it, 'a mixture of streamlining, photographic hardness and precision on the one hand, and individualistic residues, sentimentality and an already disposed and adapted romanticism on the other'.[102] As long as a product meets certain minimum requirements, a feature which distinguishes it from others, a little glamour and distinctness, marks of 'mainstream' (conventional) character, it is suitable material for popular presentation.

But it is not just 'the industry's' produce that is standardized.

Dozens of cues are provided to evince 'correct' responses. For example, in case there is any question as to what type of show a comedy is, laughter is often prerecorded. Continuous commentary is supplied on many radio and television programmes should one be uncertain what to think. Standardization 'aims at standard responses'. Apart from effects generated by promoters, cultural commodities embody 'a system of response-mechanisms which tend to automize reactions and weaken the forces of individual resistence'.[103] Frameworks for, and/or models of, interpretation are offered. These often lead back to familiar experiences; safe grounds for the reception of the culture industry. Programmes watch for their audiences as popular music hears for those who listen.

Despite the repetitiveness and ubiquity of mass culture its structure is multi-layered. In Lowenthal's well-known phrase, 'mass culture is psychoanalysis in reverse'. The culture industry appears to recognize that individuals have multi-layered personalities. This knowledge, far from being used for the purposes of emancipation, is employed in order to 'ensnare the consumer as completely as possible' and in order to embroil his or her senses in the vicissitudes of predetermined effects. A number of examples drawn from Adorno's work on television, astrology and music can usefully highlight this theme.

Examples: television, astrology and music

In 'Television and the patterns of culture' Adorno discusses the layers of meaning of an American comedy series.[104] At one level the series of shows presents an entertaining tale about the struggle for survival of an underpaid, young, very hungry school teacher. Supposedly amusing situations arise as she tries, without success, to win a free meal from friends and foes. The very mention of food becomes a stimulus for laughter. The series does not 'push' any set of ideas. Its 'hidden message' emerges as its pseudo-realism promotes identification with the charming and funny heroine. The script implies, Adorno contended:

If you are as humorous, good natured, quick-witted, and charming as she is, do not worry about being paid a starvation wage. You can cope with your frustration in a humorous way; and your superior wit and cleverness put you not only above material privations, but also above the rest of mankind. . . . In other words, the script is a shrewd method of promoting adjustment to humiliating conditions by presenting them as objectively comical and by giving a picture of a person who experiences even her own inadequate position as an object of fun apparently free of any resentment.'[105]

Patterns of reaction are set for the audience without either party's necessary awareness of them. An atmosphere of the normality of hunger (or crime and killing in detective stories and westerns) is established quite easily. Further, the show's set frames of reference suggest and reinforce certain stereotypes (for instance about how 'good girls' behave). The response formations and presuppositions of the culture industry are brought out even more clearly, with much greater detail, in Adorno's discussion of astrology.

The results of a content analysis of the daily astrological column of the *Los Angeles Times*, covering a period of about three months, along with a number of observations on astrological journals, were published under the title, 'The stars down to earth' in 1957.[106] Conventional astrology, Adorno argued, is institutionalized superstition. It is another product of the culture industry to be passively received. Astrologers offer 'authoritative' advice to individuals whose specific situation they know nothing about. Their columns are remarkable for their seriousness and practical attitude toward everyday problems. The emphasis of the *Los Angeles Times* column is always on the capacity of the private individual to 'find the right approach' to particular problems. Although fate is essentially set by the stars, a pragmatic (read 'conventional, conformist and contented') attitude to life is recommended for it can ensure satisfaction and the prospect of high rewards.

Urge to tell off official would alienate helpful partner, so keep calm despite irritation: later material benefits will follow making more cooperative deal at home.

10 November, Aries

Sulking over disappointing act of influential executive merely puts you deeper in disfavour.

10 November, Scorpio

Get away from that concern that seems to have no solution. . . .

10 November, Sagittarius[107]

The astrologer, in this case, places his 'magical authority' behind certain strategies and tactics for the day. He has to write as if the constellation of stars had endowed him with certain knowledge.

But the 'fictitious reasonableness' of the advice masks the 'arbitrary and entirely opaque' nature of his authority. The source of his knowledge is depersonalized; it remains remote and is treated as 'impersonal and thing-like'. Astrology reflects accurately that the fate of individuals is independent of their will; that the order of life appears as natural. But it does not simply register the dependence of individuals on social configurations beyond their immediate control – it further justifies this state of affairs. If you want to survive and be happy, then astrologists recommend coming to terms with your inner and outer life; they suggest you forget frustrated wants and needs and remember/accept all that cannot be changed – the nature of your job, social hierarchies, family life, etc. Thus, one can come to terms with life, the main stages of which one cannot control. To be 'rational' in astrological terms means to adjust private interests to given social configurations.

If one does not heed the stars, then one incurs a number of risks. But help is available. If you submit to the stars, if the astrologer's advice is followed, if you give in to 'the absolute power', pleasure without threat, including sexual pleasure, can be assured.[108] As a necessary result of this, communication with the stars also offers the individual increased security, the comfort of being directed and protected by another and a certain relief from responsibility. At the same time people are continually flattered and made to feel that it is their individual efforts that count! 'The individual is provided with the narcissistic gratification that he is really all-important while at the same time being kept under control.'[109]

The columnist is a homespun psychologist. His role, however, is the opposite of an analyst or therapist. He plays up to people's defences (for instance narcissism), and seeks to strengthen rather than undermine them. The continuous suggestion of threats, of grounds for anxiety – 'Drive carefully!' – ensures that the reader will seek help. Underlying destructive urges are satisfied while aid for a more pleasurable life is promised by a 'superhuman agency'. Individuals are reassured: if fate doesn't solve your problem, effort will.[110]

Astrology stresses and appears to promote individualism, independent thinking and a concern for play while, at the same time, it strengthens and reinforces dependencies, adjustment to the *status quo* and the work ethic. The columnist's approach, Adorno argued, supports what Otto Fenichel calls 'bi-phasic behaviour'; that is, the development of a reaction formation 'which embodies contradictory attitudes or actions'.[111] Bi-phasic symptoms, common, according to Fenichel, in compulsive neurosis, are presented as normal in the astrologer's column. The column takes for granted and reproduces certain antinomies in the psyche of its audience which derive from social contradictions – a world which is a social construct and yet fetishized as a result of exchange.

The general features of the astrologer's column also resemble the mentality of the 'high scorers' on the F-scale (Adorno *et al.*'s measurement device of implicit pre-fascist tendencies). The columns promote the view that the negative is essentially due to external, natural causes; the conventional is appropriate and legitimate; and 'everything is basically fine'. Dependency needs as well as compulsive attitudes are presupposed and preserved by the pseudo-rational form of astrology. The psychological syndrome expressed promotes bourgeois ideology. As Adorno put it,

It offers the advantage of veiling all deeper-lying causes of distress and thus promoting acceptance of the given. Moreover, by strengthening the sense of fatality, dependence and obedience, it paralyses the will to change objective conditions in any respect and relegates all worries to a private plane promising a cure-all by the very same compliance which prevents a change of conditions. It can easily be seen how well this suits the over-all purpose of the prevailing ideology of today's cultural industry; to reproduce the *status quo* within the mind of the people.[112]

Like other mass media products, astrology offers a spurious short-cut both to an understanding of the social order and to an escape into a supposedly different world. Its meaning appears as something new, fresh and insightful. In actuality, it is a revamp of an opaque and reified social structure.

A third illustration of the social meaning of the culture industry can be taken from Adorno's study of music. The range of his studies in this sphere has already been mentioned. I will concentrate my exposition on some of the distinctions he makes between serious and standardized/pseudo-individualized music. Adorno often explored these differences in considerable technical detail. For the sake of simplicity I will restrict my discussion to his more general statements about divergencies in musical form and the respective 'response mechanisms' he associated with different kinds of music.

Adorno thought that many different types of music had been radically altered by capitalist economic processes. The commodification of music had necessarily changed its structure and the way it was apprehended. Particularly, mass distribution and new modes of mechanical reproduction (for example radio and film) had led to the corruption of classical music; its original structure was often sacrificed to ensure immediate intelligibility (and, therefore, ease of consumption). The result was often 'quotation listening' and the repression of the listener as well as of serious music.[113] Mechanical modes of reproduction and mass distribution enhanced the tendency to fetishize music's technical structure. Experiences in live concerts were also subject to this process as conductors and impresarios sought to appeal to ever larger audiences.[114] Further, a new variety of music had developed, the structure of which was entirely determined by its exchange value. It was functional for the new techniques of reproduction and for the 'needs' of the masses seeking relief and distraction. This type of music Adorno called 'popular music', by which he meant 'light' music, or music composed purely for entertainment (including jazz, 'beat' and film music). Popular music is analysed in juxtaposition to serious music.

The categories of serious and popular music do not simply correspond to notions of classical and non-classical. Adorno stresses that there can be classical music which has many of the features of popular music. He noted, of course, that serious music can be bad.[115] It can also become 'popularized' and hence lose much of its original integrity. The differences between these two musical spheres cannot be grasped either in terms of familiar ideas such as 'lowbrow and highbrow', 'simple and complex', 'naive and sophisticated'.[116] Once again standardization and pseudo-individualization are the central categories for analysing the difference. The structural characteristics of these different kinds of music are listed in the table on page 101. In various works Adorno traced the history and changes involved in the development from the classical and romantic musical eras to the world of popular music. The history is marked by a series of transitions: from an emphasis on form and the highest technical achievement to 'structural poverty'; from the development of themes to incessant repetition of opening melodies; from the whole piece of music being the prime unit of meaning to the detail and effect taking on the most significance.[117] In popular music, styles are plugged as much as the 'personalities' of the show-business world. Popular music today, Adorno held, is like a 'multiple-choice questionnaire' – but without a correct answer. For so long as one chooses, the

The structure of production and composition of 'serious' and 'popular' music

'Serious' music	'Popular' music
Every part/detail depends 'for its musical sense on the concrete totality and never on a mere enforcement of a musical scheme'	Musical compositions follow familiar patterns/frameworks: they are stylized
	Little originality is introduced
Themes and details are highly interwoven with the whole	Structure of the whole does not depend upon details – whole is not altered by individual detail
Themes are carefully developed	Melodic structure is highly rigid and is frequently repeated
Details cannot be changed without altering the whole – details almost contain/anticipate the whole	Harmonic structure embodies a set scheme ('The most primitive harmonic facts are emphasised')
	Complications have no effect on structure of work – they do not develop themes
Consistency is maintained between formal structure and content (themes)	Stress is on combination of individual 'effects' – on sound, colour, tone, beat, rythmn
If standard schemes are employed (e.g. for dance) they still maintain a key role in the whole	Improvisations become 'normalized' (the boys can only 'swing it' in a narrow framework)
	Details are substitutable (they 'serve their function as cogs in machines')
Emphasizes norms of high technical competence	Affirms conventional norms of what constitutes intelligibility in music while appearing novel and original

culture industry is reproduced.[118] (It should be noted that it is not always clear whether the characteristics in the table describe forms of ideal or of actual types.)

The effects of the different kinds of music were centrally important to Adorno. 'Response mechanisms', he argued, are built into musical form. The table on page 103 summarizes the different responses encouraged and demands made upon the listener by the two respective types of music. Whereas the aesthetic form of serious music had ensured the transcendence of its material preconditions and a contradiction between production and prevailing consciousness, popular music affirms existing norms of intelligibility. The listeners of the music plugged by the culture industry 'become so accustomed to the recurrence of the same things that they react automatically'.[119] Repetition enforces recognition and often then acceptance of the seemingly inescapable. While in great serious music understanding involves a spontaneous act of linking elements together in ever new synthesis, in popular music understanding coincides with recognition.[120] Popular music presupposes and continually reinforces a frame of mind which is one of 'distraction and inattention'. Exhaustion and boredom conditioned by the dominant mode of production is complemented by the culture industry which distracts 'from the demands of reality by entertainment which does not demand attention either'.[121] Popular music is tailor-made for the functions of this 'industry'. It 'fits' well into the *status quo's* ideological tendencies. Whether heard on radio or in live concerts, popular music's often repeated and 'detachable' themes, exaggerated emphases, sheer volume, etc. lead to 'fetishism in music' and 'regression of the listener'.[122] Irrespective of the intent of composers and functionaries in the popular music world, the music serves to prevent criticism of the social order; it enraptures and has 'a soporific effect'. As set pieces tend to produce set responses, a 'retrogressive and sometimes even infantile type of person' is promoted; responses become impulsive, mimetic and generally child-like. Regression in listening focuses on details and melodies. 'Atomistic' and 'quotation listening' is the counterpart to the 'musical children's language' – structural poverty – of popular music. Relieved of responsibility again, the individual does not have to worry about the 'correct' reactions.

Popular music enhances predispositions to compulsive and irrational responses and, therefore, it increases susceptibility to outside influences. The atmosphere it creates is suitable for the

Differences between 'serious' and 'popular' music in responses encouraged/demands made upon listener

'Serious' music	'Popular' music
To understand a piece of serious music one must experience the whole of it	The whole has little influence on reception and reaction to parts – stronger reactions to part than whole
The whole has strong impact on reaction to details	The music is standardized into easily recognizable types, whole are pre-accepted/known prior to reception
Themes and details can only be comprehended in the context of the whole	Little effort is required to follow music – audience already has models under which musical experiences can be subsumed
The sense of the music cannot be grasped by recognition alone, i.e. by identifying music with another 'identical' piece	Little emphasis on the whole as musical event – what matters is style, rhythm (the movement of the foot on the floor)
Effort and concentration are required to follow music	Leads back to familiar experiences (themes and details can be understood out of context because listener can automatically supply framework)
Its aesthetic disrupts the continuum of everyday life and encourages recollection	A sense of the music is grasped by recognition – leading to acceptance
	Pleasure, fun gained through listening are 'transferred' to the musical object, which becomes invested with qualities that stem from mechanism of identification
	The most successful, best music is identified with the most often repeated
	Music has 'soporific effect' on social consciousness
	It reinforces a sense of continuity in everyday living – while its reified structure enforces forgetfulness
	Renders 'unnecessary the process of thinking'

promotion of other goods and services. Additional 'escapes' and 'comforts' are usually on offer. But the gratifications and reliefs available are illusionary as is the 'adjustment' effected by the musical world. In listening individuals are actually subject to the same social forces they seek to escape. This has ramifications for the attitudes of the masses. Listening habits, 'likes' and 'dislikes' which have been enforced upon audiences contain ambivalence. Crazes for the latest fashion/fad contain their opposite – 'spite and fury' – which are easily released. Frequently, when promotion pressure is reduced, revenge is provoked. People 'compensate for the "guilt" in having condoned the worthless by making fun of it' (for example laughing at pictures of old fashions.[123] The tremendous amount of energy (libido) employed in order to digest the goods of the industry can be deflected. But the relaxation of sales pressure on a particular product is made only so as to launch something 'new'. In order to sustain the illusion of satisfaction, the entertainment business has to introduce constantly 'fresh' ideas and 'different' works. The process could, Adorno thought, continue indefinitely. The autonomy of music is vanishing. 'Music today is largely a social cement.'[124]

Examples of modern art which resist assimilation

There were, however, in Adorno's and Horkheimer's opinion, certain types of modern art which resisted assimilation. In 'Art and mass culture' Horkheimer spoke of works which can still shock and provoke; works which reproduce the 'abyss' between the individual and environment.

The works in which the subject cut off from his own development still manages to find expression are those in which the abyss between him and the barbaric environment appears most insistently: poems such as those of Trakl, the *Guernica* of Picasso, a composition of Schoenberg. The sorrow and the horror which adhere to such works do not correspond to the experience of a subject who turns away from reality, for understandable reasons, or revolts against it; the consciousness to which these belong is cut off from society, thrust back on distorted, outré figures. . . . The latest works of art . . . relinquish illusion of an existing community, they are memorials of a lonely and desperate life. . . . Insofar as they still represent communication they denounce the dominant forms of intercourse as tools of destruction.[125]

Autonomous art can make the familiar unfamiliar and cast a new light upon it. Adorno agreed in principle with this view. But his analysis of particular works was, as always, more detailed and cautious. This can be seen in his studies of the 'new music' composed, notably, by Schoenberg (and in his writings on Beckett).[126]

The 'new music', Adorno maintained, reveals a mode of composition which continually produced new forms and 'honours the listener by not making any concessions to him'. The dissonance and large intervals which were articulated by the mature Schoenberg during his commitment to free atonality expressed the composer's refusal either to accept the rigid forms of traditional musical structure, or to bow to demands of conventional taste and attitudes. Schoenberg deliberately maintained unresolved tensions and refused to introduce ordering categories which might ease the task of comprehending his works. His music, Adorno noted, often seems 'fragmented and abrupt to the unnaive-naive listener'. But all aspects of his work are 'so totally formed that there is never any confusion'.[127] Although Schoenberg's works sound entirely experimental they submit classicism and romanticism to sustained criticism. In Adorno's opinion, Schoenberg 'liberated the latent structure' of these traditions while 'disposing of their manifest one'. Far from breaking with tradition, Schoenberg continued it. His works preserved 'identity in non-identity'.[128] But while the form of the atonal compositions contradicted prevailing tastes and attitudes, the meaning of the music became more and more remote from the understanding of potential and actual listeners. Thus, the critical impact of these works was diminished.

The transition in Schoenberg's style from free atonality to the twelve-tone technique also reduced the influence of the former. Schoenberg's work developed into a new system. Twelve-tone rows and relations became as explicit as key relations in traditional music.[129] Another false and premature resolution of tensions was projected. Schoenberg's disciples further rationalized the system. It became a new, all-embracing 'fixed idea', hence, 'the bad heir of tonality'. The desire for security was once more manifest. In a social order where security cannot be achieved its expression in artistic forms simply adds to the barriers to self-reflection. The effects of the culture industry are very hard to escape, interlocked as they are with the whole development of capitalist society.

The changing structure of ideology

Summarizing the effects of the culture industry, Adorno wrote, 'it impedes the development of autonomous, independent individuals who judge and decide consciously for themselves'.[130] The 'industry' appeals to, develops from and reinforces a state of dependence, anxiety and ego weakness. The message it conveys is most often one of adjustment and obedience. Its essential content can be reduced to one axiom: since things cannot be other than they are, 'become that which thou art'. Through displaced wish-fulfilment, 'substitute gratification' (*Ersatzbefriedigung*), the 'industry' seeks to meet individual needs for diversion and distraction. It provides tonics – 'pick-me-ups' – for another working day. The 'response mechanisms' embedded in its produce calls for both passivity, susceptibility and a sense of smugness about the individual's actual and potential achievements. Identification with prevailing norms and conditions is inculcated. Horkheimer and Adorno recognized that there is a rationale for light art: it does, after all, keep people going.[131] But its suppression of reason, sensuality and spontaneity promotes only 'pseudo-activity' – marginally differentiated types of social practice. The individual 'is tolerated only so long as his complete identification with the generality (the social totality) is unquestioned'.[132] The culture industry is 'anti-enlightenment'.

The transition from autonomous to standardized/pseudo-individualized cultural forms also marks a transformation in the nature of ideology. The critique of ideology, as the immanent critique of an object – a critique which (to put it crudely) assesses an object in terms of its own standards and ideals – is possible only in so far as 'ideology contains a rational element with which the critique can deal'. Capitalist exchange, for example, can be assessed in light of its own, substantial claim to be just. But when people become 'objects of calculation', as the consumers of the culture industry, then the ideology which informs this calculation is no longer simply false by its own standards – for it has none. It represents nothing other than 'manipulative contrivance'.[133] As a joint Institute publication put it in 1956:

The socially conditioned false consciousness of today is no longer objective spirit; it is not . . . crystallized blindly and anonymously out of the social process, but rather is tailored scientifically to fit the society.[134]

This is the case, the Institute claimed, whether one talks about television, film, radio or newspapers, magazines and many kinds of best-sellers. Ideology is no longer just socially necessary illusion. Rather, it is rapidly becoming a planned construct which duplicates and enforces the *status quo*.

Further differences among Institute members

It would be wrong, however, to exaggerate the similarity of style and level of agreement reached between members of the Institute on the status of the culture industry. While Horkheimer's individual works often repeated themes discussed above, he rarely explored them in depth.[135] Adorno's work was more sharply focused and deeply intertwined with the categories of Marx's theory of value. His theory of culture was most often couched in terms of an analysis of the production, distribution, exchange and consumption of cultural forms. His writings are rich in detailed elaborations and illustrations. Adorno argued, as he put it in a letter to Benjamin, that autonomous avant-garde art and popular culture are both 'torn halves of an integral freedom, to which however they do not add up'.[136] 'Genuine' art could be preserved as little in the flux of historical circumstances as popular art could be completely dismissed. Despite his negative assessment of many forms of 'mass culture' he did not completely reject the validity of new techniques of production and reproduction. Furthermore, in the 1960s Adorno added significant reservations to any thesis that maintained the total commercialization and reification of culture. In some of his very last essays he contended: 'Society remains class struggle, today as in the period when that concept originated.'[137] The fundamental contradictions of society remain 'undiminished' and, as a necessary result, consciousness is not, nor can it be, totally integrated.[138]

Although Lowenthal raises a number of questions about the legitimacy of distinctions between genuine and mass art, his *Literature, Culture and Society* and *Literature and the Image of Man* adhere to many of the same basic theoretical presuppositions as Adorno and Horkheimer. (He argued, for example, that literature designed for mass consumption – for instance, popular biographies of 'stars', politicians and businessmen – reflects a 'command psychology' which seeks to ensure that 'people live in a limbo of children and victims'.)[139] Marcuse's analysis of mass culture also has much in common with the studies outlined above. But he does, of course, introduce a series of original categories – the most important being that of 'repressive desublimation' (the systematic limitation on the scope of desublimation, the reduction of the sensual, pleasurable and erotic to specific sexual experiences).[140] As Marcuse's work is well known and accessible, it will not require detailed treatment here. It might be usefully noted, however, that he has argued, in *One Dimensional Man* and in other texts, that the development of mass culture increasingly

establishes a (false) harmony between public and private
   interests;
reinforces privatization and consumption orientations;
spreads an advertising aesthetic;
undermines indigenous working-class culture;
increases the domination of instrumental reason; and
manipulates sexuality – leading to the general pursuit of false and
   limited wants and needs, repressive desublimation.

I shall pursue some of these themes further in Chapter 4, in discussing Marcuse's and other Frankfurt theorists' analysis of the changing basis of identity formation.[141]

Benjamin, as has already been noted, defended a rather different position from any of the others. He saw in the new techniques of mechanical reproduction, and in the distraction offered, certain positive consequences.[142] Through film, radio and literature response mechanisms could be learnt which had radical implications. The new techniques could be of assistance to revolutionary struggle. The tasks 'which face the human apparatus of perception at the turning points of history cannot be solved . . . by contemplation alone. They are mastered gradually by habit . . . the ability to master certain tasks in a state of distraction proves that their solution has become a matter of habit'.[143] Consistent and reliable revolutionary habits could be learnt through a radical politicization of art.[144] Once again following Brecht, Benjamin stressed the possibility of the 'functioning transformation' (*Umfunktionierung*) of aspects of mass culture; 'the transformation of forms and instruments of production by a progressive intelligentsia – an intelligentsia interested in liberating the means of production'.[145] In contradistinction to the other members of the Institute, the central point for Benjamin is that

> a writer's production (whether it be of a novel, play or programme) must have the character of a model: it must be able to instruct other writers in their production and, secondly, it must be able to place an improved apparatus at their disposal. This apparatus will be the better, the more consumers it brings in contact with the production process – in short, the more readers or spectators it turns into collaborators.[146]

Benjamin took Brecht's epic theatre to be the model for this enterprise. Against the views of Adorno, Horkheimer, Marcuse and Lowenthal, Benjamin contended that the writer must transform himself 'from a supplier of the production apparatus, into an engineer who sees his task in adapting that apparatus to the ends of the proletarian revolution'.[147] Benjamin rejected the priority of form or style in favour of enlisting both form and content into the direct service of the revolutionary forces.

4 The changing structure of the family and the individual: critical theory and psychoanalysis

There remains [left over] from the critique of bourgeois consciousness only that shrug of the shoulders with which all physicians have manifested their secret understanding with death.

T. ADORNO, *Minima Moralia*

In order to explore questions about the relation between the individual and society, the members of the Frankfurt school proposed an integration of Marxism and Freudian psychoanalysis. From the late 1930s they defended an increasingly orthodox version of psychoanalysis and a less and less orthodox version of Marxism. They claimed that Freudian theory provided concepts and theorems which revealed a great deal about the socio-psychological formation of the individual. Psychoanalysis is argued to have shown how, as Horkheimer wrote,

the lack of independence; the deep sense of inferiority that afflicts most men; the centering of their whole psychic life around the ideas of order and subordination; their cultural achievements; are all conditioned by the relations of child to parents or their substitutes and to brothers and sisters.[1]

Marxist social theory, on the other hand, amended to take account of the Stalin–Hitler pact, provided an analysis of the structures and conditions which the theory of identity formation presupposed. Each theoretical framework supplemented the other.

The sociological and psychological, Adorno contended, in an article published in 1955, have to be drawn upon in order to analyse aspects of the social whole.[2] Their spheres are interdependent but irreducible to each other; for the individual is a 'unity of identity and difference with society'. Every society reaches into the individual, but within the individual, it is translated into a language quite distinct from that of everyday life – 'the language of the unconscious'. The languages of society and the unconscious are related but separate entities. Adorno believed, however, that the relationship between these phenomena cannot be stipulated once and for all. The relationship changes with history. In a contradictory totality, the spheres of the sociological and psychological cannot be integrated.

The separation of sociology and psychology is both correct and false. False because it encourages the specialist to relinquish the attempt to know the totality which even the separation of the two demands; and correct insofar as it registers more intransigently the split that has actually taken place in reality than does the premature unification at the level of theory.[3]

Whether or not the spheres can be integrated depends, then, on the possibility of overcoming contradictions in an alternative social order: a remote but nonetheless possible future.

Horkheimer's and Adorno's interest in Freud dates from the 1920s. References to psychoanalytic literature are scattered throughout their early writings. Leo Lowenthal, in particular, encouraged Horkheimer to pursue this interest; both underwent periods of analysis. In the late 1920s Horkheimer played a part in the establishment of an Institute of Psychoanalysis at the University of Frankfurt. Although it did not have as secure a position as the Institute of Social Research, it did become the first Freudian institute to be linked to a German university. Among other activities, it offered a series of public lectures by such figures as Anna Freud and Hans Sachs.[4] But it was Erich Fromm, a member of the new Frankfurt Psychoanalytic Institute and, after emigration, a member of the Institute of Social Research, who was perhaps the most important single stimulus to Horkheimer's recognition of the importance of Freud's discoveries. Fromm influenced Horkheimer and, indeed, Adorno also in a both positive and negative manner. His early work taught them a considerable amount about personality structure and the deeply rooted nature of sado-masochism.[5] His writings of the middle and later 1930s stimulated a great deal of discussion but led to his increasing estrangement from the others. Fromm finally left the Institute in 1939 in order to spend more time on clinical work and to develop a psychology that was at once more explicitly sociological and less Freudian. In the process of criticizing this phase of Fromm's career, Horkheimer and Adorno, and later Marcuse, sharpened their own focus on the nature of Freud's contributions. Fromm's relationship to the Institute and his differences with Institute members has received considerable attention. I will, therefore, only provide a brief synopsis of the relevant issues.[6]

Erich Fromm

Fromm's changing relationship to the Institute reflects the changing commitments of the Institute's leading members to Freud. In his earliest contributions to the *Zeitschrift*, Fromm expressed the nature of his interest in psychoanalysis and some of his earliest objections to Freud.[7] Utilizing Freud's notion of libido (the energy underlying the sexual instinct), his early view that sexual and self-preservation instincts are at the root of human psychic life, and his stress on the significance of early childhood experiences for the overall formation of the individual, Fromm sought to show how Freudian theory could enrich Marx's concept of man and the whole Marxist enterprise. Freud's work, on Fromm's account, presupposed ideas which made it compatible with Marx's sociology; these included Freud's insight that individual psychology is simultaneously social psychology. The individual, Freud maintained, must be understood in his or her relations to others.[8] But Freud, as most psychoanalysts after him, had not produced an adequate account of people's 'social being'. Freud's psychology had to be synthesized with Marx's grasp of social structure. Thus, the task of what Fromm called 'analytic social psychology' became that of understanding social phenomena in terms of 'processes involving the active and passive adaptation of the instinctual apparatus to the socio-economic situation'. In certain important respects, Fromm maintained, 'the instinctual apparatus itself is a biological given; but it is highly modifiable. The primary formative factors are economic conditions', while the family 'is the essential medium through which the economic situation exerts its . . . influence on the individual's psyche'.[9]

Fromm was not advocating a mono-causal view of the development of psychic life. One could not always predict from the economic base the future development of the individual or society. As will be noted later, Fromm also argued that character traits can take a long time to alter and, therefore, impede the development of new and radical changes in the economy.[10]

In the early 1930s, Horkheimer, along with other members of the Institute, had been sympathetic to the thrust of Fromm's writings and, especially, his critical approach to aspects of Freud's metapsychology. Fromm referred to Freud's postulation of the death instinct as a weak 'intermingling of biological and psychological tendencies'. The death instinct, a notion developed late in Freud's working life, contradicted his early view of the instincts as, according to Fromm, 'primarily wishing, desiring, and serving man's striving for life'. The early view, Fromm felt, was the correct one. Not only was the idea of a death instinct poorly supported by clinical evidence but it seemed to lead to a false view of humans – abstracted from the *status quo* – which could justify civilization in its present form.[11] However, from Fromm's earliest essays onward, the basis was set for the disagreements which were to motivate his departure from the Institute. Apart from the rejection of the death instinct – which Horkheimer, Adorno and Marcuse were all later to acknowledge as an important concept – Fromm castigated Freud for placing too great an emphasis on early childhood experiences as against the whole personality in its 'social relatedness and isolation'. Furthermore, he argued with ever more vehemence that the main elements of Freud's work are bound to bourgeois and patriarchal values.[12] Freud's neglect of social structures had led him to generalize phenomena like the Oedipus complex into universal human mechanisms; this was misleading. It failed to register the historical specificity of many of the problems Freud tackled. It also meant that Freud failed to capture the particular authority relations that were at the root of many social and individual situations.

As the 1930s progressed, Fromm became less and less committed to orthodox Freudianism. From the beginning of his career he had been interested in philosophical anthropology. In the mid 1930s he was influenced by the work of Johann Bachofen. Marx's 1844 manuscripts were to become even more important for the development of his views – more important even than Freud's ideas. By the time he published *Escape from Freedom* (1941), Fromm posited against Freud the notion of an original unity between people and nature. The seeds of both an historical and existentialist approach were laid. In the appendix of this important text, he argued that 'man is not infinitely adaptable'. In seeming contradiction to the main thesis of his work, he stated that

the striving for justice and truth is an inherent trend of human nature. . . . Man's inalienable rights of freedom and happiness are founded in inherent human qualities: his striving for life, to expand and express the potentialities that have developed in him in the process of historical evolution.[13]

In short, Fromm was more and more committed both to the idea of an essential human nature, which could, of course, be perverted and repressed, and to the view that Freud's work needed to be supplemented by a more sociological and historical approach.[14]

In a letter to Martin Jay (14 May 1971) Fromm remarked:

I consider the basic achievement of Freud to be his concept of the unconscious, its manifestations in neurosis, dreams, etc., resistance, and his dynamic concept of character. These concepts have remained for me of basic importance in all my work.

In the same letter Fromm contended that he never left Freudianism – a claim Horkheimer, Adorno and Marcuse could not accept.[15] By the time he completed *Escape from Freedom*, Fromm had rejected Freud's libido theory, the metapsychology and such central concepts as the Oedipus complex (which he radically recast).[16] The other three men came to see and defend these elements as some of the most significant of Freud's insights. As a result they became ever more critical of Fromm.

Adorno and Marcuse wrote extensive polemics against Fromm and other neo-Freudian revisionists. In a public lecture delivered on 26 April 1946, Adorno, anticipating many of the later points made by Marcuse in his famous exchange with Fromm, not only chastised Fromm and Karen Horney for misrepresenting Freud, but also criticized them for being more mechanistic and less historical in orientation than Freud himself.[17] Fromm and Horney failed to see that Freud's instinct theory, the theory of the life maintaining (sexual) instincts and the death instinct, entailed the possibility of an almost infinite number of patterns in the human psyche, and that it had a most definite relation to history and culture. In denying the validity of Freud's analysis of the id (the instinctual pole of the individual), they were unable to account, Adorno argued, for the reach of culture into the depth of human feelings and, thus, for the origin of repressions, guilt, aggressions, and needs for self-punishment. In addition, Adorno contended, the neo-Freudian postulation of (what Adorno called) 'the unity of the personality' had uncritical, conformist implications. It implied the possibility of a smooth functioning, integrated and unified ego. Now while Freud had accepted that the ego had a synthetic function, he postulated the destructive instincts to account for precisely those deep-rooted conflicts in the psyche which notions of 'inherent unity' could not account for. The impact of childhood traumas and the fragmentary impulses that he discovered, present, Adorno insisted, a more accurate picture of the personality in a contradictory totality than beliefs that imply innate harmony. Marcuse's critique, published almost ten years later (1955), pursued and elaborated upon these and other themes.[18]

On Marcuse's account, the neo-Freudian redefinition of some of Freud's most 'explosive' discoveries (the relation between the id and ego, the function of the unconscious, the scope of sexuality), along with the rejection or defusing of Freud's most speculative concepts such as the death instinct, the hypothesis of the primal horde and primal crime, had destroyed the integrity and import of Freud's work. Marcuse also claimed that the neo-Freudians had distorted Freud and over-simplified psychology with their stress on the necessity of dealing with the 'total personality' (against the particular concern with childhood) and 'sociological factors' (supposedly neglected by Freud). Such a stress revealed an ignorance of both Freud's notions of identity formation and the profoundly sociological and historical character of his thought. The de-emphasis on sexuality also led to a neglect of the antagonisms Freud uncovered between the individual and society, between the individual's search for gratification and existing forms of civilization. 'Behind all the differences among the historical forms of society', Marcuse wrote, 'Freud saw the basic inhumanity common to all of them, and the repressive controls which perpetuate, in the instinctual structure itself, the domination of man by man.' Fromm's attempt to sensitize social psychologists to 'the total individual' and changing 'social conditions' was, Marcuse concluded, 'sociologically and psychologically far more inconsequential than Freud's "neglect" of these conditions'. As a consequence, the critical nature of Freud's work was inaccessible to Fromm. Furthermore, his failure to pursue Freud's conception of the depth of the conflict between the individual and society encouraged a false political optimism and moralism.[19]

The debate with Erich Fromm maps some of the contours of the significance of Freud for critical theory. The same can be said about the Frankfurt theorists' relationship to Reich.

Wilhelm Reich

According to Marcuse, Reich's early writings represent one of the most serious attempts to elaborate 'the critical social theory implicit in Freud'.[20] Reich's attempt to avoid a reduction of Marxism to psychoanalysis or vice versa is noted and praised: in his early work social and instinctual structures specify related but distinct realms, as they do for the Frankfurt theorists. Reich's concern with sexuality, the effects of repression, authoritarianism and the mediating influence of the family between the economy and the individual influenced the thinking of most of those associated with the Institute. But the way in which he developed these concerns did not meet with uncritical enthusiasm. This was the case even in his pre-1935 writings; that is, even before he distanced himself from both Marx and Freud.

In his book *Character Analysis*, written in the 1920s and early 1930s, and in *Mass Psychology of Fascism* (1933), Reich sought to show that 'every social order creates those character forms which it needs for its preservation'. Character structure, he maintained, represents 'the crystallization of the sociological process of a given epoch'.[21] Fromm defended a similar position in a 1932 essay.[22] But unlike Fromm, who then discussed psychoanalytic characterology in fairly familiar psychoanalytic terms, Reich introduced a series of new categories. Ultimately, he understood personality in terms of three structured layers. The first, the most superficial level, consisted of a 'false, sham-social surface', an 'artificial mask' of self-control, restraint, politeness and conscientiousness. The second is 'the Freudian "unconscious" or "what is repressed"', in which 'cruel, sadistic, lascivious, predatory and envious impulses' hold dominance. The third is 'the biological core'. In this deepest layer, people's capacity for '*natural* sociality and sexuality', pleasure, love and work can be uncovered (as well as a capacity, 'if motivated', for rational hatred). Under non-capitalist and non-patriarchal institutions people could live 'honestly, industriously and co-operatively'.[23] However, in the existing order where human natural instincts are repressed, the conscious ego, split from the 'natural core', predominates, along with the unconscious. The result, Reich held, is distorted identity formation and 'maimed' character. Destructiveness and many a perverse impulse are the product of repressed libido – by which Reich essentially meant sexuality. 'It is the inhibition of sexuality . . . which makes aggression a power beyond mastery.'[24] Repressed sexuality, especially genital sexuality, blocks impulses for liberating experiences. Reflections on such experiences become infused with guilt which, Reich argued, is a crucial condition for confused thinking, submissiveness, self-abasement and fear of authority. Reich explained this process as follows:

It was not until relatively late, with the establishment of an authoritarian patriarchy and the beginning of the division of the classes, that suppression of sexuality begins to make an appearance. It is at this stage that sexual interests in general begin to enter the service of a minority's interest in material profit; in the patriarchal marriage and family this state of affairs assumes a solid organizational form. . . . The moral inhibition of the child's natural sexuality [through the formation of a strong super-ego], the last stage of which is the severe impairment of the child's *genital* sexuality, makes the child afraid, shy, fearful of authority, obedient, 'good', and 'docile'. . . . It has a crippling effect on man's rebellious forces because every vital life-impulse is now burdened with severe fear; and since sex is a forbidden subject, thought in general and man's critical faculty also become inhibited.[25]

Rigid, conservative and reactionary thinking is the result. Authoritarian patriarchy ensures 'the organization of sexuality' and the production of 'authoritarian ideologies'. Thus, ideology is 'anchored' in the character structure of the individual.

Although Reich often focused his analysis on the authoritarian and fascist tendencies of the petty bourgeoisie, he frequently generalized his findings to include other social strata in Germany and elsewhere. 'Fascism is only the politically organized expression of the average human character structure.' This structure 'has nothing to do with this or that race, nation, or party but . . . is general and international'.[26] Reich's conclusions as to what could bring about an end of this state of affairs included recommendations establishing the sexual rights of all – including children and adolescents. 'To define freedom', he declared, 'is at the same time to define sexual health.'

To Marcuse, Horkheimer, Adorno (and Fromm), Reich's notions of sexuality and sexual repression were inadequately developed. His early writings tended to reduce, unjustifiably, Freud's concern with the broadest spectrum of erotic sensibilities to a narrow focus on genital sexuality. For Marcuse this meant that Reich was unable to distinguish between different types of repression and sublimation, and their respective (historical) dynamics.[27]

The basis for the degeneration of Reich's later work into an obsession with orgasm and orgone energy was, therefore, laid at an early date. The importance Reich ascribed to sexual liberation *per se* was condemned by all as naive (especially in light of the Nazis' relative openness about sexuality).[28] Nonetheless the intentions behind some of his earlier writings were defended.

The critiques of Fromm and Reich help to clarify the conception of Freudian theory which became so important to the Frankfurt school. Unfortunately, it is difficult to define this conception precisely. Adorno's and Horkheimer's engagement with Freud's work remained incomplete. Their approach to the specific problems of the changing relationship of the individual to society, and to the individual's 'loss of autonomy' – the end of critical thinking – can, nevertheless, be specified.

Concepts of human nature

In his introductory chapter to the Institute's first major publication, *Studien über Autorität und Familie* [Studies on Authority and Family] (1936), Horkheimer specified the limits of his general approach to the notion of human nature. It is worth quoting at length.

> The term 'human nature' here does not refer to an original or an eternal or a uniform essence. Every philosophical doctrine which sees the movement of society or the life of the individual as emerging out of a fundamental, ahistorical unity is open to justified criticism. Such theories with their undialectical method have special difficulty in coming to grips with the fact that new individual and social qualities arise in the historical process. Their reaction to this fact either takes the form of mechanical evolution: all human characteristics which arise at a later point were originally present in germ; or it takes the form of some variety of philosophical anthropology: these characteristics emerge from a metaphysical 'ground' of being. These mutually opposed theories fail to do justice to the methodological principle that vital processes are marked by structural change no less than by continuous development.[29]

As is shown below, Adorno and even Marcuse sometimes expressed a similar position. But there is no simple convergence of views.

Following Freud, Adorno 'ventures the hypothesis that various historical situations and social settings favour various psychological syndromes and "bring out" and accentuate distinct types of possibilities ever present in human beings'.[30] Rational and irrational susceptibilities define part of the human condition. The introductory chapter of the *Authoritarian Personality* states a theory of personality structure which is compatible with this view. The primary forces underlying individuals' identity are, on this account, a bundle of needs, wishes and impulses which are in various states of integration and conflict. Among individuals they can vary in their quality, intensity, mode of gratification, object(s) of their attachment etc.[31] Personality, as the organization of these needs and desires, is not, however, according to the authors, 'to be hypostatized'. It evolves under changing historical conditions and 'can never be isolated from the social totality'.[32] Early childhood, the family, education, economic and political factors are crucial determinants of identity.

This means that broad changes in social conditions and institutions will have a direct bearing upon the kinds of personalities that develop within a society. . . . Although personality is a product of the social environment . . . it is not . . . a mere object of the contemporary environment . . . and is frequently very resistant to fundamental change.[33]

An adequate approach to personality 'must take into account both fixity and flexibility . . . as the extremes of a single continuum along which human characteristics may be placed'.[34] Writing alone in his section of *The Authoritarian Personality*, Adorno stressed the danger of losing sight of the fluid reality of psychological life. But he balanced this remark with the argument that more than ever one can legitimately talk of character structure and character types. For people are typified – standardized, in the present social epoch. Today, 'standardized, opaque, and overpowering social processes . . . leave the "individual" . . . little freedom for action and true individuation'.[35] How society constitutes the individual, producing social character types, became a major focus for Adorno and, indeed, for the Frankfurt school in general.

The Institute's members appeared to agree that the distinctive nature of society has a very important role in the conditioning of character traits common to its members. On this point there were no differences with Fromm. Character structures emerge, as he put it, 'from the basic experiences and modes of life common to particular groups'.[36] In fact, Fromm's early work on psychoanalytic characterology was a prime influence on Horkheimer's and Adorno's thinking in this area. In his 1932 essay on this topic,

Fromm viewed character traits as 'sublimations or reaction formations of certain instinctual drives that are sexual in nature'.[37] (Sublimations transform sexual impulses into non-sexual aims, while
reaction formations utilize the energy of a repressed wish to constitute a behaviour pattern in reaction against it.) From this position
Fromm argued that character traits are likely to remain relatively
stable and take a long time to alter. As a consequence, resistance is
set up to rapid social transformation; the superstructure is embedded in mechanisms that are slower to change than those of the
economic base. *Escape from Freedom* attempted a thorough
exploration of this theme. This idea has also, of course, been held
by Reich. In separate works Horkheimer and Adorno pursued the
same notion although they tied it to a different theory of instinct
and need.[38] The insight provided, they both believed, a foundation
for understanding why a yoke was so often borne – for so long – by
social classes. It helped shed light on why people can still cling to
ideas and behaviour patterns long after their rational justification
has been dissolved. As Horkheimer wrote,

That men preserve economic relations which they have outgrown in force
and need, instead of replacing them through a higher more rational form
of organization, is possible only because the actions of a numerically
significant social stratum are not determined by cognition, but by an
instinctual motive force that falsifies consciousness. In no way do mere
ideological manoeuvres form the root of this historically important
moment . . . on the contrary, the psychic structure of these groups, that is
the character of their members, is constantly renewed in connection with
their role in the economic process.[39]

But within this broad framework, important differences existed
between Horkheimer and Adorno, and Marcuse – differences
about which they most often remained silent. The issues can be
seen most clearly by juxtaposing the views of Adorno and Marcuse. Adorno is extremely critical of all conventional psychoanalytic ideas about the 'well-balanced' personality.[40] The ideal '"good"
Freudian uninhibited by repressions would', he commented, 'in the
existing acquisitive society, be almost indistinguishable from the
hungry beast of prey'. The psychologists' image of a 'superman' is
someone whose freedom, in fact, 'remains false, neurotically
greedy'. As long as society is constituted by structural inequality
and presupposes unfreedom, 'every "image of man" is ideological
except the negative one'.[41] The best possible resolution of the
conflict between individual and society cannot be specified: resolu-

tions that surmount existing contradictions can only be pointed to negatively. The method of immanent criticism cannot justify a positive image of utopia. Such a notion would be highly abstract and ahistorical.

Marcuse, on the other hand, explicitly defends a more elaborate theory of human beings and their potentiality. Negative thinking is important for him. But although he begins by investigating the negative in the present, he insists that history contains the possibility of negating this negation, that is, of realizing that which is constrained by the given and exists in possibility. A concern with sexuality, pleasure and the mechanisms of repression manifested itself in his early writings.[42] It was not until the late 1930s and 1940s that he pursued these interests in detail. In his classic *Eros and Civilization* (1955) and *Five Lectures* (1970), an extremely bold position is expressed.

Life and death in the works of Marcuse

Marcuse aims to develop the 'political and sociological substance of Freud's work'.[43] His analysis begins with an acceptance of some of Freud's most controversial claims. These include the theory of infantile sexuality, the centrality of the unconscious, the seemingly inevitable conflict between the individual and civilization and the notions of the life and death instincts. But Marcuse's interpretation of the significance of these ideas is original and provocative. Ultimately, he seeks to argue that Freud was wrong about the permanent necessity of the repressive transformation of human instinctual structure: under conditions of post-scarcity, the reduction of overdevelopment in the Western world and redistribution of resources, a sensuous order which integrates sexuality into work and play can be established. Marcuse's position can be stated in a number of theses.

1 The human organism develops as a result of two basic instincts: the life instinct (sexuality, *Eros*) and the death instinct (the destructive instinct). (Instincts refer to primary 'drives' which have somatic and mental dimensions; their objectives and manifestations are subject to historical change, although their basic 'location' and 'direction' remain the same.) The life instinct 'strives for the binding of living substance into ever more permanent units', while the death instinct 'desires regression to the condition before

birth, without needs and thus without pain'; it seeks the reversion of life to inorganic matter. Human beings' instincts orient them towards satisfaction without tension.[44]

2 With the beginning of life, the death instinct becomes subjected to the life instinct: destructive energy is diverted either towards the outside world in the form of 'socially useful aggression', for instance, against nature, or it is directed to help master inner impulses. *Eros* seeks pleasure. But within the environment within which the organism develops the immediate gratification of the instincts is impossible.

3 Thus, the psyche's dynamic is dependent upon the struggle between three basic forces: (*a*) *eros* (the sexual instinct), (*b*) the death instinct, and (*c*) material conditions, the 'world for us'. Corresponding to these forces there are three principles that govern mental functioning:

the pleasure principle (the search for satisfaction),

the nirvana principle (the search for the reduction of excitation to zero or as low a level as possible), and

the reality principle (the transformation of energy into goal-directed behaviour necessitated by conditions imposed by the outside environment).[45]

4 Civilization, Freud argued, rests upon the transformation of the species' orientation from the pleasure principle to the reality principle. An unrestrained search for pleasure comes into conflict with scarcity in the natural and human environment. According to Freud, although the reality principle entails the end of immediate satisfaction, it 'safeguards and modifies' pleasure. However, Marcuse argues, there is a 'transubstantiation of pleasure itself'. For gratification, if available at all, now becomes a byproduct of the organization of labour.

5 The human ego is formed and organized in accordance with the reality principle. Reason develops along with a capacity for reality testing. As a result, increased production of the 'means of satisfaction' becomes possible. The scope of wants, needs and the instrumentalities for their satisfaction, steadily increases over time. Both at the level of individual development (ontogenesis) and species development (phylogenesis) this is a major step forward. Renunciation was necessary for the progress of civilization. But the reality principle has to be continually reinforced. Within each individual and epoch, its dominance cannot be taken for granted. The pleasure principle survives in the unconscious and conscious

to affect reality. Scarcity and the 'eternal primordial struggle for existence' enforces repression but also the conditions for the 'return of the repressed' (the continuous re-experiencing and re-enactment of the repressed conflicts and traumas suffered in individual and societal development).

6 The ego is an 'outgrowth' of the primary processes of the id. It emerges in order to co-ordinate and control the id's instinctual impulses. It has to fight on two fronts: defending itself against reality and modifying instincts which might lead to its destruction. But the ego's processes remain secondary. 'The memory of gratification is at the origin of all thinking, and the impulse to recapture past gratification is the hidden driving power behind the process of thought.' The superego develops in the course of the ego's development: it represents 'external restrictions' which have been introjected into the ego (primarily through the struggle of the Oedipus complex). The superego ensures that the ego enforces the demands of the past. Thus adherence to a *status quo ante* is implanted in the instinctual structure.[46]

7 The repressive transformation of the instincts leads to systematic social restraints; restraints on the individual, on his or her labour, and on outer nature itself. Paradoxically, these limitations were necessary for a certain freedom and happiness. It is Marcuse's contention, however, that this is no longer the case today.

Freud believed that 'the price of civilization is paid for in forfeiting happiness through heightening of the sense of guilt'.

> Every renunciation ... becomes a dynamic fount of conscience; every fresh abandonment of gratification increases its severity and intolerance ... every impulse of aggression which we omit to gratify is taken over by the superego and goes to heighten its aggressiveness (against the ego).[47]

The more civilization progresses, on Freud's view, the more repressive it has to become in order to sustain instinctual order and, therefore, cultural development. While Marcuse agrees with those who argue that Freud generalizes from a specific historical form of reality to all civilization, from a particular form of the organization of the reality principle to a supposedly universal state of affairs, he thinks that Freud is right in pointing to a repressive organization of instincts that underpins 'all historical forms of the reality principle in civilization'. Freud's 'unhistorical' analysis 'contains the element of its opposite'.[48] But in order to develop the Freudian categories so that they can be used to account more adequately for changing historical situations, Marcuse introduces two notions: surplus-repression and the performance principle. The former refers to the quantitative impact of specific types of political and economic domination on sexuality, while conceding that a certain amount of (basic) repression is necessary for the reproduction of civilization. The latter denotes the particular historical form of the reality principle as it is organized, for example, by the exchange principle and instrumental reason. These notions, Marcuse argues, remain loyal to the main substance of Freud's thought while differentiating more consistently between the biological and socio-historical vicissitudes of identity formation. They add a fuller historical dimension to the relation between civilization and repression. With the aid of these categories, Marcuse feels, he is able to show both the correctness and limitedness of the Freudian position.

8 In the contemporary epoch, the instinctual constraint enforced by scarcity has been and is intensified by constraints imposed by the hierarchical distribution of scarcity and labour. The performance principle leads to surplus repression. Originally, sexuality was polymorphous-perverse (there were no temporal and spatial limits placed on its manifestation). But at the level of ontogenesis and phylogenesis there is a natural movement from 'generalized bodily eroticism to genital sexuality'. With the advent of the contemporary performance principle, however, this movement has been radically accentuated and distorted. The (capitalist) performance principle presides over the all but complete desexualization of the pre-genital erogenous zones and explores, at best, repressive desublimation: that is, the release of sexuality in ways which reduce erotic energy and remain controlled by the reality principle. The result is a body 'free' for use as labour power. 'Under the rule of the performance principle, body and mind are made into instruments of alienated labour; they can function as such instruments only if they renounce the freedom of the libidinal subject-object which the human organism primarily is and desires.'[49]

9 With the rapid development of the forces of production (especially with the development of the processes of mechanization and automation), the historical necessity for existent forms of repression is undermined. Alienated labour is increasingly rendered unnecessary. Automation promises the end of the use of the body as a mere instrument of production. The technical need

for sexual repression can be challenged. For the performance principle generates the conditions for its own negation.[50] Freud's equation of civilization with repression can be broken – and for reasons, according to Marcuse, which are consistent with Freud's own thinking. A vision of a non-repressive order now becomes possible.

10   Within the 'dialectic of civilization' the conditions have been created for a reconciliation between the pleasure and reality principles. Such a reconciliation would 'reactivate early stages of the libido which were surpassed in the development of the reality-ego', and lead to the dismantlement of existing institutions in which the reality principle exists. The goal of the new society would be to develop lasting erotic relations between conscious, mature individuals. Its conditions include the transformation of toil into play, the self-sublimation of sensuousness and the desublimation of instrumental reason, and the overcoming of time so that gratification can endure. All this adds up to the convergence of reason and happiness in a rationality of gratification.[51]

Can the sex instincts, released from the distortions imposed by surplus repression, create and sustain liberation of this kind? Marcuse clearly believes they can. Given specific preconditions – the abolition of scarcity, the transformation of relations of production, the cultivation of faculties – sexuality, he argues, can create 'highly civilized human relations'. Under the altered conditions there could be a reactivation of all erogenous zones and a resurgence of pregenital polymorphous sexuality. This does not mean simply the pursuit of genital sexuality or the release of suppressed sexuality. Previous restrictions on the aim of the object of the instinct would be relaxed: 'the organism in its entirety' would become 'the substratum of sexuality'. Sexuality would be integrated with the order of work and play. However, in this context, Marcuse further argues, sexuality would 'tend to its own sublimation: the libido would not simply reactivate precivilized and infantile stages, but would also transform the perverted content of these stages'. While the sexual instinct would not be 'deflected' from its aim it would be 'gratified in activities and relations that are not sexual in the sense of "organized" genital sexuality and yet are libidinal and erotic'.[52] What then of the death instinct? Since the death instinct operates under the nirvana principle and aims at a state of minimum tension, in a non-repressive society it can be stifled. The conflict beween life and death would progressively diminish the more society approximated the new sensuous order. With changes in social structure, Marcuse concludes, *eros* can be expected to absorb the death instinct.

The conclusions of Marcuse's analysis are a far cry from Adorno's. Adorno's emphasis on exposing the negative in reality is in marked contrast to Marcuse's defence of a positive conception of reconciliation in human affairs – a reconciliation which suggests the possible supersession of all social contradictions. Despite these differences, however, Adorno and Marcuse shared, along with Horkheimer, a number of similar opinions on the changing nature of the individual, the family and society.

The individual, family and society

The social influence on character, the Frankfurt theorists argued (especially in the mid 1930s), operates most often through the family. In liberal capitalist society, the family is the mediator between the economic structure of the order and its ideological superstructure. The family has, as Horkheimer wrote,

a very special place among the relationships which through conscious and unconscious mechanisms influence the psychic character of the vast majority of people. The processes that go on within the family shape the child from his tenderest years and play a decisive role in the development of his capabilities. The growing child experiences the influence of reality according to the mode in which the latter is reflected in the mirror of the family circle.[53]

The family, as one of the most important agencies for identity formation, 'sees to it', Horkheimer maintained, 'that the kind of human character emerges which social life requires, and imparts to human beings the indispensable capacity for authoritarian attitudes and behaviour on which the existence of the bourgeois order largely depends'.[54] On these points, Fromm, Reich and the Frankfurt school were in agreement.

Conventionally and traditionally the family is seen as either a natural and eternal formation or as an institution the structure and change of which can be directly derived from the structure of society and its change. In the former case, the 'naturalistic conception', the necessity of reproduction and child care are taken for granted and give the family a validity that is beyond question. In the latter case, the 'sociological conception', no autonomy or independence is ascribed to the family's capacity to maintain *or* promote society. The members of the Frankfurt school rejected both these conceptions.[55] The term 'family', they argued, does not refer to a given social form. It is subject to varying 'social dynamics' and it, in turn, affects these dynamics.

Throughout history, the family has, of course, had numerous and changing roles. In contradistinction to the period in which it was the predominant productive unit, the family of the twentieth century has clearly fewer and more ambiguous tasks. Horkheimer, in this introductory essay to *Studies on Authority and Family*, argued that 'not only has the family completely lost many of its former functions but even the ones left to it have been affected by changes in society as a whole'.[56] He noted that in 1911 it was still possible for one scholar of the family, Müller-Lyer, to list its functions as

the management of the household, reproduction, rearing, education of children, the control of population growth and genetic lines, the development of sociableness, the care of the sick and elderly, the accumulation and hereditary transmission of capital and other property, as well as the determination of choice of occupation.[57]

Today (1936), however, Horkheimer stressed, sociological publications are full of evidence that the family is unable to fulfil these functions adequately. Increasingly, the family is 'under the sign of crisis'. Concentration of capital in large-scale manufacturing, the increasing intervention of the state in previously private realms of determination, mobility of labour, etc., have all contributed to an alteration of the structures which condition and support family life.[58] In Horkheimer's opinion, the family still exercises necessary functions – production and nurturing of children, for instance. But it does so 'in an ever more inadequate way due to increasing contradictions and crises'. This situation can be altered only with a radical change in the organization of social relations. The adequate fulfilment of 'family tasks' depends on the creation of a non-competitive, rational society.[59] In order to examine this view more carefully three questions need to be asked. What is Horkheimer *et al*'s conception of the modern family? Why is the family held to be operating in an increasingly inadequate way? What is their conception of an alternative?

In the *Communist Manifesto*, Marx argued that the bourgeois family was founded on capital and private gain. Its form and content depended on commodity production and successful capital accumulation. The 'hallowed co-relation of parent and child' was, he held, 'bourgeois clap-trap'.[60] Hegel, writing in the *Phenomenology*, had had a very different conception. For him the family represented the 'indwelling principle of sociality'. It was a 'natural ethical community', the foundation, ultimately, for all communities.[61] Hegel recognized, however, an opposition between the family and the larger community. The family's positive purpose was 'the individual as such'; individuals are valued for their own sakes.[62] Outside the family, in civil society, individuals act 'in segregation and violation', in competition with one another. Hegel did not conceive of a resolution to this opposition. He was unable, as Horkheimer put it, 'to think of the possibility of a truly united and rational society' in which 'the individual as such' could be the centre of all social institutions.[63] The Frankfurt school's own approach drew upon Hegel's and Marx's concepts. The family, in their view, served contradictory functions and needs.

As people were being reduced to mere adjuncts of the means of production, a similar process was occurring, it was argued, within the family in so far as set sex roles were determining individuals' fates: 'the father was becoming the money-earner, the woman a sexual object or a domestic servant, and the children either heirs of the family possessions or living forms of social security who would later make up with interest . . . the effort expended upon them'.[64] But within the family itself, it was still the case, according to Horkheimer and Adorno, that the individual could find some care and protection. It was a place where suffering and injury could be given expression and where the individual could voice protest against the outside world. In contradistinction to public life, relationships were not conditioned directly by production and the market. Individuals were not simply in a competitive exchange-relation. Horkheimer made the point thus:

In contrast to public life, within the family . . . human beings always had the possibility of being effective not as a mere function but as human beings. Whilst in bourgeois life the collective interest [*gemeinschaftliche Interesse*] – even where it is not mediated through contract as in times of natural catastrophe, war or in repression of revolution – bears an essentially negative character concerning itself with defence against danger, it has in sexual love and maternal care a positive character. In this context the development and happiness of the other is the aim. . . . In the yearning of some adults for the paradise of their childhood, in the manner in which a mother speaks of her son, even if he is in conflict with the world . . . *there are notions and forces alive, which though not connected [tied] to the existence of the contemporary family – and are even in danger of atrophy in this [social] form – have no other resting place in the bourgeois order of life than in the family.'*[65]

In *Minima Moralia*, Adorno adopted a similar stance.[66]

But family life, Horkheimer and Adorno agreed, was being progressively undermined. Changes in familial relations were being forced by the transformation of liberal capitalism into a 'post-competitive', state-capitalist system. In the context of the specification of these general stages of the development of capitalism, study was focused on the relationship between family, authority and authoritarianism.

The birth of capitalism emancipated the family from serfdom. Yet the family retained a pseudo-feudal, hierarchical structure as the direct personal dependence of women and children survived in the home.[67] The power of the father was always based on the dependence of others; he had the capacity to give or withhold things that were greatly wanted. Under capitalism the basis of his authority was, at least for a period, reinforced: 'father' rules the roost not only in virtue of his physical strength but also because he is often the sole breadwinner (and, as a consequence, the one with the most experience of the 'real world' etc.). The relative isolation of women and helplessness of children in the home strengthens his position.

The seeming naturalness of father's power ensures that the restricted family is 'a first-rate schooling in the authority behaviour specific to this society'. The world in which the male child grows (most of the Frankfurt studies focus on the male child), is one of dependence. His experience and fantasies of the world, the mode in which he peoples it, his ideas, wishes and dreams are all, Horkheimer claimed, 'dominated by the thought of man's power over man, of above and below, of command and obedience'.[68] Psychoanalytic theory is drawn upon to explore the processes of the child's identity formation in this situation.

One of the corner-stones of psychoanalysis is the Oedipus complex. Freud believed that this complex constituted the fundamental mechanism in the development of the child and was the 'nucleus of neurosis'. The complex defines a crucial avenue in which the struggle for personal autonomy is or is not realized. Crudely put, the child desires (at the age of 4 or 5) the parent of the opposite sex. The desire is thwarted as the child fears the repercussions (for example castration) from the parent of the same sex. The result is various forms of identification with, and internalization of, the commands and prohibitions of the parent of the same sex. The child redirects the aim of his desire. The internalization of a previously feared outside authority figure (the father) becomes an important stage in the successful development of the ego. The relationship must be internalized and the superego thus formed. As Marcuse wrote,

through the struggle with father and mother as personal targets of love and aggression, the younger generation entered societal life with impulses, ideas, and needs which were largely *their own* . . . the formation of their superego, the repressive modification of their impulses, their renunciation and sublimation were very personal experiences.[69]

Through these experiences the child takes over the role of the father, develops a conception of self and wins autonomy. However, through these experiences the child also learns to respect what is existent and given. In this process he comes to understand and adapt to the bourgeois relationship to authority.[70] The son, Horkheimer argued,

may think what he will of his father, but if he is to avoid conflicts and costly refusals he must submit to his father and satisfy him. The father is, in the last analysis, always right where his son is concerned. The father represents power and success, and the only way the son can preserve in his own mind a harmony often shattered in the years before puberty's end, is to endow his father, the strong and powerful one, with all the other qualities the son considers estimable . . . childhood in a limited family becomes an habituation to an authority which in an obscure way unites a necessary social function with power over men.[71]

In this situation whatever autonomy the child achieves develops 'with and against the other'. But with the massive changes that have occurred with the development of capitalism, this process, Horkheimer, Adorno and Marcuse all argued, has radically altered. With the decline of the independence of the economic subject, the subject itself is threatened with the loss of its autonomy. The sociological conditions of the Oedipal situation were thought to be decisively changing and, with them, the psychodynamics of identity formation. This process was analysed in a number of different ways by the three men. But from all their analyses, two factors emerge as central: increasingly the legitimacy of the father's authority is undermined, and the child aspires ever less to become like his father.

Although they recognized that the authority structure of the family and, in particular, the father may maintain itself after its material basis has disappeared, they nonetheless contended that this structure had been severely weakened. Drawing on evidence collected from a wide variety of sources, including the Institute's own *Studies on Authority and Family*, they argued that within the family children are provided with less and less protection against the pressures of the outside world.[72] For the family's reliability as a source of economic life support is decreasing. The father's position as wage or salary earner is insecure. Particularly during times of chronic unemployment and inflation, his position as provider is severely threatened if not completely undermined. With the reduction of his authority as a transmitter of material goods, there is also a reduction of his authority as a teacher of skills and experiences. In the total schema of things, 'father' has less and less to offer. One of the foundation stones of his image as 'potent' is shattered.

The position of the father is made worse by his sons' early 'economic maturity'. In *Studies* it was found that adolescent boys are increasingly independent of their father's income. Of course, during economic crisis they are some of the first to be made redundant. Nonetheless, their sense of independence lives on and is a permanent challenge to paternal authority.[73]

The forces leading to the progressive disintegration of the family have by no means solely the 'positive aspect of liberation from heteronomous authority'. The decline of the bourgeois family does not entail that 'freer, less authoritarian forms are taking their place'.[74] In fact, more authoritarian forms took their place in Weimar and Nazi Germany and are taking hold often today. As it was expressed in *Aspects of Sociology*:

in the early phases of his development the child still undergoes the same experiences of hate and love with respect to his father, which constituted the Oedipus complex. . . . More rapidly than before, however, the child discovers that the father by no means embodies the power, justice and goodness the child had initially expected. The actual weakness of the father within society . . . extends into the innermost cells of the psychic household: the child can no longer identify with the father, no longer can accomplish that internalization of the familial demands, which with all their repressive moments still contributed decisively to the formation of an autonomous individual. Therefore there is today actually no longer the conflict between the powerful family and the no less powerful ego; instead the two, equally weak are split apart. . . . From his relationship to his father the child now carries away only the abstract idea of arbitrary, unconditional power and strength and then searches for a stronger, more powerful father than the real one, who is truly adequate to this image, a super-father, as it were, like the one produced by the totalitarian ideologies.[75]

Father's weakness means that his prohibitions do not have the force they once possessed. The superego is not formed in the usual manner; it no longer evolves in a protracted struggle with the father. Although the child still learns of father's strength and power – which is of course greater than his own – he is, as he gets older, made ever more aware of father's 'impotence' in reality. The father is unable to justify his image in the child's eyes. In this situation the child retains a concept of the powerful but searches elsewhere for its fulfilment. A general state of susceptibility is created to outside forces. Increasingly the superego is the representative of collectivities, for example the school class, the club, the state. The child has to adapt to an external authority that is 'more powerful and less spiritual, less "internalized" than parental authority ever was'.[76]

In this context the child continues to fear and submit to authority. Fear, in fact, becomes one of the main sources of motivation. The development from a state of fearing 'another' (the father), to the internalization of this outside figure and, therefore, to the negation of this fear, does not occur. The process of internalization fails. Thus, an autonomous ego is not formed. The overwhelming pressures of external forces, the culture industry and other 'authorities' become more influential in determining the demands and prohibitions with which the individual identifies.

This view of changes in the pattern of identity formation is not only consistent with aspects of Freud's work but dependent upon certain of his insights, especially those disclosed in his *Group Psychology and the Analysis of the Ego*. In this text Freud argued that, in a number of situations, the object of libidinal cathexis can be put in the place of the 'ego-ideal' (which he later replaced by the concept superego). He discussed the situation in which the ideal of the father can be transferred to secondary groups and their leaders. He interpreted this process as one in which 'the individual gives up his ego-ideal and substitutes it for the group ideal as embodied in the leader'.[77] This can occur when 'a number of individuals have put one and the same object in the place of their ego-ideals and have consequently identified themselves with one another in their ego': that is, all egos now have the same (relationship to the) ego-ideal. In such circumstances 'we have an impression', Freud points out, 'of a state in which an individual's private emotional impulses and intellectual acts are too weak to come to anything by themselves and are entirely dependent for this on being reinforced by being repeated in a similar way in other members of the group'.[78]

On the Frankfurt school's account, this is the case today. The male child does not wish to become like his father but, rather, like the image projected by the culture industry (or by fascist demagogues, as in Nazi Germany). The classical process of ego differentiation and individuation is increasingly undermined. An autonomous ego is not formed and yet there is submission to authority. The modern family, interlocked with other institutions, produces 'the ideal object of totalitarian integration'. For the 'collectivized Ego-ideal is the satanic counterpart of a liberated ego'.[79]

These developments were thought to have been exacerbated by changes in the role of the mother. Writing in 1936 Horkheimer stressed that if the present-day family remains a source of strength to resist dehumanization it is essentially because 'women still foster human relations'.[80] But, he added, 'it must also be recognized that because of her dependence woman herself has been changed'. Her dependence in the family, and in extra-familial institutions, on men ensures that her own development is lastingly restricted. Despite enforced passivity and the systematic restrictions on her wants and needs, 'mother', Horkheimer argued, strengthens the authority of the *status quo* in two ways. First, through her dependence on her husband's economic resources and earnings she is linked to his ambition. As a result, she often becomes a conservative force: her main worries often focus on the stability of her husband's work and income, thus reinforcing a 'sense of economic and social responsibility'. Struggle against given historical conditions becomes, therefore, fraught with greater anxiety.[81] Second, through her submission to the patriarchal family, women become instruments for sustaining the existing patterns of relations and authority. Since women are particularly dependent on the equation of marriage, security and family, they contribute to the social maintenance of sex roles and to the exaltation of marriage, thereby inhibiting non-monogamous sensual urges.[82]

Women's gradual admission into the economic world of the male has not helped, according to both Horkheimer and Adorno. Increasingly, she also takes over the behaviour patterns of a thoroughly reified society. She becomes 'just another mouthpiece of reality'. Her former capacity to be a 'mitigating intermediary' between her children and brute reality is sapped.[83]

These social processes had, of course, a class-specific impact. When conditions in the labour market were more or less buoyant, proletarian families took the shape, in Horkheimer's view, of the bourgeois family, although some differences remained. He felt that the fate of the proletarian families in the modern era was often similar to the case described above but he recognized that working-class families were particularly susceptible to external forces. Economic pressures quickly forced husband, wife and child (in the early stages of capitalist development) and husband and wife (in advanced capitalism) outside the home. As a consequence, home life became more difficult. With unemployment the situation was made even worse. 'There can be no longer any question of a private existence with its own satisfactions and values. In the extreme case, the family becomes the available form of sexual satisfaction and, for the rest, a source of multiplied anxieties.'[84]

In 1936, Horkheimer still maintained that

Out of the suffering caused by the oppressive conditions that prevail under the sign of bourgeois authority, there can arise a new community . . . to replace the individualistic motive as the dominant bond in relationships.'[85]

Horkheimer's view seemed to be that as the family fulfilled fewer and fewer of the tasks that sprang from its original antagonistic character, a community of men and women might arise *outside* of the family. It must be said, however, that the nature of this 'possibility' is never elaborated in his work. It is conceived only negatively. His texts are full of highly suggestive remarks but there is no full historical account.

Adorno's essays on ego weakness and narcissism

In a number of essays written during the 1940s and 1950s Adorno sought to explore further the psychoanalytic dimension of the individual's loss of autonomy.[86] He set out to examine the consequences of the failure of the process of internalization. Of these, two in particular were of importance: ego weakness and narcissism, which leave the id impulses susceptible to manipulation. According to Adorno, Freud 'clearly foresaw the rise and nature of fascist mass movements in purely psychological categories'.[87] In *Group Psychology and the Analysis of the Ego* (1922), Freud came to see, through reflection on the individual, 'traces of its profound crises and willingness to yield unquestioningly to powerful outside, collective agencies'. In his 'Freudian theory and the pattern of Fascist propaganda', Adorno registered agreement with this analysis.

Following Freud, he believed that 'the bond which integrates the individuals into a mass, is of a libidinal nature' and is to be explained in terms of the pleasure principle – in terms of the gratifications individuals obtain when they surrender to a large group. Within a group the individual is in a situation which encourages the undoing of repressions of unconscious instincts, thereby unleashing and utilizing energy 'from other psychological agencies which are pressed into the service of the unconscious' (for example, energies of destructiveness or energies which derive from the subjects' archaic inheritance).[88] The central mechanism for transformation of libido into a bond between follower and follower and between follower and leader is identification. Identification involves an essential, primitive narcissistic aspect, one which makes the 'beloved object part of oneself'. The authoritarian leader becomes, Adorno argued, 'an enlargement of the subject's own personality'. Hence strong narcissistic impulses can be absorbed and satisfied by identification and idealization of a leader. Hostility to 'out groups' can also be explained by this mechanism: for all individual and/or group characteristics which are different from the 'in-group's' own pattern of development are taken as a criticism or threat.[89] Adorno's discussion of the relationship between the id, ego and superego in circumstances such as these remains incomplete. In 'Sociology and psychology', however, he stressed that the ego's formation under modern conditions is subject to severe strain. In an analysis of the ego he pursued the theme of its present weakness and narcissistic tendencies.

The concept of ego is dialectical; 'both psychic and extrapsychic, a quantum of libido and the representative of outside reality'. The ego is 'the co-ordinator of psychic impulses'. It both 'arrests the play of inner forces' and tests them against outside reality.[90] But its cognitive activity, Adorno argued, 'performed in the interests of self-preservation, has to be constantly reversed, and self-awareness forgone in the interests of self-preservation'.[91] This is because the ego has both to understand society in order to operate within it and in order to sustain this operation it has to establish unconscious prohibitions to manage the 'often senseless renunciations imposed on it'. Further, many forms of renunciation remain unintelligible; they are prohibitions which the individual does not identify with nor internalize. Thus, the contradictory situation arises in which 'the ego is supposed to be both, *qua* consciousness, the opposite of repression, and, *qua* unconsciousness, the repressive agency itself'.[92] Freud did not, on Adorno's account, provide an adequate view of the 'life and death' nature of the ego's position. (Adorno's views on the concept of superego remain somewhat unclear in this essay. Traces of the concept remain, although it is evident that, because of the changing structure of the family etc., Adorno no longer thinks this key Freudian category can be employed in the traditional manner.)

The ego, Adorno held, is constantly 'taxed beyond its powers'. Where the ego does not develop its potential for self-differentiation, it regresses towards ego-libido – libido which cathects the ego (the ego is taken as love-object) – or, at the very minimum, it mingles its conscious and unconscious functions. The usual result is that the ego is both negated and rigidified: there is chronic ego weakness (which the *Authoritarian Personality* sought to understand) and narcissism. In fact, Adorno appears to suggest that narcissism replaces internalization. In narcissism the ego's self-preserving function is retained, but 'split off from that of consciousness and thus lost to rationality'.[93] The ego is left in a frail state both in its relation to the instincts and to outside forces. This frailty is usually experienced as 'narcissistic injury'. The ensuing experiences of helplessness gives the ego limited choices in any attempt to overcome its position: it can either change reality or retreat to the id. Retreat is frequently chosen. But the exact nature of retreat, the course of regression, is determined by objective historical factors. The individual is exposed to a variety of sources offering gratification and protection. Taking advantage of this susceptibility, particular social forces can mobilize id impulses and infantile defence mechanisms to their advantage. Fascism and the culture industry feed on and nurture regression. They determine its prevalent form.

Marcuse: the obsolescence of the Freudian concept of man?

Pursuing a number of similar ideas, Marcuse argues that as a result of the strengthening of extra-familial authority, the absorption of the ego's confrontation with father by 'social reason', there is a 'reification of the ego itself'.[94] The ego's independence is undermined. Delivered to the superego, it becomes 'all the more a subject of destruction and all the less a subject of Eros'. As individuals tend to identify with a group ideal at the expense of their own ego-ideals, external, conventional and stereotyped values replace their own thinking. The individual's psychological state becomes highly rigid and, therefore, unable to cope with the unexpected. The unpredictable and irrational remain unmastered. The ego is faced with growing anxiety, constriction and destructiveness.[95]

Marcuse's analysis, however, goes a step further than that of Adorno (and of Freud). He contends that the decline of entre-preneurial capitalism, the decline in importance of inherited skills, the rise of general education and the expansion of public and private administrations have all been so dramatic that even Freud's group psychology seems obsolete. Freud's theory requires the internalization of social control through a struggle between instinctual and social needs – a struggle which takes place within the ego and against personal authority.[96] No matter how remote this authority is from the individual's life, it must still be 'embodied' in a person, so that the ego ideal can be transferred to the leader (or an equivalent) as father image. Film stars, 'personalities' and 'leaders', of course, still have an effect in this role. But today's conditions, Marcuse declares, do not correspond to the society Freud observed; we are faced with a 'society without fathers' and, as a consequence, the threat of an enormous release of destructive energy. Even stars and leaders are increasingly caught up in the seemingly self-perpetuating authority of the pro-duction apparatus: a society of total reification. The ego-ideal becomes embodied in economic laws: 'the technical code, the moral code, and that of profitable productivity are merged into one effective whole'.[97] Society is still, of course, held together by a form of libidinal relationship. But it is a relationship constituted by reified social relations and personified things (for example automobiles). Everyday gratification remains ungratifying, unsatisfactory: it reflects repressive desublimation.

In a society tending toward one-dimensionality, the individual Freud understood is threatened with obsolescence. In summary this is because:

severe limits are placed on ego development;
there is a decline of the position of the father;
individuals do not develop an autonomous conscience;
values and prohibitions become less central to the individual's
  concerns and reflections;
there is a transference of the ego ideal to a group ideal – now itself
  being undermined;
repressive desublimation reinforces social control.

As a result regression and the transgression of old moral codes become ever more likely. A certain amount of aggression, in Marcuse's opinion, is absorbed by normalized avenues of hostility towards 'sanctioned' out-groups, for instance communists, black people. But a situation of unstable equilibrium is created. It is a situation which could be undermined by any number of events and which could well lead to the further unleashing of irrational forces.

Thus, despite themselves, the neo-Freudians registered a truth about existing society: the Freudian model of the individual is an unsatisfactory basis for understanding the individual's fate in society. However, Marcuse argues, 'psychoanalysis draws its strength from its obsolescence: from its insistence on individual needs and individual potentialities which have become outdated' in the present. 'That which is obsolete is not, by this token false ... the Freudian concepts invoke not only a past left behind but also a future to be recaptured'.[98] The neo-Freudians, therefore, are guilty of absolutizing a developmental trend in society. They take society's present for its essence. Their 'realism' marks a premature and false abandonment of the 'most provocative hypotheses' of psychoanalysis.

Studies on prejudice and authoritarianism

The Institute initiated and participated in a variety of projects to investigate the relationship between the individual, family and society. Some of its most original empirical work was executed in this area. The focus was nearly always on problems relating to prejudice, authority and authoritarianism. From the early 1930s Horkheimer sought to plan and involve himself in research in this field. In the 1940s, Adorno participated in one of the most far reaching studies ever conducted in social psychology in an effort to pursue at an empirical level many of his concerns about the individual's capacity for authoritarian behaviour. Marcuse was one of the few who did not carry out extensive empirical work on these (and, in fact, on all the other) issues.

The most well known and most important study was, of course, *The Authoritarian Personality* (1950) by Adorno, Else Frenkel-Brunswick, Daniel Levinson and R. Nevitt Sanford. But the study was only one part of a larger project entitled *Studies in Prejudice*. It consisted in its published form of five volumes. Apart from *The Authoritarian Personality*, these include: *Prophets of Deceit* (1949) by Leo Lowenthal and Norbert Guterman; *Rehearsal for Destruction* (1949) by Paul Massing; *Dynamics of Prejudice: A Psychological and Sociological Study of Veterans* (1950), by Bruno Bettelheim and Morris Janowitz; and *Anti-Semitism and Emotional Disorder: A Psychanalytic Interpretation* (1950), by Nathan W. Ackerman and Marie Jahoda. The *Studies* were directed by Horkheimer. Although he did not write extensively in any of the volumes, he shaped the overall plan of the contributions and much of the final content.[99] Project work began in 1945.

Lowenthal and Guterman's work investigated the devices employed by 'rabble-rousers', a small group of American neo-fascist demagogues, to win over and stimulate audiences. The research consisted of a series of detailed analysis of radio speeches, leaflets and pamphlets written by people often explicitly sympathetic to Hitler. It was discovered that the 'rhetorical tricks' were often the same in America and Nazi Germany. This was not simply because the Americans copied the Nazis. Rather, it was because in both countries the agitators speculated and played on similar emotions. Since few positive political programmes emerged from their speeches, it seemed clear that the conveyance of rational information was not their goal. Their often 'shrewdly emotional' oratory sought to provide surrogate satisfactions for audiences through the very nature of the oratory itself. Their whole style, Lowenthal and Guterman argued, functioned as a form of wish-fulfilment, substituting means for ends. It appealed to the individual, to the 'little man' who seeks to be less lonely, threatened and isolated. It speaks to the secretly self-ordained who wish to belong, to be powerful and great. The agitator's ceaseless repetition of clichés, and the rigid thinking that it reflected, was investigated further by some of the other studies.

While Paul Massing's text provided an account of the emergence of anti-Semitism – as a political tool and confused expression of social protest – in imperial Germany, Bettelheim and Janowitz presented a substantial analysis of prejudice among veterans. Lengthy interviews were carried out with 150 such individuals in Chicago. Although Bettelheim and Janowitz concluded that the weaker the personality the more vulnerable the individual to outside influences, they did not find positive correlations between conformity and prejudice – one of the main findings of *The Authoritarian Personality*. (It has been suggested that the discrepancy between the two studies on this issue can be explained by the different class backgrounds of those in their respective samples.)[100] But in agreement with *The Authoritarian Personality*, they found that prejudice tends to diminish with increased ego strength; an autonomous ego is more tolerant than an ego formed in processes involving inadequate internalization and differentiation. Ackerman's and Jahoda's research consisted of a secondary analysis of forty case studies collected from twenty-five analysts. Both Ackerman, a trained analyst, and Jahoda were extremely reluctant to draw generalizations about the relation between anti-Semitism and particular emotional syndromes. The psychological specificity of the anti-Semite varies, they argued, from case to case. 'The selection of anti-Semitism – from the psychodynamic point of view – ... is a more or less *accidental* manifestation of the prejudiced person's deficiencies.' A readiness to generalize, however, about the relation between aspects of personality and prejudice, was not absent from the authors of *The Authoritarian Personality*.

The authors of this study benefited greatly (as did *Studies in Prejudice* generally) from previous research conducted by the Institute – particularly from two early projects concerned with beliefs and their relation to character.[101] *The Authoritarian Personality* aimed at analysing the susceptibility of individuals to anti-democratic propaganda. It sought to investigate the socio-psychological preconditions of the potential fascist. The central question was: why do certain individuals have fascist leanings while others do not? The study endeavoured to establish interconnections between certain character traits and beliefs, such as aggressive nationalism and racial prejudice. Its authors were guided by the hypothesis that 'the political, economic, and social convictions of an individual often form a broad and coherent pattern . . . and this pattern is an expression of deep-lying trends in his personality'.[102] The study claimed to uncover a personality syndrome which is associated directly with rigid, dogmatic and prejudiced thinking.

Adorno and Sanford were the co-directors of the project. Sanford, along with Else Frankel-Brunswick and Daniel Levinson, were leading members of the Berkeley Public Opinion Study Group, with which the Institute co-operated for the duration of the project. The Berkeley contribution, not surprisingly, considerably strengthened the Institute's capacity to handle research techniques, including the creation of scales, the categorization and quantification of interview material, and the use of statistical techniques. While each of the four authors participated in many parts of the study, there was a division of labour.[103]

The project combined both quantitative and qualitative approaches: questionnaires, statistical tests, projective measures and clinical interviews. Despite Adorno's very critical attitude towards the use of quantitative methods, he felt that given a suitable theoretical framework, they could be employed fruitfully.[104] The categories which underpin quantitative research are, he insisted, always qualitative and must be derived from appropriate theoretical considerations.[105] The project's main categories were derived from psychoanalytic characterology. The study's model of the individual was influenced heavily by Freud. Academic psychology provided the approach to the more directly observable and measurable aspects of personality. But Adorno characteristically did not feel that the theory which underpinned the study was on test in the study itself. As he put it,

we never regarded the theory simply as a set of hypotheses but as in some sense standing on its own feet, and therefore did not intend to prove or disprove the theory through our findings but only to derive from it concrete questions for investigation, which must then be judged on their own merit and demonstrate certain prevalent socio-psychological structures.[106]

The Authoritarian Personality, he thought, succeeded in demonstrating the existence of such structures, although he admitted that the study as a whole was open to a number of fundamental criticisms.[107]

The subject population for the project was drawn from fairly diverse groups, though there was a very marked slant in the sample towards the middle-class. Over 2000 questionnaires were distributed. On the basis of the results, approximately one-tenth of the respondents were interviewed. In order to help clarify the meaning of the data from questionnaires, interviews, which often extended over a number of sessions, explored issues relating to both the individual's childhood and relationship to the family, and his or her 'world-view'. Both questionnaires and interview schedules were carefully drawn up so that results from each could be compared and contrasted. Interviews were designed so that they could be analysed statistically and employed to assess further the results from the questionnaires.[108]

The most famous device employed by the project was the 'F-scale', so-called because it is concerned with the measurement of 'implicit prefascist tendencies'. The scale was the result of continuous efforts to measure anti-Semitism, ethnocentrism and political and economic conservatism, and their respective relation to character structure. Research began by using three separate scales to measure each phenomenon; respectively, the A–S scale, the E scale and the PEC scale. The F-scale synthesized aspects of the three measurement devices. It had two interrelated goals: to measure prejudice without mentioning, for example, religious and ethnic groups; and to measure the character structure underlying such opinions. The aim was to reveal a 'syndrome' or 'structural unit' which its authors declared represents the potentially fascist character. The syndrome was thought to be constituted by nine basic personality variables:

Conventionalism   Rigid adherence to conventional, middle-class values.

Authoritarian submission   Submissive, uncritical attitude towards idealized moral authorities of the ingroup.

Authoritarian aggression   Tendency to be on the look-out for, and to condemn, reject and punish people who violate conventional values.

Anti-intraception Opposition to the subjective, the imaginative, the tender-minded.

Superstition and stereotypy The belief in mystical determinants of the individual's fate; the disposition to think in rigid categories.

Power and 'toughness' Preoccupation with the dominance–submission, strong–weak, leader–follower dimension; identification with power figures; overemphasis upon the conventionalized attributes of the ego; exaggerated assertion of strength and toughness.

Destructiveness and cynicism Generalized hostility, vilification of the human.

Projectivity The disposition to believe that wild and dangerous things go on in the world; the projection outwards of unconscious emotional impulses.

Sex Exaggerated concern with sexual 'goings-on'.[109]

Within the general frame of reference of the authoritarian personality a number of further types, or subsyndromes, were pointed to; they were differentiated according to an emphasis on one or another of the personality variables. The subsyndromes were analysed by Adorno on the basis of the empirical findings and theoretical developments of the study.[110] They were given a tentative status. For Adorno, they suggested the necessity of further research into each of the character traits.

A massive array of data was presented by the authors and was claimed to give 'considerable support' to the contention that the general syndrome existed. The results attained by the F-scale were found to have a .75 correlation with those of the E-scale. Although the average correlation between the F and the PEC scale was only about .57, this was explained by the prevalence of 'pseudoconservatism', a phenomenon that was thought to be 'most expressive of the personality trends which the F-scale measures'. Pseudoconservatism entails a relatively superficial identification with authoritarian patterns with considerable carry-overs of emotional conflicts (strong ambivalence and destructive countertendencies).[111] The authors refrained from drawing many generalizations about how widespread the authoritarian personality might be. No data was presented about the frequency of high and low scores within the surveyed population.[112] But despite this stance, a number of remarks can be found which suggest that the researchers had a view about the extent of the syndrome. In his section, Adorno referred to an 'indubitable mass basis' and general concluding comments suggested that the majority of the tested population are not very high but in the middle of the scale.[113] These remarks were at best, given the data base, injudicious (as critics of the study have pointed out). They do not point (nor are they, of course, intended to) to the most interesting aspects of the project: the revelation of the syndrome itself.

The classic authoritarian type emerges, Adorno argued, from a sado-masochistic resolution of the Oedipus complex. Love for the mother is placed under a severe taboo. A strict father, or a general atmosphere of coldness and little love, forces the infant to repress feelings of desire. A home of marked but often arbitrary discipline ensures that strong feelings of ambivalence and hostility to the parents have to be hidden. The child must learn to direct his feelings along socially acceptable channels. Hatred for the father is, as a result, transformed by reaction-formation into love.[114] The early rebellion against the father is thereby also repressed, but only to resurface later in the form of authoritarian aggression – aggression that is turned both into masochism and sadism.

Findings from the interviews indicated that those who were highly susceptible to fascist propaganda idealized their parents and uncritically identified with their families. The image of the parents is conventionalized and stereotyped: the father is 'stern, just, successful, detached and a (sometimes) generous disciplinarian', while the mother is 'good looking, healthy, clean and endowed with many practical skills'. A tendency to complete submissiveness to family authority in early childhood was also revealed. Repressed early resentment of parental harshness seemed to go hand in hand with the parents' idealization. But along with these attitudes, little evidence was found of genuine attachment to the parents as individuals – to their problems and weaknesses. As Horkheimer summarized the point, 'the abstract glorification of the family is paralleled by an almost complete lack of concrete emotional ties, either positive or negative, to the parents'.[115] The actual underlying 'weakness' of the parents' position was suggested by the way in which parental values remained ego-alien to the child. In these circumstances a particular type of superego is formed; one which remains over-rigid and externalized.[116] Thus, the father does not have genuine inner authority. The child's identity remains poorly integrated and susceptible to external pressures.

The authoritarian syndrome is based, then, on ego weakness. Outside forces, of suitable intensity and direction, can activate and draw upon the repressed urges. In the face of powerful social forces, the ego is unable to cope with the demands of self-determination. Unmanageable and repressed desires are dealt with by projecting them on to groups in the environment. In the search for security and escape from responsibility, the individual identifies with powerful external authorities. Submissiveness and coldness, combined with aggression (against the self but projected) against others, are the likely characteristics of this type. Relief and pleasure are gained from obedience and from the 'destruction' of those who are weak and represent qualities the individual finds intolerable in his or her self.

The syndrome is, Adorno suggested, highly characteristic of the lower-middle classes in Europe.[117] It is likely to result from conditions in which the structure of the family are rapidly changing, where there is disintegration of (petit-bourgeois) property relations, and discrepancy between actual and aspired status.[118] These conditions, themselves the result of 'the false goals of the economy', exacerbate individual propensities for sado-masochism.[119] Exaltation of the in-group, racial prejudice, a commitment to nationalism and a contempt for indecision, discussion and democracy become familiar attitudes of this type. But a pervasive confusion about political and social issues also typifies the authoritarian personality: political attitudes are often riddled with fear and uncertainty.

In an analysis of the belief structures of those interviewed, Adorno showed that although there is an 'ignorance and confusion ... when it comes to social matters beyond the range of ... immediate experience', a gap exists between individuals' 'official' ideology – what they feel (and think they ought to feel) about the conventional sphere of politics – and their ideas about issues which express more immediate problems and needs. In the discussion of everyday concerns, Adorno detected a certain progressiveness.[120] Thus, an incomplete identification with authoritarian patterns was revealed: a pseudo-conservatism. As against genuine conservatism, this type can be compatible with support for populist movements. But it most often leads to uncritical identification with higher and more powerful social groups. It has highly regressive qualities.

The authoritarian personality was contrasted to an identity pattern characterized mainly 'by affectionate, basically egalitarian, and permissive interpersonal relationships'. With a strong sense of personal autonomy and independence, this type is capable of critical thinking. He or she is a person who 'actively seeks progressive social change, who can be militantly critical (though not necessarily totally rejective) of the present *status quo*'.[121] The non-authoritarian personality directs emotions and feelings towards the other as subject. Id tendencies are not banished but synthesized with a capacity for love and compassion. As the authors of the study concluded: 'If fear and destructiveness are the major emotional sources of fascism, *eros* belongs mainly to democracy.'[122]

Anti-Semitism

It has often been said that *The Authoritarian Personality* turns authoritarianism into a phenomenon of the psyche and fails to explain it at the sociological level. It should be clear, however, that if the study is properly located within the Institute's programme, this charge misses the mark. *The Authoritarian Personality* is only one study amongst a number, many of which have complementary purposes. Furthermore, while it was being planned and executed, Horkheimer and Adorno were writing *Dialectic of Enlightenment*. In the fourth part of this latter text, they concentrated on an explication of some of the major social conditions of anti-Semitism. Their major thesis is, 'bourgeois anti-Semitism has a specific economic reason: the concealment of domination in production.'[123] Since the mechanism for the generation of structured inequality is 'hidden' in the day to day process of production and exchange, the source of misery and toil is hard to understand. Capitalists claim to be productive, to be engaged in the creation of social wealth in the national interest. Further, they often blame the non-productive for society's problems. In Nazi Germany, the Jews, among other groups, were the victims of this accusation.

Throughout the ages the Jews have often been denied access to the ownership of the means of production and to many different types of employment. They have found economic opportunities, however, in trade and commerce – in the circulation sector. The activity of this sector, in relation to manufacturing, is difficult to comprehend. The tradesman or merchant appears to be unproductive, and yet the profit taker – a thief or parasite. On Horkheimer's and Adorno's account, 'the merchant [most often the Jew] presents . . . [the workers] with the bill which they have signed away to the manufacturer. The merchant is the bailiff of the whole system and takes the hatred of others upon himself'.[124] Thus, a tendency is established to attribute the injustice perpetuated by a whole class sytem to the Jews. The situation is compounded by the growth of monopolies and trade organizations (for example, cartels) which reduce in importance the role of the 'independent' circulation sector. The middleman becomes less and less necessary and potentially dispensable. As a result, the Jews (and others in similar positions) seemed 'ready-made' to be blamed for the failures of the economic system; their economic position and symbolic significance made them easy targets for aggression and persecution.

Utilizing psychoanalytic theory, Horkheimer and Adorno tried to explain in greater detail what it was that Jews represented to the masses. Anti-Semitism, they argued, is based on a projection of fears and repressed wants. For example, feelings of inability to cope and impotence are projected onto those who appear (or are made to appear) capable and potent. The Jews were a suitable case for such treatment. They were perceived as both 'no better than animals' and a threat. For they were thought to live according to feelings and styles their tormentors envied but found intolerable and dangerous. In desperation, the anti-Semite sought to 'castrate' the feared 'castrator'. Anti-Semitism is, in part, a manifestation of unconscious, regressive processes. It could express and unite both the repressed desires of working people and the frustrations and paranoia of the bourgeoisie.

Of course, other factors were thought to be important. Many of these have already been mentioned, including changes in the family, culture and the economy. In *Dialectic of Enlightenment*, Horkheimer and Adorno also sought to trace the history of anti-Semitism back to prc-bourgeois life, particularly to early Christian beliefs and to general developments in the nature of reason.

5 The critique of instrumental reason: critical theory and philosophy of history

Developments in science, technology and production have increased the range of possibilities facing human beings. Yet, as it has turned out, only a 'real hell' (Adorno) has been distilled from these opportunities. In *Dialectic of Enlightenment*, the task Horkheimer and Adorno set themselves was nothing less than to discover 'why mankind, instead of entering into a truly human condition, is sinking into a new kind of barbarism'.[1] They attempted to focus attention on the 'nexus of rationality and social actuality, and upon what is inseparable therefrom – that of nature and the mastery of nature'.[2] For it is the fundamental intention to dominate nature which, according to Horkheimer and Adorno, increasingly underlies the way the social and natural worlds are appropriated and apprehended.

Dialectic of Enlightenment is crucially important to the development of the Frankfurt school. For the text addresses one of the school's most central concerns – the rise and domination of instrumental reason. The theme is explored with reference to the philosophy of the Enlightenment and to forms of 'enlightenment'. The Enlightenment is, of course, associated with a variety of the intellectual currents which informed and helped stimulate the political upheavals in Europe in the closing decades of the eighteenth century. The notion of 'enlightenment' does not refer to a definite period or to a particular set of intellectual currents, but, as will be shown below, to more encompassing principles. Contradictions are revealed between the philosophy of the Enlightenment and 'enlightenment'. In examining the importance of instrumental reason in this context, Horkheimer and Adorno hoped to prepare the way for a positive, emancipatory notion of enlightenment 'released from entanglement in blind domination'.

They did not define the concept of domination. However, as a minimal condition for its application, they suppose a situation in which the thoughts, wants and purposes of those affected by it would have been radically different, if it had not been for the effects created by domination. This view appears to be consistent with Marcuse's later position.

Domination is in effect whenever the individual's goals and purposes and the means of striving for and attaining them are prescribed to him and performed by him as something prescribed. Domination can be exercised by men, by nature, by things – it can also be internal, exercised by the individual on himself, and appear in the form of autonomy.[3]

Capitalist exploitation is seen as only one specific, historical form of domination. The history of civilization reveals, all three authors contended, a threefold pattern of domination:

first, domination over one's self, over one's own nature . . .; second, domination of the labour achieved by such disciplined and controlled individuals; and third, domination of outward nature, science and technology.[4]

In the *Dialectic*, the history of domination is traced back to the 'turning points' of Western civilization – from the first chapters of Genesis and Olympian religion, to the Reformation and bourgeois atheism and to the culture industry and the authoritarian state. Horkheimer and Adorno were concerned to show 'how the rational domination of nature comes increasingly to win the day, in spite of all deviations and resistance, and integrates all human characteristics'.

'Dialectic of Enlightenment': philosophical fragments towards a philosophy of history

The *Dialectic of Enlightenment* does not present a systematic reconstruction of history – and deliberately so. The authors do not intend to construct a philosophical system on the model, for example, of Hegel's philosophy. Their work clearly involves the attempt to develop concepts that contribute to a philosophy of history. But these concepts are not offered as a definitive set. Systematic philosophies of history tend, they held, to impose themselves upon, and to distort, history.[5] History becomes interesting only as the 'correlation of a unified theory' and as such it is transformed into its opposite.[6] In addition, systematic philosophies tend to legitimize acts of severe brutality. For example,

Christianity, idealism, and materialism, which in themselves contain truth, are . . . also responsible for the barbaric acts perpetrated in their name. As representatives of power – even if of power for good – they themselves became historical forces which could be organized, and as such played a bloody role in the true history of the human race: that of the instruments of organization.[7]

Belief systems like Christianity became 'fixed ideas and universal recipes'. They led, as Adorno put it elsewhere, 'to the rejection of anything not already analytically assimilated'. While dissenting, critical thought becomes irrational when measured against 'the system'; those who have privileged access to the system's content can wield it to perpetuate particular favours and interests.

The authors of the *Dialectic* present a critical rather than constructive view of history. They do not recommend particular practices as correct and beneficial. Their work is motivated by an awareness of the ever-present threat of domination. They offer, as the subtitle (curiously omitted from the English translation) promises, 'philosophical fragments'. Their philosophy of history attempts to break the grip of all closed systems of thought;[8] it is conceived as a contribution to the undermining of all beliefs that claim completeness and encourage an unreflected affirmation of society.

The *Dialectic* can be read at two different levels. At one level the notion of Enlightenment is traced from Kant's discussion of reason and freedom to Hegel's and Nietzsche's recognition of the 'dialectic of Enlightenment'. The Enlightenment's concept of reason, expressed most clearly by Kant, has, it is argued, a dual structure:

[part of which] as the transcendental, supraindividual self, . . . comprises the idea of a free, human social life in which men organize themselves as the universal subject and overcome the conflict between pure and empirical reason in the conscious solidarity of the whole. This represents the idea of true universality: utopia. At the same time, however, reason constitutes the court of judgement of calculation, which adjusts the world for the ends of self-preservation and recognizes no function other than the preparation of the object from mere sensory material in order to make it the material of subjugation.[9]

The dialectic is between these two aspects of reason: reason as universal, common to every being, and reason as domination of the particular. The first aspect has provided the ideals and legitimations which have become embedded in people's interpretations of their activities, while the second has generated the structure of conventions which have actually conditioned day-to-day practice. The Enlightenment can be seen as a unity of enlightened thought, myth and domination.

At a more fundamental level, however, the book is a study of the structure of 'enlightenment'. Liberating reason or enlightenment, like every social phenomenon, expresses the contradiction that it is both itself and at one and the same time something other than itself – a unity of opposites. The dialectic of enlightenment can be characterized in two short theses: 'myth is already enlightenment; and enlightenment reverts to mythology'. They see enlightenment, as one commentator succinctly put it, 'as subject throughout history to a dialectic wherein it all too easily gives itself an absolute status over and against its objects, thereby constantly collapsing into new forms of the very conditions of primeval repression which it earlier set out to overcome'.[10] Through the development of this thesis, Horkheimer and Adorno hoped to reassess many of the traditional problems posed by German idealist thinking. In particular they sought to recast, within a historical and dialectical context, the concern with reason and truth.

Their discussion is indebted to Hegel. The opening chapter of the *Dialectic* employs many of Hegel's insights (from *Phenomenology of mind*) into the Enlightenment's concept of reason. Particularly, Hegel's claim that there is an internal relationship between Enlightenment, an ethic of utility and terror (especially the Terror of the French Revolution) is paralled in their own discussion of the relationship between scientific consciousness (based on instrumental reason), pragmatism and ethical decisionism, and barbarism (especially the barbarism of totalitarianism).[11]

For Hegel, the Enlightenment is marked by the dominance in the intellectual world of universal scientific consciousness. The concept of science Hegel had in mind was Francis Bacon's, for whom scientific knowledge is potential power – the instrument or tool which can be used to master nature. Science is the key to the control of nature and (as Bacon well recognized) of human beings. By obeying nature one can, on Bacon's account, command her: 'for you have but to follow and as it were hound nature in her wanderings, and you will be able, when you like, to lead and drive her afterwards to the same place again'.[12]

Enlightenment consciousness, Hegel argued, objectifies the

world. It sees it as an 'absolute reality' of 'pure and simple' things – a world of 'material things', which are given to the senses with 'no further determination of any sort'.[13] Nature is perceived as neutral, disenchanted. Matter has no intrinsic significance.[14] It is, therefore, open to manipulation and alteration. Following Hegel's reference, the *Dialectic* begins with a lengthy quotation from Bacon, in which Bacon suggests that the human mind can and should overcome all forms of superstition; for the 'sovereignty of man [man's power] lieth hid in knowledge'. In drawing on Bacon, Horkheimer and Adorno sought to indicate that 'what men want to learn from nature is how to use it in order to fully dominate it and other men'. The domination of nature, they contended, is at the basis of the philosophy of the Enlightenment. The transformation of what was once liberating reason into a repressive orthodoxy, of the Enlightenment into totalitarianism, can be understood as a result of elements integral to this very form of enlightenment itself.

On Horkheimer's and Adorno's account, the Enlightenment's fundamental character is contained in the concept of nature to which most of the Enlightenment thinkers adhered. The concept suggests a 'radical disjuncture between subjectivity and nature'. In contradistinction to the Greek concept of nature which did not sharply distinguish mind or subjectivity and the world of objects, the Enlightenment concept refers to nature as essentially pure matter, structured according to laws and capable of being known through a mathematically formulated universal science. This conception of nature had one of its earliest expressions in Galileo's writings. The Galilean notion was developed in the context of a web of ideas about life and its place in the universe. But it was, Horkheimer and Adorno maintained, inextricably connected with the goal of dominating nature; 'technology is the essence of this knowledge'.

From now on, matter would at last be mastered without any illusion of ruling or inherent powers, of hidden qualities. For the Enlightenment, whatever does not conform to the rule of computation and utility is suspect.[15]

Nature is the 'sphere of pure objects'. Since consciousness and purposeful activity are attributes of humans and/or God, the use to which nature will be put depends upon human decision and/or divine bequest.

The specific categories under which nature is subsumed depend on a view as to how it can be used. Nature is useful. The concept of 'useful' follows almost naturally from the Enlightenment perspective. Nature is not valuable in and for itself and, therefore, if it is to have significance, it must serve the ends and purposes of another (human beings and/or God). Utility becomes, as Hegel noted, the ethic of the Enlightenment.[16] Acts and ideas are judged according to their usefulness which is assessed in terms of their consequences for some (variously set) goal or aim.

The development of this notion of nature pre-dates the Enlightenment (although its clearest articulation is found there). The traditions which shaped it are multifarious, as are the empirical conditions which determined its rise to prominence. Horkheimer and Adorno refer to and discuss a number of these. First, the idea can be traced in myth and magic. 'Myth intended report, naming, the narration of the Beginning; but also presentation, confirmation, explanation; a tendency that grew stronger with the recording and collection of myths.' At a very early moment in history, a strong didactic element appeared in narratives. 'Every ritual includes the idea of activity as a determined process which magic can nevertheless influence.'[17] Myth and magic represent an important stage in the development of the instrumentalist view of nature. Second, myths, in Greek culture, are already, on Horkheimer's and Adorno's account, 'characterized by the discipline and power that Bacon celebrated as the "right mark"'.

In place of the local spirits and demons there appeared heaven and its hierarchy; in place of the invocations of the magician and the tribe the distinct gradation of sacrifice and the labour of the unfree mediated through the word of command. The Olympic deities are no longer directly identical with elements, but signify them.[18]

Renunciation and sacrifice to these deities was linked to a certain degree of control over nature. Third, the domination of nature as a concept is part and parcel of the Judaeo-Christian tradition. Within it religious 'spirit' is held to be distinct from nature and endowed with capacities to shape and rule over it. God has sovereignty over the universe, and humans have God's authority to govern on earth. This rule is established by God upon the creation: 'Let us make men in our image, after our likeness; and let them have dominion over the fish of the sea, and over the birds of the air, and over the cattle, and over all the earth, and over every creeping thing that creepeth upon the earth.'[19] The story of the creation in the Book of Genesis tells us that the domination of nature is a natural part of life. Fourth, the idea of establishing and extending the domination of humanity over nature through science entered into philosophy and tradition in the late sixteenth, and seventeenth and eighteenth centuries. Most of its authors, Bacon especially, saw the quest to dominate nature as sanctioned by religion and ethics. It was conceived as a means to combat the fall from the original state of paradise.

For man by the fall fell at the same time from his state of innocency and from his dominion over creation. Both of these losses however can even in his life be in some part repaired; the former by religion and faith, the latter by arts and sciences.[20]

The Renaissance and Reformation gave an impetus to these ideas. Instrumental reason came to penetrate an increasing number of areas of everyday life. The impetus to these ideas was reinforced, of course, by economic pressures. Fifth, the development of capitalism institutionalized economic growth and led to the systematic exploitation of the new forms of knowledge. Bacon's 'formula' was easily secularized. Scientific and technical development became interdependent. The sciences were transformed into an important productive force. The domination of nature became an interest of the whole economic system.

For Horkheimer and Adorno, then, the domination of nature denotes a particular type of relationship between human beings and nature. Nature has meaning in so far as it has utility – in so far as it is instrumental to human purposes. Matter is *defined* as a possible object of manipulation.[21] People, embodying the natural, are also potentially controllable. 'Domination is potentially all-embracing.' There is a 'necessary relation', on Horkheimer's and Adorno's account, 'between our concept of nature and the domination of nature [and, therefore, of human beings]'. The history of the concept is to a large extent the history of the 'coming-to-be' of the relationship that it posits.

Both mythology and enlightenment find their roots in the same basic needs: survival, self-preservation and fear (*Angst*).

Man imagines himself free from fear when there is no longer anything unknown. This determines the course of demythologizing. . . . Enlightenment is mythic fear turned radical. The pure immanence of positivism, its ultimate product, is no more than a so to speak universal taboo. Nothing at all may remain outside, because the mere idea of outsideness is the very source of fear.[22]

Fear of the unknown in an environment which threatens survival is, according to Horkheimer and Adorno, the root of the desire to dominate nature and the basis of both ancient and modern systems of thought.

Like science, myth and magic pursue objectives, but the way in which they do so are obviously not the same. The latter seek to achieve their goal by mimesis: the re-enactment in ritual of natural processes as an attempt to control and understand them. They do not posit a radical distinction between thought and reality. Science seeks progressively to distance itself from its object domain. It is grounded in the 'sovereignty of ideas'. Myth compounds the inanimate with the animate; it is structured, to a significant degree, by the 'projection of the subjective onto nature'. For the scientific consciousness of the Enlightenment nature is disenchanted. To the Enlightenment thinkers myth is essentially superstition and unconscious error. There is an apparent asymmetry between the two modes of thought. But the dualism between humans and nature is found, in an underdeveloped form, in myth.[23] As Horkheimer's and Adorno's analysis of Homer's *Odyssey* sought to demonstrate, people acknowledged early the power of the solar system. They learnt to respect nature and uncover its 'forces of repetition'. In the struggle to come to terms with laws of nature humans *qua* subjects were born.[24] (Horkheimer's and Adorno's treatment of the *Odyssey* is elaborated in the appendix.) Myth already contained elements of enlightenment. On the other hand, the systematic exploitation of enlightened reason led to the compounding of the animate with the inanimate. Although reason originated in the struggle to come to terms with nature, it turned 'against the thinking subject'. The extension of enlightenment in practice led to the decline of critical thought. Enlightenment 'with every step became more deeply engulfed in mythology'.[25]

In societies where myth and/or magic are prominent the human subject tends to be dominated by the object; praxis is embedded in an undifferentiated unity between humanity and nature. In the Enlightenment, as in contemporary consciousness, there is a radical separation of subject and object. But as it develops and unfolds, reducing the external world to quantified objects of manipulation, the subject becomes increasingly repressed and dominated by a *second nature*, by a history which appears as 'fatefully structured, pregiven' (Adorno). The replacement of myth by empiricism and positivism and the context-bound practices of 'the medicine man by all-inclusive industrial technology', lead to the reification of the social and to what Adorno called the 'false whole'.[26] The increasing control of humanity over nature seems to bring ever greater oppression. The expansion of the productive forces has not opened the path (as orthodox Marxists expected) to a liberated society.[27] The potential for emancipation has expanded. However, the division between control and the execution of tasks, between mental and repetitive mundane labour, along with the effects of the culture industry, etc., signal the 'eclipse of reason'.

The idea of reconciliation

The recognition of the dialectic of enlightenment as a condition and continuing experience of Western civilization owes a great deal to Nietzsche, as Horkheimer and Adorno acknowledged. 'Nietzsche was one of the few after Hegel who recognized the dialectic of enlightenment.' He discerned both 'the universal movement of sovereign spirit (whose executor he felt himself to be) and a "nihilistic" anti-life force in enlightenment.'[28] Unlike Hegel, he did not succumb to the repressive and absolutist moment of the dialectic by positing a 'final universal goal' unfolding in history – a comprehensive system which is 'closed' and 'uncritical'. Nietzsche recognized that reason only enables us 'to misunderstand reality in a shrewd manner'. His instrumental theory of truth provided a basis for many critical insights, although it also led, ultimately, to substantial errors.

For Nietzsche, 'knowledge works as a tool of power'.

In order for a particular species to maintain itself and increase its power, it . . . must comprehend enough of the calculable and constant for it to base a scheme of behaviour on it. The utility of preservation . . . stands as the motive behind the development of the organs of knowledge – they develop in such a way that their observations suffice for our preservation. In other words: the measure of the desire for knowledge depends upon the measure to which the will to power grows in a species: a species grasps a certain amount of reality in order to become master of it, in order to press it into service.[29]

There is no ultimate criterion of truth. Truth is whatever is imposed as 'truth': it expresses 'will to power', which extends a capacity for prediction and control and, therefore, self-preservation. As a result, the domination of nature is, according to Nietzsche, a universal characteristic of reason. Horkheimer's and Adorno's own emphasis on the organizational power of concepts and ideas which structure our perceptions and sense-impressions points in a similar direction; their discussion of the domination of nature suggests some similar ideas to those of Nietzsche. But Horkheimer's distinction between critical and subjective (instrumental) reason, which is discussed in Chapter 6, and the implied notion in the *Dialectic* of a *reconciliation* between humankind and nature, leaves open the possibility of a fully liberating reason.[30] Adorno's own work contains the same implication (although it appears as if the idea of reconciliation only has logical status).[31] In *One Dimensional Man* and *Counterrevolution and Revolt*, Marcuse also offers a conception of an alternative to the *status quo*. He defends, as will be seen in Chapter 8, the idea of a liberated nature – a nature free from forces of domination and destruction. The writings of the Frankfurt theorists all conclude on a note which is in contrast to Nietzsche's sceptical view of reason.

Enlightenment and morality

The ideological components of the Enlightenment can be revealed most clearly, according to Horkheimer and Adorno, in the thought of Kant, the Marquis de Sade and Nietzsche. For in their works we can see how the radical separation of subject and object, humanity and nature, legitimizes the subjugation of the natural world and the treatment of men and women as objects. A continuity exists, Horkheimer and Adorno maintained, between elements of liberalism, developed and exemplified by Kant, and totalitarian thought and practice, anticipated by de Sade. Nietzsche's contributions lie between these poles. The moral teachings of these figures reveal a desperate attempt to replace 'enfeebled religion' with some *raison d'être*.[32] Their writings bear witness to the intrinsic difficulties of this enterprise.

The discussion of Kant's moral philosophy in the *Dialectic of Enlightenment* is similar to Hegel's critique of this doctrine. On Hegel's account of Kant, the most important task of practical (moral) reason is to be consistent: all that is asked is that the principle upon which one acts is universally valid. Kant had argued that there was a practical rule which was a categorical imperative. It was valid unconditionally – it was a priori. The rule which states 'Act only on that maxim *through* which you can at the same time will that it should become a universal law', was argued to determine the possible principles which could be objectively valid for decisions of the human will.[33] It determined what duty was, but solely as regards its *form*. For Hegel this sort of reason is 'dissociated'. Reason so employed remains indifferent both to the context within which a principle is applied and to the ends of practical activity. If all that is required is consistency, a justification can be offered for almost anything which can be formulated as a general rule. Moral reason remains divorced from an assessment of human wants, goals and passions.[34]

Horkheimer and Adorno endorsed this criticism of Kant. For them the extreme formalism of the Categorical Imperative leaves reason unable to evaluate substantive goals.[35] Furthermore, Kant's attempt to derive the duty of mutual respect (that men should never treat each other as mere means) from the law of reason could not, they thought, be sustained by the arguments of the *Critique of Practical Reason*. Kant's ambition 'to ground respect upon something other than material interest and force . . . is more sublime and paradoxical than . . . previous attempts'. But it remains, they bluntly stated, as 'ephemeral' as all such philosophies.[36]

While Kant, one of the most remarkable of the Enlightenment thinkers, failed to provide an adequate way of assessing competing ends, many other Enlightenment philosophers seemed content simply to sanction a utilitarian or decisionistic ethics. (Decisionism is a doctrine which teaches that there is no rational way of adjudicating between competing values other than through private individual decision.) For Horkheimer and Adorno it was de Sade, more than any other thinker, who ensured that people became aware of the large range of choices open to them within these terms of reference. De Sade did not leave it to the Enlightenment's opponents to reveal its black side. He 'mercilessly declared its shocking truth'. His *chronique scandaleuse* anticipated the fulfilment of some of the immanent possibilities of Enlightenment thinking. His 'private vices constitute a predictive chronicle of the public virtues of the totalitarian era'.[37]

Horkheimer and Adorno suggest that de Sade represents the

enbodiment of Enlightenment rationality. Following many Enlightenment thinkers, he separated mind and body, *Geist* and nature, and, as a result, the spiritual from the corporeal side of love. His *Histoire de Juliette* and *One Hundred and Twenty Days of Sodom* pursue many of the implications of this dualism. His treatment of both women and men are classic illustrations of the consequences of reason reduced to instrumentalism. Reason becomes 'the organ of calculation, of planning; it is neutral in regard to ends: its element is coordination'.[38] The form of activity – its usefulness – becomes more important than its content. For example, Juliette believes in reason and science. 'She wholly despises any form of worship whose rationality cannot be demonstrated.'[39] She is dedicated to 'tabooed activities' which she pursues efficiently and with the 'self-discipline of the criminal'. Within this framework individuals as natural beings are open to potentially total subjugation.

De Sade took his critique of solidarity with 'society, family and morality' to the point of preaching anarchy. The tale of Justine and Juliette 'is the Homeric epic [*The Odyssey*] with its last mythological covering removed: the history of thought as an organ of domination'.[40] The Marquis continually proclaims and reveals the identity of (subjective) reason and domination. As such he has one redeeming quality: he is more honest and admirable 'than those moralistic lackeys of the bourgeoisie'.[41]

The same is said of Nietzsche. His 'malicious celebration of the powerful and their cruelty' at least has honesty to commend it. Nietzsche also placed the subject in a central position. But the autonomy he bestowed on the newly formed subject is highly exaggerated. Paradoxically, people within Nietzsche's 'anti-system' find few freedoms. The ideal form of subject becomes that of unrestricted strength and authority.

Nietzsche correctly recognized, Horkheimer and Adorno maintained, that scientific-technical progress in the nineteenth century undermined claims to validity of traditional world views, for example, religious and metaphysical systems. He quite rightly saw the course of the Enlightenment as nihilistic. His non-rationalist concept of reality suggested, in harmony with the modern age, that any moral belief can maintain the same claim to validity as long as it is grounded in a want or need. 'It is our needs that interpret the world.'[42] His analysis of the will to power also revealed an important aspect of bourgeois history. He was right to argue that bourgeois liberalism and tolerance are more often than not myths masking a 'will to rule'. But he falsely generalized this insight into a theory of the source of all knowledge. 'Every drive . . . has its perspective that it would like to compel all other drives to accept as a norm.'[43] For Nietzsche, understanding 'owes its importance to the yardstick of survival';[44] it recognizes only one law of existence, namely, that the will to power predominates. All moral thinking is reduced to an effect of this law. A morality becomes, as Nietzsche put it, 'a mode of living tried and proved by long experience and testimony'. It enters social life as a law, as dominating; it becomes venerable, unassailable, true.[45] To be free, within this frame of reference, is to assume responsibility for oneself, to maintain distance from others and to become more indifferent to the difficulties of others. Ultimately, the free individual is a *warrior*; for freedom means that 'the manly instincts which delight in war and victory dominate over other instincts, for example, over those of pleasure'.[46] Despite Nietzsche's many important critical works only 'domination survives as an end in itself'.

German fascism, not Nietzsche, raised 'the cult of strength to a world-historical doctrine'. On Horkheimer's and Adorno's account 'the realization of Nietzsche's assertions both refutes his views and at the same time reveals their truth'.[47] The same thing is true of many of de Sade's statements. Both Nietzsche and de Sade anticipated the future by carefully examining the past and present. They both contributed to the affirmation of this reality but they did not directly create it. To their credit they do not try, like bourgeois apologists, 'to ward off the consequences of the Enlightenment by harmonizing theories. They have not postulated that formalistic reason is more closely allied to morality than to immorality.'[48] They both exposed and helped to sustain the unity of reason and domination.

Science, social science and positivism

According to Horkheimer and Adorno, the Enlightenment came to its fulfilment with the foundation of modern science – with the mathematization of nature. The new science established a purely rational, ideational world as the only true reality. It understood the world as a scientific universe which could be systematically comprehended only by science itself. Within this world every object, represented by means of mathematical theorems, became a possible focus of study. The development of a universal, mathematically formulated science and its emergence as the model for all science and knowledge represents a culmination of the Enlightenment's project. Although such a notion of science predates the Enlightenment, the Enlightenment gave an enormous impetus to it. With these events, European thought entered, as Marcuse put it, an 'era of positivism'.

The 'era' made itself known, in part, through systems of positive philosophy. In *Reason and Revolution*, Marcuse discusses three of these systems: Auguste Comte's *Cours de philosophie positive*, Friedrich Stahl's positive philosophy of the state, and Schelling's Berlin lectures on the *Positive Philosophie*.[49] I will restrict my exposition to Marcuse's analysis of Comte's work, which provides a useful introduction to critical theory's general assessment of positivism.

Comte, like the other philosophers mentioned above, sought to explore reality through an assessment of matters of fact available in experience. He aimed to counter the influence of purely *a priori* thinking and establish the authority of observation.[50] On Marcuse's account, Comte made few distinctions between the methods appropriate to the physical and human sciences.[51] Accordingly, sociology is to be modelled after the natural sciences and, in particular, after biology. Society is to be treated as a complex of facts governed by general laws. Comte taught that human beings and their institutions must be viewed as 'neutral objects' which can be investigated in more or less the same way as any other scientific object. The form and pattern of society is equated with that of nature. Both realms are seen as governed by natural necessity. Therefore, Comte's philosophy implies, as Marcuse expressed it, 'educating men to take a positive attitude towards the prevailing state of affairs. Positive philosophy was going to affirm the existing order against those who asserted the need for "negating" it'.[52] Comte did not, of course, deny the necessity of progressive reforms. But the form of these changes, Marcuse argues, is always given by 'the machinery of the established order'.[53]

Comte saw all social movements as subject to law-like regularities; he regarded many social institutions as unalterable through the application of rational will. Political action, therefore, must resign itself to fixed and general limits. Comte preached (in his words) 'resignation' and the 'consolidation of public order' (against the 'anarchic force of purely revolutionary principles').[54]

Central issues in social struggle are to be withdrawn from its arena and resolved by expert opinion informed by scientific investigation. Thus the 'critique of the given' gives way, in Marcuse's opinion, 'to an ideological saviour'. Comte's system surrenders metaphysics and political imagination to the existent.

Which of the principles of positive philosophy ensure that it legitimizes the existing order? On Marcuse's account, the offending principles are those which attempt to justify the authority of observation against alternative forms of reason and imagination. Resignation to the given follows from the positivist view that concepts must be grounded in observed facts, and from the notion that the real connection between facts represents an 'inexorable order'. In emphasizing the importance of natural laws of societal 'statics' and 'dynamics', human activity is subsumed under the category of objective necessity. Further, in maintaining that sociology as a positive science has no relation to value judgements, and that facts and values are quite separate entities, there is held to be no objective basis independent of science and its findings to criticize society. What is is what (with certain moderate adjustments) ought to be! But this position cannot itself be justified by positive philosophy. For questions of 'ought', of value judgement, are condemned to irrationality by the separation of fact and value. In common with later forms of positivism, discussed below, positive philosophy builds upon prejudgements and evaluations which it cannot ground, that is, rationally justify.

Marcuse's discussion of the positivist method is, however, not wholly critical. He notes that it helped undermine theological and metaphysical illusions and aided the promotion of free thought, particularly in the physical sciences.[55] Horkheimer, writing in the late 1930s, made a similar claim about the import of the tradition of Hume and Locke. He argued that the sceptical empiricism of Hume, for example, had an underlying moral impulse in its critique of prevailing dogmas.[56] Horkheimer and Adorno writing together also stressed a certain emancipatory effect from the Enlightenment's emphasis on instrumental reason and from its expression in a positivist understanding of science. The desire to impose on our assertions the responsibility of satisfying relevant independent controls was certainly justified.[57] As Adorno put it, 'numerous stalwart assertions . . . can be tested and refuted with the aid of strict investigations'.[58] Likewise, the tendency to equate legitimate knowledge with a conception of the form of knowledge derived from the natural sciences also had some justification. In the nineteenth century the natural sciences appeared to be progressing at such a rapid rate and with such spectacular results that they seemed only to be burdened by metaphysical theories. These sciences were generally thought to be the most systematic source of the type of knowledge which could be utilized to liberate humanity from natural necessity, domination by the forces of nature and drudgery in work.[59] Much attention was focused, therefore, on the nature and methodology of natural science. Biology and with time physics, as the most developed, advanced, and prestigious natural sciences, increasingly took centre stage. The other sciences, both natural and social, were regarded as poor 'seconds' and less developed. However, it was generally assumed by the (very) late nineteenth century, that all these other sciences essentially admitted of the same structure and procedure as physics and would eventually produce significant advances and benefits.

On Horkheimer's and Adorno's account, with the twentieth century, the moral impulse behind these developments faded and the developments themselves became increasingly destructive. The promises of a social science modelled on biology and/or physics had not been fulfilled. In fact, important questions in social theory, as well as various useful approaches to social phenomena, had been closed off. Capacities for a critical analysis of society were being undermined. In order to understand Horkheimer's and Adorno's opposition to this state of affairs it is necessary to examine their critique of positivism in more detail and ask what they meant by positivism itself.

'Positivism' is a term which is used to cover a range of philosophical positions. Hence it is often difficult to reach a clear understanding of the term's meaning. When Horkheimer and Adorno use it they often refer to the logical positivism of the Vienna circle (although this is not always stated with clarity).[60] From their employment of the term in this way it can be inferred that as long as a philosophy adheres to some version of the following five tenets it is, in their eyes, positivist. The tenets are:

All (synthetic) knowledge is founded in sensory experience.
Meaning is grounded in observation.
Concepts and generalizations only represent the particulars from which they have been abstracted. Conceptual entities don't exist

in themselves – they are mere names; positivism is (normally) associated with nominalism.

Sciences are unified according to the methodology of the natural sciences. The ideal pursued is knowledge 'in the form of a mathematically formulated universal science deducible from the smallest possible number of axioms, a system which assures the calculation of the probable occurrence of all events'.[61]

Values are not facts and hence values cannot be given as such in sense-experience. Since all knowledge is based on sensory experience, value judgements cannot be accorded the status of knowledge claims.

The goal of positivism is to construct an objective, empirical and systematic foundation for knowledge. Given the above five tenets, it follows that positivists would hold that the world is composed of 'facts', or 'sense data' (or 'atoms'). These facts are given directly, or indirectly, in sensory experience and are the *only* objects of knowledge.

The world of immediate sensations, experiences and perceptions appears, Horkheimer and Adorno noted, to be the ultimate foundation of knowledge. Its appearance as ultimate, however, belies its dependent and derivative status.[62] Observations, for example, do not merely present a copy of a given object world. The world of objects is always the world of *our* objects – of our interpretations. As Hegel noted, objects are always objects *for us*, the being for consciousness of an in-itself. The given is mediated in many ways by consciousness. But the structure of the world given to us through consciousness is based, in turn, for Horkheimer and Adorno, on the inner historicality of consciousness itself, which is a result and product of the whole of social practice.[63] Marcuse agrees: 'facts are the work of the historical practice of man'. As Lukács wrote in *History and Class Consciousness*:

> The desire to leave behind the immediacy of empirical reality . . . must not be allowed to become an attempt to abandon immanent (social) reality . . . to leave empirical reality behind can only mean that the objects of the empirical world are to be understood as aspects of a totality, i.e. as the aspects of a total social situation caught up in the process of historical change.[64]

There are no social 'facts' which constitute the 'substratum' of social theory, as the positivists thought. Every facet of social reality can only be understood as an outcome of the continual interplay between 'moment' (phase of, aspect of, totality) and 'totality'. The structure of the social process conditions and determines both the place and function of every particular 'thing' and the form in which it appears as an object of experience. Any given object can only be understood in the context (and in the light) of its conditions and relations. These do not appear in immediate experience but are important in the understanding and explanation of 'things'.[65] Positivists fail to comprehend that the process of knowing cannot be severed from the historical struggle between humans and the world. Theory and theoretical labour are inextricably intertwined in social life processes. The theorist cannot remain detached, passively contemplating, reflecting and describing 'society' or 'nature'.

The structure of knowledge, and, therefore, of reality is as rigid for any positivist as for any dogmatist. Despite their criticisms of the rationalist claim that there are a range of propositions which cannot be contradicted by any experience – propositions concerning the rational nature of reason and reality – positivists posit a fixed structure of being. As Horkheimer put it,

In principle, the whole world [for positivists] has its place in a fixed system ... the statement that the correct form of all knowledge is identical with physics, that physics is the great 'unity of science' in terms of which everything must be stated, posits certain forms as constant. Such an assertion constitutes a judgement *a priori*.[66]

From the outset positivism's unjustified judgement prejudices what is taken as the nature of the object of study. For example, the human subject is viewed as 'an isolated subject, a set of physical events like every other set'. Adorno made a similar point when discussing the influence of positivism on methods in sociology. Certain methods, he argued, which are indebted to a positivist understanding of science, often stipulate in advance what is to be ascertained.[67] For instance, survey methods in opinion research all too often create, through the fixed selection of questions put to the individual or through the very generality of the questions, opinions where they do not exist and an artificially limited range of responses. Frequently these opinions are then treated uncritically as 'objective accounts' of subjective attitudes. The structure of the object is neglected in favour of what is taken as a general objective method. In this way opinion research both produces its own object and hypostatizes its results.[68] Rather than prescribing their objects, Adorno maintained, methods 'must be adequate to them'.

Despite the considerable differences between critical theory and phenomenology, Horkheimer's, Adorno's and Marcuse's critique of the positivist concept of modern science parallels a number of points made by Husserl in *The Crisis of European Sciences and Transcendental Phenomenology*.[69] Some of the parallels they note.[70] A brief outline of Husserl's views and the similarities of opinion provide a useful aid to understanding Horkheimer and the others' position. In *The Crisis*, Husserl examined a model of science which makes two central claims: systematic observation is the medium for objective access to the world; the basic language of science is mathematics (and geometry). He sought to criticize the currents of thought that support the 'mathematization of nature' and idealization of reality into a 'mathematical manifold' (although it should be noted that this was not the main purpose of his book).[71] He objected to the typically unselfconscious presentation of quantified, ideational forms of nature as the only real and true forms. In a detailed discussion of the Galilean concept of science, he exposed the historicity of what is represented as pure or objective theory and method. He unfolded sciences' pre-scientific foundations in the life-world (*Lebenswelt*) – the world of human praxis, intentional activity and everyday knowledge and beliefs. The Galilean notion of science retains, in the very structure and meaning of its concepts, the ultimate purpose which it was supposed to serve – a purpose which, Husserl argued, necessarily derives from the activity of the pre-scientific life-world.[72] Science embodies the particular ends and values which aid the enhancement of practical interests and the discovery of new possibilities for 'the technical control of nature'.[73]

Modern science, according to Husserl, abstracts from the infinite world a form of knowledge capable of technical exploitation. It conceives its object domain in terms of geometric shapes and calculates the relationships between objects in mathematical formulae which allow precise measurement of motion and causality. But this picture is, ultimately, an abstraction from the concrete qualities of certain aspects of the life-world. It is the result of the constitution of the world from, Husserl sometimes suggests (and often implies on Marcuse's reading of his work), one particular standpoint; that is, from the standpoint of an interest in controlling the environment (a *lebensweltliche a priori*).[74] 'Once one possesses the formulae', Husserl noted, 'one possesses the foresight which is desired in practice' to anticipate 'the regularities of the practical

Lebenswelt' and, therefore, to better 'co-ordinate it'. However, the internal connections between science and life practice remain unacknowledged by modern science and positivist philosophy.

The *Ideenkleid* (the ideational veil) of mathematics and mathematical physics represents and [at the same time] disguises the empirical reality and leads us to take for True Being that which is only a method.[75]

What is, in fact, only one approach and method appears as the sole mode in which reality can be disclosed.

Husserl's analysis highlights, for Horkheimer, Adorno and Marcuse, the illusionary nature of modern science's claim to neutrality; the concern with exactness, calculability and foresight predisposes science to seek knowledge of a particular type and form, namely knowledge suitable for prediction and, therefore, technical control. Legitimated by a positivist philosophy, it constitutes the world solely from this standpoint. As Husserl put it, modern science operates 'like a machine, reliable in accomplishing obviously very useful things, a machine everyone can learn to operate correctly without in the least understanding the inner possibility and necessity of this sort of accomplishment'.[76] Thus the modern scientific project is seen to have, prior to the utilization of its findings, an inherently instrumental character.[77] Its *a priori* condition is its tie to a specific societal project, namely, the adaptation of nature to human purposes. Furthermore, the Frankfurt theorists agree with Husserl that this character implies that modern science has, when viewed from a positivist self-understanding, an inner core which it cannot account for or master. It is intrinsically impossible for this science to assess its own objectives, or the purposes for which it is employed. Since it regards the world as a domain of neutral objects, as one such object itself it cannot even comprehend or assess itself; for it cannot reflect upon itself. Unable to explicate the foundations of systematic thought, it remains unaware of its own origin and application. As Marcuse wrote, 'scientific experience as well as pre-scientific experience are false, incomplete inasmuch as they experience as *objective* (material or ideational) what in reality is subject-object, objectivation of subjectivity'.[78]

Positivistic consciousness objectifies the social as well as the natural world; that is, it conceptualizes the world as a field of objects open to manipulation. Under this perspective society is conceived, as Horkheimer and Adorno put it, as 'second nature'. The social world is reified: socially created rules, conventions and regularities are comprehended as 'natural', 'the ways things have been and always will be'. Social institutions and processes are taken to follow 'the order of things'. Social facts are given the status of natural facts. Historical laws are given the same status as natural laws. But these concepts of social life are inadequate to their object(s). Men and women are of nature but make history; nature is not, in any parallel sense, made by them. As a result, history embodies the possibility of nature (through human beings) attaining self-consciousness. The laws of history cannot simply be equated with the laws of nature. The differences are vital. To be sure, one can speak of laws in history (for example the law of increasing concentration of capital), laws which seem natural, to which the individual is subjected. But these laws are tied to specific modes of human organization. They cannot be abstracted from the context and peculiarity of particular epochs. They change and can be changed. The historical relation between the movement of general social structures and individuals is not a constant.[79]

For example, a society may be 'possessed', such that the individual is 'overpowered by objective mechanisms that operate with the necessity of "natural" [physical] laws . . .'.[80] Human agency, according to this account, can be reduced to a mere support, or a carrier, of general social structures. Frankfurt social theory in the late 1930s and early 1940s clearly implied that in capitalist societies this process of reduction was well under way. The prevalence of the law of exchange and the regimentation of opinion by the mass media etc., ensured that nearly everyone's behaviour became regularized and compulsive.[81] If individuals wish to survive they must adapt their lives to these processes and become agents and bearers of commodity exchange. Under these conditions social interaction does appear to be governed by 'rigid' laws. Positivists' reflections on the similarities of method appropriate for the examination of natural and social life contain, despite themselves, a certain truth.

> To the extent that the hardening of society reduces men increasingly to the condition of objects and transforms this condition into a 'second nature', there is no need to treat as sacrilegious those methods which are themselves a testimony to this very process. The unfreedom of the methods serves the course of freedom by bearing silent witness to the unfreedom that prevails in reality.[82]

But as soon as one hypostatizes this state of affairs one is contributing 'willy-nilly to its perpetuation'.[83] Instead of making the individual and the conditions under which he or she lives the object of critical reflection, positivist methods duplicate the reified consciousness of their object. In fact, they distort it through duplication itself. They give an ontological status to a specific historical relation between the particular and general, the individual and society. They abstract unjustifiably from the experience of a particular epoch a general view of the structure of the object of social science. As such, social reality is distorted on a number of accounts. There is:

an 'hypostatization of the immediately given', a 'fetishization of aspects of the social process', a 'freezing' of the *status quo*;

decontextualization of the particular, absence of understanding of the conditions under which any 'thing' can be said to exist, loss of insight into the total context to which a particular relates; and following from this

loss of the category of potentiality and possibility – the existing order is taken to exhaust all possible alternatives.

The spell of a world which appears to be administered by a *deus ex machina* – the very medium for the realization of the domination of some people over others – can be broken by critical reflection and political practice. As long as society depends for its reproduction on the consciousness and everyday practices of human beings, the possibility exists of transforming social relations. Through reification positivism forgets this. Hence as enlightenment it 'returns to mythology, which it never really knew how to elude'.[84]

Through its adherence to the principle of the uniformity of nature, the positivistic concept of science represents nature as potential instrumentality. Its concept of legitimate knowledge restricts science's findings to a technical function. This technical character of the positivist conception of science is further analysed by Horkheimer and Adorno in *Dialectic of Enlightenment*, and by Horkheimer and Adorno individually in many other writings, in terms of the positivist separation of fact and value.[85] Given this dichotomy science can judge the efficiency of means for given ends but it cannot contribute to the formation of an objective basis for values. However, the dichotomy is untenable on a number of grounds. First, the ideals of objectivity and value-freedom are themselves values. The notion that a true judgement is better than a false one implies an evaluation. 'Value and value freedom are not separate; rather, they are contained in one another.'[86] Second, in the name of its own view of science and rationality, positivism launches a critique of ideology aimed at rooting out competing theories which are supposedly value-laden and hence illegitimately used to justify scientific practice. But this form of critique is not, as positivists maintain, value-free. For it embodies a formal (means–end) rationality and centres its interests on efficiency and economy of means to given ends. In the name of value-freedom this criticism of ideologies dictates the value system for other modes of scientific practice. Science lends itself, on this account, to technical recommendations and has an in-built potential for becoming little more than a technical critique.

The belief in the fact/value, theory/practice dichotomies has, within these terms of reference, paradoxical results. In the name of value-freedom, a certain value-orientation is championed to the exclusion of all others. In the name of a separation between theory and practice, a particular form of practice is sanctioned. Seemingly passive, contemplative reason masks an underlying level of committed reason. Not being open to rational investigation and solution, practical questions become the province of the private individual and in the end can be justified only by reference to a decision or a commitment of belief or faith. By confining rational decision procedures to those utilized by the natural sciences, positivists reduce ethics to decisionism and close off ultimate principles and values from the possibility of rational justification. As a result of their own presuppositions positivists are prevented from recognizing these inconsistencies.[87]

The effect on social theory of this hidden value commitment is a conceptualization of problems and alternative solutions which *encourages* the development of a technological rationality and mentality. Only those problems which are amenable to scientific–technological solutions are rationally decidable. Ultimate goals are supposedly not accessible to rational decision and therefore are beyond the control of science and rational dialogue. The grounding of science on instrumental reason ensures the technical applicability of its findings.

With positivism instrumental reason finds its most advanced stage of expression. But its advanced development entails moments of the severest regression. For its programme of 'demythologizing the world' reaches a *reductio ad absurdum*: positivism not only condemns to irrationality the process of adjudicating between values but also the whole process of conceptual thought itself. According to one of the most classical (but early) formulations of logical positivism, the meaning of statements is specified by the 'verifiability theory of meaning'. Generally, the 'verifiability theory' maintains that a statement is meaningful only if it is capable of a particular type of empirical verification – a statement's meaning is the mode of its verification. The question is: how is this principle to be justified? If empirically verifiable (and tautologous) assertions alone are thought to be meaningful, then an disagreement or debate about the concepts of 'meaning', 'science' and 'truth' must themselves contain meaningless statements. Philosophy becomes an impotent, meaningless sphere. The whole debate as to the status of science cannot take place within the terms of reference of the positivist programme. The verifiability principle is inadequate for determining what may be justly called science and truth.[88] It guarantees positivism's inability to account for itself, let alone justify itself. If science is to be secure in its stand against obscurantism and mythology, philosophers 'must', Horkheimer argued, 'set up a criterion for the true nature of science'.[89] Positivist philosophy of science is able to elucidate neither the conditions and limits of its own validity and method nor those of modern science.

The Frankfurt theoreticians also rejected the place accorded to prediction by positivist philosophers. Within the positivist framework, all data can be classified with a view to predicting future facts and can be formulated as laws or law-like generalizations. A discipline worthy of the name science must proceed in a generalizing manner, testing generalizations made against experience. A scientific theory is tested by checking the validity of its law-like hypotheses. Since the logical structure of explanation is held to be identical with the logical structure of a prediction, tests are made by comparing the events expected with those observed. However, on Horkheimer's and Adorno's account, this manner of testing hypothesis is an insufficient test for theory. As Adorno put it, 'the cheap satisfaction that things actually come about in the manner which the theory of society has suspected' ought not to 'delude the theoretician that he has penetrated society'.[90] In fact, for Adorno, the theoretician has, in all likelihood, conflated social and natural processes and hypostatized a particular stage of development of society. Predictability, Horkheimer also asserted, does not lead to truth. Rather it highlights the extent to which social relations are relations of unfreedom. The more society takes the form of, and is perceived in, the categories of a second nature, the more it is shaped by the outcome of individual actions locked in relations of econòmic necessity, the more human agency is subjugated to 'laws' of development, the easier it is to predict societal outcomes.[91] As Marcuse wrote, 'the less a society is rationally organized and directed by the collective efforts of free men, the more it will appear as . . . governed by "inexorable" laws'.[92] From these views it follows that critical theory cannot be empirically assessed, if assessment implies verification or falsification, solely by the success or failure of predictions. Critical theory is concerned to examine the particular historical conditions that gave the present its shape. It seeks to explicate the extraordinary range of human experience that cannot be assessed within the strait-jackets of positivist (or, as we will see, interpretative) science. In refusing to dismiss the importance of a wide range of different types of experience, critical theory seeks to show the historically given potentiality for the expansion of realms of freedom.

With positivism, science is no longer understood as one possible form of knowledge but is identified with knowledge as such. 'There is no mode of thought left which may criticize the conceptual forms and the structural patterns of science.'[93] The consequence is, Horkheimer maintained, 'a ghostlike and distorted picture of the world'.[94] Positivism, restricted to a programme of investigating observable particulars, cannot grasp the 'self-formative process of man as process'. It hypostatizes the *abstract concept* of fact or datum. By declaring meaning to be revealed in sensory observation and in identifying, in the social sciences, legitimate scientific experience with the sensory observation of manifest and overt action, positivism closes off central aspects of social reality. It excludes from inquiry:

different meanings the subject-object might attach to his or her own actions;
the way dimensions of social relations might be organized to avoid certain types of actions and the expression of certain types of interests, that is the mode in which relations of domination systematically exclude (through ideology and repression) certain types of meaning (for example claims, demands) which might otherwise be present and thematized in everyday life;
the possibility of 'things being otherwise than thus': an assessment

of the potentiality of constrained and avoided actions being 'set free'.

Critical theory addresses itself directly to an investigation of these dimensions of the social world. It seeks to explicate human reality as a self-structured, self-unfolding and contradictory whole. If it is to pursue its task successfully it must proceed:

1 through the explication of the constitution of ideas in consciousness and interaction, in the dialectics of experience;
2 through the analysis of the creation, maintenance, and change of people's inter-subjective, historical *concepts*;
3 by refusing to ignore and smooth over contradictions and contradictory claims at the phenomenal level; in other words, it must observe and explain 'determinate and historical acts of negation' and grasp the dynamic movement of the subject;
4 by leaving open the possibility of a critically reflexive understanding of history and tradition. It must not only accept the importance of an understanding of the meaning structure of tradition, but also recognize that tradition must not be idealized. For it might also embody interaction based on deception and distortion (ideology).

The goal of such an approach is to be able to judge between competing accounts of 'reality' and to expose realms of ideology. Within the terms of reference of critical theory science and evaluation are united. One must be able to evaluate aspects of reality (of which ideology, myths, etc., are of course a part) in order to describe it accurately. A positivist approach cannot grasp this. It has no basis to come to terms with, or assess, competing frames of meaning. It bows to the existent as comprehended through its own epistemological and methodological strictures. The relapse of certain types of Marxism in the twentieth century into positivistic philosophy testifies to the consequences of this surrender. By reducing ideas and cultural phenomena to the status of mere epiphenomena of physical events and by elevating natural necessity to the status of the foundation of all social phenomena, orthodox Marxism can legitimate quietism and the end of critical thinking.[95] The relation of the realm of necessity to the realm of freedom becomes purely 'quantitative and mechanical'. The realization of freedom now depends on the 'necessary natural evolution' of the forces of production which drive society onwards towards its highest stage of development. History must take its course. Thus the subject is denied an active role in the making of history. Class agencies, such as the party, are ascribed a limited facility for active intervention. The party can initiate policies which might accelerate and/or manage social change; but it cannot alter the direction of this change. As a result, technocracy becomes the appropriate mode for the consummation of history and technical success the only recognized standard of thinking. Instrumental action and knowledge determine the scope of just alternatives. Thus the legitimacy of a critical theory is threatened when reason is tied to instrumental rationality.

In order to sustain their critique of positivism and positivist philosophy the Frankfurt theorists had to elaborate their own notions of 'reason', 'objectivity' and 'truth'. The rejection of positivism required the development of alternative philosophical and social foundations. There are important differences in the approach and style of Horkheimer, Adorno and Marcuse to these issues.

6 Horkheimer's formulation of critical theory: epistemology and method 1

The following three chapters are devoted to a reconstruction of Horkheimer's, Adorno's and Marcuse's positions with respect to epistemology and method. What is a *critical* theory? How is it justified? What is its structure? In seeking answers to questions such as these it will be seen that each of the Frankfurt theorists elaborated a different and original position.

Under Max Horkheimer, the Institute of Social Research was oriented to develop social theory on an interdisciplinary basis. He wanted theory to benefit both from the reflective capacity of philosophy and the rigorous procedures of the individual sciences. From his inaugural address onward, he stressed the necessity of forging a new unity between philosophy and science, science and criticism, fact and value. There are a number of different ways of gaining further insight into this approach. One of the most fruitful is through Horkheimer's understanding and assessment of Hegel.

Hegel

Horkheimer accepted and sought to re-express Hegel's critique of Kant on many occasions in the *Zeitschrift für Sozialforschung*.[1] He found in Hegel's thought, with its emphasis on historical process and change, a great deal of promise. He always distanced himself, however, from Hegel's philosophy of history. Commenting on Hegel's reflections on his own system, Horkheimer argued that

Hegel forgets a very definite part of experience. The view that this system is the completion of truth conceals from him the meaning of the time-bound interest which influences the individual dialectical presentations as regards the direction of thought, the choice of material and the use of names and words, and which turns his attention from the fact that his conscious and unconscious partiality vis-a-vis the questions of life must necessarily become operative as constitutive elements of his philosophy.[2]

Horkheimer accepted important parts of Marx's critique of Hegel. The question is: what is retrieved from Hegel's work? Conversely, what does Horkheimer reject in Hegel's programme?

Horkheimer contended that a critique of knowledge, presented as a dialectical critique of ideology, must locate all thought in its historical context, uncover its rootedness in human interests and yet (itself) avoid relativism and be distinguished from scepticism.[3] He accepted the Hegelian idea of a critique of forms of thought, as exemplified by the *Phenomenology of Mind*, but rejected Hegel's systematic intention – the mapping out of the nature and range of all forms of consciousness.

In making these distinctions Horkheimer stressed the centrality of the 'governing principle of dialectical thought', Hegel's concept of determinate (*bestimmte*) negation. This 'governing principle' Hegel called 'the soul of the dialectic'. It is a notion which manifests itself throughout Hegel's writings and is one of the major modes in which the dynamics of the dialectic is specified. At the beginning of the *Phenomenology of Mind* the subject, and thereby also reason, is conceived as a stable entity, independent of its object domain; the realm of real objects is defined in opposition to consciousness. Hegel claimed this state of affairs to be unstable, for reason discovers that its posited separateness from the object world cannot be sustained. It discovers itself 'behind the objects'; the world *qua* known is generated from its own constitutive practice. In this process of discovery, new conceptions of both subject and object emerge and hence new oppositions. The process whereby consciousness attempts to come to terms with the world around it involves continuous negation; that is, continuous criticism and reconstruction of the knowledge of subject and object and of their relation to one another. The development of consciousness through determinate negation consists precisely in the experience of surmounting old forms of consciousness and in incorporating these moments into a new reflective attitude.

Hegel sought to show how the identity of phenomena cannot be separated from history and, in the last analysis, from the genesis of the subject. The world as we understand and interpret it changes with the development of the subject. But any determinate 'thing', or concept of a 'thing', or any finite perspective, is not thereby dismissed out of hand. Rather, as Horkheimer pointed out,

through the cognition of the conditional [nature] of every view [or perspective], and the rejection of the claim on its part to unlimited truth, limited knowledge is not at all destroyed, but is taken up as limited, one-sided and isolated into the total system of truth.[4]

For Hegel, then, the critique of knowledge seeks to reveal the essential boundedness, limitedness, isolatedness, etc. of concepts and complexes of concepts through their 'progressive incorporation into the total picture of the whole'.[5] The result is not the 'simple negation' of each such view. The recognition of the conditional nature of knowledge, its partiality, does not lead to scepticism or relativism. Instead it leads, at least on Horkheimer's reading of Hegel, to the preservation of each notion, view or perspective as a 'moment of truth'.[6]

In his essay 'Montaigne and the function of scepticism', published in 1938, Horkheimer argued that Hegel's judgement about the relation between dialectical theory and scepticism should be regarded as definitive.[7] The dialectic 'contains scepsis in itself in so far as it shows the one-sided, limited and transitory in particular representations and opinions'.[8] It differentiates itself from scepticism, however, in as much as it does not consider incomplete or partial views as simply 'null and void'. Rather, it finds in them a limited validity.[9] The result is not

The view that one can . . . forget everything because it is valueless, as it were the emptyness of consciousness as ideal, but the whole process of thought with all [its] assertions, analyses, limitations, etc., within which not only particular views are taken up, but in which are also recognized the real relationships in all their relativity and temporariness.[10]

Ultimately, for Hegel, 'the true is the whole' and the 'whole', Horkheimer argued,

is not something other than the parts in their determinate structure . . . the whole process of thought which contains in itself all limited representations in the consciousness of their limitedness.[11]

What distinguishes the dialectical method is its recognition of the insufficiencies and imperfections of 'finished' systems of thought. The dialectial method is a critical method for it reveals incompleteness where completeness is claimed. It embraces that which is in terms of that which is not, and that which is real in terms of potentialities not yet realized. Through continuous criticism and reconstruction, however, the partiality of perspectives can be progressively overcome. For Hegel, every 'point of view' has a place in the unfolding of the universal, absolute Idea – the final transcendence of all subject-object differentiation. The closer our knowledge comes to this limit, the closer it is to truth.

But Horkheimer cannot ground a materialist critique on Hegel's comprehensive system. Hegel's philosophy, consonant with the 'innermost effort' of his own thought, has to be superseded, as Marcuse put it, 'not by substituting for reason some extrarational standards, but by driving reason itself to recognize the extent to which it is still unreasonable, blind, the victim of unmastered forces'.[12] To the extent that the dialectic is embedded in an idealist system, it must be recast and itself determinately negated. As Horkeimer wrote,

With Hegel the complete theory is no longer integrated into History, there is an all-enclosed [all-embracing, *umgreifendes*] thinking, the product of which is no longer abstract and changeable: The Dialectic is concluded [or closed, complete – *abgeschlossen*].[13]

Although Horkheimer rejected Hegel's 'concluded' concept of history – his philosophy of history and identity theory – it was his intention to preserve central aspects of the dialectic. He sought to defend Hegel's insight into the knowing process, the critique of forms of knowledge and the dynamism and fluidity of history against, on the one hand, an empiricist rejection of Hegel's approach and, on the other, the attempts of certain orthodox Marxists of the second and third Internationals simply to 'invert' Hegel's system and to equate Marxism with an evolutionary determinism.

In contradistinction to these Marxists and to Hegel, of course, Horkheimer formulated the dialectic – the materialist dialectic – as the 'unconcluded' dialectic (*unabgeschlossene Dialektik*). The recognition that prevailing conditions are transitory and limited does not mean, Horkheimer held, that they will necessarily be overcome by a more complete or perfect state of affairs. He rejected all notions of a predetermined abolition and overcoming of contradictions. Progress is not guaranteed in history; it depends on the productive and reproductive practices of historically acting subjects. History gives rise to a number of contradictions and a number of modes of resolving them. When and how 'immanent' possibilities will be actualized is not an issue that theory alone can resolve. It is a practical question. The materialistic dialectic is *unabgeschlossen*.

Furthermore, 'objective' reality can never be identical with, or fully grasped by, people's concepts; 'an isolated and completable theory of reality is simply inconceivable'.[14] In accord with Marx, Horkheimer argued,

There is no complete picture of reality, neither according to essence or appearance. Even the very idea of a . . . subject, who can grasp all, is a delusion. Moreover, neither does the overcoming of the onesidedness of abstract concepts lead in the art of dialectical constructs [*Konstruktion*], as Hegel believes, to absolute truth. It always occurs in the thought of particular historical men.[15]

Thought can never gain an overview of history as a pre-given totality. The central claims of identity theories (whether idealist or materialist), purporting to have insight into an essential nature which underlies the past as well as the future, are criticized as entailing an ahistorical perspective.[16] Genuine materialism does not build up 'supra-temporal concepts and abstract from the differences introduced by time'.[17] One might form complexes of concepts of events and periods of history but these are not to be interpreted as the 'ground of history in its totality'. Thus, for example, Horkheimer argued,

The scientific idea of man, as well as nature which is known and to be known by science, are elements in the dynamism of history and will play a role even in the future. But they themselves are determined and altered by the total process, just as much as they in turn . . . determine and alter it. The application, therefore, of definitions constructed in the context of the contemporary situation or, what comes to the same thing, the contemporary signification of these concepts can some day become meaningless.[18]

For Horkheimer society is a totality which is 'continuously restructuring itself'. As a consequence, the idea of a social absolute – a complete or perfect state of social phenomena – is criticized.

The claim that there is an absolute order and an absolute demand made upon men always presupposes a claim to know the whole, the totality of things, the infinite. But if our knowledge is in fact not yet final, if there is an irreducible tension between concept and being, then no proposition can claim the dignity of perfect knowledge. Knowledge of the infinite must itself be infinite, and a knowledge which is admittedly imperfect is not a knowledge of the absolute.[19]

In classical idealist metaphysics concept and object are held to be identical. Horkheimer, on the other hand, maintained that there is an 'irreducible tension between concept and object and thus . . .

[that there exists] a critical weapon of defense against belief in the infinity of the mind [*Geist*]'.[20] There is an ever present tension between the object as known and the object's actuality and development. Critical theory seeks to examine and assess this tension.

Feuerbach, Marx and materialism

Feuerbach's critique of philosophy and theology, with its emphasis on the human origin of all philosophical and theological categories, represented, for Horkheimer, a crucial turning point in the attempt to dislodge the dialectic from its idealist form. In particular, Horkheimer shared Feuerbach's stress on material human existence as the ground or foundation of all consciousness. For Feuerbach it was not 'the absolute, that is, abstract spirit' which determined the cognitive process but the 'whole essence (*Wesen*) of humanity'.[21] Reality is constituted by human beings in their sensible existence; that is, through their sensibility (*Sinnlichkeit*) – through their consciousness of their needs, wants and interests, rooted in particular physical and social conditions. Feuerbach's philosophy was, however, just the beginning of important developments in the philosophy of materialism. As Hegel had failed to adequately concretize his concepts so too had Feuerbach. The sensibility which Feuerbach takes as the domain of the dialectic is insufficiently differentiated as various types of social and political practice.[22] Feuerbach's awareness of concrete human activity was undeveloped. The concept of man which he claimed as the subject of the knowing process was an hypostatization of the dynamics of that subject. It was left to Marx to thoroughly expose this.

Marx decisively advanced the doctrine of materialism. From his early writings onward, it became possible to conceive of the subject 'as man of a definite historical epoch', and of the relation of human beings to nature and to each other in terms of their transformative, world-structuring activity.[23] The central importance of Marx's notion of praxis is emphasized. Thereby, reality is understood as constructed by practice; it can 'never be broken down into neatly separable subjective and objective elements'.[24] But this does not mean that it is arbitrarily produced by human will. From a materialistic perspective, reality is a process of interaction between society and nature, freedom and necessity, already existent and emerging cultures.[25] The 'human' and 'material' are themselves derived from concrete situations of historical human activity.[26]

As a corollary of this position, Horkheimer argued that while materialists must acknowledge as real 'what is given in sense experience' they must not 'absolutize sensation'.

The requirement that every thing manifest itself through the senses does not mean that the senses do not change in the historical process or that they are to be regarded as fixed cornerstones of the world. If the evidence of sense experience is part of the grounds for existential judgements, such experiences are far from identical with the constant elements in the world.[27]

While sense experience is a crucial basis of knowledge, it is conditioned and changeable; it is a product of the structure of human activities in various societies, and of culture and theory.[28] What people see depends on how life is produced and interpreted. Cognition is always the cognition of particular men and women, in particular social relations within a particular society: materialism, Horkheimer maintained, 'challenges every claim to the autonomy of thought'.[29]

All factors in the total societal process are held to be in 'the process of movement'. This includes the relation of 'parts' to 'whole'.[30] Through the constant interaction and development of parts – whether they be individuals, social classes, or institutions – the whole also changes, realizing some of the possibilities given in prior stages. This conception of the whole implies, as Bertell Ollman has written about dialectical and materialist conceptions of the totality, that 'flux and interaction, projected back into the origins of the present and forward into its possible future, are the chief distinguishing characteristics of the world'.[31] It is a consequence of this view, Horkheimer argued, that there is 'no general formula for handling the interaction of the forces which must be taken into account in particular theories; the formula must be searched out in each case'.[32] For example, in the understanding of a theory itself, we must grasp the relation between subject and object, part and whole, particular and universal, historically. We must grasp 'the interplay of both aspects, the human and the extrahuman, the individual and the classifiable, the methodological and the substantive, and not separate any of these, as realities, from the others'.[33] There is no linear path from ignorance to knowledge. We may posit the existence of the totality and may strive toward knowledge of it, but its terms are not constants and so it can never be made fully transparent. The image of a knowing process involving the simple realities 'knowledge' and 'object' is 'an hypostatization of abstract significations'.[34]

The structure of critical theory

Every thought, idea and particular is interwoven with the whole societal life process. Critical theory, in spite of its efforts to reflect the object in its manifold forms of development, depends in its every step on particular historical conditions.[35] Its content is ever changing. 'There are no general criteria for critical theory as a whole, for such criteria always depend on a repetition of events and thus on a self-reproducing totality . . . .'[36] This sociological radicalism, however, raises questions as to the logical structure of critical theory. In his essay 'On the problem of truth', Horkheimer contended that a dialectical theory which has given up the

metaphysical character of finality, the solemnity of a revelation, becomes itself a transitory element bound up with the destiny of men. The unconcluded dialectic does not however lose the stamp of truth. In fact, the uncovering of limitedness and onesidedness in one's own and in other's thought, constitutes an important aspect of the intellectual process. . . . The abstract reservation that one day a justified critique of one's own epistemic situation will be put into play, that it is open to correction expresses itself among materialists not in a tolerance for contradictory opinions or even in a skeptical indecision, but in a watchfulness against one's own error and in the mobility of thought. . . . The theory which we see as right may one day disappear because the practical and scientific interests which played a role in its conceptual development, and more importantly the things and conditions to which it referred have disappeared . . . but a later correction does not mean that an earlier truth was an earlier untruth, . . . the dialectic freed from the idealist illusion overcomes the contradiction between relativism and dogmatism. While it does not presume that the progress of critique and determination will end with its own standpoint, it in no way gives up the conviction that its knowledge – in the total context to which its concepts and judgements refer – is valid not only for individuals or groups but simply valid, i.e., that opposed theories are false.[37]

But how are the relationships between theory and practice, fact and value, etc., conceived to avoid scepticism or relativism? To what concept of truth does critical theory appeal?

Horkheimer's responses to these questions are complex. It should be said from the outset that his positions are not always consistent and that they changed over time. I will focus my analysis on his works written during the most productive period of the Institute, 1930 to 1945 (although reference will be made to his later writings). During this period his position contained, at least, three elements. First, there is the idea of a critique of ideology which he took to be similar in structure to Marx's critique of capitalist commodity production and exchange. Second, there is a stress on the importance of methodical research in an interdisciplinary context. Third, there is an emphasis on the central role of praxis in the ultimate verification of theories. Each of these requires comment.

The critique of ideology

Horkheimer maintained that there is an hiatus between concept and object, word and thing: these are interdependent but irreducible aspects of the total societal process. On his account, it is as false to reduce 'spirit' (or culture) to 'nature' as it is 'nature' to 'spirit'. The hypostatization of either of these polarities is, likewise, a mistake. Philosophical concepts like 'nature' and 'spirit' become 'inadequate, empty and false' when they are abstracted from the total context in which they are embedded: the processes through which they have been obtained'.[38]

The assumption of an ultimate duality is [also therefore] inadmissible. . . . The two poles cannot be reduced to a monistic principle, yet their duality too must be largely understood as a product.[39]

These ideas provide the foundation for understanding central aspects of Horkheimer's idea of truth.

Critical theory aims to assess 'the breach between ideas and reality'. The method of procedure is immanent criticism.[40] Immanent criticism confronts 'the existent, in its historical context, with the claim of its conceptual principles, in order to criticize the relation between the two and thus transcend them'.[41] For example, following Marx, Horkheimer argued that there is a contradiction between the bourgeois order's ideas and reality, between its words and deeds. The bourgeois social order places the great universal ideals, 'justice, equality and freedom', at the centre of its political and moral philosophy. It claims to put universality into practice by creating the conditions for free and just exchange. The commodity or market system is held to create a dynamic equilibrium between demand and supply, utility and disutility, individual interests and scarce resources, etc.; it is held to be the most efficient and fairest mode of satisfying individual needs and wants. Its universalistic principles are, however, negated in practice.

Through the immanent critique of capitalism, there is a transformation of

the concepts that thoroughly dominate the economy into their opposites: fair exchange into a deepening of social injustice; a free economy into the domination of monopolies; productive labour into the strengthening of relations which hinder production; the maintenance of society's life into the impoverishment [*Verelendung*] of the people's.[42]

But the process of changing concepts into their opposites is not just an abstract and logical process. The method must be 'adequate' to the object. The commodity economy, it is contended, reveals its own inherent negativity. Its development contradicts its own claims about itself and about what is possible. From this perspective, Horkheimer felt he could argue that the further bourgeois society moves from keeping its revolutionary promise of 'justice, equality and freedom', the more it can be said to fail against its own standards. The ideology of liberal capitalism which preached a harmony between 'egotistical individual interest and societal progress' conceals the 'negative dialectic, that the masses, by means of their own work "produce a reality which enslaves them to an increasing degree and threatens them with every kind of suffering"'.[43]

Social theory, developed through immanent criticism, is concerned to investigate (aspects of) the social world 'in the movement of its development'. It starts with the conceptual principles and standards of an object, and unfolds their implications and consequences. Then it re-examines and reassesses the object (the object's function, for instance) in light of these implications and consequences. Critique proceeds, so to speak, 'from within' and hopes to avoid, thereby, the charge that its concepts impose irrelevant criteria of evaluation on the object. As a result, a new understanding of the object is generated – a new comprehension of contradictions and possibilities. Thus, the original image of the object is transcended and the object itself is brought partly into flux.

To re-express the point in Horkheimer's own language: the

social investigator observes an object that is a unity of identity and difference – a unity of opposites that contains within itself contradictions. The object's view of itself is contradicted by its effective actuality. Through reflection and critique, it can become aware of its own limitations; that is, that it fails by its own standards. Through this awareness it develops and becomes open to radical change.

In confronting the existent with the claims of 'its own conceptual principles' critical theory retains the principle of negation as the mainstay of its approach. The truths to be drawn out are primarily negations. But a critique of ideology based on immanent criticism derives a certain positive character by pointing to the limits and, therefore, the closed-off possibilities, immanent in the existing order.

Negation plays a crucial role. . . . The negation is double-edged – a negation of the absolute claims of prevailing ideology and of the brash claims of reality. . . . Philosophy [developed as critical theory] takes existing values seriously but insists that they become parts of a theoretical whole that reveals their relativity. Inasmuch as subject and object, word and thing, cannot be integrated under present conditions, we are driven, by the principles of negation, to attempt to salvage relative truths from the wreckage of false ultimates.[44]

It should be noted that Horkheimer does not imply that the understanding of negativity in existing social life is co-extensive with the praxis of freedom. The practice of reflection and critique is a necessary but by no means sufficient condition for the overcoming of particular historical situations.

To assume this would be to confound true philosophy with the idealistic interpretation of history, and to lose sight of the core difference between the ideal and the real, between theory and practice.[45]

Therefore, there is a gap between theory and practice, precisely that which must be filled by a conscious, revolutionary politics (early Horkheimer!). Only such a practice can create the conditions of real material freedom. By disclosing contradictions in the social totality, especially those between the existent and ideology, critical theory, Horkheimer held, can contribute to the development of this practice.

Ideologies, on this account, are not to be confused with the necessarily limited and conditioned validity of propositions.

The conditional nature of a proposition and ideology are two quite different things. The limit of what we may rightly call ideology is always set by the present state of affairs and our knowledge. Insight into the historically conditioned [nature of a proposition or general perspective] is never identical with the proof that it is ideological. Rather, for this there is needed . . . [understanding] of its societal function.[46]

Whether or not ideas and modes of cognitively appropriating reality are ideological, depends on their roles and functions in *particular historical contexts*. Individual (or sets of) claims, perspectives and philosophies can be regarded as ideological if they conceal or mask social contradictions on behalf of a dominant class or group. For example, forms of consciousness are ideological in so far as they claim to represent generalizable interests but conceal the particular and sectarian interests of the ruling class; and/or in so far as they maintain that societal outcomes represent natural ones, when they are the result of particular constellations of social relations; and/or in so far as they glorify the social situation as harmonious, when it is, in fact, conflict ridden. Ideologies are not, however, merely illusions. They are embodied and manifested in social relations. The ahistorical and asocial character of certain kinds of interpretation of social life may itself be a reflection of the transformation of social relations into impersonal and reified forms. Ideologies can express 'modes of existence'. Therefore, ideologies are often also packages of symbols, ideas, images and theories through which people experience their relation to each other and the world. The degree to which ideologies mystify social relations or adequately reflect distorted social relations (but thereby mystify the possibility of non-distorted social relations) is a question for inquiry in particular cases and contexts.

While critical theory aims to expose and thematize contradictions between society's performance and legitimating ideologies, this does not imply, on Horkheimer's view, any dogmatism as to moral principle.

Social theory may be able to circumvent a skeptical spurning of value judgements without succumbing to normative dogmatism. This may be accomplished by relating social institutions and activities to the values they themselves set forth as their standards and ideals. . . . If subjected to such an analysis, the social agencies most representative of the present pattern of society will disclose a pervasive discrepancy between what they actually are and the values they accept. To take an example, the media of public communication, radio, press, and film, constantly profess their adherence to the individual's ultimate value and his inalienable freedom, but they operate in such a way that they tend to forswear such values by fettering the individuals to prescribed attitudes, thoughts, and buying habits. The ambivalent relation between prevailing values and the social context forces the categories of social theory to become critical and thus to reflect the actual rift between the social reality and the values it posits.[47]

The activities of a social institution can be investigated in light of its avowed aims and ends without the acceptance of these aims and ends as valid. But the categories and concepts of critical theory are not simply descriptive. Through immanent criticism 'they come alive and enter an indictment of society' (Marcuse). Thus, there is a unification of science and criticism.

The standards upon which critique is founded are always culture and time bound. This fact, however, does not prevent adoption of a grounded critical stance. It does not imply, Horkheimer contended, radical relativism. Rather it implies the recognition that justified positions for critique will not be justified 'for all time', and will not have the same connotation 'for all time'. Such standards and values are relative to certain contexts but, nevertheless, can, within these, be objective. As a consequence, the original and classical notion of truth, the 'adequation of name and thing', can be preserved.[48] Through immanent criticism and its central vehicle, negation, 'things can be called by their right names'.[49]

The importance of immanent criticism is emphasized also in the work of Adorno and Marcuse. They share a commitment to certain of the above methodological tenets, although they develop them in different ways. They all agree, furthermore, on one central point; that is, that in developing the methods of immanent criticism they are developing a key element of Marx's method. This view is illustrated most clearly in Adorno's writings and will be discussed in the following chapter.

Interdisciplinary research

Throughout his essays in the 1930s, Horkheimer maintained that although theories and methods are always (to be understood as) embedded in historical and societal processes, every theoretical claim must 'submit' itself to, or 'subordinate' itself to, the results of relevant, individual empirical sciences. Critical theory must ensure a congruence with the most advanced 'traditional' theories. (Although the term 'traditional theory' carries a pejorative connotation for Horkheimer – this type of theory, he held, uncritically affirms society by treating, for example, social phenomena as if they had the qualities of given and unchanging forms – he recognized that it often provides ideas of interest: ideas which should be critically appropriated.) The limitations and one-sidedness of the individual, empirical sciences are to be superseded not by rejecting out of hand experiences won through methodical research, but by reconstructing and reinterpreting their works in the total context to which their concepts and judgements refer. Conventional criteria specifying standards of adequacy for scientific theory and research (for example, logical consistency, methodological clarity, reproducibility of results or intersubjective validity; capacity to explain problems and issues other theories and modes of proce-dure cannot account for) are to be respected. This respect, how-ever, is not to be taken as implying any unremitting and exclusive attention to given, individual facts as the sole basis of generating knowledge. It must not exclude systematic reflection – employing philosophical, theoretical and interdisciplinary perspectives – on the nature of the phenomena under scrutiny.

The gulf between the individual social sciences and critical theory is to be overcome by distinguishing between two inter-related but distinct phases of investigation: the processes 'rep-resentation' or 'presentation' (*Darstellungsweise*) and 'research' (*Forschung*). All the relevant concepts, definitions and proposi-tions advanced on the basis of available scientific experience must be heeded. These concepts form an essential part of the material for the comprehension of socio-historical events. But in the con-text of the process of representation, i.e. theoretical reconstruc-tion, they are taken up and reinterpreted. As a result, they obtain a new meaning in a larger frame of concepts and theories. Concepts gain new functions, senses, and referents. Their new character contradicts the abstract – the partial and one-sided – context within which they arose and were previously understood. 'Representation' can, Horkheimer contended, relocate an analysis of a 'part', a 'something', in the context of totality. Particular perspectives constituted by particular standpoints are to find their place in the reconstruction of the whole carried out by a philosophically astute, interdisciplinary programme.[50] Only after this work is done can the real movement of history be adequately characterized. In the early days of the Institute there was, in fact, a remarkable homology between the organizational structure of the

Institute and this methodological framework.[51] Horkheimer, as
director, often saw himself as the synthesizer of the findings of the
research conducted under the Institute's auspices.

In a short article published in 1941, Horkheimer asserted that
critical theory can, in the final analysis, only arrive at adequate
categories for the understanding of society inductively. This
appears to represent a change in his position, although his notion
of induction is not the traditional one. For Horkheimer, following
the influence of Walter Benjamin, induction suggests a method of
examining 'the universal within the particular, not above or
beyond it': for 'society is a "system" in the material sense that
every single social field or relation contains and reflects, in various
ways, the whole itself'.[52] Critical social research 'should delve
deeper and deeper into the particular and discover the universal
law therein'. To the extent that the historical totality can be
grasped, it is a result of detailed theoretical and empirical investigation of particular social phenomena.[53] Instead of 'moving from
one particular to another and then to the heights of abstraction',
the proposal seems to be that supportive evidence for theory can
only be uncovered by analysing, in an interdisciplinary context, the
way in which particular phenomena are mediated; that is, the way
in which they are formed and their identities sustained in interdependence with other phenomena. The claims of immanent criticism must be assessed in this context.

Theory and practice

The third element in Horkheimer's writings on the essential features of critical theory emphasizes the central role of praxis in the
ultimate verification of theories. The assessment and confirmation
of ideas which relate to people and society is said to depend on
historical struggles. This idea is best understood with reference to
Marx's work.

In the first of the *Theses on Feuerbach*, Marx summarized his
critical stance with respect to materialism and idealism.

The chief defect of all materialism up to now (including Feuerbach's) is,
that the object, reality, what we apprehend through our senses, is understood only in the form of the object or of contemplation [*Anschauung*];
but not as sensuous human activity, as practice; not subjectively. Hence in
opposition to materialism the active side was developed abstractly by

idealism – which of course does not know real sensuous activity as such. . . .[54]

Marx interpreted 'sensuous human activity' in juxtaposition with the abstract side of idealism. In the second thesis on Feuerbach, he pointed to the epistemological import of this category: 'the dispute over the reality or non-reality of thinking which is isolated from practice is a purely *scholastic* question'. The question is a *practical* one; 'man must prove the truth, i.e. the reality and power, the this-sidedness of his thinking in practice'.[55] The suggestion appears to be that theory is tested and verified in and through practice.

Marx's historical materialism entails a rejection of objectivism and subjectivism. For him social reality is neither something wholly 'outside' of the subject nor is it simply a creation of human thought. Rather, reality is conceived as formed and constructed through practice and labour. Through practice and labour the human species synthesizes and alters the material world and thereby transforms nature *qua* known as well as itself. The objects of human perception are themselves the products of the self-generative and self-formative activity of the species. What we understand by nature or the human species changes over time as both are actively transformed. The process of knowing cannot be separated from historical being.

But, as Marx often suggested, history is not made as actors might consciously and immediately wish. Circumstances exist, generated prior to any given instance of history in the making, which condition the social act and limit the extent to which any co-ordinated action may be fully explained as the pursuit of rational ends. Reality impinges upon, constrains individuals: it remains something seemingly 'non-human', objectified and reified. This situation, however, can be altered. While it cannot be changed by the subject simply appropriating its 'other', people can come to understand how society operates, understand it as a social product, and understand that it is open to transformation. What is true of the existing order need not be true of the next. But more than this, Marx argued, for true consciousness to exist, not only must consciousness grasp reality, but reality must be changed so that it no longer (through the production of ideology) systematically distorts consciousness. For this to be achieved a 'genuinely free life' must be created (that is, one in which – at least on one reading of Marx – the fundamental, unfulfilled potentiality contained in human beings is realized). Of course, whether or not such a life can be achieved is not a question that can be decided independently of practice. As Marx put it in his speech to the Second Congress of the Communist International,

... we must ... note two widespread errors. ... Revolutionaries sometimes try to prove that there is absolutely no way out of the crisis. This is a mistake. There is no such thing as an absolutely hopeless situation. ... To try to 'prove' in advance that there is 'absolutely' no way out of the situation would be sheer pedantry, or playing with concepts and catchwords. Practice alone can serve as real 'proof' in this and similar questions.[56]

Horkheimer's position could claim to be an extension of this view. He refused to ground critical theory outside of the historical process. Throughout his *Zeitschrift* essays he refers to a type of *historico-practical* confirmation. For example, he wrote:

It is not history which takes care of the correction and further determination of the truth, so that the knowing subject ... would only have to look and see; rather the truth is carried forward insofar as the men who have it stand firm by it, apply and support it, act according to it, bring it to power against all resistance from regressive, limited, one-sided standpoints. The process of knowledge involves real historical willing and acting as well as experiencing and conceiving. The latter cannot progress without the former.[57]

For Horkheimer there is no objective reality which social theorists can passively reflect upon. The social theorist is at every moment a part of the societal process analysed as well as 'its potential critical self-awareness'.

Theory is intertwined with history. Its concepts and categories refer to the development and formation of social relations, practical human activities and historical struggles. Therefore, if a theory is correct, this will be indicated in history. It will be confirmed in so far as 'men who have it ... bring it to power'. Praxis is, on Horkheimer's account, an historical, political and epistemological category. The point was made clearly in an essay published in 1935.

The verification and confirmation of ideas, which relate to men and society, does not consist in laboratory experiments or in the search for documents, but in historical struggles, in which conviction itself plays an essential role. The false view that the present is ... harmonious, forms a moment in the renewal of disharmony and downfall . . . itself becoming a factor in its own practical refutation. The correct theory of the prevailing circumstances, the teaching of the deepening of the crisis and of the imminence of catastrophes are, to be sure, constantly confirmed in full detail, but the picture of a better order which is inherent [*einwohnt*] in it and by means of which the claim for the 'evil' [*schlechtigkeit*] of the present is oriented – the immanent representation of mankind and its possibilities – is determined, corrected and confirmed in the course of historical struggles.[58]

In the same essay Horkheimer stated bluntly: truth inheres in and is a moment of correct practice.[59]

This description of critical theory gives rise to a number of further questions. If all knowledge is regarded as culture and time bound, and if cognitive processes are understood as a moment (aspect or phase) of practice, the question arises, as previously stated, as to how we can demarcate valid and true knowledge. Horkheimer argued that it is in historical struggles that ideas and theories are tested. But truth, he wrote, is not carried forward by just any social group. The groups he pointed to were said to be *progressive*.

The value of a theory is not decided alone by the formal criteria of truth . . . the value of a theory is decided by its connection with the tasks, which in the particular historical moment are taken up by *progressive social forces*. But not [even] this value is immediately valid for the whole of mankind, but in the first instance only for those groups which are interested in the tasks.[60]

How can this notion be justified? In what sense are tasks of particular social groups and classes progressive? Horkheimer's view appears to be that the struggles of social groups are progressive to the extent that they carry forward, through 'correct practices', the truth. 'Truth is a moment of correct practice.' But if his position is to avoid circularity, then the question becomes, how can correct practices, the practices that critical theory might be grounded upon, be distinguished from partial or sectarian practices and interests which, he claimed, underlie ideological theories?[61]

While all thought and theory is tied to human interests, critical theory, Horkheimer argued, expresses and is guided by a 'particular' practical interest – an interest in the emancipation of men and women from the constraints of class society and domination in all its forms:

despite all its insights into individual steps and the agreement of its elements with those of the most advanced traditional theories, critical theory has no specific instance for itself other than its inherent interest in the supersession of class domination. . . .[62]

This is not a sectarian interest but rather, on his account, a generalizable interest, the interest of the 'general public' (*Allgemeinheit*).[63] In the early 1930s Horkheimer emphasized that a materialistic and critical theory, in the formation of its categories, concepts and in all phases of its development, makes this general interest its own. During these years, he was particularly concerned to show how in a class society (or in a society dominated by a despotic, political group), the 'general interest' cannot be fulfilled because *individual* autonomy is negated in practice. He clarified the seemingly paradoxical nature of this position as follows.

Conventional capitalist social relations depend on, among other things, the freedom of the individual to pursue certain self-defined goals and interests. The importance of individual choice is at the very centre of bourgeois theory and practice.[64] The progress of society is said to depend on the interaction of divergent wants and interests in a free market. To this idea belongs a fundamental principle of liberalism – 'that the individual, pursing his own interests, at the same time automatically serves the common interest of the whole'.[65] Horkheimer refers to these notions as the doctrine of individualism.

Under the conditions of capitalist production and exchange people are conditioned to work for themselves. The individual is the focus of all existence. But the individual's subjectivity is both emphasized and denied. It is emphasized because the individual, freed from the political bondages of feudalism, has become free to buy or sell on the market – the 'fine instrument of social organization'. The individual's success becomes a guideline for judging right and wrong: practical success becomes both the sign and reward of individual development.[66] The individual's subjectivity is denied because he or she is isolated in the context of buying and selling. Exchange processes are the mode in which individuality is organized. The pursuit of self-interest becomes synonymous with the pursuit of material interests.[67] Within the context of the bourgeois order, the liberal defence of 'individual freedom' becomes ideology: it masks sectional interests, the interests of the bourgeois class.

The reproduction of this state of affairs is held to be a result, in the system of private property, of the principle that individuals should 'look out for themselves'.[68] But the efforts of nearly all individuals in competitive isolation are self-defeating. The single-minded pursuit of economic gain and profit, ultimately, negates individual self-interests. At the centre of this view (the view, that is, of the 'young' Horkheimer) is an agreement with Marx's analysis of the commodity economy.[69] The endeavours of individuals, structured by the wage labour/capital relation, result in 'exploitation, impoverishment, unemployment, inflation and crises'. Thus, on the one hand, society is created and changed by the labour of individuals in given social relations. But on the other hand, it takes on a dynamic of its own. Society becomes the 'world of capital'. The competitive relation between individuals creates a 'blind and anarchistic' (Marx) process of societal development which is increasingly beyond the individual's control. This is true for entrepreneurs as well as proletarians.

> At the heart of the freedom and seeming originality of the entrepreneur . . . is adaptation to a social situation in which mankind does not control its own destiny . . . subjection to a purposeless process instead of rational regulation of it, dependence on an irrational condition of society which one must try to profit by instead of shaping it in its totality. . . . It is not their boasted inner decision that motivates the apparently free entrepreneurs but a soulless economic dynamism, and they have no way of opposing this state of affairs except by surrendering their very existence.[70]

In short, the individual negates his or her own individuality in individualism. In the context of capitalist social relations, the needs of the whole community as well as those of the individual are distorted and denied. The era of large economic combines and the culture industry simply reinforces these trends. Therefore, the political task is to liberate the individual from the conditions of individualism.[71]

> If today the interest of the 'general public' [*Allgemeinheit*] is confronted by the blind persecution of itself, then the reason for this truth is to be found in that society in its present form is in contradiction to the self-interest of most of its members. The overcoming of this contradiction, not the repression of individual interests, is the task which . . . is to be solved only through a definite change in the relations of production, the foundation of the whole of society.[72]

This task is represented by Horkheimer as the struggle to realize the standpoint ('interests', 'needs') of 'most of society's members'.

In a number of aphorisms in *Dämmerung*, in 'Remarks on science and crisis' (1932) and in 'The dispute over rationalism in contemporary philosophy' (1934), Horkheimer implied that this standpoint is the standpoint of the 'progressive social forces' who have become progressive by virtue of their position in the productive process. Theory must conform to the 'mental (*geistigen*) and materialistic situation . . . of a particular social class' – the proletariat.[73] It can be noted that this position is not unlike Lukács's, as developed in *History and Class Consciousness*.[74] For the young Horkheimer, the important thing about the proletariat is that it is developing needs which cannot be satisfied by capitalism's rigid distribution of scarce values – needs which, if adequately articulated, can be fulfilled only through the realization of capitalism's promise of 'justice, equality and freedom'. Hence if those needs are transformed into militant class consciousness, they can become the basis for the actualization of the universalistic principles on which capitalism was founded.[75] For as Marcuse wrote, the proletariat's particular interest in its own liberation 'is at the same time the general interest: it cannot free itself without abolishing itself as a class, and all classes. . . . the goals of the proletariat *as revolutionary class* are self-transcendent: while remaining historical, concrete goals, they extend, in their class context, beyond the specific class content'.[76] Until the very late 1930s Horkheimer believed that the critical intellectual's thinking could be a 'stimulating, active factor . . . in the development of the masses'. By making its own the interest in emancipation, the interest in the transcendence of all class societies, critical theory could help to promote greater awareness about societal contradictions and thus an objective improvement in human existence.[77]

With the late 1930s Horkheimer became more and more disillusioned about the potential development of the working class. Although he still stressed that the standpoint critical theory makes its own is conditioned by the productive process and the position of the proletariat, he emphasized, increasingly, that this position can be less and less associated with the practice of the working class.[78] As a result, he sought to justify the objectivity of critical theory's standpoint by reference to

an interest in a rational organization of human activity which it [critical theory] has set itself to elucidate and legitimize. For it is not only concerned with goals as they have been prescribed by pre-existent life-forms, but with mankind and all its possibilities.[79]

The goal of a rational society 'which today, of course, only appears to arise in the imagination, is really invested', he added, 'in every man'. It is given in human beings as potential.[80]

For Horkheimer the concept of a rational society can only be gained *ex negativo*: it is a society pointed to by immanent critique, a society free of the contradictions of the existing order. But he says little, if anything, positive about the nature of such a society. This is deliberate. 'In regard to the essential kind of change at which critical theory aims, there can be no . . . concrete conception of it until it actually comes about. If the proof of the pudding is in the eating, the eating here is still in the future.'[81] The dialectic is necessarily negative. A 'rational society' can only emerge in 'the struggle for the future', in the struggle against 'the world of capital' (early Horkheimer) and 'the domination of technical rationality in all its forms' (later Horkheimer). It is only through the struggle against existing contradictions that the notion of a rational society can become more clearly defined.

Horkheimer, however, discussed not only the idea of a rational society but also *an interest* in such a society which is embedded 'in man': it is, as he sometimes put it, 'immanent to human labour'. What are the grounds for the claim that an interest in a rational society is 'immanent in man' or given in humans 'as potential'? What is the status of this interest? The critic of society might well be able to point out 'alternatives', 'closed-off possibilities'. But if these are to be taken as something other than the product of utopian thinking, they need a justified basis. If the charge of utopianism is to be dismissed, Horkheimer must, as he himself realized, assess the actual potentiality for a rational society. If the idea of a rational society is to be united with an actual historical movement, the latter's possibility must be revealed.[82]

Horkheimer's response to these issues in his pre-1937 writings involves, I think, two interrelated sets of arguments.[83] First, there is a claim that there are new needs developing which cannot be satisfied under the present system of labour and which represent, potentially, generalizable interests. This claim is defended by reference to Marx's account of the development of capitalist economies. This account provides, to a large extent, the basis of his argument that individual self-interests are negated in capitalist society. Bourgeois society denies and limits 'self-fulfilling praxis'. Following Marx, Horkheimer suggested that the proletariat can potentially transcend this condition. It has been prepared for this task by its position in the productive process. In the position of wage labourer it is apparent that the pursuit of individual 'profit' (at the expense of other's interests) is a self-defeating strategy. The isolated pursuit of individual interests denies the worker the power to pursue claims against capital. A strategy of collective action is, therefore, the only basis for the pursuit of certain basic needs and wants (increased material benefits, control over every-day life, satisfying work, for instance). It is only through collective action that *individuals* can establish the conditions for a fulfilling life. Ultimately, it is only through the abolition of the 'economic structure which underlies all social change', class relations, that 'individuality can be set free'. The collective struggle for the real-ization of greater individual freedom and happiness *is part of the experience* of many people. The struggle must be carried forward and developed if the 'general interests' of the masses are to be enhanced; that is, if 'the *free* development of individuals, a *just* allocation of scarce values, *equality* in community' are to be actual-ized.

Second, there is the view that some phenomena which critical theory interprets can be shown to be natural properties of the species, which under certain conditions can be developed. Follow-ing Freud, especially his libido theory, Horkheimer argued that the instinctual structure of the species is directed toward the release of tension and the fulfilment of needs.[84] As previously noted, libido theory, for Horkheimer, demonstrates that human beings share a striving for pleasure and self-preservation. Thus, there is a stratum of human existence which is 'an ever-flowing source of stimuli'.[85] Although materialism reveals that the structure of human needs is changeable it recognizes, on Horkheimer's account, that

man's striving for happiness is to be regarded as a natural fact requiring no justification . . . the satisfaction of desire, unlike 'higher' motives, requires no reasons, excuses, or justifications . . . men are determined by elemen-tary reactions of pleasure and pain.[86]

But capitalism enforces restrictions on libidinal drives and, there-fore, perpetuates repressions, feelings of guilt and general suffer-ing. It does, however, through its massive increase in productive forces, create the possibility of the liberation of human potential-ity. Whether or not this potentiality will be realized is not a ques-tion that can be settled by a priori reasoning. The negation of the negation, the abolition of existing limitations and restrictions on human development, is dependent on the autonomous acts of human beings.

Post-war developments

In light of the failure of revolution in the West, the absence of proletarian revolutionary consciousness, the growth of monopoly capitalism, the expansion of the (authoritarian) state and bureaucracy, Horkheimer frequently acknowledged the need to revise his position.[87] He became more and more concerned to preserve a past in danger of being forgotten – the history of struggles for emancipation – and maintain a capacity for independent, critical, thinking.

By the early 1940s, there was little in Horkheimer's work to suggest the imminent emergence of needs compatible with universal moral principles. There was less discussion of the relation between theory and revolutionary practice. The strategy of justifying critical theory's project by reference to generalizable interests represented by the position of the proletariat, became less and less important. Horkheimer concentrated on immanent criticism in the context of interdisciplinary research – although these two strands in his thinking often diverged. For example, projects in philosophy (on the philosophy of history) carried out simultaneously with empirical research (for example on authoritarianism) lacked the 'dynamic unity' which he had argued was necessary in the *Zeitschrift* essays. Throughout the 1950s and 1960s these trends became more marked as Horkheimer's interests underwent a number of alterations.

Perhaps the most important development was his re-evaluation of certain metaphysical and theological traditions. By the mid 1960s he felt he could not defend any philosophy or critical stance that lacked a theological moment; that is, an awareness of the transcendent, or the infinite, or the 'Wholly other'.[88] His thought became increasingly speculative as he sought to develop an areligious conception of theology – a theology which, while rejecting all links with any kind of organized church or cultus, focused attention on dimensions of experience that transcend the empirically given world. For Horkheimer, theology was the expression of humanity's unappeasable longing to go beyond its immediate reality and to establish a free and just community.[89] While traces of his earlier concerns with the 'interest of the general public' (*All-gemeinheit*) – the 'interest in a rational society' – are retained in this idea, they are very faint. It is hard to recognize Horkheimer's original programme for a critique of ideology in his later works.

7 Adorno's conception of negative dialectics: epistemology and method 2

Differences between Horkheimer and Adorno

From the early 1930s, according to Horkheimer, philosophy was in a state of disarray. The great philosophical attempts to grasp the totality of life had failed. Classical German philosophy had degenerated into a set of competing systems, highly abstract and equally arbitrary. In reaction, the Vienna circle (among other contemporary schools) led philosophy along a new path – a path, however, which was yet another *cul-de-sac*. From the position of the Vienna circle, it proved impossible to give an adequate account of the meaning of the 'given' and of the nature of philosophical and scientific activity.

Horkheimer believed that many traditional philosophical concerns ought not to be completely rejected; they ought instead to be recast. He tended to emphasize the capacities of the social sciences to provide answers to important philosophical questions. Adorno sympathized with this position but tried to strengthen Horkheimer's 'anti-positivistic, speculative bent'.[1] For Adorno, the primary task was an immanent critique of philosophy. Only the systematic critique of philosophy could adequately dispense with old problems and set the limits for new projects. As he argued in his inaugural address to the University of Frankfurt, seven years before he became a full member of the Institute,

> only an essentially undialectical philosophy, one which aims at ahistorical truth, could maintain that the old problems could simply be removed by forgetting them and starting fresh from the beginning. Only in the strictest dialectical communication with the most recent. . . . philosophy. . . . can a real change of philosophical consciousness prevail.[2]

As art expressed social contradictions and antinomies in a mediated form, so, on Adorno's account, philosophy embodied similar objective structures. And as certain forms of art could preserve a critical perspective, so could particular philosophies. By examining the antagonisms and tensions of other theories, Adorno sought to develop a philosophy and style which would contribute to the establishment of a 'critical social consciousness'.[3] Horkheimer was also interested in this enterprise. But while much of the latter's effort was spent examining the social functions of systems of thought – exposing the way in which these systems, perhaps valid at a certain level, serve to conceal or legitimate particular interests – Adorno concentrated his effort on an examination of the way philosophy expresses the structure of society. Unlike Horkheimer, Adorno proceeded to investigate a variety of philosophies in considerable technical detail.[4]

Apart from these differences of emphasis, there were differences in the two men's notions of how one could legitimately adjudicate between competing theories of society. Horkheimer's early position was closer to the Lukács of *History and Class Consciousness* than Adorno could have ever found acceptable. From his earliest philosophical works onward, Adorno was concerned with a re-examination of the concept of truth.[5] For him the truth of theory rested upon a particular type of dialectical criticism. This divergence, however, became less marked over time, as did the differences between the two men's orientations. By the very early 1940s there was sufficient common ground for *Dialectic of Enlightenment*. Horkheimer's position on the determination of the validity of theory drew closer to Adorno's. This was a result of both Horkheimer's growing pessimism about the potential of the proletariat and the growing influence of Adorno in the Institute. Horkheimer's summary of critical theory published in *Studies in Philosophy and Social Science*, 1941, bears Adorno's mark, particularly in the treatment of immanent criticism.[6] Although Adorno's general philosophical positions changed relatively little throughout his working life, he became more and more interested in the nature and practice of research. His growing willingness to extend the sphere of his activities to empirical research created more common ground with Horkheimer. None of this is to say that their style and orientations ever became the same. The differences were still sufficiently great to ensure that the two men did quite different work when writing independently.

The critique of philosophy: initial orientation

Adorno's views developed through an immanent critique of philosophy.[7] Most philosophies, he contended, fail to provide an adequate account of the relation between subject and object.[8] In his view, this relation is 'neither an ultimate duality nor a screen hiding ultimate unity'.[9] Subject and object are constituted by one another but are irreducible to each other – neither can be wholly subsumed by the other. They are internally related, interdependent structures within which the cognitive process unfolds. Yet many philosophies, as will be illustrated below, reduce subject to object or vice versa and thereby proclaim false identities. Adorno was most concerned to assess this state of affairs as it was manifested in the history of bourgeois philosophy. He was particularly anxious to expose the fallacies of subjectivism, the result of too great an emphasis, although it is often hidden or denied, on the role of the subject. Subjectivism finds one of its classical expressions in bourgeois idealism – as represented, for instance, in Hegel's work – with its emphasis on constitutive subjectivity, or crudely put, on the idea that the subject's concepts produce the world. Along with quite different philosophical approaches (such as empiricism), bourgeois idealism embraces what Adorno called 'identity thinking'. Identity thinking (discussed in detail later in the chapter) aims at the subsumption of all particular objects under general definitions and/or a unitary system of concepts. The tendency in contemporary social institutions to 'total' organization is, Adorno claimed, the historical counterpart to this mode of thinking; the particular is subsumed under the general concept as the individual is subsumed under 'the plan'. This type of thinking, Adorno tried to show, correctly registers but falsely affirms dominant ideologies.

A second classical expression of subjectivism is philosophical scepticism – as manifested, for example, in the empiricist tradition. On inquiry into its various guises, philosophical scepticism is shown to be internally inconsistent. But more importantly, it serves to block the critical assessment of social existence. For in the characteristic forms of its social and political philosophy the authority of the individual alone is thought to be justified. Individuals are left 'free' to believe whatever they will. Both the prominence and illusory freedom of the bourgeois subject are sanctioned by these ideas. Philosophical scepticism is the reverse side of identity thinking, but it is equally unacceptable to Adorno.

Hegel, Benjamin and Nietzsche

In order to grasp the distinctive characteristics of Adorno's thought, it is necessary to understand a number of the determining influences on his thinking.[10] Among them are three crucial sources of ideas: first, his acceptance of aspects of Marx's critique of Hegel's notion of history; second, his concern with Benjamin's criticism of conceptual thinking, Benjamin's stress on the impossibility of universal history, the importance of the particular and the difficulties of comprehending it; third, his adherence to Nietzsche's views on the absence of ultimate foundations in epistemology, the falsity of identity thinking and the importance of method and style. Each of these formative elements in Adorno's thinking deserves some comment.

Like Horkheimer, Adorno thought he could draw a distinction between aspects of Hegel's work which could be legitimately employed for the development of a materialistic and dialectical method and those which had to be discarded. He was impressed by, and sought to utilize, in a recast form, Hegel's method, his emphasis on process – on mind as activity – and his notion of determinate negation. He rejected Hegel's concept of philosophy, his system, his notions of the identity of subject and object and of the Absolute Idea. *Negative Dialectics,* Adorno's most mature statement of his position, sets out to free dialectics from affirmative traits which are entailed in Hegel's notion of the negation of the negation,[11] free our understanding of history from the fallacies which follow from too great an emphasis on subjectivity, and free our thinking from systemic approaches. In some ways Adorno's position represents a series of inversions of Hegel's approach.

Hegel's *Phenomenology of Mind*, especially the section on the Master and Slave, shows the origins of the 'I', the ego, in the 'Not I', the non-ego.[12] The analysis reveals the genesis of consciousness and self-consciousness. Specifically, it reveals the way in which all forms of consciousness develop and are inextricably intertwined with socio-life processes. For Adorno these insights are crucial. Following Hegel, he maintained that a central task of philosophy is to reflect upon these processes and describe their structure and development. Cognition is to be understood in light of its development in actual social processes, not by 'describing in advance the cognitive achievement in accordance with a logical or scientific model to which, in truth, productive knowledge in no way corresponds'.[13] However, Adorno held, Hegel failed to pursue the logic of this kind of perspective. For he 'hypostatized the mind'.[14] Not only did he falsify 'the object ideologically, calling it a free act of the absolute subject; he also recognized in the subject a self-representing objectivity', thus failing to appreciate the degree to which ideology impinges upon the individual.[15] (By 'objectivity' Adorno is not referring to a notion in the philosophy of social science, but to the structure of reality – 'the conditions, institutions and forces of society'.)[16]

In opposition to Hegel, Adorno argued that reality cannot be grasped from a single standpoint.[17] The idea that there is a vantage point outside the sway of socio-cultural development – that is, the standpoint of that development's completion – from which one can assess history as a whole is illegitimate. The illusion that the mind has privileged access to such an Archimedean point and can, as a result, achieve self-sufficiency, forgets the 'effort of conceptualization'. It fails, moreover, to understand the nature of this effort. Thinking is a form of praxis, always historically conditioned; as physical labour transforms and negates the material world under changing historical circumstances, so mental labour, under changing historical conditions, alters its object world through criticism. The illusion also leads invariably to a highly abstract (misleading and arbitrary) categorization of the world. Against Hegel's notion of a cognitive process that unfolds into a unity in the absolute idea (the complete identity of subject and object), Adorno's understanding suggests only negativity – that the difference between subject and object cannot be abolished. He rejects the representation of the cognitive process as a series of developmental oppositions which reach new syntheses only to be dissolved by new oppositions until a harmonious reconciliation is attained. The poles within which the cognitive process works do not admit of a simple harmonious resolution. The capacity of dialectics to transcend opposition is limited. Critique cannot escape the terms of reference of its object. The grounds for transcendence in history are strictly (and tragically) circumscribed – by particular historical conditions. Clearly, philosophy cannot transform these conditions. But it can help to create the precondition for their alteration.

The power of reflection is inadequate to 'grasp the totality of the real'. Hegel's notion of universal history, of grasping the whole of social development, eternalizes history in categories of the present. For reason is not simply autonomous. Adorno's critique of Hegel's notion of history as the manifestation of World Spirit parallels Marcuse's. Reason is bound by historical circumstances which constrain thinking.[18] The only way in which the historical process might be conceived as a whole is negatively.

Universal history must be construed and denied. After the catastrophes that have happened, and in view of the catastrophes to come, it would be cynical to say that a plan for a better world is manifested in history and unites it. Not to be denied for that reason, however, is the unity that cements the discontinuous, chaotically splintered moments and phases of history – the unity of the control of nature, progressing to rule over men, and finally to that over men's inner nature. No universal history leads from savagery to humanitarianism, but there is one leading from the slingshot to the megaton bomb.[19]

If history has any unity, it is that given by suffering.

The 'desire to control' the world, Adorno believed, lies beneath all philosophical attempts – particularly those attempts which lead to the construction of systems – to represent the totality. Disorder in reality leads to the desire for order in thought. From the seventeenth century philosophical systems played a very important compensatory role. Motivated by fear of chaos and impotency in the world, they produced within themselves what bourgeois reason failed to produce outside of itself.[20] The 'desire to control', Adorno thought, is a necessary feature of everyday life which is made more acute by capitalism. But such a desire does not lead by itself to truth, as an examination of the great philosophical systems of the bourgeois era reveals.[21] As Adorno put it, 'the philosophical systems were antinomical from the outset. Their rudiments entwined with their own impossibility'.[22] Systems try to interpret the world. They call for an 'orderly organization and presentation of thoughts'. Most often they claim their concepts to be adequate to their object: they claim to have identified their object fully. The great systems were accompanied by a 'paranoid zeal' to embrace the whole, to tolerate nothing outside of themselves. For 'the slightest remnant of non-identity sufficed to deny an identity conceived as total'.[23] But systems enter into an inevitable conflict with the objectivity they pretend to have grasped. The many qualitative dimensions of the object disappear in the system – but only to arise later to contradict it. History defies systems. The fate of Hegel's system presents a classic example of such defiance. His identity thinking proved inadequate to comprehend the past and future path of human reason. He failed to grasp the 'object's point of view'. For Adorno 'the matters of true philosophical interest at this point in history are those in which Hegel, agreeing with tradition, expressed his disinterest. They are non-conceptual, the individual, and the particular . . .'.[24] To understand these phenomena, Adorno argued, 'we are not to philosophize about concrete things; we are to philosophize, rather, out of these things'.[25] Adorno drew similar conclusions in his major studies on Kierkegaard, Husserl and Heidegger.[26]

Adorno's critique of Hegel bears the influence of both Benjamin and Nietzsche. Benjamin's influence was central. For example, a number of the main categories of Benjamin's *Ursprung des Deutschen Trauerspieles* [Origin of German Tragic Drama], found their way into Adorno's work. However, these categories were not simply borrowed and utilized in a straightforward fashion. On the contrary, Adorno recast them within the terms of reference of a philosophy that is, unlike Benjamin's early writings, materialistic and dialectical.[27]

In the *Origin of German Tragic Drama* Benjamin was critical of identity theory on a number of grounds. First, he rejected the claim that an individual phenomenon could be grasped and its truth known by subsuming it under general concepts. Second, he maintained – contrary to most classical German philosophy – that the universal could only be grasped within the particular. Concrete individual phenomena expressed the universal within their very structure. Third, he argued that discrete and disparate phenomena could be grasped only through the recovery of the 'Ideas' – the symbolic representations – they embody. Crudely put, 'ideas' can be represented by concepts of particular configurations of concrete elements. Ideas are timeless. They represent the objective interpretation of 'historical crystallizations' which emerge from the 'process of becoming and decay' in history. Benjamin compared ideas to monads. Every idea, he argued, 'contains an image of the world' and expresses 'unintentional truth' (*intentionslose Wahrheit*) – that is, subjectively unintended truth – about aspects of the world's structure.[28] Fourth, Benjamin stressed the difficulties involved in all efforts to comprehend unique concrete elements and ideas. In his texts he sought to determine and exemplify the method and style most suitable to his task. As the representative of truth, philosophy, he thought, must remain true to the form of its object. Benjamin utilized 'constellations' – sets of concepts, clusters of juxtaposed words and terms – to assist in the reconstruction of particulars, and, thus, in the representation of ideas. Constellations were created to characterize a phenomenon while not suggesting that concept and object are identical. Benjamin often presented his material in a fragmentary and aphoristic style in order to underline its inevitable incompleteness.

Benjamin's emphasis on the uniqueness, importance and complexity of the particular, his highly unconventional concept of induction (reversing the standard relation of particular to general) and many other of his concepts (for instance, 'constellation') had a profound impact on Adorno's earliest works. Benjamin's later reflections, in his more materialistic phase, on the question of the relation between ideas and material reality also left important traces on Adorno's writings. In his *Passagenarbeit* (the uncompleted study of Paris in the nineteenth century), Benjamin formulated the issue in the following terms:

The question is namely: if the substructure determines the superstructure to a certain degree, its thought and experience material, yet this determination is not one of simply copying or reflection, how is it then – totally apart from the question of its causal origins – to be characterized? As its expression. The superstructure is the expression of the substructure. The economic conditions under which society exists come to expression in the superstructure.[29]

The superstructure was the expression, on Benjamin's account, of objective, historical circumstances. The task of the critic was to reveal the 'unintentional' truth about socio-cultural formations embodied within it. Adorno agreed. The level of Adorno's agreement can be measured by his continual attempt to show how in philosophical thought, antinomies, illegitimate abstractions and the one-sided treatment of problems, express aspects of the structure of society. Benjamin and Adorno disagreed, however, on how the 'truth' was to be grasped. Unlike Benjamin, Adorno always emphasized that interpretation and theory are necessary in order to uncover the meaning of objects. As he put it in one of his earliest statements on the subject:

In this remains the great, perhaps everlasting paradox: philosophy persistently, and with the claim of truth, must proceed interpretively without ever possessing a sure key to interpretation; nothing more is given to it than fleeting, disappearing traces within the riddle figures of that which exists and their astonishing entwinings. The history of philosophy is nothing other than the history of such entwinings. Thus it reaches so few 'results'. It must always begin anew and therefore cannot do without the least thread which earlier times have spun, and through which the lineature is perhaps completed which could transform the ciphers into a text.[30]

Sometimes Benjamin seemed to suggest that the mere juxtaposition of concrete elements was enough to release the truth of particulars. Although Benjamin's positions change he often denied the necessity of theoretical intervention.[31] Adorno rejected this view. True interpretations could only be achieved through the confrontation between individual phenomena and the particular linguistic act of the interpreter. He readily granted that many types of superstructural phenomena contained objective truths. But these truths were often inadequately interpreted by their creators and were not self-explanatory. To be grasped fully, the intervention of the theorist was necessary. The nature of Adorno's procedures for interpretation will be clarified below.[32]

Nietzsche's influence on Adorno is no less significant. In fact, Nietzsche's ideas constitute one of the most important sources for the development of Adorno's views.[33] It is useful to draw out some of the connections between the two men's work. Adorno does not accept Nietzsche's claim that all beliefs can maintain the same validity as long as they are grounded in some want or need.[34] Ultimately, he rejects Nietzsche's non-rationalist concept of reality and his notion of truth. However, many of Nietzsche's arguments against other philosophers and many of his positions, for example, on the problem of grounding, the validity of identity theory, the import of style, are admired and employed by Adorno throughout his writings. References to Nietzsche are numerous.

Nietzsche's profound scepticism of all values and ideas which are taken for granted and thought to be legitimate, his critical stance and commitment to a revaluation and transformation of all values and concepts, impressed Adorno. Adorno's critique of philosophy, sociology and culture shares many aspects of Nietzsche's radical perspective. It also shares Nietzsche's rejection of idealism, of notions of the self-sufficiency of mind, of ideas which suggest the inferiority of the 'not-I' and of thinking which can only express itself in systems. Nietzsche 'refused homage to the speculative concept, the hypostasis of the mind' and this for Adorno was 'a liberating act, a true turning point of Western thought'.[35] Nietzsche's criticisms of philosophical categories that fail to grasp the dynamic processes of the world are also taken up by Adorno. Nietzsche maintained that the world is in a state of continual transition and development.[36] Reality is process; it is becoming. Becoming is 'invention, willing, self-denial, overcoming of oneself: no subject, but an action, a positing, creative, no "cause and effects"'.[37] Hence reality cannot be explained by reference to final states and goals. Nor can it be assessed, Nietzsche also argued, from any 'ultimate standpoint'.

> Becoming is of equivalent value every moment; the sum of its values always remain the same; in other words, it has no value at all, for anything against which to measure it, and in relation to which the word 'value' would have meaning, is lacking. *The total value of the world cannot be evaluated*.[38]

For Nietzsche, to comprehend aspects of the continually changing world requires a method adequate to this dynamic structure.[39] To a large extent, Adorno agreed. He continually emphasized, following Nietzsche as well as Hegel and Marx on this point, that the motion of history is 'internalized in the structure of thinking', and that in order to grasp history we must develop methods suitable to its changing structure.[40] He employed a notion of becoming, of a continuous dynamic in history, in his critique of philosophies and sociologies that hypostasize the world. He often utilized similar notions in his critique of all attempts to uncover an ultimate origin, or to establish ultimate foundations in philosophy. There is no foundation for the cognitive process independent of history. This position, he hoped to demonstrate, does not entail a commitment to historicism or radical relativism. A critical perspective can be preserved.

Nietzsche's method of asking and answering questions is dependent on his critical stance and his belief that there are no ultimate criteria to which we can appeal. He intends his criticisms as criticisms of particular phenomena. He claimed, for example, that one cannot assess humanity *per se* (although some of his comments and works contradict this). The critique of humanity can only be a critique of what constitutes humanity at a particular point in time.[41] Adorno's emphasis on negative dialectics shared this sense of the limits of criticism. He also shared Nietzsche's sense of the power of this approach.[42] For both thinkers the criticism of beliefs, ideas and modes of thinking is at one and the same time the criticism of society and/or nature *as known*. Both sought to examine – albeit very differently – the way in which we construct and represent the real. Both hoped to reveal, thereby, the fallacious nature of many interpretations of reality and to expose certain underlying neglected factors. For example, Nietzsche argued:

In the formation of reason, logic, the categories, it was *need* that was authoritative: the need, not to 'know', but to subsume, to schematize, for the purpose of intelligibility and calculation. (The development of reason is adjustment, invention, with the aim of making similar, equal – the same process that every sense impression goes through!) No pre-existing 'idea' was here at work, but the utilitarian fact that only when we see things coarsely and made equal do they become calculable and usable to us.[43]

On Nietzsche's account, the categories of everyday life as well as the categories of classical philosophy have an instrumental value – they are valid in so far as they serve some purpose or need. Nietzsche often interpreted these needs as an expression of the 'will to power'. Ultimately, in his opinion, it is this 'will' which constitutes the real. Adorno rejected this view. Nonetheless, his thought is permeated by some of Nietzsche's views in this area. Adorno agreed, as *Dialectic of Enlightenment* reveals, that what is taken as true is often a result of instrumental reasoning and/or imposition. He recognized, moreover, in all thoughts that seek to identify, a pragmatic dimension, an effort to bring objects under control.[44] His notions of different types of thinking, however, suggest other dimensions which Nietzsche's thought did not embrace.

Nietzsche's lack of concern for social and economic questions is striking.[45] He absolutized the 'will to power' without detailed consideration of power. Despite dissent from the teachings and attitudes of the day, Nietzsche's thought reflects resignation to 'the powers that be' – to the 'nature-like process of social fate'.[46] He was finally 'brought under the sway . . . of bourgeois society'.[47] His critical views were not critical enough. But his style taught Adorno an immense amount. Adorno is consistent in his admiration of the way Nietzsche's writings had sought to refuse 'complicity with the world'.[48] For Adorno, following Nietzsche (and, of course, Benjamin), the preservation of independent thinking requires defiance of society's language.[49]

Style

The meaning of Adorno's thought cannot be fully comprehended if one concentrates simply on content at the expense of form.[50] Adorno strove for a consistency between the style of his writings and their themes. The structure of many of his works *enact* his concern with the development of repressive systems of thought and organization. He sought to disclose and express the situation of the individual in contemporary society – a situation moulded ever more by the exchange process, bureaucracy and the culture industry.

Adorno's writings emphasize the disparity – often hidden or denied – between an object's claim for itself and its actual performance. His works investigate and display discontinuity, disharmony and contradiction within the social whole. While a society by virtue of its continual development defies exact definition, the non-identical, if it is to be revealed, must, Adorno insisted, be made apparent in the form and the content of a work.[51] In order to break the grip of all closed systems of thought (Hegelian idealism, for example, or orthodox Marxism) and to prevent an unreflected affirmation of society typical of bourgeois ideology, Adorno conceived of his writings as a series of analyses and interventions. His frequent preference for an aphoristic style or the essay form reflects his concern, on the one hand, to undermine all systems of thought that claim completeness and, on the other, to preserve the uniqueness of the particular. The contradictions and antinomies of the object were reproduced in the structure of his text. On his account it could not be otherwise. For their resolution is dependent on history, not philosophy.

Further, there is more involved in the reading of a text, Adorno argued, than gleaning information. Reading involves and evokes complex experiences which can to some extent be effected by careful composition. Through 'provocative formulation' and 'dramatic emphasis', Adorno hoped to create conditions under which the social world could be reappraised. The battery of techniques he employed to stir the reader include careful choice of verb tenses, a mass of references and cross-references, the use of irony and ironic inversion, hyperbole, chiasmus (a grammatical figure which inverts in a second clause the word order of the first), repetition of the familiar, seemingly endless repetition of some themes and glaring omissions of others.[52] Adorno did not believe, of course, that he could provide all the cues for the interpretation of his texts. He sought above everything else to sustain and create the capacities for new and genuine critical thinking. His comments on Schoenberg's music could equally well be applied to the demand that his own writing lays upon the reader: 'it requires the listener spontaneously to compose its inner movement and demands of him not mere contemplation but praxis'.[53] The reader has to struggle for the meaning of phenomena in a context in which the validity of traditional categories has been severely undermined. In a 'total' society, a reified social world, Adorno presented his themes so as to register and evoke dissonance and difference. He hoped thereby to write in a way that would prevent his texts from being integrated and co-opted.

Adorno's style, however, does vary. It varies with the method he employed, the telos of a work and the audience he addressed. There are aphorisms, essays, monographs and lengthy texts. Sometimes he expressed himself simply and at other times in a very complicated manner. Despite these differences, his writings maintain a distinctive form. Given his rejection of philosophical first principles Adorno could not present his writings around a continuous chain of deductive argument. His theory of identity thinking and reification, his view that 'objects do not go into their concepts without leaving a remainder', ensured that he had to develop a special way of presenting his object of inquiry if he was to sustain his claim to be going beyond conventional methods. He tried to do this by constructing 'the whole from a series of complexes of parts' – the set of which produces insight.[54] Only a number of representations of the object can lead to an approximation of it. Adorno often referred to these as a 'constellation'.[55] None of this means that the 'complexes of parts' can be arranged in an *ad hoc* manner. 'Properly written texts', he stated, 'are like spiders' webs: tight, concentric, transparent, well-spun and firm.'[56] They should be organized around a middle point which is articulated by the constellation. In a philosophical text all statements 'ought to be equally close to the centre'.[57] Adorno often presents his findings as 'figures', 'images', 'prisms', 'models' in order to underline their inevitable incompleteness. Style is an important weapon in the fight for truth against philosophical and social absolutes.

Negative dialectics: non-identity thinking

The struggle for emancipation depends upon particular material and historical conditions, which Adorno believed are less and less favourable to its success. 'No recollection of transcendence is possible any more, save by way of perdition; eternity appears, not as such, but diffracted through the most perishable.'[58] Yet, within Adorno's terms of reference a glimmer of hope remains. *Negative Dialectics*

is a critique of the fact that critique itself, contrary to its own tendency, must remain within the medium of the concept. . . . It lies in the definition of negative dialectics that it will not come to rest in itself, as if it were total. This is its form of hope.[59.]

Adorno does not see much room for optimism. But historical circumstances, within which all metaphysics and belief systems are anchored, might change. History does not and cannot provide a stable foundation for any thought system. If thinking can continually be dissolved into a critical process, at least receptivity to a moment of transcendence can be preserved. Negative dialectics alone cannot lead to change. But it can help to break the grip of all conceptual systems which would freeze the object and ignore its genesis. Ultimately, it is the position of the particular, changing configurations of objects (whether natural or social things, or human practices), which Adorno sought to explicate. In *Negative Dialectics* he aimed to demonstrate the priority of the object and, at one and the same time, confirm the mediation of subject and object. As he wrote:

An object can be conceived only by a subject but always remains something other than the subject, whereas a subject by its very nature is from the outset an object as well. Not even as an idea can we conceive a subject that is not an object, but we can conceive an object that is not a subject. To be an object also is part of the meaning of subjectivity; but it is not equally part of the meaning of objectivity to be a subject.[60]

Adorno's goal was to show how the history of mind, which he conceived as the attempt of the subject to gain distance from the object, continually reveals the 'superiority of objectivity'.[61] Objects exist *for us*.[62] Without conceptuality we could not grasp them. But objects do not therefore dissolve into concepts. Over time concepts disappear, as a result of their own inevitable insufficiency, into the flux and process of objects. The history of the subject is a history of it giving way to the predominance of objectivity. By means of the concept, Adorno sought to transcend the concept and reach the 'non-conceptual'.[63] In salvaging the particular through remembrance, the hold of all-embracing rationalities might be broken and a space for freedom – creative, spontaneous thought and action – might be created. How is this to be done?

To comprehend something we must, to begin with, perceive it in its immanent connections with other things and examine the conditions under which it exists and becomes.[64] The history 'locked in the object can only be delivered by a knowledge mindful of the historic positional value of the object in its relation to other objects'.[65] Adorno's materialism insists upon the necessity of tracing out the inner history of the object – the way it is mediated in history. The central category in negative dialectics for the comprehension of the object is 'possibility', which reality has cheated the object of, but which is nonetheless visible.[66] In exploring possibility with 'constellations', we can explore the historical process stored in the object – its actualization and limitation.[67]

Knowledge is embedded in tradition. Tradition serves, Adorno recognized, to mediate between known objects. It is contained in the simplest of questions and in the most complex of answers. The question is, how is critical theory, embroiled in tradition, able to transcend it?[68] For Adorno the answer lay in non-identity thinking which depends upon, and yet alters, existent convention. Adorno elaborated non-identity thinking juxtaposed with identity thinking. The essential differences between the two types of thinking are summarized in the table on page 215.[69] Negative dialectics is non-identity thinking which Adorno often also referred to as immanent criticism or the immanent method. It operates within the 'force-field' between concept (*Begriff*) and object, idea and material world. It confronts its object with norms which the object itself has formed. It examines contradictions between the object's idea of itself and its actual existence. In this process it surpasses the object's self-image, and brings the object into flux. Thus the immanent method, through its capacity to produce a 'heightened perception of the thing itself', cannot escape a certain 'transcendent' quality.[70] The transcendent element of this approach does not, of course, lead to a once and for all grasp of the totality.

Identity and non-identity thinking

Identity thinking	Rational identity	Negative dialectics, non-identity thinking
Identity thinking aims at the subsumption of all particular objects under general concepts. As a result, the particular is usually dissolved into the universal.	'The supposition of identity is . . . the ideological element of pure thinking . . . but hidden in it is also the true moment of ideology.' For there is a utopian aspect in concepts. In a judgement of identification we claim that an object is adequate to its concept (*Begriff*). However, concepts comprehend more than a given particular object. They refer also to the central or guiding idea of the object. They point to a set of ideal properties – conditions and relations – held to be essential to the object and yet other than it. Under the present conditions of society, the object may fail to fulfil its concept. An object only does justice to its concept if it meets the specifications of its ideal characteristics. This Adorno called rational identity.	The falseness of the claims of identity thinking can be revealed by negative dialectics, the thinking that explores non-identity. Negative dialectics assesses the relation between concept and object, between the set of properties implied by the concept and the object's actuality.
		In assessing its object, negative dialectics employs the standards and criteria the object has of itself in its concept. The historically crystallized standards suggest what the object sought and perhaps seeks to be. They also suggest possibilities which are rarely, if ever, realized and present an image of (logically entailed) unfulfilled potentialities.
		Non-identity thinking employs language, through the construction of 'constellations' of concepts, as a connotative or indicative device. Thus specific sides of objects are revealed which are inaccessible to identity thinking and the dogmatic application of classificatory schema.

On Adorno's account, 'to define identity as the correspondence of the thing-in-itself to its concept is *hubris*; but the ideal of identity must not simply be discarded.'[71] For the idea of rational identity (see page 215), contained within the ideal, preserves 'a place for utopia', a notion of the possible, which is always in danger of being overlooked or suppressed. Non-identity thinking can uncover this moment. At one level it is not difficult to point to the non-identical element which a judgement of identity fails to grasp; 'every single object subsumed under a class has definitions not contained in the definitions of that class'.[72] But it is also the case, more importantly, that within a certain range of concepts (for example freedom, justice or beauty) – concepts which are not simply abstractions from 'the characteristic unit of individual objects' (for example triangle) – definitions are contained which the object itself might fail to fulfil. These concepts embody ideas which are more and less than the particular. They are less because the object always has qualities which its concept fails to grasp. They are more because the concept comprehends more than a particular thing. For these concepts point to a set of ideal properties – conditions and relations – held to be essential to the object and yet other than it. Concepts thereby can connote what the particular object is and is not.[73] They can become means to reveal the difference between the actuality and potentiality of a given thing. Cognition of non-identity thus allows identification of an object but in more ways and to a greater extent than identity thinking.[74] The general conditions referred to in an object's concept highlight the state of existence of the object. Through the object's concept access is provided to an understanding and evaluation of the object. For example,

the judgement that a man is free refers to the concept of freedom; but this concept in turn is more than is predicated of the man, and by other definitions the man is more than the concept of his freedom. The concept says not only that it can be applied to all men defined as free; it feeds on the idea of a condition in which individuals would have qualities not to be ascribed to anyone here and now.[75]

This condition would be one in which men and women meet and fulfil all the properties and conditions contained in the notion of freedom.[76] In the so-called free society in which we live the inequality of social power ensures that the claimed identity between concept (freedom) and object (the present state of affairs) is false. The negation of the concept of freedom in practice points to aspects of society which aid, restrict and restrain freedom's actualization.

In the analysis of a particular entity we start with its concept and reveal non-identity (where identity all too often is assumed). Through this immanent method, Adorno argued, the individuality of the particular can be uncovered – through categories which are intrinsic to it rather than through notions which are imposed from without. Negative dialectics depends on the internally related employment of the categories of concept and object, appearance and essence, particular and universal, and part and whole (totality). Through the examination of the formation of concepts and the disjuncture between them and the objects they seek to cover, Adorno's dialectical method aims to disclose the processes of mutual constitution and alteration between object and totality. In this examination the object is also assessed in terms of what it appears to be and what it is (its essence) – revealing the universal within the particular, i.e. the nature of the particular as constituted in the totality. It is important to note that Adorno's notion of totality is 'decentered'. Totality cannot be reduced, as in Hegel or Lukács, to a specific 'genetic centre' or 'creator subject'; for it is, in Jay's words, 'a constellation of interactions without a specific origin'.[77] As Adorno became more and more sceptical about the chances of the proletariat acting as revolutionary subject, he continually sought to uncover and clarify a foundation for critique in configurations of objects and relations.

Most other approaches to the study of society (for example those typical of conventional sociology) duplicate, Adorno argued, the reified and opaque nature of society. They perceive society as an object which is to be understood through methods similar to those of the natural sciences. In contrast, critical theory seeks to understand, analyse and *enact* in its very structure the subjective ground of society: society is not simply an object; it is a subject-object. It is both the subject of knowledge and the object.

Society is subjective because it refers back to the human beings who create it, and its organizational principles too refer back to subjective consciousness and its most general form of abstraction – logic, something essentially subjective. Society is objective because, on account of its underlying structure, it cannot perceive its own subjectivity, because it does not possess a total subject and through its organization it thwarts the installation of such a subject.[78]

To comprehend society we must know it from the inside; we must know its formative processes. If society is treated as a 'neutral object', these processes will not be grasped and society *qua* subject-object will be violated. The object will be attributed qualities it does not have of itself. It will be reconstructed (hence comprehended) with categories which are imposed from without. Adorno refused to define the concepts he employed. For to do so would be to suggest rational identity. The history and process that constitutes the genesis of objects ensure that they cannot be simply defined. To avoid such definitions he constructed constellations of concepts in order to 'indicate', to 'gesture' the particularity of the object. He did concede, however, that some concepts (the authoritarian personality, for example) might well have to be introduced (with definitions) in order to grasp an 'ontology of the wrong state of affairs'; that is, a state in which illusions are produced and social contradictions reproduced.[79] To interpret such a state, the introduction of theory is unavoidable. But this does not mean that theory is unconstrained.[80] As Adorno wrote,

Theory . . . must transform the concepts which it brings, as it were, from the outside into those which the object has of itself, into that which the object would, left to itself, like to be, and confront it with what it is. It must dissolve the rigidity of the temporally and spatially fixed object into a field of tension of the possible and the real: each one, in order to exist, is dependent upon the other. . . . [In this sense] theory is indisputably critical.[81]

The development of such theory is the telos of social science.[82]

Negative dialectics and Marx's theory of value

Subject and object, mind and material world are relational concepts: they presuppose each other. Yet the process of their mutual constitution, Adorno contended, takes place in the formation of the object. Subject and object are differentiated by objectivity. Their separation is a feature of the object. In order to comprehend the object we must grasp its development; in order to assess it we must grasp the standards it crystallizes. There is no method independent of the object; no strict separation between reality and method can be sustained.

Anyone who wishes to follow the structure of his object and conceptualizes it as possessing motion in itself does not have at his disposal a method independent of the object.[83]

Methods themselves must be adequate to the character of social forms.

From this perspective one can understand the importance Adorno placed on Marx's work and particularly the theory of value. In a number of places throughout his writings he used Marx's analysis of exchange as an example of non-identity thinking. Exchange, on Marx's account, is claimed to be exchange of equivalents, yet it is unequal. As Adorno expressed it:

The assertion of the equivalence of what is exchanged, the basis of all exchange, is repudiated by its consequences. As the principle of exchange, by virtue of its immanent dynamics, extends to the living labours of human beings it changes compulsively into objective inequality, namely that of social classes. Forcibly stated, the contradiction is that exchange takes place justly and unjustly.[84]

But the significance of Marx's work goes beyond its use as an example; aspects of it provide the *model* for Adorno's own method. 'In a grand manner', he wrote, 'the unity of the critique of scientific and meta-scientific sense is revealed in the work of Marx.' Unwilling to accept traditional modes of grounding knowledge, Adorno adopted the critical procedure which has most successfully disentangled bourgeois ideology, namely the method Marx employed in his analysis of exchange value and commodity fetishism. He claimed, therefore, that his approach was historically relevant and, more important, adequate to history's dynamic.

Marx's analysis exposed, Adorno maintained, the prime source of illusion in capitalism and the necessity of immanent criticism to overcome it.[85] Through the exchange process and its subsequent fetishization, unlike phenomena are equated. This occurs in two ways: social phenomena are reified on the one hand and, on the other, inanimate things are treated as if they had the qualities of the social. Both processes create and sustain identity thinking. As a result of reification definite relations between human beings appear in the form of characteristics of, or relations between, material objects, and concepts of things are applied to social relations. With the attribution of properties of social relations to 'things', a deceptive equation of concept and object also occurs. It is important not to conceive of these phenomena as simple errors of consciousness. They are socially created illusions which project images about the world which contain both truth and error. They contain truth in so far as they reflect the process of commodity exchange, a process which does equate unlike things:

the exchange principle, the reduction of human labour to its abstract universal concept of average labour-time, is fundamentally related to the principle of identification. Identification has its social model in exchange and exchange would be nothing without it.[86]

It is through the universalization of exchange that the dissimilar becomes comparable. But identity thinking as, for instance, reified thinking, is unable to penetrate the appearances of society and perceive the 'non-identical' underlying it. Thus, it cannot comprehend the nature of the social relations of production which, in their many complex forms, determine society's character.

According to Adorno, Marx showed that conceptuality is immanent to reality not merely as 'the constitutive conceptuality of the knowing subject' but as 'a conceptuality which holds sway in reality [*Sache*] itself'.[87] The latter is an illusion immanent to the bourgeois social world and created by the exchange process. Marx also demonstrated, in Adorno's opinion, that some of the effects of exchange and fetishism can be dissolved with an examination of the specific conditions under which concepts and things exist and evolve. Adorno adopted Marx's approach and applied it to the study of cultural phenomena in the bourgeois world.

Following this perspective one can understand Adorno's view that

The study of ideology, of false consciousness, of socially necessary illusion would be nonsense without the concept of true consciousness and objective truth. Nevertheless, genesis and validity cannot be separated without contradiction. . . . They must certainly be critically distinguished in the individual cognitive acts and disciplines. But in the realm of . . . constitutional problems they are inseparably united.[88]

The meaning of phenomena cannot be simply given. It changes historically. The truth and/or untruth of a phenomenon, of what that phenomenon 'would like to be', can, however, be judged. The truth and falsity of capitalist society can be assessed according to whether or not it is adequate to its concept.[89] Marx's work on exchange, or Adorno's on culture, shows that it is not. For bourgeois society to be true, it would have to have rational identity; it would have to meet its claim to represent a free and just process of exchange; it would have to fulfil its promise of liberty and equality. To be rationally identical with these concepts, society would have to undergo radical transformation. In the end, 'the idea of scientific truth cannot be split off from that of a true society. Only such a society would be free from contradiction and lack of contradiction.'[90] Negative dialectics points to unfulfilled potentialities for emancipation. It uncovers values which are immanent to its object and yet, most often, negated by the object's actuality. As such, negative dialectics is neither simply a method nor reality. It is not simply a method because its object is contradictory, has no unambiguous starting and ending points, resists complete interpretation, and itself drives thought to dialectics. On the other hand, negative dialectics is not simply a reality for it recasts the real in the process of reflection; 'contradictoriness is a category of reflection, the cogitative confrontation of concept and thing'. To understand and express this contradiction is to contradict reality (the fetishized bourgeois world). To contradict reality is not to leave everything as it is. Negative dialectics represents a 'practical challenge'.[91]

'Meditations on metaphysics'

Negative Dialectics closes with a series of 'Meditations on metaphysics'. As always Adorno emphasized the centrality of the 'objectivity' of history, the contradictory character of social reality and the poverty of identity theory. Within these anti-Hegelian terms of reference Adorno's final position draws closer to aspects of the spirit of Kantian philosophy than to the spirit of many other philosophical positions. The antinomies of Kant's metaphysics are said to represent accurately the position of metaphysics in a contradictory historical situation. Adorno praised Kant for having contributed to 'forestalling the mythology of the concept' and for having appreciated that the mind does not and cannot exhaust 'what it touches upon'. Adorno did not, of course, accept Kant's transcendental method. But he felt that Kant's stress on the import of what lies beyond the mind must be saved.[92] For Adorno, the preservation of this moment is the preservation of the moment of possibility, of possible transcendence – the inspiration of genuine thought.

It is the possible, never the immediately existing, that contains locked up within itself a place for Utopia – which is why in the midst of the actually existing it appears abstract. . . . The colour that cannot fade comes from the nonexistent. . . . Thought is its servant, a piece of existence extending – however, negatively – to that which is not. The utmost distance alone would be proximity; philosophy is the prism in which its colour is caught.[93]

Although negative dialectics continually evokes the possibility of the transcendence of existing belief systems and material conditions, it does not give an absolute status to this idea. As Adorno put it, 'dialectics allow us to think the absolute'; but 'the absolute as transmitted by dialectics remains in bondage to conditioned thinking'. Dialectics cannot escape this bondage. 'No absolute can be expressed other than in topics and categories of immanence, although neither in its conditionality nor in its totality is immanence to be deified.'[94] The concept of immanence is itself historical. Negative dialectics seeks to be the self-consciousness of the context of ideology. It does not claim to have entirely escaped this context – though it does hope 'to break out of the context from within'.

8 Marcuse's notions of theory and practice: epistemology and method 3

Differences with Horkheimer and Adorno

Marcuse shares Adorno's concern with the critique and transcendence of reification and fetishism. In a similar vein to Horkheimer, he stresses the unconcluded nature of the dialectic, a potential in man that is yet to be realized, the centrality of human practice in the constitution and assessment of knowledge, and the importance of interdisciplinary approaches to the comprehension of the social totality. But despite considerable overlaps, there are also major differences in position.

While the importance of the writings of the 'early Marx' is acknowledged by Horkheimer and Adorno, Marcuse places a greater emphasis on them and, in particular, on the *Economic and Philosophical Manuscripts*: he is more willing to defend the discoveries of the 'young Marx' and to argue that they are presupposed and refined in works like *Capital*. A general theory of labour and alienation provides a backdrop to all his writings. In light of this it is not surprising that in some ways Hegel had a more profound impact on Marcuse than on either Horkheimer or Adorno. Marcuse is directly indebted to some of Hegel's central ideas, for instance, Hegel's notions of reason, dialectics and understanding of the structure of history. Hegel is also relevant because Marcuse sees in his work early formulations of a number of Marx's most challenging ideas – the nature of labour, alienation and the anarchic state of civil society.

Marcuse's writings engage more fully than those of Horkheimer and Adorno with the interests of classical Marxism. Politics plays a key, if not the central role in his life and work. His career represents a constant attempt to examine, defend and reconstruct the Marxist enterprise. A preoccupation with the fate of revolution, the potentiality for socialism and the defence of 'utopian' (seemingly unobtainable) objectives, is apparent in his work. The goals of his critical approach to society are the emancipation of consciousness, the nurturing of a decentralized political movement and the reconciliation of humanity and nature. Further, unlike Horkheimer and Adorno, Marcuse has, as one commentator accurately observed, 'continually striven to relate the comprehensive picture of the social process offered by critical theory to currently existing and emerging forms of opposition, no matter how fragmented, distorted, or hopeless they may seem at the moment'.[1]

There are other differences that mark off Marcuse's interests from those of the other two men. For example, while he always adopts an interdisciplinary perspective, he has undertaken less empirical work than the other Institute members. He is primarily a philosopher and a social and political theorist. He has also been more positively influenced by certain twentieth-century philosophical developments.[2] As a student of both Heidegger and Husserl, he was sympathetic to their enterprises. For a period he worked closely with Heidegger and the latter's concerns and language are manifest in most of his early publications, including his *Habilitationschrift – Hegels Ontologie und die Grundlegung einer Theorie der Geschichtlichkeit* [Hegel's Ontology and the Foundation of a Theory of Historicity].[3] But the extent of Heidegger's influence has sometimes been exaggerated.[4] There is little unqualified approval of Heidegger's phenomenological programme even in Marcuse's earliest writings. For instance, in an essay published in 1928, Marcuse wrote: 'a phenomenology of human existence falls short of the necessary clarity and completeness' as it 'bypasses the material condition of historical existence'.[5] In 1932, in a review of *Hegels Ontologie*, Adorno noted with approval Marcuse's movement away from 'the Meaning of Being to an openness to being-in-the-world [*Seienden*], from fundamental ontology to philosophy of history, from historicity [*Geschichtlichkeit*] to history'.[6]

The concept of critical theory

Critical theory is oriented, according to Marcuse, toward the understanding of all forms of social practice and the factors which hinder their self-consciousness and free development. As such, it is concerned with both 'preventing the loss of truths which past knowledge laboured to attain' and the 'critique of current conditions and the analysis of their tendencies'.[7] Through an inquiry into the structure of society present in all social phenomena, 'present in all particular facts and conditions and determining their place and function', it seeks to show that this structure contains unrealized potentialities – potentialities created by a gulf between prevailing human existence and human essence (the unfulfilled historically constituted abilities and capacities of human beings). This gulf can be grasped by examining what exists in opposition to the established order: social struggles; concepts which transcend conventional patterns of description (the dominant use of language); and wants and desires which reflect frustration and longing for a 'different order of things'.

Despite a belief in the historical rootedness of all knowledge, Marcuse firmly believes that the array of potentialities and possibilities projected by thought can be rationally adjudicated. But in agreement with Horkheimer and Adorno, he holds that historical rather than purely epistemological conditions determine the meaningfulness and truth of propositions. The conditions of, as he put it in his early work, 'being-in-the-world' generate the criteria for the assessment of the validity of statements. For the Marcuse writing before the late 1940s, it is in reason and labour that these criteria are revealed.

Marcuse defends a rationalist and, therefore, critical approach to society. This approach has two main guidelines:

first, the given situation of man as a rational organism, i.e. one that has the potentiality of freely determining and shaping his own existence, directed by the process of knowledge and with regard to his worldly happiness; second, the given level of development of the productive forces and the (corresponding or conflicting) relations of production as the criterion for those potentialities that can be realized at any given time in men's rational structuring of society.[8]

Marcuse does not regard reason as the 'absolute ground or essence of what is'. Rather, he comprehends reason as 'the reason of concrete individuals in their specific social situations', situations which place limits on human knowledge and on the extent to which action may be explained as the pursuit of rational ends. But these situations themselves, he argues, 'are to be comprehended rationally and, on the basis of this comprehension, to be transformed'.[9] Marcuse's critique of society is both theoretical and practical.

Stages of development

Marcuse's work demonstrates both continuity in direction and a number of fairly striking stages of development. It is worth describing the latter briefly, for they provide a useful point of contrast to Horkheimer's and Adorno's interests. The first stage can be characterized as an attempt to synthesize Heideggerian phenomenology and Marxism and to lay a critical foundation for theory. In the first long essay he published, 'Contribution to a phenomenology of historical materialism' (1928), Marcuse struggled to work out the relation between ontology, historicity and dialectics. The second phase of his work was marked by a re-examination of Hegel's *oeuvre*, a discovery of the radical and political nature of Hegel's concepts of, among things, reason and labour, and the development of his understanding of Marxism in light of the 'early Marx'. During this time Marcuse engaged in sustained criticism of empiricism, positive philosophy and positivism. The period culminated with the publication of *Reason and Revolution* (1941). This book represents one, if not the most significant, attempt to establish the revolutionary character of Hegel's thought. (The views it promulgated were in direct opposition to most standard Anglo-American commentaries which claimed Hegel to be a precursor of twentieth-century right-wing totalitarianism.)

From 1942 to 1950 Marcuse published very little, working for part of the war and a number of years thereafter in United States government offices. But with the publication of *Eros and Civilization* in 1955, a crucial new dimension was added to his thinking. This derived, of course, from his reading of Freud. His approach to Freud demonstrates similar tactics to those employed in his assessment of Hegel. As one commentator aptly put it,

With both he attempted to make his case by disregarding their explicit political pronouncements and turning instead to an analysis of their basic philosophical or psychological conceptions. In each case Marcuse found a revolutionary message, which remained intact despite all overt concessions to historical pessimism, authoritarianism, the status quo. . . . And in both instances the result was to uncover beneath an apparently conservative veneer the same critical impetus which achieved explicit formulation in the writings of Karl Marx.[10]

With the aid of instinct theory, Marcuse sought to explore the relation between the individual and society and the possibility for the exercise of rationality in history.

The late 1950s and early 1960s saw the publication of Marcuse's critical analyses of Soviet Marxism and industrial capitalism. In these works his concern with the multiple roots of domination (economic, political, cultural, intellectual, sexual) was given its most elaborate expression. Both *Soviet Marxism* (1958) and *One Dimensional Man* (1964) had an explicitly polemical intent: they are best understood as particular historical interventions designed to analyse (and project) tendencies in the most highly developed societies, on the one hand, and expose the factors which paralyse social criticism and block the possibility of a truly democractic society, on the other.

In the last few years Marcuse devoted a great deal of time to aesthetics, uncovering in autonomous art a critical spirit. It is this spirit which he has continually sought to examine and express.

Heidegger and history

The structure of Marcuse's concerns was laid down in his earliest published work in which Heidegger's *Being and Time* was juxtaposed with Marx's programme. Through phenomenological investigation, a process of 'letting things reveal themselves', Heidegger showed, according to Marcuse, that 'the problems of transcendence, reality, and the demonstrability of the world in their traditional contexts turn out to be pseudo-problems', for human existence is always 'being-in-the-world' (*In-der-Welt-Sein*).[11] Marcuse was sympathetic to this finding and to some of Heidegger's main preoccupations, including establishing the extent to which philosophy express the struggles, the truths and deceits, of being-in-the-world; examining the meaning and essence of humankind in terms of concrete existence; exploring the nature of authentic existence and the conditions for its possibility. Here, however, Marcuse's interest in Heidegger's enterprise ended; for Heidegger's whole approach stopped short of concreteness, of an understanding of the material constitution of historicity, that is, of 'the boundaries of concrete historical conditions under which concrete existence exists, and in which this existence and the totality of the relationships in its world are rooted'. It is meaningless, Marcuse insisted, to answer questions concerning, for example, concrete authentic existence in terms of 'existence itself'. The division of society into classes necessitates a carefully differentiated analysis

of the social totality. Only an historical analysis, such as that provided by Marx, can be adequate for this purpose.

Marx's approach, Marcuse noted, is historical in two fundamental senses. First, its object is historical and is treated historically.
Second, it is itself embedded in concrete historical situations: it is
an active factor in history. The approach is dialectical. This term,
Marcuse argued, does not connote a 'rattling scaffold' or 'ready-
made schema' to be imposed on social forms. Rather, it 'frees
historical categories abstracted into rigid one-sidedness by uncovering them as "forms and determinations of actual existence", thus
bringing them back ... to their concrete, living foundations'.[12]
Therein, Marcuse emphasized, is the methodological relevance of
the Marxist dialectic: to pursue a dialectical analysis is to grasp and
investigate the context of relations and mediations, the developments and transformations, the whole of human practice, of which
any given object is a part. But the examination of these processes
must not, in turn, neglect certain Heideggerian concerns. On the
one hand, Marcuse demanded that

Heidegger's phenomenology of human existence be driven to dialectical
concreteness so that it can be fulfilled in a phenomenology of concrete
existence and of the historically concrete act demanded of it. And, on the
other hand, the dialectical method of knowing must go the other way and
become phenomenological so as to incorporate concreteness *in a complete account of its object.* In the analysis of the given, it must not simply
locate it historically, or indicate its roots in an historical existential situation. It must also ask *whether the given is thereby exhausted,* or whether it
contains an authentic meaning which, although not a-historical, endures
through all historicity.[13]

Reason and dialectics: Hegel

The issues raised by the confrontation of Heideggerian
phenomenology and Marxism were pursued in many of Marcuse's
writings. They were clearly articulated in his efforts to come to
terms with dialectics, which he understood as an attempt to
express the nature of 'true being'. In 'On the problem of the
dialectic', published in 1930, he traced a number of the most
important formulations of the concept. His intention, as in all his
discussions of concepts, was not to write the history of an idea.
Instead, his goal was to grasp the meaning of the concept and to
examine its critical potentiality. The analysis began with Plato.

The Platonic dialectic, in its earliest form, expressed an 'ability' or 'capacity' of human reason to uncover the nature of 'true being' or the 'unity of being' (the Ideas) discernible within the world of 'movement', 'multiplicity' and 'opposition'. But the notion failed to capture, in Marcuse's words, 'the problematic of becoming'; that is, the development of new forms of being in opposition to, but within the boundaries set by, old forms of being. In his later writings Plato sought to address this issue. But while his analysis pointed to the historicity of being (its historic quality or character), and the necessity of grasping it, his views remained, as a result of the inclusion of the dialectic in the theory of Ideas, the product of an *a priori* intuition which lacked concrete historical foundation. Hegel and Marx decisively altered Plato's perspective; and Marcuse adopted aspects of both their contributions.

For Hegel, the dialectic is, as it had been for Plato, 'a cognitive power and a cognitive method, because . . . reality itself is dialectical'.[14] The most important principle of the dialectic is 'to surrender to the life of the object' (Hegel), to express and represent the 'coming-into-being' of reality itself. Dialectical method, on this account, seeks to free all being from the appearance of rigidity and from ahistorical interpretations. It treats all objects as 'many-faced, coming-into-being, acting and passing away in time'.[15] As a result, reality is comprehended as a process of becoming, in which reality as a whole, as well as each particular, individual part, is understood as developing out of an earlier stage of its existence and as evolving into something else. This entails grasping not only an object's positive features but also its negative qualities – 'what the historical object has been . . . what it is becoming, and what it is not' – for all these things contribute to its character.[16]

In *Reason and Revolution*, Marcuse explained the constitutive elements of Hegel's dialectic at considerably greater length. As he put it, 'the driving power of the dialectic . . . is the power of negative thinking, used as a tool for analysing the world of facts in terms of its internal inadequacy'.[17] The 'inadequacy' is disclosed by uncovering the way in which the real opposes and denies potentialities inherent in itself – potentialities which represent its possible 'determinate negation'. (In Marcuse's view, the negation is determinate if it refers to forces which make for the destruction of the established state of affairs and lead to alternatives beyond it.) As such, negative thinking is historical thinking and historical thinking is critical thinking for it 'reveals modes and contents of thought which transcend the codified pattern of use and validation'.

Hegel focused on the triad subject, object and their synthesis; it is 'the true form of thought'. He did not understand this, however, in terms of a mechanistic scheme – thesis, antithesis, and synthesis – to be applied to the historically given. Rather, the triad (*Triplizität*) is the appropriate form of thought because it expresses the dynamic unity of reality; that is, the dynamic unity of opposites – 'a reality in which every being is the synthetic unity of antagonistic conditions'. To know what a thing really is, we have, then,

> to get beyond its immediately given state . . . and follow out the process in which it turns into something other than itself. . . . Its reality is the entire dynamic of its turning into something else and unifying itself with its 'other'. The dialectical pattern represents, and is thus 'the truth of', a world permeated by negativity, a world in which everything is something other than it *really* is, [that is, the present state of things differs from their essence], and in which opposition and contradiction constitute the laws of progress.[18]

Dialectics has both a negative and a positive character. Its negative character arises from a twofold process. In the attempt to reflect the actual nature of reality dialectics first negates the fixed categories of common sense and, second, reveals the limitations of the world designated by these categories. It shows that the existence of 'things' taken as isolated particulars is basically negative or incomplete. Everything is because it is both itself and its opposite. Thus, any 'finite thing', or concept of a thing, is said to contain within itself a contradiction; that is, it is constituted both by what it is and by what it is not. Non-A (what is excluded or repelled by A) belongs to the identity of A. Therefore, every particular must be grasped, according to (Marcuse's account of) Hegel, as 'transgressing' its given state, as 'negating' its negativity.[19]

The positive character of the dialectic emerges from the attempt to grasp the negativity of the real. The particular exists only in and through the totality of relations of which it is a part. To grasp its nature is, therefore, to grasp the complete set of its relations or the universal that makes it what it is. Human beings, to take an example, are constituted as such only in the context of groups, classes and institutions. It is not as isolated particulars, but by virtue of their relations (such as being a father, worker, citizen), that they are what they are. Thus, the true form of reality is not the unity of the particular as such but the universal – the universal that comes-to-be in and through particulars. Dialectical thinking is positive because, in Hegel's words, 'it is the source of the Universal in which the Particular is comprehended'.

But Hegel maintains, according to Marcuse, that the universal is not only the totality of relations but is further the 'rational structure of being'. The content of the universal is preserved in the notion or concept. The notion gives us the truth about phenomena: it captures their 'essence' or 'nature'.[20] In other words, it grasps the dynamics of being – being as becoming. In expressing the essence of a phenomenon the 'notion' refers not only to what is the case, but also to the phenomenon's potentiality.

Every state of existence is comprehended in its movement and formation as 'something negative, which things ... desert for another state, which again reveals itself as negative'.[21] The real meaning of the finite exists only as a passing, as a 'passing beyond itself'. To be what it really is, each thing must become what it is not: it must overcome its limitations and realize its potentialities. A particular's identity can only be uncovered by thought which must reconstruct the process whereby every being or entity becomes its own opposite and then negates this opposition by transforming itself. The 'motor of all change' is, of course, in this view, 'contradiction'. As Marcuse put it,

By virtue of the inherent negativity in them, all things become self-contradictory, opposed to themselves, and their being consists in that 'force which can both comprehend and endure Contradiction'. *'All things are contradictory in themselves'* – this proposition, which so sharply differs from the traditional laws of identity and contradiction, expresses for Hegel 'the truth and essence of things'. 'Contradiction is the root of all movement and life', all reality is self-contradictory. Motion especially, external movement as well as self-movement, is nothing but 'existing contradiction'.[22]

But contradiction is not the end of all life processes. It is as much historical as ontological: it perishes as the negative is gradually abolished and potentialities are progressively realized in reality. Hegel believed that in his age the discrepancy between the possible and the actual would be steadily overcome and truth would be realized. It is worth elaborating what Hegel (at least on Marcuse's reading) means by truth for it has a direct bearing on Marcuse's own position.

The fulfilment of potentialities inherent in reality is called 'the truth'. Truth, therefore, is not just an attribute of propositions and judgements but of the process of reality itself. It is a category of being. 'Something is true if it is what it can be, fulfilling all its objective possibilities.'[23] Something becomes true only as a result of a *process*, a process of overcoming the negativity in a given state of affairs. In its developed state, a phenomenon can be said to fulfil, and be identical with, its notion. For Hegel, the realization of truth depends on the comprehensive process of the subject's development.[24] He did not claim that truth is complete – that everything exists in conformity to its potentiality – but rather argued that 'mind has attained the self-consciousness of its freedom, and become capable of freeing nature and society from the restrictions on their development'.[25]

Foundations of historical materialism

For over a century prior to the development of Hegel's system, philosophy had taken reason as its banner. Many philosophers maintained that the natural and social world could – indeed must, if it was to be adequately grasped – be understood and steered by reason. The realization of reason promised the eventual dissolution of all arbitrary and external authority – the freedom of men and women to act according to their will and the reconciliation of reality to human endeavour.[26] Hegel was the last to interpret both nature and history in terms of the standards of thought and to comprehend the world as reason. But because he understood that the fulfilment of reason was dependent upon the social and political order, he, according to Marcuse, 'brought philosophy to the threshold of its negation'. It required only a few steps to change the direction and form of the critical tradition.[27] By revealing the nature of the proletariat, Marx, in Marcuse's opinion, took one of the most important of these steps and successfully refuted Hegel's claim to have confronted the world of (the coming-into-being of) truth: 'the existence of the proletariat contradicts the alleged reality of reason, for it sets before us an entire class that gives proof of the very negation of reason'.[28] The truth of Hegel's philosophy was negated by historical reality itself. The critique of society could no longer be carried forward merely by philosophical discourse. The 'negation of philosophy' became necessary for the realization of its concerns. It was now apparent that 'the truth' could only be uncovered and fulfilled in the historical process and through the collective practice of men and women.

While Hegel's social and economic categories are all philosophical concepts, the philosophical concepts of Marx's thought are all, Marcuse stresses, social and economic categories.[29] But Marx's categories are by no means all original. As previously noted, many of them derive from Hegel. The most significant of these is the concept of labour, a 'decisive contribution' (according to both Marx and Marcuse). Hegel's use of the concept points directly to a process of 'practical, human-sensuous activity' (Marx) – a dynamic process of creation.[30] By focusing his theory on the labour process, Marx, Marcuse contends, 'consummated the principle of the Hegelian dialectic that the structure of the content (reality) determines the structure of the theory'.[31] He established the labour process, 'the foundations of society', as the foundation of his theory of society. This was achieved from his earliest works onward.

Marcuse affirms the significance of the *Manuscripts* not only for the whole of Marx's development but also for Marxist studies and for the general theory of 'scientific socialism'. In his now-famous introduction to these early writings, Marcuse argues that orthodox Marxism violates the essence of some of Marx's most central ideas.[32] Far from entailing an 'economistic' view of history and an image of a society which simply resolves, at a technical level, the contradiction between the forces and relations of production, the categories (of Marx's political economy) evaluate

reality with a view to what it has made of man, of his faculties, powers, and needs. Marx summarizes these human qualities when he speaks of the 'universal essence' of man; his examination of the economy is specifically carried on with the question in mind whether that economy realizes man's *Geltungwesen (universelles Wesen)*.[33]

In this, Marcuse thinks, lies the decisive justification of revolution. It is because capitalist society threatens the very existence of 'human reality' and the qualities of the human species that a 'total and radical revolution' is both necessary and defensible.[34] If revolution fails to further human fulfilment, it betrays its purpose and, as a consequence, cannot justify itself as progressive.

In order to explore the basis of this view one needs to ask: what is meant by 'universal essence' or, as Marx (and Marcuse) sometimes express it, 'human essential powers', 'man's essential being'?

234 The Frankfurt School

Individuals become what they are, in Marcuse's interpretation of Marx, in the labour process. The labour process is 'man's act of self-creation', a process in which, struggling to fulfil anticipated needs, humanity is formed – a knowing and conscious activity in which the human world is created. It is a process of *becoming*, a process with a central meaning – the satisfaction of need. Any account of the 'essential being' of men and women has to capture this in its categories. Any assessment of Marx's contributions has to begin from this consideration; for the essential premise of his work, of historical materialism, is a specific conception of human essence and human development.

The starting point of Marx's analysis is the human being as a 'species being'. In Marcuse's interpretation of the *Manuscripts*, what are the species' characteristics? Humans are not restricted to exist in a particular state. Their being and their object world are not exhausted by their immediate circumstances. They can 'recognize and grasp the possibilities contained in every being . . . can exploit, alter, mould, treat, and take further . . . any being'.[35] It is precisely this quality that distinguishes humans as *universal* animals and, therefore, *free* beings. Human beings treat themselves as the 'actual, living species': all being becomes objective *for them*. The universality of humankind constitutes its freedom.[36]

Human beings mould their lives through 'real, sensuous objects'. The power of their being is dependent upon their enactment – through and in external objects – of everything they are.[37] The world of objects is objective, that is, material, only *for them*; it is 'the "self-objectification" of man, or human objectification'. Humans are *objectifying* animals: objectification constitutes the unity of humanity and nature.

But people not only create and posit objects; they are also posited by them. This is the fundamental determinant of *sensuousness*, 'the quality of having senses, which are affected by objects'.[38] Men and women are born into a world of pre-established objectivity on which they depend for the satisfaction of needs and cares. It is through the 'sensuousness' of their own material being that they relate to this world and develop as 'universal' and 'free' beings. The mode of 'relating' and 'developing' is given by human activity, that is, by labour.

It is in and through labour that they know and possess the world.

In his labour man supersedes the mere objectivity of objects and makes them into 'the means of life'. He impresses upon them the form of his being, and makes them into 'his work and his reality'. . . . The objective piece of finished work *is* the reality of man; man *is* as he has realized himself in the object of his labour . . . it is precisely in labour that . . . specifically human *universality* is realized.[39]

It is not the single, isolated individual who is active in this process. All labour is within the sphere of community: it is *social*, always 'with and for and against others'. Hence, the world is always a social world and, as such, an historical reality. The given and pre-established is the medium and means for all acts of labour and appropriation.

In sum, Marx's concept of humanity depicts a 'natural' and 'sensuous' (objective) being, a being that is 'universal' and 'free'. The condition of this being is labour: men and women realize themselves only through labour in which they produce themselves and their own reality. This, according to Marcuse, is the core of Marx's concept of species being. Species being, therefore, does not refer to some abstract human essence, which remains valid at all stages of history. The 'essentials of man and history' (essence) and 'the situation of factual history' (facticity) are not separate and autonomous spheres. Rather, the historical experience of 'man is *taken up into the definition of his essence* . . . essence . . . can be defined in *history* and *only* in history'.[40] Social inquiry, on this account, is directed to explore how people, their social relations and their object world have developed as they have. It becomes a critical analysis in so far as it discloses the extent to which existence is a 'means' or a 'block' to free self-realization.

In an essay published in 1933 and in subsequent works, particularly *Reason and Revolution*, Marcuse made this analysis his own.[41] In these writings labour is made an *a priori* category of human existence, for 'only in labour, and not before, man becomes historical and acquires his determinate position in the historical process'.[42] Following Marx, Marcuse argues that labour is not a mere economic activity (*Erwerbstätigkeit*). He reaffirms the view that labour is 'the becoming-for-itself of man within externalization [*Entäusserung*]' – the 'self-creating or self-objectifying act of man' (Marx).[43] In his view, labour is the condition of human existence independent of all social forms, the foundation of every activity. As such, it is characterized by duration and permanence. What is created becomes part of the environment of the labourer – 'it becomes actual, existent, historical "objectivity" [*Objectivität*], which acquires an objective form in the becoming [*Geschehen*] of the "world"'.[44] In his essay of 1933, Marcuse also characterizes labour as intrinsically burdensome, because it is directed towards things which impose alien conditions on human activity. This position, however, is modified in *Reason and Revolution*, where Marcuse can conceive of labour, free from capitalist relations of production, as potentially a self-directed and free activity.[45]

Through labour, irrespective of its form, every situation people encounter they make their own, by mediating it themselves – by producing and reproducing it.

Production and reproduction do not simply refer to the becoming of 'material existence' in economic doing, but to the active process of human existence as a whole: appropriation, overcoming, transforming and further developing all of human existence in all of its vital spheres.[46]

This 'doing' is essentially a conscious, purposeful set of activities which is shaped by a particular goal – the creation and development of human existence, and of an ever more suitable world for human beings.[47] This goal is, Marcuse maintains, the ground of labour and basis of all becoming.

The driving force of human activity is 'need'. Drawing on the work of Friedrich von Gottl, Marcuse argues that 'the remedy of wants always leaves something to imagine and that some unfulfilled want always remains behind'.[48] This derives from the very structure of being human and explains, in part, an incapacity to remain inactive and an ability to be constantly involved in a process of self-making. Being human always involves more than humanity manifests in its present form – a situation which demands constant labour.

This essential excess of being over existence constitutes the primordial and ineliminable human 'necessity for life' (Gottl). Man's very structure of need is grounded in it and its fulfilling is the final meaning of labour:the need for an enduring and lasting self-fulfilment of . . . existence in the actuality of all its possibilities – a task in whose service the economy ultimately is also engaged.[49]

Labour, therefore, cannot be conceived as an end in itself. Its meaning is inextricably tied to the advancement of human existence. It is an expression of desire, a lack, and is oriented toward the overcoming of this through creation and appropriation. Labour always takes place, of course, within the boundaries set by past accomplishments. It is frequently, at the level of everyday life, a mundane activity. But all labour is, at least as Marcuse boldly stated it in the early 1930s, subordinated to 'the final intention . . . the goal and end of labour, the real fulfilment of human existence in its duration and permanence'. Labour is, Marcuse concluded in accord with Marx, the means for the development of humankind's 'universal nature'.[50]

An understanding of labour in general is not a substitute, Marcuse stresses, for understanding its determinate social forms. Clearly, these vary with natural and historical circumstances. Labour can only be adequately comprehended through concrete investigations of the distinct form it takes in each *mode of production*. Through an inquiry of this kind the basic patterns and processes of society, as well as the potentiality for change, can be grasped.[51] For the process of labour determines the essential structures of society and, therefore, the conditions for the possibility of the realization of reason and freedom.

In *Reason and Revolution*, Marcuse accepts the basic findings of Marx's work on capitalism. (He even sees his more recent work, *One Dimensional Man*, as a development of this analysis.) Relations such as those of labour and capital, capital and commodity, are understood in terms of human relationships, which determine a particular form of social existence. This existence, dominated as it is by the mechanisms of the labour process and the 'laws of the economy', is seen to 'mortify the worker's body and ruin his mind'.[52] As the accumulation of capital exacerbates poverty, and rapid technological change leads to 'the rule of dead matter over the human world', the fundamental nature of workers' alienation is exposed; that is, their alienation from their product, process of work, 'fellow-man', and species being. The situation is one in which the product of labour becomes a force independent of the producer; the worker has little, if any, control over the labour process; individuals are divided against each other by competition and possession; and men and women are in danger of losing their capacity to be universal and free in all the spheres of life.[53]

In the analysis of the wage labour/capital relation, Marcuse sees the origin of the Marxian dialectic. Comparing aspects of Hegel's and Marx's approach to dialectics, he wrote:

For Marx, as for Hegel, the dialectic takes note of the fact that the negation inherent in reality is 'the moving and creative principle'. Every fact is more than a mere fact; it is a negation and restriction of real possibilities. Wage labour is a fact, but at the same time it is a restraint on free work that might satisfy human needs. Private property is a fact, but at the same time it is a negation of man's collective appropriation of nature. . . .'[54]

Marx's concepts grasp the negativity of the existing order – the alienation of labour – with an eye to its positive resolution. The concepts embrace two interrelated dimensions: the existing pattern of social relationships and the tendencies inherent in it toward revolutionary change. A dialectical approach is necessary for the study of these phenomena because their very structure is dialectical.

The Marxian dialectic

Marx detached Hegel's dialectic from its ontological base. His analysis focuses on the inherent contradictions of a particular stage of the historical process. The totality he discloses is the totality of class societies. The negativity he portrays is the product of this type of society. It is a *'historical* condition . . . which cannot be hypostatized'.[55]

Following Marx, Marcuse holds that the antagonisms of capitalism are unique. Capitalism not only denies and opposes real possibilities; it also, by virtue of its very structure, creates the possibility of the negation of the negation – the overcoming of alienated social relationships. This possibility has a very special character: it marks the establishment of the conditions for human fulfilment. While Hegel's philosophy was based on the idea of the universality of reason – in which every 'part' or 'thing' was integrated into a structural and comprehensive whole – Marx showed, Marcuse contends, that it was capitalist society that 'first put such a universality into practice'.

Capitalism developed the productive forces for the totality of a uniform social system. Universal commerce, universal competition and the universal interdependence of labour were made to prevail and transformed men into 'world-historical, empirically universal individuals.[56]

Furthermore, capitalism created a subject whose interest is essentially universal: 'the proletariat is distinguished by the fact that, as a class, it signifies the negation of all classes'. Marcuse justifies this claim, in part, by reference to the structural position and potential consciousness of the proletariat.

The universality of the proletariat is . . . a negative universality, indicating that the alienation of labour has intensified. . . . The labour of the proletarian prevents any self-fulfilment; his work negates his entire existence. This utmost negativity, however, takes a positive turn. The very fact that he is deprived of all assets of the prevailing system sets him beyond this system. He is a member of the class 'which is really rid of the old world and at the same time stands pitted against it'. The 'universal character' of the proletariat is the final basis for the universal character of the communist revolution. . . . The proletariat is the negation not only of certain particular human potentialities, but also of man as such. All specific distinguishing marks [property, culture, religion, nationality] by which men are differentiated lose their validity. . . . His concern to exist is not the concern of a given group, class or nation, but is truly universal and 'world historical'.[57]

The universality that capitalism puts into practice is created by dint of circumstances in an uncontrolled and alien manner. The realization of control, of freedom and reason, requires a transformation of the situation – a universal revolution which ensures that the universal will no longer operate as a 'blind natural force', but rather, as 'a general plan formulated by freely combined individuals'.[58]

The negation of the negation, however, is not, as it was for Hegel in the last analysis, an inevitable process; the liberation of the possibilities immanent in the existing order requires 'man's historical action to fulfil them'.[59] The dialectic remains unconcluded so long as autonomous, emancipatory action is not forthcoming. Although dialectical analysis describes a system that will necessarily perish and must necessarily be superseded by a socialist society, this does not mean, Marcuse insists, that it describes an inevitable and positive transformation of capitalism, as Marx himself sometimes assumed.[60] What is necessary and inevitable is capitalism's demise. What is necessary but not inevitable is a genuinely socialist society. And it itself is necessary, Marcuse points out, 'only in the sense that it is necessary to use available productive forces for the general satisfaction of all individuals'.[61]

The concept of truth Marx works with in this context is similar in nature to Hegel's. Despite the emphasis in historical materialism on the determination of consciousness by being and, in particular, by material circumstances, an epistemological and ethical relativism is not, Marcuse argues, entailed. 'There is only one truth and one practice capable of realizing it.' Theory has revealed the tendencies, and demonstrated the conditions, that make possible a rational society – a society free of the contradictions of the existing order. It has formulated the broad goals of the 'new' and 'necessary' social practice: the progressive eradication of alienated labour, and the planned use of collectively owned means of production for the satisfaction of all individual potentialities.[62] In defending the interest in a rational society, critical theory, from Marx onward, preserves 'the truth of the present order' – the vision of a society in which existing potentialities are fulfilled. The correct theory, therefore, is the one that retains the consciousness of the practice necessary for the progressive attainment of this ideal society.[63]

The interest in a rational society is also, however, the interest in the creation of the conditions for the realization of the species' capacities. In this lies, in fact, its foremost significance. Accordingly, the rational society represents the true, just and virtuous life – the unity of theory and practice. The foundation of the unity is given in labour. In labour, theory finds its ultimate ground, a ground which can only be articulated by theory and realized by practice. In the analysis of labour, theory finds a criterion of truth that is both internal to practice and independent of its given form. Labour contains its own critical criterion. For every moment of labour anticipates the 'good life' – fulfilment of species being, an enduring and lasting fulfilment of existence 'in the actuality of all its possibilities'.[64]

It is a central tenet of Marcuse's analysis that the capacity of human beings to realize their essence evolves and changes over time. It is only with capitalism that a social form is created which might genuinely lead to the progressive dealienation of men and women. From this position one can understand Marcuse when he wrote,

Theory accompanies the practice at every moment, analysing the changing situation and formulating its concepts accordingly. The concrete conditions for realizing the truth may vary, but the truth remains the same and theory remains its ultimate guardian. Theory will preserve the truth even if revolutionary practice deviates from its proper path.[65]

Marcuse's position until the 1950s can be summarized as follows. The labour process is pivotal in the constitution of being; it discloses the unfolding of human powers in history. It determines both the basic structure of human existence and society's basic patterns; it involves a process defined by negativity, contradiction and change – a dialectical process. But the dialectic is, as it was for Horkheimer, unconcluded and open. The opportunities for human beings to realize their essence are not part of any 'iron laws'. As manifest in capitalism, 'productive activity' is thought to have created the possibility of realizing the species' nature. The truth of this process is the world constitutive activity of labour. The key element in the overcoming of capitalism is the proletariat. The truth claims of critical theory are, thus, intertwined with 'man's historico-practical activity'. The interest in freedom and a rational society is grounded in every act of labour. Every moment of labour anticipates the fulfilment of the species' capacities. As a consequence, we can assess what exists in terms of its potentiality. The analysis of particular modes of labour and production can be empirical, analytical and critical.

The integration of Freud

Marcuse's relation to Freud and psychoanalytic theory has already been discussed in Chapter 4. The introduction of Freud complicates the picture of the foundations of historical materialism. While a marriage seems possible between the theory of labour and Freud's insights, the exact relation between the two is never outlined by Marcuse at any length.

In *Eros and Civilization*, it was argued that civilization has of necessity been antagonistic to the demands for immediate happiness; it has continuously modified these impulses. The fate of happiness (and freedom) is held to depend on the life and death struggle of the instincts in which 'soma and psyche, nature and civilization participate'. But this struggle, and the subsequent development of the individual and society, cannot be adequately conceived without reference to the process of labour. For Marcuse interprets Freud's categories and theories both in terms of their explicit and implicit socio-historical content and in terms of the main tenets of historical materialism. The development of civilization is argued to rest on sublimation and continuous labour. It is only as a result of the products of labour that non-repressive desublimation becomes a real possibility. The dialectics of labour remains at the centre of Marcuse's theory of social development.

A major change occurs, however, in the concept of species being. Marx's notion is enriched by Freudian categories; his view of the species as a 'universal' and 'free' being is supplemented by the theory of instincts – a conception of the essence of being as eros.[66] Marcuse interprets Freud's work as having a general ontological meaning. Being, thereby, can be conceived in terms of the striving for pleasure.

This striving becomes an 'aim' in human existence: the erotic impulse to combine living substance into ever larger and more durable units is the instinctual source of civilization. The sex instincts are *life* instincts: the impulse to preserve and enrich life by mastering nature in accordance with the developing vital needs is originally an erotic impulse. Ananke [scarcity] is experienced as the barrier against the satisfaction of the life instincts, which seek pleasure, not security. And the 'struggle for existence' is originally a struggle for pleasure: culture begins with the collective implementation of this aim.[67]

Human existence is grounded in eros. Cultural development is shaped by this aim. But eros is dependent on, and interlocked with, labour. It is only through labour that scarcity can be sufficiently overcome so that the life instincts are satisfied. In terms of their orientation to the satisfaction of individual potentiality, eros and labour are one.

In its exploration of thoughts, dreams and wishes, psychoanalysis is, of course, able to penetrate much further than historical materialism. In these phenomena psychoanalysis discloses a 'drive for integral gratification' which is often tabooed by the present society. Through therapeutic activity, the many manifestations of the drive can be uncovered. The vehicle for this is memory. Its importance derives from its truth value which 'lies in the specific function of memory to preserve promises and potentialities which are betrayed and even outlawed by the mature, civilized individual, but which had once been fulfilled in his dim past and which are never entirely forgotten'.[68] Through remembrance psychoanalysis yields a range of (additional) critical standards that the existing order systematically abrogates.

Fantasy occupies a special place within the psyche. It has, on Marcuse's account, a truth value of its own. Here, perhaps more clearly than anywhere else, a longing for reconciliation – between desire and reality, happiness and reason – can be found. Behind 'illusion lies knowledge', a knowledge which overcomes the antagonisms of reality and expresses 'the claim of the whole of the individual, in union with the genus and the archaic past'.[69] For Marcuse, art reveals a similar cognitive dimension: the aesthetic form preserves 'the repressed harmony of sensuousness and reason'. The development of critical theory depends on its capacity to draw as readily from these domains as from political economy. For the struggle for socialism involves not only a struggle for a rational economy but also for an individual free from surplus repression and repressive desublimation. The standards for the latter struggle can only be derived from the psychology sensitive to history: psychoanalysis.

Nature and natural science

'History is the negation of nature.' Through labour the negative in nature (including human nature) can be overcome; that is, nature can be freed of insufficiency.[70] This process of change, however, Marcuse believes, has been fundamentally distorted by modern science and technology, both of which have developed under an *a priori* of 'technical usefulness'.[71] Science is, Marcuse contends, in one of his most controversial statements, *a priori* technology, 'the *a priori* of a *specific* technology – namely, technology as a form of social control and domination'. It projects an image of nature as the 'stuff of control and organization'.[72] For prior to all actual use, it is tied to a specific societal project – the technical control of nature.

The organization of nature under these circumstances (organized by instrumental reason and usually by profit as well), offers greater capacity for control, but 'deprives man from finding himself in nature, beyond and this side of alienation; it also prevents him from recognizing nature as a *subject* in its own right – a subject with which to live in a common universe'.[73] To refer to nature as a subject and to speak, as Marcuse often does, of its necessary liberation, is not to attribute a plan or intention to nature itself: liberation, Marcuse emphasizes, is always the plan or goal of human beings. It is, however, to conceive of nature as a subject-object: 'as a *cosmos* with its own potentialities, necessities and chances'. It is to insist that nature is susceptible to the project of emancipation, and that there are forces in nature which could support and reinforce the liberation of human beings.[74] The realization of human potentiality is linked directly to the realization of nature's inherent possibilities. A free society, Marcuse holds, may well have 'a very different *a priori* and a very different object; the development of the scientific concepts may be grounded in an experience of nature as a totality of life to be protected and "cultivated", and technology would apply this science to the reconstruction of the environment of life'.[75]

The nature of concepts: appearance and essence

Marcuse's approach to history and society, as analytical, empirical and critical, is revealed clearly in one of his early *Zeitschrift* essays, 'The concept of essence' (1936). The essay expresses many of Marcuse's main doctrines and, thus, provides a useful basis for highlighting his position.

Critical theory functions at two fundamental levels. It seeks, first, to grasp the social world in its immediacy – the reified and fetishized world of appearances. Second, it 'abstracts from these abstractions' and centres its analysis on essential social relations and practices which ensure the production of society. In pursuing this investigation, its concepts aim to embrace 'the essence of the social whole'. This essence can be unfolded by examining the way in which the 'totality of the social process is organized in a particular epoch'; various levels of social reality are 'grounded in a fundamental level' (for example the economy); constellations of social relationships condition the difference between the appearance of society and its core structures; the individual is restricted, by real need and suffering, from 'the liberation of becoming himself'.[76] Appearance and essence are the constitutive elements of particular historical structures. They are members of a real antithesis which reveals differences between what things are in their immediate existence and what they are in themselves as historical being and becoming. From an assessment of this antithesis objective possibilities can be uncovered – possibilities which suggest paths for social development.

These possibilities, projected by thought, can be systematically evaluated. Marcuse proposes a number of criteria for deciding their 'truth value'. What humans can be in a given historical situation depends on:

the measure of control of natural and social productive forces, the level of the organization of labour, the development of needs in relation to possibilities for their fulfilment . . ., the availability, as material to be appropriated, of a wealth of cultural values in all areas of life.[77]

A concern with people's capacity to fulfil themselves through labour, to integrate culture and play, and to act with self-determination without depriving others of their ability to do the same can be distinguished from utopian thinking.[78] For theory can show, Marcuse argues, the 'concrete roads to their realization and can adduce as evidence those attempts at realization which are already under way'. But the knowledge wielded by critical theory, like all knowledge, cannot be guaranteed:

it . . . can have recourse neither to evidence afforded by mere perception nor to . . . [an eternal] system of values. . . . The truth of . . . [the] . . . model of essence [of man's existence and potentiality] is preserved better in human misery and suffering and the struggle to overcome them than in the forms and concepts of pure thought. This truth is 'indeterminate' and remains necessarily so as long as it is measured against the idea of unconditionally certain knowledge. For it is fulfilled only through historical action, and its concretion can thus result only *post festum*.[79]

The truth that theory discloses cannot be confirmed through thought alone. For while its adequate expression requires a consistent system of concepts and statements, its confirmation depends on historical struggles: 'only in them can the essential theoretical truths be ultimately verified'.[80]

The very way the concept of essence is derived is determined, furthermore, by 'historical and practical presuppositions'; that is, it is determined by the framework of 'historical goals with which materialist theory is linked'. Critical theory understands all knowledge to be rooted in interests; by making those interests conscious and by distinguishing between particular and general interests, critical theory makes its own an interest in the objective advancement of humankind. In this way it 'moves beyond historical relativism in linking itself with those social forces which the historical situation reveals to be progressive and truly "universal"'.[81] In expressing and clarifying 'the general interest', critical theory distinguishes its goals from sectarian interests and allies itself with those social groups and individuals who are part of the struggle for a rational society. Its concepts are intertwined with the consciousness of these forces.

A similar view was defended by Marcuse thirty years after 'The concept of essence' was written. In discussing how one judges between various 'transcendent projects', he argued that the criteria for their historical truth can best be formulated as criteria of rationality. As he wrote,

The transcendent project, in order to falsify the established totality, must demonstrate its own *higher* rationality in the threefold sense that

(a) it offers the prospect of preserving and improving the productive achievements of civilization;

(b) it defines the established totality in its very structure, basic tendencies, and relations;

(c) its realization offers a greater chance for the pacification of existence, within the framework of institutions which offer a greater chance for the free development of human needs and faculties.[82]

Notions like 'the chance for the free development of human needs and faculties' can be empirically assessed, Marcuse believes, in light of the attained level of material and intellectual culture. On this basis, the 'truth value' of various social practices can be assessed. The historical negation of the existing order can be anticipated. It cannot, of course, be simply predicted; for it represents a possibility, a 'determinate choice', which future historical action alone can realize. While dialectical theory transcends the given facts, defines options, and even necessities, it is only in theoretically guided practice that these can be fulfilled. All the facts are there Marcuse maintains, which suggest that a rational society is necessary: 'the increasing irrationality of the whole; waste and restriction of productivity; the need for aggressive expansion; the constant threat of war; intensified exploitation; dehumanization'.[83] The material basis is there that makes a rational society possible. But these are torn pieces of a whole that does not, as yet, add up to a movement that would forge a new society. It is critical theory's ultimate objective to help create this movement and bind these pieces together.

Part Two

Critical Theory: Habermas

The human interest in autonomy and responsibility is not mere fancy, for it can be apprehended *a priori*. What raises us out of nature is . . . *language*. Through its structure, autonomy and responsibility are posited for us. Our first sentence expresses unequivocally the intention of universal and unconstrained consensus.

JÜRGEN HABERMAS, *Knowledge and Human Interests*

9 Introduction to Habermas

The thought of the Frankfurt school has been a major source of stimulus to the man who has now become the leading spokesman for a new generation of critical theorists – Jürgen Habermas. Born in 1929, and brought up in Nazi Germany, Habermas did not become radicalized until the late 1950s. Under the influence of, among others, Adorno (to whom he became an assistant), Habermas discovered the systematic use that could be made of Marx and Freud. After teaching at Heidelberg, he took up a chair in 1964 in philosophy and sociology at the University of Frankfurt. He left the post in 1971 and moved to the Max Planck Institute in Starnberg, West Germany, where he is currently working. Although his *oeuvre* should not simply be regarded as the outcome of a path of progressive development that begins with the earliest writings of Horkheimer and Adorno, his efforts have been directed, from the late 1950s onward, to the remoulding of critical theory.

The works of Jürgen Habermas, and the debates they have stimulated, are gradually becoming familiar to the Anglo-American world. But the reception of his thought has not been without difficulties. Like those of the Frankfurt school, his writings are steeped in German traditions which often remain undiscussed and untranslated in the English speaking world. As a result, the import of his work has often been missed.[1] Problems of interpretation have also arisen due to the appearance of only some of his writings in English and to the time lapses between publications. Further, the work of many of Habermas's past and present collaborators (including Claus Offe, Albrecht Wellmer, Klaus Eder, Rainer Döbert and Ulrich Oevermann) as well as the thought of contemporaries who have influenced him (most notably Karl-Otto Apel) remain largely unknown in Britain and America. In the discussion below the work of these individuals will be drawn upon, wherever helpful, to elucidate Habermas's views.

Habermas conceives of his project as an attempt to develop a theory of society with a practical intention: the self-emancipation of people from domination. Through an assessment of the self-formative processes of the human species, Habermas's critical theory aims to further the self-understanding of social groups capable of transforming society. While the status he ascribes to his enterprise has changed, and a greater emphasis has been placed in recent times on what he calls its 'empirical-theoretical' or 'empirical reconstructive' tasks, critical theory remains designed to help in the making of history 'with will and consciousness'. In order to defend the idea of a critical theory of society, Habermas has been concerned systematically to develop its philosophical underpinnings. This involves a reconstruction of some of the central theses of classical Greek and German philosophy: the inseparability of truth and virtue, of facts and values, of theory and practice. The project is defined as a 'struggle for the critical soul of science' and 'the scientific soul of criticism'.[2]

The imperative to reformulate critical theory derives its force, for Habermas, from the 'course of history'. He maintains that twentieth-century history is characterized by a number of major developments in socialist and capitalist societies. The degeneration of the Russian revolution into Stalinism and technocratic social management; the failure hitherto of mass revolution in the West; the absence of mass proletarian revolutionary class consciousness; the frequent collapse of Marxist theory into either a deterministic, objectivistic science or a pessimistic cultural critique: all, he holds, are important features of recent times. He sees structural changes in capitalist society as having altered both its appearance and its essence. State intervention grows; the market-place is supported and replaced; capitalism is increasingly 'organized'; instrumental reason and bureaucracy, seeming ever to expand, threaten the public sphere, the sphere in which political life is discussed openly by a reasoning public.[3] Habermas contends that in light of these events, doubt can be cast on the validity of Marx's work, the general Marxian framework and on many other well known theories of society. He finds it necessary, therefore, to assess, and in fact reformulate, the major traditions of social thought.

The events of the 1960s, particularly the advent of the student movement, also had a significant impact on his thinking. Initially, Habermas was a leading spokesman for the movement and, in fact, for all those who sought a radical democratization of society.

However, by the late 1960s, he had become estranged from the movement's leading groups. He was critical of what he saw as their departure from their original democratic and non-authoritarian goals. Instead of struggling for an expansion of the sphere of freedom and initiative, they were working, he believed, to impose new restrictions on thought and action. The students in turn criticized Habermas for, among other things, failing to become involved in actual struggles, retreating into theoretical reflection, and for uniting theory and practice in theory only. Since this time Habermas appears to have put less emphasis on the practical-political aspects of his programme. He has sought to defend and elaborate his theoretical interests, only pointing occasionally to their practical implications. His work at Starnberg reflects this changed emphasis.

Continuities and discontinuities with the Frankfurt school

Many of the ideas and theories of members of the Frankfurt school can be found, in a recast form, in Habermas's early writings on social theory. In *Strukturwandel der Öffentlichkeit* [Structural transformation in the Public Sphere] – (1962) and *Towards a Rational Society* (a selection of essays written in the latter half of the sixties but not published in English until 1970), he documented the growth of large-scale economic and commercial organizations, the increasing interdependence of science, technology and industry, the increasing interdependence of state and society, the commercialization of the media, and the extension of means-end rationality to more and more areas of life. These developments, he argued (in accord with a central Frankfurt school position), have created a new constellation of economics and politics; 'politics is no longer *only* a phenomenon of the superstructure'.[4] The expansion of the state – symptomatic of the crisis tendencies of capitalist society – leads to an ever greater involvement of administrators and technicians in social and economic affairs.[5] It also leads, in conjunction with the fusion of science, technology and industry, to the emergence of a new form of ideology; ideology is no longer simply based on notions of just exchange but also on a technocratic justification of the social order.[6] Practical issues, underpinned by particular historical class interests, are defined as technical problems: politics becomes the sphere for the technical elimination of dysfunctions and the avoidance of risks that threaten 'the system'.

This conception of industrial capitalist societies can still be found in Habermas's more recent works – in *Legitimation Crisis* (1973) and *Zur Rekonstruktion des Historischen Materialismus* [The Reconstruction of Historical Materialism] (1976). But in these writings his analysis of the key elements of capitalism radically departs from the 'Frankfurt' view. The framework in which Horkheimer and the others understood modern society is recast. Important differences with, for example, Marcuse are already evident in Habermas's 'early writing'.[7] However, the range of material over which they differ has extended and now includes interpretations of science, technology, culture, crisis tendencies and the prospects for revolutionary change. Habermas is not as optimistic about radical social transformation as the Marcuse who defends the possibility of a non-repressive desublimated society, although he is certainly not as pessimistic as Horkheimer or Adorno were in the latter part of their lives.

Unlike most of the members of the Institute of Social Research, Habermas has not been much concerned with aesthetics and with the study of, for example, contemporary popular culture. But he stresses the importance of psychology for explicating the links between the institutional framework of society and individual identity formation. He agrees that the 'heritage of natural history, consisting of unspecified impulse potentials [that are both libidinal and aggressive], determines the initial conditions of the [conflict-ridden] reproduction of the human species'.[8] Although he employs psychoanalytic concepts to explore the relations between power and ideology he does not, as did the earlier critical theorists, make direct use of many of Freud's categories. It is striking, for instance, that Habermas rarely discusses the central psychosexual dimensions of Freud's work. The sensual and erotic do not play a key role in his writings. (It is unclear how much of Freud's substantive contributions Habermas would defend.) His interest in psychoanalysis seems to be mainly methodological.[9] On the other hand, Habermas has sought to develop the psychological dimension of critical theory by drawing on and integrating a range of contributions to contemporary individual and social psychology, including the symbolic interactionist theory of action (Mead, Goffman), role theory (Parsons), and cognitive developmental psychology (Piaget, Kohlberg). He has recently set out the basis for an analysis of ego development (the integration of 'inner nature' into the universal structures of language, thought and action) and identity formation (the capacity to produce a continuity in life history).

Habermas does not share the views of Horkheimer, Adorno and Marcuse on philosophy. For instance, while Adorno maintained that there are no ultimate foundations for knowledge and values, Habermas defends a position which suggests the opposite. He rejects Adorno's (and Horkheimer's) antipathy for systematic thought. The whole emphasis in his work – on engaging *and* appropriating competing traditions of philosophy and social thought, reformulating the foundations of social theory, and demonstrating the superiority of his stance over others – contrasts markedly with the main interests of the Frankfurt theorists. A series of public debates with, for example, Hans-Georg Gadamer, in relation to hermeneutics, and Niklas Luhmann, in relation to systems theory, has both stimulated the development of his thought and led to the alteration of some of his ideas. His work is marked by a general eclecticism.

Habermas's project: an overview of fundamental concepts

Despite an overlap of concerns with the Frankfurt school Habermas develops his ideas in a framework which is significantly different from the positions outlined in Part One. Before reconstructing this framework in detail I will provide a brief overview of his key concepts and theories. This should help to show both the extent to which he differs from Horkheimer and the others and how the various parts of his project fit together. One cautionary note is necessary: Habermas's views have changed over time and, indeed, are still in the process of development. He often gives his positions a tentative and programmatic status – they are part of an on-going project. The positions he elaborated and defended in his important *Knowledge and Human Interests* (1968) have been modified and, in many cases, substantially reworked.[10] His conception of the logical structure of critical theory has altered and with it his view of the nature of social science. The influence of Hegelian ideas has diminished and this has had important consequences.[11] These, along with other recent changes, will be highlighted in later sections, but they will be largely passed over in the following introductory sketch.

A major concern of Habermas since *Strukturwandel der Öffentlichkeit* has been the spread of instrumental reason to many areas

of social life. The rise of technocratic consciousness, with its disin-
tegrative effect on the public sphere, is discussed at two fundamental levels. At the level of social theory Habermas argues that the
increasing tendency to define practical problems as technical issues
threatens an essential aspect of human life; for technocratic consciousness not only justifies a particular class interest in domination, but also affects the very structure of human interests.[12]
Accordingly, reflection on this state of affairs must, on Habermas's
account, 'penetrate beyond the level of particular historical class
interests to disclose the fundamental interests of mankind as
such'.[13]

At the level of the theory of knowledge, Habermas investigates
the way instrumental reason has dominated modern thought.
Focusing on the dissolution of epistemology and the ascendance of
positivism during the last century, he examines the way the
significance of the epistemic subject – and the capacity for
reflection by the subject on his or her activities – has been gradually eclipsed. Today, he argues, if emancipation from domination
is to remain a project of humanity, it is essential to counter this
tendency and to reaffirm the necessity of self-reflection for self-
understanding. This Habermas tries to do by a systematic investigation of the nature of human interests, action and knowledge. The
investigation takes the form of an immanent critique of writers
from a wide range of traditions: from Kant and Hegel to Mach,
Peirce and Freud.

Like Horkheimer, Habermas contends that knowledge is historically rooted and interest bound. But he understands this in quite
different terms from his predecessor. In *Knowledge and Human
Interests* and *Theory and Practice*, Habermas develops the theory
of cognitive interests (or knowledge-constitutive interests), the
important first stage in his elaboration of the relationship of knowledge to human activity.[14] In more recent work he has extended
this inquiry and formulated the theory of 'communicative competence'. These complex theories have been developed in order to
justify the critical enterprise.

The theory of cognitive interests is concerned with uncovering
the conditions for the possibility of knowledge. While accepting
the need to understand knowledge as the result of the constituting
activity of the cognizing subject, Habermas rejects the Kantian
approach of locating such activity in an ahistorical, transcendental
subject. Rather, starting with an essential tenet of historical mater-

ialism — that history, social reality and nature (as known) are all a product of the constituting labour of the human species – Habermas understands knowledge in light of the problems man encounters in his efforts to 'produce his existence and reproduce his species being'. The conditions of the constitution of knowledge which determine 'the structure of objects of possible experience', are the historical material conditions in which the development of the species has occurred.

It is Habermas's contention that the human species organizes its experience in terms of *a priori* interests, or cognitive interests/or knowledge-guiding interests. That there is a 'basis of interests' follows, he argues, from an understanding of humans as both toolmaking and language-using animals: they must produce from nature what is needed for material existence through the manipulation and control of objects and communicate with others through the use of intersubjectively understood symbols within the context of rule-governed institutions. Thus, humankind has an interest in the creation of knowledge which would enable it to control objectified processes and to maintain communication. There is, however, on his account, a third interest: an interest in the reflective appropriation of human life, without which the interest-bound character of knowledge could not itself be grasped. This is an interest in reason, in the human capacity to be self-reflective and self-determining, to act rationally. As a result of it, knowledge is generated which enhances autonomy and responsibility (*Mündigkeit*); hence, it is an emancipatory interest. Cognitive interests, which are the transcendental conditions of knowledge, are themselves naturalistically grounded. That is, the rule systems governing the activities of the species 'have a transcendental function but arise from actual structures of human life'. Habermas accords to the category of 'cognitive interests' a somewhat problematic status as 'quasi-transcendental'.

The end point of this analysis – of the mode in which reality is disclosed, constituted and acted upon – is a trichotomous model of the human species' *interests* ('anthropologically rooted strategies for interpreting life experience'), *media* (means of social organization) and *sciences*. The interests are the technical, the practical and the emancipatory. These unfold in three media, work (instrumental action), interaction (language) and power (asymmetrical relations of constraint and dependency) and give rise to the conditions for the possibility of three sciences, the empirical-analytic, the historical-hermeneutic and the critical. It is one of Habermas's central claims that these three sciences only systematize and formalize the procedures required for the success of human activity.

The theory of cognitive interests, as developed in *Knowledge and Human Interests*, represents Habermas's initial attempt to specify the relation between knowledge and human activity. He has recently recognized, however, the need to examine this relation further – particularly, the distinction between processes of constitution and justification. This he attempts to do in the theory of communicative competence.

In this theory Habermas argues that all speech is oriented to the idea of a genuine consensus – a discursively achieved consensus – which is rarely realized.[15] The analysis of consensus, he claims, shows this notion to involve a normative dimension, which is formalized in the concept of what he calls 'an ideal speech situation'. A consensus attained in this situation, referred to as a 'rational consensus', is, in Habermas's opinion, the ultimate criterion of the truth of a statement or of the correctness of norms. The end result of this argument is that the very structure of speech is held to involve the anticipation of a form of life in which truth, freedom and justice are possible. On Habermas's account, the critical theory of society makes this its starting point. Critical theory is, therefore, grounded in a normative standard that is not arbitrary, but 'inherent in the very structure of social action and language'. It is just this anticipation of an ideal form of discourse which can be used as a normative standard for a critique of distorted communication. It is Habermas's contention that in every communicative situation in which a consensus is established under coercion or under other similar types of condition, we are likely to be confronting instances of systematically distorted communication. This is, in his view, the contemporary formulation of ideology. On this account ideology is, as Trent Schroyer put it, 'those belief systems which can maintain their legitimacy despite the fact that they could not be validated if subjected to rational discourse'.[16] The process of emancipation, then, entails the transcendence of such systems of distorted communication. This process, in turn, requires engaging in critical reflection and criticism. It is only through reflection that domination, in its many forms, can be unmasked.

In his latest work, Habermas explores the acquisition of communicative competence – of cognitive, linguistic and interactive abilities – in ontogenesis and phylogenesis. By examining the major stages of individual development and social evolution, he hopes to show that at both levels there is a growing capacity to master theoretical and practical discourse, respectively discourse about statements that make problematic truth claims and discourse about the rightness or correctness of norms. A reconstruction of communicative competence is needed for self-reflection and criticism – in order that an adequate basis be provided for an historically relevant critique and the exploration of developmental possibilities.

Human beings' capacity for freedom is dependent, on Habermas's account, on cumulative learning in theoretical and practical activity. Through such learning, knowledge is generated that makes possible the technical mastery of the natural and social world and the organization and alteration of social relations; that is, the expansion of the sphere of 'sensuous human activity' or praxis. Habermas analyses praxis (both in his early and later writings, but more clearly in his later writings) as a complex consisting of two key parts – work (or instrumental action, purposive-rational action) and interaction (or communicative interaction).[17] He also refers sometimes to a third type of action – strategic action – which is both instrumental (means–end oriented) and bound to a context of interaction. But, as Thomas McCarthy has pointed out, it is

	Work	*Interaction*
Orientation	technical control over objectified processes	mutual understanding
Co-ordinating elements	rational decision procedures (involving e.g. preference rules, decision maxims) and efficient use of technical knowledge	intersubjectively recognized norms and rules (reciprocity and consensus predominate)

	Work bounded by interaction: strategic action
Orientation	calculated pursuit of individual interests
Co-ordinating elements	rational decision strategies interlocked in a framework of norms and intersubjectively recognized rules of procedure

misleading to present strategic action (as Habermas sometimes does) as a wholly distinct type of action.[18] Unless otherwise stated I will, therefore, understand Habermas's basic action categories – work and interaction – as shown in the diagram on page 257.

Under the categories of 'work' and 'interaction' attention is directed to issues concerning, respectively, the technical mastery of the natural and social worlds and the organization of social relations.

Habermas takes as central to his theory of social evolution the claim that through work and interaction the human species evolves in two separate but interrelated dimensions, namely the development of the forces of production and the development of normative structures of interaction.[19] In both these dimensions 'cumulative processes are involved which allow a direction to be perceived'. The table on page 259 outlines some of the main elements of this process.

Habermas's ideas about social evolution provide the framework within which he examines the development of specific societies or social formations. Part of this project involves the identification of first, the 'possibility spaces' – the potential avenue of development – which a society's 'core structures' open to evolution; and second, the crisis tendencies to which such structures are vulnerable. Although Habermas is concerned to investigate pre-civilization (primitive communities) and traditional societies, his main focus hitherto has been on modern capitalism. He explores, in particular, the way 'advanced' (or, as he sometimes calls it, 'late' or 'organized') capitalism is susceptible to 'legitimation crisis' – the withdrawal from the existing order of the support or loyalty of the mass of the population as their motivational commitment to its normative basis is broken. It is Habermas's contention that the seeds of a new evolutionary development – the overcoming of capitalism's underlying class contradiction – can be uncovered in this and other related crisis tendencies.

From the above sketch it can be seen that Habermas's work covers an extraordinary range of problems. It is his ultimate objective to provide a coherent framework within which a large number of apparently competing approaches to the social sciences can be integrated; these include, the critique of ideology, the perspective of action theory, the analysis of social systems and evolutionary theory. It is also his hope that the framework will provide a basis for bringing together the interests and findings of the ever more

Learning and evolution

Marx's category of 'sensuous human activity', or praxis, involves two types of structured activities:

Work, or purposive-rational action (the dimension of activity in which the human species – through the manipulation and control of objects – produces from nature what is needed for its material existence)

Language, or communicative action (the dimension of activity in which the human species communicates through the use of intersubjectively understood symbols, within the context of rule-governed institutions)

The human species has the capacity to learn. It is unable not to learn:

through the generation and application of technical knowledge there is development of the forces of production

through the generation and application of practical and moral knowledge there are changes in structured interaction (the relations of production, for instance)

The human species evolves in these two dimensions. In each there is a logic of development which has its own dynamic and which cannot be reduced to the other. The logics can be reconstructed in terms of:

cumulative growth in technical and scientific knowledge

the pattern of reflexivity, universality of beliefs, and discursiveness in the sphere of practical life

fragmented, individual disciplines within the social sciences. The following chapter will examine Habermas's contributions to the theory of society. The next two will deal with problems of epistemology and method.

10   Discourse, science and society

The public sphere and the scientization of politics

From his earliest published writings Habermas has been concerned with the development and disintegration of the 'public sphere' and with the principle of 'discursive will-formation' (constraint free discussion) on which it was founded. By public sphere Habermas refers to 'a realm of social life in which something approaching public opinion can be formed'.[1] It is a sphere in which citizens can 'confer in an unrestricted fashion – that is, with the guarantee of freedom of assembly and association and the freedom to express and publish their opinions – about matters of general interest'.[2] It is a realm in which, in principle, political life can be discussed openly; debate proceeds in accordance with standards of critical reason and not by simple appeal to traditional dogmas and authorities (the divine right of kings, for instance). The procedures and presuppositions of free argument are the basis for the justification of opinions. It is these conditions of argument that lend public opinion its legitimizing force; 'public opinion' becomes distinguished from mere 'opinion' (for example cultural assumptions, customs and collective prejudice).[3]

In a detailed historical study (*Strukturwandel der Öffentlichkeit*) Habermas traces the emergence of 'public opinion' to the eighteenth century. Forums for public discussion (clubs, newspapers, journals) developed rapidly in Europe to mediate the growing division between the state and civil society, a division which followed from the expansion of market economies.[4] These centres of debate and information nurtured opposition to the traditional and hierarchical forms of feudal authority. The public sphere anticipated the replacement of the rule of tradition with the rule of reason.

Public discussions, Habermas argues, grew out of a specific phase of the development of bourgeois society; a particular constellation of interests lay at the roots of this type of interchange. A large number of 'private individuals' (merchants, etc.), excluded from the (then) dominant political institutions, became concerned about the government of society because 'the reproduction of life in the wake of the developing market economy had grown beyond the bounds of private domestic authority'. These individuals promoted and shaped the public sphere by, among other things, maintaining as many newspapers and journals as possible in order to further debate about the nature of authority. As a result, 'newspapers changed from mere institutions for the publication of news into bearers and leaders of public opinion – weapons of party politics'.[5] Until the establishment of a more open and accountable authority structure, large numbers of papers and journals joined the struggle for freedom, public opinion and the principle of the public sphere.

The public sphere was thought to represent the general interest, although those who participated in it were generally of 'high standing' (people with education and property). Members of the bourgeoisie were the 'reasoning public'; armed with what they took to be knowledge of the general interest they sought to change society into a sphere of private autonomy free of political interference, and to transform the state into an authority restricted to a limited number of functions and supervised by the 'public'. The earliest modern constitutions reflected this desire directly.

In the first modern constitutions the catalogues of fundamental rights were a perfect image of the liberal model of the public sphere: they guaranteed the society as a sphere of private autonomy and the restriction of public authority to a few functions. Between these two spheres, the constitutions further insured the existence of a realm of private individuals assembled into a public body who as citizens transmit the needs of bourgeois society to the state, in order, ideally, to transform political into 'rational' authority within the medium of the public sphere. The general interest, which was the measure of such a rationality, was then guaranteed.[6]

The social basis of the public sphere meant, however, that its commitment to rational self-determination was never fully actualized either within its own boundaries or in politics generally. The bourgeois or liberal idea of free speech and discursive will formation was always at some distance from reality: the discrepancy increased with the development of the capitalist economy.

The press gradually became less and less involved in political struggles: journalism altered from an occupation motivated by conviction to one stimulated primarily by commerce.[7] The general commercialization of the media eventually excluded political and practical questions from large areas of the public sphere. The growth of large-scale economic organizations, the increase in state intervention to stabilize the economy, the expanding influence of science and, more generally, of instrumental reason in social life, furthered the process of depoliticization. Under these conditions the public realm was transformed. In industrially advanced mass democracies the public sphere was reduced and compressed.

Group needs that can expect no satisfaction from a self-regulating market tend to be regulated through the state. The public sphere, which now mediates these demands, becomes a field for the competition of interests ... With the interweaving of the public and private realms, not only do political authorities assume certain functions in the sphere of commodity exchange and social labour, but conversely social powers now assume political functions. This leads to a kind of 'refeudalization' of the public sphere. Large organizations strive for a kind of political compromise with the state and with one another, excluding the public whenever possible. But at the same time they must secure at least a plebiscitary support among the mass of the population through the development of demonstrative publicity (*domonstrative Publizität*).[8]

As a result of these processes, the original notion of 'public opinion' was undermined. The creating and probing of public opinion through 'publicity', 'public relations work' and 'public opinion research' replaced discursive will formation. The critical functions of the public sphere were thoroughly weakened.

Habermas notes a number of counter tendencies to these developments. For instance, 'the weakening of the public sphere as a principle is opposed by the extension of fundamental rights in the social welfare state. The demand that information be accessible to the public is extended from organs of the state to all organizations dealing with the state'. To the extent that this is actualized aspects of the public sphere can be upheld. But the public sphere could only be fully realized today on an altered basis – 'as a rational organization of social and political power under the mutual control of . . . organizations committed to the public sphere in their internal structure as well as in their relations with the state'.[9] The rise of 'technocratic consciousness' and the institutions that support it, make this, Habermas concluded in his early work, an unlikely possibility.

Towards a Rational Society and several essays in *Theory and Practice* outline some of the major social forces which have combined in recent times to alter the structure of society and state.[10] In particular, Habermas stresses two developmental trends which have become marked in advanced Western capitalism in the last quarter of the nineteenth century: an increase in state intervention in order to stabilize economic growth, and the growing mutual dependence of research and technology, which has turned the sciences into a leading force of production.[11] The permanent regulation of the economic process arose to combat and correct the dysfunctional tendencies – dysfunctional, that is, for the private utilization of capital – which are generated through the business cycle. With the advent of large-scale investment in research and development, science, technology, and industrial production were interlocked. Since then 'industrial research has been linked with research under government contract, which primarily promotes scientific and technical progress in the military sector. From there information flows back into the sectors of civilian production'.[12] Thus technology and science contribute significantly to productivity and production. Surplus value is no longer simply dependent on labour power; it is generated also by scientific technical innovation. As a consequence, Marx's labour theory of value is undermined: his theory of base and superstructure, as well as his theories of ideology and class struggle, are also affected by these developments.[13]

The base and superstructure of society could only be analysed separately while the polity and civil society were distinct spheres. As civil society is no longer 'autonomously' regulated through the market, the relationship between base and superstructure must be reassessed. To do this it is no longer sufficient to restrict attention to economic analysis; for the burgeoning of state intervention has altered both economic and political life. It has altered the former by restructuring economic activity and displacing economic crisis tendencies (an idea which I will return to later). It has altered the latter by transforming the structure of ideology and communication. The classical capitalist ideology of fair exchange is eroded as the exchange process increasingly operates under direct political regulation. This amounts to a repoliticization of many social institutions: the power that once operated indirectly over the exchange process is superseded by the more 'visible hand' of the state.[14] A new form of legitimation is required – one that ensures sufficient latitude for state intervention to secure both the private utilization of capital and mass loyalty to the system. This requirement is met to a considerable extent by the depoliticization of practical issues.

The immanent development of the capitalist economy produces 'objective exigencies' which must be met if social and political stability is to be maintained.[15] Accordingly, politics takes on a peculiarly 'negative character'. It becomes oriented towards the avoidance of risks and the eradication of dangers to the system: 'not, in other words, towards the *realization of practical goals* but towards the *solution of technical problems*'.[16] The tasks governments face appear as if they can be solved only by science and technology. Propaganda can then refer to the necessary role of the experts and the important position of science in the economy 'in order to explain why in modern societies the process of democratic decision-making about practical problems loses its function and "must" be replaced by plebiscitary decisions about alternative sets of leaders of administrative personnel'.[17] The legitimation system of advanced capitalism, thus, tends to become a technocratic one, based upon the ability of groups of administrators, technicians and politicians to guarantee a minimum level of welfare, manage the economy successfully and sustain economic growth.

Technocratic consciousness is both more and less ideological than all previous ideologies. It is 'less ideological' because it does not have the 'opaque force of a delusion that only transfigures the implementation of interests'. It does not express, in any straightforward sense, an interpretation of interaction grounded in an idealized view of life. On the other hand, it is 'more ideological' than its predecessors for it is 'more irresistible and farther-reaching'.[18] In veiling practical problems it 'severs the criteria for justifying the organization of social life from any normative regulation of interaction'. By apparently eliminating the distinction between the practical and the technical it represses '"ethics" as such as a category of life' and blocks reflection on the many factors and practical orientations which determine social processes.[19] Technocratic consciousness fulfils the ideological function of legitimating the pursuit of particular interests. It conceals behind a facade of objective necessity the interests of classes and groups that actually determine the function, direction and pace of technological and social development.[20]

At the core of technocratic consciousness is instrumental reason. At the centre of technocratic domination is the creeping erosion of the institutional framework of society, the realm of symbolic interaction, by systems of purposive-rational action. The growth of technological control in society ultimately implies, Habermas argues, 'an entire organization of society: one in which technology, become autonomous, dictates a value-system – namely, its own – to the domains of praxis it has usurped'.[21] Specifically, Habermas notes four levels of progressive rationalization of technical control.[22] The first is in the application of techniques generated by science to social problems for the realization of specific goals. The second emerges when there is a conflict between competing technical solutions on the first level. This type of conflict is rationalized in decision theory. On the first two levels, values are isolated from rational decision procedures and enter into the process as subjectively given goals. The technical values of efficiency and economy tend to dominate the selection of means. The ends as such cannot be questioned within the terms of the procedures: they admit only of compromise between competing parties. As decision theory rationalizes choice of techniques, however, the operative value systems also change; for values themselves are subject indirectly to a pragmatic test of their validity.[23] This testing of values becomes particularly necessary when a system is confronted with a conflict situation in which there is a rationally operating opponent who has a choice between various plans of action. At this point, a third level of rationalization becomes relevant – technical rationality is extended directly to values themselves. Here all previous value orientations are measured against a basic formalized value – survival or successful self-assertion. Actor strategies are then clarified in terms of a specific technical task, namely standing up to the opponent. All other value systems are discounted. This type of strategic decision-making framework can be widened to subsume all decision situations. At this point, a fourth level of rationalization becomes possible, a level on which decision-making could be completely delegated to computers. A cybernetically centered systems theory (oriented around the primary goal of reproduction and self-maintenance) can, Habermas speculates, become the basis for the automatic analysis and steering of action systems in complex environments.

Habermas regards this fourth level of rationalization as the stage towards which modern technocratic politics is moving. Its ideal is a cybernetically self-regulated organization of society – 'a negative utopia of technical control over history'. He notes, of course, that this technocratic goal has nowhere been realized; the institutional framework of society is not fully absorbed by systems of purposive-rational action. But he sees the removal of decisions from the bulk of humanity's control as a distinct possibility. As a consequence, he is extremely critical of systems theory (although he adopts aspects of it for his own programme). His debate with Niklas Luhmann must be understood in this light.[24]

While class and privilege still remain integral elements of advanced capitalism, class conflict, Habermas argues, recedes behind conflicts which, although often explosive, do not affect the central structures of society. Following an analysis by Claus Offe, Habermas holds that 'open conflicts about social interests break out with greater probability the less their frustrations have dangerous consequences for the system'.[25]

State-regulated capitalism, which emerged from a reaction against the dangers to the system produced by open class antagonism, suspends class conflict. The system of advanced capitalism is so defined by a policy of securing the loyalty of the wage earning masses through rewards, that is, by avoiding conflict, that the conflict still built into the structure of society in virtue of the private mode of capital utilization is the very area of conflict which has the greatest probability of remaining latent. It recedes behind others, which, while conditioned by the mode of production, can no longer assume the form of class conflicts. This means *not* that class antagonisms have been abolished but that they have become latent. The political system has incorporated an interest – which transcends latent class boundaries – in preserving the compensatory distribution facade.[26]

There are, of course, conflicts over wages, conditions of work, etc., but these are quickly resolved in most cases. While more violent and destructive forms of conflict do erupt, they are, Habermas holds, usually a result of uneven development, disproportionately scattered state intervention (which produces areas in need of urgent development), and the general 'displacement of the conflict zone from the class boundary to the underpriviliged regions of life'.[27]

These developments have significance, Habermas maintains, not only for the relevance of Marx's ideas and theories but also for his emphasis on political economy as the most suitable approach to the study of society. Political economy, Habermas concludes, is an insufficient basis for the development of a theory of society. Many of Marx's basic assumptions require new formulations. In order to understand the alternative positions Habermas has in mind it is useful to examine his works which discuss Marx directly. Through his critique of Marx (and, as is revealed in the next section, Freud) one can grasp why and how he sets out to reconstruct social theory.

Marx and historical materialism

Habermas engages with Marx's work in a number of his major writings. Of these his comments in *Knowledge and Human Interests* and *Zur Rekonstruktion des Historischen Materialismus* are the most important.[28] In *Knowledge and Human Interests* he explores 'a fundamental unresolved tension' in Marx which, he claims, has contributed to the positivist atrophy of Marx's social theory, on the one hand, and to the justification of technocratic social management in, for example, East European societies, on the other. In *Zur Rekonstruktion des Historischen Materialismus* he seeks to reconstruct historical materialism. By *reconstruction* he means 'taking a theory apart and putting it back together again in a new form, in order to attain more fully the goal that it has set for itself'.[29] I shall begin by elaborating his position in *Knowledge and Human Interests*.

In his empirical investigations and in his work on historical materialism, Marx, in Habermas's view, always takes account both of productive labour and practical activity or, as Habermas most often expresses it, both of work and interaction. Marx incorporates an analysis of the way human beings reproduce the material conditions of their lives (transforming their material world) with an analysis of the mode in which they interpret and alter their institutions in historical struggles (establishing and changing their identities).[30] His concrete social inquiries embrace both the material (economic) basis of society and the institutional framework, the structure of symbolic interaction and the role of cultural tradition. Marx draws on analytic distinctions between two, dialectically related, 'dimensions' of the reproductive process of society. On the one hand, there is the realm of scientific-technical progress which is characterized by 'epochal innovations' – the forces of production. On the other hand, there is the institutional realm – the relations of production – which distributes rewards, obligations, and charges. The latter comprises forms of social integration (domination) and social conflict (class struggle). The course of institutional change is marked by stages of reflection through which the 'dogmatic character of surpassed forms of domination and ideologies are dispelled'.[31]

The human self-formative process is viewed, then, as dependent on both confrontation with nature in production and on the transformation of society in social struggles. Marx's theory of capitalism develops within this frame of reference; it attempts to take account of both technical and practical activity. It is at one and the same time an analysis of the crisis-ridden dynamics of capitalism and a critique of ideology; it is both an analysis of political economy (*qua* political-economic activity) and a critique of political economy (*qua* an incorrect theory of such activity). It is both science and criticism, a theory of exploitation, etc., which *also* conceives of itself as the critical consciousness of revolutionary practice.

But Marx's self-understanding, Habermas argues, is inconsistent with this categorial framework. In reflection on his own work in, for instance, his preface to *A Contribution to the Critique of Political Economy*, Marx had a strong tendency to reduce practical to technical activity: technical activity (or productive labour or instrumental action) becomes the paradigm for the analysis of sensuous, practical activity.

Marx does not actually explicate the interrelationship of interaction and labour, but instead, under the unspecific title of social praxis, reduces the one to the other, namely communicative action to instrumental action . . . the productive activity which regulates the material exchange of the human species with its natural environment, becomes the paradigm for the generation of all the categories, everything is resolved into the self-movement of production. Because of this, Marx's brilliant insight into the dialectical relationship between the forces of production and the relations of production could very quickly be misinterpreted in a mechanistic manner.[32]

On the level of philosophical anthropology and epistemology Marx's 'brilliant insight' would require a concomitant distinction between humans as tool-making and as language-using animals. In contrast, however, at both levels Marx has a strong tendency to incorporate the latter in the former.

The reductionist tendency in Marx's thought is complemented by his misunderstanding of the epistemological and methodological status of his own enterprise. On Habermas's account, although Marx himself 'established the science of man in the form of critique and not as a natural science, he continually tended to classify it with the natural sciences',[33] Marx makes frequent analogies between the status of his work and that of the natural sciences. Habermas regards this demand for a natural science of man, with its positivist overtones, as astonishing – although not difficult to explain. It is a logical consequence of a framework restricted to instrumental action. If patterns of interaction are tied to a feedback relation with production, then it is possible to describe these patterns in the same terms as those used for the productive process. If interaction is not an independent dimension of human activity, if it is reduced to technical activity, then knowledge of social processes can be developed by searching out laws which operate 'independently' or 'over the heads' of human agents. The emphasis on critique in Marx's concrete studies is displaced by a concern for nomological knowledge: an emphasis on the interplay between freedom and necessity gives way to an exclusive emphasis on necessity (determinism). Marx failed, Habermas contends, to work out a satisfactory metatheory which would relate work and interaction and the respective forms of knowledge that are generated in each domain. There is an unresolved tension in his work between the reductionism and positivism (or scientism, as Habermas sometimes writes) of his general theoretical approach and the critical, dialectical character of his concrete social investigations.[34]

In the work of Engels, Lenin, Bukharin and Stalin, among others, Habermas claims, this tension was resolved in favour of reductionism and positivism. Dialectics uncovered (guaranteed) the unity of humans and nature.[35] The objective workings of every branch of life were thought to be accessible. Accordingly, knowledge of the laws of motion of history made possible the control of social processes in a manner analogous to the control exercized by the natural sciences. With knowledge (apparently) available about the outcomes of social processes, the possibility existed of taking the objectively correct course of action in any given situation. Prediction allows control in accord with the facts. Thus science – developed as dialectical materialism – legitimizes technocratic activity and centralized management by 'experts'. The import of the subject's own reflections on his or her activity or on the practices of the party and state is eclipsed. Indeed, from the point of view of those that wield 'objective knowledge' these reflections are superfluous; for the emancipation of the subject follows, in principle, automatically from the scientific control of the objective structures of history.

Habermas's own notion of critical theory, elaborated in the following chapters, seeks to reformulate the philosophical and methodological foundation of Marxism so as to unambiguously prevent the critical enterprise from becoming a support of technocratic ideology. But he is not just concerned, as previously indicated, with the philosophical problems of Marxism. In *Zur Rekonstruktion des Historischen Materialismus* he assesses some of the basic concepts and assumptions of historical materialism as they were explicated by Marx and subsequent orthodox Marxists.[36] In his view, Marx's theory of capitalist development (worked out in the *Grundrisse* and *Capital*) is a 'subtheory' of historical materialism. Accordingly, historical materialism is not a guide or a method but rather 'a theory of social evolution, which, owing to its reflective status, is also informative for purposes of political action'.[37] Although Habermas feels that the 'stimulus from historical materialism has not yet been exhausted', he thinks that it 'requires revision in many respects'. Many of the difficulties derive from Marx's emphasis on the forces of production as the motor of history:

Whereas Marx localized the learning processes important for evolution in the dimension of . . . the *productive forces* – there are in the meantime good reasons for assuming that learning processes also take place in the dimension of moral insight, practical knowledge, communicative action, and the consensual regulation of action conflicts – learning processes that are deposited in more mature forms of social integration, in new *productive relations*, and that in turn first make possible the introduction of new productive forces.[38]

Habermas focuses his discussion of historical materialism on what he takes to be its two basic concepts –'social labour' and the 'history of the species' (which is linked to the idea of 'developmental sequences of modes of production') – and its two fundamental theorems – the theory of 'base and superstructure' and the theory of (crisis) development, that is, the 'dialectic of the forces and relations of production'.

For Marx the concept of 'socially organized labour' specifies the way human beings (as opposed to animals) reproduce their lives. According to Habermas, however, recent anthropological findings contradict this thesis; socially organized labour and economic life forms characterize not only *Homo sapiens* but also *hominids*.[39] Marx's notion 'reaches too deeply into the evolutionary scale'. While social labour is fundamental to *Homo sapiens*, it is their form of social organization – along kinship lines – that marks, Habermas argues, their distinctiveness. The institutionalization of a *father role* (with the establishment of the incest taboo between father and daughter and a familial social structure) created the specifically human form of reproducing life. This evolutionary development was dependent on the emergence of linguistic communication which enabled the formulation of a system of social roles and norms.

Habermas stresses that language is one of the crucial media through which the social life of the human species unfolds. The evolutionary disjuncture between human and animal occurs because at the socio-cultural stage of development (human) animal behaviour is reorganized by the structure of linguistic communication. Linguistically produced intersubjectivity cannot be achieved without interchange about both particular experiences and patterns of interpersonal relations. This, Habermas suggests, is an expression of the specifically human interpenetration of cognitive abilities, action motives and linguistic intersubjectivity. In this process language functions as a kind of transformer; 'since psychic processes such as sensations, needs, and feelings are fit into the structures of linguistic intersubjectivity, inner episodes of experiences are transformed into intentional contents, that is, cognitions into statements, needs, and feelings into normative expectations (precepts and values)'. The transformation produces a distinction 'rich in consequences' between the 'subjectivity of opinion, of wanting, of pleasure and pain on the one hand, and the utterances and norms which appear with a claim to generality [*Allgemeinheitsanspruch*] on the other'. Social systems reproduce themselves, Habermas maintains, through actions incorporating claims to generality and validity.[40] Production and socialization, social labour and systems of roles (the familial principle of organization) are, he concludes, 'equally important for the reproduction of the species'.

Marx conceives the historical process as a discrete series of stages of development. Social labour produces both the material conditions of life and a particular historical dynamic. The key to the reconstruction of the 'history of the species' is, on this account, the concept of 'mode of production'. A mode of production is characterized, according to Habermas, by a specific state of development of the forces of production – forces comprising the labour power of producers, technical knowledge in so far as it is converted into means and techniques of production, and organizational knowledge in so far as it is used for the deployment of labour – and a specific form of social intercourse (relations of production) – those institutions and social mechanisms that regulate access to the means of production and determine indirectly the distribution of social wealth and the 'interest structure' of society.[41] In the orthodox Marxist version of historical materialism (most clearly elaborated by Stalin), social evolution is seen as passing through five stages of development, from the primitive communal to the ancient, feudal, capitalist and socialist modes of production.[42] The course of history, in this view, 'sets down the *unilinear, necessary, uninterrupted, and progressive development of a macro [or species-] subject*'. Habermas has strong analytical and empirical objections to this position.

He argues, first, that historical materialism must reject (and does not need) the notion of an evolving macro-subject. 'The bearers of evolution are rather societies and the acting subjects integrated into them.'[43] Second, it is important to distinguish 'the rationally reconstructible *pattern* ['rules for possible problem-solving'] of a hierachy of more and more comprehensive structures [of purposive-rational and communicative action], from the *processes* through which the empirical substrates develop'.[44] He does not reject the idea of teleology in history but aims to develop an acceptable formulation of it. He seeks to defend the thesis that *if* a society is involved in evolution – a matter which itself depends on empirical circumstances – there is development of a cumulative kind which 'exhibits direction'. Both in the spheres of technical and practical activity progressive rationalization can occur. New technically useful knowledge and moral-practical knowledge can be employed to develop and advance the forces of production and the basic institutions of society. The complex claims embedded in this view will be elaborated later. Third, Habermas maintains that recent anthropological and historical research creates important difficulties for the schema of modes of production because many different societies combine elements of several different 'modes'; the concept is often hard to apply and leaves unresolved significant questions (for example, can paleolithic societies be distinguished from neolithic'societies on the basis of the primitive communal mode of production? Does state-regulated capitalism mark 'the last phase of the old [capitalist] mode of production or the transition to a new one?'); the concept of mode of production is an insufficient basis for distinguishing some of society's most important characteristics (for instance, the complex patterns of interaction which are not in a simple feedback relation to production).[45]

These and other considerations, Habermas concludes, require the development of an approach to the 'history of the species' which would allow both the grasp of developmental-logical structures and the analysis of complex historical conditions. This, he believes, can be achieved by working, on the one hand, at higher levels of generalization than Marx, and, on the other, by paying more attention to specific empirical mechanisms. In order to lay the basis for this programme the Marxian concept of social formation is introduced along with the notion that each formation is 'determined by a principle of social organization'. By principle of organization Habermas understands those innovations which institutionalize levels of societal learning. The organizational principle of a society determines 'ranges of possibility' within which: particular dimensions of institutions can be changed; available productive forces can be utilized; new productive forces can be developed; and system complexity can be heightened.

A principle of organization consists of regulations so abstract that within the social formation which it determines a number of functionally equivalent modes of production are possible. Accordingly, the economic structure of a given society would have to be examined at two analytic levels; firstly in terms of the modes of production that have been concretely combined in it; and then in terms of that social formation to which the dominant mode of production belongs.[46]

Habermas attempts a tentative classification of social formations and organizational principles in both *Legitimation Crisis* and *Zur Rekonstruktion des Historischen Materialismus*. In the former this is undertaken through an analysis which seeks to pinpoint the 'institutional core' that determines the dominant forms of social integration, for instance, kinship in primitive societies, class domination in a political form in traditional societies. In the latter this is achieved by bringing societies under the perspective of a developmental logical series; that is, by classifying, according to evolutionary features, the forms of social integration determined by principles of social organization.[47] (By a 'form of social organization' Habermas means, following Durkheim, the establishment of 'the unity of a social life-world through values and norms'.)

The theory of base and superstructure was elaborated by Marx in order to uncover the social forces which play a leading role in social evolution. For Marx the 'basic domain' of society is constituted by the forces and relations of production; they form an economic structure that delimits the realm in which the most testing problems for a society are generated. The identification of the 'base' of society with economic structures is, however, according to Habermas, inadequate for the comprehension of many different forms of society. The 'base' need not be the *economic* realm. For if relations of production are understood as the mechanisms that regulate access to the means of production and indirectly determine the distribution of social wealth, then it can be seen that they have, in the past, been rooted in non-economic social institutions. 'In primitive societies this function was performed by kinship systems, and in civilizations by systems of domination. Only in capitalism,, when the market, along with its steering function, also assumed the function of stabilizing class relationships, did the relations of production come forth as such and take on an *economic* form'.[48] It was only at this point that the 'base' actually coincided with the economic subsystem.

The institutional nucleus around which the relations of production are formed determines a particular 'form of social integration'. If problems emerge which cannot be solved within a society's dominant framework of integration, its identity is threatened: it is in crisis. In Marx's analysis, societal crises develop as a result of the 'dialectic of forces and relations of production'; the endogenous development of the productive forces create structural incongruities with the relations of production. Habermas has both an empirical and analytic objection to this position. He notes, first, that the events which led to the first civilizations and to the rise of European capitalism 'were not conditioned but followed by the significant developments of productive forces'.[49] In other words, the forces of production did not in these cases create the conditions for an evolutionary thrust. Second, the theorem of forces and relations itself fails to explain *how* and *why* the structural problems facing a mode of production are solved – how and why the 'evolutionary step' to new forms of social integration is taken. Habermas proposes the following answer: the species learns both in the dimension of technically useful knowledge and in the dimension of moral–practical consciousness decisive for, respectively, the development of productive forces and the structures of interaction.[50] Social evolution comprises a 'learning process' which can be reconstructed on the basis of a developmental logic. The notion of a developmental logic is taken from the cognitive-developmental approach to psychology (Piaget) and moral consciousness (Kohlberg). It implies a structured sequence of development in which there are qualitatively distinct stages, each of which must be passed through if development is to be fully advanced. Individual elements of a particular stage comprise a structured whole: they represent, as Kohlberg puts it, 'an underlying thought–organization which determines responses to tasks which are not manifestly similar'.[51] The schemata of each stage

are ordered in an *invariant and hierarchically structured sequence*. This means that no later phase can be attained without passing through all those preceding it; further, that in later stages of development the elements of earlier phases are transformed [*aufgehoben*] and re-integrated at a higher level; and moreover that for the sequence as a whole a direction of development can be specified.[52]

Although there does, on Habermas's account, seem to be a pattern of development of technology, one can 'get behind the level of the history of technology'.[53] Taking his cue once more from Piaget, he suggests that the evolution of technology might well be explained, in part, by reference to the developmental sequence of formal structures of thought – 'from preoperational through concrete-operational to formal-operational thought'.[54] (So far he has only offered a number of clues as to how this idea might be further elaborated.) If this strategy were successful one would have an account of the logic of technical development – the logic behind the development of the productive forces. This would not yet be, however, an analysis of the actual historical development of these forces; for the genesis of them, Habermas insists, cannot be understood independently of changing patterns of world views. 'The evolution of world views mediates between the stages of development of interaction structures and advances in technically useful knowledge.'[55]

The rationality structures that find expression in world views, and which become a practical force in social movements and institutions, have 'a strategically important position from a theoretical point of view'.[56] The approach Habermas takes to their analysis has changed over time, particularly from *Knowledge and Human Interests* to *Legitimation Crisis* and more recent work. It is important to outline his position in the early as well as the later writings in order to understand more fully: the emphasis on belief systems and moral representations; how he develops these issues; why he draws extensively on social psychology.

Freud, social psychology and normative structures

In *Knowledge and Human Interests* Habermas takes Freudian psychoanalysis as an exemplar for critical theory.[57] His interest in Freud's work is first and foremost in its theoretical and methodological structure. However, he stresses that certain elements of Freud's substantive theory can be usefully employed to supplement and enrich Marx's conception of the nature of social organization.[58] Specifically, he argues that in Freud's later work – in his contributions to social theory and social psychology – there are systematic insights into the origins and functions of social institutions which aid the elucidation of the concepts of social power and ideology.

According to Habermas, Freud understood institutions as the manifestation of 'historically required repression of instinctual drives' which result from 'the conflict between surplus impulses and conditions of collective self-preservation'.[59] Faced with conditions of scarcity, human beings – in order to survive – are forced to adapt to their environment in ways which prevent 'complete gratification of instinctual desires'. The process of adaptation is the central principle behind Freud's conception of social organization. On Habermas's interpretation, Freud held that there are important similarities between the development of the individual and the development of the species.[60]

As long as the pressure of reality is overpowering and ego organization is weak, so that instinctual renunciation can only be brought about by forces of affect, the species finds collective solutions for the problem of defense, which resemble neurotic solutions at the individual level. The same configurations that drive the individual to neurosis move society to establish institutions.[61]

The effectiveness of social institutions in facilitating survival occurs at the cost of repression of wants and needs. This repression is operationalized through the development of patterns of distorted communication on a social scale.

Freud distinguished, Habermas claims, the forces and relations of production, in a way similar to Marx. He understood that the level of necessary social repression was a function of the level of development of productive forces; as the technical power of a society to control the forces of outer nature increases, the constraints of scarcity are progressively overcome, thus decreasing the degree of socially necessary repression. As the level of repression diminishes, the institutional framework of a society *can* be changed to accommodate a higher level of needs gratification. The impetus for such a change emerges from the experience of members of a given society who suffer as a result of repression. Beyond the level of general repressions which are imposed on all members alike, there are, Habermas points out (in accord with Marcuse), class-specific privations and denials. Hence the classes who experience the most deprivation and suffering are potentially the least integrated into society and the most likely source of radical change.

It is Habermas's contention that by conceiving of social institutions as the result of repressed needs and, therefore, as the source of distorted and limited communication, Freud was able to give a better account of ideology than Marx. Marx was unable, given his focus on production and labour, to develop a satisfactory conception of ideology and power as distorted communication. This is reflected in his tendency to conceive the development of social organization in terms directly dependent on the productive process. Freud, on the other hand, by focusing on the development of socially expressible needs and motivational patterns, was able to perceive that the power of social norms 'is based on a defence which enforces substitute-gratifications and produces symptoms as long as it is a result of unconscious mechanisms and not of conscious control'.[62] Accordingly, although a precondition of emancipation is 'the extension of objective possibilities by the productive forces, there is no certainty that emancipation will follow automatically from greater technical progress.'[63] For emancipation entails not only overcoming constraints of nature, like scarcity, but also dissolving systems of distorted communication. In Habermas's view, historical materialism must be supplemented by a theory of ideology understood in terms of distorted communication.

In order to investigate capacities for the eradication of barriers to self-reflection and communication Habermas has turned his attention to the study of linguistic, cognitive, moral, interactive and psychosexual development.[64] He thinks that a developmental-logic for the ontogenesis of action competence – particularly of moral reasoning – has already been plausibly established. His aim is to elaborate both a general model of individual development and a model of the development of forms of social integration. This is clearly an enormous project which, Habermas recognizes, is only at a very early stage in its formulation. But he hopes to establish an integrated framework for the analysis of communicative competence and, thus, for the analysis of the conditions and possibilities of individual and social development. It is only in such a framework, he believes, that systematic answers can be given to questions concerning human capabilities.

Habermas thinks that ontogenetic models of developmental processes provide a number of important clues for the unravelling of social evolution, although, he stresses, one cannot draw from them any direct conclusions about developmental levels of societies.[65] The models provide insights into the structures of consciousness of socialized individuals and into the structures of social institutions ('the infrastructure of action systems'); for 'individuals acquire their competencies not as isolated monads but by growing into the symbolic structures of their life-worlds'.[66] It is Habermas's view that within the history of the individual and the species homologous structures of consciousness can be uncovered in three domains: ego development and the evolution of world views, ego and group identities, and moral judgements and actions of individuals and legal and moral systems. The investigation of the evolution of forms of social integration requires analysis and study of these different areas before a framework can be developed for their interrelation. The first two areas, Habermas notes, have had little systematic attention. In *Zur Rekonstruktion des Historischen Materialismus* he devotes some space to their consideration.

Ontogenesis can be examined by focusing on the capability for cognition, speech and action. These three aspects of individual development can, Habermas maintains, 'be brought under one unifying idea of ego development – the ego is formed in a system of demarcations. The subjectivity of internal nature demarcates itself in relation to the objectivity of a perceptible external nature, in relation to the normativity of society, and in relation to the intersubjectivity of language'.[67] Habermas analyses the process –

'very tentatively' – into a number of stages of development: the 'symbiotic' (where there are no clear indications of a demarcation of subjectivity); the 'egocentric' (subject and object are differentiated but judgements are linked to a 'body-bound perspective'); the 'sociocentric-objectivistic' (clear differentiation of the environment into physical and social domains, awareness of the 'perspectival character of one's own standpoint'), and the 'universalistic stage' (subject can become free of the 'dogmatism of the given and existing', systems of ego demarcation become reflective).[68] A similar series of stages of demarcation can, Habermas conjectures, be found in world views.

In both dimensions, development apparently leads to . . . an ever clearer categorical demarcation of the subjectivity of internal nature from the objectivity of external nature, as well as from the normativity of social reality and the intersubjectivity of linguistic reality.[69]

At the level of world views he distinguishes a number of stages of development from the 'magical – animistic representational world' of paleolithic societies (which are centered in tribal life) to the establishment of universalistic forms of intercourse in contemporary society (governed by rules which can, in principle, be subjected to reflection and transformation). To date Habermas claims only that his work has rendered plausible the idea that there are 'homologies between the structures of the ego and world views'.[70]

From a more socio-psychological viewpoint he has examined the formation of ego and group identities.[71] He distinguishes three essential stages of the development of the former: 'natural identity' (based on the temporal continuity and the character of the child's body); 'role identity' (based on intersubjectively recognized, stable expectations) and 'ego identity' (based on the individual's capacity to construct identities and integrate them into an 'unmistakable life history').[72] Habermas contends that the pattern of development of individual identity is a key to uncovering the change of collective identities. 'In both dimensions identity projections apparently become more and more general and abstract, until finally the projection mechanism as such becomes conscious, and identity formation takes on a reflective form.'[73] Although he qualifies the comparison, he clearly sees parallels between the genesis of individual and collective identity. The development of societies from the neolithic to the modern world displays similar stages to those of the histories of the individual.[74]

However, Habermas's main concern hitherto has been with an examination of what he calls one of the 'core domains of interaction' – law and morality. Law and morality represent arrangements and orientations to resolve action conflicts on the basis of agreement. They mark both the moral consciousness of the individual and the regulations of society. Following Kohlberg, who has studied patterns of moral consciousness in ontogenesis, he outlines three important stages or structures of consciousness: the preconventional, conventional and postconventional.[75]

At the *preconventional stage*, at which actions, motives, and acting subjects are still perceived on a single plane of reality, only the consequences of action are evaluated in cases of conflict. At the *conventional stage*, motives can be assessed independently of concrete action consequences; conformity with a certain social role or with an existing system of norms is the standard. At the *postconventional stage*, these systems of norms lose their quasi-natural validity; they require justification from universalistic points of view.[76]

The different stages represent modes of problem solving, the ability to make moral judgements. Habermas appears to be in little doubt that the different stages of moral consciousness uncovered in cognitive developmental pyschology can be found in the social evolution of moral and legal systems.

As in the behaviour of individuals, different 'stages' can be present simultaneously in a given social formation. In order to grasp this Habermas stresses that it is necessary to distinguish the core structures that underlie and serve to maintain the consensual regulation of conflict from the general structures (the institutions and norms) that underpin 'normal interaction' (for example routines of daily life) with relatively little conflict. If one also distinguishes the expression of moral consciousness in the judgement of conflicts from processes of actively resolving them, then one is in a position, he suggests, to offer a tentative sketch of levels of social integration. These can be summarized as follows:

1 In Neolithic societies normal interaction is conventionally structured mythical world views, which are still interlaced with the action system, contaii, conventional patterns of conflict resolution; the legally institutionized regulation of conflicts is, however, tied to preconventional points of view (such as assessment of the consequences of action ... restoration of the status quo ante).

2 In archaic civilizations normal interaction is conventionally structured; mythical world views, set off from the system of action, take on the

function of providing legitimation for the occupants of dominant positions; conflicts are regulated from the standpoint of a conventional morality tied to the dominant figure who administers the law or represents justice (evaluation according to intentions, transition from retaliation to punishment, from group to individual liability).

3   In developed civilizations normal interaction is conventionally structured; there is a break with mythical thought and the formation of rationalized (cosmological and monotheistic) world views containing postconventional moral representations; conflicts are regulated from the point of view of a conventional morality disengaged from the person of the ruler (expanded system of legal administration, law dependent on tradition but systematized).

4   In early modern societies certain spheres of interaction are structured postconventionally – spheres of strategic action (such as capitalist enterprise) are regulated universalistically, and there are the beginnings of political will-formation grounded on principles (formal democracy); legitimating doctrines are developed along universalistic lines (rational natural law, for example); conflicts are regulated from the point of view of a strict separation of legality and morality (general, formal, and rationalized law; private morality guided by principles).[77]

Reconstruction of historical materialism

On Habermas's account, therefore, learning takes place in two central dimensions: moral-practical insight and empirical-analytic knowledge. The results of learning are passed down in cultural traditions. These traditions provide the essential resources for social movements; a cognitive potential for dealing with disturbances and crises in the reproductive process of society. Cultural traditions are the basis of the rationalization of action. The table on page 283 outlines Habermas's conception of the essential elements of the rationalization process.[78] Despite his emphasis on the centrality of both these dimensions Habermas holds that the development of normative structures 'is the pacemaker of social evolution, for new principles of social organization mean new forms of social integration; and the latter, in turn, first make it possible to implement available productive forces or to generate new ones'.[79]

Habermas is quick to point out that his description of patterns of normative structures (and of the development of productive forces) is not in itself a theory of social evolution – it is a depiction of a '*development logic* inherent in cultural traditions and institutional change'. It says nothing about the '*mechanisms* of development'; it tells us only 'something about the range of variations within which cultural values, moral representations, norms and the like – at a given level of social organization – can be organized'. The actual developmental dynamics of normative structures are dependent upon system problems conditioned by economic circumstances, and the learning processes that emerge in reaction to them.[80] In this sense culture remains, on Habermas's account, 'a superstructural phenomenon, even if it does seem to play a more prominent role in the transition to new developmental levels than many Marxists have heretofore supposed'. As a consequence, he claims, his approach remains materialist and historical.

The analysis of developmental dynamics is 'materialist' insofar as it makes reference to crisis-producing systems problems in the domain of production and reproduction; and the analysis remains 'historically orientated' insofar as it has to seek the causes of evolutionary changes in the whole range of those contingent circumstances under which (a) new structures are acquired in the individual consciousness and transposed into structures of world views; (b) systems problems arise, which overload the steering capacity of a society; (c) the institutional embodiment of new rationality structures can be tried and stabilized; and (d) the new latitude for the mobilization of resources can be utilized. Only after rationalization processes (which require explanations that are both historical and materialist) have been historically completed can we specify the patterns of development for the normative structures of society. These developmental logics betoken the independence – and to this extent the internal history – of the spirit.[81]

It is important to keep in mind that social evolution proceeds at two levels: 'in processes of learning and adaption *at each given* level of learning (until its structural possibilities are exhausted) and in those unlikely evolutionary thrusts that lead to new learning levels'.[82] The emergence of problems which overload the 'adaptive capacity' of society is a contingent matter. If such problems do arise whether and how they are resolved depends on 'access to new stages of learning'. Solutions to severe crises require both attempts to alter existent forms of social integration, and a social environment that can sustain such attempts.[83] Evolutionary learning, the constructive movement to new stages, is subject to, at least, two initial conditions:

on the one hand, unresolved system problems that represent challenges; on the other, new levels of learning that have already been achieved in

Rationalization of action

	Purposive-rational action	Communicative action
Learning dimension	Objectivating thought	Moral-practical insight
Action can be rationalized in terms of	*a* empirical efficiency of technical means *b* consistency of choices between means	*a* moral-practical aspect of responsibility of acting subject *b* Justifiability of underlying norms
Rationalization of action requires	*a* technically utilizable, empirical knowledge *b* testing of inner consistency of value systems and decisions maxims and correct derivation of choices	*a* truthfulness of intentional expressions *b* justification of rightness of norms
Rationalization of action affects	productive forces	normative structures, forms of social integration
Rationality embodied in	technology, strategies, organizations, qualifications	mechanisms of regulating conflict (law and morality), world views, identity formation
'Rationalization'	growing capacity to control outer nature, development of productive forces	expansion of realm of consensual action, overcoming of systematically distorted communication

world views . . . but are not yet incorporated in action systems and thus still remain institutionally inoperative.[84]

Crisis and the development of capitalism

For Habermas, the history of the species can be reconstructed as the history of humanity's increasing capacity for freedom from the vicissitudes of both environmental and personal conditions: people's autonomy is dependent upon developments in the spheres of production and normative structures of interaction. This history, however, is also the history of crises. There is no guarantee that these crises will be resolved – there is no guarantee of progress.

Habermas reinforces this point in his discussion of the 'dialectic of progress'. Whilst maintaining the existence of developmental stages, he points out that 'the extent of exploitation and repression by no means stands in inverse proportion to these levels of development.' New stages of learning expand both choices and the range of possible problem solutions. A higher level of, for example, productive forces does remove certain burdens. But new problems arise which can (to the extent that they are comparable with the older problems) increase in intensity.

The dialectic of progress can be seen in the fact that with the acquisition of problem solving abilities new problem situations come to consciousness . . . suffering from the contingencies of an uncontrolled process gains a new quality to the extent that we believe ourselves capable of rationally intervening in it. This suffering is then the negative of a new need. . . . At every stage of development the social-evolutionary learning process itself generates new resources, which mean new dimensions of scarcity and thus new historical needs.[86]

Habermas develops his programme through the application of the general theory of social evolution to the development of specific societies or social formations. In particular, he focuses on the emergence of class societies organized around a state and on the possibilities of a 'post-modern' society. In his discussion of the development of class societies he draws heavily on the work of his associate Klaus Eder. Since this material has already been summarized in a recent article (and in *Zur Rekonstruktion des Historischen Materialismus*) by Habermas himself I will not repeat it here.[86] The second focus is essentially the topic of *Legitimation*

Crisis. The key themes of this text will be elaborated in the remainder of the chapter.

The analysis of late capitalism offered by Habermas is set within the terms of his theory of evolution. Before turning to this analysis it is useful to explicate briefly his concept of social crisis. In a brief history of the concept he suggests that the idea is often associated with an objective force which deprives subjects of part of their sovereignty; resolution of the crisis implies a liberation of the subject caught in it. A scientifically useful concept of crisis, Habermas argues, must retain this idea while grasping the connection between social integration and system integration.

We speak of social integration in relation to the systems of institutions in which speaking and acting subjects are socially related (*vergellschaften*). Systems are seen here as *life-worlds* that are symbolically structured. We speak of system integration with a view to the specific steering performance of a self-regulated *system*. Social systems are considered here from the point of view of their capacity to maintain their boundaries and their continued existence by mastering the complexity of an inconstant environment. Both paradigms, life-world and system, are important.[87]

The notion of crisis implies, when used with respect to social systems, a change in the identity of the system itself. The question is, how do we know when a society has changed its identity?

The identity of a society can, Habermas thinks, be regarded from two points of view. From the perspective of a systems theoretic approach, identity change involves alterations of structures essential to the stability and maintenance of a particular social configuration, for example the wage–capital structure in capitalism. The difficulty for systems theorists is that they must be able to distinguish which are in fact the essential structures of a given society. Obviously, not all changes of structural elements endanger the system's identity. From a different point of view, that taken by action theory (or an interpretative theory), we can talk of the identity of a society as it is experienced and understood by the members of that society. Social systems appear here under the aspect of a 'life-world' which is symbolically constituted in terms of normative structures, values, and institutions. On the level of social integration, crises are felt as a threat to the social identity of an individual or as an impetus for an individual to actively change that identity. The difficulty here, of course, is that 'a society does not plunge into crisis when, and only when, its members so identify the situation'.[88] To rely exclusively on either approach would be a mistake.

If the paradigm of systems theory is reduced to that of the life world of action theory, the issues of systems steering and control of essential structures are screened out; investigations stay at the level of commonsense or everyday knowledge of social procedures. If, on the other hand, there is an attempt to reduce the life-world to a systems theoretic approach, we are faced with the danger of losing sight of the realization that social reality is constituted through the meaningful interaction of social agents who, in the last instance, determine the tolerance levels of social conditions. What is needed, Habermas therefore maintains, is the integration of the two approaches in a historically oriented analysis of social systems.[89]

Using the concept of an organization principle, Habermas claims that it can be determined for a given social formation first, if and how 'system and social integration can be functionally differentiated'; second, 'when dangers to system integration must result in dangers to social integration'; and third, how problems of control and maintenance develop into dangers to identity, 'that is, what type of crisis predominates'.[90]

Given this conceptual framework we can turn to Habermas's examination of capitalism in *Legitimation Crisis*. He first provides an analysis of liberal capitalism which follows Marx closely. He explicates the organization principle as the *relationship of wage labour and capital*. The fundamental contradiction of capitalism is formulated as that between social production and private appropriation, namely social production for non-generalizable interests. But here, in Habermas's view, a number of questions arise. Have events in the last one hundred years altered the mode in which this contradiction affects the dynamic of society? Has the logic of crisis changed (from the path of crisis growth, unstable accumulation, to something fundamentally different)? Does the developmental dynamic of advanced capitalism ward off economic crises permanently? If so, are there consequences for patterns of social struggle? Several of these questions informed Habermas's early writings. However, the way he now addresses them represents a marked development of his earlier views.

The model of advanced capitalism Habermas uses follows many well known recent studies.[91] He begins by delineating three basic sub-systems, the economic, the political-administrative, and the socio-cultural. The economic sub-system is itself understood in terms of three sectors: a public sector and two distinct types of private sector. The public sector – industries such as armaments and space – is oriented towards state production and consumption. Within the private sector, a distinction is made between a sector which is still oriented towards market competition and an oligopolistic sector which is much freer of market constraints. Advanced capitalism, it is claimed, is characterized by capital concentration and the spread of oligopolistic structures.

Habermas contends that crises specific to the current development of capitalism can arise at different points. These he lists as follows:

Point of origin	System crisis	Identity crisis
(Sub-systems)		
economic	economic crisis	
political	rationality crisis	legitimation crisis
socio-cultural		motivation crisis

His argument is that late-capitalist societies are endangered from at least one of four possible crisis tendencies. It is a consequence of the fundamental contradiction of capitalist society that, other factors being equal, there is either an economic crisis because the 'requisite quantity' of consumable values are not produced; or a rationality crisis because the 'requisite quantity' of rational decisions are not forthcoming; or a legitimation crisis because the 'requisite quantity' of 'generalized motivations' are not generated; or a motivational crisis because the 'requisite quantity' of 'action-motivating meaning' is not created. The expression 'the requisite quantity' refers to the extent and quality of the respective sub-system's products: 'value, administrative decision, legitimation and meaning'.[92]

The reconstruction of developmental tendencies in capitalism are pursued in each of these dimensions of possible crisis. For each sphere theorems concerning the nature of crisis are discussed, theories which purport to explain crisis evaluated, and possible strategies of crisis avoidance are considered. 'Each individual crisis argument, if it proves correct, is a sufficient explanation of a possible case of crisis.' But in the explanation of actual cases of crises,

Habermas stresses, 'several arguments can supplement one another'.[93]

At the moment, in Habermas's opinion, there is no way of cogently deciding questions about the chances of a self-transformation of advanced capitalism. He does not exclude the possibility that economic crises can be permanently averted, although only in such a way that contradictory steering imperatives, which assert themselves in the pressure of capital utilization (social production for non-generalizable interests), produce a series of other crisis tendencies. That is *not* to say economic crises will be avoided, but that there is no '*logically necessary*' reason why the system cannot mitigate the crisis effects as they manifest themselves in one subsystem. The consequences of controlling crises in one subsystem are, however, achieved only at the expense of displacing and transforming the contradictions into another. What is presented is a typology of crisis tendencies, a logic of their development and, ultimately, a postulation that the system's identity can only be preserved at the cost of individual autonomy – with the coming of a totally administered and manipulated world.

Two theorems of economic crises are mentioned but only the first is important and will be discussed here. This is the orthodox Marxist thesis that the crisis tendency is still determined by the law of value; 'that is, the structurally necessary asymmetry in the exchange of wage labour for capital'. Under these conditions 'the state cannot compensate for the tendency of the falling rate of profit'.[94] The state cannot intervene substantially in the economic process 'without setting off an "investment strike"; nor can it avoid, in the long run, cyclical disturbances of the accumulation process . . . nor can it even control crisis substitutes, that is, chronic deficits in the public budget and inflation'.[95]

Habermas has two objections to this orthodox view. The first is that by uncritically utilizing the conceptual strategy of value theory, the economic theory of crisis is deprived of a possible empirical test. It cannot dogmatically be assumed that the law of value still holds; that is, that commodities still exchange at their value. The increasing role of the state has, Habermas argues (as he did in *Towards a Rational Society*), altered the form of the production of surplus value. In particular, governmental support of the material and non-material infrastructures indirectly contributes to the production of surplus value by increasing the productivity of human labour. This is expressed in the cheapening of constant capital and a rise in the rate of surplus value. An important element of this problem is whether reflexive labour, e.g. research, administration (much of which is non-productive in the classical Marxist definition), should be regarded as productive. Habermas's position is that such labour does contribute to the production of more surplus value by altering the conditions under which surplus value can be appropriated; it is 'indirectly productive'. As a result, he concludes: 'the classical fundamental categories of the theory of value are insufficient for an analysis of governmental policy in education, technology, and science'. Furthermore, 'it is an empirical question whether the new form of production of surplus value can compensate for the tendential fall in the rate of profit, that is, whether it can work against economic crisis' – a question which has been insufficiently explored.[96]

The second argument against the continued applicability of the law of value has to do with what Habermas calls the 'quasi-political nature of the wage structure' – a wage structure determined by bargaining between opposing parties. The erosion of the free competition of the labour market has, he contends, had an effect on the price of labour taken as a commodity. The theory of value can allow for commodities other than labour to be sold above their value. Labour as a commodity, however, presents special difficulties; for it is used as the unit measure against which the deviations of other commodities are gauged. To dogmatically take the average wage, as many orthodox Marxists do, as equal to the cost of reproduction of labour power is, in Habermas's opinion, to prejudice

at the analytical level the (no doubt) empirically substantial question of whether the class struggle, organized politically and through unionization, has perhaps had a stabilizing effect only because it has been successful in an economic sense and has visibly altered the rate of exploitation to the advantage of the best organized parts of the working class.[97]

In light of these objections, Habermas holds that the nature of economic crisis cannot be established without more evidence concerning productivity and government intervention. His belief seems to be that this evidence will demonstrate the inadequacy of a purely economic analysis of crisis. For economic crisis can, in his opinion, be averted – but only through increased activity on the part of the state. This activity in turn generates its own crisis tendencies: 'rationality crises'.

Increased state activity in the interest of avoiding economic crisis forces the government to shoulder an increasing share of the costs of socialized production.[98] In addition, in order to fulfil its increasingly diversified roles, the state has to expand considerably its bureaucratic structures, thus increasing its own internal complexity. This growing complexity, in turn, entails an increased need for co-operation and more importantly, requires an ever expanding state budget. The state must finance itself through taxation, but it cannot do this in a way which will interfere with the accumulation process and jeopardize economic growth. These constraints have helped to create a situation of almost permanent inflation and crisis in public finances. If the state cannot develop adequate policy strategies within the systematic constraints it encounters, the eventual result is a breakdown in policy and planning operations. Such a breakdown can exacerbate economic situations; it can lead back to an economic crisis. But rationality crises themselves cannot be analysed simply in economic terms.

If the state is conceived of as a system on which various demands are made (for policy and administrative decisions and action), then a rationality crisis can be said to occur when 'the administrative system does not succeed in reconciling and fulfilling the imperatives received from the economic system'.[99] These imperatives are essential to maintain steady growth and accumulation. The major theorem of the rationality crisis which Habermas discusses claims that the crisis results from the anarchistic, unplanned nature of commodity production being transferred onto the administrative system. This situation arises from the position of the state in the accumulation process. 'On the one hand, the state is supposed to act as a collective capitalist.' In this role, it acts to safeguard the accumulation process as a whole. 'On the other hand, competing individual capitals cannot form or carry through a collective will as long as freedom of investment is not eliminated.'[100] Thus particularized interests of capital press for competing policy decisions, none of which may coincide with the general interests of the whole. In this situation, the state supposedly cannot initiate coherent and consistent planning measures and thus lapses into a 'rationality deficit'. But rationality crises are not, Habermas argues, inevitable. He has three objections to a belief that they are.

First, in the administrative system contradictions are expressed as policy failures, but these lie within thresholds of tolerance which are hard to determine; there are no clear criteria of failure as there are in the economic realm (for example unemployment, bankruptcy). Thus we cannot prejudge the state's ability or inability to adjust to a contradictory environment. Second, the state can make its policy alternatives visible to its conflicting clients, thereby opening up a possible bargaining, compromise opportunity. Third, since the state can consciously formulate its objectives and alternatives, it is less likely to fall prey to unintended consequences. That is to say, the anarchy of the market cannot be directly transferred into the administrative system. Therefore, the possibility of avoiding a rationality crisis cannot be ruled out.[101].

The state's decisions, of course, are not merely based on economic considerations. Whilst on the one hand, the state has the task of sustaining the accumulation process, on the other, it must also maintain a certain level of 'mass loyalty'. In order for the system to function, there must be a general compliance with the laws, rules, etc. Although this compliance can be secured to a limited extent by coercion, societies claiming to operate according to the principles of bourgeois democracy depend more on the existence of a wide spread belief that the system adheres to the principles of equality, justice and freedom. Thus the capitalist state must act to support the production process and at the same time act, if it is to protect its image as fair and just, to conceal what it is doing. If mass loyalty is threatened, a tendency toward a legitimation crisis is established.

As the administrative system expands in late capitalism into areas traditionally assigned to the private sphere, there is a progressive demystification of the nature-like process of social fate. The state's very intervention into the economy, education, etc., draws attention to issues of choice, planning and control. The 'hand of the state' is more visible and intelligible than 'the invisible hand' of liberal capitalism. More and more areas of life are seen by the general population as politicized, as falling within its (via the government's) potential control. This development, in turn, stimulates ever greater demands on the state. If the administrative system cannot fulfil these demands within the potentially legitimizable alternatives available to it, while at the same time avoiding economic crisis, that is, 'if governmental crisis management fails . . . the penalty . . . is the withdrawal of legitimation'.[102] The underlying cause of the legitimation crisis is the contradiction between class interests. 'In the final analysis, this class structure is the source of the legitimation deficit.'[103] The state must secure the loyalty of one class while systematically acting to the advantage of another. As the state's activity expands and its role in controlling social reality becomes more transparent, there is a greater danger that this asymmetrical relation will be exposed. Such exposure would only increase the demands on the system. The state can ignore these demands only at the peril of further demonstrating its non-democratic nature.

To this point the argument establishes only that the advanced capitalist state might experience legitimation problems. Is there any reason to expect that it will be confronted by a legitimation crisis? It can be maintained that since the second world war, Western capitalism has been able to buy its way out of its legitimation difficulties (through fiscal policy, the provision of services etc.). While demand upon the state may outstrip its ability to deliver the goods, thus creating a crisis, it is not necessary that this occurs. In order to complete his argument, therefore, and to show – as he seeks to – that the legitimation crisis is the central and predictable form of crisis confronting advanced capitalism, Habermas must demonstrate that needs and expectations are being produced (on the part of at least a section of the population) which will 'tax the state's legitimizing mechanisms beyond their capacity'.

Habermas's position, in essence, is that the general development of late capitalism, and in particular, the increasing incursion of the state into formerly private realms, has significantly altered the patterns of motivation formation. The continuation of this tendency will lead, he contends, to a dislocation of existing demands and commitments. Habermas analyses these issues under the heading 'motivation crisis'. 'I speak of a motivation crisis when the socio-cultural system changes in such a way that its output becomes dysfunctional for the state and for the system of social labour.'[104] This crisis will result in demands that the state cannot meet.

The discussion of the motivation crisis is complex. The two major patterns of motivation generated by the socio-cultural system in late capitalist societies are, according to Habermas, civil and familial-vocational privatism. Civil privatism engenders in the individual an interest in the output of the political system (steering and maintenance performances) but at a level demanding little participation. Familial-vocational privatism promotes a family orientated behavioral pattern centred on leisure and consumption, on the one hand, and a career interest orientated towards status competition, on the other. Both patterns are necessary for the maintenance of the system under its present institutions. Habermas argues that these motivational bases are being systematically eroded in such a way that crisis tendencies can be discerned. This argument involves two theses: (1) that the traditions which produce these motivations are being eroded, and (2) that the logic of development of normative structures prevents a functionally equivalent replacement for the eroded structures.

The motivational patterns of late capitalism are produced, Habermas suggests, by a mixture of traditional pre-capitalist elements (for example the old civic ethic, religious tradition) and bourgeois elements (like progressive individualism and utilitarianism). Given this overlay of traditions, thesis (1) can itself be analysed into two parts: (*a*) that the pre-bourgeois components of motivational patterns are being eroded and (*b*) that the core aspects of bourgeois ideology are likewise being undermined by social developments. Habermas acknowledges that these theses can only be offered tentatively; they are intended as aids for future research.[105]

The process of erosion of traditional (pre-bourgeois) world views is argued to be an effect of the general process of rationalization. This process results in, among other things: a loss of an interpretation of the totality of life; and the increasing subjectivizing and relativizing of morality. With regard to thesis (1) (*b*), that the core elements of bourgeois ideology are being undermined, Habermas examines three phenomena: achievement ideology, possessive individualism, and the orientation towards exchange value.[106] The idea of endless competitiveness and achievement seeking is being destroyed gradually as people lose faith in the market as a fair distributor of scarce values (as the state's very intervention raises issues of distribution and as the increasing level of education provides aspirations and expectations that cannot be co-ordinated with occupational opportunity etc.). Possessive individualism, the belief that collective goals can only be realized by private individuals acting in competitive isolation, is being undermined as the development of the state, with its contradictory functions, is (ever more) forced into socializing costs and goals of urban life. Additionally, the orientation to exchange value is weakening as larger segments of the population – for instance, welfare clients, students, the criminal and sick, the unemployable – no longer reproduce their lives through labour for exchange value (wages), thus 'weakening the socialization effects of the market'.

The second thesis – that the logic of development of normative structures prevents a functionally equivalent replacement of eroded traditions – also has two parts. They are (*a*) that the remaining residues of tradition in bourgeois ideology cannot generate elements to replace those of destroyed privatism; but (*b*) that the remaining structures of bourgeois ideology are still relevant for motivation formation. With regard to (*a*), Habermas looks at three elements of the contemporary dominant cultural formation: scientism, post-auratic or post-representational art, and universalistic morality. He contends that in each of these areas, the logic of development is such that the normative structures no longer promote the reproduction of privatism and that they could only do so again at the cost of a regression in social development, that is, in increased authoritarianism. In each of these areas the changing normative structures embody tendencies towards universality and critique. It is these last and developing elements which undermine privatism and which are potentially threatening to the inequalities of the economic and political system.

But the undermining of privatism does not necessitate that there will be a motivation crisis. If the motivations being generated by the emerging structures are dysfunctional for the economic and political systems, one way of avoiding a crisis would be to 'uncouple' (an obscure notion in Habermas's writings) the socio-cultural system from the political-economic system so that the latter would no longer be dependent on the former.[107] To complete his argument Habermas must make plausible the contention that the uncoupling process has not occurred and that the remaining structures are still relevant for some type of motivation formation. His claim is that evidence from studies of adolescent socialization patterns (from Kenniston and others) and such phenomena as the students' and women's movements indicate that a new level of consciousness involving a universalistic (communicative) ethic is emerging as a functional element in motivation formation. On this basis he argues that individuals will increasingly be produced whose motivational norms will be such as to demand a rational justification of social realities. If such a justification cannot be provided by the system's legitimizing mechanisms, on the one hand, nor bought off via distribution of value on the other, a motivational crisis is the likely outcome – the system will not find sufficient motivation for its maintenance.

Habermas's conclusion, then, is that, given its logic of crisis tendencies, organized capitalism cannot maintain its present form. If his argument is correct, then capitalism will either evolve into a kind of 'brave new world' or it will have to overcome its underlying class contradiction. To do the latter would mean the adoption of a new principle of organization. Such a principle would involve a universalistic morality embedded in a system of participatory democracy, providing the opportunity for discursive will-formation. What exact institutional form the new social formation might take Habermas does not say; nor does he say, in any detail, how the new social formation might evolve.

11   Interests, knowledge and action

If emancipation is to remain a project for humanity, if a 'brave new world' is to be avoided, it is essential, Habermas argues, to counter the influence of 'scientism' in philosophy and other spheres of thought. 'Scientism means . . . that we no longer understand science as *one* form of possible knowledge, but rather identify knowledge with science.'[1] Habermas's critique of scientism focuses on its relation to positivism, since positivism provides scientism's most sophisticated defence. Although positivism began life as a critique of ideology (of religion, dogma, speculative metaphysics, etc.), it became a central element of technocratic consciousness and a key aspect of modern ideology. While Habermas's treatment of this issue recalls a familiar Frankfurt school theme – the critique of instrumental reason – his analysis is original, as is his formulation of the relationship between knowledge and human activity. In outlining his position a variety of his writings will be drawn upon, particularly those published in the 1960s. *Knowledge and Human Interests*, perhaps the best known of these works, explicates some of the key themes in this area. But other works which examine the relationship between knowledge, interests and action, for example, *Zur Logik der Sozialwissenschaften*, will also be consulted.

Knowledge and Human Interests investigates the 'dissolution of epistemology' in the last two centuries. Since Kant, Habermas argues, epistemology as the critique of knowledge has been progressively undermined. As a result, science can no longer be comprehended by philosophy; science can no longer be understood as merely one category of knowledge. For the rise of scientism resulted in a radical de-emphasis of what had been the traditional concern of the critique of knowledge – inquiry into conditions of possible knowledge as well as into the meaning of knowledge as such. Epistemology became increasingly restricted to an examination of questions internal to methodology, thereby losing sight of the significance of the role of the epistemic subject (the knower) and of reflection by the subject on his or her activities.[2] The possibility of philosophy taking a critical approach to knowledge dissolved.[3] From an epistemological standpoint there could be no attempt to question the meaning or function of science because there was no source of knowledge held to be independent of science by which to criticize its results. As Habermas puts it, 'the meaning of knowledge itself becomes irrational – in the name of rigorous knowledge'.[4]

If critical theory is to remain a possibility, it is necessary, Habermas contends, to understand the activity of the knowing subject and, in particular, the moment of reflection and of self-understanding. In *Knowledge and Human Interests* he seeks to do this by analysing the connections between knowledge and human interests. On his account, knowledge must discard the illusion of objectivism – the idea that 'the world appears objectively as a universe of facts whose lawlike connection can be grasped descriptively'.[5] The illusion conceals the processes in which facts are constituted, and thereby 'prevents consciousness of the interlocking of knowledge with interests from the life-world'.[6] For Habermas, it should be recalled, knowledge is formed in virtue of three interests: 'information that expands our power of technical control; interpretations that make possible the orientations of action within common traditions; and analyses that free consciousness from its dependence on hypostatized power'.[7] The knowledge-constitutive, or knowledge-leading, interests are *general* interests; they are underlying modes through which reality is disclosed and acted upon. They delineate a general orientation which yields a *viewpoint* from which reality is constituted. The basic cognitive strategies of the human species are determined by the conditions and problems governing its reproduction; that is, 'by the sociocultural form of life *as such*'.[8] It is Habermas's contention that 'the critique of knowledge is possible only as social theory'.[9]

The critique of knowledge

Kant understood science as one category of possible knowledge. But the framework within which he comprehended the different types of knowledge was problematic. His successors criticized the framework, focusing in particular on what he took as given: the transcendental conditions (categories and forms of intuition) and his concept of the subject constituted within these conditions.[10] Hegel sought to supersede Kant's project by reflection on the forms of knowledge that emerge in human experience. Such reflection aims, on Habermas's interpretation, to reveal the 'dimension within which transcendental determinations themselves take form', that is, the process in which the conditions of knowledge are themselves generated.[11] But although Hegel successfully revealed weaknesses in Kant's project – weaknesses connected with Kant's ahistorical conception of the epistemic subject and the knowing process – he failed to provide an adequate basis on which science and knowledge generally could be understood. In accord with Horkheimer and Adorno, Habermas argues – although for somewhat different reasons – that Hegel's project is severely flawed. For in asserting philosophy itself to be the authentic science, it mischaracterized the relation between science and philosophy. Instead of understanding the empirical sciences as one category of possible knowledge, it dissolved their independent status in a philosophy of Absolute Spirit. The claim, however, that philosophy represents 'universal scientific knowledge' was not made good by Hegel; indeed, it was unmasked, Habermas contends, by 'the actual fact of scientific progress, as bare fiction'.[12]

Marx provided the 'guide' to appropriating Hegel's insights while demythologizing them. By tracing the genesis of possible experience to social labour, to 'the process of social reproduction of the species', he uncovered, according to Habermas, the basis for comprehending the epistemic subject, the knowing process, and social change. But the ambiguity in Marx's *epistemological* categories – the reduction of 'practical activity' to labour, of praxis to *techne* – meant that he too failed to satisfactorily ground epistemology in social theory.[13] 'All the elements of a critique of knowledge radicalized by Hegel's critique of Kant are present in Marx and yet not combined to construct a materialist epistemology.' Habermas elaborates the ambiguity in Marx's theory of knowledge by reference to what he calls its Kantian and Fichtean strains.

Kantian residues can be found in Marx's view that humans have an invariant relation to nature in which they struggle to satisfy their needs and reproduce themselves in the realm of necessity. For Marx the labour process represents 'the perpetual natural necessity of human life'. The conditions of possible objects of experience are rooted in 'a deep-seated structure of human action' – the 'universal structure of mediation constituted by labouring subjects'. The Kantian dimension of Marx's thought suggests that people are engaged in a trial-and-error encounter with nature in everyday life, acquiring, inquiring and learning in the realm of feedback-controlled action. The resultant knowledge increases the range of control over nature and the capacity to transform the world. But the instrumental relation to nature does not alter in this process; it is invariant, for the natural processes over which humans must secure control to reproduce life cannot be overturned. As Marx wrote in a letter to Kugelmann: 'natural laws can absolutely not be abolished. What can change in different historical states is only the forms in which these laws take effect'.[14] The historically changeable effect of natural laws is conditioned by the level of productive forces.

While dependent on the 'labour of the entire previous course of world history', the human subject achieves its identity only through the comprehension of its 'self-positing struggles'.[15] The struggle for identity, according to Habermas, represents the *Fichtean* moment of Marx's analysis. For Marx this moment refers, of course, to a self-conscious positing in historical struggles, not to a logical relation between ego and nonego (as Fichte understood the elements of the self-formative process). The mechanisms for the achievement of self-consciousness are not those determined by the extension of technical control; rather, they involve a complex struggle for reflection and understanding. Habermas holds that the Fichtean moment of self-formative activity is logically irreducible to the Kantian dimension of human action. However, since Marx reduced the self-constituting act of reflection to a feedback relation to the productive process, he deluded himself about the nature of reflection and critical activity. Although, in Habermas's view, Marx retained important insights from the philosophy of reflection at the level of social theory, he failed to recognize its implications for the epistemological and methodological status of his own work. Natural science becomes his basic paradigm for knowledge; the technical interest becomes the key knowledge-guiding interest. The sciences of humans – instead of appearing under the categories of knowledge for the enhancement of self-reflection – appear under categories of knowledge for control.[16] In the materialist synthesis Marx relegates the Fichtean moment to an area bounded by the Kantian, on the one hand, and Darwin's theory of evolution, on the other. Marx failed to distinguished between the logical status of the empirical-analytic sciences and the sciences of humankind as critique. On Habermas's account the elaboration of this distinction is crucial to the adequate development of a science of human beings.

Positivism and the empirical-analytic sciences

In *Knowledge and Human Interests* Habermas engages in a critique of positivism. Its main purpose is to retrieve 'a *dimension* of the problem of knowledge which [positivism] had effaced', namely, the dimension in which it is acknowledged that knowing subjects play an active role in constituting the world they know.[17] But Habermas does not offer a simply negative assessment of this school of thought. He recognizes that positivist philosophy had an initially liberating intent; its concern to provide a criterion for a strict separation between science and metaphysics was motivated by the desire to dispel all dogmas – all modes of thought that placed themselves beyond empirical test and relevant independent controls. The exclusive concern with science, and in particular, natural science, had, he thinks, a certain plausibility in the eighteenth and nineteenth centuries. The results of scientific activity were impressive; science appeared to offer the road to salvation. But the preoccupation with science and, in philosophy, with an examination of its methodology, impaired the understanding of the 'meaning' and 'import' of knowledge. This tendency reinforced technocratic consciousness. On Habermas's account, scientific knowledge, while a necessary condition, is certainly not sufficient for human emancipation.

Habermas regards the critique of positivism as a necessary prolegomenon to the re-establishment of philosophy as critique. In order to place positivism, both its advances and limitations, in perspective, it is necessary, he argues, to examine the position as it has developed over the last one hundred years. He takes as his task the reconstruction of 'the prehistory of modern positivism'.[18] He focuses on the thought of Comte, Mach and Peirce.[19] He believes that by systematically examining the works of these men and by exploring certain questions within the philosophy of science, positivism can be brought to the point of transcending its own limitations. The discussion of Mach and Peirce is particularly significant; the exposition below will concentrate on Habermas's interpretation of their thought. It is his contention that positivism, as expounded by individuals like Mach, cannot understand science and scientific activity. He thinks that Peirce's writings in the prag-matist tradition provide a more adequate conception of scientific inquiry and a basis for uncovering the *conditions* of scientific knowledge.

In Comte's writings positivism did not appear in its purest form; for it was interlaced with a philosophy of history which gave an account of the development of science in the evolution of the human species. Such a philosophy was held to be necessary in order to 'interpret the meaning of positive knowledge'.[20] As sci-ence developed in the nineteenth century, however, it became less and less important to justify its status by reference to its relation to other things. Positivism 'shed' its philosophy of history and became increasingly scientistic. Although there is a tension in Mach's work between an evolutionary perspective and an adher-ence to phenomenalism (crudely, the doctrine that phenomena – the immediately perceived – are the only objects of science), his writings on the latter were extremely influential and were often thought to provide a relevant epistemology for science.[21]

Mach's phenomenalism was inspired by a particular science, a new science, 'energetics'.[22] Following ideas from this developing discipline, he argued that a scientific object exists if 'its symbol is the name of a set of particular perceptions'. Scientific entities are uncovered in ordered bundles of observations abstracted from the flux of immediate sense experience.[23] Although this notion served to aid both the elimination of cherished metaphysical (unobserv-able) aspects of scientific theories, and to provide a basis for the unification of various sciences into a general science of sensed experiences, it had several other important, but unexplicated, con-sequences. Of these, the conflation of appearance and reality is central.

Facts (Mach's term) are given in sensory experience. Since sci-ence is held to merely describe and correlate these facts, it is objectivistic – it is assumed that it 'adequately describes reality as it is'.[24] But the facts which constitute the world on this view have, according to Habermas, an ambiguous status. On the one hand, they are subjective. They are given in sensory experience and expressed in terms of individual observation reports. On the other hand, they must be established as intersubjectively valid, if science is to be viewed as objective. The ambiguity was not resolved by Mach. If the objective, intersubjective aspects of the facticity of the world are emphasized, then positivism falls into a circle. 'If

science describes facts and their relations, and if we use this criterion to demarcate science from metaphysics, then we need a criterion of facticity in order to know if a science is genuine. One way
to avoid this demand is to ontologize facts or sensations and, with
Mach, make them the given in experience. Subjectivism is then
ruled out *a priori*.'[25] But if science is distinguished principally as a
methodological procedure for correlating assortments of facts – as
it was by Mach – the status of the ontology is problematic. Habermas expresses the difficulty as follows:

> How. . . *prior* to all science, can the doctrine of elements [facts] make
> statements about the object domain of science as such, if we only obtain
> information about this domain *through* science? [26]

In order to guarantee the objectivity of science Mach was led to
assume an objectivistic perspective and to posit an ontology of
facts. Since these assumptions cannot be justified (except circu-
larly) science itself remains ungrounded.[27]

Habermas's position implies that Mach's philosophy generates
difficulties which render it incapable of understanding science. The
world of intersubjectivity and social practice remains unthematized, much less accounted for. However, it is insufficient to found a
critique of positivism merely on an examination of phenomenalism; not all positivist programmes are of this type. The logical
positivists, for example, realized the inadequacies of their early
commitment to phenomenalism. By the mid 1930s, Carnap, one of
the leading figures of the school, accepted a physicalist position.[28]
This position allowed for observation reports to be made in terms
of physical objects and coordinates which were supposedly intersubjectively accessible. The physicalist thesis made possible the
doctrine of the unity of science – the possible reduction of all
knowledge to a single conceptual framework. But while this version of positivism avoids some of the difficulties facing Mach's
position, it too, Habermas argues, is open to a number of objections.

In trying to establish a single framework for knowledge, positivists must either presuppose as unproblematic the availability of an
intersubjectively constituted language, or assume, as Karl-Otto
Apel expresses it, a position of 'methodical solipsism'. This
amounts to 'the tacit assumption that *objective* knowledge should
be possible without *intersubjective* understanding by communication being presupposed'.[29] In either case, positivists are unable,

within their own terms of reference, to account for the possibility and nature of ordinary language and of intersubjective agreement in general. While adhering to the programme of a unified science, positivists could not, Habermas argues, recognize that there are methodological procedures appropriate to understanding communicative interaction and intersubjectivity, procedures which differ from those utilized to gain knowledge of objectified processes of nature. The import of these differing procedures arises from the fundamental difference, previously mentioned, between the interaction of a subject with an object, which can be regarded as another subject, and that of a subject with an object which cannot be so construed. In the former case, we have dialogic or communicative interaction; in the latter case monologic or instrumental activity.

Insofar as the employment of symbols is constitutive for the behavioural system of instrumental action, the use of language involved is monologic. But the communication of investigators requires the use of language that is not confined to the limits of technical control over objectified natural processes. It arises from symbolic interaction between societal subjects who reciprocally know and recognize each other as unmistakable individuals. This *communicative action* is a system of reference that cannot be reduced to the framework of *instrumental action*'.[30]

In a position parallel to Habermas, Apel argues that the fundamental shortcomings of positivism spring from a lack of reflection 'upon the fact that all cognition of objects presupposes understanding as a means of intersubjective communication'.[31] Science, he contends, is unintelligible *qua* human activity, if one cannot understand the implicit and explicit conventions and rules, or more generally, the communication community or language game, which it presupposes. On his account, even tacit conventions about the use of words – 'not to mention explicit conventions about definitions, theoretical frameworks, or statements of facts in empirical science' – imply 'an intersubjective consensus about situational meanings and aims of practical life'.[32] Science, in its adoption of procedural conventions, goes beyond the

scientific rationality of operations on objects which could be performed in a repeatable way by exchangeable human subjects . . . and passes into the realm of a . . . *pre-* and *meta-scientific rationality* of intersubjective discourse mediated by *explication of concepts* and interpretation of intentions.[33]

The additional dimension of rationality needed to understand science entails the presupposition of what Apel calls, under the inspiration of Wittgenstein's later philosophy, the '*a priori* of communication' – a dimension of communication that is both a condition of the possibility of science, and the basis for the understanding of science as a particular mode of activity.[34]

In *Knowledge and Human Interests*, Habermas argues that Peirce was one of the first philosophers to realize the need to systematically reflect on science and to go beyond a limited positivist position in order to understand the logic of science and its relation to action.[35]

What separates Peirce from both early and modern positivism is his understanding that the task of methodology is not to clarify the logical structure of scientific theories but the logic of the procedure with whose aid we obtain scientific theories.[36]

While Habermas argues that Peirce, ultimately, failed to appreciate that the intersubjective basis of scientific beliefs cannot be understood within the terms of a science of objectified processes, he is fundamentally in agreement with the spirit of Peirce's project – to uncover the connections between knowledge, inquiry and action, and to reveal thereby science's foundations in human beings' practical activity.

Central to his interpretation of Peirce is the idea that science only systematizes and formalizes the procedures required for the successful completion of certain types of activity. On this account, the knowledge generated by the methods of natural science, or by the methods of all empirical-analytical sciences, is to be understood as the reflected form (*Reflexionsform*) of learning processes already posited within the framework of instrumental action (activity used for the control of the external conditions of existence).[37] Scientific inquiry represents a refinement of the conceptual framework according to which reality is constituted in relation to purposive-rational, feedback-monitored action.

The process of inquiry . . . (1) isolates the learning process from the life process. Therefore the performance of operations is reduced to selective feedback controls. (2) It guarantees precision and intersubjective reliability. Therefore action assumes the abstract form of experiment mediated by measurement procedures. (3) It systematizes the progression of knowledge. Therefore as many universal assumptions as possible are integrated into theoretical connections that are as simple as possible.[38]

Empirical-analytic science is the necessary outcome of disturbances or disruptions in routinized intercourse with nature; it aims to eliminate problematic situations which emerge from disappointed expectations.

The theoretical connections made within this type of science have the form of hypothetico-deductive systems. Particular phenomena are conceived in terms which allow their subsumption under hypothetically proposed general concepts. Through the use of such concepts, knowledge is generated which makes possible the duplication of conditions and the reproducibility of results. Thus, empirical-analytic knowledge is predictive knowledge.

Theories compromise hypothetico-deductive connections of propositions, which permit the deduction of lawlike hypotheses with empirical content. The latter can be interpreted as statements about the covariance of observable events; given a set of initial conditions, they make predictions possible.[39]

Theory is connected to action by means of certain operations and activities, in particular, systematic observation, experimentation, and operations of measurement.[40] These actions and the (monologic) language required to express them objectify reality under the conditions of a 'restricted mode of experience'.[41] Objects constituted as observable are at one and the same time objects whose behaviour can be described in causal laws and objects which are instrumentally manipulable. Observation or basic statements, therefore, 'are not simple representations of fact in themselves', but rather expressions of 'the success or failure of operations'.[42] Facts are constituted through particular structures of experience and action. In the empirical-analytic sciences they are generated through 'an *a priori* organization of our experience in the behavioural system of instrumental action'.[43] The logical structure of admissible propositions and the conditions of their corroboration suggest that, within this type of science, theories 'disclose reality subject to the constitutive interest in the possible securing and expansion, through information, of feedback-monitored action. This is the cognitive interest in technical control'.[44] There is a systematic relationship between the form of knowledge claims and the uses to which such knowledge can be put.

In his discussion of Peirce, Habermas attempts to demonstrate that natural science is oriented toward the production of technically useful information: although Habermas does not reduce natural science to a simple or crude instrumentalism, he claims that it can be understood as oriented toward the production of knowledge which can be used for the manipulation and control of the environment. While not every study or inquiry in the natural (or behavioral) sciences need produce technically utilizable results, nor need have as a conscious intent the production of such knowledge,

nevertheless, with the structure of propositions (restricted prognoses concerning observable behaviour) and with the type of conditions of validation (imitation of the control of the results of action . . .) a methodical decision has been taken in advance on the technical utility of information. . . . Similarly the range of possible experience is prejudiced, precisely the range to which hypotheses refer and upon which they can founder.[45]

The interest in technically useful knowledge and the rationality which it embodies are values implicit in science – although they are frequently not recognized as such. Positivists especially do not regard them as values which need to be defended; for they identify rationality with purposive rational procedures. The methods which positivism considers scientific and therefore rational are those which allow for the gathering of knowledge useful for prediction and feedback-control operations. Theoretical knowledge and questions of scientific inquiry are, as a result, made co-extensive with technically useful knowledge. Questions of practical reason are ruled out of the range of science and beyond rational investigation. Practical questions become the province of the private individual and in the final analysis can be justified only by reference to a decision or a commitment of belief or faith. The effect on social consciousness, on interaction, is a conceptualization of problems and solutions which encourages the development of a technocratic rationality and mentality.[46] Positivism fails, however, to grasp this; it is prevented by its own presuppositions from an adequate interpretation of its own status.

In conclusion, therefore, it is Habermas's claim that science cannot be fully comprehended merely as a formal abstract system, but must be understood as a product of concrete, social activity. To view science in this way forces us not only beyond the limits of positivist presuppositions, but also beyond the framework of the empirical-analytic sciences. For the approach of empirical-analytic science – its concepts, methods and theories – is an insufficient basis from which to understand the very element of scientific activity that it presupposes, namely, human interaction and language. To grasp this domain more fully we require a different form of knowledge which, Habermas claims, is grounded in a different orientation to life.

To the extent that actions are causally produced as the effects of social and natural forces beyond the knowledge and/or control of actors, it is possible to consider them in an objectified manner. Habermas, it should be noted, does not argue that it is never appropriate to study human subjects with the methods of a causal, nomological science. Rather, the claim is that a science that restricted itself to this procedure would – by itself – be incapable of understanding social reality.

The hermeneutic sciences

In his investigation of the hermeneutic sciences, Habermas is concerned to disclose their methodological framework and constituting interest.[47] It should be borne in mind that he is not describing an ontologically distinct sphere of objects. Rather he is attempting to delineate another viewpoint from which reality is disclosed. While knowledge claims of the empirical-analytic sciences '*grasp reality with regard to technical control that, under specified conditions, is possible everywhere and at all times*', knowledge claims in the hermeneutic sciences, Habermas holds, '*grasp interpretations of reality with regard to possible intersubjectivity of action-orienting mutual understanding specific to a given hermeneutic starting point*'.[48]

Individuals act within a matrix of intersubjective meanings. These require controlled appropriation if key aspects of behaviour – not the least of which are motives, purposes and beliefs about action – are to be understood.[49] In *Knowledge and Human Interests* Habermas focuses his analysis on Dilthey's approach to these phenomena. He finds in this an important attempt to uncover the basis of the cultural sciences, although he also discovers a number of crucial limitations – limitations which lead to descripticism, objectivism and relativism and, consequently, to the loss of a critical perspective. In *Zur Logik der Sozialwissenschaften* he assesses a number of more recent attempts to lay the foundations for an interpretative approach to social life including various schools of phenomenological, hermeneutic and linguistic analysis. He discovers similar limitations in these schools. The following discussion

will focus on Dilthey and the writings of Hans-Georg Gadamer –
the men who, Habermas thinks, have provided the most important
statement on hermeneutics. The other positions, which have been
well expounded elsewhere, will only be briefly mentioned.[50]

Dilthey sought to distinguish the foundations of *Geisteswissenschaften* from those of the natural sciences. He contended that the
categories of the cultural sciences had to be sufficient to understand humans: to analyse their consciousness as expressed and
shaped in symbolic systems.[51] The respective domains of the *Geisteswissenschaften* and the natural sciences overlap only in so far as
nature enters into social interaction; but then 'nature' is viewed
from a different standpoint, as socially meaningful. While explanation, on Dilthey's account, is the cognitive task of the natural
sciences, which pursue the questions 'why?' and 'how?', the cultural sciences have a different cognitive goal – *Verstehen* (understanding). *Verstehen* attempts to answer the questions: 'What?'
'What is this item of behaviour?' 'What is this object?' Initially,
Dilthey conceptualized *Verstehen* in terms of empathy – the re-
enactment or reliving of the psychological state of one's past self
or of others. Through the use of this technique, he claimed, the
historical world could be reconstructed.[52]

Dilthey himself came to appreciate that his early formulation of
Verstehen contained a number of fundamental problems. In his
later writings he sought to address these. The following questions,
among others, were posed: how can the idea of reliving the
experience of another be made sense of? Can the problem of
Verstehen be reduced to the attempt to re-experience psychological states?[53] Gradually, Dilthey turned against the psychologism
inherent in his early works. From his revised position he argued
that the attempt to recapture a former experience was not dependent on having the same experience, but on our capacity to reconstruct the same intentional or symbolic object. The cultural scientist must recapture the meaning of social objects and of agents'
actions. Since these things are objective in the sense that they have
a publicly accessible structure, it is possible to have objective
knowledge of them. Experience does not reflect 'fundamental
organic states'; rather, it is formed by 'publicly established symbolic structures' – by language. In order to develop knowledge of a
socio-cultural phenomenon, the scientist must, at least according
to Habermas's interpretation of Dilthey, penetrate the language
and the social context of the object. Knowledge can only be

enhanced through the establishment of intersubjective understanding.[54]

But the specific meanings of experiences and actions are not determined merely by linguistic communication. The realm of the cultural sciences is more complicated than this. In Habermas's view, Dilthey postulated the 'community of life unities' – defined by the process of self-formation and ego identity, on the one hand, and a dialogic relation between subjects who reciprocally recognize each other as intentional subjects sharing meanings, on the other – as the objective framework of the *Geisteswissenschaften*. Individual life histories are constituted in the cumulative experiences of individuals over time (the diachronic dimension), and in the intersubjectivity of communication common to different subjects (the synchronic dimension). The 'community of life unities' is formed in the multitude of overlapping structural connections in which the two dimensions merge. The cultural sciences must explicate these connections if the meaning of life practices is to be grasped.[55]

Through his reading of Dilthey Habermas affirms that social scientists must learn the language of their subject/object – they 'must learn to speak the language that they interpret'.[56] But all interpretation, it is stressed, should be given the status of hypotheses; for they can be tested and changed in light of further information. As experiences, linguistic acts have a significance beyond their role as carriers of meaning within systems of grammatical structures. Since ordinary language is intertwined with practice, the meanings and experiences that an interpretation attempts to grasp can be seen as part of a 'stream of life'.[57] Linguistic analysis, therefore, also reveals 'the empirical context of indirectly communicated life experiences'.[58] If there is a manifest discrepancy between the posited interpretation and its object, it will be uncovered as a 'gap' between actions anticipated and the actual resultant actions. An interpretation fails when there is a disappointment of expectations.

Within a given social context, a disappointment of expectations takes the form of a disturbance of a certain mutuality or consensus. Such a consensus is essential to interaction and to the integration of society. Habermas quotes Dilthey with approval:

Understanding first arises in the interests of practical life. Here people are dependent on intercourse with one another. They must make themselves understandable to one another. One must know what the other wants Thus the elementary forms of understanding come into being.[59]

The possibility of creating and maintaining successful mutual interaction between two or more individuals depends on a 'bridge-head' of shared expectations and linguistic skills, and on the possibility of understanding. Without these prerequisites, the likelihood of severe conflict is enhanced. Thus knowledge of language and action – of communication structures – is directly tied to an interest in successful social action, in what Habermas calls humankind's 'practical interest'.

According to Habermas, however, Dilthey was ambiguous on the status of hermeneutics' relation to practical activity. Rather than seeing it as laying down the conditions for the possibility of knowledge, he saw in it dangers for the scientific character of hermeneutics. In a bid to maintain the ideal of pure objectivity, he fell back into objectivism and a conception of *Verstehen* which retains traces of his early psychologism.[60]

The result was a position which restricted the cultural sciences to a merely descriptive function. The link between 'science' and 'life', theory and practice, as well as between fact and value, was broken. A critical approach to a given object of study was ruled out. The categories of the cultural sciences became those of the people or social objects being studied. If all that is demanded is that interpretations of the texts (persons, cultures, or traditions) be descriptive, nothing can be said about the truth-content or possible deception (ideology) expressed by the subject. Discussion is restricted to questions concerning logical consistency and problematic areas of interpretation.

Dilthey also claimed that the process of interpreting 'another' has no necessary effects on the self-understanding and practice of the interpreter. As reality is unaffected by an 'interpretative intervention', so too is the interpreter. This position depends for its validity on, amongst other things, the possibility of a context-free, neutral observer. But such a notion contradicts the central realization of contemporary hermeneutics: that 'there is no neutral standpoint outside of history upon which the cultural scientist could base himself'.[61] Interpretations, people like Gadamer have forcefully argued, cannot escape the language, the preconceptions embedded in it, the background life-contexts, of their authors. The relation between social analysts, their language, and their subject-objects and the effects on all these of an interpretative intervention, were insufficiently explored by Dilthey.

In his investigations of more recent attempts by, for example,

Alfred Schutz, Peter Winch and Harold Garfinkel, to uncover the nature of interpretative inquiry in the social sciences, Habermas argues that many of the issues which Dilthey failed to resolve remain unsatisfactorily dealt with. In the work of these individuals there is a lapse into a form of descriptivism and relativism and the subsequent loss of ability to assess the nature of ideological distortion and the truth content of tradition; an inadequate treatment of history – of how, for instance, meaning complexes are created and renewed; an ineffective treatment of the objective context of action as social reality is essentially derived from individual activities or language games; an insufficient account of the nature and conditions of the interpretative process.[62] Clearly, a satisfactory treatment of these issues is crucial to Habermas's programme in epistemology and methodology. The plausibility of critical social theory depends on an acceptable explication of the relation between language, action and history. Habermas takes Gadamer's work to be a particularly important step towards the resolution of these problems.

Against Dilthey and others who thought that *understanding* follows life, as a method to gain access to a subject matter, Gadamer conceives it as essential 'to the original character of the being of human life itself'.[63] It is, in his view, the condition and mode of human intersubjectivity as such. The medium in which understanding itself is realized is language.[64] For Gadamer language 'is not just one of man's possessions in the world; for on it depends the fact that man has a world at all'.[65] Following Heidegger, Gadamer argues that 'language speaks its own being'; it is 'a universal ontological structure'.[66] The truth of objects 'comes-to-be' in the activity of language. The 'being that can be understood is language'. Language is the possibility-condition of truth.[67]

Language mediates between the finite historical nature of humankind and the world; it is the mechanism through which people can come to understand themselves and their relation to others. The mastery of language, referred to by Gadamer as an 'accomplishment of life' (*Lebensvollzug*), is the precondition of *Verstehen*. The problem of *Verstehen*, on Gadamer's account, emerges after language has already been learnt. Translation presents the clearest expression of what is taken as the essence of *Verstehen*: the attempt to achieve understanding in dialogue.

Verstehen is inextricably tied to the process of interpretation. It involves the interpreter's attempt to articulate in his or her own language meanings constituted in another universe of discourse. According to Gadamer 'interpretative understanding' has both a hypothetical and circular dimension. The hermeneutician or social investigator makes an initial interpretation of the meaning as a whole of, for example, a text or social institution. With further reflection and research, the conjectured interpretation can be revised and developed.[68] The process is continuously one of understanding the parts in terms of a conjectured sense of the whole, and altering the latter in light of better knowledge of the former. A 'unity of sense' can be achieved if, and only if, our detailed knowledge of the parts can be integrated without being 'pulled up short' by the subject-matter.[69] Interpretations can be tested in dialogue (between the interpreter and the interpreted). For hermeneuticians, Gadamer contends, there are no standards of objectivity which can be recognized independently of the attainment of intersubjective agreement by the partners in the dialogic process. The scientists' interpretations must be based on understanding held in common with their subject-objects and expressed through the mutual satisfaction of expectations on both sides, that is, through continuing agreement on the level of both interpretation and practice.

The ideal of a neutral, detached observer is, in Gadamer's view, a myth. In contradistinction to Dilthey he accepts as unavoidable the engagement of the scientist-interpreter in a socio-historical context. Each party enters the dialogue situation with a framework of concepts, beliefs and standards – a horizon of expectations – which is the product of tradition. Tradition represents an 'effective-historical consciousness' constituted by a language community.[70] *Verstehen* entails the mediation of traditions. Interpretation renders a given subject intelligible in relation to our present horizon of understanding. A successful interpretation, however, not only makes the subject comprehensible *for us* but also preserves the subject's unique meaning. Thus, in the process of understanding 'there always takes place a real fusing of horizons'.[71] Understanding involves the interpretation of the past *as well as*, in Gadamer's words, 'something like the application of the text to be understood to the present situation of the interpreter'.[72] *Verstehen* is necessarily concerned with the 'claims to truth' of its subject matter; for this subject matter embodies answers to questions we hold. To understand at all hermeneuticians must relate the text, for instance, to their situations, their lives. Application 'co-determines understanding as a whole from the beginning'.[73] In the dialogue of understanding, description and evaluaton are inevitably intertwined.

The appreciation of the tradition-bound nature of understanding means not only that hermeneutics cannot be restricted to a purely descriptive role but that texts, experiences, actions, etc., have to be understood in their historical contexts. For once the historical dimension of understanding is established, it becomes possible to transcend the 'surface level' of intended meaning. Since tradition is the medium in which meaning is created and transmitted through time, the actions and expressions of a person can only be properly grasped within this context. As tradition lends significance to phenomena it becomes possible to conceive of them as having a meaning beyond or in conflict with that subjectively intended by their creators. Therefore, in an interpretative analysis it is necessary for the scientist-interpreter to examine whether or not there are discrepancies between manifest and intended meaning. Such discrepancies can become apparent to the analyst even in cases where the actor was not, or is not yet, aware of it. Gadamer has expressed this point forcefully.

I maintain that the hermeneutical problem is universal and basic for all interhuman experience, both of history and of the present moment, precisely because of the fact that meaning can be experienced even where it is not actually intended.[74]

There are a number of important principles that follow from Gadamer's work. First, tradition and its 'foremeanings', 'prejudgements' or 'prejudices' are not barriers to understanding but integral elements of it. Second, understanding cannot escape the historicity of traditions. Knowledge is generated within the framework of traditions; the discernment of truth has a temporal structure. As a consequence, there can be no such thing as the correct or final understanding of a phenomenon. The meaning of a text, for example, is always open to future interpretations from new perspectives. Third, since we are ourselves constituted by history and tradition the process of understanding aspects of the world contributes simultaneously to our self-formation and self-understanding. *Verstehen has an irreducible practical dimension*. Fourth, the process of self-understanding, like the process of understanding other things, can never be complete. 'History does not belong to us, but we belong to it. The self-awareness of the individual is only a flickering in the closed-circuits of historical life.'[75] Fifth, understanding is neither an ideal of human experience nor a method; rather it is 'the original form of . . . being-in-the-world'.[76] Hermeneutics is the universal principle of human thought.

In an extensive exchange with Gadamer, Habermas outlined the degree to which he accepts these views.[77] Habermas agrees that the process of coming-to-an-understanding is context-dependent; history is and remains effective in all understanding of tradition; social analysts are necessarily immersed in and engaged with their socio-historical contexts; a hermeneutical procedure is required when there is a breakdown of an action expectation; interpretative understanding has significance for self-understanding. But he rejects fundamental aspects of Gadamer's characterization of communicative action and of the condition and limits of interpretative understanding. In particular, he expresses serious reservations about the analysis of the discrepancy between experienced/manifested meaning and intended meaning, and of the nature of tradition. Within the debate between the two men these points are merged into a discussion about the authority of tradition. He also disagrees – while recognizing the importance of historicity, communication, and understanding – with Gadamer's methodological conclusions.

For Gadamer, the fact that interpretation always presupposes the supporting consensus of an ongoing tradition – a structure of forejudgements or prejudices (*Vorurteilsstruktur*) – means that there is no independent ground from which to criticize the tradition. Habermas summarizes the position as follows:

Any attempt to suggest that this (certainly contingent) consensus is false consciousness is meaningless since we cannot transcend the discussion in which we are engaged. From this Gadamer deduces the ontological priority of linguistic tradition before all possible critique: at any given time we can thus carry on critique only of individual traditions, inasmuch as we ourselves belong to the comprehensive tradition-context of a language.[78]

The underlying consensus must be treated as an authentic and legitimate domain of agreement and authority, since in Gadamer's opinion there is no way to step outside it, no standard from which to consider it otherwise, no language available that will allow us to step beyond its bounds in order to see how reality ultimately is or should be constituted. This implies that when a discrepancy is uncovered between intended and manifested meaning, the intended meaning must be interpreted within the given conceptual system of the ongoing tradition. The tradition's supporting consensus provides the standards from which the experienced meaning must be understood; for from Gadamer's point of view, theoretical and practical questions only admit of truth within the terms of reference of tradition.

Habermas takes issue with this position by challenging as dogmatic its uncritical acceptance of the underlying consensus of tradition. For him,

> every consensus, in which the understanding of meaning terminates, stands fundamentally under suspicion of being pseudo-communicatively induced. . . . the prejudgmental structure of the understanding of meaning does not guarantee identification of an achieved consensus with a true one.[79]

He is critical of Gadamer for failing to come to terms with what the Enlightenment knew, 'that the "dialogue" which (according to Gadamer) we *"are"* is also a relationship of coercion and, for this very reason, *no* dialogue at all'.[80] Gadamer fails to see the fundamental 'opposition between authority and reason'. Habermas contrasts his critical standpoint toward authority, which he considers (in agreement with Weber) as legitimized force, with what he refers to as Gadamer's dogmatic acceptance of the authority of tradition. 'Reason in the sense of the principle of rational discourse is the rock on which hitherto factual authorities are smashed rather than the rock on which they are founded.'[81]

A 'depth hermeneutics' is needed, Habermas thinks, in order to grasp the history of tradition in such a way as to reveal sources of domination and distortion in communication. Before discussing directly what this amounts to, it is worth clarifying the essential ingredients that are missing, in his opinion, from Gadamer's approach to *Verstehen* and the cultural sciences. By treating tradition and culture as self-sufficient or absolute, Gadamer fails, he maintains, to conceptualize their dependency on other social processes. Habermas agrees that 'it makes good sense to conceive of language as a kind of metainstitution on which all social institutions are dependent'. He has little difficulty with the idea that 'social action is constituted in ordinary language communication'.[82] But language can, he argues, conceal as well as reveal the conditions of social life:

[the] metainstitution of language as tradition is evidently dependent in turn on social processes that are not reducible to normative relationships. Language is *also* a medium for domination and social power; it serves to legitimate relations of organized force. In so far as the legitimations do not articulate the power relations whose institutionalization they make possible, in so far as these relations manifest themselves in the legitimations, language is *also* ideological.[83]

A systematic critique of ideology is necessary in order to comprehend the power relations which are embodied in the communicative process and actually constitute the authority relation in tradition. Tradition must be put in context by taking into account the boundaries and empirical conditions under which it develops and changes. By reducing social reality to the world of 'intersubjectively intended and symbolically transmitted meaning', Gadamer fails to appreciate that this world is 'part of a complex' that, however symbolically mediated, is also shaped by the constraint of material conditions – 'by the constraint of outer nature that enters into procedures for technical mastery and by the constraint of inner nature reflected in the repressive character of social power relations'.[84]

Social action can only be fully understood, Habermas contends, in a framework 'that is constituted conjointly by language, labour and domination'. A purely interpretative sociology cannot grasp this. An approach is required that, on the one hand 'does not suppress the symbolic mediation of social action in favour of a naturalistic view of behaviour that is merely controlled by signals and excited by stimuli' and, on the other, does not 'succumb to an idealism of linguisticality (*Sprachlichkeit*) and sublimate social processes entirely to cultural tradition.'[85] Tradition must be comprehended in relation to other aspects of life; its conditions and functions in the social totality must be explicated so that its subjectively intended content and its objective meaning can be distinguished.[86] What is missing in Gadamer is a critical approach to tradition – a critique of ideology – and an historically orientated analysis of social systems which locates tradition in the social whole.

The limitations of an approach based solely upon the speakers of natural languages can be transcended, in Habermas's view, by recognizing that human life unfolds in a framework of language, labour and domination, and by developing theoretical and empirical accounts of these domains. The theory of social evolution and the theory of communicative competence are crucial stages in this programme. They represent an attempt to mitigate the context-dependency of understanding by, as one commentator usefully put it, providing 'a theoretically grounded and methodologically secured' account of the 'preunderstanding that functions in any attempt to grasp meanings'.[87] In the remainder of this chapter, and in the next, I will outline how these ideas and others fit with his conception of critical theory.

Psychoanalysis and emancipation

Besides the technical interest in controlling objects in the environment and the practical interest in furthering mutual, intersubjective understanding, human beings have, Habermas argues in *Knowledge and Human Interests*, a third interest, an emancipatory interest, in securing freedom from hypostatized forces and conditions of distorted communication. This interest is rooted in their capacity to act rationally, to self-consciously reason and to make decisions in light of available knowledge, rules and needs. The human species' self-formative process is, potentially, a process in which history is made with will and consciousness. But once it is acknowledged that history embodies domination, repression and the ideological framing of action, it becomes apparent that self-understanding is often limited by unacknowledged conditions. If the rational capabilities of human beings are to be released, a particular type of knowledge becomes necessary to guide the elucidation and abolition of these conditions. The form of knowledge most appropriate for this is self-knowledge generated through self-reflection.

Self-reflection brings to consciousness those determinates of a self-formative process of cultivation and self-formation (*Bildung*) which ideologically determine a contemporary practice and conception of the world . . . [It] leads to insight due to the fact that what has previously been unconscious is made conscious in a manner rich in consequences: analytic insights intervene in life.[88]

By bringing to consciousness the determinates of the self-formative process, structures of distortion can be revealed, isolated and, under the proper, specifiable conditions, eradicated.

The impetus to achieve self-understanding and autonomy of action is identified with the emancipatory interest in knowledge; it is in human beings' ability to reflect on their own development and, as a consequence, to act with greater consciousness and autonomy that the basis of the emancipatory interest can be uncovered. The interest is an interest in reason, in human beings' capacity to be self-reflective and self-determining.[89]

In self-reflection, knowledge for the sake of knowledge comes to coincide with the interest in autonomy and responsibility (*Mündigkeit*). For the pursuit of reflection knows itself as a moment of emancipation. Reason is at the same time subject to the interest in reason. We can say that it obeys an *emancipatory cognitive interest*, which aims at the pursuit of reflection.[90]

The relation between knowledge and interest is of a different order for the emancipatory interest than it is for the other two interests. With the latter, the act of knowing is not immediately connected with the utilization of knowledge – with the satisfaction of the needs which gave rise to an interest in such knowledge. But theory and practice are intimately connected in the process of self-reflection. Through self-reflection, individuals can become aware of forces which have exerted a hitherto unacknowledged influence over them. Thus, the act of knowing coincides with the act which achieves the goal of the interest, namely emancipation from hypostatized forces. Furthermore, it is only through the act of reflection on the self-formative process of the species that human beings, Habermas claims, can become aware of the connection between knowledge and interest. The true unity of knowledge and interest is only achieved in the emancipatory interest. '*It is in accomplishing self-reflection that reason grasps itself as interested.*'[91]

The interest in reason – the emancipatory interest – follows from the 'exigencies of man's struggle for self-preservation'. But the actual historical form the interest takes is conditioned by the stage of development of technical activity and by the conditions of symbolic interaction; it is dependent on the interests in possible intersubjective action-orientation and in possible technical control.[92] The emancipatory interest has a 'derivative status'.

Compared with the technical and practical interests in knowledge, which are both grounded in deeply-rooted . . . structures of action and experience – i.e. the constituent elements of social systems – the emancipatory interest in knowledge has a derivative status. It guarantees the connection between theoretical knowledge and an 'object domain' of practical life which comes into existence as a result of systematically distorted communication and thinly legitimized repression. The type of action and experience corresponding to the object domain is, therefore, also derivative.[93]

Habermas's formulation of the emancipatory interest is, however, ambiguous (particularly in *Knowledge and Human Interests*). The basic conditions of human existence are sometimes specified as work, language and domination: the conditions for three cognitive orientations of equal standing. On other occasions, work and language alone are designated as the fundamental conditions of existence.[94] Domination is then conceived as a systematic distortion of interaction or language; and the interest in emancipation becomes an interest in the transcendence of such structures of communication. In his more recent works Habermas appears to have adopted the second of these formulations (although some ambiguity remains). Accordingly, systematically distorted communication is seen as the condition of the emancipatory interest: the interest only develops to the extent that domination is institutionalized. (Whether or not the empirical conditions will exist for the realization of undistorted communication is, in Habermas's opinion, an open question.)[95]

The emancipatory interest is the guiding interest of the critically oriented sciences and of all systematic reflection, including philosophy.[96] The goal of the critical sciences is to facilitate the process of methodical self-reflection and to dissolve barriers to the self-conscious development of life. An adequate understanding of all social practices, including scientific inquiry, depends ultimately on these sciences; for by disclosing deformations of communication they attempt to restore to men and women a true awareness of their position in history.

While the empirical-analytic sciences are structured to generate knowledge in the form of laws and theories which can account for regularities in 'observable' phenomena and the hermeneutic sciences are structured to allow the recovery of a particular meaning of an action or expression, the critical sciences, Habermas maintains, unite an interest in nomological and interpretative knowledge with a framework aimed at facilitating the process of self-reflection. The model of a critical science that Habermas turns to is that of psychoanalysis as developed by Freud.[97] Psychoanalysis is, he argues, 'the only tangible example of a science incorporating methodical self-reflection'.[98] Although Freud misunderstood the nature of his own discipline by frequently ascribing the status of a natural science to his enterprise, psychoanalysis reveals, in Habermas's view, the logic of a reflective science and important guidelines for the construction of a critical social theory.

Freud developed an interpretative framework for the examination of the self-formative process of the individual, particularly of the individual in need of 'therapeutically guided self-reflection'. At first sight, psychoanalysis appears, according to Habermas, to be a process of methodical interpretation (of behaviour, dreams, etc) and therefore a hermeneutical science; it 'provides theoretical perspectives and technical rules for the interpretation of symbolic structures'. However, by recognizing the presence of neurotic symptoms which disrupt language games at the level of speech, action and non-verbal expression, psychoanalysis goes beyond the procedures of traditional hermeneutics. By aiding the analysand to reconstruct his or her life history, the analyst attempts to bring to consciousness the latent content of symbolic expression – a portion of life history that has been systematically repressed. The need for psychoanalysis to penetrate the world of surface meanings and appearances and to recover unconscious wishes and motives, 'distinguishes the peculiar task of a hermeneutics that cannot be confined to the procedures of philology but rather *unites linguistic analysis with the psychological investigation of causal connections*'.[99] The methods and procedures which Freud used are called by Habermas 'depth hermeneutics'.[100]

In the process of depth hermeneutics, the analyst seeks to interpret speech and behaviour both on the level of the subject's conscious intentions and on the level of repressed needs and wants. The meaning of observed actions, symbols, etc., can only be adequately understood in terms of the underlying unconscious factors which caused the actor to act as he or she did. A correct interpretation of an action or expression can be supplied only with the successful uncovering of relevant unconscious factors. Systematic reference must be made to experiences which are initially opaque to the patient.

In the therapeutic process, however, it is not enough for the analyst to merely present a correct interpretation; rather analysands must come to accept the reconstruction of their past, as they relive the 'original scenes' which lie at the base of their disturbances. This re-experiencing is awakened during the course of the therapeutic process. Mechanisms of repression which banish particular need interpretations – splitting off individual symbols which represent, at one level, undesired needs and wants from public communication – are weakened through techniques which induce relaxation.[101] The patient is aided to relive experiences in such a way that the emotions involved are felt as immediately present and real. Freud calls this process transference. Under the conditions of a 'transference neurosis', the patient is confronted by the analyst with an interpretation of crucial experiences and an attempt is made to induce the patient to reflect upon this interpretation:

the physician's constructions can be changed into actual recollections of the patient only to the degree that the latter, confronted with the results of his action in transference . . . sees himself through the eyes of another and learns to reflect on his symptoms as offshoots of his own behaviour.[102]

Thus, for Habermas, Freud's psychoanalysis is concerned with the construction of interpretations. As in Gadamerian hermeneutics, 'dialogue' is the medium to gain access to data and test conjectured interpretations. But unlike the interpretations of the hermeneutic sciences, adequate interpretations in psychoanalysis can only be developed with, among other things, the aid of explanations involving causal connections. Such explanations can only be developed, in turn, with reference to a general theory of neurosis, etc., such as that provided by Freud.[103] In order to see this point more clearly, it is useful to delineate the three levels into which Habermas analyses the theoretical structure of psychoanalysis.[104]

The first level is that of metapsychology or metahermeneutics. This comprises the 'basic categories . . . of the discipline, the conceptual constructions, the assumptions about the functional structures of the psychic apparatus and about mechanisms for both the genesis of symptoms and the dissolution of pathological compulsions'.[105] On this level one finds, according to Habermas, Freud's theory of neurosis – that is, an explication of 'the connection between *language deformation* and *behavioural pathology*' – as well as the ego-id-superego model and the theory of instincts. 'Metapsychology unfolds the logic of interpretation of the analytic situation of dialogue.' Its basic categories are derived from reflection on the conditions of psychoanalytic knowledge; that is, on the very form of communication in which analyst and patient participate. They cannot be explicated independently of this context. Nor can they be assessed directly by empirical test; 'they can be confirmed or rejected only indirectly, with regard to the outcome of, so to speak, an entire category of processes of inquiry'.[106]

The metapsychological level is to be distinguished from that of general interpretation. On this latter level, 'empirically substantive interpretations of self-formative processes can be developed within the framework provided by the metapsychology'.[107] The general interpretations are drawn from data collected from clinical experience and operate like theories in the empirical sciences. Thus a general interpretation 'is "fixed" and, like a general theory, must prove itself through predictions deduced from it'. In psychoanalysis, a general interpretation provides a systematically generalized narrative of the psychodynamic development of the child. By addressing itself to patterns of interaction between child and parent, development of motivational syndromes and learning mechanisms (for example object choice), etc., it allows individual case histories to be understood in terms of a series of causal connections; although its application must be modified, of course, in light of initial conditions and the particularity of the case.

The third level involves '*reconstructions of individual life histories* with a therapeutic intent'.[108] The actual events of the patient's life are pieced together using the general interpretive scheme, on the one hand, and the fragmentary information obtained in the analytic dialogue, on the other. Each reconstructed individual life history can be viewed as a hypothesis generated by the theory. Verification, however, is *not*, as in the empirical-analytic sciences, merely a matter of establishing agreement concerning the result of an observation in light of a prediction; nor is it, as in the hermeneutic sciences, simply a question of reaching a consensus about an interpretation. Rather, in psychoanalysis, verification means acceptance by the analysand of the reconstruction of his or her life history – acceptance on a level of self-reflection such that the obstacles to memory, etc., are apprehended and dissolved by the patient, such that his or her neurotic symptoms are for all practical purposes overcome. If self-reflection is successful, the patient can gain a conscious understanding of his or her process of development.[109] Thus, in the end, the ultimate criterion of assessment is emancipatory reflection achieved in and through practice: 'only the context of the self-formative process as a whole has confirming and falsifying power'.[110]

At this point it is useful to note briefly how Habermas conceives the respective roles of *Verstehen* and explanation in psychoanalysis. Psychoanalysis presents a way of understanding neurosis as the consequence of sequences of lawlike developments which act, prior to therapy, as a form of 'second nature'. While understanding cannot be accomplished without explanation, the role of explanation is to mediate between distorted self-understanding and a posited state of self-consciousness.[111] Explanation, in the form of a reconstructed life history, is used both to understand and overcome the pressures of second nature. The complementary utilization of explanation and understanding is necessary, therefore, only while there is a gap between the patient's self-understanding and his or her behaviour (as manifest, for instance, in neurotic symptoms).[112] Once the therapy has been successfully concluded and the patient is well, explanation of actions will coincide with the patient's own understanding and the process of explanation itself will become superfluous to the recovery of meaning. Apel sums up the use which he, in accord with Habermas, sees in the psychoanalytical model.

I think that this methodological pattern of *dialectically mediating communicative understanding by causal explanation* is, in fact, the model for a philosophical understanding of all those types of *critical social science* which have their relation to the practice of life, not in the realm of social engineering, but in provoking public self-reflection and in emancipation of men as subjects.[113]

While taking psychoanalysis as the prototype of a critical science, Habermas transposes the model to the realm of social analysis and political practice. The position developed in *Zur Logik der Sozialwissenschaften* and *Knowledge and Human Interests* suggests that historical materialism can and must be reformulated as a critical theory of society which incorporates the insights of the psychoanalytic model, particularly its insights into the significance of self-reflection. Seen in this context, historical materialism becomes a critique of ideology with a practical intent. According to Habermas:

the critiques which Marx developed *as a theory of society* and Freud as metapsychology are distinguished precisely by incorporating in their consciousness an interest which directs knowledge, an interest in emancipation going beyond the technical and the practical interest of knowledge.[114]

As in psychoanalysis, so in critical theory we:

begin with an object the nature and meaning of which is in question;

employ 'dialogue', as in traditional hermeneutics, as an essential means of gaining data and exploring possible interpretations;

move beyond traditional interpretative techniques, because subjects' accounts of their behaviour include meanings which remain opaque due to distortion and repression;

explain the opaqueness through explanations involving causal connections. Such explanations can only be constructed with reference to a general theory (itself formulated within terms provided by a metatheory – systematic reflections on the nature of the object domain under review, for instance identity formation and ideology);

test the general theory by reconstruction of individual cases (life histories in psychoanalysis, specific societies for critical theory) and examine whether or not it has the capacity to reveal and dissolve distortions of communication.

Ultimate verification of the entire 'empirical-theoretical' enterprise is dependent upon practice – on the eradication of barriers to self-reflection and the overcoming of structures which support such barriers.

The methodological character of psychoanalysis provides systematic insight into the levels at which critical theory must be developed: metatheory; general interpretation; and application of the general interpretation to the development of specific societies. These levels correspond in Habermas's work to: his theories of interests and communication; 'theoretically generalized history', or as he now calls it, the theory of social evolution; and the attempt to reconstruct the life history of a given society in order to uncover and dissolve ideological formations. On this latter level the aim is to identify potential crisis points in the social structure and thereby social groups amenable to the process of enlightenment.[115]

Rational reconstruction and critical self-reflection

To summarize, it is Habermas's view that there are three knowledge-constitutive interests and three categories of knowledge. Each of the interests is expressed in a distinct methodological approach to the generation of knowledge. Each is rooted in life – in a complex of activities which is basic to the survival and development of the species. It is only in light of these interests that knowledge can be comprehended. As Habermas writes: 'as long as these intersets of knowledge are identified and analysed by way of reflection on the logic of inquiry that structures the natural and the human sciences, they can claim a "transcendental" status'.[116]

But Habermas's epistemology is not transcendental in the traditional Kantian sense: there is no ahistorical transcendental subject which provides the preconditions for the constitution of possible experience. Rather, the subject of the constituting activity is the human species; the conditions of the constitution of knowledge are historical, material conditions. Cognitive interests are, thus, transcendental from the point of view of the generation of human knowledge, but are themselves naturalistically grounded. That is, the rule systems governing the cognitive activities of the species,

have a transcendental function but arise from actual structures of human life: from structures of a species that reproduces its life both through learning processes of socially organized labour and processes of mutual understanding in interactions mediated in ordinary language.[117]

The category 'cognitive interest' is neither merely transcendental nor simply empirical. Human knowledge can be conceived of as neither wholly instrumental in regard to an organism's adaptive strategies toward its environment nor as 'the act of a pure rational being removed from the context of life in contemplation'.[118] The cognitive interests exemplify both human continuity with nature and power over nature, in the sense that nature (*qua* nature as known) is the product of the constituting activity of people. 'Thus "interests" can be neither classed with those mechanisms of steering animal behaviour that we can call instincts nor entirely severed from the objective context of a life process.'[119] In recognition of this tension, Habermas refers to them as 'quasi-transcendental'.

Knowledge and Human Interests has been the object of a great deal of criticism. It is worth exploring now some of the issues raised, for they have directly influenced Habermas's most recent line of inquiry.[120] Among other things, Habermas has been accused of defending a questionable version of pragmatism. It should be noted, however, that despite the connections he draws between knowledge and interests, between knowledge and emancipatory practice, he rejects the view that 'the success of . . . action is a sufficient criterion of the truth of propositions'.[121] He acknowledges that 'the basis of knowledge in interest affects the possibility of knowledge as such'. But he argues in a postscript to *Knowledge and Human Interests* that the truth of a proposition 'is not established by means of interest gratification [through 'successful' action] but only by an argumentative redemption of the truth claim itself'.[122] The difference between problems of object constitution and problems of truth was, nonetheless, insufficiently worked out, as Habermas readily admits, in *Knowledge and Human Interests*.[123] It is not only the context of a successful self-formative process, he now argues, that has confirming or falsifying power.

The relation between reflection and emancipation also generates difficulties. Habermas's formulation frequently seems to entail the view that the achievement of self-consciousness is the total concern of the process of emancipation: that self-reflection is co-extensive with the struggle for freedom. This clearly questionable position has been commented upon by many of his critics. Karl-Otto Apel, for instance, has criticized him for conflating reflection and practical engagement.[124] In recent writings, Habermas has made it quite clear that it was never his intention to conflate these phenomena: the practice of self-reflection, he contends, is a necessary but by no means sufficient condition for the achievement of real, material freedom.[125] The interrelation between self-reflection and freedom must be understood historically. The theory of social evolution (developed for the most part after *Knowledge and Human Interests*) seeks to go some way towards the specification of this interrelation. But the epistemological import of emancipatory reflection is not thereby clarified; for there is a fundamental ambiguity in the notion of 'reflection' itself. Transcendental reflection on the general conditions of knowledge and action is inadequately distinguished from critical self-reflection.

In the postscript to *Knowledge and Human Interests* Habermas himself notes that:

It occurred to me only after completing the book that the traditional use of the term 'reflection' which goes back to German Idealism, covers (and confuses) two things: on the one hand, it denotes the reflection upon the conditions of potential abilities of a knowing, speaking and acting subject as such; on the other hand, it denotes the reflection upon unconsciously produced constraints to which a determinate subject (or a determinate group of subjects, or a determinate species subject) succumbs in its process of self-reflection.[126]

The distinction between these two modes of reflection, which

Habermas now calls *rational reconstruction* and *self-reflection* (or self-criticism) respectively, is at the heart of his most recent work. His goal is to develop a 'materialistically transformed transcendental philosophy' – a rational reconstruction of universal competencies. Such a 'philosophy' would, in his view, provide an adequate basis for both a historically relevant critique of social life and the exploration of actual developmental possibilities.[127]

A rational reconstruction explicates general rules of human competency in a given area or context, for example linguistics, or cognitive development. While reconstructions depend on reflection, this reflection is not limited to a particular subject.

> Rational reconstructions . . . deal with anonymous rule systems, which any subjects whatsoever can comply with in so far as they have acquired the corresponding competence with respect to these rules. Reconstructions thus do not encompass subjectivity, within the horizon of which alone the experience of reflection [in the sense of self-criticism] is possible.[128]

Self-knowledge is enhanced by rational reconstructions in that one 'becomes familiar with the range of inevitable subjective conditions' which both make human action possible and limit its scope. Such reconstructions can tell us what is entailed in a successful participation in a functioning rule-governed context; that is, they can render explicit 'know-how' – the intuitive knowledge we employ with respect to cognition, speech and action.

The impetus to develop a rational reconstruction of a particular area of competence emerges, Habermas thinks, only in the context of a theoretical discourse; that is, it is only when we bracket or suspend the imperatives of everyday action and reflect on 'the conditions normally assumed in ordinary interaction' that we can engage in this type of activity. But while rational reconstruction highlights *a priori* conditions for the possibility of knowledge and interaction, it remains, Habermas stresses, unlike its ancestors, empirical in so far as it explains the development and acquisition of empirical competencies by empirical subjects.

Self-criticism, on the other hand, is a mode of reflection which 'brings to consciousness those determinants of a self-formative process (*Bildung*) which ideologically determine a contemporary praxis and conception of the world'.[129] Thus self-criticism is the mode of reflection which the analysand is encouraged to engage in during psychoanalysis. Unlike rational reconstruction, self-criticism is directly tied to practice in so far as it is:

(a) brought to bear on objects of experience whose pseudo-objectivity is to be revealed;
(b) brought to bear on something particular – on the particular self-formative process of an ego, or group, identity;
(c) characterized by its ability to make unconscious elements conscious in a way which has *practical consequences*.[130]

In a therapeutic dialogue a rational reconstruction is required in order to facilitate the understanding of developmental processes. Likewise within the context of a critical social science, the self-criticism which becomes a critique of ideology requires a theory of normal communication as well as a reconstructed history which locates sources of ideology. As Habermas puts it:

If critique, moving beyond the interpretative understanding of a context meaning, accepts as its task the explanation of a systematically distorted communication, then it must have the mastery of the idea of undistorted communication.[131]

Habermas's interest in rational reconstructions has developed, in part, as a result of the fruitfulness of this approach in, for example, linguistics (phonetic and syntactic theory), anthropology (the analysis of mythological world views), psychology (ontogenesis of thought and of moral consciousness). In each of these spheres, he believes, elementary deep structures – basic systems of rules – have been successfully isolated.[132] There has been less success in areas where several such structures intermesh, for instance in the investigation of processes of uttering and understanding or in the analysis of the conditions of systematically distorted communication. But it is precisely here, Habermas argues, that attention must be focused: rewards from this, he clearly thinks, would be substantial.

Habermas's programme of reconstruction develops, as outlined in the last chapter, at the levels of both the individual and society. On the level of the individual, reconstructions are pursued in three dimensions: cognition (operations of thought, of cognitively processing reality); speech (production of well formed sentences); and interaction (including, the capacity for the regulation of conflict). On the level of society, distinctive elementary deep structures are analysed for productive forces (in terms of the organizational and technical knowledge embodied in them), and for forms of social integration (in terms of the various types of practical knowledge they incorporate). Hypotheses advanced in the 'empirical-reconstructive' process are understood as theoretical statements which are open to test in discourse. Reconstructions appear to represent a 'pure form of knowledge'; for they are not directly dependent on any of the three interests.[133] Unlike 'critical self reflection', which directly connects to the emancipatory interest, the transformed 'transcendental reflection' seems to break the links between reason, enlightenment and emancipation, in other words, between theory and practice. But Habermas has not given up the claim that such a link exists. He has, however, substantially altered his conception of it.[134] The new conception is uncovered in the process of rational reconstruction itself; it is presented in the theory of communicative competence.

Habermas's emphasis on the importance of things like the reconstruction of fundamental competencies and the elaboration of a theory of social evolution, should not be taken as evidence of a single-minded concern with theory at the expense of all practical considerations. For these 'empirical-theoretic' tasks have, in his view, an immediately practical reference in so far as they serve to aid the diagnosis of contemporary development problems.[135] Furthermore, although the construction of a satisfactory account of *past* development is essentially an empirical and theoretical problem, the analysis of present circumstances has, Habermas stresses, an unavoidable practical-political moment. Since the future cannot be known, a purely theoretical attitude obviously cannot be taken to it. The theorist's 'provinciality with regard to the future' underlines the creative role he or she has in the making of history. The analyst of the present must assume 'the fictive standpoint of an evolution-theoretic explanation of a future past' and explore society in terms of possibilities that are not yet realized. An historical and practical orientation are an inescapable aspect of any attempt to grasp the formative processes of society. Habermas's conception of the critical standpoint one may legitimately take towards the social world is elaborated in the following chapter.

12   The reformulation of the foundations of critical theory

To date, some of Habermas's most important contributions have been on the problem of foundations – the problem of providing a justified normative basis for critical theory in light of the rejection of the possibility of pure *theoria*. One of the key presuppositions of this work is that moral validity claims are capable of being grounded in a similar way to statements about 'states of affairs': that is to say, that moral, or practical, questions can be decided with reason.[1] This position is important not only for epistemology and methodology but also for the discussion of legitimation.

If a belief in legitimacy is tied to a claim to 'rightness' or 'correctness', then beyond the mere motivational (psychological) justification of the belief, questions concerning the rationality of the belief can be raised. If legitimacy is not related to such claims, then the only important factor is that there be a positively constituted procedure in whose legality the participants (citizens) believe. In this case, the belief in legality is all that is required to legitimize. The second position leads to a decisionistic ethics according to which ultimate moral (and legal) principles cannot be rationally grounded but must be accepted purely on the basis of individual decision. In order to refute this view and make good his case for the first of the alternatives, Habermas must sustain the possibility of a cognitive ethics (an ethics which upholds the notion that moral questions admit of rational justification).

The difficulty with non-cognitive ethics, according to Habermas, is that it cannot account for the binding quality of the moral 'ought'. In the terms of the discussion of legitimation, this means that such an ethics cannot provide 'an account of the decisive *difference between obeying concrete commands and following intersubjectively recognized norms*'.[2] For Habermas the only way to explain the particular qualities of intersubjectively recognized norms is by recourse to the notion of a consensus based on the primacy of rational criticism. What is needed is recognition of the procedures by which rationally motivated agreement is and can be attained. While no procedures exist which can guarantee a lasting consensus, or which can supply the 'truth' once and for all, there are procedures, Habermas thinks, which generate good reasons to accept or reject competing knowledge claims. These are located in the notion of a discourse. It is Habermas's contention that the presuppositions and procedures of discourse are the basis for establishing both the truth of statements and the correctness of norms. The rationality of discourse resides in 'the fact that the reciprocal behavioural expectations raised to normative status afford validity to a *common* interest ascertained *without decep-tion*'.[3] By stipulating that the consensus arrived at must be con-straint free (if one is possible on a given issue), there is a guarantee that the consensus expresses the desires of all – the common interest. Such a consensus requires that interests be both generalizable and shared communicatively.

The force of discourse rests on the principle of universalization (both, as is shown below, on the level of generalizability of inter-ests and of access to participation in discourse). But how can this principle be established in a non-decisionistic, non-circular way; that is, how can we justify the norm which is used to justify all other norms? Habermas's solution is that this principle is embed-ded in the very nature of speech. As he argues in the theory of communicative competence, an analysis of 'universal pragma-tics' – 'rules for using sentences in utterances' – discloses the 'transcendental' nature of all such acts and, in particular, demon-strates that 'the expectation of discursive redemption of normative-validity claims is already contained in the structure of intersubjectivity and makes specially introduced maxims of uni-versalization superfluous'.[4] The theory of communicative com-petence, the centrepiece of Habermas's current work, needs to be carefully elaborated.

The twentieth century has witnessed the transformation of the philosophy of consciousness into the philosophy of language. Since the philosophy of the later Wittgenstein in particular, it has been realized by many that consciousness is linguistically organized and is only accessible in and through language. The implications of the 'linguistic turn' for a critical social theory are pursued by Haber-mas. 'Today', as he puts it, 'the problem of language has replaced the traditional problem of consciousness; the transcendental critique of language supersedes that of consciousness.'[5] After critically examining a number of approaches to the study of language and language use, Habermas attempts to set out a highly novel programme for the analysis of 'the general presuppositions of communicative action', or as he sometimes calls it, 'the reconstruction of the universal conditions of possible understanding'.[6] In a major paper entitled 'What is universal pragmatics?', he seeks to defend this programme. In a number of related essays on communication and truth the import of this approach is drawn out.[7]

It is Habermas's contention that conflict, competition, and strategic action in general, as well as other forms of social action, 'represent derivatives of action oriented to reaching understanding (*verständigungsorientiert*)'; they are 'derivatives' because they involve a 'suspension' or 'putting out of play' of certain of its dimensions (validity claims).[8] Since language is the key distinguishing characteristic of human life, and since it cannot be fully comprehended independently of the process of communication, Habermas feels it is particularly important to focus his analysis on explicit speech actions. Although he ignores non-verbalized actions and bodily expressions in his discussion of universal pragmatics, his aim is to produce (eventually) a general analysis of action types. The stages of inquiry seem to be first, the reconstruction of the universal conditions of possible understanding through the investigation of 'consensual speech' and 'speech that is oriented toward reaching an understanding'; second, the analysis of derivative and deformed modes of communication, such as deceit, manipulation; third, the examination of other related types of action. Hitherto, most of Habermas's attention has been concentrated upon the first part of this project.

Universal pragmatics

Drawing upon ideas developed by, among others, Chomsky in linguistics and Austin and Searle in the theory of speech acts, Habermas argues that 'communicative competence' can be rationally reconstructed.[9] He states the core idea behind this as follows:

[Universal pragmatics] thematizes the elementary units of speech (utterances) in an attitude similar to that in which linguistics does the units of language (sentences). The goal of reconstructive language analysis [such as that initiated by Chomsky] is an explicit description of the rules that a competent speaker must master in order to form grammatical sentences and to utter them in an acceptable way.... It is ... assumed that communicative competence has just as universal a core as linguistic competence. A general theory of speech actions would thus describe exactly that fundamental system of rules that adult subjects master to the extent that they can fulfil *the conditions for a happy employment of sentences in utterances*, no matter to which individual language the sentences may belong and in which accidental contexts the utterances may be embedded.[10]

Habermas is concerned, in particular, to investigate the 'validity basis' of speech; for successful communication is underpinned, in his view, by a rational foundation – by a series of validity claims that have a cognitive character. He develops the thesis that anyone acting communicatively 'must raise universal validity claims and suppose that they can be vindicated [or redeemed: *einlösen*]'.[11] To the extent that interlocutors aim at reaching an understanding, they raise four different types of claims (*Geltungsansprüche*): comprehensibility (*Verständlichkeit*), truth (*Wahrheit*), rightness/correctness (*Richtigkeit*) and truthfulness/sincerity (*Wahrhaftigkeit*). Communicative interaction can be continued only to the degree to which participants credibly sustain these four types of validity claim: that the utterance is comprehensible or intelligible; that its propositional content (or its existential presupposition) is true; that it is legitimate and appropriate in the context and that it is sincerely spoken. In everyday interaction these claims are usually taken for granted and naively accepted (as, for instance, in gossip). But the assumption is made by interacting subjects that they could, if the background consensus is brought into disrepute, vindicate their beliefs. Habermas realizes, of course, that the assumption of accountability is usually counterfactual. But, he wants to contend, the assumption nevertheless persists – it is a reciprocal presupposition unavoidable in speech.

The goal of coming to an understanding is a genuine consensus. This involves bringing about an agreement that culminates in 'the intersubjective mutuality of reciprocal understanding, shared knowledge, mutual trust, and accord with one another'. But understanding is an ambiguous notion; it has a maximal meaning – the genuine consensus referred to above – as well as a minimal meaning – implied when two subjects simply understand a linguistic expression in the same way.[12] The analysis of universal pragmatics is pursued in order to comprehend the elements and general conditions of understanding.

Universal pragmatics directs attention to the 'infrastructure of speech situations in general' (the 'rules for using sentences in utterances'). This infrastructure can be unfolded, albeit crudely, by examining the 'relations to reality' in which every sentence is embedded through its being uttered. Each sentence is situated in relation to external reality (the world of perceived and potentially manipulable objects), normative reality (the realm of socially recognized expectations, values, rules, etc.) and inner reality (the arena of intentions). Through language the subject is involved in a process of demarcation:

(1) from an environment that he objectifies in the ... attitude of an observer; (2) from an environment that he conforms to or deviates from in the ... attitude of a participant; (3) from his own subjectivity, that he expresses or conceals in a first person attitude; and finally (4) from the medium of language itself.[13]

Habermas refers to these domains of reality as 'external nature', 'society', 'internal nature' and 'language', respectively. On his account, these domains appear simultaneously in every speech action as a result of the unavoidable raising of validity claims.

Of all the validity claims that can be attached to a sentence only intelligibility or comprehensibility can be 'fulfilled immanently to language' – a sentence must be grammatical, it must conform to an established system of recognized rules for the use of language. By contrast,

the validity of the propositional content of an utterance depends ... on whether the proposition stated *represents* a fact (or whether the existential presuppositions of a mentioned propositional content hold); the validity of an intention *expressed* depends on whether it corresponds to what is actually intended by the speaker; and the validity of the utterance performed depends on whether this action *conforms* to a recognized normative background.[14]

The expression of communicative competence is not dependent on particular epistemic presuppositions and concepts, but rather upon the extent to which a speaker causes 'sentences in general to be engaged in the universal pragmatic functions of representation, expression and legitimate interpersonal relations'.

The universal pragmatic functions of 'representation, expression and legitimate interpersonal relations' have already been the subject of research, although not all have benefited from the same degree of attention. The study of the conditions that have to be met for the representation of experiences and facts – the examination of the logic of the use of predicates and expressions that identify objects – has been a long-standing interest of analytic philosophy.[15] By comparison, the study of the expressive function of utterances is underdeveloped. A particular need exists, Habermas stresses, for theoretical work in this area.[16] For a theory of communicative competence, however, the investigation of the third dimension of utterances – the establishment of interpersonal relations – is particularly important; it is this that is at the centre of Habermas's most recent concerns. In the investigation of the 'interactive' function of language, speech act theory provides vital clues.

A speech act is the employment of a sentence in an utterance under certain conditions. Speech act theory is directed to understanding the performative status of linguistic utterances – the way in which 'we do things in saying something'. The sense in which one can utter sentences in speech acts – do things in saying – was analysed by Austin as the 'illocutionary force' of speech actions. This notion attempts to grasp the way in which 'every utterance must, at least implicitly, establish and bring to expression a certain relation between the speaker and his counterpart'. Habermas seeks to distinguish two communicative levels on which speaker and hearer must, if they want to communicate their intentions and needs, come to an understanding:

(a) the *level of intersubjectivity* on which speaker and hearer, through illocutionary acts, establish the relations that permit them to come to an understanding with one another, and

(b) the *level of propositional content* which is communicated.[17]

Participants in dialogue have to combine 'communication of a content with communication about the role in which the communicated content is used'. The propositional content, p, can be expressed in a variety of different ways, for example in assertions, promises and commands. The proposition, 'he is in the car', can be articulated as an assertion: 'he is in the car'; as a promise: 'I promise that he is in the car'; and in many other forms. If there is to be communication through an utterance its content must be understood 'as something' and the sense in which the propositional content is employed must be established. The 'double structure' and 'inherent reflexivity' of ordinary language communication are two of its most important features.

While the details of Habermas's position need not be elaborated here, it is important to grasp the questions which underlie his concern with the 'double structure' of speech: What is the source of the illocutionary force of an utterance? In what does this force consist? How does the speaker influence the hearer to take up an interpersonal relation with him? What is the basis of a speech act's 'generative power'?[18] He seeks to address these problems with special reference to a particular class of speech acts: 'propositionally differentiated and institutionally unbound speech actions'. These are speech acts that do not presuppose specific institutions (or sets of institutions) where quite explicit rules and norms determine the conditions of speech action (as in, for instance, betting, marrying, christening). The challenge to speech act theory, Habermas believes, is to work out the basis of 'institutionally unbound' speech actions.

Austin and Searle sought to examine 'illocutionary force' by focusing on the conditions of the success or failure of speech acts. By the 'success' of a speech act Habermas understands a situation in which the hearer not only grasps 'the meaning of the sentence uttered but actually enters into the relationship intended by the speaker'. While Austin's work on this issue is most often restricted to institutionally bound speech acts (cases of explicit rule or norm violation), Searle's deals more directly with those types of speech act which most concern Habermas. Searle points to four types of condition that have to be met by 'unbound' speech acts: 'propositional rules'; 'preparatory rules' (which specify the 'generalized or restricted *contexts* for possible types of speech action'); 'essential rules' (which require that the utterance offered 'counts as' an offer of a certain kind); and 'sincerity rules' (which demand a discernable readiness to enter into a specific kind of interpersonal bond).[19] The relationship which the speaker enters into with an illocutionary act means, on this account,

a guarantee that, in consequence of his utterance, he will fulfil certain conditions – for example, regard a question as settled when a satisfactory answer is given; drop an assertion when it proves to be false; follow his own advice when he finds himself in the same situation as the hearer . . . and so on. *Thus the illocutionary force of an acceptable speech act consists in the fact that it can move a hearer to rely on the speech-act-typical commitments of the speaker.*[20]

As a result 'of the binding force of established norms which constitute the background and medium of institutionally bound speech acts, a particular pattern of relations is created. Institutionally unbound speech acts cannot draw their force from such normative contexts. The creation of a pattern of interaction under these conditions appears to depend on the speaker's power of suggestion and capacity to move and influence the hearer, on the one hand, and the hearer's willingness to make assumptions about the seriousness of the speaker's engagement, on the other. It is Habermas's contention, however, that the illocutionary force in the 'unbound situation' can be fully comprehended only if 'we take into consideration sequences of speech actions that are connected with one another on the basis of a reciprocal recognition of validity claims'.[21] The basis on which the hearers are 'moved' to enter into specific relations is not simply dependent on the apparent sincerity of the speaker.

With their illocutionary acts, speaker and hearer raise validity claims and demand they be recognized. But this recognition need not follow irrationally, since the validity claims have a cognitive character and can be checked. I would like therefore to defend the following thesis: *In the final analysis, the speaker can illocutionarily influence the hearer and vice verse, because speech-act-typical commitments are connected with cognitively testable validity claims*, that is, because the reciprocal bonds have a rational basis. The engaged speaker normally connects the specific sense in which he would like to take up an interpersonal relationship with a thematically stressed validity claim, and thereby chooses a specific mode of communication.[22]

In sequences of speech acts the content of the engagement is determined by specific reference to, and emphasis upon, universal validity claims. Each act carries specific meaning; but it puts forward general claims.[23] Thus, speech-act-typical commitments are linked to (implicit and sometimes explicit) obligations to provide grounds or justifications. Consequently, the hearer can be *'rationally motivated'* to accept the content of the speaker's engagement. Habermas elucidates this by reference to the three modes of communication – the cognitive, interactive and expressive. He does not claim that every speech action can be unambiguously classified under these headings; rather, his view is that 'every competent speaker has in principle the possibility of unequivocally selecting one mode, because with every speech act he *must* raise [given that

comprehensibility is already fulfilled] three universal validity
claims, so that he *can* single out one of them to thematize as a
component of speech'.[24] The relationship between different types
of language use and validity claims is set out in the table below.

Language use and validity claims

| | Mode of communication | | |
	cognitive	interactive	expressive
Types of speech action	constantives (e.g. assertions, descriptions, explanations)	regulatives (e.g. commands, advice, recommendations)	avowals (e.g. revelation, admission, deception)
Implied validity claim	truth	rightness, appropriateness	sincerity, truthfulness
Theme	propositional content	interpersonal relation	speakers' intention
Speech-act-immanent obligation to provide	grounds	justifications	confirmations

Every speech-act-immanent obligation can 'be made good at two
levels, namely immediately, in the context of utterance – whether
through recourse to experiential certainty, through indicating a
corresponding normative background, or through affirmation of
what is evident to oneself – and mediately, in discourse or in the
succession of consistent actions'. The mediate satisfaction of validity claims is different for each mode of communication. In the
cognitive use of language, if an initial statement is found uncon-
vincing, the truth claim can be tested in a theoretical discourse. In
the interactive use of language, if the rightness of an utterance is
doubted, it can become the subject of a practical discourse. In the
expressive use of language, if the truthfulness or sincerity of an
utterance is questioned, it can be checked against future action.

But no matter what emphasis is placed in speech on these
respective claims, the possibility is given of examining every utterance to find out whether it is true or untrue, justified or unjustified,
truthful or untruthful, because, as Habermas puts it, 'in speech . . .
grammatical sentences are embedded in relations to reality in such
a way that in an acceptable speech action segments of external

nature, society, and internal nature always come into appearance together'.[25]

Theoretical and practical discourse

Behind all smoothly functioning communication is a background consensus based on the mutual recognition by all interlocutors of validity claims. It is assumed that all participating subjects could, if the background consensus is brought into disrepute, justify their views and attitudes. What is the status of this assumption?

It is obvious, Habermas holds, that 'institutionalized actions do not as a rule fit this model of pure communication'. But, he goes on to argue, we cannot avoid 'counterfactually proceeding as if the model were really the case – on this unavoidable fiction rests the humanity of intercourse among men'.[26] The supposition of accountability is a necessary feature of ordinary language communication; without it the nature of ordinary language could not be comprehended. That this supposition persists as an expectation, despite its counterfactual status, gives rise to a crucial question, a question which must be answered if the argument is to be advanced – how is this counterfactual stabilized? Habermas's position is that

this can be achieved only through legitimation of the ruling systems of norms and through the anchoring of the belief in legitimacy in systematic barriers to will-forming communication. The claim that our norms can be grounded is redeemed through legitimizing world-views. The validity of these world-views is in turn secured in a communication structure which excludes discursive will-formation ... the barriers to communication which make a fiction precisely of the reciprocal imputation of accountability, support at the same time the belief in legitimacy that sustains the fiction and prevents its being found out. That is the paradoxical achievement of ideologies, whose individual prototype is the neurotic disturbance.[27]

A theory of systematically distorted communication is required to explain the actual pattern of communication. But before discussing the elements of such a theory a number of further issues have to be addressed: How can we distinguish a true from a false consensus? How can we exempt discourse itself – the arena in which knowledge claims are tested – from distortion? What are the criteria for distinguishing non-distorted from distorted communication?

The 'immanent obligations' of speech remain unfulfilled so long as people unreflectively adopt a 'frame of meaning'. But should one (or more) of the validity claims be challenged, as frequently occurs, communicative interaction can continue only if the claim is redeemed. (If it is not, there is always, of course, recourse to other types of action, for example struggle and conflict.) Each claim requires, Habermas argues, a different mode of redemption to restore consensual interaction. Of the four types of validity claim, two – *Wahrheit* and *Richtigkeit* – require specific forms of discursive justification. *Verständlichkeit*, as the basic condition of all ordinary language communication, is either factually redeemed/negotiated or it is not, while *Wahrhaftigkeit* depends for its redemption on an assessment of actual behaviour – the demonstration of 'good intent'. The validity of questioned and problematic truth claims or norms can be redeemed only through argumentation in, respectively, a 'theoretical-empirical' and 'practical' discourse.[28]

In discourse our relation to action is transformed. As opposed to other forms of communicative interaction this speech situation depends, Habermas maintains, upon the 'suspension of the constraints of action'. There is only one form of compulsion permissible – 'the force of the better arguement'. There is only one acceptable motive – 'the co-operative search for truth'.[29] By drawing a distinction between the conditions and problems of the constitution of reality, on the one hand, and the redemption of truth claims about reality, on the other, Habermas seeks to clarify this bold (and seemingly unrealistic) view of the discursive process. It is his intention to demonstrate that the *a priori* of experience (which lays down the objects and structure of possible action-related experience) is independent of the *a priori* of argumentative reasoning (which lays down the conditions of possible discourse). The theory of cognitive interests specifies the *a priori* of experience – the structure of a given object domain. The theory of communication (which connects directly, as is shown below, to a theory of truth) specifies the *a priori* of argumentative reasoning – the conditions of discourse. These theories together combine to define 'the limits of theories which are built up from accumulated evidence'. Theories can only, on Habermas's account, 'be constructed, and progressively reconstructed, in the context of conditions pertaining to the nature of argumentation and within the limits of prior objectivation of experienceable occurrences'.[30]

In everyday interaction statements are generated about the objects of experience. These statements imply truth claims. Experiences *support* these claims; but the truth of opinions and norms can be redeemed only through argumentation. 'A claim *founded* in experience is', Habermas contends, 'by no means a *grounded* claim.'[31] The grounding of claims 'has nothing to do with the relation between individual sentences and reality, but above all with the coherence between sentences within systems of speech.'[32] For when statements about objects of possible action-related experience are found to be in need of corroboration they break their connections with practical life in one fundamental respect: 'their truth claims, which in practical life are simply *presupposed*, are now suspended and tested'.[33] Statements in need of assessment become sentences in a discourse. In discourse facts can be established. Following Strawson, Habermas argues that facts do not correspond to things and happenings. Facts 'are what statements (when true) state'.[34] They are not 'constituted since they are not entities *in the world* but correlates of propositions on the level of argumentative reasoning'.[35] When a statement becomes part of a discourse it 'focuses on a state of affairs, trying to make explicit and to question a truth claim'. In so doing it presupposes, of course, identifiable objects: statements need not be simply about linguistic phenomena. But we cannot 'break out', as the correspondence theory of truth attempts, 'of the sphere of language'.[36] In asserting a state of affairs, 'I precisely do not assert an experience. . . . I can only draw upon structurally analogous experiences as data in an attempt to ground the truth claim embodied in my statement.'[37] In asserting what is the case the claim is made that the *asserted statements* are true. 'Truth belongs categorically to the world of thoughts (in Frege's sense) and not to that of perception.'[38] The meaning of 'facts' and 'states of affairs', therefore, cannot be established without reference to the process whereby the truth claims of statements are tested.[39] In order to uncover the meaning of truth implied in the 'pragmatics of assertions', an analysis of the argumentative corroboration of validity claims, of the logic of discourse, is required.[40]

The analysis of discourse is dependent on an explication of the notion of 'providing rational grounds' or 'rational motivation' for the acceptance, suspension, or rejection of a validity claim. This is done in terms of 'the formal (not in the sense of syntactical or semantical sense, but in the pragmatic sense) properties of argumentation'. Habermas distinguishes a number of levels of argument for the two arenas of discourse, which are outlined in the table on page 342.[41]

	Theoretical-empirical discourse	*Practical discourse*
Conclusions	statements	precepts/evaluations
Controversial validity claim	truth	correctness/propriety
Demanded from opponent	explanations	justifications
Data	causes (of events) motives (of behaviour)	grounds
Warrant	empirical uniformities, hypothetical laws, etc.	behavioural/evaluative norms or principles
Backing	observations, results of surveys, factual accounts, etc.	interpretations of needs (values), inferences, secondary implications, etc.

Drawing on the work of Stephen Toulmin, he argues that statements or evaluative judgements can only be grounded as elements of a hierarchy of concepts and considerations; that is, as elements embedded in a structure of argument. This hierarchy can be analysed in terms of: the conclusion that is to be grounded (particular statements in theoretical discourse, commands or evaluations in practical discourse); the data that is submitted as pertinent (causes, grounds); the warrant which establishes the link between data and conclusions (general laws, moral principles), and the backing which makes this link plausible (observation reports, considerations of secondary implications of following a particular norm).[42] The form of a theoretical-empirical discourse is illustrated by Habermas with an example adapted from Toulmin.

The assertion, 'Harry is a British subject' (conclusion), can be explained by the identification of a cause: 'Harry was born in Bermuda' (data). This explanation is reached through the deductive application of a generalization: 'A man born in Bermuda will generally be a British subject' (warrant). The plausibility of this generalization is justified . . . 'on account of the following statutes and other legal provisions' (backing).[43]

Practical discourse, as should be clear from the table above, has a parallel structure.

In order to ensure that the process of argumentation is affected by nothing other than 'the force of the better argument', Habermas argues that the conditions of discourse must make possible a progressive 'radicalization of argument'. There must be freedom to move to increasing levels of reflection. The levels involved can be depicted as follows:[44]

Steps in radicalization	Theoretical discourse	Practical discourse
acts	statements	commands/prohibitions
grounding	theoretical explanations	theoretical justifications
substantive language-criticism	metatheoretical	metaethical/metapolitical
	transformation of language and conceptual systems	
self-reflection	critique of knowledge	formation of rational critical will

In theoretical discourse there must be freedom to enter a discourse; check questioned claims; evaluate explanations; modify a given conceptual framework; and reflect on the nature of knowledge as such. In practical discourse it must be possible to let commands or prohibitions enter discourse when they can no longer be taken for granted; assess justifications; alter conceptions of norms, etc.; and reflect on the nature of political will.

A validity claim can only be adequately redeemed if it is possible to enter freely into discourse and move between its different levels. A consensus reached in this situation is a grounded (justified) consensus. The conditions of this situation – the conditions of discourse free of constraint or systematically distorted communication – can be specified formally, Habermas maintains, in terms of the pragmatic structure of communication itself; that is, it can be formalized in the concept of *an ideal speech situation*. The condition for a grounded consensus is a situation in which there is mutual understanding between participants, equal chances to select and employ speech acts, recognition of the legitimacy of each to participate in the dialogue as 'an autonomous and equal partner' and where the resulting consensus is due simply 'to the force of the better argument'. In other words, the conditions of the ideal speech situation must ensure equal opportunity for discus-

sion, free from all domination, whether arising from conscious
strategic behaviour and/or systematically distorted communication
(internal and/or external constraints). A consensus attained in this
situation, referred to by Habermas as a 'rational consensus', is the
ultimate criterion of the truth of a statement or the correctness of
norms. The criterion is 'not the fact that some consensus has been
reached; but rather that at all times and all places, if only we enter
a discourse, a consensus can be arrived at under conditions which
show the consensus to be grounded'.[45]

The conditions of the ideal speech situation represent, Habermas recognizes, an ideal. But this does not of itself undermine its
significance. For, as he explains it,

the ideal speech situation is neither an empirical phenomenon nor simply
a construct, but a reciprocal supposition unavoidable in discourse. This
supposition can, but need not be, counterfactual; but even when counterfactual it is a fiction which is operatively effective in communication. I
would therefore prefer to speak of an anticipation of an ideal speech
situation. . . . This alone is the warrant which permits us to join to an
actually attained consensus the claim of a rational consensus. At the same
time it is a critical standard against which every actually realized consensus can be called into question and tested.[46]

The conclusion of Habermas's analysis of discourse is that it rests
on a normative foundation. In systematic argument we assume the
reality of an ideal speech situation; it is 'anticipated, but as anticipated . . . also effective'.[47] Without such an anticipation, Habermas contends, we would not and could not enter discourse. In
attempting to 'rationally motivate' and justify a line of argumentative reasoning we must, he insists, presuppose that the outcome of
the debate will rest simply on the force of the better argument, and
not on accidental or systematic constraints. If the assumption was
not made, then the very meaning of discourse would be radically
changed. Each time we pursue a theoretical or practical argument
with the intention of reaching a rational agreement, we presuppose
an ideal speech situation: we assume its reality. It is constitutive of
the meaning of discourse. The 'anticipated situation', however, is
rarely, if ever, approximated in actual speech situations. But
despite this the ideal can serve as a standard for the critique of
systematically distorted communication and as a guide for the institutionalization of discourse: where it is clearly violated doubt
can be cast on the genuineness of the consensus and the legitimacy
of all that is derived from it. Whether or not the empirical conditions can be practically created for the realization of this ideal of

reason and life·is a separate question and it is not one, in Habermas's opinion, that 'admits of an *a priori* answer. The fundamental norms of rational speech which arc built into universal pragmatics contain . . . a practical hypothesis'.[48]

In his work on ontogenesis and phylogenesis, Habermas is exploring, as is indicated in Chapter 10, the changing nature of theoretical and practical reason over time. By examining the major stages of individual development and social evolution, he hopes to show that at both levels there is a growing capacity to master theoretical and practical discourse. But the attempt to realize the conditions of an ideal speech situation can be imagined by Habermas only as a 'self-controlled learning process'.[49] There is no set of institutions which can be specified as the only legitimate basis of social organization. What type of institutions prevails depends on a multiplicity of social and political conditions. The concern motivating Habermas's analysis is less to discover the correct forms of social organization (for example direct democracy), but rather to find concrete arrangements which would 'ground the presumption that the basic institutions of . . . society and the political decisions would meet with the unforced agreement of all those involved, if they could participate, as free and equal, in discursive will-formation '.[50]

In summary, therefore, it is Habermas's view that the analysis of speech shows it is oriented to the idea of understanding, to the idea of a genuine consensus – which is rarely realized; the analysis of the consensus shows it to be based on four types of validity claim; the analysis of validity claims shows that they can only be established by, among other things, discourse; the analysis of discourse ties it to the idea of a situation in which agreement is reached simply on the basis of 'the better argument' – an ideal speech situation; the analysis of the ideal speech situation shows it to involve assumptions about the institutional context of interaction.[51] The end point of this argument is that the structure of speech is held to involve 'the anticipation of a form of life in which truth, freedom and justice are possible'. Critical theory is, therefore, grounded on a normative standard that is not arbitrary, but 'inherent in the very structure of social action and language'. With this reconceptualization of the basis of critique Habermas seeks to defend the claim that truth and virtue, facts and values, and theory and practice are inseparable. For 'the truth of statements is linked in the last analysis to the intention of the good and true life'.[52]

The argument for the 'unity of argumentation' must not be

conflated with arguments for the unity of scientific theories. 'The *unity of reasoning*', Habermas states in the postscript to *Knowledge and Human Interests*, 'is compatible with *a differential meaning-constitution of the object domains*.'[53] There is, however, a certain unity between the *a priori* of experience and the *a priori* of argumentative reasoning, between action, experience and discourse. This unity is maintained by the knowledge-constitutive interests themselves. 'They preserve the *latent nexus between action and theoretical knowledge*. They are responsible for the transformation of opinions into theorems and for the retransformation of theorems into action-oriented knowledge.'[54]

Critique and practical action

As a consequence of the positions outlined above, the critique of ideology can take as a framework, Habermas argues, 'a model of the suppression of generalizable interests'.[55] The critique would involve a comparison of the existing, historical normative structures of a society with those which hypothetically would be the case if norms were arrived at discursively. This would allow a measure of the degree and nature of ideology in a given society.

Such a counterfactually projected reconstruction . . . can be guided by the question [justified, in Habermas's view, by considerations from universal pragmatics]: how would the members of a social system, at a given stage of development of productive forces, have collectively and bindingly interpreted their needs (and which norms would they have accepted as justified) if they could and would have decided on the organization of social intercourse through discursive will-formation, with adequate knowledge of the limiting conditions and functional imperatives of their society.[56]

The fruitful employment of the model also requires certain assumptions from conflict theory, namely that conflict concerning action oriented to institutionalized norms arises only when the consensus governing the distribution of opportunities for satisfying needs breaks down; the conflict can come to consciousness only within the categories of the interpretative system obtaining at that specific historical time; at such time, action oriented to norms gives way to interest-oriented (strategic) action. Habermas needs two further assumptions for his model of a critique of ideology. One is the empirical assumption that the interests that actually emerge in conflict situations coincide sufficiently with the interests that the same parties would express if they were to enter into a discourse at that time. The second is the methodological assumption that hidden interests can be reconstructed even in cases where there is no manifested conflict, and that these interests could be brought to consciousness in such a way that it would lead to conflict and strategic action. (Marx, Habermas asserts, was working with these or equivalent assumptions in his theory of class conflict.)

The above assumptions give Habermas the framework for what he calls the 'advocacy model'.

The advocacy role of the critical theory of society would consist in ascertaining generalizable, though nevertheless suppressed, interests in a representatively simulated discourse between groups which are differentiated (or could be non-arbitrarily differentiated) from one another by an articulated, or at least virtual, opposition of interests.[57]

Using such indicators of potential conflict as discrepancies between level of claims, and politically permitted level of satisfaction, or differences between legal norms and legal reality, or codified rules of exclusion which distinguish one political system from another, a result could be obtained which would indicate the nature of ideological repression and the level of generalizable interests possible at a given historical point. But the result would, of course, be a hypothetical one. 'The social scientist can only hypothetically project this ascription of interests; indeed a direct confirmation of this hypothesis would be possible only in the form of a practical discourse among the very individuals or groups involved.' Indirect confirmation is possible on the basis of observable conflicts 'to the extent that the ascribed interest positions can be connected with predictions about conflict motivations'.[58] But when this model is applied to an assessment of contemporary normative structures and their interpretations, and reveals ideological elements in the *de facto* consensus about the existing distribution of scarce values, then it becomes (is) a force in the process of enlightenment – an advocate for a society based on democratic, discursive will-formation. In the final analysis,

The theory serves primarily to enlighten its addressees about the position which they occupy in an antagonistic social system, and about the interests of which they could become conscious as objectively their own in the situation. Only to the extent that the organized enlightenment and counsel lead to the target group recognizing itself in the preferred interpretations does the analytically proposed interpretation become an actual consciousness, and the objectively attributed interest situation the interest situation of a group capable of action.[59]

The question now arises, how, in light of the theory, is the political struggle for emancipation to be organized and carried out? What is Habermas's conception of the relationship between theory and practice *in* practice? In order to answer these questions we need to turn back to the model of psychoanalysis as a critical science. For Habermas, psychoanalysis links theory with practice through methodically incorporating self-reflection. But how can the psychoanalytic model be transferred to the level of social and political interaction? Are there safeguards that can be applied to aid its application and sanctions that would help avoid its abuse?

In political struggles, there does not seem to be any overriding authority that can impose sanctions. Nor does it appear that we can easily speak, when reflecting on conflict between classes, of the voluntary submission of one class to a group, party, etc., for the purpose of systematic enlightenment. In recognition of these problems, Habermas was led to make a number of distinctions about the function and organization of enlightenment. Three levels are differentiated. The first is 'the formation and extension of critical theorems, which can stand up to scientific discourse'.[60] On this level theory is established via scientific procedures, the aim of which is the generation of true claims about the socio-historical world. The validity of these claims rests ultimately on their redeemability in a discursively generated consensus. The second level is 'the organization of processes of enlightenment'.[61] This is the level on which the theory generated is therapeutically applied to eradicate the repressive structure of communication which blocks the capacities of individuals (or groups or classes) to locate themselves in history and to articulate their interests. Through the systematic application of the theory developed in discourse, and self-reflection on the part of the subject/object of investigation, the theorems can be tested in the only way which can lead to their genuine confirmation.

The third and final level is concerned with 'the selection of appropriate strategies, the solution of tactical questions, and the conduct of the political struggle'.[62] This level must be clearly differentiated, Habermas emphasizes, from the second level. While the theory which is developed on the first level can be used to legitimize the organization of the process of enlightenment, it cannot in a like manner be used to justify *particular political actions*. That is, theory cannot dictate and justify action. Theory can be used to create agents capable of full participation in decisions concerning action and it can be used to support arguments in favour of certain courses of action. But it cannot be used, in any automatic or mechanistic way, to generate strategy or to ensure the success of strategic action. For strategic movement contains an irreducible element of uncertainty and risk – an element which can only be fully taken account of in the context in which it arises. While aspects of human 'being-in-the-world' provide the conditions for the possibility of theory as well as the basis for its justification, theory does not provide the grounds, conditions or justifications, for day to day political decisions.[63]

The structure of norms in advanced capitalism

In his discussion of motivation crises Habermas explores whether in the complex societies of advanced capitalism norms are still connected to a process of justification. If it is the case that they are not then it can be supposed that the socio-cultural system has been successfully uncoupled from the political-economic system, at least as concerns legitimation and motivation formation. While the logic of development of world views, according to Habermas, does not indicate that practical reason must be divorced from a concern with justification, the steering problems of complex societies might create a situation in which this happens; then, 'legitimation problems *per se* would cease'.[64]

In *Legitimation Crisis*, Habermas notes that there is, at the present time, a perceptible change in bourgeois consciousness along with an attack on the values of the bourgeois individual. This phenomenon can be viewed in at least two ways. It might be a retreat on the part of the bourgeoisie from its own values in light of increasing pressure to make good its ideals. Or, it might be viewed as the collapse of what had been a generally pervasive culture – a culture now dysfunctional for socialization. This latter interpretation Habermas calls, in recognition of the Frankfurt school's work, 'the thesis of the "end of the individual".'[65] But whether or not we are witnessing the destruction of the traditional individual cannot, in Habermas's view, be answered at this point; there is no clear-cut evidence which would allow one to settle the issue.[66] This very lack of evidence, however, throws doubt upon the claim that changes in socialization are systematically destroying people's ability to recognize and put forward practical claims. As Habermas points out, such a world has obviously not yet been realized; the process of destruction – if such process is taking place – can still be halted. To this end, he contends, an ever greater adherence to, and partiality for, reason and critique is required.

Habermas seeks to give this commitment still clearer and more detailed expression. His writings on social evolution and crisis tendencies provide a framework for further studies into patterns of social development. His reformulation of the notion of critique lays a basis for the criticism of domination – a criticism which he intends to develop. His writings on epistemology and method provide a re-examination of the links between social science and emancipation – links which he continues to affirm and explicate. Habermas's work to date ends on a note of guarded optimism; while the reality of advanced capitalism is ambiguous, reason can – with the right support – preserve its cunning.

13 An assessment of the Frankfurt school and Habermas

The issues raised by the members of the Frankfurt school and Habermas are of profound importance. Their criticisms of traditional approaches to philosophy, of conventional schools of social science and of orthodox Marxism provide a major challenge to writers in these areas. Horkheimer's thought on ideology, Adorno's work on reification and fetishism, Marcuse's writings on labour and repressive desublimation and Habermas's reflections on distorted communication recast the terms of reference of critique and reinforce the emancipatory intent of Marx's enterprise. Although the various models of critical theory do not satisfactorily resolve many of the questions which they raise, nevertheless the way connections are established between apparently disparate traditions of thought and fields of inquiry, the constant attention to both philosophical and empirical problems, the concern with theory and practice – all indicate, in my opinion, that critical theory constitutes one of the major sources for contemporary social and political thought.

A number of common, but erroneous views about critical theory were outlined in the Introduction.[1] The work of the critical theorists seems especially prone to hostile and inadequate polemic. It is interesting to speculate as to why this is so. By criticizing and drawing upon a variety of seemingly quite different schools of thought, they break out of the protected positions often given to established members of a tradition. By recasting the terms of reference of philosophical and social inquiry they risk pleasing no established parties. By working with a critical intent against various forms of domination and by simultaneously refusing to specify 'what is to be done', they antagonize all those who seem to require a hard and fast doctrine to guide their action.

Before raising criticisms of the substantive contributions of critical theory in this chapter, I would like to examine a number of objections often made by those who have been strongly influenced by Leninism or Trotskyism and/or by Louis Althusser's understanding of Marxism. Of all the attacks on critical theory those launched from this direction have been perhaps the harshest and most misconceived.

A reply to Marxist critics

In a number of short works Perry Anderson and Göran Therborn, for example, have sought to provide a 'balance sheet' of critical theory's achievements and limitations.[2] Despite the occasional generous comment Anderson and Therborn are unequivocal in their assessment: not only do the limitations of critical theory far outweigh the achievements, but to remain within the 'problematic' of critical theory is to risk intellectual paralysis and a failure to produce a genuine reconciliation of theory and practice, Marxism and revolutionary politics.[3] Summing up the position of the Frankfurt school (and all those whom he calls 'Western Marxists') Anderson writes: 'method as impotence; art as consolation, pessimism as quiescence'.[4] Therborn expresses his views of the Frankfurt school thus: 'there is an underlying structure . . . which involves *a double reduction of science and politics to philosophy*', Further, Adorno's and Horkheimer's involvement in the *Authoritarian Personality* marks, at the level of social analysis, 'a complete capitulation to bourgeois social psychology in theory, method and political conclusions'.[5] Another recent critic of the Frankfurt school, Slater, argues that while 'the Frankfurt school of the 1930s and early 1940s made a serious contribution to the elucidation and articulation of historical materialism . . . [it] failed to achieve the relation to praxis which is central to the Marxist project'.[6] On Slater's reading, the leading members of the Institute of Social Research failed to 'relate concretely to the praxis and theory of the class-struggles in Germany' and their work lacks 'economic concreteness', that is, a thorough analysis of the economic base.[7] The result is that their attempts to develop, for example, a historical materialist aesthetics, miss the vital 'practical class standpoint'.[8] Yet another critic writes in a discussion of Habermas: 'critical theory does not . . . possess concepts necessary to discern let alone comprehend class relations at the general systemic level'.[9] Critical theory 'makes impossible the systematic identification and analysis of class-structural phenomena in relation to the development of the forces and relations of production'.[10] In the opinion of such authors, critical theory represents, at best, a diversion both from the 'path of true science' (Therborn) and from 'a *close connection* with the *practical activity* of the proletariat' (Anderson).

The charges made against critical theory fall into four main areas (although not all of the critics raise issues in each of them). I would like to mention these briefly and then assess them; for such an assessment provides a useful backdrop against which the major achievements of critical theory can be located. First, there is the view that critical theory, far from breaking with the heritage of classical German idealism, reproduces idealist positions.[11] Its radical break is not with idealism but with real, materialist science. The epistemological basis of critical theory is 'metaphysical humanism'. In a position saturated with the influence of Hegel, history is portrayed as 'an all-embracing process, in which an historical subject realizes itself'. Society is reduced to 'a creator-subject'. Truth becomes objective only 'in the metaphysical sense of being inherent in the essence of human reality'.[12] Several consequences are said to follow from this, including the neglect of the scientific specificity of Marx's critique of political economy; the subordination of analyses of concrete situations to a general assessment of reality in terms of the degree to which human 'essence' is realized; and the loss of a view of social totalities as structures of irreducible complexity involving processes of discontinuous development.[13]

Second, the charge is made that critical theory shows undue concern for philosophical and theoretical problems, problems pursued at the expense of Marxist topics. A 'constant concourse with ... thought systems outside of historical materialism' (various types of idealism, psychoanalysis) is claimed to be a 'striking feature' of the critical theorists' work.[14] Critical theory turns attention away from classical Marxist issues; it neglects the essential concerns of historical materialism: 'scrutiny of the economic laws of motion of capital as a mode of production; analysis of the political machinery of the bourgeois state, strategy of the class struggle necessary to overthrow it'.[15] Critical theory's interest in philosophy betrays a distance from practical-political concerns – a sad but inevitable result, Anderson contends, of the rift between theory and practice, science and proletarian insurgency, which characterized the period in which it developed.[16] Third, connected with the above is the view that an excessive amount of time was spent studying 'superstructural phenomena' – aesthetics and culture – thus further detracting from serious engagement with the key determinants of social life. Finally, a general remoteness from, rather than involvement with, working-class politics, is said to characterize the life of Horkheimer and the others. They were 'isolated' in academic settings, increasingly concerned with a 'second-order' discourse – 'on Marxism, rather than in Marxism'.[17] Instead of moving as Marx did from philosophy to economics and politics, they turned back to ever more abstract issues.

The above portrayal of critical theory is for the most part inaccurate and misleading. It is worth examining not only the nature of the misrepresentations but also some of the alternative positions suggested by the critics – their claims about the core structures of reality, science and the key issues in politics. For critical theory developed, in part, as a critique of precisely that kind of view which claimed to have fully captured these phenomena. The debate over what constitutes Marxism, the essential structures of society, the nature of scientific inquiry, etc. is inseparable from the genesis of critical theory itself.

It is striking that the characterization of critical theory by, for instance, Therborn and Slater, rests on an insufficiently differentiated analysis of the positions of each of the critical theorists.[18] Therborn, for example, explicates Horkheimer's concept of history with a quotation from Marcuse.[19] Slater elaborates Horkheimer's notion of critical theory through Marcuse's critique of Hegel and Marx.[20] The 'Frankfurt school's' analysis of fascism is expounded by Therborn with a brief summary of one of Marcuse's articles (thus leaving aside the diverse contributions of the Institute members discussed in the first five chapters of this book). The general conflation of positions has a number of serious consequences. First, the very different views of, for instance, Adorno and Marcuse on Hegel and Marx remain unexplicated. Yet these two men stressed quite different aspects of Hegel and Marx. Second, the various models of critical theory expounded by Horkheimer, Adorno and Marcuse are ignored. As a result, the real break between, for example, Adorno's final stage of development, exemplified by works like *Negative Dialectics*, and Marcuse's notion of critique, which directly preserves many of Hegel's ideas, is bypassed. While an argument might be made that Marcuse's work resembles the position outlined in the first of the four sets of criticisms, Adorno's bears no such resemblance. Adorno fre-

quently attacked the notion of a general subject in history, an-
thropocentric conceptions of the historical process, and the concept of the negation of the negation. He affirmed the primacy of
the object. He fiercely criticized attempts to articulate the 'fundamental structure of being' as well as all thought-systems that
claimed privileged access to 'human destination'.[21]

Many of Horkheimer's views, especially from the late 1930s,
were similar to Adorno's. But even Horkheimer's earlier works,
which were expounded in some detail in Chapter 6, there is no
evidence that history is being described simply as a process
in which 'a historical subject realizes itself'. It is precisely because
Adorno and Horkheimer saw no inescapable path for human
history and no inevitable transformation of capitalism, that they
were so concerned with critique – with criticizing ideology and thus
helping to create awareness of the possibility of a break with the
existing structure of domination. Even Marcuse's work, which
clearly affirms the concept of the negation of the negation and a
(materialistically transformed) version of Hegel's concept of truth,
resembles only superficially the portrait offered by critics. His writings on the concepts of species-being and labour seek to capture
the dynamic character of sensuous, practical activity and make it
the foundation of the notion of essence.[22] His formulation of the
latter leads, in his early writings at any rate, 'into history rather
than out or it'. Further, the conception of 'human' as 'natural' and
'sensuous' beings, beings that are 'universal' and 'free', does not
prevent examination of the way in which, in a capitalist mode of
production, the laws of the economy become the primary determinants of social and political conditions. On the contrary, it
allows inquiry into the nature of these laws (their appearance as
natural but their actual dependence on particular social practices)
and their many effects (not just on economy-state relations but on
the nature of social relations themselves). To reflect on historically
constituted human capacities, on unfulfilled needs and wants is not,
moreover, to 'collapse' into a 'metaphysical humanism'. Rather, it
is to treat seriously the claim – the claim of all those who believe
'things might be otherwise than they are' – that potentialities for
radical change exist. The presuppositions entailed in this view,
including the belief that certain groups have the capacity and
desire to organize their lives differently, require investigation. It is
one of Marcuse's merits to have pursued issues such as these.
Although there are pronounced difficulties with some of Marcuse's

positions, difficulties that I will come to later, a critique of his work requires, as a minimum precondition, sensitivity both to the kinds of questions he was concerned with and to the different stages of development of his thought.

Third, the accusation of 'idealism' rests, as has been pointed out in one recent reply to Anderson, on the unsubstantiated assumption that the influence of idealism was completely negative.[23] The Frankfurt school's and Habermas's concern with idealism (and with a variety of other traditions of social thought and philosophy) was not motivated by a retreat to non-Marxist thinking, but by an ambition to revitalize Marxism. As Marx had turned to Hegel for a method that can be a 'scandal and an abomination to the bourgeoisie and its doctrinaire spokesmen', and for ideas that would bring to life 'hitherto existing materialism', so the critical theorists looked to Hegel for similar reasons. They were faced with an orthodoxy in Marxism (established by the Third International in particular) that reduced the Marxian project to an ideology that could legitimate Stalinism, a science that could steer an all powerful state, and a body of ideas that ran directly contrary to the revolutionary, emancipatory and fundamentally democratic dimensions of Marx's programme. At a theoretical level the reduction of Marxism to dialectical materialism trivialized the significance of human agency, and, at a political level, justified the exclusion of the mass of people from active participation in decisions that affect their lives. As Marx indicated in the *Theses on Feuerbach*, idealism restores insight into the 'active side' of materialism.[24] The retrieval of precisely this aspect of materialism – the interplay between sensuous human activity and nature, between human subjectivity and second nature – enabled the critical theorists, at various stages in their careers, to restore to the centre of Marxism some of the most radical and subversive elements of Marx's work. The latter are encapsulated by the view, defended by Horkheimer, Adorno, Marcuse and Habermas, that the process of emancipation is inseparable from the struggle for self-emancipation. Or, as Habermas put it, 'democratization, greater popular participation and decentralization of the process of formation of the collective will are essential because the *market + administration* cannot satisfy a whole series of collective needs'.[25]

Therborn argues that critical theory's real 'innovation' lies in its 'radical break with science'. In this he sees one of its most serious failings and the source of many of its deficiencies. But while it is true that each of the critical theorists launched attacks on various models of science (positivism), on science and technology as ideology, and very clearly in Marcuse's case, on modern science and technology as such, Therborn's criticism is wholly ungrounded. For it relies on a dogmatic assertion – an assertion stemming from Althusser – that science can be neatly demarcated from ideology. The assertion is dogmatic because Althusser and Therborn provide no plausible criteria to settle disputes over what constitutes the 'scientific' and what does not.[26] Critical theorists have contributed extensively to debates on this issue. Therborn does not assess their contributions. He merely calls for science against 'critical theory'. The readiness with which he dismisses Habermas's interest in 'scientific theory' is astonishing.[27]

The charge that critical theorists had an 'excessive interest' in philosophy and the theoretical traditions of non-Marxists is also ill considered. There are a number of separate issues involved here. Philosophical concerns, obviously, were at the heart of part of the critical theorists' project. But their interest in philosophy, like their interest in idealism was not just, as Therborn implies, an interest in the philosophical *per se*. It stemmed from a direct concern with major problems in theory and in practice. For example, Horkheimer and Adorno were anxious to resist the degeneration of Marxism into a form of technocratic consciousness, the increasing pervasiveness of instrumental reason in many spheres of life, and the influence of idealism, positivism and crude materialism. In resisting these things, furthermore, they were not simply concerned to dismiss them out of hand. They were well aware of the contradictions involved in rejecting the dogmatic dogmatically. The engagement with philosophy and non-Marxist traditions of thought was, therefore, a necessity – a necessity for the struggle against misleading and pernicious doctrines.

But there are other important reasons for engaging with authors who draw their inspiration from non-Marxist perspectives. The acknowledgement that Marxism in its Stalinist manifestation became a repressive ideology – thereby confirming that as a body of ideas it is not the sole key to truth – constitutes one of the crucial premises of critical theory. It allows recognition not only of the fact that 'classical' Marxist concepts are inadequate to account for a range of phenomena (fascism, Stalinism), but also of the fact that the ideas and theories of, for example, Weber and Freud, provide vital clues to problems that face Marxists – why revolution in the West was expected and why it had not occurred. The critical theorists' concern to assess and, where applicable, develop non-Marxist thought was, again, not an attempt to undermine Marxism, but an attempt to reinvigorate and develop it. Whether or not critical theory is adequate to this task is, of course, another question, a question I will return to later.

It should, in addition, be clear from my exposition of critical theory that the pursuit of philosophical problems was not at the expense of certain classical Marxist concerns. The central importance of Marx's contributions to political economy was acknowledged by each of the critical theorists. In fact, they tended to take its validity for granted.[28] While Horkheimer and Adorno did not pursue detailed analyses of the economy themselves, such analyses were encouraged in the Institute. The work of Pollock, Neumann and Gurland is often ignored by critics of the Frankfurt school. If it were properly addressed, the charge that the school neglected political economy would lose a great deal of its force. Any view that Habermas ignores the essential concerns of political economy also appears rather thin in light of his analysis of, for example, crisis tendencies.

But the very objection that key Marxist problems were neglected needs to be examined carefully. For when the point is made it is usually taken for granted that these problem areas are synonymous with political economy and with the theory and practice of Leninist (or Trotskyist) politics. Yet this equation was rejected by each of the critical theorists. Their positions, however, are rarely confronted by their critics. With respect to political economy the position of critical theory is clear: political economy is crucial but too narrow a base when taken alone for the development of Marxist concerns. I shall return to this point again in the discussion of the focus on aesthetics and culture. The supposed equation between Marxist politics and a Leninist (or Trotskyist) programme raises additional questions. While it is the case that critical theory has not provided an extended discussion of 'the strategy of the party necessary to overthrow the bourgeois state', this is not an oversight or a rejection of the importance of practical concerns. Instead, it must be understood as a result both of an explicit hostility to Leninist forms of organization as the mode of political intervention and as an explicit and urgent attempt to uncover and expose the factors which currently make positive claims about the possibility of revolutionary change in the West appear a mere fantasy. Leninist vanguard organizations were looked upon critically because it was thought they reproduced a chronic division of labour, bureaucracy and authoritarian leadership. Although it is true that the critical theorists did not produce a sustained political theory, they stand in the tradition of those who maintain *the unity of socialism and liberty* and who argue that the aims of a rational society must be embedded in the means used to establish that society. Horkheimer *et al.* hoped that their work would help to compel changes in consciousness and political action in a similar way to the effects generated by *Capital*. Their project was a form of political praxis with significant political implications. Far from reflecting a distance from practical-political problems, their interest in theory and critique was directly related to an ambition to analyse new forms of domination, undermine ideology, enhance awareness of the material conditions of life circumstances, and to aid the creation of radical political movements.

The view that the Frankfurt school's studies of aesthetics and culture constitute, in part, a distraction from the key determinants of social and political life is also questionable in a number of respects. First, it fails to confront their arguments that the critique of political economy does not provide a sufficient basis to investigate the increasing encroachment of the market and bureaucratic organizations into areas of life hitherto free of them, and that the general interlocking of 'base' and 'superstructure', of civil society and the polity, seems to make radical alternatives to the present society remote. Second, it assumes that if only the Frankfurt school had grasped 'the objective nature of the contradiction between the social character of the productive forces and the private character of the relations of production' (the nature of the capitalist mode of production), then the collapse of their analysis into an obsession with the 'subjective' could have been avoided.[29] In the critiques of critical theory launched from an Althusserian perspective the concept of 'mode of production' is presented as if the Frankfurt school and Habermas had never heard of it and as if it can unlock all the core dimensions of capitalism. But a careful reading of critical theory would reveal that in most of the Frankfurt school's substantive analysis the concept of the capitalist mode of production is central; that Habermas seeks to develop an array of analytic tools which include this concept; that all the critical theorists had the strongest objections to the use of an hypostatized notion of 'modes of production'. Their work sought to expose the complex relations and mediations which prevent the forces and relations of production from being characterized simply as objective – as things developing 'over the heads' of human agents. An analysis of the components of culture, of identity formation, etc. is necessary because 'history is made' – by the 'situated conduct of partially knowing subjects'. The contradiction between the forces and relations of production does not give rise to a fixed crisis path. The course of the crisis, the nature of its resolution, depends on the practices of social agents, and on how they understand the situation they are part of. Critical theory does not downplay structure, but seeks to examine the interplay between structure and social practices, the mediation of the objective and subjective in and through particular social phenomena.

It is quite wrong to suggest that 'in place of the complex unity of mode of production . . . Habermas proposes the dualism of instrumental action and communicative action'.[30] Habermas's distinction between two types of action is meant to capture the differences between the types of action that underpin – produce and reproduce – the 'complex unity'. Although Habermas clearly thinks that the notion of mode of production is insufficient to analyse social formations this is not because, as Chapter 10 makes clear, action concepts are substituted for it. To infer this is simply to mistake the different levels of analysis at which he works.

Finally, the objection that critical theory developed in an academic setting isolated from working-class politics, and that it became increasingly embroiled in 'abstract issues' and 'second-order' discourse, requires comment. It is true that critical theory did develop, as has most of the criticism of critical theory, in an academic context. It is also the case that critical theory developed largely in isolation from working-class politics. Given that the most active years of the Institute of Social Research were also the years of fascism, Stalinism and the second world war, this is hardly surprising (though it must be added that such isolation clearly suited Horkheimer as he grew more conservative in the years following the second world war). But the criticism of 'lack of involvement' itself presupposes an attachment to the view that the only form of legitimate political involvement is active participation in day to day working class politics. One of the significant achievements of critical theory is, in my view, to have shown that there are many ways of contributing to the project of human emancipation and that the terms of reference of the political are wider than is often thought. The Frankfurt school and Habermas sought to extend and adapt the insights of Marx's work in order to reveal the complex factors which hinder people coming to consciousness of themselves as capable of different action. The Frankfurt school's criticisms of contemporary culture, authoritarianism, bureaucracy and so on were intended to help foster independent thinking and the strugle for emancipation. They directed attention to the effects of domination not only in production but in the family, the environment and other areas of life. Consequently, their work transformed the concept of the political; it directed attention to issues such as the division of labour, sexism, ecological problems as well as the central question of ownership and control. This has crucial potential significance which was recognized by sections of the New Left in the 1960s. In short, critical theory took Marxism into a range of new areas. The extension of the focus of critique, the expansion of the domain of political reflection, helped to open up many dimensions of life to critical social analysis and active intervention.

Critical theory's leading spokesmen made important independent contributions to these issues. Horkheimer's attempts to develop a critique of ideology, to focus attention on the necessity of interdisciplinary research in the comprehension of cultural, political and economic phenomena, and to pursue the analysis of the antagonisms of society into the depths of the individual's psyche, provide lessons for social inquiry which have by no means been exhausted.[31] Adorno's unfolding of the logic of commodity production and exchange value, his development of immanent critique, his use of negative dialectics in cultural criticism (especially in his studies on music), and his critique of all philosophies which try to establish indubitable first principles, stand as an enduring challenge to all those who would seek to understand society and science within the framework of traditional approaches.[32] The retrieval and defence by Marcuse of negative thinking in the writings of Hegel, Marx and Freud represents a major achievement in light of the existing interpretations which have neglected or distorted their emphasis on negation.[33] His examination of the obstacles to negative thinking in contemporary capitalist and socialist societies – which are, of course, recognized to be immense – with the simultaneous commitment to utopian thinking, are a provocative challenge to the dominant orthodoxies in liberalism and Marxism.

Habermas's achievements cannot easily be placed alongside those of the earlier critical theorists, although they often address similar problems. His criticisms of nineteenth- and twentieth-century philosophy – especially scientism and hermeneutics – offer original interpretations along with radically new proposals for epistemology. The theories of knowledge-constitutive interests and of communicative competence rank as bold achievements in philosophy. His review of the philosophy of social science provides one of the most systematic and coherent accounts of the field. His explication of the scientization of politics and his reworking of crisis theory in the context of an analysis of social evolution is a novel framework for posing basic questions about past and contemporary society. And Habermas has, perhaps more than anyone else, contributed to the fruitful comparison and assessment of Continental and Anglo-American philosophy and social theory.

The thought of the critical theorists marks one of the major sources of stimulus in twentieth century philosophical and social thought. It sets out an array of ideas and theories which invite debate and assessment, but given the diversity of the work, it is necessary to circumscribe the range of issues that will be dealt with here. I would like to pose a series of questions about the cogency of some of the critical theorists' views on the economy, polity and the factors which shape social struggle in the remaining space of this chapter; I will focus on the notion of critical theory itself in Chapter 14. It should be emphasized that the discussion is not exhaustive. My critical remarks are intended to have a tentative status, indicating certain limitations and raising issues which require, in my view, further attention.

The economy, the polity and social struggle

The Frankfurt school

Although I have defended critical theory against the general position advanced by critics such as Anderson and Therborn, a number of their points converge with my own views. I agree, for example, that critical theory fails to grasp adequately the pattern of conflicts and tensions in society and that it maintains an exaggerated notion of the cohesion of capitalism. I agree, moreover, that the level at which some of the critical theorists work often makes the relevance of their ideas to social and political events hard to grasp.

(This does not entail endorsing the view that many of the critical theorists' concerns are merely abstract.) But points such as these must be detached from the *framework* in which they are posed by those essentially dismissive of critical theory.

The work of the Frankfurt school and of the Institute of Social Research does not lead, I want to argue, to an adequate theory of economics, politics, or of their relation to one another. Their conception of capitalist (and socialist) development is excessively influenced by their experience of fascism and Nazism. While categories of conflict – including class and class conflict – remain even in the Frankfurt theorists' late work, they are not adequately elaborated. A conception of society is presented which overestimates its internal homogeneity; society appears in their writings as steered from above rather than as the outcome, as I believe it to be, of a continuous process of struggle over rules and resources.[34]

From the late 1930s onward in particular, Horkheimer, Adorno and Marcuse postulated an overharmonious relation between the state, administrative apparatuses and the economy. While none of these men defended a straightforward theory (in the conventional sense of a hierarchy of interrelated propositions) about the state–economy relation, a series of claims were made about this domain. Many of the generalizations were based on Pollock's writings about pre-Nazi and Nazi Germany. The economy in Weimer and Nazi Germany was subjected to massive political intervention. But it would be wrong to infer from this, as Pollock did, that the various regimes supporting the intervention had a highly defined sense of purpose and a straightforward capacity to execute their will. Recent research has strongly suggested, for example, that even the workings of the Nazi government 'were characterized by an extreme diffusion and dislocation of authority, and a highly disordered proliferation of agencies and hierarchies'.[35] The research has tended to bear out the position taken by Neumann in *Behemoth*, not adhered to for the most part by Horkheimer or Adorno, that the Nazi period, like the decade in Germany before it, was marked by an absence of clear structure and central political control.

If one looks beyond the Nazi regime and, indeed, beyond the framework of nation-states in general, then the relations between the economy and polity appear even more complex, and anything but a simple unity or carefully controlled and closed relation

– as Marcuse, in particular, sometimes suggests.[36] The economic and political dynamics of the 1970s are a clear testimony to this: despite massive state intervention, economic crises persist. They may not take a simply economic form as various crisis tendencies are interlaced, but they manifest few signs of being brought under the sway of centralized administrations and bureaucracies.[37]

Four points need to be made about the Frankfurt school's view that the economy and state are deeply interlocked in capitalist societies.[38] First, it leads to an unsatisfactory notion of domination; that is, a notion which suggests a rigid relation between various public and private bureaucracies, and a conception of administrative and/or bureaucratic and/or class domination as seemingly inescapable. The mechanisms which lead to this state of affairs are poorly elaborated and documented – especially the configurations of social relations and conflicts that underlie these apparent developments. As a consequence, the power of the ruling class and the 'control centre' of the system appear as an obvious and/or necessary outcome, rather than one that has been – and is – a focus of struggle.[39] Second, by failing to examine the development of particular policies and reforms (regarding, for instance, national health, nationalization) and by treating them as, more or less, the outcome of manoeuvres from above, the positions developed by Horkheimer *et al.* (especially after 1940) seem to deny several important possibilities: the possibility of conflict and struggle over state activities; of the state being conceived as an arena of class and other types of struggle; and the possibility of reforms being instituted which work to circumscribe and perhaps undermine (in the long run) the accumulation process.[40] Recent research on the constant pressure on government and state to legitimate their activities and on the unintended consequences of state intervention in the material and non-material infrastructure of society (fiscal crisis) testify to the importance of not closing off these perspectives from analysis.[41]

Third, there are policies that are put into effect by public administrations, for example, internal reforms of their own organization structures, which cannot simply be explained, as the Frankfurt school thought, by reference to the pursuit of profit and production maximization and/or the commitment to instrumental reason and/or various forms of direct corporate pressure.[42] To explain policies such as these it is necessary to have an account of the 'structuration' (production and reproduction) of state organizations, both in terms of their internal operations and their relations to the economy and other social realms.[43] The preliminary work done in this area suggests that the positions developed by the Frankfurt school are insufficient accounts of this complex reality.[44]

Fourth, the work of the Institute's economists is inadequate to explain the persistence of political-business cycles and the unemployment and inflation facing advanced capitalist societies. The interrelation of economic outcomes with everyday understandings of them is also inadequately developed. It has been shown in a recent analysis by Douglas Hibbs that not only are objective economic interests – class interests – at the basis of the political-business cycle (generated as it is, in large part, by cyclical movements in labour costs, the struggle over national income), but also that a fairly high degree of awareness exists, amongst all parties involved, as to who wins and who loses at the macroeconomic level.[45] Objective economic outcomes, in so far as they are reflected in the movement of wages, profits and the distribution of personal income over the business cycle, are understood and transformed into various (class based) preferences. This degree of class conflict and consciousness, while not to be confused with revolutionary activity, cannot be explained satisfactorily with the Frankfurt school's terms of reference.[46]

The school's tendency to hold an exaggerated view of the integration, or unity, of economy and state relations is complemented by an overestimation of the significance of instrumental reason, technique and technology in the shaping of political attitudes and demands. The stress Adorno put on reification and fetishism in the analysis of consciousness and ideology, along with Marcuse's strong emphasis on the pressures towards depoliticization, contain many insights; but they cannot account, I believe, for the diversity in the levels of awareness of social conditions. This point can best be illustrated by reference to the whole notion of society's reach into the individual. To the extent that generalizations can be made about social consciousness – and most historical and comparative work suggests great caution is needed here – they might suggest, as Michael Mann and Anthony Giddens, amongst others, have argued, that a 'dual consciousness' is often expressed in communities and work places.[47] This implies a quite radical interpretation of many everyday events but a relatively conservative, privatistic interest in dominant political parties and processes.

Many institutions and processes are perceived and hypostatized as 'natural', 'the way things have been and always will be'; but the language used to express and account for immediate needs and their frustrations often reveals a marked penetration of ideology or dominant interpretative systems. (Ideology is understood here as a set of beliefs that mask or conceal aspects of reality, particularly social contradictions, in the interests of dominant social groups or classes.)[48] Social structures may mould the individual but meaning systems do not in any straightforward sense reflect the stamp of the production process or the culture industry. Nor is there much evidence to suggest, as Marcuse sometimes does, that consumption patterns foster a strong identification with the Establishment. While many members of the Frankfurt school clearly recognize this, at a theoretical level it is not taken systematically into account. If it were, they would not have asserted so strongly that the superego is increasingly representative of collectivities, e.g. the (school) class and/or state. Rather, they would understand some of the key constitutive elements of identity formation as the result of interaction between active, reflective and critical participants – the result of social struggle – and not simply, as the Frankfurt school sometimes suggests, the outcome of imposition.

Although there is evidence of dissensus and various levels of class consciousness, it is clear that there has also been widespread compliance to dominant ideas. The question is: what does this compliance mean? What does it entail? Does it reflect normative integration (as Habermas, amongst others, might suggest) or depoliticization (as Marcuse has forcefully argued)? There are strong reasons and evidence to suggest that, in many cases, this 'compliance' is best interpreted as a combination of pragmatic acceptance of existing institutions and false consciousness. Pragmatic acceptance or acquiescence is involved because few alternatives are seen to the status quo and it is recognized that one must participate in it, if comfort and security in life are to be achieved. False consciousness can be argued to be involved (though this is clearly a more contentious claim) because the asymmetrical distribution of power ('transformative capacity') in contemporary society is mobilized (albeit often unintentionally) to prevent working people from properly understanding the reality they experience. The notion of dual consciousness lends important support to this idea. Frames of meaning often utilized to articulate needs and account for everyday life frequently diverge from the interpretative schemes employed to make sense of traditional political institutions. The mode in which the latter are understood can be traced back, in part, to the family, to schooling, and to the culture industry – to socialization processes which embody ideas and theories about life which do not coincide with many people's own accounts of the 'realities of working life'.[49] The conservative ideology often expressed by these processes does not, however, simply replace everyday interpretations – dissensus and seemingly deviant frames of meaning remain.[50]

The Frankfurt school's analysis (especially Adorno's) of contemporary culture represents one of the most important areas of their work. It helps explain, more clearly than all conventional sociological accounts, the ways in which dominant ideologies penetrate everyday interpretative schemes. But assumptions are made in this analysis which, in light of my discussion above, need to be questioned. Particularly, a homology is often assumed, quite unjustifiably, between the form and content of the culture industry and the actual consciousness of working people. This assumption is most often found in Horkheimer's, Lowenthal's and Marcuse's writings, though it also exists in Adorno's thought. Their work often shifts quite sharply, as one commentator has aptly noted, 'from an internal aesthetic analysis of capitalist commercial culture to its assumed effects on mass behaviour and consciousness'. This shift in position neglects the important consideration that 'the cultural media function through a complex of mediating factors and influences so that the cultural object itself is grasped, understood and assimilated through the influence of peer groups, occupational and professional groups, family, and other social institutions'.[51] Reactions to the 'culture industry', along with the actual effects of 'cultural consumption', remain under-researched.

Connected with this is a tendency for the Institute's members to overlook the need for a differentiated historical analysis of the development of different aesthetic forms – art, literature, music.[52] The development of 'mass culture' has been uneven. Their work underestimates the degree to which contemporary culture often combines a variety of impulses and elements. For example, it is not at all clear that Adorno's characterization of popular music (see pages 99-104) holds for a variety of very popular musical innovations. The complexity and subtlety of much of the Beatles' music is a case in point. Nor can the different type of reactions to popular music simply be placed under the rather fixed categories Adorno tended to elaborate.[53] A case could be made, more systematically than Adorno does, that the appeal of some kinds of popular music (certain strains of soul, blues, rock and jazz), can be traced to a subversive or critical element. Their style and 'message' sometimes create rhythms and events which are in contradiction with most people's rather more passive involvement in other areas of life. Adorno failed to differentiate adequately the variety of possible reactions to popular music. It is at least an open question as to the effects on thought and action of the latter and certainly more research and analysis is required to settle the issue.

Reliance on the immanent method itself is perhaps directly responsible for some of the problems in the Frankfurt school's account of contemporary culture. The importance of national and local cultures for individual and social identity is underestimated. Their approach to culture could have been considerably enriched if they had supplemented immanent critique with a comparative historical perspective. For in taking certain national or local historical trajectories as the units of analysis and comparison, one can uncover some of the elements unique to particular constellations of social relations and cultural practices – elements which are vital in explaining the very different histories (political and cultural) which persist across nations, despite the fact that they have in common a capitalist mode of production. This same point can be made with respect to the Frankfurt school's treatment of industrial and political organizations and collectivities.

A different series of issues arise when we consider the framework employed to investigate socio-psychological questions. The framework was, of course, adopted in large part from Freud and, as Habermas points out, with good reason:

If one considers the normative implications of notions like ego-strength, dismantling the ego-distant parts of the super-ego and reducing the domain in which unconscious defense mechanisms functions, it becomes clear that psychoanalysis singles out certain personality structures as ideal. . . . In the . . . work of the Institute of Social Research. . . . basic psychological and sociological concepts can be interlaced because the perspective projected in them of an autonomous ego and an emancipated society reciprocally require one another.[54]

An autonomous ego can be sustained only if the structures which support the authoritarian state are undermined. But this notion of an autonomous ego is ambiguous. For it seems to harbour assumptions about identity as a property of the individual – assumptions which imply, in the last analysis, that identity comprises a given set of qualities and potentialities for smooth-functioning integration.[55] Now Adorno, in particular, was scathing about assumptions such as these – at least, as they were manifest in Fromm's writings. Yet in the work of most of the Institute's members they reappear. In Marcuse these notions are explicit and boldly explicated. He maintains the very un-Freudian idea of the 'self-sublimation of sexuality': the 'obstructions and limitations' upon libido can, in the good society, be 'set and accepted by the instinct itself', rather than by conflict between *Eros* and external reality.[56] In Horkheimer's writings and even in Adorno's (especially in the *Authoritarian Personality*), a not altogether dissimilar idea is alluded to; an idea which appears to preserve the heritage of idealist philosophy – a heritage which holds out the possibility of an 'uncoerced ego that is potentially identical with itself'. A notion like this is employed as a benchmark to assess societies that fail to produce, as Habermas wryly put it, 'upright individuals'.[57] But it is hard to grasp the precise content of notions such as these. For they are frequently expressed as part of a paradoxical thesis: on the one hand, history, as manifest through specific social conditions, is granted primacy as the crucial determinant of character structure; while on the other hand, a unitary human nature is postulated. In my view, Adorno most successfully brought together these two tenets by interpreting Freud's instinct theory as a basis for a large variety of patterns in the human psyche. Horkheimer and, in particular, Marcuse (in the latter half of his career) are less convincing in their attempt to extricate themselves from the problems entailed by this thesis. Horkheimer's notion of what is 'immanent in man' or 'immanent in human labour', and Marcuse's concept of individual needs and potentialities (developed in the context of the thesis of the obsolescence of the Freudian notion of man), seem to ascribe to human beings certain qualities which, however distorted or repressed, somehow remain the basis for hope (Horkheimer), the ultimate source of progressive change (Marcuse). As a consequence, they often fall back on a concept of critique which they themselves, in other contexts, rejected: an ahistorical essence becomes the criterion for the evaluation of the present.[58]

A number of issues concerning Freud's interpretation could be raised. But one issue above all others deserves to be mentioned, for it has implications for the thesis of the end of the individual and the explanation given for authoritarian behaviour. A strong case can be made that, for Freud, it is less the *father in reality* (the actually strong or weak man) and more the *symbolic father* that is crucial for the passage of the Oedipus complex.[59] There are several implications of this, but one is of special importance: a weak father in reality can 'produce' children with strong superegos. In *Civilization and its Discontents* Freud footnotes Melanie Klein's work in support of this view.[60]

This whole issue might not be so significant if it were not for a series of studies of socialization which appear to lend considerable support (albeit indirectly) to this emphasis of Freud's. The studies reveal low correlations and/or marked inconsistencies across research findings between individual and cultural differences in parental practices and differences in children's motivational behaviour. Many of these studies have focused on 'conscience strength' (the superego) through measures of 'resistance to temptation' and measures of guilt.[61] They have attempted to relate childhood and adolescent differences in 'conscience strength' to early experiences of restraint of gratification; amount and type of moral discipline; and parent attitudes and power structures.[62] As Kohlberg points out in a survey of this literature, 'in general no correlations have been found between parental modes of handling infantile wants, needs, drives and later moral behaviours or attitudes'. Nor have significant relations been found between 'amounts of various types of discipline [for example 'love withdrawal'] and moral views and actions'.[63] It appears, therefore, that one of the Frankfurt school's bases for explaining authoritarianism is problematic: the reach of society into the individual may not depend directly on the socio-economic position of the father and particular parental practices. This conclusion is reinforced by a consideration of the time period in which the authoritarian personality is said to have emerged. The generation that most actively participated in the rise of fascism and Nazism were born in the years preceding and during the first world war. This was not a time of mass unemployment in which the father's potency (as socio-economic provider) was wholly shattered. Mass unemployment (unemployment affecting 26 per cent of the population) was a feature of the late 1920s and early 1930s. The children born during this period were not pivotal in the rise of authoritarianism.[64]

The *Authoritarian Personality* itself has been subject to an array of criticisms. These include the charges that: the personality syndrome is not just associated with right-wing political views (intolerance of ambiguity, stereotyping and suggestibility can be associated with a wide spectrum of political positions); the key questionnaires, designed so that a 'yes' answer indicates a high score in all cases, gives rise to a 'response bias' (since some people tend to answer survey questions positively); the F-scale cannot be claimed to be correlated with, for example, ethnocentrism (since the F-scale contains many reworded elements of the E and A–S scales).[65] All these criticisms have some substance. The postulated relation of the personality syndrome to specific political convictions must be rejected (although relations between the syndrome and a tendency to express authoritarian attitudes appear to have been confirmed).

There is something to be made of the oft-repeated charge that the Frankfurt school failed, ultimately, to integrate studies of the individual and social consciousness with political economy and institutional analysis. Because so many of the most important features of contemporary capitalist society are seen as the result of initiatives from public and private bureaucracies (Marcuse) or as the outcome of illusion (reification) (Adorno), the importance of analysing particular patterns of social relations, the labour process (the experiences people have of it as well as its structure) and political organizations, is downgraded. Adorno's thesis of increasing reification, for example, fails to develop a detailed theory of the ways in which reification is produced and experienced by individuals in various social settings. Many changes are postulated to have occurred in the organization of production, consumption and in the structure of the labour force; but these are only pointed to in a general way. Without more detailed accounts of these phenomena the alleged opaqueness of society remains unpenetrated. Reification becomes a 'synonym for an all-embracing power structure', which appears to affect everyone in an equal manner.[66] Without systematic reflection on the contexts in which it is produced and reproduced, it remains – when used so generally – a less than compelling notion. An image of society is projected which can be read as a left counterpart to the discredited 'end of ideology' thesis. Marcuse's *One Dimensional Man* is open to a similar objection. Many of his claims about changes in production, productivity and state intervention give the impression of an increasingly homogeneous and depoliticized society. These views, however, are, at best, only loosely supported by evidence and fail to capture the seemingly irreducible conflicts and tensions in society.[67]

This last series of points is connected with what, I think, is an insufficient approach to, or use of, techniques of historical investigation. Despite the Frankfurt school's continual emphasis on history and the importance of historical inquiry, their work lacks sufficient historical detail on the ways in which social forms are created, sustained and changed. Despite the intention, most clearly articulated by Horkheimer, to bring together theoretical considerations and empirical research, many of their boldest claims are under-researched. Precisely that which they sought to grasp – the 'fluid reality' of sociological and psychological life – is neglected. This occurred, I would like to suggest, for two reasons. First, models of societal development were too readily drawn from experiences of fascism, Nazism, and Stalinism. Second, as confidence in the possibility of fundamental social change was gradually lost (particularly by Horkheimer and Adorno) hopes were increasingly vested in the individual as the fount of freedom – despite all the arguments they made against such a position. As a consequence, there is a tendency, most notable in Horkheimer's and Marcuse's work, to lose touch with the essential referent of Marxian and Freudian concepts. Each of these respective systems of thought is concerned, at its centre, with relations – with relations between individuals, groups and other collectivities, with relations characterized by irreducible conflicts and contradictions. It is these that one loses sight of in, for instance, Horkheimer's use of concepts like 'mode of production' in his writings of the 1940s onward, and in Marcuse's use of the ego, superego, id system.

Habermas

Habermas's approach to the analysis of capitalism raises a number of parallel considerations. These can be seen most clearly in the crisis argument developed in *Legitimation Crisis*. This argument relies on many system-theoretic concepts and assumptions; accordingly, the practical activity of social agents tends, as McCarthy has noted, 'to recede into the background'.[68] The same tendency is fostered by Habermas's gradual 'deemphasis of hermeneutic motifs in favour of a more strongly theoretical programme. As the universalistic elements in the theories of communication and social evolution have come to the fore, the situa-

tional and practical aspects of social inquiry have declined in systematic importance.'[69] This shift in direction has implications
which merge with some of those of the Frankfurt analysis. Critique
is addressed to 'mankind as such' and not to any particular class or
group. While this position follows, in part, from some convincing
arguments against orthodox Marxist expectations, it also follows,
much more disconcertingly, from the categorial system itself.
Habermas' programme, at least as it is articulated to date, diverts
attention away from the analysis of concrete social and political
situations (where particular interests weigh rather more heavily
than universal species' capacities).

Central to the arguments of *Legitimation Crisis* is the view that
the ideology of advanced capitalism is being undermined. This
argument is crucial to the contention that in the changing structures of consciousness the grounds for a new principle of organization can be located. For just as Marx argued that in the womb of
the old mode of production a new mode is born and develops, so
Habermas argues that a new and more developed form of consciousness is emerging which will not support capitalist value relations. But within the terms of Habermas's characterization of the
structure of consciousness there is a tendency to overestimate the
degree to which liberal capitalist ideology has been eroded, and
generalize too readily about complex empirical phenomena. If one
examines the substantial number of studies analysing the nature of
the social cohesion of capitalist societies, one thing emerges with
clarity: patterns of consciousness, especially class consciousness,
vary significantly across and within specific cultures and countries.[70] At the empirical level there is no ready evidence to support
Habermas's contention of the potentially imminent realization of a
communicative ethics – the highest stage of 'man's inner cognitive
logic'. On the available evidence (and in light of there being no
substantial evidence in his own work), there does not seem to be a
sufficient basis to locate the emergence of a principle of organization of a 'post-modern' society. Contemporary changes in normative structures have, it seems, a very ambiguous relationship to
discursive will-formation, universality and critique.

This point connects to another difficulty with the argument.
Habermas refers to groups of, amongst others, students and
women as evidence that 'the system' is failing to produce the
requisite amounts of necessary motivation. Apart from the fact
that the argument sounds a little like a (new) left-over from the

1960s, the further conclusion that this phenomenon will spread to other segments of the population is, as it is currently formulated, not very convincing.[71] There is little approaching a revolutionary subject in Habermas's argument; and this despite the fact that he recognizes the need for a theory such as his to be able to identify the subject of emancipation. Processes of actual transformation remain unthematized: we remain very much in the dark as to the nature of political processes and events. As a consequence, it is difficult to draw any political conclusions from the crisis argument. The practical implications of the theory are undeveloped.

Different problems arise in Habermas's discussion of actual and potential system crises. System crises (economic and rationality) can, on his account, be potentially contained (although it does not follow that they will be). Containment occurs, however, only at the cost of increasing legitimation pressures on the state: the state is the interface at which the tensions of both system integration and social integration meet. Habermas's argument rests, of course, on the claim that organized capitalism can control its potential system crises (as opposed to social identity crises). Can this claim be supported? Most of Habermas's remarks on system crises, like those of the Frankfurt school, centre around considerations of the nation state; that is, the focus is on the changing relation between the state and economy within an ideal-typical capitalist country. His discussion of past and present economic tendencies pays little, if any, systematic attention to developments of international capitalism. He raises important considerations in connection with the law of value; but the referent and context is usually that of the nation-state. It is crucially important to explore the development of capitalism in one country in the context of international political economy. The capitalist world was created in dependence on an international market and is ever more dependent on international trade. Before one can conclude that economic crises can be contained (on either a national or international level), the relationship between economic crises in the nation-state and crisis tendencies in the international market must be better analysed and explained. These issues deserve a much more substantial treatment than Habermas gives them.[72] Without an analysis of them, Habermas's conception of the logic of crisis development can be questioned; for the political-economic constraints on capitalist development might be much less open to control and manipulation than he suggests.

Habermas's claim that there are logics of development in history treads a fine line between the stronger claims of Hegelian teleology and historical relativism; but there are problems here too. The argument for the importance of cognitive development is enormously suggestive, and – as he himself readily admits – highly problematic. Any discussion of a logic (or logics) of development carries with it certain dangers. In a somewhat different context Adorno pointed out that:

To suppose, if only methodologically, anything like an independent logic of culture is to collaborate in the hypostasis of culture, the ideological proton pseudos. The substance of culture, according to this argument, resides not in culture alone but in its relation to something external, to the material life-process. Culture, as Marx observed of juridical and political systems, cannot be fully 'understood either in terms of itself . . . or in terms of the so-called universal development of the mind.' To ignore this . . . is to make ideology the basic matter and thus to establish it firmly.[73]

Habermas would hope to avoid the weakness to which Adorno refers. But obviously he does want to defend the idea of a logic of development of key components of communicative interaction (world views, for instance) that cannot be reduced to the logic of the development of work. In so doing, his argument carries with it a tendency to accept certain forms of distorted communication and hence certain levels of social repression, as unavoidable at various stages in history. (I believe that this position was also held by Marx.) Given this view it is extremely important to elaborate when in any given society systematically distorted communication is unavoidable and when it is not. If criteria for these judgements are not provided we risk, as Adorno put it, 'making ideology the basic matter' and thus reinforcing it. Habermas's conception of critical theory, as I indicate below, does not address these issues satisfactorily.

Further, the rather formal nature of Habermas's current enterprise makes it very hard to see what explanatory force his theories and arguments have. It is not at all clear, for instance, how the diversity of cultures (China, India, the West) can be made sense of within the terms of the theory of social evolution. The same can be said even if attention is restricted to the application of his ideas to capitalism. Concepts like rationality crisis, legitimation crisis are not easy to employ; for they are elaborated without detailed reference to specific instances of crises and the conditions which have generated them. The relation of rationality crisis to, for example, class structure and its related patterns of struggle remains unexplicated. Theoretical categorization is combined with an insufficient regard for historical analysisof evolving social relations.[74]

14 The concept of critical theory

In recent discussions of critical theory, especially those in the literature of the social sciences, Habermas's work is often presented as if it were self-evidently the pinnacle of critical theory. The general emphasis on Habermas's ideas has a number of unfortunate consequences. First, the differences in scope of the various types of critical theory remain unexplicated. Second, there is a tendency to ignore the fact that some of the writings of the Frankfurt school offer alternative positions to those defended by Habermas. For instance, in one introduction to critical theory, the Frankfurt school is said to have evolved through four 'stages of development' – stages which appear to comprise a path of cumulative and progressive development from the earliest writings of Horkheimer and Adorno to Habermas's most current works.[1] As should be quite clear from Parts One and Two of this book, views such as these fail to do justice to the very considerable differences that exist between, for example, the standpoint developed by Adorno in *Negative Dialectics*, and that of Habermas in *Knowledge and Human Interests*. Inaccurate views of this genre, however, are overshadowed by the highly misleading impression of critical theory created by studies which appear motivated merely by a desire to discredit it theoretically. It is worth mentioning briefly two such studies in order to illustrate the insubstantial nature of the cases often made against the positions of the critical theorists. They provide a useful background to my own commentary on the concept of critical theory as understood by each of its authors.

Zoltan Tar, in a book published in 1977, seeks to assess the contributions of Horkheimer and Adorno.[2] In Tar's opinion, critical theory 'is the document of the disintegration of old Central European bourgeois society' – the expression of 'a certain sociohistoric condition and the situation of a social group, the marginal bourgeois-Jewish intelligentsia'.[3] His main conclusion is that critical theory cannot qualify either as Marxism or as 'scientific sociology'; it made precious few, if any, contributions to either of these and is, 'in the last analysis . . . another existential philosophy'.[4] Tar frequently accuses Horkheimer and Adorno of not defining their key terms (like 'reflection') and for failing to support – with argument and evidence – their philosophy and sociology. Yet Tar himself neither defines the concept of existentialism nor provides arguments as to its main flaws. Without this, one of his major conclusions remains devoid of critical content.[5]

The view that Horkheimer and Adorno are neither Marxists nor 'scientific sociologists' is derived by comparing their work to 'ideal-types' of Marxism and 'scientific sociology'.[6] These types are presented without argument, without discussion of their relation to one another, and as if there were a consensus as to the basic elements of these doctrines. The debate over what precisely constitutes these doctrines – a debate which was vital to critical theory – is simply by-passed. As a consequence, the significance of much of critical theory is missed. Tar's use of biographical information in the book in order to 'explain' a number of Horkheimer's and Adorno's positions further detracts from serious argument. To establish a connection, for instance, between Horkheimer's Jewish background and his philosophy is not enough to bring the latter into disrepute. Nor can the language which Horkheimer used to express himself be disparaged by simply saying that it is 'saturated with biblical terminology such as true, truth, false . . . suffering. . .'![7] Tar sets up a straw man and then, from a variety of positions which are unrelated to each other, tries to knock it down.

Karl Popper, in a well-known article, 'Reason or revolution' (1970), says of the critical theorists generally that they were 'simply talking trivialities in high-sounding language'.[8] Of Habermas he writes: 'most of what he says seems to me trivial; the rest seems to me mistaken'.[9] It is striking that Popper, a putative champion of open discussion and argument, presents these harsh assessments after only a most cursory reference to critical theory. He fails to analyse any of the major works of Horkheimer, Adorno or Habermas. The little he says about Adorno and Habermas is itself mistaken. (He does not discuss Horkheimer.) This can be illustrated by reference to his remarks on Habermas.

Popper characterizes Habermas's views as follows:

Professor Habermas seems to think that only one who is a practical critic of existing society can produce serious theoretical arguments about society, since social knowledge cannot be divorced from fundamental social attitudes.[10]

Popper's 'reply' to this position is, in his own words, 'very simple'. He welcomes discussion about the problems of society but adds:

I certainly do not think that the debate about the reform of society should be reserved for those who first put in a claim for recognition as political revolutionaries, and who see the sole function of the revolutionary intellectual in pointing out as much as possible that is repulsive in our social life (excepting their own social roles).[11]

Popper clearly misrepresents Habermas's position. Habermas's writings continuously indicate how seriously he takes the views of those with whom he disagrees. His reformulation of Marx's theories – drawing as it does on a variety of non-Marxist thinkers – makes any suggestion that he thinks 'one must be a practical critic of existing society' to produce 'serious arguments', appear quite absurd. Moreover, Popper fails to differentiate a position like that of Habermas (which focuses on 'cognitive interests') from that of the sociology of knowledge (which directly relates knowledge to 'social attitudes'). Further, Popper's 'reply' to Habermas compounds the errors. It is a striking feature of Habermas's work that far from 'first putting in a claim as revolutionary' and using this in some sense to justify a critique of society, he continuously asks himself if a critical standpoint can be justified and, if so, in what form. Habermas's work is distinguished by a concern for 'rational criticism'.

My critical commentary below focuses on the main tenets of each of the models of critical theory and on grounds given for them. Issues are also raised about the fundamental nature of the critical enterprise. Since Horkheimer's position in the early 1940s grew closer to Adorno's, I shall begin with remarks on Adorno's views and keep my comments on Horkheimer brief.

Adorno

Adorno's work has a style and character which marks it off from the rest of critical theory. His thought is much harder to expound than that of the others: to try to summarize its qualities is to take a considerable risk. Adorno's work is often elusive – and deliberately so. This is a source of both strength and weakness. It is a source of strength because the intricate nature of many of

Adorno's studies ensures that practically each time one reads them, something new is gleaned. It is a source of weakness because it is often not apparent whether Adorno is offering, for example, an explanation of a phenomenon, or an elaborately spun metaphor, or a deliberate hyperbole to stir political action. The problem – a severe problem for anyone who seeks to come to grips with Adorno's thought – is to know what kind of assessment Adorno's work requires; that is, the status of his theories and claims.

Fundamental questions can, I believe, be raised about Adorno's method. Unable to accept as the foundation for social investigation classical Hegelian views, the standpoint of the proletariat, the position of the party and its leadership, or the claims to rigour of various models of the natural sciences, hermeneutic philosophy and so on, Adorno gave priority to immanent criticism. The continuous process of flux and change in history, Adorno consistently stressed, undermines most conventional methods of philosophical and social reflection – and all approaches, in fact, which have a pretence to universality. Horkheimer and, indeed, Marcuse often expressed a similar position, but many of their own ideas are quite inconsistent with it. The immanent mode of inquiry is held to be capable of scrutinizing social and cultural phenomena and simultaneously generating its own foundations. It is only through the enactment of immanent criticism, according to Adorno, that traditional questions concerning, for example, the relation of theory and practice, or the nature of what exists, can be answered. Yet, as I illustrate below, this view is questionable.

Immanent criticism depends for its validity on the discovery of a discrepancy between a subject/object's concept and its actuality. Such an analysis rests on being able to uncover the guiding idea of a phenomenon and to disentangle the self-contradictions which the phenomenon displays in itself. As Adorno put it, 'theory . . . must transform the concepts which it brings, as it were, from the outside into those which the object has of itself, into that which the object would, left to itself, like to be, and confront it with what it is'. The analysis requires the acceptance of certain views of the concept of the object, whether the object be a society or musical work. But what happens when there are competing views as to the object's concept? What standards should a critique of ideology then employ? The objection that the choice of standards becomes arbitrary has a certain force.

Now Adorno recognized a fundamentally contingent dimension in the relation of subject and object. Against Hegel he maintained that there is no basic starting or ending point to the cognitive process. For Adorno there is no foundation for cognition independent of particular configurations of concepts and objects. This position, he hoped to demonstrate, does not entail a commitment to epistemological and ethical relativism. But it is hard to accept the latter point.[12] It is not clear how one can judge, for example, within his terms of reference, between competing claims about an object. At a certain level negative dialectics seems to do little more than reflect the rift between social reality and the concepts it posits. When Adorno argued that the truth or falsity of capitalist society can be assessed according to whether or not it fulfils its concept, he presupposed that we can specify this concept. Yet even if there is some degree of historical agreement as to the nature of this – bourgeois society claiming, for example, to represent a free and just process of exchange, to sustain liberty and equality – these concepts will not point to a basis for critique unless their content is carefully unfolded. To do this is to reveal fundamental disagreements – even if we restrict attention to bourgeois political theorists – about the nature of equality and liberty. Each different understanding of the term could give rise to different critiques, thus opening up such questions as: Which standards should we choose? How do we judge between them? These are the very kinds of questions Adorno's analysis sought to circumvent. Yet an historical account cannot avoid them.[13]

Adorno's focus on objective illusion, however, and, in particular, his concern with reification give his approach an unambiguous critical stance – the exposure of the social relations and processes which underpin the making of 'unlike things alike'. While his 'disjunctive' approach seeks to reveal truth and error contained in various views about the world, it is difficult to see how, within his terms, one can go beyond criticism of inadequate perspectives to develop concrete alternative accounts and theories. For the possibility of negative dialectics is intimately tied to the object's concept. The problems which result are highlighted by an examination of the status of the 'utopian moment' – the unfulfilled potentialities – which negative dialectics seeks to reveal. Leaving aside the issue that many types of concepts do not refer to such a moment and that Adorno did not clarify at any length the nature of concepts that do, it may be asked whether or not the 'vision of potentialities' has anything more than a formal or logical status (a mere registration that reality and concept do not coincide and that reality is not all it might be). Or, to put the point differently, what kind of historical import and relevance does Adorno's dialectical criticism have? The revelation of non-identity is also the relevation of that which is 'not yet'. What is represented by this notion?

Marx was able to avoid the charge of utopianism in his day by being able to identify the subject of revolutionary activity with a class which, he argued, had the potential power to transcend conditions of domination. Adorno did not accept many aspects of this analysis. For him history did not indicate that a revolutionary working class movement was likely to materialize in the future. Yet, if he and, indeed, Horkheimer are to avoid the charge of utopianism, then the nature of the 'not yet' – the emancipatory potential – must be analysed, while a subject of possible emancipation must be identified. In my view, too little attention is paid to these concerns and to *how* one might address them. While Adorno refused, for good reason, to offer a static, ahistorical vision of 'utopia' – of unfulfilled possibilities – he did not give the 'utopian moment' sufficiently precise content. Without such precision, the force of critique is weakened. The diffuse nature of the utopian moment implies diffuse criticism; for the 'not yet' remains an unspecified 'wishful image'.

Adorno succeeded, perhaps better than anyone else, in elaborating the critical, negative aspects of Marx's political economy. But his philosophy of criticism is too unsystematic to provide a foundation for the construction of a theory of capitalist and socialist development. Negative dialectics does not capture the positive or constructive dimension of a work like *Capital* which depends on the systematic elaboration of new concepts and generalizations. It must of course be remembered that Adorno did not intend to provide such theories. He never linked his enterprise to such an objective. Nevertheless, his critical stances do depend, in part, on a stock of social theory and criticisms of it. Although he made a major contribution to the development of Marxian viewpoints in the arts and humanities, the social theorist will not find in his work a developed theory of contemporary society nor a basis for constructing such a theory.

Both Marcuse and Horkheimer, at certain times of their lives, expressed their conception of critique and hopes for social transformation in relatively positive terms. Adorno eschewed a similar

approach for fear of losing the capacity to experience the non-identical. But he did so not only at the cost of the ability to reformulate creatively theories of society but also at the cost of taking a positive stance in relation to social struggles. For as the specification of the 'not yet' runs the risk of diverting attention from 'the open range of possibilities', the pursuit of actual goals creates the danger, on Adorno's account, of 'being consumed, swallowed up'.[14] Paradoxically, Adorno's 'reflections on damaged life', which contain insights full of practical implications, tied him to a position which prevents recognition of the relation of these reflections to concrete historical problems. Adorno's work stands as a sober reminder of the risks and difficulties involved in elaborating a constructive approach to society and philosophy.

Horkheimer

The possible convergence of reason and freedom was said, by Horkheimer (in the late 1920s and 1930s), to be immanent to man, or as he sometimes put it, to human labour. On this account, critical theory makes its own the idea of a rational society, the goal of 'a community of free human beings'. To avoid the charge that this version of critical theory represents and defends an arbitrary ethical ideal 'forcing itself on history', or is nothing more than the product of speculation, the onus is on Horkheimer, if he is to complete his case, to provide arguments and evidence for what might be immanent or potential in the human species (for example, a capacity of a given kind for self-knowledge, self-fulfilment, dialogue, etc.), or of what is imminent and possible in social developments (for example in struggles or crises). For this to be done, the phenomena which such a theory interprets must be shown in some sense to be:

(a) historically developing (for example, needs which cannot be satisfied under the present system of labour and which represent, potentially generalizable interests); and/or
(b) historically necessary (for example, to the survival of human beings); and/or
(c) natural-historical properties of the species (for example, qualities of species-being, or species needs), which under certain conditions can be realized.

Horkheimer's essays written throughout the 1930s suggest that he

intended to argue along the lines of strategy(a) and, but to a lesser
extent, strategy(c). In his later work (*Dialectic of Enlightenment*
onward) strategy(b) appears to underpin his approach. But in all
cases there are only bits of an argument (which are often, especially in the essays, inconsistent with one another).

What is required, for instance, if strategy(a) is to be persuasive,
is a theory of the development of needs which reveal them to be
compatible with universal practical principles. Horkheimer's
argument about how in a capitalist mode of production the needs
of the members of the community as a whole remain unfulfilled (as
individuals' individuality is distorted and denied), is an interesting
step towards meeting this requirement.[15] But the connections, in
actual social movements, between needs, interests and the universal principles of equality and liberty, remain unexplored. Horkheimer does not demonstrate why the interest in a rational society is universal. Nor does he demonstrate, a further necessary step,
why critical theory is the correct theoretical expression of this
interest.[16] None of these points receives adequate attention in his
writings.

The notion of what constitutes a 'rational society' is (like
Adorno's notion of 'unfulfilled possibilities') undeveloped. On
Horkheimer's view this is inevitable: the truths to be drawn out are
primarily negations. Yet the unpacking, concretization and elaboration of the idea of a rational society seems of central importance if it is to become something more than an abstract standard
accessible only to isolated theorists. How can we or might we recognize the 'interest in rational society', know its content, let alone
deduce institutional structures compatible with its principles? How
are we to differentiate what Horkheimer held to be immanent and
potential from those who claim to represent an alternative view –
the party, intellectuals, other critical theorists? Are there criteria
that make such distinctions possible? Or are there a multitude of
competing moral and political standpoints compatible with 'the
general interest in a rational society'? Horkheimer had an unfortunate tendency to avoid these questions or to treat answers to them
as self-evident. The critical thrust of his work is, as a result,
diminished. Marcuse, on the other hand, gives more attention to
issues such as these.

Marcuse

In his account of historical materialism, his defence of a philosophy of labour, his elaboration of a Marxian dialectic and his integration of aspects of Marx's and Freud's work, Marcuse develops a
distinctive view of the relation of theory and practice, human
potentiality, the possibilities contained in the present and the contours of a rational society. While he resolutely refuses to state
'what is to be done', he does suggest alternative modes of organiz-
ing human relationships – a suggestion which is grounded in a
theory of the relation between human needs, the material conditions of life, and social organization. There are several directions
one could take in commenting on Marcuse's position. For example, much could be said about the relationship between causality,
teleology and unfreedom and about what is referred to as the
dialectic.[17] However, I will restrict attention here to his concept of
critical theory.

First, difficulties arise in Marcuse's thought because it is not
always clear at what level his arguments are developed.[18] Arguments move between, for example, strong metaphysical statements
about the nature of Being (conceiving of human existence as
grounded in *eros*), bold reflections on human nature (on the conditions of human life and social reproduction), and sweeping
generalizations about historical development (as, for instance, in
Eros and Civilization). My point here is less that Marcuse uses
inconsistent arguments and poor evidence – although, as indicated
in the previous chapter, this is sometimes the case – but more that
it is not always apparent what criteria should be applied in assessing texts like *One Dimensional Man*. On the one hand, this work
might be read as a political tract; on the other, it could be understood as a set of propositions about the actual and potential
development of capitalist society. At the latter level it is inadequate; at the former level it was extremely effective.

A more fundamental issue is raised by Marcuse's oft asserted
position that it is historical rather than purely epistemological conditions which determine the meaningfulness and truth of propositions, that 'history itself' generates criteria for the assessment of
the validity of statements. For this position assumes what it has, in
fact, to prove; namely, that history is the final court of appeal for
the justification of assertions. The general view that 'whatever
exists or happens is completely explicable by categories wholly
continuous with, immanent within, and restricted to the empirical

domain of objects and events' is itself in need of philosophical justification.[19] Yet a thesis such as this is hard for Marcuse to defend; for he is committed to the view that from Marx onward the essential problems of philosophy have been successfully dissolved into social theory. Philosophy culminates with Hegel; and Marx's innovations demonstrate that the formal and substantive, the logical and evaluative, can no longer be treated as separate languages. To defend this thesis arguments would have to be provided which cannot, at least in any obvious sense, be reduced to social analysis.[20]

A number of problems follow from Marcuse's conception of philosophy. For example, he says that in a rationally organized society labour can win back its 'originally libidinous' character and become a joyful experience. Marx, on the other hand, attacked the thesis that labour can become play in a free society. In the *Grundrisse*, he chastised Fourier's romantic ' "naive, dreaming shopgirl's view" that labour must become fun: really free labour, e.g. composing, is at the same time grimly serious, the most intensive effort'.[21] The question arises: how do we decide which interpretations of labour are correct and which are distortions? In even posing this question within the theoretical framework of Marcuse's early work, we are caught in a circle. For the only criterion of truth he uses in these texts is derived from a conception of labour – precisely the standpoint that is here problematic and questioned. To what standards and criteria can one appeal in determining whether the original (Marcusian) notion of labour is false, or that some of its premises are erroneous? As the criterion of truth, the standpoint derived from labour does not allow us to challenge it without undermining the entire theoretical structure. The theory can only answer its critics by restating its premises.

Marcuse accepts, of course, certain key Hegelian ideas but transposes them on to a historical and materialist basis. This leads to another dilemma. From one perspective, history is the arena for the realization of human potentiality (the negation of all negativity) and on this basis critical theory gains its transformative power. However, from another perspective critical theory exposes history as the history of repression. The problem is: how can history at once provide the criterion for critical theory and be the history of repression which critical theory claims it to be?

Marcuse seeks to resolve this antinomy through his philosophical reading of Marx's concept of labour and of Freud's theory of individual and social development. Given his extremely bleak picture of the actual state of society, what basis can be provided for the theory of what exists in potentiality? While Marcuse does point, for example, to certain cultural forms and social struggles as evidence that the promise of the good life has not been entirely eclipsed, he tends to understand these phenomena as the manifestation of the structure of human potentiality uncovered in his anthropology. As such, he relies on a general theory of 'man' to understand the specific actions of human beings and yet, at the same time, claims the specific actions of human beings are the locus of the general theory of 'man'. The position tends toward an essence which is a fugitive among its own historical manifestations.[22] While concrete materialist history is the locus for the normative anthropology, it is hard to see how, especially on Marcuse's account, the concrete history bears out the anthropology. The claim to be theoretically situated in concrete materialist history is heavily compromised by the introduction of an objectivistic conception of human potentiality (of instincts, etc.) and by the lack of a sufficiently differentiated, concretely grounded, empirical analysis of historical conflicts and struggles.

Ultimately, Marcuse locates reason or rationality in human instincts: that which is rational reconciles the pleasure and reality principles.[23] What people really want is intuitively accessible. Theory accounts for why what is really desired often goes unrecognized. But one cannot simply appeal, as Marcuse does, to instincts to settle questions about real wants; for wants cannot be articulated independently of the circumstances of their development and of the way in which they are conceived. Marcuse's analysis is both too general and too specific. It can be demonstrated to be too general because it is compatible with a vast number of conceptions of what is good or desirable. It is too specific because it does not refer adequately to the formation of needs in history. What is required and what is missing is a more detailed examination of human wants and their relationship to historical developments. How wants emerge and how they are recognized and conceived, need analysis.

Habermas

Habermas's project is also open to a number of criticisms. His attempts to sustain the distinctions between labour and interaction, the various knowledge-constitutive interests, distinct types of knowledge and inquiry, discourse and the ideal speech situation, are not wholly convincing. It is worth pointing to a few of the problems as they have implications for the very nature of his enterprise.[24]

Habermas's work proceeds at a number of different levels. Frequently, he seeks to set out a number of fundamental analytic distinctions which elucidate certain logical relations and which, he hopes, provide the terms which enable the reconstruction of historical materialism. Beside the fact that it is often difficult to follow the nature of the argument that provides the basis for these categories (for example, it is unclear in *Knowledge and Human Interests* what precisely the mode of argument is that establishes the interests as 'quasi-transcendental'), the validity and utility of the categories themselves often remains questionable.

For example, the distinction between work and interaction, or purposive-rational action and communicative action, is fundamental to his writings. Work is understood as instrumental activity through which nature is transformed. By communicative interaction Habermas understands symbolic interaction governed by consensual norms which define reciprocal expectations. The contrast, as it is sometimes formulated, is between two distinct types of action: one which is grounded in intersubjectivity and is dependent upon convention and institutional structures (interaction) and one which is not (work). But in this formulation it is hard to see how the distinction can be sustained. For work is always also interaction. Work presupposes community: it is governed by socially interpreted relations. It is dependent for its organization on (dialogical) rules – on knowing 'how to go on' – which are grounded in complexes of speech and action. Although technical rules are crucial elements of instrumental action they are always articulated within the framework of communication – the *a priori* of communication.[25] The appropriation of nature on the part of the individual is, as Marx put it in the *Grundrisse*, 'within and through a specific form of society'. The category of work can only be adequately articulated as a subcategory of interaction.

But the category of interaction is also, in a number of its formulations, unsatisfactory. For it often appears to refer to a realm of language, gesture and action, independent of any reference to 'external nature' (which is confronted by individuals through work). Thus communicative interaction seems to unfold in isolation from the world of things. Yet individuals interact through frameworks of social relations which are inextricably tied to the production and distribution of resources. How these spheres are connected is problematic in Habermas's writings. If the category of interaction is to be useful it also has to be recast – incorporating these various dimensions in an alternative conceptual framework.

Habermas could reply to the above criticism by arguing, as in fact he has done, that he is 'analysing parts of a complex'. As he put it in the postscript to *Knowledge and Human Interests*:

I do not mind at all calling both phenomena [work and interaction] praxis. Nor do I deny that normally instrumental action is embedded in communicative action. . . . But I see no reason why we should not adequately *analyze* a complex, i.e. dissect it into parts.[26]

Expressed like this, Habermas's earlier formulation of the work/ interaction distinction is somewhat misleading. But even the new formulation leads to difficulties. For it remains unclear as to whether instrumental action is to be understood as an element of all human activity – governed by socially interpreted relations – or as a distinct type of human action – isolated from social contexts. If it is the latter then the problems posed above re-emerge. If it is the former then the interconnections between means-ends elements of action and the integration of nature into practical life and symbolic interchange, remain to be carefully specified. The category of praxis, in other words, requires explication. None of this is to say that for analytic purposes it is entirely unhelpful to examine instrumentally oriented action. But it is to say that such action cannot be adequately described without reference to the social context which is produced and reproduced *in* and *through* its enactment.

In the Marxian perspective, as Marcuse has convincingly shown, labour cannot be simply represented by the concept of instrumental action.[27] The concept of instrumental action simplifies the changing relations between people and nature effected by different patterns of productive forces.[28] Accordingly, given problems with the work/interaction distinction, aspects of Habermas's critique of Marx run into difficulties. While Marx does often appear to assume unjustifiably that changes in the relations of production are directly dependent on developments in the productive forces, he cannot be accused, at a metatheoretical level, of reducing interaction to work. For his concept of labour is not synonymous with the concept of work. While Marx does understand the unfolding of human powers and needs in history in relation to labour, this does not entail the collapse of interaction into a narrow instrumentalist framework. The referent of labour is always a form of social activity.

The difficulty of making a categorical distinction between types of action is paralleled by the problem of sustaining a radical distinction between different types of science and forms of knowledge. For although there are significant differences between understanding a natural object as an instance of a particular type of phenomenon and understanding what a fellow human being says – as there are between predicting the behaviour of a natural object and a social agent – it seems readily apparent from post-Kuhnian philosophy of science that no straightforward separation can be made between what Habermas calls the 'empirical-analytic' and the 'hermeneutic sciences'. The respective forms of knowledge of these sciences cannot be adequately grasped by reference to the hypothetico-deductive model of explanation and interpretative accounts. Hermeneutic problems are central to all attempts to comprehend law-like regularities in natural or social phenomena, while a knowledge of regularities and a capacity for prediction seems an important constitutive element of most forms of interpretative knowledge.[29] A strong argument can be made that the mediation of understanding by explanatory procedures is the typical structure of many scientific disciplines. The case for this has been made recently by some of those who defend a network model of science.[30]

Habermas's conception of the relationship between knowledge and interests is also problematic. To begin his argument he has to establish at least three things. In the first place he must establish that the 'action and interest structure' of the species is of the form he claims; but given the difficulty with the distinction between work and interaction the distinctions between types of 'action and interest structure' become equally questionable. Second, Habermas must show that the structure of knowledge and explanatory claims is as he suggests; but it is hard to see – given the problems with his conception of the empirical-analytic and hermeneutic sciences – how he could sustain his position. However, even if there were no problems with these issues, there would be with the third: the need to establish that the 'action and interest structure' provides the conditions for the possibility of knowledge. For to argue, as Habermas does, that humans have an interest in controlling and manipulating objects in their natural environment and that to fulfil this they require knowledge of regularities, etc., is not enough to establish that this interest is the crucial condition of knowledge, or that it is the constitutive basis of an object domain. Certain forms of empirical-analytic knowledge do not have any obvious relation to technical control. As Mary Hesse has pointed out, 'many theories enlarge our pragmatic knowledge (for example, about fossils or quasers), without necessarily forming the basis of technology'.[31] An interest in prediction is not necessarily an interest in technical control. There does not seem to be a link between predictive knowledge and the technical interest in certain sciences and theories.

Further, Habermas has not provided sufficient arguments to demonstrate that a range of orientations we can and do take toward nature – contemplative, playful, poetic, mimetic, communicative – are noncognitive.[32] Why should an attitude to our own body or to aspects of the external environment which is, for example, contemplative or playful, have no cognitive status? Cannot aspects of nature be disclosed subject to an interest in pleasure and/or sensuous activity and/or non-technical use? It is not at all clear that there are three and only three cognitive interests. To say this is not to deny that an interest in prediction and/or control has a place in the natural sciences. Nor is it to deny the constitutive role of need and desire in knowledge. But to recognize these things is quite different from granting a transhistorical role to any particular interest(s).

The whole notion of a 'quasi-transcendental' interest can, moreover, be called into question. For in attempting to bring together a transcendental and naturalistic approach to knowledge, Habermas is caught in a dilemma: 'either nature has the transcendental status of a constituted objectivity and cannot, therefore, be the ground of the constituting subject; or nature is the ground of subjectivity and cannot, therefore, be simply a constituted objectivity'.[33] His approach appears to grant primacy simultaneously to the natural conditions of life – the source of interests and the origins of the structure of action – and to the historical world in which nature is socially constructed. The theory of cognitive interests appears to entail both an objectivistic ontology of nature and a conception of nature as a mere abstraction required by thought. Habermas's attempts to unite these prespectives are not convincing.[34]

A number of objections of a different kind can be made to the use of psychoanalysis as the model of critical social science. First, it is not apparent how far the analogy between psychoanalysis and critical social science can be pushed. For example, it may be noted that there are problems with Habermas's conception of the organization of enlightenment as it is envisaged on the model of the psychoanalytic dialogue. Central to Freud's theory of 'enlightenment' is the process of transference. It is not enough for the therapist merely to present a correct interpretation; only if a re-experience occurs (of the experiences that caused neurosis), can the analysand successfully transcend his or her distorted self-understanding and neurotic behaviour. The crucial question here is: what political or social experience can be taken as analogous, on the level of social enlightenment, to transference within the psychoanalytic situation? Habermas does not analyse this problem.

One can similarly question the comparability of the structure of neurosis and ideology. The production of ideology, unlike that of neurosis, requires the concealment or masking of aspects of reality in the interests of particular social groups or classes. By seeing both ideology and neurosis through a communications paradigm, Habermas risks deflecting attention from the specificity of each; that is, from the link of neurosis with the dynamic of desire and the necessity of repression in the achievement of self-identity, on the one hand, and, on the other, the connection of ideology with the clash of material interests.

At a more fundamental level the general applicability of the psychoanalytic model can be doubted. In what ways can a dialogue between individuals become a model for the analysis of relations between classes and groups? How can a relationship which is essentially voluntary become the methodological model for understanding and changing social situations characterized by unequal distribution of scarce resources, discrepancies in material interests and power relations? As has been noted by one commentator,

the psychoanalytic encounter . . . places an *epoché* upon the interests (in the usual sense) and involvements of everyday life, and reconstitutes them on a symbolic level as components, or deformations, of dialogue. Such a framework is thus peculiarly apposite to Habermas's conceptualization of interaction, as 'communicative interaction' or symbolic interchange, which also abstracts from the 'material' context of practical day-to-day conduct.[35]

But, given the difficulties with the work/interaction distinction, this model of the communicative process is unsatisfactory. Communication in society cannot be conceived in isolation from the 'world of things'. An *epoché* on this world makes the object of Habermas's critical science unclear. In his recent work, *Legitimation Crisis* and *Zur Rekonstruktion des Historischen Materialismus*, it is readily apparent that he does not focus his analysis of advanced capitalism on the labour process. Is this because the labour process is assigned to the sphere of work and, therefore, not subject to domination understood as systematically distorted communication? There is much in Habermas's writings to suggest that he does *not* hold this view. Yet this highly questionable position is an implication of his thought as it is currently developed.

It is necessary for a theory such as Habermas's to identify the subject of emancipation. The questions arise: To whom is critical theory addressed? How, in any concrete situation, can critical theory be applied? Who is to be the instigator or promoter of enlightenment? It is clear that a discussion of these issues is important if Habermas is to argue successfully that the organization of enlightenment at the social level can be fashioned after critical theory. His model of the critical project requires that a catalyst and agent of social transformation be specified. Yet these issues are only discussed at a most abstract level, for instance, in relation to the theory of political organization.[36] The theory of the relationship between theory and political and moral life is undeveloped, as are the modes in which this relationship might be enacted.

Since the development of the theory of communicative competence, the relationship between truth claims sustained in discourse and those vindicated in the process of enlightenment has become obscure. It appears now that a 'rational consensus' – a consensus attained in a context that approximates the ideal speech situation –is, for Habermas, the ultimate criterion of truth or of the correctness of norms. In *Knowledge and Human Interests*, however, the process of assessing problematic truth claims is tied directly to practice. Theory is tested in and through practice – in the struggle to overcome and dissolve barriers to self-reflection. Clearly, our capacity to enter a genuine discourse is conditioned by emancipatory practice of this kind. But while critical self-reflection might be argued to be a necessary condition for discourse (though how much self-knowledge one requires is itself a controversial issue), it is not a sufficient condition. For the requirements of a rational consensus involve assumptions not only about the individual's knowledge-states, but also about the relations between individuals. The successful continuation of self-formative processes represents only one condition for the realization of the 'symmetry requirement' and, therefore, of a genuine discourse.

The issues raised by the discrepancy between the position of *Knowledge and Human Interests* and the later views are not put to rest by simply adopting the position taken up by the theory of communicative competence. For the ideal speech situation itself is not a sufficient condition for a fully open discourse, nor, by extension, for the critical assessment of barriers to this type of discourse in society. The conditions of the ideal speech situation fail to cover a range of phenomena, from the nature (content) of cultural traditions to the distribution of material resources, which are obviously important determinants of the possibility of discourse – and, more generally, of a rational, free and just society.[37] The difficulties with the category of communicative interaction – the problems of connecting interaction with the world of things – are reproduced here.

There are other shortcomings with the theory of communicative competence. The supposition of the ideal speech situation and, therefore, the presence of the ideas of truth and freedom as anticipations in speech, are argued to be operative in discourse. While it seems clear that the idea of an unrestrained discourse is a regulative ideal in discourse – it would be a *contradictio in adjecto* to enter discourse without this goal – the claim that all speech is oriented to the idea of a genuine consensus is hard to sustain. It is not at all obvious, as one critic put it, 'that anything within the various other language games of ordinary language [for example poetry, banter] can be said to impel speakers to enter discourse'.[38] For what counts as competent rule usage has been shown by Garfinkel and others to vary across social settings.[39] The expected level of accountability changes with different types of everyday practice. The conditions of understanding, one might conjecture, are closely tied to the practical purposes and ordinary interests of hearers, speakers and other participants; it appears that understanding is always the understanding of something for particular purposes. Why we should take discourse as the model of communicative action and why we should employ criteria from it for the assessment of other spheres of ordinary language communication, remains obscure.

Additional problems can also be raised concerning the relation of action and discourse. As a form of communication in which the constraints of action are suspended, Habermas holds that it is possible for individuals in discourse to 'step outside' of their web of everyday beliefs and commitments. This implies a capacity for a complete transformation in psychic states and interests – a capacity which would lead one to expect that people could adopt wholly new concerns and attitudes in systematic argument. Not only is such an expectation unrealistic but it is also fundamentally irrelevant.[40] The conduct of various forms of discourse, say mathematics, seems compatible with a large range of psychological states and belief systems. Discourse can proceed if one claim, or a set of claims, is picked out from the range of presuppositions one inevitably holds in a non-discursive or discursive attitude. Although Habermas's model of discourse and action can be altered to take this objection into account, the whole issue links to another serious difficulty.[41]

While the idea of unconstrained discourse as the regulative principle of discourse is important, it is not apparent that it generates criteria that actually aid the resolution of disputes between competing theoretical systems or value positions. How does the approach, as one critic put it,

> help us in the face of the great ideological struggles of the age, involving religious and anti-religious creeds, nationalist and pan-nationalist doctrines of all kinds, and all varieties of socialism, liberalism and conservatism? How does it help even when trying to decide between the views of, say, Herbert Marcuse and John Rawls? For it is precisely the claim of such contending doctrines that each advances views which are reasonable and rational.[42]

Habermas's conception of discourse and the ideal speech situation does not provide a basis or procedure which would unambiguously lead to the adoption of one of these positions. At a certain level, however, this is *not* a criticism; since Habermas would argue that he is less concerned with particular theoretical and value positions which are relative to social and historical contexts, and more with the conditions for the possibility of argument as such. That is, his project of developing a theory of communication is directed to the explication of the nature of understanding, the structure of human reason and the conditions of discourse. He is concerned with why and how it is that argument and learning are unavoidable in human life, and with why and how certain positions are established as true or correct. But to the extent that he claims that from the theory of communicative competence one can specify the contours of the good and true life, and resolve disputes between, for example, Marcuse and Rawls, the questions posed above do raise critical issues. For once we have opted for argument, and discourse has begun, the old questions re-emerge: Does the symmetry requirement (the requirement that there should be a symmetrical distribution in chances to select and employ speech acts) set bounds on the kinds of theoretical and practical positions that can be established? How do we judge the force of the better argument? What kinds of evidence can legitimately be employed? How do we solve disputes between competing positions claiming to establish objective moral and political stances? The symmetry requirement and the notion of the force of the better argument do not, as currently elaborated, resolve these vital concerns.

Unresolved problems

Two central problems are manifest throughout the writings of the Frankfurt school and of Habermas. The first concerns the relation of critique and history. How can the possibility of critique be sustained, if the historical contextuality of knowledge is recognized? Or, to put the question somewhat differently, how can critical theory at once acknowledge its historicality and yet be critical? How can critical theory be part of the movement of history and a means of enlightenment? Each of the critical theorists thought it was possible to locate a basis for critique – a basis which is both part of historical reality and yet not identical with this reality. The means for doing this was, as I have tried to show, different for each of the theorists. The Horkheimer of the early 1930s pointed to a subject that was both a central part of society and yet not identifiable with the *status quo*. By articulating and clarifying the emerging consciousness of this subject – the proletariat – critical theory conceived itself as an agent of enlightenment in the historical process. For Adorno (as well as for Horkheimer from the forties) the 'concept' provided the critical wedge for both grasping the real and revealing its limitations. Marcuse's model of critique is grounded in human instincts and theory. The former provides access to what human beings really desire, while the latter explains why at present they cannot recognize their desires. In Habermas's model, the ideal speech situation is the foundation for criticism; it is both anticipated in discourse and yet marks an unrealized actuality.

There are difficulties, as I have indicated, with each of these conceptions of critical theory. While the critical theorists have convincingly exposed some of the major flaws of certain traditional and conventional approaches to philosophy and social investigation, they have not, in my assessment, adequately demonstrated that critical theory has a special theoretical status; that is, they have not resolved a whole series of epistemological and methodological issues they intended to settle or render redundant. The difficulties embodied in each of the models of critical theory should not be taken to imply that the critique of ideology, or critique generally, has no place in social inquiry. The nature of the difficulties do point, however, to the necessity of rethinking the way in which critique is understood.

The second problem concerns theory and practice. It is striking that critical theory acknowledges no central revolutionary agent, while its proponents seek to develop Marxism. They present a revolutionary theory in an age which, on their account, is non-revolutionary. In so doing, their work exhibits a paradox, particularly embarrassing since they maintain that the potentialities for human and social change must be historically based: they offer a theory of the importance of fundamental social transformation which has little basis in social struggle.

The critical theorists' expansion of the terms of reference of critique and the notion of the political constitute an important step in holding together the tensions of their position. But the tensions in the main arise from a questionable thesis – a thesis which leads them to underestimate both the significance of certain types of political struggle and the importance of their own work for these struggles.

One of the main concerns of Frankfurt social theory is to explain why revolution, as envisaged by Marx, has not occurred in the West. Habermas's contributions to social theory are predicated, much less strongly, on a similar concern. In trying to account for the absence of revolution the critical theorists tend, in my view, to underrate the complexity of political events. Their assumption that change should have occurred through a decisive break with the existing order, leads them to give undue weight to the power of the forces operating to stabilize society. In attempting to explain why what they expected was absent, they exaggerate the capacity of 'the system' to absorb opposition. As a consequence, critical theory loses sight of a range of important social and political struggles both within the West and beyond it – struggles which have changed and are continuing to change the face of politics. The struggles, for instance, between labour and capital, while not constituting a revolutionary situation, show no signs of abating in countries like Britain. They continue to impinge on the successful reproduction of capitalism. Further, the massive political changes in China, Cuba and Vietnam point to a range of political circumstances which cannot be encompassed within a theory that focuses on the Western capitalist nation-state. Neither the implications of diverse and changing political movements, nor the importance of non-European societies in world politics, are adequately recognized by the critical theorists.

I do not think it is surprising, therefore, that some of the leading spokesmen of critical theory were taken aback when they encountered the radical movements of the 1960s. Horkheimer and Adorno, in particular, did not recognize the political significance of some of the demands of the New Left. (This was not true, of course, of Marcuse, for reasons which I hope have become clear in the course of this book.) Nonetheless, although they were not always able to appreciate the changing constellation of political events, their interest in theory and critique, in analysis of the many forms of domination which inhibit radical political movements, had considerable practical impact. Their work in these domains stands, I believe, as an integral and important part of the Marxist tradition.

Appendix   The Odyssey

In the second part of *Dialectic of Englightenment*, Horkheimer and Adorno discuss Homer's *Odyssey*. The choice of subject appears at first a curious one. But, as I want to show briefly below, it is quite consistent with the general concerns, outlined in Chapter 4 above, of their text.

Nietzsche's insight into the dialectic of enlightenment provides the basis for Horkheimer's and Adorno's interpretation of the *Odyssey*. For them the *Odyssey* represents an enactment of the dialectic – it is not a mere epiphenomenon. There is 'no work which offers more eloquent testimony of the mutual implication of enlightenment and myth'. Their hope is to reveal the 'primal powers' celebrated in the poem, display its concerns with domination and exploitation, and show how, since the beginning of Western thought, the struggle for self-preservation and autonomy has been linked to sacrifice, renunciation and repression. Within the German idealist tradition the Homeric tale was often thought to anticipate or portray an ideal unity of subject and object, culture and nature, universal and particular. For Horkheimer and Adorno, the *Odyssey* is a tale about the development of human subjectivity and culture and about the trials which face enlightened reason. The poem's central character exemplifies both the general and a particular form of the struggle for liberation from nature – the self-positing, autonomous subject and the bourgeois individual. In demonstrating, in contradistinction to a host of classical interpretations, that Homer did not simply describe and praise the life and times of a Greek hero, they sought to emancipate the writings of the first great poet of the Western world from ideology.

Odysseus is the poem's hero. He represents the individual struggling for a life independent of the immediate vicissitudes of fate and temptation. His 'lot' is a continuous fight against the diversity which threatens all unity – that is, the individual ego is constantly tested in a variety of situations. His adventures and confrontations with, for example, the beautiful goddess Circe, the temptations of the Sirens or of the Lotus and the cattle of Hyperion are continual challenges to his potential autonomy. Where there are allurements and dangers, and where impulse or instinct governs action, the would-be developed subject is threatened with destruction. To insure his self-preservation he must pursue a purely pragmatic policy of self-interest. Only through repression of instincts and continual sacrifice – a 'denial of nature in man for the sake of domination over non-human nature and over other men' – can Odysseus survive. This very denial, 'the nucleus of all civilizing rationality', is the 'germ-cell' of the bourgeois individual. In fact, Odysseus is its prototype.[1] He is the self who saves his life by always restraining himself and 'forgetting' his immediate needs.[2] He survives through repression of inner nature and consciously contrived adaptation to outer nature.

The nimble-witted survives only at the price of his own dream, which he wins only by demystifying himself as well as the powers without. He can never have everything; he has always to wait, to be patient, to do without; he may not taste the lotus or eat the cattle of the Sun-god Hyperion, and when he steers between the rocks he must count on the loss of the men whom Skylla plucks from the boat. He just pulls through; struggle is his survival; and all the fame that he and the others win in the process serves merely to confirm that the title of hero is only gained at the price of the abasement and mortification of the instinct for . . . undivided happiness.[3]

He masters nature by rational calculation. The formula for his cunning is that of the 'instrumental spirit'. Odysseus represents rationality against the power of fate. But his rationality assumes a restrictive form – it meets the constant presence of nature only through subjective (instrumental) reason.

The voyage from Troy to Ithaca reveals the 'space whose measure the self must take'. Odysseus might be thought of as powerless when faced with domination of the gods of mythic fate on the one side, and temptation, the weakness of the will on the other. Both threaten the individual's course. But both are not simply givens. Odysseus, as rational individual and as captain of his ship, acts 'as sacrifice and priest at one and the same time. By calculating his own sacrifice, he effectively negates the power to whom the sacrifice is made. In this way he redeems the life he had forfeited'.[4] Sacrifice represents, on Horkheimer's and Adorno's account, one of the earlist forms of rational exchange. Through it people gain a device by 'which the gods may be mastered'. Odysseus never chooses to engage in direct conflict with the mythic forces. Rather, he engages with them through sacrificial ceremonies which he dares not contravene. The ceremonies are preconditions of his own rational decision. The 'magical pattern of rational exchange' renders possible a certain degree of control over nature, over its forces of repetition. The gods 'are overthrown by the very system by which they are honored'.[5]

For Horkheimer and Adorno, Odysseus' behaviour is also 'reminiscent of the casual barterer', who takes a risk, steps outside tradition and the domestic economy (the casual process of exchange between private households), and embarks for unknown lands and possible riches. His adventurous spirit, when measured against the prevailing agricultural mores, contains elements of apparent unconventionality. Yet, 'the wily solitary is already *homo oeconomicus* . . . hence the *Odyssey* is already a Robinsonade'.[6] Like Robinson Crusoe, Odysseus makes the most of his weak position. Through reason and wit he survives and pursues his goals. Furthermore, the very weakness of his position acts as an ideology to advance his interests. His

defencelessness against the breakers is of the same stamp as the traveller's justification of his enrichment at the expense of the . . . savage. . . . the possibility of failure becomes the postulate of a moral excuse for profit. From the standpoint of the developed exchange society and its individuals, the adventures of Odysseus are an exact representation of the risks which mark out the road to success.[7]

As a result of ceremony and sacrifice, death is staved off. As a result of self-control and the fulfilment of the moral code (aristocratic and familial purity), temptation is overcome. As a result of both economic and military risk, glory is pursued and Odysseus becomes a hero.

The hero of the *Odyssey* 'lives by the original constitutive principle of civil society'. The other side of the coin of his success and knowledge is other people's misery and ignorance. Nowhere is this better illustrated than in the encounter with the Sirens.[8] In legend it was held to be impossible to escape the allurement of their beautiful song: once the song of pleasure is heard the self is lost. For Homer, the Sirens know 'everything that has ever happened'. In exchange for their knowledge they 'demand the future'. It is the price that has to be paid for one who seeks to live in the memories of the past. The Sirens represent one of the great temptations that threaten the 'I' in all stages of development. The temptation 'to lose the self has always been there with the blind determination to maintain it'.[9] The boundary between self and destruction has always been fragile. Odysseus, warned by Circe, knows of the dangers ahead. He discovers two ways to escape. For his men he prescribes the plugging of their ears with wax. When his ship passes the Sirens they are prevented from hearing the song. They must simply 'row with all their strength'. Odysseus, of course, listens and escapes. He hears the melody of temptation but is tied to the mast and impotent to respond. The Sirens episode symbolizes the mode in which crews, servants and labourers produce their oppressor's life together with their own.[10] Odysseus' men 'must be fresh and concentrate as they look ahead, and must ignore whatever lies to one side. They . . . cannot enjoy their labour because it is performed under pressure, in desperation, with senses stopped by force. The servant remains enslaved in body and soul'.[11] Their master neither labours nor succumbs to the temptation of immediate gratification. He indulges in the beauty of the song. But the Sirens' voices become 'mere objects of contemplation – become art'. He is a passive listener at a concert. Thus while Odysseus can enjoy culture and art his pleasure doesn't lead to action. The capacity for the appreciation of culture and manual labour 'break apart'.

If Odysseus is a prototype of the bourgeois individual a great deal of the *Odyssey* is an anticipation of things to come. Phases of the journey homeward can be taken to represent stages in the history of civilization and the 'introversion of sacrifice'. Odysseus struggles to master nature and people. He seeks access to treasures and bounty through *mimesis*. By imitating nature he learns to adapt to it. But the 'subjective spirit [instrumental reason] which cancels the animation of nature can master a despiritualized nature only by imitating its rigidity and despiritualizing itself in turn'.[12] In learning to imitate, Odysseus learns renunciation. Survival depends on the suppression of a range of needs and on the frequent treatment of fellow humans as objects. As he becomes aware of some of nature's regularities he also learns of some of its violence. In imitating nature's rigidity he himself becomes rigid. He treats his crew as he treats his knowledge of the weather – they are all, ultimately, means to his end. His enlightenment 'enters into the service of domination'. A few examples can usefully illustrate this theme.

One of Odysseus' first encounters is with the Lotus-eaters. Their land offers many of the opportunities Marx associated with primitive communism. Once the lotus has been eaten people sink into a harmonious relationship with their environment. But the harmony and happiness created are not the work of self-conscious labour. Rather they reflect an organic, impulsive unity between man and nature. As Horkheimer and Adorno put it, 'for adherents of the rationale of self-preservation . . . this kind of idyll . . . is impermissible'. For Odysseus the happiness offered by the lotus is 'more illusion, a dull vegetation . . . and at best only the absence of the awareness of misfortune'.[13] But for his crew the illusion promises, at least, a certain contentment. Some want to stay. Odysseus' response is immediate. He forces them back to the boats. He acts in the interest of self-conscious preservation: he seeks a reflected unity between men and nature – a genuine homecoming. Admirable as his enterprise may seem one cannot but be ambivalent about his achievement. The goal which he pursues will never be within the grasp of the ordinary crewmen, and in forcing them to submit to his will, he denies them one of the few opportunities they have encountered to escape from misery and toil.

Odysseus' ship sails on. The next island to which they are driven is the home of the Cyclops Polyphemus – the giant with a 'cartwheel-sized' eye. Cyclops embodies aspects of the prehistoric world. Yet, in terms of history, he represents 'in comparison to Lotus-eaters . . . a later stage in world development – the barbaric age proper, one of hunters and herdsmen'.[14] For Homer Cyclops is a 'lawless-minded monster'. The giant cave-dweller lives according to brute egoism. He is part of a 'society' which is already patriarchical, grounded on the subjection of the physically weaker; it is a disorderly world which is not yet organized, albeit in an alienated manner, 'by the yardstick of fixed property and its hierarchy'.

By refusing to leave the island early, a result of Odysseus' stubborn curiosity, Cyclops captures our 'hero' and some of his best men. Odysseus only escapes by trickery. He attempts to befriend the giant and tells him his name is 'No-man'. He offers the giant wine. When Cyclops is drunk and asleep, Odysseus and his crewmen blind him. Cyclops cries out in pain and, as Odysseus calculated, he answers his tribesmen's inquiry 'as to the source of his anguish' by saying that 'No-man' had hurt him. Thus, the other giants return home and Odysseus avoids punishment and slips away.

In myth 'the word must have direct power over fact, expression and intention penetrate one another'.[15] To the giant 'No-man' was Odysseus' name. The adventurer cunningly exploits the distinction between name and object, word and thing. The trick worked. But Odysseus' self-assertion is also – as it has been for Western people – a form of self-denial. He only establishes an identity by denying his identity and, once again, does this at the expense of the lives of some of his crew.

The *Odyssey* provides many illustrations of the way in which reason collapses into repressive and mythical forms. Odysseus' encounter with the magical goddess Circe reveals aspects of these forms and explores them in relation to sexuality. Circe symbolizes much of what is attractive and fearful for men in women. She is ascribed magical qualities. Magic has often been a symbol of the power (the 'secret' power) of women. Circe's beauty enthralls those of Odysseus' crew that have been sent to explore her island. She tempts them to 'give themselves up to instinct'.[16] She promises happiness and fulfilment but threatens autonomy. Those who give themselves up to Circe's powers are transformed into peaceful, wild animals. ('The animal form of the tempted man has always been associated with a reversion to basic impulse.')[17] They are not actually hurt or injured.

The mythic commandment to which they succumb liberates at the same time the repressed nature in them. The repression of instinct that makes them individuals . . . and separates them from animals, was the introversion of repression in the hopelessly closed cycle of nature. . . . But because they have already been men, the civilized epic cannot represent what has happened to them as anything other than unseemly degradation.[18]

The temptress is, however, vulnerable; her power 'comes to her only by male mediation'. As such she is open to male domination. Odysseus resists her magic (on the advice of another goddess). Eventually he sleeps with her but only after he has extracted an oath that secures his protection. Thus the goddess 'shows herself to be the first female character'.[19] Through a 'contractually protected exchange' she becomes powerless. Marriage itself represents a later stage in the development and stabilization of the patriarchical order. Odysseus' ultimate return to his wife, Penelope, marks a return 'to pleasure in the fixed order of life and property'. The encounter with Circe marks an early but clear stage in women's (and Odysseus') homecoming.

Homeland, is of course, the *telos* of the Homeric journey. It symbolizes 'the state of having escaped'. The idea of being home is a primary source of Odysseus' motivation and drive. Throughout the *Odyssey* homeland is opposed to myth. Odysseus longs for 'oneness', a sense of 'wholeness' and the 'settled life'. In philhellenic and fascist interpretations the longing has often been associated with an impulse to return 'to a lost antiquity'. But for Horkheimer and Adorno this interpretation is quite wrong. The 'law of Homeric escape' reveals 'eloquent discourse itself . . . and the possibility of retaining in memory the disaster that has occured'.[20] This is why the 'hero' is so frequently introduced as narrator. Reason, reflection and remembrance ultimately triumph over the repressive forms they have taken. Odysseus' return, anticipating the possible homecoming of Western human beings, is to a life 'wrested from myth'. His home, however, does not allow us to forget the horror of his journey. Nor do we forget that the home is *his*. The Odyssean homecoming might promise reconciliation between people and nature, and between people and one another, but it remains a promise – it awaits actualization.

Notes and references

Abbreviations

GS   *Gesammelte Schriften*
ZfS   *Zeitschrift für Sozialforschung*
SPSS *Studies in Philosophy and Social Science*

Introduction

1 See Martin Jay, *The Dialectical Imagination: A History of the Frankfurt School and the Institute of Social Research, 1923–1950* (Boston: Little, Brown 1973). cf. Russell Jacoby, 'Marxism and the critical school', *Theory and society*, vol. 1, no. 2 (1974), and Douglas Kellner, 'The Frankfurt School revisited: a critique of Martin Jay's *The Dialectical Imagination*', *New German Critique*, no. 4 (Winter 1975).

2 Erich Fromm can be added to this list only if one focuses on the early years of the Institute under Horkheimer's directorship.

3 Walter Benjamin was never a close member of this group. He played a relatively marginal part in the Institute's activities as a whole. But he had considerable intellectual influence, especially on Adorno. For interesting discussions of the relation between Benjamin and Adorno see Susan Buck-Morss, *The Origin of Negative Dialectics* (Hassocks, Sussex: Harvester 1977), and Andrew Arato's introduction in A. Arato and Eike Gebhardt (eds), *The Essential Frankfurt School Reader* (Oxford: Basil Blackwell 1978), pp. 207–19.

4 An objectivistic perspective maintains, among other things, that there is, in the last analysis, a realm of brute data, accessible through a neutral observation language, which is the foundation of all empirical knowledge.

5 A. J. Ryder, *The German Revolution of 1918* (Cambridge: Cambridge University Press 1967), pp. 1–8 (and foreword). See also Werner Angress, *Stillborn Revolution* (Princeton, N.J.: Princeton University Press 1963), Arthur Rosenberg, *The History of the German Republic*, trans. F. D. Morrow and L. Marie Sieveking (New York: Rusell & Rusell 1963), and Perry Anderson, *Considerations on Western Marxism* (London: New Left Books 1976).

6   See especially Gwyn A. Williams, *Proletarian Order: Antonio Gramsci, Factory Councils and the Origins of Communism in Italy* (London: Pluto Press 1975).

7   cf. Paul Breines, 'Praxis and its theorists: the impact of Lukács and Korsch in the 1920s', *Telos*, no. 11 (1972), pp. 67–105.

8   Bernstein to Bebel, 20 October 1898, cited in Dick Howard, 'The historical context', in *The Unknown Dimension; European Marxism since Lenin*, ed. Dick Howard and Karl Klare (New York: Basic Books 1972), p. 46.

9   See Franz Neumann, *Behemoth: The Structure and Practice of National Socialism, 1933–1944*, rev. ed. (London: Gollancz 1944), ch. 1. (The references in this chapter amount to a useful bibliography on the topic.) cf. A. J. Nicholls, *Weimer and the Rise of Hitler* (London: Macmillan 1968).

10 Neumann, *Behemoth*, p. 21. For a more detailed account of the Social Democratic Party's policies and legislation that 'unwittingly strengthened the monopolistic trends in German industry', see A.R.L. Gurland, Otto Kirchheimer and Franz Neumann, *The Fate of Small Business in Nazi Germany* (New York: Howard Fertig 1975).

11 Georg Lukács, *History and Class Consciousness* (1923), trans. Rodney Livingstone (Cambridge, Mass.: MIT Press 1971), and Karl Korsch, *Marxism and Philosophy* (the title essay was published in 1923), trans. Fred Halliday (London: New Left Books 1970).

12 For an excellent discussion of the treatment of Lukács and Korsch in the early 1920s see Breines's 'Praxis and its theorists . . .'.

13 Lukács remained committed to a number of tenets of orthodox Marxism, especially those governing the role of the party. See George Lichtheim, *Marxism: An Historical and Critical Study* (New York: Praeger 1961), and Russell Jacoby, 'Towards a critique of automatic Marxism: the politics of Philosophy from Lukács to the Frankfurt School', *Telos*, no. 10 (Winter 1971), for an introduction to orthodox Marxism.

14 See Jay, *The Dialectical Imagination*, chs. 1 and 2, and Buck-Morss, *The Origin of Negative Dialectics*, ch. 2.

15 Lukács, *History and Class Consciousness*, p. 3.

16 See James Schmidt, 'Lukács' concept of proletarian Bildung', *Telos*, no. 24 (1975), for an excellent discussion of these views.

17 The responsibility for initiating this is put squarely on the shoulders of the party. It is assigned the 'sublime role of *bearer of the class consciousness of the proletariat and the conscience of its historical vocation*' [*History and Class Consciousness*, p. 41].

18 ibid., p. 83.

19 For an elaboration of the theory of reification see A. Arato, 'Lukács' theory of reification', *Telos*, no. 11 (Spring 1972), pp. 25–65.

20 Lukács's concept of politics – which, ultimately, justified the supre-

macy of the party – was also quite antithetical to any Frankfurt school position.

21 It was not, however, as will be shown below, built upon with same force by all of them.

22 cf. Jay, 'The Frankfurt school's critique of Marxist humanism', *Social Research*, vol. 39, no. 2 (Summer 1972).

23 Göran Therborn, 'A critique of the Frankfurt School', *New Left Review*, vol. 63 (1970), p. 77. I discuss Therborn's critique of the Frankfurt school along with similar positions, at greater length in ch. 13.

24 Max Horkheimer, 'Bermerkungen zur philosophischen Anthropologie' [Remarks on philosophical anthropology], *Kritische Theorie*, vol. 1 (Frankfurt: S. Fischer Verlag 1968) p. 202.

25 This view has been expressed by Perry Anderson: see his *Considerations on Western Marxism*. Ch. 13 below contains a critique of Anderson's assessment of critical theory.

1 The formation of the Institute of Social Research

1 For a detailed account of the foundation of the Institute of Social Research see Martin Jay, *The Dialectical Imagination* (Boston: Little Brown 1973), ch. 1.

2 ibid., p. 10.

3 P. Anderson, *Considerations on Western Marxism* (London: New Left Books 1976), p. 21.

4 Henryk Grossmann to Paul Mattick, a letter included in the appendix of Grossmann's *Marx, die Klassiche Nationalökonomie und das Problem der Dynamic* [Marx, the Classical Political Economist and the Problem of the Dynamic], pp. 85–6, quoted in Jay, *The Dialectical Imagination*, p. 14.

5 Carl Grünberg, 'Festrede, gehalten zur Einweihung des Institute für Sozialforschung an der Universität Frankfurt am Main am 22.6.1924' [Inaugural address, given on the occasion of the opening . . .], *Frankfurter Universitätsreden* (Frankfurt 1924), pp. 3–6, 10.

6 ibid., p. 11.

7 Walter Benjamin, 'Ein deutsches Institut freier Forschung' [A German Institute of Free Research], in *GS*, vol. 3 (Frankfurt: Suhrkamp 1972).

8 Benjamin died in 1940. Adorno joined the Institute in 1938 in New York.

9 Horkheimer, 'Die gegenwärtige Lage der Sozialphilosophie und die Aufgaben eines Instituts für Sozialforschung' [The present situation of social philosophy and the tasks of an Institute of Social Research], *Sozialphilosophische Studien* (Frankfurt: Athenäum Fischer Taschenbuch Verlag 1972).

10   ibid., p. 33. Social philosophy, as Horkheimer understands it, 'concerns itself above all with phenomena which can only be understood in connection with the social life of people: state, law, economy, religion, in short, with the entire material and spiritual culture of humanity' (ibid., p. 33).
11   ibid., p. 40.
12   ibid.
13   cf. M. Horkheimer, 'Observations on science and crisis' (1932), in *Critical Theory*, trans. Matthew J. O'Connell (New York: Herder & Herder 1972).
14   Horkheimer, 'Die gegenwärtige Lage', pp. 39–40.
15   Anderson, *Considerations on Western Marxism*, pp. 32–3.
16   Horkheimer, 'Die gegenwärtige Lage', p. 41. cf. Adorno's discussion of the 'intrinsic tension' between philosophical ideas and their 'empirical substantiations' in his 'The actuality of philosophy' (1931), *Telos*, no. 31 (1977).
17   Horkheimer, 'Die gegenwärtige', p. 43.
18   ibid., p. 44.
19   See, for example, his 'Vorwort', *Zeitschrift für Sozialforschung*, no. 1 (1932), pp. i–iv.
20   Horkheimer proposed to pursue some of the tasks he had set the Institute in the context of an empirical study of the everyday attitudes of skilled and salaried workers. Empirical material was to be gathered (with the use of survey questionnaires) and then interpreted in light of relevant theoretical material.
21   H. Marcuse, *Reason and Revolution* (New York: Oxford University Press 1941), p. xii.
22   See T. Adorno, 'Scientific experiences of a European scholar in America', in Donald Fleming and Bernard Bailyn (eds.), *The Intellectual Migration: Europe and America, 1930–1960* (Cambridge, Mass.: Harvard University Press 1969), and Franz Neumann, 'The social sciences', in Neumann, H. Peyre *et al.*, *The Cultural Migration: The European Scholar in America* (Philadelphia: University of Pennsylvania Press 1953) for two personal accounts. cf. Jay, *The Dialectical Imagination*, chs. 2 and 7.
23   cf. Jay, 'The Frankfurt school in exile', *Perspectives in American History*, vol. 6 (Cambridge, Mass., 1972), especially pp. 358–9.
24   Neumann, 'The social sciences', p. 19.
25   The clash of cultural traditions is discussed at some length by Neumann, 'The social sciences', and Paul Lazersfeld, 'An episode in the history of social research: a memoir', in Fleming and Bailyn (eds.) *The Intellectual Migration: Europe and America 1930–1960*, especially pp. 319–37.
26   Adorno, 'Scientific experiences of a European scholar', p. 369.

27   Jay, *The Dialectical Imagination*, pp. 219–21.
28   ibid., pp. 205–6.
29   Marcuse, *Soviet Marxism* (Boston: Beacon Press 1964), p. 106. cf. his foreword to *Negations: Essays in Critical Theory* (Boston: Beacon Press 1968).

2   Class, class conflict and the development of capitalism

1   For an example of this type of criticism, see Paul Mattick's critique of Marcuse's *One Dimensional Man*, 'The limits of integration', in Kurt H. Wolff and Barrington Moore (eds.), *The Cultural Spirit: Essays in Honor of Herbert Marcuse* (Boston: Beacon Press 1968). cf. Martin Jay, *The Dialectical Imaginaton* (Boston: Little Brown 1973) pp. 256, 294.
2   See, for instance, Galvano della Volpe, *Opere*, vol. 6 (Rome 1973), pp. 345–49.
3   H. Grossmann, *Das Akkumulations- und Zusammenbruchsgesetz des Kapitalistichen Systems* (Frankfurt; Neue Kritik 1967) has not been translated. cf. Russell Jacoby, 'The politics of the crisis theory', *Telos*, no. 23 (Spring 1975), pp. 29–38, and Paul Sweezy, *The Theory of Capitalist Development* (New York: Monthly Review Press 1956), pp. 209–13, for a summary of the main arguments.
4   H. Grossmann, 'The evolutionist revolt against classical economics', *Journal of Political Economy*, vol. 51, nos. 5 and 6 (1943), p. 520.
5   M. Horkheimer, 'Traditionelle und kritische Theorie' [Traditional and critical theory (1937)] *Kritische Theorie*, vol. 11, pp. 175–6.
6   M. Horkheimer, 'Traditional and critical theory', in *Critical Theory*, trans. M. J. O'Connell (New York: Herder & Herder 1972), p. 213 (amended translation).
7   M. Horkheimer, 'Egoismus und Freiheitsbewegung' [Egoism and the movement for freedom (1936)], *Kritische Theorie*, vol. 11, pp. 73–81, and 'Zum Rationalismusstreit in der gegenwärtigen Philosophie' [The dispute over rationalism in contemporary philosophy (1934)], *Kritische Theorie*, vol. 1, pp. 164–7. Writing in 1961, Horkheimer drew on Schopenhauer's theory of consciousness to emphasize the 'dynamic' and 'irrepressible' character of this substratum of human existence. 'The basis for his [Schopenhauer's] theory is the . . . unappeasable will. Each breath is followed by a silence that is already the desire for the next breath, and each movement which passes without satisfying this desire increases the need and its awareness, until they finally fade out. Breathing stands for life. So do eating and drinking: those cut off from them must fight for them, and the higher the stage of development of the living creature, the more subtle and insatiable the struggle becomes. Need and endless striving, kindled again and again, make up the content

of history and determine man's relationship to nature' ('Schopenhauer today', in *Critique of Instrumental Reason*, trans. M. J. O'Connell, New York: Seabury 1974, p. 74).

8 This can be seen, I think, if one examines the presuppositions of, for example, Adorno's 'Über den Fetischcharakter in der Musik und die Regression des Hörers' [On the fetishism in music and the regression of the listener], *ZfS*, vol. 8 (1938), and 'A social critique of radio music', *Kenyon Review*, vol. 7, no. 2 (Spring 1945).

9 M. Horkheimer, *Notizen 1950 bis 1969 und Dämmerung* (Frankfurt: S. Fischer Verlag, 1974).

10 ibid., p. 225.

11 M. Horkheimer, Preface (1968), *Critical Theory* (amended translation), p. v.

12 M. Horkheimer, 'The authoritarian state', *Telos*, no. 15 (Spring 1973), p. 10.

13 ibid., p. 17.

14 M. Horkheimer, *Notizen 1950 bis 1969 und Dämmerung*, p. 295. I am indebted to Helmut Dubiel for pointing out a number of Horkheimer's most interesting early statements on the Soviet Union.

15 See, for example, O. Kirchheimer, 'Marxismus, Diktatur und Organisationsformen des Proletariats' [Marxism, dictatorship and the organization of the proletariat], *Die Gesellschaft*, vol. 10 (March 1933), pp. 230–9; reprinted (along with other relevant essays) in his *Politics, Law, and Social Change*, ed. Frederic S. Burin and Kurt L. Shell (New York: Columbia University Press 1969). References are to this edition.

16 O. Kirchheimer, 'Marxism, dictatorship and the organization of the proletariat', in *Politics, Law, and Social Change*, pp. 28–9.

17 ibid., pp. 30–2.

18 For example, M. Horkheimer and T. Adorno, *Dialectic of Enlightenment*, pp. xii, 41.

19 H. Marcuse, *Soviet Marxism: A Critical Analysis* (Harmondsworth: Penguin 1971) p. 32.

20 M. Horkheimer, 'Die Ohnmacht der Deutschen Arbeiterklasse' [The powerlessness of the German working class], in *Notizen 1950 bis 1969 und Dämmerung*.

21 ibid., p. 282.

22 ibid., p. 283.

23 ibid., p. 284.

24 ibid., p. 283.

25 Grossmann to Paul Mattick, in his *Marx, die Klassische Nationalokonomie und das Problem der Dynamik* (Frankfurt: Europäisher Verlagsanstalt 1969), p. 98.

26 Horkheimer, 'Traditional and critical theory', in *Critical Theory*, p. 214.

27 Adorno to Lowenthal, quoted in Jay, *The Dialectical Imagination*, p. 66.
28 Adorno, 'Zur gesellschaftlichen Lage der Musik' [The social situation of music], *ZfS* vol. 1 (1932), p. 106.
29 T. Adorno, *Minima Moralia* (London: New Left Books 1974), p. 44.
30 H. Marcuse, 'The affirmative character of culture', in his *Negations*, (Boston: Beacon Press 1968), p. 132.
31 For Marcuse's concept of socialism see pp. 124–6 and ch. 8.
32 H. Marcuse, *Counterrevolution and Revolt* (Boston: Beacon Press 1972), pp. 44–5.
33 M. Horkheimer, 'Die Juden und Europa' [The Jews in Europe], *ZfS* vol. 8, no. 1/2 (1939), p. 115.
34 H. Marcuse, 'The struggle against liberalism in the totalitarian view of the state', in *Negations*, p. 19.
35 See, for example, T. Adorno (with George Simpson), 'On popular music', *SPSS*, vol. 9 (1941), p. 29.
36 See T. Adorno, 'Reflexionen zur Klassentheorie' [Reflections on the theory of classes (1942)], in *GS*, vol. 8, and 'Individuum und Organisation' [The individual and organization (1953)], in ibid.
37 See, for example, M. Horkheimer, 'Authority and the family', in *Critical Theory*, pp. 80–1.
38 M. Horkheimer, Preface, *SPSS*, vol. 9, no. 2 (1941), p. 196. cf. his 'Marx heute' [Marx today (1968)], in *Gesellschaft in Übergang* (Frankfurt: Athenäum Fischer 1972), pp. 152–62.
39 F. Neumann, *Behemoth: The Structure and Practice of National Socialism, 1933–1944* (London: Gollancz 1944), especially the introduction and pt 2.
40 A. R. L. Gurland, Otto Kirchheimer and Franz Neumann, *The Fate of Small Business in Nazi Germany* (New York: Howard Fertig 1975), p. 1.
41 A. R. L. Gurland, 'Technological trends and economic structure under National Socialism', *SPSS*, vol. 9, no. 2 (1941), p. 230.
42 ibid.
43 cf. Paul Baran and Paul Sweezy, *Monopoly Capital* (New York: Monthly Review Press 1966).
44 Gurland, 'Technological trends and economic structure', p. 227. Gurland supports his view by the evidence available from the hearings of the investigation committee established by the German Reichstag: *Enqueteausschuss zur Untersuchung der Erzeugungs – und Absatzbedingungen der deutschen Wirtschaft*. He also cites Robert A. Brody, *The Rationalization Movement in German Industy* (Berkeley, Calif.: University of California Press 1933).
45 Neumann, *Behemoth*, pp. 289–90.
46 Marcuse, 'The struggle against liberalism in the totalitarian view of

the state,' *Negations*, p. 19.

47   Otto Kirchheimer, 'Changes in the structure of political compromise', *SPSS*, vol. 9, no. 2 (1941).

48   Neumann, *Behemoth*, p. 295. cf. Gurland, 'Technological trends and
economic structure'.

49   Gurland, 'Technological trends and economic structure', p. 248.

50   ibid., p. 241.

51   Neumann, *Behemoth*, p. 229.

52   cf. Neumann, *Behemoth*, pt 2, and Gurland, 'Technological trends
and economic structure'.

53   Gurland, 'Technological trends and economic structure', p. 254.

54   Neumann, *Behemoth*, p. 230. cf. H. Marcuse, *Reason and Revolution: Hegel and the Rise of Social Theory* (Boston: Beacon Press
1960), p. 59.

55   Pollock's most important essays in political economy, written between 1932 and 1941 (for the *ZfS* and *SPSS*), have been republished in *Stadien des Kapitalismus* [Stages of Capitalism], ed. and
with an introduction by Helmut Dubiel (München: Beck 1975).
Dubiel's introduction presents an excellent summary of Pollock's
work and role in the Institute.

56   F. Pollock, 'Die gegenwärtige Lage des Kapitalismus und die
Aussichten einer planwirtschaftlichen Neuordnung' [The present
situation of capitalism and the prospects of a new planned order],
ZfS, vol. 1 (1932), and 'Bemerkungen zur Wirtschaftskrise' [Obser-
vations on the economic crisis], *ZfS*, vol. 2 (1933). Both essays are
reprinted in his *Stadien des Kapitalismus*.

57   F. Pollock, 'Die gegenwärtige Lage des Kapitalismus und die
Aussichten einer planwirtschaftlichen Neuordnung', *ZfS*, vol. 1
(1932), p. 12, or in *Stadien des Kapitalismus*, p. 24.

58   ibid., pp. 12–13, or pp. 24–5.

59   F. Pollock, 'State capitalism', *SPSS* vol. 9 (1941), p. 202 (also in
Stadien des Kapitalismus).

60   The National Socialist regime rescued the tottering cartel system by
statutes enacted on 15 July 1933 (introducing compulsory carteliza-
tion). Groups which had struggled with each other for the maximum
profits now assumed collective responsibility for co-ordinating the
economic system. See Gurland *et al.*, *The Fate of Small Business in
Nazi Germany*, pp. 90–1.

61   F. Pollock, 'Is National Socialism a new order?', *SPSS*, vol. 9
(1941), p. 451.

62   ibid., p. 450.

63   ibid., p. 445, and cf. p. 451.

64   Pollock, 'State capitalism', p. 201.

65   Pollock, 'Is National Socialism a new order?' p. 453.

66   'In analysing the structure of state-capitalism I am unable to dis-

cover such,inherent economic forces as would prevent the functioning of the new order. The command economy possesses the means
for eliminating the economic causes of depression, cumulative destructive processes and unemployment of capital and labor.
Economic problems in the old sense no longer exist when the co-
ordination of all economic activities is effected consciously instead
of by the "natural laws" of the market' (Pollock, 'Is National Socialism a new order?', p. 454).

67 Neumann, *Behemoth*, p. 186.
68 ibid., p. 389.
69 ibid., p. 385.
70 See, *Behemoth*, pp. 314–15, 356, 385.
71 ibid., p. 386.
72 ibid., p. 385.
73 ibid., p. 183.
74 ibid., p. 5.
75 O. Kirchheimer, 'The legal order of National Socialism', *SPSS*, vol.
   9 (1941).
76 Neumann, *Behemoth*, p. 184.
77 See ibid., pp. 181–6. Pollock's work is only one among the many
   Neumann is concerned to refute. In this section it is only noted once.
   It seems fairly clear, however, that Neumann was directing many of
   his criticisms directly at Pollock.
78 See Pollock, 'Is National Socialism a new order?', pp. 442–3.
79 Jay, *The Dialectical Imagination*, ch. 5, for a discussion of the personal and political differences between Neumann, Horkheimer and
   Adorno.
80 Horkheimer, 'Die Juden und Europa', pp. 121–2.
81 Horkheimer, 'The authoritarian state', p. 14.
82 ibid., p. 15.
83 ibid., pp. 12–13.
84 ibid., pp. 13–14.
85 See, for example, M. Horkheimer, 'The end of reason', *SPSS*, vol. 9,
   1941, pp. 373–4. In this essay, Horkheimer seems to adopt many of
   Weber's arguments from the *Protestant Ethic and the Spirit of Capitalism* for his own position. See also H. Marcuse 'Some social implications of modern technology', *SPSS*, vol. 9 (1941), pp. 414–39, and
   his later 'Industrialization and capitalism in the work of Max Weber'
   (1964), in *Negations*. cf. Adorno, 'Society', trans. F. Jameson, *Salmagundi*, nos. 10–11 (1969–70). (Generally, Adorno's discussion of
   Weber focuses on his methodological writings.) Nietzsche's
   engagement with concerns like rationalization, the impact of science
   and of technology seems to have had a significant influence on
   Adorno's substantive writings in this area.
86 Max Weber, *From Max Weber: Essays in Sociology*, ed. and trans.

H. Gerth and C. W. Mills (New York: Oxford University Press 1972), pp. 293–4. cf. Anthony Giddens, *Politics and Sociology in the Thought of Max Weber* (London: Macmillan 1972), pp. 44–5.

87 Weber, quoted in ibid., p. 44.

88 Neumann and Gurland would not have agreed with all these tenets. For example, Neumann argued that the extension of rationalization and the technological revolution originated with the mechanisms of capitalist production.

89 Marcuse, 'Industrialization and capitalism in Max Weber', p. 215.

90 The Frankfurt Institute, *Aspects of Sociology*, pp. 94–5.

91 This summary is based on material from Marcuse's 'Some social implications of modern technology', *SPSS*, vol. 9 (1941). The position Marcuse adopts in this essay is generally consistent with Horkheimer's and Adorno's work (on these issues) of the same period. See also Pollock, *Automation*, trans. W. O. Henderson and W. H. Chalmer (Oxford: Basil Blackwell 1957). Pollock's book contains a substantial elaboration of some of these themes and a fairly careful discussion of the relevant, available empirical material.

92 Marcuse, 'Some social implications of modern technology', p. 417.

93 ibid., p. 422.

94 ibid, p. 430.

95 ibid., p. 431, and quoting from Max Weber, *Wirtschaft und Gesellschaft* (Tübingen 1922), p. 669.

96 cf. Adorno, 'Reflexionen zur Klassentheorie', and 'Anmerkungen zum sozialen Konflikt heute' [Remarks on Social Conflict Today' (1968)], *GS*, vol. 8, and M. Horkheimer, 'The end of reason', especially pp. 377–8.

97 Horkheimer and Adorno, *Dialectic of Enlightenment*, p. 25.

98 ibid., p. 7.

99 Marcuse, 'Some social implications of modern technology', p. 424.

100 ibid., p. 426.

101 O. Kirchheimer, 'Party structure and mass democracy in Europe' (1954), 'The waning of opposition in parliamentary regimes' (1957), 'The transformation of the western European party system' (1966), all reprinted in his *Politics, Law and Social Change*.

102 Kirchheimer, 'The transformation of the western European party system', in *Politics, Law and Social Change*, pp. 360–1.

103 Kirchheimer, 'Private man and society', in *Politics, Law and Social Change*.

104 Adorno, 'Reflexionen zur Klassentheorie', and 'Anmerkungen zum sozialen Konflikt Heute'.

105 Adorno, 'Reflexionen zur Klassentheorie', p. 380.

106 Adorno, 'Society', pp. 148–9.

107 ibid., p. 149.

108 ibid., p. 150, and cf. 'Reflexionen zur Klassentheorie' for a discus-

sion of the impoverishment of the working class.
109 Adorno, 'Society', p. 152.
110 ibid., p. 153.
111 Adorno, 'Spätkapitalismus oder Industriegesellschaft?', *GS*, vol. 8, pp. 358–9. The universal application of science and the immense increase in technical potential has, in Adorno's view, created an increasingly anonymous form of economic domination by radically reducing the share of 'living labour' in the production process (from which alone, according to classical Marxist theory, surplus value flows) without affecting the productive process dramatically (ibid., p. 359).
112 Horkheimer, 'The concept of man' (1957), in *Critique of Instrumental Reason*, p. 28.
113 Horkheimer, Preface (1968), in *Critical Theory*, p. vi. cf. 'Marx heute', in *Gesellschaft in Übergang*.
114 Horkheimer, 'Preface', in *Critical Theory*, pp. vii, viii.
115 Horkheimer, *Die Sehnsucht nach dem ganz Anderen, ein interview mit Kommentar von Helmut Guimnior* (Hamburg: Furche-Verlag 1970). cf. Horkheimer's interview in *Der Spiegel*, 5 January 1970. In these interviews Horkheimer reveals a growing commitment to the preservation of many of the central elements of liberalism and a quasi-religious belief in something other than the present. Similar themes are expressed in 'The concept of freedom', trans. Victor A. Velen, *Diogenes*, vol. 53 (Paris 1966).
116 Horkheimer, Preface, in *Critical Theory*, p. xviii. Kirchheimer's conclusions were not radically different. In 'Private man and society' (published posthumously in 1966) he surveyed many contemporary studies of individuals' perceptions of their everyday lives. One finding emerged as crucial to nearly all of these studies – a consciousness of isolation and the inability to control one's job is typical of most working people. This consciousness, he argued, is the measure of the individual's capacity to withstand those forces that would engulf him or her: its development is of central importance to freedom and genuine democracy.
117 H. Marcuse, *One Dimensional Man* (Boston: Beacon Press 1964), p. xv.
118 ibid., especially, chs. 1–4.
119 ibid., p. 35.
120 Marcuse, *Counterrevolution and Revolt*, p. 37.
121 ibid., p. 30.
122 ibid., p. 7.
123 ibid., p. 21.
124 ibid., p. 124.
125 Marcuse, *Five Lectures*, pp. 84–94.
126 Marcuse, *One Dimensional Man*, pp. 240–1. In an essay published in

1967, Marcuse defended a more radical position than that outlined in his books of the late 1960s and early 1970s. He maintained that the victories of national liberation movements, for example in Vietnam, the slow but progressive actions of the 'new strategy' labour movements in Europe (seeking extended influence and power over key industrial and other establishments), the protests of all those underprivileged in capitalist societies and the criticisms of the oppositional intelligentsia, all constitute a major threat to the reproduction of the *status quo*. He argued, furthermore, that the threat would be gradually strengthened as it was revealed that capitalist contradictions – 'between a) the growing productivity of labour and the ever growing social wealth on the one side, and b) between the social character of the means of production . . . and their private ownership and control' – can only be temporarily solved. No long-run solutions are available to crises within capitalist societies because 'the competitive drive for armament production profit leads to a vast concentration of economic power, aggressive expansion abroad, conflicts with other imperialist powers and finally to a recurrent cycle of war and depressions'. Marcuse believes these cycles are progressively exacerbated due to (as Marx anticipated in the *Grundrisse*) 'internal technological-economic tendencies in capitalism'; that is, automation. See 'The obsolescence of Marxism', in H. Marcuse, *Marx and the Western World*, ed. N. Lobkowicz (Notre Dame, Indiana, University of Notre Dame Press 1967), pp. 409–17.

3 The culture industry: critical theory and aesthetics

1   For programmatic statements about this shift cf. H. Marcuse, *Five Lectures*, trans. J. Shapiro and S. M. Webber (Boston: Beacon Press 1970), ch. 3; M. Horkheimer, 'Art and mass culture', *SPSS*, vol. 9, no. 2 (1941), and 'The end of reason', *SPSS*, vol. 9, no. 3 (1941); T. Adorno, with the assistance of George Simpson, 'On popular music', *SPSS*, vol. 9, no. 1 (1941).

2   See Gillian Rose, *The Melancholy Science: An Introduction to the Thought of Theodor W. Adorno* (London: Macmillan 1978), ch. 6.

3   For a history of the development of Institute members' concern for culture and aesthetics, see Martin Jay, *The Dialectical Imagination* (Boston: Little Brown 1973), ch. 6.

4   Adorno wrote monographs on Berg, Mahler and Wagner. These are published in *Die musikalischen Monographien* [The monographs on music], *GS*, vol. 13. His most central work on Schoenberg and Stravinsky is *Philosophie der neun Musik* [The Philosophy of New Music], originally published in 1949, published in translation (incorrectly) as *Philosophy of Modern Music*, trans. Anne G. Mitchell and Wesley V. Blomster (London: Sheed & Ward 1973); this work includes interesting comments on Beethoven.

5 T. Adorno, 'Versuch über Wagner' [Study of Wagner (1952)], *GS*, vol. 13, for comments on the violin (see the opening pages of this monograph). For observations on the saxophone, see his *Moments musicaux* (Frankfurt: Suhrkamp 1964), p. 123.

6 See T. Adorno, *Prisms*, originally published 1955, trans. S. and S. Weber (London: Spearman 1967).

7 For example, 'Notes on Kafka' in *Prisms*, pp. 243ff. For comments on Thomas Mann, see 'Erpresste Versöhnung' [Forced reconciliation], and 'Zu einem Porträt Thomas Mann' [A portrait of Thomas Mann] in *Noten zur Literatur* [Notes on literature], *GS*, vol. 11, pp. 251–80, 335–44. On Brecht and Beckett, see 'Engagement', *GS*, vol. 11; 'Commitment', trans. Francis McDonagh, *New Left Review*, nos. 87–8 (1974).

8 Adorno, 'Erpresste Versöhnung', pp. 251–80.

9 T. Adorno, *Ästhetische Theorie* [Aesthetic theory], eds. G. Adorno and R. Tiedmann, *GS*, vol. 7 (1970).

10 See Rolf Tiedemann, *Studien zur Philosophie Walter Benjamins* (Frankfurt: Suhrkamp 1965).

11 These essays are collected and translated in Walter Benjamin, *Illuminations*, ed. with an introduction by Hannah Arendt, trans. Harry Zohn (New York: Schocken Books 1969; London: Fontana 1973). Subsequent references below are to the American edition.

12 These works are listed in the bibliography.

13 For further details see 'Editor's note', *Illuminations*, pp. 265–7.

14 See Frederic Jameson, *Marxism and Form* (Princeton, NJ: Princeton University Press 1971) for a general introduction. Essays by Andrew Arato, Sandor Radnoti and Heinz Paetzoldt in a special issue of the *International Journal of Sociology*, vol. 7, no. 1 (Spring 1977), provide an excellent account of Benjamin's work. Rose, *The Melancholy Science*, ch. 6, is a very good study of Adorno's work in this area.

15 M. Horkheimer and T. Adorno, *Dialectic of Enlightenment* (New York: Herder & Herder 1972), pp. 120–67.

16 Adorno, *Philosophy of Modern Music*, p. xiii.

17 W. Benjamin, 'The work of art in the age of mechanical reproduction' (1936), in *Illuminations*, pp. 217–52.

18 M. Horkheimer, 'Art and mass culture', and 'Philosophie als Kulturkritik' [Philosophy as cultural criticism], in *Sozialphilosophische Studien* (Frankfurt: Athenäum Fischer Taschenbuch Verlag 1972), pp. 90–108.

19 See especially, Leo Lowenthal, *Literature, Popular Culture and Society* (Palo Alto, Calif.: Pacific Books 1967), and *Literature and the Image of Man* (Boston: Beacon Press 1957). *Literature, Popular Culture and Society* is a collection of essays and monographs most of which were written and published in the 1940s and 1950s.

20 For a useful introduction to orthodox Marxist approaches to culture, see Stanley Aronowitz, 'Culture and politics', *Politics and Society*, vol. 6, no. 3 (1976), pp. 347–96.

21 Adorno, 'Cultural criticism and society', in *Prisms*, p. 29.

22 Sigmund Freud, *Civilization and its Discontents*, ed. and trans. James Strachey (New York: W. W. Norton 1962), p. 67. cf. *Future of an Illusion*, p. 2, and the Frankfurt Institute's *Aspects of Sociology*, trans. John Viertel (London: Heinemann 1973), pp. 89–100.

23 Marcuse's general notion of culture follows Horkheimer's. Marcuse writes: 'There is a general concept of culture that can serve as an important instrument of social research because it expresses the implication of the mind in the historical process of society. It signifies the totality of social life in a given situation, in so far as both the areas of ideational reproduction (culture, in the narrower sense, the 'spiritual world') and of material reproduction ('civilization') form a historically distinguishable and comprehensible unity' ('The affirmative concept of culture', in his *Negations: Essays in Critical Theory* (Boston: Beacon Press 1968), p. 94). cf. Horkheimer's essay in *Studien über Autorität und Familie* (Paris: Felix Alcan 1936), pp. 7ff.

24 H. Marcuse, *Counterrevolution and Revolt* (Boston: Beacon Press 1972), p. 83.

25 'Ten years on Morningside Heights: a report on the Institute's history, 1934–44' (1944, unpublished; in Leo Lowenthal's collection), quoted in Jay, *The Dialectic of Imagination*, p. 177.

26 Benjamin's work is more complicated on this issue.

27 Adorno, 'Culture industry reconsidered', trans. Anson G. Robinbach, *New German Critique*, vol. 6 (Fall 1975); it was first written in 1963 and first published in his *Ohne Lietbild Parva Aesthetica* (1967).

28 T. Adorno, 'Kultur und Verwaltung' [Culture and administration], in *Soziologische Schriften* [Sociological writings], *GS*, vol. 9.1, p. 128.

29 The Frankfurt Institute for Social Research, 'Sociology of art and music', in *Aspects of Sociology*, p. 110 (this essay was almost certainly written by Adorno). The community remains, while confronted with the music, 'a community of listeners, an audience, and thus without any consequence'.

30 Horkheimer and Adorno, *Dialectic of Enlightenment*, p. 130. cf. pp. 129–33.

31 ibid.

32 Adorno, 'Commitment', p. 86–7.

33 Adorno, *Ästhetische Theorie*, pp. 336–7 (cf. 86–8). The views outlined in the following two paragraphs are given much fuller treatment in this text. See particularly *Ästhetische Theorie*, pp. 401,

408–9, 474–5, 480.

34 Adorno, 'Commitment', p. 86. Adorno notes that autonomous works of art have never really existed in a pure form; they are always 'permeated by a constellation of effects'.

35 ibid., p. 76.

36 Horkheimer makes a series of parallel points in *Dämmerung* (1932) when discussing the revolutionary potential of the theatre.

37 Adorno, 'Commitment', p. 86. In Adorno's opinion, this ideal was achieved by Beckett in some of his plays.

38 Adorno, *Ästhetische Theorie*, p. 218.

39 Adorno, *Prisms*, p. 23.

40 cf. T. Adorno, 'Theses upon art and religion today', *Kenyon Review*, vol. 8, no. 4 (Autumn 1945), p. 678; and Adorno's discussion of this theme in relation to music, 'Zur gesellschaftlichen Lage der Musik' [The social situation of music], pt 1, *ZfS*, vol. 1 (1932), especially p. 105.

41 Adorno, *Prisms*, p. 32.

42 Adorno, *Ästhetische Theorie*, p. 358 cf. p. 359.

43 Horkheimer, 'Art and mass culture', pp. 291–2. cf. Adorno, 'Kultur und Verwaltung', *GS*, vol. 8, p. 128.

44 Horkheimer, 'Art and mass culture', p. 292.

45 ibid., pp. 294–5.

46 Horkheimer does develop some more specific views about certain contemporary artists and the role of art in mass culture. These will be referred to later.

47 H. Marcuse, 'Affirmative character of culture', in *Negations*, p. 95.

48 ibid., pp. 118–24.

49 ibid., p. 114.

50 H. Marcuse, *An Essay on Liberation* (Boston: Beacon Press 1969) pp. 42–3.

51 H. Marcuse, *Counterrevolution and Revolt* (Boston: Beacon Press 1970), p. 96.

52 ibid.

53 ibid., pp. 98–9. In *Eros and Civilization* Marcuse connects the subversive character of art – its truth function – to its capacity to rekindle unconscious life processes. On this account art is grounded in, and reflects, fantasy; it is the sublimated expression of fantasy (see *Eros and Civilization*, Boston: Beacon Press 1966, ch. 8). I discuss this idea further in Chapter 8.

54 ibid., p. 99. Marcuse's position, it should be emphasized, has changed in the last few years. In his most recent book, *The Aesthetic Dimension* (Boston: Beacon Press 1978), Marcuse, for example, no longer contemplates, as he did in 'The affirmative character of culture', the possible 'end of art' – an end that would follow from the realization in everyday life of the ideals and visions preserved in art.

Today, he argues, 'the talk of the end of art belongs . . . to the ideological arsenal'. See *The Aesthetic Dimension* for a discussion of this idea.

55   Marcuse, *One Dimensional Man* (Boston: Beacon Press 1964), p. 66.

56   ibid., p. 240. Marcuse cites Hegel's *Vorlesungen über die Aesthetik*, in *Sämtliche Werke*, ed. H. Glockner (Stuttgart: Frommann 1929) vol. 12, pp. 217ff., in support of this view.

57   Marcuse, *Counterrevolution and Revolt*, p. 86.

58   H. Marcuse, *One Dimensional Man*, p. 60. cf., ibid., pp. 87–8, 97.

59   For a discussion of this effect in drama see Leo Lowenthal, *Literature and the Image of Man* (Boston: Beacon Press 1957).

60   Marcuse, *Counterrevolution and Revolt*, pp. 103–4.

61   For a more developed treatment of Benjamin's views see Tiedemann, *Studien zur Philosophie Walter Benjamins*; the essays by Arato, Radnoti and Paetzoldt in the *International Journal of Sociology*; the introductory paper by Hannah Arendt in Benjamin's *Illuminations*; and the paper by Stanley Mitchell in Benjamin's *Understanding Brecht*, trans. Anna Bostock (London: New Left Books 1973).

62   W. Benjamin, 'The work of art in the age of mechanical reproduction', in *Illuminations*, pp. 224–5.

63   ibid., p. 221.

64   ibid., p. 226.

65   ibid., p. 221. cf. W. Benjamin, 'Eduard Fuchs: collector and historian', trans. Knut Tarnowski, *New German Critique*, vol. 5 (1975), pp. 29–30 (this essay was originally published in *ZfS*, vol. 6 [1937]).

66   'The work of art', p. 224.

67   ibid., pp. 229–34. There are some essays and passages in Benjamin's work which suggest that auratic art and perception anticipate a utopian reconciliation of people and nature in a non-authoritarian, communal relation. For a discussion of this view see A. Arato, 'Introduction: the antinomies of the neo-Marxian theory of culture', *International Journal of Sociology*, vol. 7, no. 1 (1977), pp. 9–11, and H. Paetzoldt, 'Walter Benjamin's theory of the end of art', in ibid., pp. 44–6, 56–9.

68   'The work of art', pp. 224–5.

69   ibid., p. 238.

70   ibid., p. 234.

71   In 'The storyteller' (1936), in *Illuminations*, pp. 83–110, and in 'Some motifs in Baudelaire' (1938), in ibid., pp. 155–200, Benjamin's argument is more developed and subtle. In these writings he distances himself somewhat from the technological determinism implicit in his 'The work of art', and concentrates more attention on the loss of community and the basis for shared experience in the

contemporary age. The decline of aura – the notion is also recast in these essays – is explained by reference to more general non-technical social factors that have created an atomized, bourgeois society. For an analysis of Benjamin's changing position over time see Arato, 'Introduction: the antinomies of the neo-Marxian theory of culture'.

72 Adorno to Benjamin, London, 18 March 1936, trans. Harry Zohn, reprinted in *New Left Review*, no. 81 (1973), p. 66. For Adorno's more general assessment of Benjamin see his *Über Walter Benjamin* [On Walter Benjamin], ed. Rolf Tiedemann (Frankfurt: Suhrkamp 1970).

73 Horkheimer, 'Art and mass culture', p. 294.

74 'A product of popular culture', Lowenthal maintained, 'has none of the features of genuine art, but in all its media, popular culture proves to have its own genuine characteristics.' These Lowenthal lists as standardization, stereotyping, conservatism, mendacity and a capacity to manipulate. cf. 'Popular culture in perspective', in *Literature, Popular Culture and Society*.

75 Adorno, 'Arnold Schoenberg, 1874–1951', in *Prisms*, pp. 147–72. Adorno's views on Schoenberg are discussed later in this chapter.

76 cf. Marcuse *Counterrevolution and Revolt*, pp. 101ff.; *One Dimensional Man*, p. 65; 'Affirmative character of culture', in *Negations*, pp. 124–5, 133.

77 cf., for example, T. Adorno, 'Über den Fetischcharakter in der Musik und die Regression des Hörers' [On the fetishism in music and the regression of the listener], *ZfS*, vol. 7 (1938), and 'A social critique of radio music', *Kenyon Review*, vol. 7, no. 2 (Spring 1945).

78 Horkheimer and Adorno, *Dialectic of Enlightenment*, p. 158.

79 Adorno, 'Culture industry reconsidered', p. 13. For an interesting case study on this theme see Lowenthal, with Marjorie Fiske, 'The debate over art and popular culture: English eighteenth century as a case study', in *Literature, Popular Culture and Society*.

80 Adorno, 'Culture industry reconsidered', p. 13.

81 M. Horkheimer and T. Adorno, 'The culture industry: enlightenment as mass deception', in *Dialectic of Enlightenment*, pp. 120–67.

82 Adorno, 'Culture industry reconsidered'. There was a broadcast of this essay in 1963.

83 ibid., p. 12.

84 For a history of literary and philosophical debate about the notions of art and popular culture see L. Lowenthal, 'The debate over art and popular culture: a synopsis', in his *Literature, Popular Culture and Society*, pp. 14–51. For a background to the extensive inter-linked academic debates about mass behaviour, mass society and mass culture in the late nineteenth and twentieth centuries (from Gustave le Bon and Gabriel Tarde to Robert Park and Herbert

Blumer), see Leon Bramson's very useful book, *The Political Context of Sociology* (Princeton, NJ: Princeton University Press 1961). It is important to bear in mind that these debates were part of the 'stock of knowledge' of the time.

85   Horkheimer, 'Art and mass culture', pp. 302–3.
86   Adorno, 'Culture industry reconsidered', p. 14.
87   Marcuse, *Counterrevolution and Revolt*, p. 115.
88   Horkheimer to Lowenthal, 14 October 1942, quoted in Jay, *The Dialectical Imagination*, pp. 213–14.
89   For example, by the Fascists (Horkheimer and Adorno, *Dialectic of Enlightenment*, p. 159).
90   See Adorno's analysis in 'The stars down to earth: the *Los Angeles Times* astrology column', *Telos*, no. 19 (Spring 1974), especially pp. 28–41. (Also published in *Soziologische Schriften*, *GS*, vol. 9.2, pp. 7–120; references below are to the *Telos* publication.)
91   ibid., p. 83.
92   Horkheimer and Adorno, *Dialectic of Enlightenment*, pp. 136–40. cf. Adorno, 'On popular music', pp. 37–9.
93   Adorno, 'On popular music', p. 38.
94   Adorno, 'The stars down to earth', p. 32.
95   ibid., pp. 16–19.
96   Adorno, 'On popular music', p. 38.
97   Marcuse, *Counterrevolution and Revolt*, pp. 101ff.
98   Horkheimer and Adorno, *Dialectic of Enlightenment*, pp. 129–44.
99   Adorno, 'On popular music', pp. 21ff. cf. Horkheimer, 'Die Juden und Europa' [The Jews in Europe], *ZfS*, vol. 8 (1939), p. 115.
100 Adorno, 'On popular music', p. 25.
101 Horkheimer and Adorno, *Dialectic of Enlightenment*, p. 125.
102 Adorno, 'Culture industry reconsidered', p. 15.
103 See, for example, Adorno, 'On popular music', p. 22; 'The stars down to earth', p. 32; 'Television and the patterns of mass culture', in *Mass Culture: The Popular Arts in America*, ed. B. Rosenberg and D. Manning White (London 1957), p. 476.
104 ibid.
105 Adorno, 'Television and the patterns of mass culture', pp. 480–1.
106 See note 90. The study was carried out between November 1952 and February 1953. A useful theoretical background to this study is provided by Adorno's 'Theses against occultism', *Telos*, no. 19 (Spring 1974).
107 Quoted in 'The stars down to earth', p. 35.
108 ibid., pp. 20–1. Adorno makes the further suggestion that 'communion with stars is an almost unrecognizable and therefore tolerable substitute of the forbidden relation with an omnipotent father figure' (ibid., p. 21).
109 ibid., p. 34.

110 ibid., pp. 30–7.
111 ibid., pp. 41–7. See Otto Fenichel, *Psychoanalytic Theory of Neurosis* (New York: W. W. Norton 1945). In bi-phasic behaviour, on Fenichel's account 'something positive is done which, actually or magically, is the opposite of something which, again actually or in imagination, was done before'.
112 'The stars down to earth', pp. 88–9.
113 See T. Adorno, 'The radio symphony', *Radio Research* (1941), and 'A social critique of radio music', p. 213. cf. 'Über den Fetischcharakter in der Musik und die Regression des Hörers', pp. 330–2.
114 Adorno, 'Zur gesellschaftlichen Lage der Musik', pt. 2, particularly pp. 356–7.
115 See, for example, his comments on Stravinsky and Hindemith in 'On popular music', pp. 39–42. Adorno discusses Stravinsky's compositions at much greater length in his *Philosophy of Modern Music*.
116 Adorno, 'On popular music', p. 21.
117 cf. Frankfurt Institute, 'Sociology of art and music', in *Aspects of Sociology*, pp. 107–14; Adorno, 'Zur gesellschaftlichen Lage der Musik'; 'The Radio Symphony'; *The Philosophy of Modern Music*.
118 Adorno, 'On popular music', p. 26. Adorno's view that popular music must have these features seems dubious. Certain types of music which are popular might well have a critical and subversive content, although if subject to continuous 'sale' (commercialization) this could well be eroded. Adorno does maintain, however, as previously mentioned and as will be emphasized below, that genuine, serious music is still, though rarely, produced today.
119 ibid., p. 27. See Malcolm McDougald, 'The popular music industry', *Radio Research* (1941), for what Adorno calls the 'first circumstantial demonstration' of the theory of the manipulability of musical taste.
120 Adorno analysed this process in some detail in a theory about the listener. For a summary see his 'On popular music', pp. 32–7.
121 ibid., p. 30.
122 Adorno, 'A social critique of radio music', p. 213, and the classic 'Über den Fetischcharakter in der Musik und die Regression des Hörers', pp. 330–1.
123 Adorno, 'On popular music', pp. 42–8.
124 ibid., p. 39.
125 M. Horkheimer, 'Kunst und Massenkultur', in *Die Umschar, Internationale Revue*, vol. 3 (1948), p. 455, quoted in 'Sociology of art and music', in *Aspects of Sociology*, pp. 105–6.
126 For useful background knowledge to Schoenberg see Charles Rosen, *Schoenberg* (Glasgow: Fontana 1976), and Anthony Payne, *Schoenberg* (London: Oxford University Press 1968). cf. Adorno,

Philosophy of Modern Music; 'Arnold Schoenberg, 1874–1951', in *Prisms*; 'Musik und neue Musik', in *Quasi una Fantasia* (Frankfurt: Suhrkamp 1963); and 'Der Dialektische Komponist', *Impromptus* (Frankfurt: Suhrkamp 1968).

127   Adorno, 'Arnold Schoenberg', in *Prisms*, p. 154.

128   ibid., pp. 154–60.

129   ibid., p. 167.

130   Adorno, 'Culture industry reconsidered', p. 19.

131   Horkheimer and Adorno, *Dialectic of Enlightenment*, p. 137.

132   ibid., p. 154.

133   Frankfurt Institute, 'Ideology', in *Aspects of Sociology*, p. 190.

134   ibid., p. 200 (amended translation).

135   See, for example, Horkheimer, *Eclipse of Reason* (New York: Oxford University Press 1947), pp. 142–4, 156–61.

136   Adorno to Benjamin, London, 18 March 1936, *New Left Review*, vol. 81 (1973), p. 66.

137   T. Adorno, 'Gesellschaft' [Society (1966)], in *Soziologische Schriften, pt 1*, *GS*, vol. 8; and trans. Frederick Jameson, in *Salmagundi*, nos. 10–11 (1969–70), p. 249.

138   T. Adorno, 'Freizeit' [Free time] in *Stichworte: Kritische Modelle 2* [Catchwords, Critical Models 2] (Frankfurt: Suhrkamp 1969), p. 65. cf. *Dialectic of Enlightenment*, p. 143.

139   Lowenthal, *Literature, Popular Culture and Society*, pp. 4–5, 10–11, 45–51, 125, 129. cf. his discussion of Ibsen in *Literature and the Image of Man*. Popular biographies, Lowenthal shows, embody an emphasis on fate and the necessity of the individual to come to terms with existing conditions. He finds that while popular literature supports the image of an individualistic society, individuality is tolerated and thought to be effective only within narrow limits. The individual is always said to be master of history – history and social structure are always personalized – and yet individual development is presented as a series of chances and lucky breaks. On Lowenthal's account, mass culture presents 'souls without history' and history without serious consideration of the relations between souls.

140   Marcuse, *Eros and Civilization*, ch. 10.

141   In an *An Essay on Liberation* and other works of the late 1960s and 1970s Marcuse discussed the emergence of what he called a 'new sensibility' which 'expresses the ascent of the life instincts over aggressiveness and guilt' and fosters 'the vital need for the abolition of injustice and misery' (Boston: Beacon Press, pp. 23–4). The foundation of this view is Marcuse's interpretation of psychoanalysis. This is discussed in the following chapter.

142   For a detailed analysis see Paetzoldt, 'Walter Benjamin's theory of the end of art', pp. 51ff.

143   Benjamin, 'The work of art', p. 240.

144 In the mid 1930s Benjamin conceived this radicalization in fairly orthodox Communist terms. Near the end o his life, however, he rejected this political stance. He was greatly shocked by the Hitler–Stalin pact and the history and extent of the Stalin purges and trials.

145 W. Benjamin, 'The author as producer' (1934), in his *Understanding Brecht*, p. 95. This is a crucial text for understanding the relation between the two men.

146 ibid., p. 98.

147 ibid., p. 102.

4 The changing structure of the family and the individual

1 M. Horkheimer, 'Authority and the family', in his *Critical Theory*, trans. M. J. O'Connell (New York: Herder & Herder 1972), pp. 108–9 (amended translation).

2 T. Adorno, 'Zum Verhältnis von Soziologie und Psychologie', *Soziologische Schriften*, pt 1 (1955), *GS*, vol. 8. References are to the English translation by Irving N. Wohlfarth, 'Sociology and psychology', *New Left Review*, nos. 46 (1967) and 47 (1968).

3 ibid., *New Left Review*, no. 46 (1967), p. 78.

4 Martin Jay, *The Dialectical Imagination* (Boston: Little Brown 1973), pp. 87–8.

5 See especially E. Fromm, 'The method and function of an analytic social psychology', and 'Psychoanalytic characterology and its relevance for social psychology', in his *The Crisis of Psychoanalysis: Essays on Freud, Marx and Social Psychology*: Greenwich, Conn.: Fawcett Publications 1971), pp. 137–87. Both essays were published originally in 1932 in the *ZfS*. See also E. Fromm, 'Sozial-psychologischer Teil: Der autoritärmasochistische Charakter' [The sociopsychological section: the sado-masochistic character], in Max Horkheimer (ed.), *Studien über Autorität und Familie* [Studies on Authority and Family] (Paris: Alcan 1936), pp. 110–35.

6 See Jay, *The Dialectical Imagination*, ch. 3. For a discussion of Marcuse's intellectual relationship to Fromm see Paul Robinson, *The Sexual Radicals* (London: Temple Smith 1969), pp. 195–200.

7 Fromm, *The Crisis of Psychoanalysis*, pp. 137–87, and 'Die gesellschaftliche Bedingtheit der psychoanalytischen Therapie' [The social conditions of psychoanalytic therapy], *ZfS*, no. 3 (1935).

8 Fromm, *The Crisis of Psychoanalysis*, p. 143.

9 ibid., p. 149.

10 Fromm, 'Psychoanalytic characterology and its relevance for social psychology'. See also his *Escape from Freedom* (New York: Avon 1965). The latter text was originally published in 1941.

11 Fromm, *The Crisis of Psychoanalysis*, pp. 138–40.

12 cf. Fromm, 'Die gesellschaftliche Bedingtheit'.

13 Fromm, *Escape from Freedom*, pp. 316–17.
14 For a summary of Fromm's objections to Freud, see *Escape from Freedom*, appendix.
15 This letter is quoted in Jay, *The Dialectical Imagination*, pp. 89–90.
16 Fromm, 'The Oedipus complex and the Oedipus myth', in Ruth Nanda Anshen (ed.), *The Family: Its Function and Destiny* (New York: Harper 1949).
17 See T. Adorno, 'Die revidierte Psychoanalyse' [Revisionist psychoanalysis], *Soziologische Schriften, 1*, *GS*, vol. 8, pp. 20–41.
18 H. Marcuse, 'The social implications of Freudian "revisionism" ', *Dissent*, vol. 2, no. 3 (Summer 1955), pp. 221–40. cf. E. Fromm, 'The human implications of instinctive "radicalism" ', *Dissent*, vol. 2, no. 4 (Autumn 1955), pp. 342–9. Also see H. Marcuse, 'A reply to Erich Fromm', *Dissent*, vol. 3, no. 1 (Winter 1956), pp. 79–81, and E. Fromm, 'A Counter-rebuttal', in ibid., pp. 81–3.
19 The significance of these and other points is brought out at greater length in the discussion below of Marcuse's *Eros and Civilization* (New York: Vintage Books 1962).
20 Marcuse, *Eros and Civilization*, p. 218. See Robinson, *The Sexual Radicals*, for a good introduction to Reich's work.
21 Wilhelm Reich, *Character Analysis*, 3rd ed. (New York 1949), pp. xxii and xxv, quoted in Russell Jacoby, *Social Amnesia* (Boston: Beacon Press 1975), p. 86.
22 Fromm, 'Psychoanalytic characterology and its relevance for social psychology'.
23 cf. Reich, *Character Analysis*, and *Mass Psychology of Fascism*, trans. Vincent R. Carfagno (Harmondsworth: Pelican 1975), pp. 13–14.
24 Reich, *Character Analysis*, p. 290.
25 Reich, *Mass Psychology of Fascism*, pp. 64–5.
26 cf. Reich, preface, *Mass Psychology of Fascism*, pp. 13–31.
27 Marcuse, *Eros and Civilization*, p. 218.
28 See, for example, M. Horkheimer, 'Egoismus und Freiheitsbewegung' [Egoism and the movement for freedom], *Kritische Theorie*, vol. 2, and Marcuse, *Eros and Civilization*, p. 218.
29 Horkheimer, 'Authority and the family', p. 66.
30 T. Adorno, 'The stars down to earth', *Telos*, no. 19 (Spring 1974), pp. 88–9.
31 T. Adorno, Else Frenkel-Brunswik, Daniel J. Levinson and R. Nevitt Sanford, *The Authoritarian Personality* (New York: Norton 1969), p. 5.
32 ibid.
33 ibid., p. 6.
34 ibid., p. 7. cf. Horkheimer, 'Authority and the family', in *Critical Theory*, for a similar position.

35 Adorno *et al.*, *The Authoritarian Personality*, pp. 747–50.
36 Fromm, *Escape from Freedom*, pp. 304–5.
37 Fromm, 'Psychoanalytic characterology and its relevance for social psychology', pp. 164–5.
38 Horkheimer, 'Authority and the family', in *Critical Theory*, especially pp. 47–68. cf. Adorno, *The Authoritarian Personality*, pp. 744–83.
39 M. Horkheimer, 'Geschichte und Psychologie' [History and psychology], reprinted in *Kritische Theorie der Gesellschaft* (Frankfurt 1968), vol. 1, pp. 19–20, and quoted in Russell Jacoby, *Social Amnesia*, p. 86.
40 Adorno, 'Sociology and psychology', *New Left Review*, no. 47 (1968), pp. 83–4.
41 ibid., p. 84.
42 See, for example, 'The affirmative character of art' and the essay on hedonism in H. Marcuse, *Negations* (Boston: Beacon Press 1968).
43 Marcuse, *Eros and Civilization*, p. ix.
44 H. Marcuse, *Five Lectures* (Boston: Beacon Press 1970). In *Eros and Civilization*, Marcuse explores certain ambiguities in Freud's posited dualism between eros and *thanatos*, sexuality and death. He notes regressive tendencies common to both instincts. As *thanatos* seeks a return to 'the primal unity of the inorganic world', eros seeks – through the release of libidinal energy – a reduction in tension. The apparent dualistic character of the instincts threatens, Marcuse notes, to give way to a 'monism of death' (pp. 27–8). Yet, following Freud, Marcuse argues: 'The primacy of the Nirvana principle, the terrifying convergence of pleasure and death, is dissolved as soon as it is established. No matter how universal the regressive inertia of organic life, the instincts strive to attain their objective in fundamentally different modes. The difference is tantamount to that of sustaining and destroying life. Out of the common nature of instinctual life develop two antagonistic instincts' (*Eros and Civilization*, p. 23).
45 Marcuse, *Five Lectures*, pp. 7–8.
46 Marcuse, *Eros and Civilization*, pp. 27–9.
47 S. Freud, *Civilization and its Discontents* (London: Hogarth Press 1949), p. 114, quoted in Marcuse, *Eros and Civilization*, p. 72.
48 Marcuse, *Eros and Civilization*, pp. 31–2.
49 cf. ibid., pp. 20–70.
50 ibid., pp. 117–26. cf. *Five Lectures*, especially ch. 4.
51 Marcuse, *Eros and Civilization*, pp. 157ff.
52 ibid., p. 190.
53 Horkheimer, 'Authority and the family', in *Critical Theory*, p. 98 (amended translation).
54 Horkheimer, 'Autorität und Familie' [Authority and the family], *Kritische Theorie*, vol. 1, pp. 325–9.

55 See 'The family', in Institute of Social Research, *Aspects of Sociology*, trans. J. Viertel (London: Heinemann 1973).
56 Horkheimer, 'Authority and the family', in *Critical Theory*, p. 101.
57 ibid., pp. 101–2.
58 ibid., p. 102.
59 ibid., pp. 96–7, 102.
60 K. Marx, *The Communist Manifesto* (Moscow: Progress 1967), p. 70.
61 G. W. F. Hegel, *The Phenomenology of Mind*, trans. J. B. Baillie (London: Allen & Unwin 1966), pp. 466–74.
62 ibid., p. 469.
63 Horkheimer, 'Authority and the family', in *Critical Theory*, p. 115.
64 ibid., p. 114 (amended translation).
65 Horkheimer, 'Autorität und Familie', *Kritische Theorie*, vol. 1, p. 346 (emphasis added).
66 T. Adorno, *Minima Moralia*, trans. E. F. N. Jephcott (London: New Left Books 1974), p. 23.
67 cf. Horkheimer, 'Authoritarianism and the family today', in Ruth Nanda Anshen (ed.), *The Family: Its Function and Destiny*, p. 360.
68 Horkheimer, 'Authority and the family', in *Critical Theory*, p. 106.
69 Marcuse, *Eros and Civilization*, p. 88.
70 Institute for Social Research, 'The family', in *Aspects of Sociology*, p. 136.
71 Horkheimer, 'Authority and the family', pp. 107–8.
72 cf. Horkheimer (ed.) *Studien über Autorität und Familie*, and Frankfurt Institute, *Aspects of Sociology*, pp. 137–8.
73 Horkheimer (ed.), *Studien über Autorität und Familie*, pp. 321–2.
74 Frankfurt Institute, *Aspects of Sociology*, p. 138.
75 ibid., pp. 141–2.
76 M. Horkheimer, 'Sociological background of the psychoanalytic approach', in Ernst Simmel (ed.), *Anti-Semitism: A Social Disease* (New York: International Universities Press 1946), p. 9. Jessica Benjamin, 'The end of internalization: Adorno's social psychology', *Telos*, no. 32 (Summer 1977), provides a useful clarification of this process.
77 S. Freud, *Group Psychology and the Analysis of the Ego* (London: Hogarth Press 1974), p. 61.
78 ibid., pp. 48–9.
79 Frankfurt Institute, *Aspects of Sociology*, p. 143.
80 Horkheimer, 'Authority and the family', in *Critical Theory*, p. 118. cf. his *Critique of Instrumental Reason*, trans. M. J. O'Connell (New York: Seabury 1974), p. 16.
81 Horkheimer, 'Authority and the family', pp. 118–20.
82 ibid., pp. 120–1. cf. Horkheimer, 'Authoritarianism and the family today', p. 363.

83 Horkheimer, 'Authoritarianism and the family today', p. 366. cf. Adorno, *Minima Moralia*, p. 92.

84 Horkheimer, 'Authority and the family', p. 124.

85 ibid.

86 T. Adorno, 'Anti-Semitism and fascist propaganda' (1946), in *Anti-Semitism: A Social Disease*; 'Freudian theory and the pattern of fascist propaganda' (1951), in Geza Roheim (ed.), *Psychoanalysis and the Social Sciences*, and 'Sociology and psychology' (1955).

87 Adorno, 'Freudian theory and the pattern of fascist propaganda', p. 281.

88 ibid., pp. 283–4.

89 ibid., pp. 287–97.

90 Adorno, 'Sociology and psychology', *New Left Review*, no. 47 (1968), pp. 86–7.

91 ibid., p. 87.

92 ibid.

93 ibid., p. 88.

94 Marcuse, *Five Lectures*, pp. 13–17.

95 ibid., p. 24.

96 ibid., p. 53.

97 ibid., p. 54.

98 ibid., pp. 60–1.

99 T. Adorno, 'Scientific experiences of a European scholar in America', in Donald Fleming and Bernard Bailyn (eds.), *The Intellectual Migration: Europe and America 1930–1960* (Cambridge, Mass.: Harvard University Press 1969), p. 348.

100 See Jay, *The Dialectical Imagination*, p. 237. cf. Nathan Glazer, '*The Authoritarian Personality* in profile: report on a major study of race hatred', *Commentary*, no. 6 (1950).

101 The most important of these, *Studies on Authority and Family*, anticipated many of the main concerns of *Studies in Prejudice*. The first of the projects (developed out of suggestions made by Horkheimer in his inaugural address), was never published. Had publication plans made in 1939 gone ahead, it would have been called *The German Workers under the Weimar Republic*. Significantly, findings from both the two early projects suggested that a commitment to radical ideology is not always enough to ensure that those so committed will be unsusceptible to right-wing political movements. It is the nature of the commitment – the relation between belief and the mode in which it was acquired and articulated – that is fundamental. This theme was taken up in *The Authoritarian Personality*.

From 1943, for a period of about two years, the Institute pursued research for the Jewish Labor Committee on anti-Semitism in the US labour force. The prime responsibility for the collection of data was shared by Pollock, Gurland, Lowenthal, Massing and Weil. The

1300-page report was not published. This was due to disagreements among its main researchers, sensitivity to possible reactions about its main findings (anti-Semitic tendencies were found in a very large number of the surveyed workers), and the impact of *Studies*. In particular, the report's findings were overshadowed by those of *The Authoritarian Personality*. For a useful survey of this material see Jay, *The Dialectical Imagination*, ch. 7.

102 Adorno *et al.*, *The Authoritarian Personality*, p. 1.

103 ibid., p. xii.

104 Adorno's views on quantification in social science are discussed further in Chapters 5 and 7.

105 Adorno, 'Scientific experiences of a European scholar in America', p. 350.

106 ibid., p. 363.

107 ibid. The role of empirical investigations in the Institute's work is discussed further in later chapters.

108 For a discussion of these methods see Adorno *et al.*, *The Authoritarian Personality*, pp. 11–30 and pt 1. For a sustained criticism of the methodology of the study see Herbert H. Hyman and Paul B. Sheatsley, '*The Authoritarian Personality*: a methodological critique', in R. Christie and M. Jahoda (eds.) *Studies in the Scope and Method of 'The Authoritarian Personality'*, (Glencoe, Ill.: Free Press 1954).

109 Adorno *et al.*, *The Authoritarian Personality*, p. 228.

110 ibid., pp. 744–83.

111 ibid., pp. 682–3.

112 The reasons for this are not always clear, although the limitations of the sample are cited at one point as a barrier to generalization (ibid., p. 23).

113 ibid., pp. 23, 676, 976.

114 ibid., p. 751.

115 Horkheimer, 'Authoritarianism and the family today', pp. 368–9.

116 Adorno *et al.*, *The Authoritarian Personality*, pp. 754–62.

117 ibid., p. 759.

118 ibid. cf. Frankfurt Institute, *Aspects of Sociology*, p. 176.

119 Frankfurt Institute, *Aspects of Sociology*, p. 170.

120 Adorno *et al.*, *The Authoritarian Personality*, pp. 671ff.

121 ibid., p. 176.

122 ibid., p. 976. *The Authoritarian Personality* was subjected to an array of criticism, from a concern with sampling, construction of measuring instruments and use of clinical materials to the implication that the syndrome was associated only with right-wing political views. For a survey of some of the relevant issues see Christie and Jahoda (eds), *Studies in the Scope and Method of 'The Authoritarian Personality'*; and Jay, *The Dialectical Imagination*, ch. 7. See also

Part Three below.

123 M. Horkheimer and T. Adorno, *Dialectic of Enlightenment*, trans. J. Cumming (New York: Herder & Herder 1972), p. 173. cf. Horkheimer, 'Die Juden und Europa' [The Jews in Europe], *ZfS*, vol. 8, no. 1/2 (1939).

124 Horkheimer and Adorno, *Dialectic of Englightenment*, p. 174.

5 The critique of instrumental reason: critical theory and philosophy of history

1 M. Horkheimer and T. Adorno, *Dialectic of Enlightenment*, trans. J. Cumming (New York: Herder & Herder 1972), p. xi. It is interesting (but not surprising) to note that Marcuse regarded *Dialectic of Enlightenment* as Horkheimer's and Adorno's best work. See Martin Jay, 'The Frankfurt school in exile', *Perspectives in American History*, vol. 6 (1972), p. 376.

2 ibid., p. xvi.

3 H. Marcuse, *Five Lectures*, (Boston: Beacon Press 1970) pp. 1–2.

4 ibid., p. 12.

5 See M. Horkheimer and T. Adorno, 'On the critique of the philosophy of history', in Horkheimer and Adorno, *Dialectic of Enlightenment*, pp. 222–5.

6 ibid., p. 224.

7 ibid.

8 Despite the gulfs that separate Karl Popper and the Frankfurt school, this theme finds direct parallels in his work. cf. Popper, *The Open Society and Its Enemies* (London: Routledge & Kegan Paul 1966), and *The Poverty of Historicism* (London: Routledge & Kegan Paul 1961).

9 Horkheimer and Adorno, *Dialectic of Enlightenment*, pp. 83–4.

10 James Bradley, 'Frankfurt views', *Radical Philosophy*, vol. 13 (Spring 1975), pp. 39–40. Despite its brevity, Bradley's review essay of the *Dialectic of Enlightenment* is the best introduction in English to the themes of the book.

11 cf. Horkheimer and Adorno, *Dialectic of Enlightenment*, chs 1 and 2, and G. W. F. Hegel, *The Phenomenology of Mind*, trans. J. B. Baillie (London: Allen & Unwin 1966) especially pp. 514–15, 559–610. For a useful and clear summary of Hegel's discussion of the enlightenment see Charles Taylor, *Hegel*, pp. 178–88.

12 Francis Bacon, *The Advancement of Learning* (trans. of *De Augmentis Scientiarum*), vol. 4, p. 296, quoted in William Leiss, *The Domination of Nature* (Boston: Beacon Press 1974); p. 59.

13 Hegel, *The Phenomenology of Mind*, p. 590.

14 ibid., p. 593.

15 Horkheimer and Adorno, *Dialectic of Enlightenment*, p. 6.
16 Hegel, *The Phenomenology of Mind*, pp. 594–8.
17 Horkheimer and Adorno, *Dialectic of Enlightenment*, p. 8. cf. Leiss, *The Domination of Nature*, ch. 2.
18 Horkheimer and Adorno, *Dialectic of Enlightenment*, p. 8.
19 Genesis, 1:26.
20 F. Bacon, 'The new organon', in *The Works of Francis Bacon*, vol. 4, pp. 247–8; quoted in Leiss, *The Domination of Nature*, p. 49. For an elaboration of these views see Leiss, pp. 48–57.
21 C. F. von Weizsäcker, *The History of Nature* (Chicago: University of Chicago Press 1949), p. 71, and Marcuse, *One Dimensional Man* (Boston: Beacon Press 1964), p. 155.
22 Horkheimer and Adorno, *Dialectic of Enlightenment*, p. 16 (amended translation). For a similar view and perhaps one of the main sources of the idea see F. Nietzsche, 'Thus spoke Zarathusa', in *The Portable Nietzsche* (Harmondsworth: Penguin 1976), p. 414.
23 It can be noted again that Horkheimer's and Adorno's discussion parallels Hegel's. See the latter's comparision of enlightenment and belief (*Glaube*) in his *Phenomenology of Mind*, pp. 561–89.
24 A precondition for the development of humanity and civilization was the recognition of the 'autonomy of ideas in regard to objects'. This was the achievement of the reality-adjusted ego. The repression of nature in people themselves, creating specific sorts of repressions and sustaining the division between the id and the ego, was crucial to the project of the rational control of nature. See Horkheimer and Adorno, *Dialectic of Enlightenment*, p. 22.
25 ibid., p. 12.
26 Adorno's actual words were, 'The whole is the false' (*Minima Moralia*, London: New Left Books 1974, p. 50), inverting Hegel's 'the whole is the true'.
27 Horkheimer and Adorno, *Dialectic of Enlightenment*, p. 41.
28 ibid., p. 44. On Horkheimer's and Adorno's account, Nietzsche's pre-fascist followers 'retained only the second aspect and perverted it into an ideology'.
29 F. Nietzsche, *The Will to Power*, ed. W. Kaufmann (New York: Vintage Books 1968), sect. 480, pp. 266–7.
30 See, for example, M. Horkheimer, *Eclipse of Reason* (New York: Seabury 1974), ch. 5.
31 Adorno, *Minima Moralia*, pp. 155–7. cf. Habermas, 'Urgeschichte der Subjektivität und verwilderte Selbstbehauptung', *Philosophisch-politische Profile* (Frankfurt: Suhrkamp 1971), p. 195.
32 Horkheimer and Adorno, *Dialectic of Enlightenment*, p. 85. See Marcuse, 'The struggle against liberalism in the totalitarian view of the state', in his *Negations* (Boston: Beacon Press 1969), for a discussion of similarities in the foundation of liberalism and

totalitarianism.

33 I. Kant, *Grundlegung zur Metaphysik der Sitten* [The Groundwork of the Metaphysics of Morals], *Immanuel Kants Werke*, vol. 4 (Hildesheim: Gerstenberg 1973), p. 252.

34 Hegel, *The Phenomenology of Mind*, pp. 446–53. It has been argued that Hegel's argument is unfair to Kant. See Judith N. Shklar, '*The Phenomenology*: beyond morality', *Western Political Quarterly*, vol. 27, no. 4 (December 1974), for a useful discussion of the limited value of Hegel's critique of Kant's conception of practical reason.

35 The formal nature of the Categorical Imperative does not mean that it has no content. See Julius Ebbinghaus, 'Interpretation and misinterpretation of the categorical imperative', *Philosophical Quarterly*, vol. 4 (1954), pp. 97–108; reprinted in *Kant: A Collection of Critical Essays*, ed. R. P. Wolff (Notre Dame: University of Notre Dame Press, 1968).

36 Horkheimer and Adorno, *Dialectic of Enlightenment*, p. 85.

37 ibid., p. 118.

38 ibid., p. 88.

39 ibid., p. 96.

40 ibid., p. 117.

41 ibid., p. 119.

42 Nietzsche, *The Will to Power*, p. 267.

43 ibid.

44 Horkheimer and Adorno, *Dialectic of Enlightenment*, p. 99.

45 Nietzsche, *The Will to Power*, pp. 277–8.

46 F. Nietzsche, 'Twilight of the idols or, how one philosophizes with a hammer', in *The Portable Nietzsche*, pp. 541–2.

47 Horkheimer and Adorno, *Dialectic of Enlightenment*, p. 101 (amended translation).

48 ibid., pp. 117–18.

49 H. Marcuse, *Reason and Revolution* (New York: Oxford University Press 1941), pp. 323–88.

50 ibid., p. 324.

51 Marcuse's treatment of Comte is sometimes too polemical and not always accurate. For a more balanced treatment see Anthony Giddens, 'Positivism and its critics', in his *Studies in Social and Political Thought* (London: Hutchinson 1977).

52 Marcuse, *Reason and Revolution*, p. 327.

53 ibid., p. 343.

54 Auguste Comte, *Cours de philosophie positive* (Paris 1975), pp. 138–42. See Marcuse's *Reason and Revolution*, pp. 345–7, for a more detailed analysis of the intrinsic connections between Comte's concepts of science and social order.

55 Marcuse, *Reason and Revolution*, p. 327.

56 M. Horkheimer, 'Der neueste Angriff auf die Metaphysik', *Kritische*

Theorie, vol. 2 (1968), pp. 82–137; trans. as 'The latest attack on metaphysics, in his *Critical Theory*, trans. M. J. O'Connell (New York) pp. 132–87.

57 cf. Horkheimer and Adorno, *Dialectic of Enlightenment*, ch. 1.
58 T. Adorno, 'Sociology and empirical research', in Adorno *et al.*, *The Positivist Dispute in German Sociology*, trans. G. Adey and D. Frisby (London: Heinemann 1969), p. 79.
59 For one such view see Frederick Engels, *Anti-Dühring*.
60 Horkheimer and Adorno use the term 'positivism' to refer to
  1 the phenomenalist tendency in the empiricist tradition, for example, the position of Mach or the early Carnap;
  2 the physicalist position of, for example, Carnap in the mid 1930s;
  3 the logical atomist position of Russell;
  4 the position of various positive philosophers such as Comte.
They sometimes fail to distinguish which of these (and other) positions they are referring to. Adorno also uses the term to refer to the views of Karl Popper (see Adorno's contributions to Adorno *et al.*, *The Positivist Dispute in German Sociology*). For a useful introduction to 'positivism' and 'positivist' philosophy see Leszek Kolakowski, *Positivist Philosophy* (Harmondsworth: Penguin 1972).
61 Horkheimer, 'The latest attack on metaphysics', in *Critical Theory*, p. 138.
62 ibid., p. 157.
63 ibid., p. 146. cf. Adorno's introduction to Adorno *et al.*, *The Positivist Dispute in German Sociology*, pp. 1–68.
64 Lukács, *History and Class Consciousness*, trans. Rodney Livingstone (Cambridge, Mass.: MIT Press 1971), p. 162.
65 Marcuse, *One Dimensional Man*, pp. 105–7, 146.
66 Horkheimer, 'The latest attack on metaphysics', in *Critical Theory*, p. 146.
67 T. Adorno, 'Sociology and empirical research', in Adorno *et al.*, *The Positivist Dispute in German Sociology*, p. 78.
68 ibid., pp. 68–86. cf. Pollock, 'Empirical research into public opinion', in Paul Connerton (ed.), *Critical Sociology*, pp. 225–36.
69 Edmund Husserl, *The Crisis of the European Sciences and Transcendental Phenomenology: An Introduction to Phenomenological Philosophy*, trans. David Carr (Evanston, Ill.: Northwestern University Press 1970).
70 cf. Marcuse, 'On science and phenomenology', in A. Giddens (ed.), *Positivism and Sociology* (London: Heinemann 1974), pp. 225–36; Horkheimer and Adorno, *Dialectic of Enlightenment*, pp. 24–5; and Horkheimer, 'The latest attack on metaphysics', in *Critical Theory*, p. 146. Marcuse's article contains useful remarks on the limitations

of Husserl's general approach. For a much more detailed and critical treatment of Husserl's project see T. Adorno, *Zur Metakritik der Erkenntnistheorie. Studien über Husserl und die phänomenologishen Antinomien* [The metacritique of epistemology: studies of Husserl and the antinomies of phenomenology] (Frankfurt: Suhrkamp 1956).

71 Husserl, *The Crisis of the European Sciences*, pp. 23ff. The main purpose of Husserl's work is to provide an introduction to the main tenets of phenomenology. See ibid., pp. 16–18.

72 ibid., p. 50.

73 ibid., p. 271, where Husserl notes: 'The result of the consistent development of the exact sciences in the modern period was a true revolution in the technical control of nature'. cf. Husserl's comments in ibid., p. 66 and his remarks, pp. 24–8, on the relationship between classic geometry and the surveying and measuring of land.

74 See ibid., pp. 48–53, 65–7. cf. Leiss, *The Domination of Nature*, pp. 125–35, for a more elaborate interpretation of Husserl along the lines suggested above.

75 Husserl, *The Crisis of the European Sciences* . . ., p. 51, quoted in H. Marcuse, 'Science and phenomenology', in *Positivism and Sociology*, p. 232.

76 Husserl, *The Crisis of the European Sciences*, p. 52.

77 Horkheimer, Adorno and Marcuse draw somewhat different conclusions from this analysis. These differences are discussed in Chapters 6, 7 and 8 below. Controversy has arisen, of course, over these views, particularly as they have been expressed by Marcuse. See pp. 243–4 of this book. cf. Leiss, *The Domination of Nature*, pp. 199–212, for a useful introduction to the debate between Marcuse and his critics.

78 Marcuse, 'Science and phenomenology', in *Positivism and Sociology*, p. 234.

79 T. Adorno, 'Sociology and empirical research', in Adorno *et al.*, *The Positivist Dispute in German Sociology*, pp. 77–8. For a useful elaboration of Adorno's views on the status of laws in history see J. Habermas, 'The analytic theory of science and dialectics', in *The Positivist Dispute*, especially pp. 136–40.

80 Marcuse, *Reason and Revolution*, p. 316.

81 Adorno, in *The Positivist Dispute*, pp. 14 and 74.

82 Adorno, 'Sociology and empirical research', in Connerton (ed.), *Critical Sociology*, p. 243.

83 ibid., p. 244.

84 Horkheimer and Adorno, *Dialectic of Enlightenment*, p. 27.

85 See, for example, Horkheimer, *Eclipse of Reason*, and Adorno, introduction to Adorno *et al.*, *The Positivist Dispute*.

86 Adorno, ibid., pp. 61–2.

87 The argument in the last two paragraphs is compatible with Hork-heimer's position in *Eclipse of Reason*. I have reconstructed the position, however, with the aid of J. Habermas, 'Analytic theory of science and dialectics', in T. Adorno *et al.*, *The Positivist Dispute*, pp. 144–9, and Gerard Radnitzky, *Contemporary Schools of Metascience* (Chicago: Henry Regnery Company 1970), p. 325.

88 Horkheimer, *Eclipse of Reason*, p. 76. cf. Husserl, *The Crisis of the European Sciences*, pp. 7–10.

89 Horkheimer, *Eclipse of Reason*, p. 77.

90 T. Adorno, 'Sociology and empirical research', in Adorno *et al.*, *The Positivist Dispute*, p. 69.

91 M. Horkheimer, 'Zum Problem der Voraussage in den Sozialwis-senschaften' [The problem of prediction in the social sciences], *Kritische Theorie*, vol. 1, pp. 112–17.

92 Marcuse, *Reason and Revolution*, p. 315.

93 Horkheimer, 'The latest attack on metaphysics', in *Critical Theory*, p. 145.

94 ibid., p. 155.

95 Horkheimer and Adorno, *Dialectic of Enlightenment*, p. 41. cf. Mar-cuse, *Reason and Revolution*, p. 399.

6 Horkheimer's formulation of critical theory

1 See, for example, M. Horkheimer, 'Materialismus und Moral' [Mat-erialism and morality], *Kritische Theorie*, vol. 1, p. 236.

2 M. Horkheimer, 'Zum Problem der Wahrheit' [The problem of truth], *Kritische Theorie*, vol. 1, p. 240.

3 It is important to note that when Horkheimer republished his *Zeitschrift* essays in *Kritische Theorie* he 'toned down' the radicalism expressed in his early work. For example, the concept 'social injus-tice' has sometimes been substituted for 'class domination' (*Klas-senherrschaft*). In this chapter I will interpret his early work in the spirit in which it was written. Later developments in his thinking will be indicated toward the end of the chapter.

4 Horkheimer, 'Zum Problem der Wahrheit', p. 236.

5 ibid.

6 ibid., p. 237.

7 Horkheimer, 'Montaigne und die Funktion der Skepsis' [Montaigne and the function of scepticism], *Kritische Theorie*, vol. 2, p. 256.

8 ibid.

9 cf. G. F. W. Hegel, *The Phenomenology of Mind*, trans. J. B. Baillie (London: Allen & Unwin 1966), pp. 241–67, where he argued that scepticism contains within itself its own negation. It cannot meet or justify its own standards.

10 Horkheimer, 'Montaigne und die Funktion', pp. 256–7.

11 Horkheimer, 'Zum Problem der Wahrheit', p. 237.
12 H. Marcuse, *Reason and Revolution* (Boston: Beacon Press 1960), p. xiii.
13 M. Horkheimer, 'Zum Rationalismusstreit in der gegenwärtigen Philosophie' [The dispute over rationalism in contemporary philosophy), *Kritische Theorie*, vol. 1, p. 145.
14 Horkheimer, 'Zum Problem der Wahrheit', pp. 242–3.
15 Horkheimer, 'Zum Rationalismusstreit', p. 145.
16 M. Horkheimer, 'Materialism and metaphysics', in *Critical Theory*, trans. M. J. O'Connell (New York: Herder & Herder 1972), p. 25.
17 ibid., p. 25.
18 ibid., p. 31. The 'time-bound interest' operative as a constitutive element of concepts and theories is illustrated by Horkheimer through discussions of, for example, the notions of 'knowledge', the 'people' (*das Volk*), 'freedom' and 'justice'. See, for example, ibid., pp. 22–3, 31–46, and 'Egoismus und Freiheitsbewegung', *Kritische Theorie*, vol. 2, pp. 240–2.
19 Horkheimer, 'Materialism and metaphysics', p. 27.
20 ibid., p. 28.
21 Ludwig Feuerbach, 'Grundsätze der philosophie der Zukunft', §50, in *Sämtliche Werke* (Stuttgart 1904), vol. 3, p. 313, quoted in Horkheimer, 'Zum Rationalismusstreit', p. 145.
22 cf. Marx W. Wartofsky, *Feuerbach* (Cambridge: Cambridge University Press 1977), p. 21, for the development of a similar view.
23 Horkheimer, 'Zum Rationalismusstreit', p. 145.
24 Horkheimer, 'Materialism and metaphysics', p. 33.
25 M. Horkheimer, 'Authority and the family', in his *Critical Theory*, p. 51.
26 These themes are developed below.
27 Horkheimer, 'Materialism and metaphysics', pp. 42–3.
28 ibid., p. 42. Horkheimer employed a number of arguments to sustain this view including those derived from the then-recent developments in psychology.
29 ibid., p. 26.
30 'Zum Rationalismusstreit', pp. 161–4
31 B. Ollman, 'Marxism and political science', *Politics and Society*, vol. 3 (1973), p. 496.
32 Horkheimer, 'Materialism and metaphysics', p. 29.
33 ibid.
34 ibid., p. 31.
35 'Zum Rationalismusstreit', pp. 150–1.
36 Horkheimer, 'Traditional and critical theory', in *Critical Theory*, p. 242 (amended translation).
37 Horkheimer, 'Zum Problem der Wahrheit', pp. 246–7, trans. and quoted in T. McCarthy 'On the problems of truth and objectivity in

the early writings of Max Horkheimer' (Boston: Department of Philosophy, Boston University, mimeographed), pp. 7–8.

38   M. Horkheimer, *Eclipse of Reason* (New York: Seabury Press 1974), p. 171.

39   ibid.

40   Horkheimer's notion of immanent criticism changed, especially during the 1930s and early 1940s. It came to reflect Adorno's influence and his more precise understanding of the term (see Chapter 7). The notion of immanent criticism presented here draws on Horkheimer's views as developed throughout his early writings but attempts to place them in a systematic framework – the framework of Horkheimer's position in the late 1930s and early 1940s.

41   Horkheimer, *Eclipse of Reason*, p. 182.

42   M. Horkheimer, 'Nachtrag', *Kritische Theorie*, vol. 2, p. 195.

43   Friedrich W. Schmidt, 'Hegel in der Kritischen Theorie der "Frankfurt School" ', in Oskar Negt (ed.), *Aktualität und Folgen der Philosophie Hegels* (Frankfurt: Suhrkamp 1971), p. 24 (and quoting Horkheimer).

44   Horkheimer, *Eclipse of Reason*, pp. 182–3.

45   ibid., p. 183.

46   M. Horkheimer, *Anfänge der bürgerlichen Geschichtsphilosophie*, (Frankfurt 1930), p. 74, quoted by Helmut Dubiel in his helpful 'Ideologiekritik versus Wissenssoziologie', *Archiv für Rechts- und Sozialphilosophie*, vol. 61, no. 2 (1975), p. 234.

47   M. Horkheimer, 'Notes on Institute activities', *Studies in Philosophy and Social Science*, vol. 9, no. 1 (1941), p. 122.

48   This notion of truth finds its origin in the classical systems of objective reason, such as Platonism. But it cannot simply be taken over from these systems since they are founded on 'glorifications of an inexorable order of the universe' which are mythological. See Horkheimer, *Eclipse of Reason*, pp. 179–83.

49   ibid., pp. 179–80.

50   cf. Horkheimer, *Kritische Theorie*, vol. 1, pp. 31–66, 118–74, 228–76.

51   This has been well documented by Helmut Dubiel in 'Dialektische Wissenschaftskritik und Interdisziplinäre Sozialforschung: Theorie und Organisationsstruktur des Frankfurter Instituts für Sozialforschung (1930ff)'. *Kölner Zeitschrift für Soziologie und Sozialpsychologie* (26 Jahrgang 1974), pt 2.

52   Horkheimer, 'Notes on Institute activities', p. 123.

53   Representation and research merge in grasping the proper nature of the particular.

54   K. Marx, 'Theses on Feuerbach', included as an appendix in Marx and Engels, *The German Ideology* (New York: International 1970), p. 197.

55 ibid.
56 K. Marx, *Collected Works*, vol. 31, pp. 226–7, quoted in Georg Lukács, 'N. Bukharin: historical materialism', in his *Political Writings* (London: New Left Books 1972), pp. 141–2.
57 Horkheimer, 'Zum Problem der Wahrheit', p. 247.
58 ibid., pp. 244–5.
59 ibid., pp. 256.
60 Horkheimer, 'Zum Rationalismusstreit', pp. 146–7 (my emphasis). There is an important distinction to be made between the value of a theory and its truth. A theory may be true, yet be dismissed as of little interest according to some value. Horkheimer occasionally made this distinction but did not pursue its implications.
61 Circularity would be involved if Horkheimer held that truth is a moment of correct practice, correct practice is practice that carries forward the truth.
62 M. Horkheimer, 'Traditionelle und kritische Theorie', *Kritische Theorie*, vol. 2, p. 190.
63 See, for example, 'Zum Rationalismusstreit', p. 156.
64 The position set out in the preceding five paragraphs is based on Horkheimer's views as variously developed in 'Egoismus und Freiheitsbewegung' (1936), 'Zum Rationalismusstreit' (1934), and 'Traditional and critical theory' (1937).
65 Frankfurt Institute, *Aspects of Sociology*, trans. J. Viertel (Heinemann 1973), p. 51.
66 Horkheimer, 'Egoismus und Freiheitsbewegung', *Kritische Theorie*, vol. 2, pp. 62ff.
67 A concept of the subject as self-seeking and egotistical becomes a dominant force in society.
68 Horkheimer, 'Traditional and critical theory', p. 213.
69 Following Marx's theory of value, Horkheimer contended that the dominant relations of exchange create and conceal exploitation. For capitalism extracts surplus value from those who reproduce it.
70 'Authority and the family', pp. 82–3.
71 'Zum Rationalismusstreit', pp. 150ff.
72 ibid., p. 156.
73 ibid., p. 146.
74 But it would be wrong to claim that their positions were the same. Horkheimer warned against the hypostatization of any single class standpoint. As he wrote in 'Traditional and critical theory', 'it is possible for the consciousness of every social stratum today to be limited and corrupted by ideology, however much, for its circumstances, it may be bent on truth'. Horkheimer refused to simply associate the vantage point of the proletariat with the vantage point of a critique of ideology.
75 cf., for example, 'Zum Rationalismusstreit', pp. 146–7 and 156, and

'Zum Problem der Wahrheit', pp. 244–5, 247 and 256. See also 'Traditionelle und kritische Theorie', p. 190.

76 H. Marcuse, *Counterrevolution and Revolt*, (Boston: Beacon Press 1972), p. 124.

77 Horkheimer, 'Traditionelle und Kritische Theorie', pp. 162–4.

78 Horkheimer, 'Zum Problem der Wahrheit', p. 256.

79 Horkheimer, 'Nachtrag', p. 193.

80 ibid., p. 198. cf. 'Montaigne und die Funktion', p. 259.

81 Horkheimer, 'Traditional and critical theory', in *Critical Theory*, pp. 220–1.

82 Critical theory makes its own the goal of 'a community of free human beings' in so far as such a community is possible, given the present technical capacities. cf. Horkheimer, 'Traditionelle und kritische Theorie', pp. 165–6, 168.

83 These arguments are neither well developed nor are they clearly interrelated in his works. This problem is discussed in the concluding chapter.

84 In his early writings, Horkheimer, while rejecting a number of concepts Freud developed in his later life (for example the death instinct), accepted the validity of libido theory. See Horkheimer, 'Egoismus und Freiheitsbewegung', pp. 73–81, and 'Zum Rationalismusstreit', pp. 164–7.

85 This view was discussed on pp. 43–4.

86 Horkheimer, 'Materialism and metaphysics', pp. 44–5 (amended translation).

87 For example, in a new preface to *Dialectic of Enlightenment*, written in April 1969, Horkheimer and Adorno wrote: 'We would not now maintain without qualification every statement in the book: that would be irreconcilable with a theory which holds that the core of truth is historical' (trans. J. Cumming, New York: Herder & Herder 1972).

88 cf. Horkheimer, *Die Sehnsucht nach dem ganz Anderen*.

89 For an excellent discussion of Horkheimer's approach to theology and religion see Rudolf Siebert, 'Horkheimer's sociology of religion', *Telos*, no. 30 (1976), and Julius Carlebach, 'Marx and the sociologists: Max Horkheimer' in *Karl Marx and the Radical Critique of Judaism* (London: Routledge & Kegan Paul, 1978), pp. 234–57.

7 Adorno's conception of negative dialectics

1 T. Adorno, 'Offener Brief an Max Horkheimer' [Open letter to Max Horkheimer], *Die Zeit*, 12 February 1965, p. 32.

2 T. Adorno, 'The actuality of philosophy', *Telos*, no. 31 (1977), p.

132. This paper was delivered by Adorno on 7 May 1931 to the philosophy faculty of Frankfurt University. It was published for the first time in 1973, in *Philosophische Frühschriften*, *GS*, vol. 1, pp. 325–44.

3 T. Adorno, *Negative Dialectics*, trans. E. B. Ashton (New York: Seabury Press 1973), p. 323 (published in London by Routledge & Kegan Paul 1973). First published in 1966 by Suhrkamp, *Negative Dialektik* is now also in *GS*, vol. 6.

4 cf. Benjamin Snow, 'Introduction to Adorno's "The actuality of philosophy"', *Telos*, no. 31 (1977), pp. 115–16.

5 T. Adorno, *Philosophische Frühschriften*, *GS*, vol. 1, pp. 325–71.

6 See M. Horkheimer, 'Notes on Institute activities', *SPSS*, vol. 9, no. I (1941), pp. 121–3.

7 This chapter has benefited considerably from discussions with Gillian Rose. Its argument is indebted to her book, *The Melancholy Science: An Introduction to the Thought of Theodor W. Adorno* (London: Macmillan 1978), chs 2, 3 and 4.

8 Adorno, *Negative Dialectics*, p. 167. The term 'subject' may refer (for the purpose of initial orientation) to a specific human agent, or to a social agent independent of any given individual. Object may refer to the social or natural world, or to aspects thereof.

9 ibid., p. 174.

10 For a more extensive discussion of these influences on Adorno, see Rose, *The Melancholy Science*. cf. Susan Buck-Morss, 'The Dialectic of T. W. Adorno, *Telos*, no. 14 (Winter 1972), and *The Origin of Negative Dialectics* (Hassocks, Sussex: Harvester 1977); Martin Jay, *The Dialectical Imagination* (Boston: Little Brown 1973), pp. 21–5, and 'The Frankfurt school's critique of marxist humanism', *Social Research*, vol. 39, no. 2 (Summer 1972), pp. 296–9.

11 Affirmative traits are also entailed in Plato's understanding of dialectics (see Adorno, *Negative Dialectics*, p. xix). Adorno discussed Hegel's notions of dialectics in several places. See, for example, 'Drei Studien zu Hegel' [Three studies on Hegel] in *GS*, vol. 5, especially pp. 251–94, and *Negative Dialectics*, pp. 334–8.

12 G. F. W. Hegel, *The Phenomenology of Mind*, trans. J. B. Baillie (London: Allen & Unwin 1966), pp. 228–40. See Adorno, *Negative Dialectics*, pp. 198–202.

13 T. Adorno, 'On the logic of the social sciences', in Adorno *et al.*, *The Positivist Dispute in German Sociology*, trans. G. Adey and D. Frisby (London: Heinemann 1969), p. 111.

14 Adorno, *Negative Dialectics*, p. 198.

15 ibid., p. 350.

16 Adorno, 'Sociology and empirical research', in *The Positivist Dispute*, p. 71.

17 cf. Adorno, 'The actuality of philosophy', and *Negative Dialectics*, pt

3.2.
18 Adorno, 'The construction of world spirit', in *Negative Dialectics*, pp. 303–5. cf. H. Marcuse, *Reason and Revolution* (Boston: Beacon Press 1960), pp. 251ff.
19 Adorno, *Negative Dialectics*, p. 320.
20 ibid., pp. 20–2.
21 This is also one of Adorno's arguments against Nietzsche's theory of truth.
22 Adorno, *Negative Dialectics*, p. 21.
23 ibid., p. 22.
24 ibid., p. 8 (amended translation). Adorno maintains a negative interest in systems. 'Philosophy retains respect for systems to the extent to which things heterogeneous to it face it in the form of a system. The administered world moves in this direction' (ibid., p. 20).
25 ibid., p. 33.
26 Adorno's studies of these philosophers are listed in the bibliography.
27 The differences between the 'early' Benjamin and Adorno can be quickly gleaned by comparing Benjamin's *The Origin of German Tragic Drama*, trans. John Osborne (London: New Left Books 1977) with Adorno's 'The actuality of philosophy'.
28 Benjamin's notion of 'ideas' is complicated and often difficult to comprehend. Aspects of its meaning are drawn from the ideas of Plato, Leibniz and the Cabbala. See his *The Origin of German Tragic Drama*, pp. 27–48.
29 Benjamin, manuscript of *Passagenarbeit*, cited in Rolf Tiedemann, *Frankfurter Beitraege zur Soziologie*, vol. 16: *Studien zur Philosophie Walter Banjamins* (Frankfurt 1965), p. 106; quoted and trans. Susan Buck-Morss in 'The dialectic of T. W. Adorno', p. 139. Susan Buck-Morss's article is a useful introduction to the relation between Benjamin and Adorno.
30 Adorno, 'The actuality of philosophy', p. 126.
31 cf., for example, Adorno/Benjamin correspondence, *New Left Review*, no. 81 (1973).
32 Adorno discussed these themes in several places. See, for example, 'The actuality of philosophy'; his introduction to *The Positivist Dispute*, pp. 1–68; and *Negative Dialectics*, especially pp. 3–55, 134–207.
33 See Rose, *The Melancholy Science*, ch. 2.
34 For a concise formulation of this position see F. Nietzsche's *The Will to Power*, ed. W. Kaufmann (New York: Vintage Books 1968), pp. 266–7.
35 Adorno, *Negative Dialectics*, p. 23.
36 Nietzsche, *The Will to Power*, pp. 278–9.
37 ibid., p. 331.

38 ibid., p. 378; cf. pp. 377–8.
39 For an illustration of these views see Nietzsche's critical discussion of the concepts of subject and object in *The Will to Power*, pp. 266ff., and his analysis of the notions of cause and effect, free will and reason in *Twilight of the Idols*, in *The Portable Nietzsche*, selected and trans. Walter Kaufmann (New York: Viking 1954, and Harmondsworth: Penguin 1976).
40 Adorno, *Negative Dialectics*, p. 54.
41 Nietzsche, *The Anti-Christ*, and *Twilight of the Idols*, in *The Portable Nietzsche*, especially pp. 486–91, 501–4, 513ff.
42 See, for example, his appraisal of Nietzsche's approach to morality in T. Adorno, *Minima Moralia* (London: New Left Books 1974), pp. 95–7.
43 Nietzsche, *The Will to Power*, p. 278.
44 Adorno, *Negative Dialectics*, pp. 144–54.
45 Karl Löwith, *From Hegel to Nietzsche*, trans. David E. Green (New York: Doubleday 1967), pp. 173–232.
46 cf. Adorno's discussion of Nietzsche's doctrine of *amor fati* (thou shalt love thy fate), in *Minima Moralia*, p. 98. Nietzsche's position cannot be appreciated properly without understanding the notion of the 'eternal recurrence'. For a useful discussion of these ideas see Löwith, *From Hegel to Nietzsche*, pp. 191–232.
47 Adorno, *Minima Moralia*, p. 98.
48 T. Adorno, *Prisms*, trans. S. Weber and S. Weber (London: Spearman 1967), p. 65.
49 ibid., p. 225. For Nietzsche's account of the importance of style see, for example, *The Gay Science*, pp. 343–6. See also Walter Kaufmann, *Nietzsche* (Princeton, NJ: Princeton University Press 1974), ch. 2. cf. Benjamin, *The Origin of German Tragic Drama*, pp. 27–34.
50 Adorno wrote a number of essays and aphorisms on style. See expecially 'Der Essay als Form', *Notizen zur Literatur* [Notes on Literature], *GS*, vol. 11, pp. 9–33 (there are a number of other relevant essays in this volume), and 'Momento' and 'Juvenal's error' in *Minima Moralia*, pp. 85–7, 209–12.
51 cf. Adorno, *Negative Dialectics*, p. 18.
52 For a further discussion of some of these devices see Adorno, *Minima Moralia*, pp. 85–7.
53 Adorno, *Prisms*, p. 150.
54 Adorno to Rolf Tiedemann, quoted in the very useful 'Editorische Nachwort', *GS*, vol. 7, p. 541.
55 Adorno, *Negative Dialectics*, pp. 162–6.
56 Adorno, *Minima Moralia*, p. 87.
57 ibid., p. 71.
58 Adorno, *Negative Dialectics*, p. 360.

59   ibid., p. 406.

60   ibid., p. 183.

61   Adorno, introduction to Adorno *et al.*, *The Positivist Dispute*, p. 21.

62   To grant priority to the object does not mean, Adorno reminds us, 'that objectivity is something immediate, that we might forget our critique of naive realism' (*Negative Dialectics*, p. 184).

63   ibid., p. 9.

64   Adorno, *Negative Dialectics*, pp. 25, 52.

65   ibid., p. 163.

66   ibid., p. 52.

67   The method, Adorno contended, 'inherits some of the hope of the name' (a reference to Benjamin's idea, which Adorno regarded as quasi-mystical and rejected, that it is possible to uncover 'the real and original' name of each object).

68   Adorno, *Negative Dialectics*, pp. 54–5.

69   Adorno discussed the basic differences between identity and non-identity thinking in *Negative Dialectics*, pp. 146–61.

70   Adorno, *Prisms*, p. 32.

71   Adorno, *Negative Dialectics*, p. 149.

72   ibid., p. 150.

73   Adorno noted that this is not true of all types of concepts (although he did not discuss this important issue systematically). See his *Negative Dialectics*, pp. 11, 149–50.

74   ibid., p. 149.

75   Adorno, *Negative Dialectics*, p. 150.

76   For another example, see Adorno, 'On the logic of the social sciences', in *The Positivist Dispute*, p. 115.

77   M. Jay, 'The concept of totality in Lukács and Adorno', *Telos*, no. 32 (Summer 1977), p. 134.

78   Adorno, introduction to *The Positivist Dispute*, p. 33.

79   *Negative Dialectics*, p. 11. For a fuller treatment of Adorno's understanding of concepts see G. Rose, 'How is critical theory possible?', *Political Studies*, vol. 24, no. 1 (1976), pp. 82–4.

80   Adorno, *Negative Dialectics*, p. 31.

81   Adorno, 'Sociology and empirical research', in Adorno *et al.*, *The Positivist Dispute*, p. 69 (amended translation).

82   Adorno, 'On the logic of the social sciences', p. 112.

83   Adorno, introduction, *The Positivist Dispute*, pp. 47–8.

84   ibid., p. 25.

85   See, for example, ibid., pp. 25, 69, 115, and *Negative Dialectics*, pp. 52, 146–8.

86   ibid., p. 146 (amended translation).

87   Adorno, 'Sociology and empirical research', p. 80.

88   Adorno, introduction, *The Positivist Dispute*, pp. 21–2.

89   Adorno recognized, of course, that many statements can be tested

and falsified with the help of strict research procedures. But the successful employment of these procedures depends on the provision of well elucidated 'key categories' which must be carefully constructed through 'trial arrangement'. cf. 'The actuality of philosophy' and Adorno's essays in *The Positivist Dispute*.

90 Adorno, introduction, *The Positivist Dispute*, p. 60.
91 Adorno, *Negative Dialectics*, pp. 144–5.
92 ibid., pp. 384–93.
93 ibid., pp. 56–7 (amended translation).
94 ibid., p. 407.

8   Marcuse's notions of theory and practice

1   William Leiss, 'The critical theory of society: present situation and future tasks', in Paul Breines (ed.), *Critical Interruptions: New Left Perspectives on Herbert Marcuse* (New York: Herder & Herder 1972), p. 93.

2   For an account of Marcuse's early intellectual development see M. Jay, *The Dialectical Imagination* (Boston: Little Brown 1973), pp. 71–80. cf. Jürgen Habermas, 'Zum Geleit', in Habermas (ed.)' *Antworten auf Herbert Marcuse* (Frankfurt: Suhrkamp 1968).

3   This work was published in Frankfurt, 1932. Other relevant works include: 'Contributions to a phenomenology of historical materialism' (originally published in *Philosophische Hefte*, no. 1, Berlin 1928), *Telos*, no. 4 (Fall 1969); 'On the philosophical foundations of the concept of labour in economics' (first published in *Archiv für Sozialwissenschaft und Sozialpolitik*, vol. 69, no. 3, 1933), trans. Douglas Kellner, *Telos*, no. 16 (Summer 1973); and 'On the problem of the dialectic' (which appeared in two parts in *Die Gesellschaft*, vol. 8, 1930, 1931), trans. Morton Schoolman and Duncan Smith, *Telos*, no. 27, (Spring 1976).

4   The nature of this influence has been subject to considerable debate. See, for example, Paul Piconne and Alexander Delfini, 'Herbert Marcuse's Heideggerian Marxism', *Telos*, no. 6 (Fall 1970); Pier Aldo Rovatti, 'Critical theory and phenomenology', *Telos*, no. 15 (Spring 1973); and Alfred Schmidt, 'Existential-Ontologie und historischer Materialismus bei Herbert Marcuse', in Habermas (ed.), *Antworten auf Herbert Marcuse*. For a well-balanced account see M. Schoolman's 'Introduction to Marcuse's "On the problem of the dialectic"', *Telos*, no. 27 (1976).

5   Marcuse, 'Contributions to a phenomenology of historical materialism', p. 21.

6   T. Adorno, review in *Zeitschrift für Sozialforschung*, vol. 1, no. 3 (1932), quoted in Jay, *The Dialectical Imagination*, p. 28.

7   H. Marcuse, 'Philosophy and critical theory', in his *Negations* (Bos-

ton: Beacon Press 1968), pp. 152, 145.

8   H. Marcuse, 'The struggle against liberalism in the totalitarian view of the state', in *Negations*, p. 15.

9   ibid., p. 272.

10   Paul Robinson, *The Sexual Radicals* (London: Temple Smith 1969), p. 156.

11   Marcuse, 'Contribution to a Phenomenology', p. 13. Existence does not encounter the world as 'rigid, independent, abstract physical things'. Rather, things are related to an 'existence that uses them, orients itself towards them, and deals with them; thus ascribing to them meaning, time and place'. The world is, first and foremost, made sense of in light of 'practical and necessary concern' (*praktisch-brauchenden Besorgen*). Ordinary objects have the character of 'stuff' (*Zeug*) or of 'availability' (*Zuhandenheit*). Their 'objectivity' is unproblematic – it is taken as self-evident (cf. ibid., pp. 13–14).

12   ibid., p. 19.

13   ibid., p. 22.

14   Marcuse, 'On the problem of the dialectic', p. 18.

15   ibid., p. 21.

16   ibid.

17   H. Marcuse, *Reason and Revolution* (Boston: Beacon Press 1960), p. viii.

18   ibid., p. 49.

19   ibid., p. 124.

20   ibid., p. 128. Marcuse points out that 'the notion' also has other meanings for Hegel. See ibid., pp. 128–9.

21   ibid., p. 136.

22   ibid., p. 147.

23   ibid., p. 25.

24   ibid., p. 27.

25   ibid., p. 26.

26   ibid., pp. 253–5.

27   Marcuse discusses at considerable length the important contributions Feuerbach and others made to the transition from Hegel to Marx. See his *Reason and Revolution*, pp. 251–73.

28   ibid., pp. 260–1.

29   ibid., p. 258.

30   For Hegel labour derives from desire which directs human activity to appropriate and mould the object environment in order to satisfy wants. During this process objects become 'manifest as "the otherness" of man' (Hegel). Human beings are overpowered by the things they have known and made. The result is, at least initially, that the world of objects is transformed into a realm of independent things 'governed by uncontrolled forces and laws in which man no longer

recognizes his own self' (ibid., p. 23). This world of alienation (*Entfremdung*) is also a world in which consciousness is estranged from reality. For the process of labour, on Hegel's account, determines the nature of consciousness. The 'life and death struggle' between master and slave described in *Phenomenology* further reveals the central social dimensions of this process and the conditions necessary for the subject to overcome its separation from itself and its objects. But by making the claim that the unity of subject and object had already been achieved, Hegel prematurely ended his critical studies. As Marx showed, the antagonisms of civil society can be as little overcome in a monarchic state as social contradictions can be resolved in the realm of thought (ibid., p. 260).

31 ibid., p. 272.
32 H. Marcuse, 'The foundations of historical materialism' (1932), in his *Studies in Critical Philosophy*, trans. Joris de Bres (Boston: Beacon Press 1973), p. 4.
33 Marcuse, *Reason and Revolution*, p. 275 (and quoting Marx, *Ökonomisch-Philosophische Manuskripte* [1844] in K. Marx and F. Engels, *Gesamtausgabe*, Berlin, 1932, vol. 3, pp. 87–8).
34 Marcuse, 'The foundation of historical materialism', pp. 10–12.
35 ibid., p. 16.
36 ibid., pp. 15–17.
37 ibid., p. 18.
38 ibid., pp. 18–21.
39 ibid., p. 23.
40 ibid., p. 28.
41 cf. Marcuse 'On the philosophical foundations of the concept of labour in economics', and *Reason and Revolution*, pp. 273–312.
42 'On the philosophical foundations of the concept of labour', p. 27. This essay contains a number of ambiguities and difficulties. These concern, first, the status of labour: it is not always clear whether labour is an ontological category *per se* or a category of human existence. Second, the differences between Hegel's and Marx's concepts of labour are not always well stated. Third, Marcuse mistakenly juxtaposes labour, a 'product of necessity', with play, an 'expression of freedom'. As a result, alienation and reification are seen as ahistorical characteristics of labour, rather than phenemona created by particular socio-historical conditions which can be changed so as to create a realm of freedom *in* work. While residues of these (and other) problems can be found in Marcuse's later work, they are generally treated more satisfactorily in these writings (that is, from *Reason and Revolution* onward). Hence, I shall not discuss these (albeit important) questions here at any length. Instead, I shall focus on the positions developed in the later writings bringing out in the earlier papers the themes which seem most consistent with them.

For a discussion of some of the problems in 'On the philosophical foundations of the concept of labour', see Douglas Kellner's introduction to the essay in *Telos*, no. 16 (Summer 1973), and Morton Schooman's introduction to 'On the problem of the dialectic'.

43 Marcuse, 'On the philosophical foundations of the concept of labour', pp. 12, 10.

44 ibid., p. 16.

45 See Marcuse, *Reason and Revolution*, pp. 292–4. cf. Marcuse, *Five Lectures*, trans. J. Shapiro and S. Weber (Boston: Beacon Press 1970), p. 63.

46 'On the philosophical foundations of the concept of labour', p. 18.

47 ibid., p. 18.

48 ibid., p. 22.

49 ibid., p. 23.

50 ibid., p. 29. This conclusion was modified in the late 1940s and 1950s in light of Marcuse's encounter with Freud. The concept of labour was enriched by psychoanalytic categories.

51 Marcuse, *Reason and Revolution*, p. 295.

52 ibid., p. 276.

53 For a discussion of these notions, ibid., pp. 273–87. cf. Bertell Ollman, *Alienation* (Cambridge: Cambridge University Press 1973). Marcuse's discussion focuses on the worker's alienation from his or her product and activities.

54 Marcuse, *Reason and Revolution*, p. 282.

55 ibid., p. 314.

56 ibid., p. 287 (and quoting Marx, *The German Ideology*, p. 64).

57 Marcuse, *Reason and Revolution*, pp. 261–92.

58 ibid., pp. 288–9. Marx's idea of a rational society is one in which, according to Marcuse, 'the universal satisfaction of all individual potentialities . . . constitutes the principle of social organization'.

59 ibid., p. 315.

60 ibid., p. 317.

61 ibid., p. 313.

62 ibid., pp. 321–2. The rest, Marcuse states, cannot be specified in advance: 'it is the task of man's liberated activity'. It belongs to the project of self-creation.

63 ibid., p. 321.

64 Critical theory is, then, grounded in a notion of truth that is both of practice – an expression of the essence of labour – and irreducible to its manifestations at any given historical moment. Marcuse's claim seems to be that if one has a theory of labour that is based on a conception of the essence of human beings as free, on creative labour, and on a theory of history which demonstrates that history is the progressive development toward the realization of the (potential) essence, then a theory which shows how and why history is as it

is and why human beings can (and should) fulfil their essence, is a better or truer theory.

65 ibid., p. 322.
66 *Eros and Civilization*, pp. 113–14.
67 ibid.
68 ibid., p. 18.
69 ibid., p. 130.
70 H. Marcuse, *One Dimensional Man* (Boston: Beacon Press 1964), p. 236.
71 cf. ibid., pp. 157–8. This has occurred, in Marcuse's opinion, since Galileo's time. See my earlier discussion of instrumental reason and positivism for the background to this view (pp. 160–74 above).
72 Marcuse, *One Dimensional Man*, p. 158.
73 Marcuse, *Counterrevolution and Revolt* (Boston: Beacon Press 1972), p. 60.
74 ibid., p. 66.
75 ibid., p. 61.
76 Marcuse, 'The concept of essence', in *Negations*, pp. 70–1. Marcuse reminds his reader that 'in truth, an *a priori* element is at work here, but one confirming the historicity of the concept of essence. It leads back into history rather than out of it. The immemorially acquired image of essence was formed in mankind's historical experience, which is preserved in the present form of reality, so that it can be 'remembered' and 'refined' to the status of essence. All historical struggles for a better organization of the impoverished conditions of existence, as well as all of suffering mankind's religious and ethical ideal conceptions of a more just order of things, are preserved in the dialectical concept of the essence of man, where they have become elements of the historical practice linked to dialectical theory' (ibid., p. 75).
77 ibid., p. 72.
78 cf. Marcuse's 'Freedom and the historical imperative' (1969) in his *Studies in Critical Philosophy*, p. 213.
79 Marcuse, 'The concept of essence', p. 73.
80 ibid., p. 74.
81 ibid., p. 78.
82 Marcuse, *One Dimensional Man*, p. 220.
83 ibid., p. 252.

9 Introduction to Habermas

1 There are a number of important exceptions to this. See particularly Thomas McCarthy, *The Critical Theory of Jürgen Habermas* (London: Hutchinson 1978), and Anthony Giddens, 'Habermas' critique of hermeneutics', in his *Studies in Social and Political Theory* (Lon-

don: Hutchinson 1977). During the winter of 1975 I wrote a monograph with Larry Simon entitled 'Understanding Habermas'. If it
were not for this joint work I would not have had the opportunity to
clarify many of the problems Habermas addresses.

2 Albrecht Wellmer, *Critical Theory of Society*, trans. John Cumming
(New York: Seabury Press 1974), p. 53.

3 For an elaboration of these arguments see chapter 10 below. cf. J.
Habermas, *Towards a Rational Society: Student Protest, Science and
Politics*, trans. Jeremy J. Shapiro (London: Heinemann 1971);
Theory and Practice, trans. John Viertel (abridged edition of 4th
German ed. of *Theorie and Praxis*) (London: Heinemann 1974),
especially pp. 3–6, 195–9; and *Legitimation Crisis*, trans. Thomas
McCarthy (London: Heinemann 1976). One of Habermas's earliest
works, as yet untranslated, *Strukturwandel der Öffentlichkeit* [Struc-
tural transformation of the Public Sphere] (Neuwied: Luchterhand
1962), is an important source of many of these views.

4 Habermas, *Towards a Rational Society*, p. 101.

5 ibid., pp. 63–4, 106–7. As Habermas put it (in words which could
have been written by either Horkheimer, Adorno or Marcuse), 'the
manifest domination of the authoritarian state gives way to the manipulative compulsions of technical-operational administration'
(ibid., p. 107).

6 ibid., p. 103.

7 In his important essay, 'Technology and science as "ideology"', published in *Towards a Rational Society*, Habermas rejects Marcuse's
view of modern science and technology as inherently ideological. He
finds in this a romantic element which cannot be justified. In contradistinction to Marcuse, Habermas interprets science and technology as part of the 'project' of the human species *as a whole* which
cannot be historically surpassed.

8 J. Habermas, *Knowledge and Human Interests*, trans. J. Shapiro
(London: Heinemann 1971), p. 285.

9 See Habermas's 'Moralentwicklung und Ich-Identität' [Moral
development and ego identity], in his *Zur Rekonstruktion des Historischen Materialismus* (Frankfurt: Suhrkamp 1976), pp. 63–91. cf.
Alfred Lorenzer, *Sprachzerstörung und Rekonstruction* [Speech
Destruction and Reconstruction], (Frankfurt: Suhrkamp 1970), and
Kritik des psychoanalytischen Symbolbegriffs [Critique of the
psychoanalytical concept of symbols] (Frankfurt: Suhrkamp 1970),
for the basis of Habermas's interpretation of Freud.

10 *Knowledge and Human Interests* appeared in 1973 with a postscript
which highlights some of the new positions. The postscript was also
published in *Philosophy of the Social Sciences*, vol. 3 (1975), pp.
157–89. (References below are to this publication.)

11 His changing relation to Hegel can, I think, be detected by compar-

ing his two contributions to Adorno *et al.*, *The Positivist Dispute in German Sociology*, trans. Glyn Adey and D. Frisby (London: Heinemann 1969).

12 Habermas, *Towards a Rational Society*, p. 113.

13 ibid.

14 See Habermas, *Zur Logic der Sozialwissenschaften* (Frankfurt: Suhrkamp 1970); *Knowledge and Human Interests*; and *Theory and Practice*. *Knowledge and Human Interests* is the most important text for the development of the theory of cognitive interests. See also, however, 'A Postscript to *Knowledge and Human Interests*', for important clarifications to the theory. For a concise statement of a position close to Habermas, see Apel, 'The *a priori* of communications and the foundations of the humanities', *Man and World*, vol. 5 (February 1972).

15 See Habermas, 'On systematically distorted communication', *Inquiry*, vol. 13 (1970), and 'Towards a theory of communicative competence', *Inquiry*, vol. 13 (1970). (These two articles are reprinted H. P. Dreitzel (ed.), *Recent Sociology*, New York 1972, vol. 2). Of particular importance for recent developments of the theory are *Legitimation Crisis*, pt 3; 'Wahrheitstheorien' [Theories of truth] in Helmut Fahrenbach, *Wirklichkeit und Reflexion: zum sechzigsten Geburtstag für Walter Schulz* (Pfüllingen 1973); 'Was heisst Universal Pragmatik?' [What is universal pragmatics?], in Karl-Otto Apel, *Sprachpragmatik und Philosophie* (Frankfurt: Suhrkamp 1976). For an English version of part of the latter, see 'Some distinctions in universal pragmatics', *Theory and Society*, no. 3 (1976). An excellent summary of the (as yet developed) theory of communicative competence, with some useful criticism, is Thomas A. McCarthy, 'A theory of communicative competence', *Philosophy of Social Science*, vol. 3, no. 2 (1973); reprinted in Paul Connerton (ed.), *Critical Sociology* (Harmondsworth: Penguin 1976).

16 Trent Schroyer, *The Critique of Domination* (New York: George Brazillier 1973) p. 163.

17 See the 'Postscript to *Knowledge and Human Interests*', *Philosophy of Social Science*, pp. 161–8, 186. These are extremely complex terms which Habermas does not always use consistently. I will discuss them at greater length throughout the next three chapters.

18 See McCarthy, *The Critical Theory of Jürgen Habermas*, pp. 16–40, for an excellent discussion of these categories.

19 cf. 'Historical materialism and the development of normative structures' and 'Toward a reconstruction of historical materialism', now in Habermas, *Communication and the Evolution of Society*, trans. Thomas McCarthy (Boston: Beacon Press 1979; London: Heinemann).

10 Discourse, science and society

1 See J. Habermas, *Strukturwandel der Öffentlichkeit* (Neuwied: Luchterhand 1962). For a useful summary of some of the main themes of this book see 'The public sphere: an encyclopedia article' (1964), trans. Sara Lennox and Frank Lennox, *New German Critique*, no. 3 (Fall 1974), pp. 49–53.

2 'The public sphere', p. 49.

3 In his more recent work on truth Habermas develops this idea. He holds that it is the formal conditions of possible consensus formation, rather than ultimate reasons or grounds, which possess the legitimatory force for statements and opinions. See 'Legitimationsprobleme im modernen Staat' [Legitimation problems in the modern state] in *Zur Rekonstruktion des Historischen Materialismus* (Frankfurt: Suhrkamp 1976), pp. 271–303, and in *Communication and the Evolution of Society*. cf. chapter 12 below.

4 The particular courses this took in different European societies are traced by Habermas in chapter 3 of *Strukturwandel der Öffentlichkeit*.

5 'This transformed the newspaper business. A new element emerged between the gathering and publication of news: the editorial staff. But for the newspaper publisher it meant that he changed from a vendor of recent news to a dealer in public opinion' (Karl Bücher, quoted by Habermas in 'The public sphere', p. 53).

6 'The public sphere', pp. 52–3.

7 This change, Habermas claims, began in England, France and the United States in the 1830s.

8 'The public sphere', p. 54 (amended translation).

9 ibid., p. 55.

10 The relevant essays in *Theory and Practice*, trans. J. Viertel (London: Heinemann 1974), include, 'Between philosophy and science: Marxism as critique', and 'Dogmatism, reason and decision: on theory and praxis in our scientific civilization'.

11 *Towards a Rational Society*, trans. J. Shapiro (London: Heinemann 1971), pp. 100ff.

12 ibid., p. 104.

13 It is no longer meaningful, Habermas writes, 'to calculate the amount of capital investment in research and development on the basis of the value of unskilled (simple) labour power, when scientific-technical progress has become an independent source of surplus value, in relation to which the only source of surplus value considered by Marx, namely the labour power of the immediate producers, plays an ever smaller role' (ibid., p. 104).

14 ibid., p. 102.

15 ibid., p. 105.

16 ibid., pp. 102–3.
17 ibid., p. 105.
18 ibid., p. 111.
19 ibid., p. 112.
20 ibid., pp. 59–60. cf. p. 105.
21 Habermas, 'Dogmatism, reason and decision: on theory and praxis in our scientific civilization', p. 270.
22 ibid., pp. 270–6.
23 ibid., p. 272.
24 Luhmann maintains that, given the increasing complexity of the social world and the ever widening range of alternatives open to societies to deal with their problems, only on the level of systems analysis can a theory and methodology be found which is adequate to the rational control of society. The real danger facing society is, according to him, systems overload. For Luhmann this means that (a) systems integration be treated as independent of social integration, (b) the administrative system be freed of restrictions from the legitimation system, and (c) the administrative system not be required to respond to participatory input (since democracy is no longer rational). This programme leads to a comprehensive-non-participatory planning approach according to which '. . . there is no class of problems whose solution would, in principle, force the administration to run against the limits of its capacity'. See J. Habermas, *Legitimation Crisis*, trans. T. McCarthy (London: Heinemann 1976), pp. 130–42, for a summary of his response to Luhmann's position. See also J. Habermas and N. Luhmann, *Theorie Der Gesellschaft oder Sozialtechnologie – Was leistet die Systemforschung?* [Theory of Society or Social Technology – What does Systems Analysis Contribute?] (Frankfurt: Suhrkamp 1971), for the original exchange of views. Several volumes of commentary and discussion by others were stimulated by this exchange.
25 *Towards a Rational Society*, p. 108. cf. Claus Offe, 'Political authority and class structure', in P. Connerton (ed.), *Critical Sociology* (Harmondsworth: Penguin 1976), pp. 388–421.
26 *Towards a Rational Society*, pp. 107–9 (my emphasis).
27 ibid., p. 109.
28 cf. Habermas, *Knowledge and Human Interests*, trans. J. Shapiro (London: Heinemann 1971), chs. 2, 3, and 'Historical materialism and the development of normative structures', and 'Toward a reconstruction of historical materialism' in *Communication and the Evolution of Society*, trans. T. McCarthy (London: Heinemann 1979).
29 'Historical materialism and the development of normative structures', p. 95.
30 Habermas analyses these two strands in Marx's account of the self-formative process in terms of what he calls, respectively, the Kantian

and Fichtean moments. I shall discuss these in the next chapter.

31   Habermas, *Knowledge and Human Interests*, p. 55.
32   Habermas, 'Labour and interaction: remarks on Hegel's Jena *Philosophy of Mind*', in *Theory and Practice*, pp. 168–9.
33   Habermas, *Knowledge and Human Interests*, p. 45.
34   'Scientism', as Habermas uses the term, connotes the equation of knowledge with science.
35   cf. 'Literaturbericht zur philosophishen Diskussion um Marx und Marxismus' [Literature report on the philosophical discussion about Marx and Marxism (1957)], in *Theorie und Praxis* (Frankfurt: Suhrkamp 1974), pp. 387–463.
36   Habermas is particularly anxious to confront the codification of historical materialism presented by such figures as Stalin. See 'Toward a reconstruction of historical materialism', pp. 130–1. cf. J. Stalin, *Dialectical and Historical Materialism*.
37   Habermas rejects the view that Marx and Engels only attached to this doctrine 'the claim to a heuristic'. Its status as a theory of evolution was, he asserts, suggested by them as well as by subsequent Marxian thinkers. See 'Towards a reconstruction of historical materialism'.
38   Habermas, 'Historical materialism and the development of normative structures', pp. 97–8.
39   Habermas, 'Towards a reconstruction of historical materialism', p. 133.
40   cf. Habermas, *Legitimation Crisis*, pp. 10–11. Habermas's analysis of language will be elaborated in Chapter 12.
41   'Toward a reconstruction of historical materialism', p. 139.
42   A sixth – the Asiatic mode of production – was later inserted into the scheme. See ibid., p. 139.
43   ibid., p. 140. How exactly Habermas conceives this will be clarified below.
44   ibid., p. 141.
45   ibid., pp. 150–2.
46   ibid., pp. 153–4.
47   ibid., p. 154.
48   ibid., p. 144 (my emphasis).
49   ibid., p. 146.
50   ibid., p. 148.
51   Lawrence Kohlberg, 'Stage and sequence: the cognitive-developmental approach to socialization', in David A. Goslin (ed.), *Handbook of Socialization Theory and Research* (Chicago: Rand McNally 1969), p. 353.
52   Habermas, 'Moral development and ego identity', in *Communication and the Evolution of Society*, pp. 220–1, n. 9. Habermas is well aware that the insights of ontogenesis cannot be simply applied to

social evolution. See pp. 278 ff. below, and 'Historical materialism and the development of normative structures'.

53 Habermas cites the work of Arnold Gehlen as providing a plausible starting point for an account of the logic of technological development. cf. A. Gehlen, 'Anthropologische Ansicht der Tecknik' [Anthropological perspective on Technology] in H. Freyer *et al.* *Tecknik im technischen Zeitalter* (Dusseldorf: Schilling 1965).

54 See Jean Piaget, *The Principles of Genetic Epistemology* (Chicago: Chicago University Press 1972).

55 'Toward a reconstruction of historical materialism', p. 169.

56 'Historical materialism and the development of normative structures', p. 98.

57 See *Knowledge and Human Interests*, chs. 10–12.

58 ibid., pp. 214–90. In particular, Habermas draws on Freud's *Civilization and Its Discontents*, *The Future of an Illusion*, and the *New Introductory Lectures*.

59 T. Schroyer, *The Critique of Domination* (New York: George Braziller 1973), p. 154.

60 This is a point Habermas makes a good deal of in his most recent writing.

61 Habermas, *Knowledge and Human Interests*, p. 276.

62 ibid., p. 279.

63 Schroyer, *The Critique of Domination*, p. 155.

64 See Habermas, 'Moral development and ego identity'.

65 Several reasons are given for thinking that ontogenetic models are useful. First, the reproduction of society, Habermas argues, is dependent upon the reproduction of competent members of society; and individual identity formation is inextricably intertwined with forms of social integration. Second, although ontogenetic models are more satisfactorily corroborated than their evolutionary counterparts, 'it should not surprise us', Habermas holds, 'that there are homologous structures of consciousness in the history of the species, if we consider that linguistically established intersubjectivity of understanding marks that innovation in species history which first made possible the level of socio-cultural learning. At this level the reproduction of society and the socialization of its members are two aspects of the same process; they are dependent on the same structures' ('Historical materialism and the development of normative structures', p. 99). The structures of linguistically established intersubjectivity are conditions of both personality and social forms. While personalities can be thought of in terms of abilities to speak and act, social systems can be regarded 'as networks of communicative actions'. Following Piaget, Habermas holds that abilities and action competencies are 'formed in a simultaneously constructive and adaptive confrontation of the subject with his environment'.

Third, if we examine the competencies of socialized individuals and social institutions for general characteristics, the same structures of consciousness are, Habermas contends, revealed. (Illustrations of this are given below.) cf. 'Historical materialism and the development of normative structures', pp. 98ff.

66 'Towards a reconstruction of historical materialism', p. 154. There is, in fact, Habermas maintains, an interdependence between 'societal learning' which is crystallized in social structures – in principles of organization – and individual learning. The cognitive development of individuals takes place under specific social conditions. Rationality structures embodied in institutions like the family are, at least initially, absorbed and adapted to by children. On the other hand, social structures are changed by socialized individuals. As a consequence, the basic concepts of Habermas's approach to the study of action systems can be thought of in two ways: 'they can be understood either as concepts of competence – acquired in stages – of speaking and acting subjects who grow into a symbolic universe, or as concepts of the infrastructure of the action system itself' (ibid., p. 155).

67 'Historical materialism and the development of normative structures', p. 100.

68 ibid., pp 100–2.

69 ibid., pp. 106.

70 ibid. The discussion of *Legitimation Crisis* at the end of this chapter will elaborate on these issues.

71 By group or collective identity Habermas means 'reference groups which are essential to the identity of their members, which are in a certain way "ascribed" to individuals, cannot be freely chosen by them, and which have a continuity that extends beyond the life-historical perspectives of their members' (ibid., p. 108).

72 ibid., pp. 106–11.

73 ibid., p. 116.

74 cf. ibid., pp. 111–14.

75 cf. L. Kohlberg, 'From is to ought: how to commit the naturalistic fallacy and get away with it in the study of moral development', in T. Mischel (ed.), *Cognitive Development and Epistemology* (New York: Academic Press 1971), especially pp. 163–80.

76 'Toward a reconstruction of historical materialism', p. 156.

77 T. McCarthy, *The Critical Theory of Jürgen Habermas* (Hutchinson, pp. 252–3). This is a summary of Habermas's view as set out in 'Toward a reconstruction of historical materialism', pp. 156–8.

78 'Historical materialism and the development of normative structures', pp. 117–22.

79 ibid., p. 120.

80 ibid., p. 98.

81 ibid., p. 123. The methodological framework employed to support this position is discussed in the next section and in the following two chapters.

82 Habermas, 'Geschichte und Evolution' [History and Evolution], in *Zur Rekonstruktion des Historischen Materialismus*, p. 235.

83 cf. 'Historical materialism and the development of normative structures', p. 122.

84 ibid., pp. 121–2.

85 'Toward a reconstruction of historical materialism', pp. 164–5.

86 See especially 'Toward a reconstruction of historical materialism', *Theory and Society*, vol. 2, no. 3 (Fall 1975), pp. 294–300.

87 Habermas, *Legitimation Crisis*, p. 4.

88 ibid.

89 In the analysis of social life, particularly at the level of social systems, Habermas draws inspiration from a variety of approaches, including structuralism, genetic structuralism and functionalism. Structuralism supplies a number of important insights about the logic of deep structures, although it is criticized for failing to grasp 'the pattern of structure-forming processes; ('Toward a reconstruction of historical materialism', p. 169). Genetic structuralism, as elaborated by Piaget, contributes a number of key ideas. Piaget's investigations of the 'development-logic behind the process in which structures are formed, builds a bridge', on Habermas's account, 'to historical materialism'. Important clues are provided as to how different modes of production can be brought under 'abstract developmental-logical viewpoints' (ibid., p. 169). Functionalism offers 'useful instruments' for analysing 'systems problems that overload a structurally limited steering capacity and trigger crises that endanger the systems continued existence' ('Historical materialism and the development of normative structures', p. 125). As such it aids the investigation of the conditions which make possible the transition from one stage of development to another and, generally, of the objective conditions of action. (Habermas cites Offe's work as having shown how systems-theoretic concepts and hypotheses can be used precisely for the analysis of crises.) The functionalist model, however, cannot be simply appropriated; for its validity, Habermas stresses in a number of essays, is severely undermined by a series of unreflected presuppositions about central aspects of social life.

In order to explain an element by reference to the function it fulfils in the maintenance of a system it is necessary to be able to: identify precisely the boundaries and goal-states of the system; determine the system's functional prerequisites as well as the alternative ways these can be satisfied (cf. Habermas, *Zur Logik der Sozialwissenschaften*, pp. 164–84). While these conditions can be met for certain natural organisms they cannot be accurately outlined for social and historical systems. The standards of life, the boundaries and goal-states of societies, are dependent on the experiences and interpretations of human agents. The 'control values' of a society (the values of the state variables the system maintains) are not simply – as Parson supposes – given; they are subject to controversy – to social and political struggle. If functionalism is to serve as a 'useful tool' for social inquiry it has to be integrated, in Habermas's view, with hermeneutic and critical procedures.

While Habermas has been very critical of functionalism, he has stressed the necessity for unifying systems-theoretic and action-theoretic perspectives with insights from other approaches. But he has not, as yet, formulated an integrated framework for inquiry. This task appears to be the topic of his current research. But until it is published the methodological framework of his work will remain unclear. Various approaches are given various emphasis in his texts; but many ideas and assumptions from (predominately) systems theory, action theory and genetic structuralism are intermingled in a manner which is often difficult to follow.

90 *Legitimation Crisis*, pp. 23–4.
91 cf., for example, James O'Connor, *The Fiscal Crisis of the State* (New York: St Martin's Press 1973); Andrew Schonfield, *Modern Capitalism* (London: Oxford University Press 1965); and the work of C. Offe on the capitalist state, e.g. 'Political authority and class structure'.
92 *Legitimation Crisis*, p. 49.
93 ibid., pp. 49–50.
94 ibid., p. 46. cf. Paul Mattick, *Marx and Keynes* (Boston: Porter Sargent 1969).
95 ibid., pp. 51–2.
96 ibid., pp. 56–7.
97 ibid., p. 57.
98 The state acts both to maintain the economic process through avoidance of instabilities and to replace the market mechanism where the economic process has produced unintended dysfunctional consequences. In its maintenance function the state utilizes such measures as price control, interest regulation, tax rebates, etc. The replacement functions of the state include bolstering non-competitive sectors through government consumption, acting to improve both the material and non-material infrastructure of society (transportation, communication, education) relieving the costs of social damages due to private enterprise (welfare, unemployment, pollution) and helping to maintain foreign markets.
99 Habermas, *Legitimation Crisis*, p. 46.
100 ibid., p. 62.
101 ibid., p. 64.

102 ibid., p. 69.
103 ibid., p. 73.
104 ibid., p. 75.
105 cf. ibid., pp. 81–4.
106 cf. ibid., pp. 84–92.
107 ibid., p. 90, 117ff.

11 Interests, knowledge and action

1 J. Habermas, *Knowledge and Human Interests*, trans. J. Shapiro (London: Heinemann 1971), p. 4.
2 Two tasks became important for such an 'epistemology'. The first was to examine the methodological procedures of science in order to understand how knowledge was generated by science. The second was to analyse scientific knowledge itself to demonstrate how such knowledge was constructed out of sensory experience. cf., ibid., pp. 68–9.
3 ibid., p. 68.
4 ibid., pp. 68–9.
5 ibid., p. 304.
6 ibid., pp. 305–6.
7 ibid., p. 314.
8 J. Habermas, 'A postscript to *Knowledge and Human Interests*', *Philosophy of the Social Sciences*, vol. 3 (1975), p. 178.
9 Habermas, *Knowledge and Human Interests*, p. vii.
10 Habermas, 'A postscript to *Knowledge and Human Interests*', p. 164.
11 Habermas, *Knowledge and Human Interests*, p. 19.
12 ibid., p. 24.
13 The position was elaborated in the previous chapter on pp. 267–70.
14 Quoted by Habermas, ibid., p. 36.
15 T. Schroyer, *The Critique of Domination* (New York: George Braziller 1973), p. 139.
16 See *Knowledge and Human Interests*, chs. 2, 3, 6, and Wellmer 'Communication and emancipation', in John O'Neill (ed), *On Critical Theory* (London: Heinemann 1977), for an elaboration of this position.
17 Habermas, 'A postscript to *Knowledge and Human Interests*', p. 158.
18 Habermas, *Knowledge and Human Interests*, p. vii.
19 These figures may seem at first sight to constitute a rather out-of-date concern for a modern critique of positivism; the developments in Anglo-American philosophy in the last twenty-five years are largely ignored. But to accuse Habermas of this is to misunderstand his intent and the progress of his research. He is less interested in

criticizing contemporary philosophy than he is in examining a major tendency in modern thought in order to uncover what has been neglected by its development – the capacity to reflect upon the relationship between knowledge and human activity and to understand the actual conditions of the empirical-analytic sciences (those sciences that aim to produce nomological knowledge). Furthermore, he recognizes that the critique of positivism has been advanced by various lines of thought in recent years, thus making the extension of his arguments – which he initially planned – unnecessary ('A postscript to *Knowledge and Human Interests*', pp. 159–60). Habermas mentions four such tendencies including (*a*) the work of various German philosophers including Apel, Wellmer, Giegel and Tugenhat; (*b*) developments by a variety of Anglo-American philosophers of science, in particular, Kuhn, Feyerabend, Lakatos and Toulmin; (*c*) the Erlangen school of methodical philosophy; (*d*) developments in linguistics and the philosophy of language, for instance, the work of Searle.

20   *Knowledge and Human Interests*, p. 71.
21   This tension has been discussed at length by Robert Cohen. See his 'Ernst Mach: physics, perception and the philosophy of science', *Synthese*, vol. 18 (1968), pp. 152–70.
22   For those who adhered to this new science it was of considerable importance that 'natural phenomena might be described as varying appearances of energy'. cf. R. Cohen, 'Dialectical materialism and Carnap's logical empiricism', in Paul A. Schilpp (ed.), *The Philosophy of Rudolph Carnap* (LaSalle, Ill.: Open Court Publishing Company 1963), p. 120.
23   The ordering process was held to be describable by laws of physiological psychology.
24   Habermas, *Knowledge and Human Interests*, p. 89. This position was not maintained consistently by Mach. See Cohen, 'Ernst Mach: physics, perception, and the philosophy of science'.
25   David Held and Larry Simon, 'Understanding Habermas' (unpublished monograph), ch. 2, p. 9. It should be noted that Mach did not simply claim, as Habermas seems sometimes to suggest, that scientific objects have an independent existence, which sensations show. See Cohen, 'Ernst Mach'.
26   Habermas, *Knowledge and Human Interests*, p. 89.
27   ibid., p. 83.
28   See A. J. Ayer (ed.), *Logical Positivism* (New York: Free Press 1959).
29   Karl-Otto Apel, 'The *a priori* of communication and the foundation of the humanities', *Man and World*, no. 5 (February 1972), p. 10.
30   Habermas, *Knowledge and Human Interests*, p. 137. Habermas has also discussed more recent formulations of the philosophy of sci-

ence. See 'The analytical theory of science and dialectics', and 'A positivistically bisected rationalism' in T. Adorno *et al.*, *The Positivist Dispute in German Sociology* (London: Heinemann 1969). cf. McCarthy, *The Critical Theory of Jürgen Habermas*, pp. 40–52.

31 Apel, 'The *a priori* of communication', p. 26.

32 ibid., p. 7.

33 ibid., p. 8.

34 ibid., p. 10. The principal metaphysical presupposition of positivism that prevented the recognition of the *a priori* of communication was, Apel maintains, 'methodological solipsism'. Any philosophy which postulates a physicalistic-behaviouristic language for objectifying human intersubjectivity involves methodical solipsism. The communicative function of language is ignored, or rather 'leapfrogged', by the postulation of a language which is held to be *a priori* intersubjective by virtue of its possible universal application. Apel contends that methodical solipsism was assumed by positivism in its phenomenalistic and in its physicalistic stages.

35 See Habermas, *Knowledge and Human Interests*, ch. 5.

36 ibid., p. 91.

37 ibid., p. 124.

38 ibid.

39 ibid., p. 308.

40 The most important operations are those of measurement; 'they permit the reversibly univocal correlation of operatively determined events and systematically connected signs. . . . Only a theory of measurement, therefore, can elucidate the conditions of the objectivity of possible knowledge for the nomological sciences' (ibid., p. 192).

41 ibid., p. 191.

42 ibid., p. 308.

43 ibid., p. 309.

44 ibid.

45 'A positivistically bisected rationalism', p. 209 (amended translation).

46 cf. Gerard Radnitzky, *Contemporary Schools of Metascience* (Chicago: Henry Regneny Co. 1973), p. 325.

47 See, in particular, Habermas *Knowledge and Human Interests*, chs. 7–8, and *Zur Logik der Sozialwissenschaften*, chs. 6–8.

48 Habermas, *Knowledge and Human Interests*, p. 195.

49 cf. Habermas, *Zur Logik der Sozialwissenschaften*, p. 220f.

50 See McCarthy, *The Critical Theory of Jürgen Habermas*, pp. 137–93, for a very detailed summary of Habermas's position with respect to Husserl, Weber, Schutz, Wittgenstein, Winch, Garfinkel and Gadamer.

51 Habermas, *Knowledge and Human Interests*, p. 323.

52　Dilthey's conception of *Verstehen* corresponds to certain formulations of the notion by a number of Logical Empiricists. For Nagel and Theodor Abel, the operation of *Verstehen* amounts to the attempt by a social scientist to 'project himself by sympathetic imagination into the phenomena he is attempting to understand'. However, unlike Dilthey, Nagel rejects the notion that *Verstehen* is a method of verification, capable of generating knowledge of social phenomena. For him it is, at best, a useful tool which can aid the generation of *hypotheses*. Nagel's rejection of a position akin to that of the early Dilthey is based, among other things, on the view that such a position entails an intractable problem of evidence. Habermas would grant this point but still defend the centrality of *Verstehen* in the human sciences. He believes that the concept of *Verstehen* can be reformulated to avoid objections such as these; see his *Zur Logik der Sozialwissenschaften*, pt 3. cf. Nagel, 'The subjective nature of social subject matter', in Brodbeck (ed.), *Readings in the Philosophy of the Social Sciences*; and Theodor Abel, 'The operation called *Verstehen*', in Marcello Truzzi (ed.), *Verstehen: Subjective Understanding in the Social Sciences* (Reading, Mass.: Addison-Wesley 1974), pp. 40–56.

53　Habermas, *Knowledge and Human Interests*, pp. 146–7.

54　All social communication generally presupposes this type of understanding. 'Hermeneutic understanding is only a methodically developed form of the dim reflexivity or semi-transparency with which the life of prescientifically communicating and socially interacting men takes place in any case.' The *a priori* of communication implies that each individual must interpret his or her own feelings, needs and intentions in accordance with the available structures of linguistic intersubjectivity. cf. ibid., p. 148.

55　ibid., p. 154–8.

56　ibid., p. 172.

57　Habermas takes Wittgenstein's concept of a language game as a refinement of this idea. cf. *Knowledge and Human Interests*, p. 168, and *Zur Logik der Sozialwissenschaften*, pp. 220–51.

58　Habermas, *Knowledge and Human Interests*, p. 172.

59　Dilthey, *GS*, vol. 7, p. 207, quoted in Habermas, *Knowledge and Human Interests*, pp. 173–4.

60　Habermas, *Knowledge and Human Interests*, pp. 180ff.

61　Radnitzky, *Contemporary Schools of Metascience*, pp. 224–5.

62　cf. Habermas, *Zur Logik der Sozialwissenschaften*, pp. 188–251.

63　Hans-Georg Gadamer, *Truth and Method*, trans. and ed. Garrett Barden and John Cumming (London: Sheed & Ward 1975), p. 230.

64　ibid., p. 350.

65　ibid., p. 401.

66　ibid., p. 431.

67 ibid., p. 432.

68 ibid., pp. 235–7.

69 ibid., p. 237.

70 ibid., p. 267.

71 ibid., p. 273.

72 ibid., p. 274.

73 ibid., p. 289.

74 H-G Gadamer, 'On the scope and function of hermeneutical reflection', trans. G. B. Hess and R. E. Palmer, *Continuum*, vol. 8, nos. 1 and 2 (Spring and Summer 1970), p. 87.

75 Gadamer, *Truth and Method*, p. 245.

76 ibid., p. 230.

77 cf. Gadamer, 'On the scope and function of hermeneutical reflection', pp. 77–95; and Jürgen Habermas, 'Summation and response', *Continuum*, vol. 8, nos. 1 and 2 (Spring and Summer 1970), pp. 123–33. The key papers in the exchange are published in K.-O. Apel *et al.*, *Hermeneutik und Ideologiekritik* (Frankfurt: Suhrkamp 1971). Habermas's original assessment of Gadamer's work, 'A review of Gadamer's *Truth and Method*', can be found in Fred R. Dallmayr and Thomas A. McCarthy (eds.), *Understanding Social Inquiry* (Notre Dame, Indiana: The University Press 1977). Habermas's most recent work entails, as the following chapter indicates, a further critical departure from Gadamer's views.

78 Habermas, 'Summation and response', p. 125 (amended translation).

79 ibid.

80 Wellmer, *Critical Theory of Society*, p. 47.

81 Habermas, 'Summation and response', p. 127.

82 Habermas, 'A review of Gadamer's *Truth and Method*', p. 360.

83 ibid.

84 ibid., p. 361.

85 ibid.

86 Habermas, *Zur Logik der Sozialwissenschaften*, pp. 305–6.

87 McCarthy, *The Critical Theory of Jürgen Habermas*, p. 191–3. cf. Habermas, 'A review of Gadamer's *Truth and Method*', pp. 356–7.

88 Habermas, *Theory and Practice*, pp. 22–3 (amended translation).

89 cf. Habermas, *Knowledge and Human Interests*, especially ch. 9.

90 ibid., pp. 197–8.

91 ibid., p. 212.

92 ibid., p. 211.

93 Habermas, 'A postscript to *Knowledge and Human Interests*', p. 176.

94 cf. Habermas, *Theory and Practice*, p. 9, and *Knowledge and Human Interests*, ch. 9.

95 Habermas, 'Wahrheitstheorien', in H. Fahrenbach (ed.), *Wirchlich-*

468   *Notes and references to pages 319–23*

keit und Reflexion (Pfüllingen: Neske 1973), pp. 258ff.
96   Habermas, *Knowledge and Human Interests*, pp. 310–10.
97   cf. ibid., 10–12.
98   ibid., p. 214.
99   ibid., p. 217.
100 ibid., p. 218.
101 ibid, p. 241. Freud failed to clarify, Habermas maintains, what rules – other than *grammatical* rules – can be used to connect unconscious ideas with verbal residues. For Habermas it seems plausible 'to conceive the act of repression as a banishment of need interpretations themselves. The degrammaticized and imagistically compressed language of the dream provides', he holds, 'some clues to an *excommunication model* of this sort. . . . The *splitting-off of individual symbols from public* communication would mean at the same time the *privitization of their semantic content*. Nevertheless, some logical connection of deformed and public language remains possible – it is in this that the therapist's activity of linguistic analysis consists' (ibid., pp. 241–2). For a position close to Habermas's see Lorenzer, 'Symbols and Stereotypes', in Connerton (ed.), *Critical Sociology*.
102 Habermas, *Knowledge and Human Interests*, p. 232.
103 It should be noted here that Habermas criticizes Freud for failing in the end to understand the status of psychoanalysis as a critical science. Habermas suggests that Freud lapsed into a positivistic misunderstanding of his own work. This positivist tendency is indicated, according to Habermas, in Freud's attempt to interpret psychoanalysis in terms of an energy distribution model, thus eliminating the hermeneutic dimension. For the critique of Freud, see Habermas, *Knowledge and Human Interests*, pp. 284–86.
104 cf. T. McCarthy, 'Philosophy and social theory', *Stony Brook Studies in Philosophy*, vol. 1 (1974), pp. 108–10, and *The Critical Theory of Jürgen Habermas*, pp. 196–203. See Habermas, *Knowledge and Human Interests*, pp. 252–73.
105 Habermas, *Knowledge and Human Interests*, p. 252.
106 ibid., p. 254.
107 ibid., p. 258.
108 McCarthy, 'Philosophy and social theory', p. 109.
109 *Knowledge and Human Interests*, p. 260.
110 ibid., p. 269.
111 Radnitzky, *Contemporary Schools of Metascience*, pp. 236–7. Radnitzky provides an interesting and wide-ranging discussion of the psychoanalytic model and the role of explanation and understanding in a critical science.
112 Habermas, *Knowledge and Human Interests*, p. 271.
113 Apel, 'The *a priori* of Communication', p. 34.
114 Habermas, *Theory and Practice*, p. 9 (my emphasis).

115 Habermas believes that the organization of political enlightenment can be fashioned after critical theory. His reasons for this are outlined in the following chapter.

116 Habermas, *Theory and Practice*, p. 21.

117 Habermas, *Knowledge and Human Interests*, p. 194. Understood in this way, cognitive interests 'assume an "empirical" status as soon as they are being analysed as the result of natural history – analysed, that is, in terms of a cognitive anthropology, as it were'. 'Empirical', must be placed in quotation marks; for the recovery of these interests as emergent properties of human history is dependent upon a theory of evolution. This theory itself, however, cannot escape the cognitive framework of the constituting interests; it cannot 'wholly divest itself of the form of a reflection on the pre-history of culture that is dependent on a prior understanding of the socio-cultural life form.' Habermas is aware of the circularity which thus appears in the interpretation of his theory of interests; see his *Theory and Practice*, p. 285.

118 Habermas, *Knowledge and Human Interests*, p. 197.

119 ibid., p. 134.

120 For a discussion of some of these problems see Fred R. Dallmayr, 'Critical theory criticized', *Philosophy of Social Science*, vol. 2, no. 3 (1973), and 'Reason and emancipation: notes on Habermas', *Man and World*, vol. 5, no. 1 (1972). Dallmayr's articles contain a useful survey and bibliography of the critical literature. See also Anthony Giddens, 'Habermas's critique of hermeneutics', in his *Studies in Social and Political Theory* (London: Hutchinson 1977). *Cultural Hermeneutics*, vol. 2 (1975) conducts a fairly full review of some of these issues. The critical literature in German is extensive. Among the most important sources are Rüdiger Bubner *et al.*, *Hermeneutik und Dialektik* (Tübingen: J. C. B. Mohr 1970); Karl-Otto Apel *et al.*, *Hermeneutik und Ideologiekritik* (Frankfurt: Suhrkamp 1971); Habermas and Niklas Luhmann, *Theorie Der Gesellschaft oder Sozialtechnologie* (Frankfurt: Suhrkamp 1971).

121 Habermas, 'A postscript to *Knowledge and Human Interests*', p. 179.

122 ibid.

123 ibid., pp. 166–72.

124 See his essay in F. Dallmayr (ed.), *Materialien zu Habermas' 'Erkenntnis und Interesse'* (Frankfurt: Suhrkamp 1974).

125 cf. Habermas, 'Introduction' to *Theory and Practice*.

126 Habermas, 'A postscript', p. 182.

127 Although this programme implies that a central claim of *Knowledge and Human Interests* must now be recast – reflection on the conditions of a knowing and acting subject does not *per se* entail emancipatory practice – Habermas believes that the critical thrust of this

text can be preserved.

128 Habermas, *Theory and Practice*, p. 22.
129 ibid.
130 Habermas, 'A postscript', p. 183 (emphasis mine).
131 Habermas, 'Summation and response' (amended translation).
132 cf. 'Toward a reconstruction of historical materialism', pp. 169–74.
      This should not be taken to mean that Habermas agrees with all the
      details and claims of these disciplines. He has, in fact, serious disag-
      reements with the pioneers of each of these areas, namely with
      Chomsky, Levi-Strauss and Piaget.
133 cf. McCarthy, *The Critical Theory of Jürgen Habermas*, pp. 100–2.
134 ibid., p. 102.
135 'Geschichte und Evolution', p. 250.

12   The reformulation of the foundations of critical theory

1 J. Habermas, *'Wahrheitstheorien', in H. Fahrenbach (ed.), Wirchlichkeit und Reflexion* (Pfüllingen: Neske 1973), pp. 226–7.
2 Habermas, *Legitimation Crisis*, trans. T. McCarthy (London:
   Heinemann 1976), p. 104.
3 ibid., p. 108.
4 ibid., p. 110.
5 Habermas, *Zur Logik der Sozialwissenschaften* (Frankfurt: Suhrkamp 1970), p. 220.
6 Habermas, 'What is universal pragmatics?', in his *Communication
   and the Evolution of Society*, trans. T. McCarthy (London:
   Heinemann 1979), p. 1.
7 See, in particular, Habermas, 'Wahrheitstheorien'; *Legitimation
   Crisis*, pt 3, especially pp. 102–11; and (with N. Luhmann), *Theorie
   der Gesellschaft oder Sozialtechnologie?*, (Frankfurt: Suhrkamp
   1971), pp. 101–41.
8 'What is universal pragmatics?', pp. 1–2.
9 See Noam Chomsky, *Aspects of the Theory of Syntax* (Cambridge,
   Mass.: MIT Press 1965); Austin, *How To Do Things with Words*
   (Oxford: Oxford University Press 1962); and John R. Searle,
   Speech Acts (Cambridge: Cambridge University Press, 1969).
10 'What is universal pragmatics?', p. 26.
11 ibid., p. 2.
12 ibid., p. 3.
13 ibid., p. 66.
14 ibid., pp. 28–9 (My emphasis).
15 ibid., pp. 29–30.
16 ibid., p. 30–1.

17 ibid., p. 42.
18 T. McCarthy, *The Critical Theory of Jürgen Habermas* (London: Hutchinson 1978), pp. 272–91, for a thorough account of Habermas's position.
19 Searle, *Speech Acts*, pp. 54ff. 'What is universal pragmatics?', pp. 59–64.
20 'What is universal pragmatics?', p. 62.
21 ibid., p. 63.
22 ibid., p. 63.
23 Against Austin Habermas thinks it is important, when analysing speech acts, to distinguish among:
    '(a) the implicitly presupposed conditions of generalized contexts,
    (b) the specific meaning of the interpersonal relation to be established, and
    (c) the implicitly raised, general validity claims.'
A full account of speech actions must work at each of these levels: 'Whereas (a) and (b)', in Habermas's opinion, 'fix the distinct classes (different in different languages) of standardized speech actions, (c) determines the universal modes of communication, modes inherent in speech in general' ('What is universal pragmatics?', p. 57).
24 ibid., p. 59.
25 ibid., p. 68.
26 Habermas, 'Vorbereitende Bemerkungen zu einer Theorie der kommunikativen Competence' [Preparatory remarks on a theory of communicative competence], in *Theorie der Gesellschaft oder Sozialtechnologie*, p. 120, quoted in T. McCarthy, 'A theory of communicative competence', *Philosophy of Social Science*, vol. 3, no. 2 (1973), p. 140.
27 ibid.
28 See Habermas, 'Wahrheitstheorien', pp. 252ff., for the analysis of these two types of discourse.
29 Habermas, 'A postscript to *Knowledge and Human Interests*', *Philosophy of the Social Sciences*, vol. 3 (1975), p. 168.
30 ibid., 171.
31 Habermas, 'Wahrheitstheorien', p. 218.
32 ibid., p. 245.
33 Habermas, 'A postscript', p. 175.
34 P. F. Strawson, 'Truth', in G. Pitcher (ed.), *Truth* (Englewood Cliffs, NJ: Prentice-Hall 1964), p. 38, quoted by Habermas in 'A postscript', p. 167.
35 Habermas, 'A postscript', p. 175.
36 'Wahrheitstheorien', p. 216.
37 'A postscript', p. 169.
38 'Wahrheitstheorien', p. 232.

39 'A postscript', p. 168.
40 'Wahrheitstheorien', p. 219.
41 The table is taken from ibid., p. 243.
42 cf., ibid., pp. 238–52. See Toulmin, *The Uses of Argument* (Cambridge: Cambridge University Press 1964).
43 'Wahrheitstheorien', p. 242.
44 ibid., p. 254.
45 ibid., pp. 239–40.
46 ibid., p. 258.
47 ibid.
48 ibid., pp. 258–9.
49 Habermas, 'Legitimation problems in the modern state', in his *Communication and the Evolution of Society*, p. 186.
50 ibid.
51 cf. McCarthy, 'A theory of communicative competence', p. 154.
52 Habermas, *Knowledge and Human Interests*, p. 317.
53 'A postscript', p. 172.
54 ibid., p. 175.
55 See *Legitimation Crisis*, pp. 111–17.
56 ibid., pp. 112–13.
57 ibid., p. 117. A discourse can be used to separate those norms which express a generalizable interest from those which do not. But if certain interests cannot be resolved into a generalizable form, one can speak of a compromise which allows for an indirectly justified agreement on a non-generalizable interest. 'A normal adjustment between particular interests is called a compromise if it takes place under conditions of a balance of power between the parties involved.' It is necessary to distinguish between a justified and a non-justified or pseudo-compromise. In order to be justified, a compromise must meet, Habermas holds, two conditions: there must be a balance of power among the parties involved and the compromised interests must be non-generalizable. If one or both of these conditions is not met, it is a pseudo-compromise. See Habermas, *Legitimation Crisis*, pp. 111–13.
58 ibid., p. 114.
59 Habermas, *Theory and Practice*, p. 32, quoted and trans. McCarthy in 'A theory of communicative competence', p. 148.
60 Habermas, *Theory and Practice*, p. 32.
61 ibid.
62 ibid.
63 Habermas is concerned to avoid, at all costs, the degeneration of political organization into elitist or mechanistic practice. He stresses this point by distinguishing different preconditions which he argues must be present on the three levels. On the first level, that of theory, it must be accepted that '. . . those engaged in scientific work have

the freedom to conduct theoretical discourse'. Only under this condition can a scientific theory be developed in the most rational way.
On the second level, that of the process of enlightenment, practice
must be organized so that '. . . those who carry out the active work of
enlightenment commit themselves wholly to the proper precautions
and assure scope for communication on the model of therapeutic
"discourse"'. This condition must be met if deception and exploitation are to be avoided. On the third level, that of political struggle,
there is yet a different precondition if it is to be legitimate, namely
'. . . that all decisions of consequence will depend on the practical
discourse of the participants – here too, and especially here, there is
no privileged access to truth'. It is Habermas's contention that a
political organization or party must adhere to these differentiated
functions and preconditions if it is to achieve its goals. Not to recognize that strategy must be decided upon under conditions different
from those of the practice of enlightenment or theory is to run the
risk of conceiving of practice instrumentally and to fall into a 'science of apologetics'. As Habermas says: 'The autonomy of theory
and enlightenment . . . is required for the sake of the independence
of political action.' cf. his *Theory and Practice*, pp. 25–40.
64 Habermas, *Legitimation Crisis*, p. 122.
65 ibid., pp. 124ff.
66 ibid., p. 141.

13 An assessment of the Frankfurt school and Habermas

1 Weaknesses in recent attempts to come to grips with the contributions of the critical theorists are also examined in my 'The battle
over critical theory', *Sociology*, vol. 12, no. 3 (September 1978).

2 cf. P. Anderson, *Considerations on Western Marxism* (London: New
Left Books 1976), and Therborn, 'The Frankfurt school', in *Western
Marxism: a Critical Reader* (London: New Left Books 1977), pp.
83–139. The level of sophistication of the critics of critical theory
varies considerably. Anderson, for example, presents a more
informed account than Therborn. Both present a more informed
assessment than Zoltan Tar's *The Frankfurt School: the Critical
Theories of Max Horkheimer and Theodor W. Adorno* (New York:
John Wiley 1977). Comments on Tar's book are included in the next
chapter.

3 See, for example, Therborn, 'The Frankfurt school', p. 120.

4 Anderson, *Considerations on Western Marxism*, p. 93.

5 Therborn, 'The Frankfurt school', pp. 92, 108.

6 Phil Slater, *Origin and Significance of the Frankfurt School: A Marxist Perspective* (London: Routledge & Kegan Paul 1977), pp. xiii–
xiv.

7 ibid., pp. 47, 63. What is needed, Slater declares, 'is a theory of *organization* and *political* action . . . a *practical–critical* theory' (ibid., p. 28). Precisely what this amounts to Slater does not say.

8 Marcuse is partly exempted from this charge.

9 Tony Woodiwiss, 'Critical theory and the capitalist state', *Economy and Society*, vol. 7, no. 2 (May 1978), p. 189.

10 ibid., pp. 188–9.

11 cf. Therborn, 'The Frankfurt school', pp. 87–92.

12 ibid., p. 88.

13 ibid., pp. 96–9.

14 Anderson, *Considerations on Western Marxism*, p. 58. Anderson makes this remark not just about critical theory, but about Western Marxism in general.

15 ibid., pp. 44–5. Again it should be noted that Anderson claims this is true of Western Marxism in general (excepting Gramsci).

16 ibid., and ch. 5.

17 ibid., p. 53.

18 This is also true of Tar's portrayal of critical theory in *The Frankfurt School: the Critical Theories of Max Horkheimer and Theodor W. Adorno*.

19 Therborn, 'The Frankfurt school', p. 99.

20 Slater, *The Origin and Significance of the Frankfurt School*, pp. 31–3.

21 See, for example, T. Adorno, *The Jargon of Authenticity* (London: Routledge & Kegan Paul 1973), and my chapter on Adorno above (pp. 200–22).

22 See my discussion of Marcuse, pp. 232–8.

23 See Jeffrey Herf, 'Science and class or philosophy and revolution: Perry Anderson on Western Marxism', *Socialist Review*, no. 35, vol. 7 (1977), pp. 129–44. I found this article extremely helpful in assessing Anderson's work.

24 ibid., p. 138.

25 J. Habermas, 'Conservatism and capitalist crisis', *New Left Review*, no. 115 (May–June 1979), p. 81.

26 cf. Gregor McLennan *et al.*, 'Althusser's theory of ideology', in Centre for Contemporary Cultural Studies, *On Ideology* (London: Hutchinson 1978).

27 Therborn, 'The Frankfurt school', p. 125.

28 See pp. 41 ff. above.

29 For example, see the discussion in Therborn, 'The Frankfurt school', pp. 124–5, and in Woodiwiss, 'Critical theory and the capitalist state', pp. 188–91.

30 Woodiwiss, 'Critical theory and the capitalist state', p. 188.

31 I elaborate this in 'Critical theory and social science', in John Law (ed.), *The Language of Sociology* (forthcoming as a *Sociological*

Review Monograph).

32 cf. G. Rose, *The Melancholy Science* (London: Macmillan 1978), pp. 138–48.

33 For an excellent discussion of this in relation to Freud see R. Jacoby, *Social Amnesia – A Critique of Conformist Psychology from Adler to Laing* (Boston: Beacon Press 1975).

34 cf. A. Giddens, *New Rules of Sociological Method* (London: Hutchinson 1976), and *Studies in Social and Political Theory* (London: Hutchinson 1977), especially pp. 126–34.

35 Jane Caplan, 'Theories of fascism: Nicos Poulantzas as historian', *History Workshop*, no. 3 (1977). As Caplan points out, 'a regime of terror may derive its effect precisely from the absence of . . . central political control, in that this leaves so many interstices open for the invasion of prerogative power, as well as radicalising the political process (though this is not to suggest that individual units within the general structure will not be organizationally "rational")' (ibid., p. 99).

36 See Paul Mattick, 'The limits of integration', in Kurt H. Wolff and Barrington Moore (eds.), *The Critical Spirit: Essays in Honor of Herbert Marcuse* (Boston: Beacon Press 1968).

37 See, for example, James O'Connor, *The Fiscal Crisis of the State* (New York: St Martin's Press 1973); Claus Offe, *Strukturprobleme des Kapitalistischen Staates* [Structural Problems of the Capitalist State](Frankfurt: Suhrkamp 1972); Mike Best and William Connolly, *The Politicized Economy* (Lexington, Mass.: D. C. Heath 1976); Douglas Hibbs, 'Economic interest and the politics of macroeconomic policy' (Cambridge, Mass.: MIT Center for International Studies Monograph 1976); J. Habermas, *Legitimation Crisis*, trans. T. McCarthy (London: Heinemann 1974).

38 These points are adapted from 'Some recent developments in the Marxist theory of the state', a paper prepared by the San Francisco Kapitalistate Group for the winter conference of the Union for Radical Political Economy, San Francisco (December 1974). The points were made in connection with a critique of instrumentalist theories of the state. (A version of this article appeared in *Monthly Review*, vol. 27, nos. 5–6 [October–November 1976].

39 The political business cycle theory elaborated by Hibbs in 'Economic interest and the politics of macroeconomic policy', and by Raford Boddy and James Crotty in 'Class conflict and macropolicy: the political business cycle'. *Review of Radical Political Economics*, vol. 7 (Spring 1974), lends support to this position.

40 San Francisco Kapitalistate Group, 'Some recent developments in the Marxist Theory of the state', p. 4.

41 See Offe, *Strukturprobleme des Kapitalistischen Staates*, and O'Con-

nor, *The Fiscal Crisis of the State*. For a summary and discussion of Offe's work see John Keane, 'The legacy of political economy: thinking with and against Claus Offe', *Canadian Journal of Political and Social Theory*, vol. 2, no. 3 (1978).

42 See, for instance, Stephan Leibrfied, 'US central government reform of the administrative structure during the Ash period (1968–1971)', *Kapitalistate*, no. 2 (1973).

43 For an elaboration of the notion of structuration see A. Giddens, 'Agency, structure', in his *Central Problems in Social Theory* (London: Macmillan 1979).

44 In particular, see Offe, *Berufsbildungsreform: eine Fallstudie über Reformpolitik* (Frankfurt: Suhrkamp 1975). cf. his 'Political authority and class structure; an analysis of late capitalist societies', *International Journal of Sociology*, vol. 2, no. 1, and 'The theory of the capitalist state and the problem of policy formation', in L. Lindberg *et al.*, *Stress and Contradiction in Modern Capitalism* (Lexington, Mass.: Lexington Books 1975).

45 Hibbs, 'Economic interest and the politics of macroeconomic policy', pt 3. An abridged version of this paper appeared in the *American Political Science Review*, vol. 71 (1977).

46 A distinction, as I outline below, needs to be made between various levels of class-consciousness. cf. John Legget, *Class, Race, and Labour* (New York and Oxford 1971), pp. 40–2; A. Giddens, *The Class Structure of Advanced Societies* (London: Hutchinson 1977), pp. 112–13, and Michael Mann, *Consciousness and Action Among the Western Working Class* (London: Macmillan 1973), especially chs. 1–3.

47 Mann, *Consciousness and Action*, and 'The social cohesion of liberal democracy', *American Sociological Review*, vol. 35 (1970); Giddens, *The Class Structure of Advanced Societies*, ch. 11.

48 See Jorge Larrain's discussion of ideology in his *The Concept of Ideology* (London: Hutchinson 1979). For an interesting treatment of the notion of social contradictions see Jon Elster, *Logic and Society – Contradictions and Possible Worlds* (Chichester: John Wiley 1978). But cf. Giddens, 'Contradiction, power, historical materialism', in his *Central Problems in Social Theory*, for an appraisal of Elster's position.

49 cf., for example, Mann, 'The social cohesion of liberal democracy', and Paul Willis, *Learning to Labour* (Westmead: Saxon House 1977).

50 Willis, *Learning to Labour*.

51 Alan Swingewood, *The Myth of Mass Culture* (London: Macmillan 1977), p. 113. While I think this criticism holds, Swingewood's treatment of Horkheimer *et al.* misrepresents their positions and neglects the differences between the various members of the Frank-

furt school. As an exposition and critique of the Frankfurt school's approach to culture this book is highly unsatisfactory.

52 See the 'Introduction to Adorno's letters to Benjamin', *New Left Review*, no. 81 (1973), p. 52.

53 See pp. 99–105 for an introduction to these categories. But cf. T. Adorno, *Introduction to the Sociology of Music*, trans. E. B. Ashton (New York: Seabury Press 1976).

54 J. Habermas, 'Moral development and ego identity', in *Communication and the Evolution of Society*, trans. T. McCarthy (London: Heinemann), pp. 70–1.

55 See pp. 114–15 for Adorno's criticisms of this view.

56 Herbert Fingarette, 'Eros and utopia', *Review of Metaphysics*, vol. 10, no. 4 (June 1957), pp. 663–5.

57 Habermas, 'Moral development and ego identity', p. 71.

58 Therborn's 'The Frankfurt school' notes similar problems but fails to separate them adequately from other issues, for example, those relating to the notions of history that Horkheimer and Marcuse defend. See my critique of his views above, pp. 354–62.

59 I owe this point to discussion with John Forrester.

60 S. Freud, *Civilization and its Discontents*, trans. Joan Riviere, rev. and ed. James Strachey (London: Hogarth Press 1969), p. 67, *n*. 1.

61 For a survey of these studies see Lawrence Kohlberg, 'Moral development and identification', in H. Stevenson (ed.), *62nd Yearbook of the National Society for the Study of Education* (Chicago: The University Press 1963) and 'A cognitive developmental analysis of children's sex-role concepts and attitudes', in E. Maccoby (ed.), *The development of sex differences* (Stanford, Calif.: The University Press 1966).

62 L. Kohlberg, 'Stage and sequence', in David A. Goslin (ed.), *Hand-book of Socialization Theory and Research* (Chicago: Rand McNally 1969), p. 362.

63 ibid., p. 363.

64 Jane Caplan pointed this out to me.

65 R. Christie and J. Jahoda (eds.), *Studies in the Scope and Method of 'The Authoritarian Personality'* (Glencoe, Ill.: Free Press 1954) contains a number of relevant papers which elaborate on these and other related themes.

66 Rose, *The Melancholy Science*, p. 141.

67 Marcuse's failure to illuminate the actual processes of late capitalist reproduction is stressed by C. Offe in his 'Technik und Eindimensionalität; eine Version der Technokratiethese?', in J. Habermas (ed.), *Anworten auf Herbert Marcuse* (Frankfurt: Suhrkamp 1968).

68 T. McCarthy, *The Critical Theory of Jürgen Habermas* (London: Hutchinson 1978), p. 379.

69 ibid.

70 Mann, *Consciousness and Action Among the Western Working Class*, particularly ch. 4.

71 It might be objected that Habermas's case could be made stronger by reference to his theory of social evolution and his theory of the logic of the development of normative structures. These theories would lend support to his contention that the disaffected groups he picks out are harbingers of the future and not merely temporary side products of the present system. But these theories are yet to be adequately developed and therefore cannot be drawn upon until they are more fully elaborated.

72 Some of the problems neglected by Habermas are addressed in Immanuel Wallerstein, *The Modern World-System* (New York: Academic Press 1974).

73 T. Adorno, *Prisms*, trans. S. Weber and S. Weber (London: Neville Spearman 1967), p. 29.

74 But cf. Boris Frankel, 'State of the state after Leninism', *Theory and Society*, vol. 7, no. 1/2 (March 1979) for a discussion of the importance of Habermas's work in relation to contemporary theories of the state.

14   The concept of critical theory

1 See Paul Connerton's introduction to the volume edited by him, *Critical Sociology* (Harmondsworth: Penguin 1976).

2 Zoltan Tar, *The Frankfurt School: the Critical Theories of Max Horkheimer and Theodor W. Adorno* (New York: John Wiley 1977). cf. the review of this text by Gillian Rose in *History and Theory*, vol. 8, no. 1 (1979).

3 Tar, *The Frankfurt School*, p. 205.

4 ibid.

5 Tar does not discuss Adorno's criticisms of existentialism and related philosophies. See, for example, Adorno's *Jargon of Authenticity* (London: Routledge & Kegan Paul 1973).

6 Tar, *The Frankfurt School*, pp. 40–3, 166–9.

7 ibid., p. 59.

8 Karl Popper, 'Reason or revolution', in Adorno *et al.*, *The Positivist Dispute in German Sociology*, p. 296.

9 ibid., p. 297.

10 ibid., p. 248.

11 ibid.

12 One of the central dilemmas facing a position like Adorno's has been succintly posed by Habermas: 'to what sources of experience can critical theory appeal, if in the materialist manner it renounces philosophy as first philosophy and yet cannot be reduced to a positive science? Must it not open itself to the historically variable

source of experience provided by the socially concrete life-world, prior to all methodological objectivations, in order to legitimize the critical initiative as such? And do not, on the other hand, quantities of experience from this source flow into . . . forms of . . . consciousness, into art, religion, and philosophy, which have been devalued by the critique of ideology?' (*Theory and Practice*, trans. J. Viertel, London: Heinemann 1974), p. 241.

13 Although Adorno mounted a fierce critique of historicism (the interpretation of things in terms of their historical contextuality), his own approach does not entirely escape the problems associated with the position; for he presupposes a definite, albeit negative, relation between cognition and social and economic conditions.

14 cf. S. Buck-Morss, *The Origin of Negative Dialectics* (Hassocks, Sussex: Harvester 1977), ch. 12.

15 See Chapter 6, pp. 193–5.

16 It is important to remember that Horkheimer's position changed over time. See 'Spiegel-Gespräch mit dem Philosophen Max Horkheimer', *Der Spiegel*, 5 January 1970.

17 On the former issue see the commentary by MacIntyre in *Marcuse* (Glasgow: Fontana/Collins 1970), pp. 38–9. For an alternative view of dialectics see Charles Lewis, 'Hegel's critique of reason' (Unpublished doctoral dissertation, Cambridge University 1979).

18 Habermas shows this well in 'Technology and science as "ideology"', in *Towards a Rational Society*, trans. J. Shapiro (London: Heinemann 1970), pp. 81–90.

19 cf. James Bradley, 'Feuerbach's relevance to modern thought', in S. W. Sykes and D. Holmes (eds.), *New Studies in Theology* (London: Duckworth 1979). This paper offers some interesting critical remarks on naturalism – whether it be of an anthropological or historical-materialist kind.

20 Marcuse's position creates a number of misunderstandings about various schools of contemporary philosophy. Some of these are pointed to by MacIntyre in *Marcuse*, ch. 7. (MacIntyre's polemical and at times vitriolic style should not be allowed to detract from the seriousness of the points he is trying to make in this chapter.)

21 K. Marx, *Grundrisse* (Penguin 1973), p. 505. cf., also, pp. 595–9 (this passage is quoted in A. Schmidt, *The Concept of Nature in Marx*, London: New Left Books 1971).

22 I am indebted to a conversation with James Bradley for this point.

23 'Theory and politics: a discussion with Herbert Marcuse, Jürgen Habermas, Heinz Lubasz and Telman Spengler', *Telos*, no. 38 (Winter 1978), especially pp. 131–40.

24 For a discussion of some of these issues see Fred R. Dallmayr, 'Critical theory criticized', *Philosophy of Social Science*, vol. 2, no. 3 (1973), and 'Reason and emancipation: notes on Habermas', *Man*

and World, vol. 5, no. 1 (1972). Dallmyr's articles contain a useful survey and bibliography of the critical literature on Habermas. See also A. Giddens, 'Habermas' critique of hermeneutics', in his *Studies in Social and Political Theory* (London: Hutchinson 1977). *Cultural Hermeneutics*, vol. 2 (1975) conducts a fairly full review of some of the issues. The critical literature in German is extensive. Among the most important sources are Rüdigner Bubner *Hermeneutik und Dialektik* (Tübingen: J. C. B. Mohr 1970); Karl-Otto Apel *et al.*, *Hermeneutik und Ideologiekritik* (Frankfurt: Suhrkamp 1971); and Habermas and Niklas Luhmann, *Theorie Der Gesellschaft oder Sozialtechnologie* (Frankfurt: Suhrkamp 1971).

25 See K-O Apel, 'The *a priori* of communication and the foundation of the humanities', *Man and World* (5 February 1972).

26 Habermas, 'A postscript to *Knowledge and Human Interests*', *Philosophy of the Social Sciences*, vol. 3 (1975), p. 186.

27 This position was elaborated in Chapter 8.

28 It is not only changes in the stock of technical knowledge which alter the relationship between human beings and nature; although on Marcuse account, capitalist industrialism and bureaucratic socialism enforce such an image of human–nature relations.

29 See Giddens, 'Habermas' critique of hermeneutics', pp. 148–54. Understanding is a fundamental goal of science which 'is precisely why it is a rival to other types of religious or magical cosmology against the backdrop of which interaction, prior to the development of Western industrial culture, has been carried on' (ibid., p. 150).

30 ibid., pp. 29–88, and Mary Hesse, *The Structure of Scientific Inference* (London: Macmillan 1974).

31 M. Hesse, 'Theory and value in the social sciences', in Christopher Hookway and Philip Pettit (eds.), *Action and Interpretation* (Cambridge: Cambridge University Press 1978), p. 6.

32 cf. T. McCarthy, *The Critical Theory of Jürgen Habermas* (London: Hutchinson 1978), pp. 66–8.

33 ibid., p. 111.

34 This issue is elaborated at length in ibid., pp. 111–25. See also the critique of critical theory by Michael Theunissen, *Gesellschaft und Geschichte: Zur Kritik der Kritischen Theorie* [Society and History: The Critique of Critical Theory] (Berlin: de Gruyter 1969).

35 Giddens, 'Habermas' critique of hermeneutics', p. 160.

36 D. Howard, 'A politics in search of the political', *Theory and Society*, vol. 1, no. 3 (1973).

37 Habermas's most recent work on ontogenesis and phylogenesis seeks clearly to confront these issues.

38 James Schmidt, 'Offensive critical theory', *Telos*, no. 39 (Spring 1979), p. 69.

39 This point is elaborated by Jeff Coulter, 'The Ethnomethodological

programme in contemporary sociology', *Human Context*, vol. 6, no. 1 (1974).

40 T. McCarthy, 'A theory of communicative competence', *Philosophy of the Social Sciences*, vol. 3, no. 2 (1973), p. 152.

41 ibid., pp. 152–3.

42 Steven Lukes, 'The critical theory trip', *Political Studies*, vol. 25, no. 3 (1977), p. 411. cf. Lukes's 'Relativism: cognitive and moral', in his *Essays in Social Theory* (London: Macmillan 1977), for a discussion of related issues.

Appendix

1 M. Horkheimer and T. Adorno, *Dialectic of Enlightenment*, trans. J. Cumming (New York: Herder & Herder 1972), p. 43.

2 ibid., p. 55.

3 ibid., p. 57.

4 ibid., p. 50.

5 ibid., p. 49.

6 ibid., p. 61.

7 ibid., pp. 61–2.

8 cf. Homer, *Odyssey*, trans. Robert Fitzgerald (New York: Doubleday 1963), book 12, and Horkheimer and Adorno, *Dialectic of Enlightenment*, pp. 32–6, 58–9.

9 Horkheimer and Adorno, *Dialectic of Enlightenment*, p. 33.

10 ibid., p. 34.

11 ibid., pp. 34–5.

12 ibid., p. 57.

13 ibid., p. 63.

14 ibid., p. 64

15 ibid., p. 60.

16 ibid., p. 69.

17 ibid. (amended translation).

18 ibid., pp. 70–1.

19 ibid., p. 72.

20 ibid., p. 78.

Select bibliography

The following list of works is highly selective. I have listed only those works of the main authors examined (see pp. 485–95), which are cited in the text and notes. In the section 'Secondary sources relating to one or more of the critical theorists' (pp. 496–9), I have restricted attention to those works I found especially helpful in understanding critical theory. For further bibliographical references see the following:

Adorno

Buck-Morss, Susan, *The Origin of Negative Dialectics: Theodor W. Adorno, Walter Benjamin and the Frankfurt School*, Hassocks, Sussex: Harvester 1977, pp. 307–15.
Rose, Gillian, *The Melancholy Science: An Introduction to the Thought of Theodor W. Adorno*, London: Macmillan 1978, pp. 193–200.
Schultz, Klaus, 'Vorläufige Bibliographie der Schriften Theodor W. Adornos', in Hermann Schweppenhäuser (ed.), *Theodor W. Adorno zum Gedächtnis*, Frankfurt: Suhrkamp 1971, pp. 178–239

Benjamin

Buck-Morss, S., *The Origin of Negative Dialectics*, Hassocks, Sussex: Harvester 1977, pp. 315–16
Tiedemann, Rolf, 'Bibliographie der Erstrucke von Benjamins Schriften', in Siegfried Unseld (ed.), *Zur Aktualität Walter Benjamins*, Frankfurt: Suhrkamp 1972

Habermas

Görtzen, Rene and van Gelder, Frederick, 'Jürgen Habermas: the complete oeuvre: a bibliography of primary literature, translations and reviews', in *Human Studies*, vol. 2, no. 4 (1979)
McCarthy, Thomas, *The Critical Theory of Jürgen Habermas*, London: Hutchinson 1978, pp. 442–5

Horkheimer

Jay, Martin, *The Dialectical Imagination: A History of the Frankfurt School and the Institute of Social Research, 1923–1950*, Boston: Litttle, Brown 1973, pp. 359–60
Schmidt, Alfred, *Zur Idee der Kritischen Theorie*, München: Carl Hanser 1974

Kirchheimer

Kirchheimer, O., *Politics, Law and Social Change*, ed. Frederic S. Burin and Kurt L. Shell, New York: Columbia University Press 1969, pp. 479–83

Lowenthal

Lowenthal, L., *Literature, Popular Culture and Society*, Palo Alto, Calif.: Pacific Books 1967

Marcuse

Leiss, William, *et al.*, 'Marcuse bibliography', in Kurt H. Wolff and Barrington Moore Jr (eds.), *The Critical Spirit: Essays in Honor of Herbert Marcuse*, Boston: Beacon 1967, pp. 427–33

For useful general bibliographies on the Institute of Social Research see:

Arato, Andrew, and Gebhardt, Eike (eds.), *The Essential Frankfurt School Reader*, Oxford: Basil Blackwell 1978, pp. 530–41
Jay, M., *The Dialectical Imagination*, Boston: Little Brown 1973, pp. 355–70

Works of the Institute of Social Research

Institute of Social Research publications

Journals and other series
1910–30   *Grünbergs Archiv*, vols. 1–15
1932–39   *ZfS*, vols. 1–8, no. 2
1939–41   *SPSS*, vol. 8, no. 3–vol. 9, no. 3

In 1955 the Institute began to publish a series of *Frankfurter Beiträge zur Soziologie* (Frankfurt: Europäische Verlagsanstalt). The first volume was a *Festschrift* for Horkheimer's sixtieth birthday. In 1956, *Soziologische Exkurse nach Vorträgen und Diskussionen*, vol. 4 of the *Frankfurter Beiträge*, was published; it is translated by John Viertel as

Aspects of Sociology (London: Heinemann, 1973). Other volumes in the series are listed below next to their authors' names.

Collective works

1936 *Studien über Autorität und Familie*, Paris: Felix Alcan
1945 'Anti-Semitism within American labor: a report to the Jewish Labor Committee', 4 vols. (unpublished)

Institute's own histories and reports

1935 *International Institute of Social Research: A Short Description of its History and Aims*, New York
1938 *International Institute of Social Research: A Report on its History and Activities, 1933–1938*, New York

The writings of individual figures associated with the Institute of Social Research

Theodor W. Adorno

A complete edition of Adorno's writings is being published: *Gesammelte Schriften*, ed. Rolf Tiedemann, 23 vols., Frankfurt: Suhrkamp (1970–). The volumes referred to in the text are listed below (although I have not included individual listings of all the articles contained in these volumes).

1931 'Die Aktualität der Philosophie', *GS*, vol. 1 (1973) and trans. as 'The actuality of philosophy', *Telos*, no. 31 (1977)
1932 'Die Idee der Naturgeschichte', *GS*, vol. 1 (1973)
1932 'Zur Gesellschaftlichen Lage der Musik': pt 1, *ZfS*, vol. I, no. 1/2 (1932); pt 2, *ZfS*, vol. 1, no. 3 (1932)
1933 *Kierkegaard: Konstruction des Ästhetischen*, Tübingen: J. C. B. Möhr
1936 'Über Jazz' (published under pseudonym 'Hektor Rottweiler'), *ZfS*, vol. 5, no. 3 (1936), and *Moments Musicaux* (1964)
1938 'Über den Fetischcharacter in der Musik und die Regression des Hörers', *ZfS*, vol. 7, no. 3 (1938), and *GS*, vol. 14 (1973). A translation has been published in Andrew Arato and Eike Gebhardt (eds.), *The Essential Frankfurt School Reader* (Oxford: Blackwell 1978), pp. 270–99
1940 'On Kierkegaard's doctrine of love', *SPSS*, vol. 8, no. 3 (1939–40)
1940 'Husserl and the problem of idealism', *Journal of Philosophy*, vol. 37, no. 1 (1940)
1941 With the assistance of George Simpson, 'On popular music', *SPSS*, vol. 9, no. 1 (1941)
1945 'A social critique of radio music', *Kenyon Review*, vol. 7, no. 2 (Spring 1945)

1945   'Thesis upon art and religion today', *Kenyon Review*, vol. 7, no. 4 (Autumn 1945)

1946   'Anti-Semitism and fascist propaganda', in Ernst Simmel (ed.), *Anti-Semitism: A Social Disease*, New York: International Universities Press, and in *GS*, vol. 8 (1972)

1946   'Die revidierte Psychoanalyse' (written 1946), *GS*, vol. 8 (1972)

1947   With Horkheimer, *Dialektik der Aufklärung: Philosophische Fragmente*, Amsterdam: Querido, and trans. John Cumming as *Dialectic of Enlightenment*, New York: Herder & Herder 1972

1949   *Philosophie der neuen Musik* (Tübingen: J. C. B. Mohr). Also published in *GS*, vol. 12, and trans. Anne G. Mitchell and Wesley V. Blomster as *Philosophy of Modern Music*, London: Sheed & Ward 1973

1950   With Else Frenkel-Brunswick, Daniel J. Levinson, and R. Nevitt Sanford, *The Authoritarian Personality*, New York: Harper 1950; Norton 1969

1951   *Minima Moralia: Reflexionen aus dem beschädigten Leben*, Frankfurt: Suhrkamp, and trans. E. F. N. Jephcott as *Minima Moralia: Reflections from Damaged Life*, London: New Left Books 1974

1952   *Versuch über Wagner* (written 1939–1940, originally published 1952), *GS*, vol. 13

1954   'How to look at Television', *The Quarterly of Film, Radio and Television*, vol. 8 (Spring 1954), and reprinted as 'Television and the patterns of mass culture', in B. Rosenberg and D. Manning White (eds.) *Mass Culture: The Popular Arts in America*, New York: Free Press 1957

1955   *Prismen: Kulturkritik und Gesellschaft*, Frankfurt: Suhrkamp, and trans. Samuel and Shierry Weber as *Prisms*, London: Neville Spearman 1967

1955   'Zum Verhältnis von Soziologie und Psychologie' (first published 1955), *GS*, vol. 8 (1972), and trans. Irving N. Wohlfarth as 'Sociology and psychology', *New Left Review*, nos. 46 (1967) and 47 (1968)

1957   'The stars down to earth: the *Los Angeles Times* astrology column', *GS*, vol. 9 (1975), and *Telos*, no. 19 (Spring 1974)

1959   'Contemporary German sociology', trans. Norman Birnbaum, *Transactions of the Fourth World Congress of Sociology*, London, vol. 1 (1959)

1963   *Quasi una Fantasia*, Frankfurt: Suhrkamp

1964   *Jargon der Eigentlichkeit*, Frankfurt: Suhrkamp; also published in *GS*, vol. 6 and trans. Knut Tarnowski and Frederic Will as *Jargon of Authenticity*, London: Routledge & Kegan Paul 1973

1964   *Moments Musicaux: Neu gedruckte Aufsätze, 1928 bis 1962*, Frankfurt: Suhrkamp

1965   'Offener Brief an Max Horkheimer', *Die Zeit*, 12 February 1965

1966 *Negative Dialektik*, Frankfurt: Suhrkamp. Also in *GS*, vol. 6 (1973), and trans. E. B. Ashton as *Negative Dialectics*, New York: Seabury Press 1973

1967 *Ohne Leitbild: Parva Aesthetica*, Frankfurt: Suhrkamp

1969 Introduction and two essays in *The Positivist Dispute in German Sociology*, trans. Glyn Adey and David Frisby, London: Heinemann

1969 'Scientific experiences of a European scholar in America', trans. Donald Fleming *et al.*, in D. Fleming and B. Bailyn (eds.), *Intellectual Migration: Europe and America, 1930–1960*, Cambridge, Mass.: Harvard University Press

1969 *Stichworte: Kritische Modelle 2*, Frankfurt: Suhrkamp

1969–70 'Society', trans. Frederick Jameson, *Salmagundi*, vols. 10–11 (1969–70); also in *GS*, vol. 8 (1972). It was originally published in 1966

1970 *Ästhetische Theorie*, ed. Gretel Adorno and Rolf Tiedemann, *GS*, vol. 7

1971 *Die musikalischen Monographien: Wagner; Mahler; Berg*, ed. Gretel Adorno and Rolf Tiedemann, *GS*, vol. 13

1971 *Zur Metakritik der Erkenntistheorie; Drie Studien zu Hegel*, ed. Gretel Adorno and Rolf Tiedemann, *GS*, vol. 5

1972 *Soziologische Schriften 1*, ed. Rolf Tiedemann, *GS*, vol. 8

1973 *Frühe philosophische Schriften*, ed. Rolf Tiedemann, *GS*, vol. I

1973 *Negative Dialektik; Jargon der Eigentlichkeit*, ed. Rolf Tiedemann, *GS*, vol. 6

1974 'Commitment', trans. Francis Mcdonagh, *New Left Review*, nos. 87–8 (1974); also in *GS*, vol. 11 (1974). (First published in 1965)

1974 *Noten zur Literatur*, ed. Rolf Tiedemann, *GS*, vol. 11

1975 'Culture industry reconsidered', trans. Anson G. Rabinach, *New German Critique*, vol. 6 (Fall 1975) (Written in 1964 and originally published in 1967)

1975 *Soziologische Schriften 2* (2 vols.), eds. Susan Buck-Morss and Rolf Tiedemann, *GS*, vol. 9

1976 *Introduction to the Sociology of Music*, trans. E. B. Ashton, New York: Seabury Press (First published by Suhrkamp, 1973)

Walter Benjamin

A complete edition of Benjamin's work is currently being compiled: *Gesammelte Schriften*, eds. Rolf Tiedemann and Hermann Schweppenhäuser, 6 vols., Frankfurt: Suhrkamp (1972–   ). The volumes referred to in the text are listed below.

1928 *Ursprung des deutschen Trauerspiels*, Berlin: Rowohlt, and trans. John Osborne as *Origin of German Tragic Drama*, London: New Left Books 1977

488   *Select bibliography*

1955   *Schriften*, eds. Theodor W. Adorno and Gretel Adorno, 2 vols., Frankfurt: Suhrkamp
1966   *Briefe*, eds. Gershom Scholem and Theodor W. Adorno, 2 vols., Frankfurt: Suhrkamp
1968   *Illuminations*, ed. and intro. Hannah Arendt, trans. Harry Zohn, New York: Harcourt, Brace; paperback ed., New York: Schocken Books 1969, and London: Fontana
1970   'Paris, capital of the nineteenth century', *Dissent*, vol. 17, no. 5 (1970)
1972   *Kritiken und Rezensionen*, ed. Hella Tiedemann-Bartels, *GS*, vol. 3
1973   *Charles Baudelaire: a Lyric Poet in the Era of High Capitalism*, trans. Harry Zohn, London: New Left Books
1973   *Understanding Brecht*, trans. Anna Bostock, London: New Left Books
1975   'Eduard Fuchs: collector and historian', *New German Critique*, no. 5 (1975)

Bruno Bettelheim and Morris Janowitz

1950   *Dynamics of Prejudice: A Psychological and Sociological Study of Veterans*, New York: Harper

Erich Fromm

1932   'Die psychoanalytische Charakterologie und ihre Bedeutung für Sozialpsychologie', *ZfS*, vol. 1, no. 3 (1932), and trans. in *The Crisis of Psychoanalysis* (1971)
1932   'Über Methode und Aufgabe einer analytischen Sozial-psychologie', *ZfS*, vol. 1, no. 1/2 (1932), and trans. in *The Crisis of Psychoanalysis* (1971)
1935   'Die gesellschaftliche Bedingtheit der psychoanalytischen Therapie', *ZfS*, vol. 3 (1935)
1936   'Sozialpsychologische Teil: Der autoritärmasochistische Charakter', in Max Horkheimer (ed.), *Studien über Autorität und Familie*, Paris: Felix Alcan
1941   *Escape From Freedom*, New York: Farrar & Rinehart; and Avon 1965
1955   'The human implications of instinctive "radicalism"', *Dissent*, vol. 2, no. 4 (1955)
1956   'A counter-rebuttal', *Dissent*, vol. 3, no. 1 (Winter 1956)
1971   *The Crisis of Psychoanalysis: Essays on Freud, Marx and Social Psychology*, Greenwich, Conn: Fawcett Publications

Henryk Grossmann

1943 'The evolutionist revolt against classical economics', 2 pts, *The Journal of Political Economy*, vol. 51, nos. 5 and 6 (October 1943)
1948 'W. Playfair, the earliest theorist of capitalist development', *Economic History Review*, vol. 18, no. 1 (1948)
1967 *Das Akkumulations – und Zusammenbruchsgesetz des Kapitalistischen Systems* (originally published 1929), Frankfurt: Neue Kritik
1969 *Marx, die klassische Nationalökonomie und das Problem der Dynamic*, afterword by Paul Mattick, Frankfurt: Europäisher Verlagsanstalt

Carl Grünberg

1924 'Festrede, gehalten zur Einweihung des Instituts für Sozialforschung an der Universität Frankfurt am Main am 22.6.1924', *Frankfurter Universitätsreden*, vol. 20 (1924)

Arkadij R. L. Gurland

1941 'Technological trends and economic structure under National Socialism', *SPSS*, vol. 9, no. 2 (1941)
1943 with O. Kirchheimer and F. Neumann, *The Fate of Small Business in Nazi Germany*, Washington, DC; New York: Howard Fertig 1975

Max Horkheimer

Most of Horkheimer's contributions to the *ZfS* have been republished in *Kritische Theorie: Eine Dokumentation*, ed. Alfred Schmidt, 2 vols., Frankfurt: S. Fischer Verlag 1968.
1930 *Anfänge der bürgerklichen Geschitsphilosophie*, Stuttgart: Kohlhammer
1931 'Die gegenwärtigen Lage der Sozialphilosophie und die Aufgaben eines Instituts für Sozialforschung', *Frankfurter Universitätsreden*, vol. 37 (Frankfurt am Main 1931), reprinted in *Sozialphilosophische Studien* (1972)
1932 'Bemerkungen über Wissenschaft und Krise', *ZfS*, vol. 1/2 (1932), trans. as 'Observations on science and crisis', in *Critical Theory* (1972)
1932 'Vorwort', *ZfS*, vol. 1 (1932)
1933 'Materialismus und Metaphysik', *ZfS*, vol. 2, no. 1 (1933), trans. as 'Materialism and Metaphysics', in *Critical Theory* (1972)
1933 'Materialismus und Moral', *ZfS*, vol. 2, no. 2 (1933), reprinted in *Kritische Theorie*, vol. 1 (1968)

490   *Select bibliography*

1933   'Zum Problem der Voraussage in den Sozialwissenschaften', *ZfS*, vol. 2, no. 3 (1933), reprinted in *Kritische Theorie*, vol. 1 (1968)
1934   'Zum Rationalismusstreit in der gegenwärtigen Philosophie', *ZfS*, vol. 3, no. 1 (1934), reprinted in *Kritische Theorie*, vol. 1 (1968)
1935   'Bemerkungen zur philosophischen Anthropologie', *ZfS*, vol. 4, no. 1 (1935), and in *Kritische Theorie*, vol. 1 (1968)
1935   'Zum Problem der Wahrheit', *ZfS*, vol. 4, no. 3 (1935), reprinted in *Kritische Theorie*, vol. 1 (1968), trans. in A. Arato and E. Gebhardt (eds.), *The Essential Frankfurt School Reader*
1936   'Autorität und Familie', first published 1936, reprinted in *Kritische Theorie*, vol. 1 (1968), trans. as 'Authority and the family', in *Critical Theory* (1972)
1936   'Egoismus und Freheitsbewegung', *ZfS*, vol. 5, no. 2 (1936), reprinted in *Kritische Theorie*, vol. 2 (1968)
1937   'Der neueste Angriff auf die Metaphysik', *ZfS*, vol. 6, no. 1 (1937), reprinted in *Kritische Theorie*, vol. 2 (1968), trans. as 'The latest attack on metaphysics', in *Critical Theory* (1972)
1937   'Traditionelle und Kritische Theorie', *ZfS*, vol. 6, no. 2 (1937), reprinted in *Kritische Theorie*, vol. 2 (1968), trans. as 'Traditional and critical theory', in *Critical Theory* (1972)
1938   'Montaigne und die Funktion der Skepsis', *ZfS*, vol. 7, no. 1 (1938), reprinted in *Kritische Theorie*, vol. 2 (1968)
1939   'Die Juden und Europa', *ZfS*, vol. 8, no. 1/2 (1939)
1939   'The social function of philosophy', *SPSS*, vol. 8, no. 3 (1939), reprinted in *Critical Theory* (1972)
1940   'The relation between psychology and sociology in the work of Wilhelm Dilthey', *SPSS*, vol. 8 (1940)
1941   'Art and mass culture', *SPSS*, vol. 9, no. 2 (1941), and reprinted in *Critical Theory* (1972)
1941   'The end of reason', *SPSS*, vol. 9 (1941)
1941   'Notes on Institute activities', *SPSS*, vol. 9, no. 1 (1941)
1941   'Preface', *SPSS*, vol. 9, no. 2 (1941)
1946   'Sociological background of the psychoanalytic approach', in Ernst Simmel (ed.), *Anti-Semitism: A Social Disease*, New York: International Universities Press
1947   with T. Adorno, *Dialektik der Aufklärung*, trans. as *Dialectic of Enlightenment* (1972)
1947   *Eclipse of Reason*, New York: Oxford University Press; reprinted Seabury Press 1974
1949   'Authoritarianism and the family today' in R. N. Anshen (ed.), *The Family: Its Function and Destiny*, New York: Harper
1950   'The lessons of Fascism', in Hadley Cantril (ed.), *Tensions that Cause Wars*, Urbana: University of Illinois Press 1950
1952   *Survey of the Social Sciences in Germany*, Washington, DC
1957   'The concept of man', in *Critique of Instrumental Reason* (1974)

1964 'On the concept of freedom', trans. Victor A. Velen, *Diogenes*, no. 53 (1964)
1967 'Schopenhauer Today', originally published in 1962, trans. Robert Kolben, in Kurt H. Wolff and Barrington Moore Jr (eds.), *The Critical Spirit: Essays in Honor of Herbert Marcuse*
1970 interview, *Der Spiegel*, 5 January 1970
1970 *Die Sehnsucht nach dem ganz Anderen*, an interview with commentary by Helmut Gumnior, Hamburg: Furche-Verlag
1972 *Critical Theory: Selected Essays*, trans. Matthew J. O'Connell *et al.*, New York: Herder & Herder
1972 *Gesellschaft im Übergang: Aufsätze, Reden und Vorträge, 1942–1970*, ed. Werner Brede, Frankfurt: Athenäum Fischer Taschenbuch Verlag
1972 *Sozialphilosophische Studien: Aufsätze, Reden und Vorträge, 1930–1972*, ed. Werner Brede, Frankfurt: Athenäum Fischer Taschenbuch Verlag
1973 'The authoritarian state', *Telos*, no. 15 (Spring 1973). It was actually written in 1942
1974 *Critique of Instrumental Reason* (lectures and essays since the end of the second world war), originally published 1967, trans. Matthew J. O'Connell *et al.*, New York: Seabury Press
1974 *Notizen 1950 bis 1969 und Dämmerung*, Frankfurt: S. Fischer Verlag. *Dämmerung* was originally published in 1934 (Zurich: Verlag Oprecht und Helbling) under the pseudonym Heinrich Regius

Otto Kirchheimer

1933 'Marxismus, Diktatur und Organisationsformen des Proletariats', *Die Gesellschaft*, vol. 10 (March 1933), reprinted and trans. in *Politics, Law and Social Change* (1969)
1939 'Criminal law in Nationalist Socialist Germany', *SPSS*, vol. 8, no. 3 (1939)
1939 with George Rusche, *Punishment and Social Structure*, New York: Columbia University Press
1941 'Changes in the structure of political compromise', *SPSS*, vol. 9, no. 2 (1941)
1941 'The legal order of National Socialism', *SPSS*, vol. 9, no. 2 (1941)
1943 with A. R. L. Gurland and F. Neumann, *The Fate of Small Business in Nazi Germany*, Washington, DC; New York: Howard Fertig (1975)
1957 'Franz Neumann: an appreciation', *Dissent*, vol. 4, no. 4 (Autumn 1957)
1961 *Political Justice: The Use of Legal Procedure for Political Ends*, Princeton, NJ: Princeton University Press

1969   *Politics, Law and Social Change: Selected Essays of Otto Kirch-heimer*, ed. Frederic S. Burin and Kurt L. Shell, New York: Columbia University Press

Leo Lowenthal

1946   'Terror's atomization of man', *Commentary*, vol. 1, no. 3 (January 1946)
1949   with Norbert Guterman, *Prophets of Deceit*, New York: Harper
1957   *Literature and the Image of Man*, Boston: Beacon Press
1967   'German popular biographies: culture's bargain counter', in Kurt H. Wolff and Barrington Moore Jr (eds.), *The Critical Spirit: Essays in Honor of Herbert Marcuse*
1967   *Literature, Popular Culture and Society*, Palo Alto, Calif.: Pacific Books. (First published 1961)

Herbert Marcuse

1928   'Contributions to a phenomenology of historical materialism', originally published in *Philosophische Hefte* (Berlin), vol. 1 (1928), trans. and republished in *Telos*, no. 4 (1969)
1929   'Zur Wahrheitsproblematik der soziologischen Methode', *Die Gesellschaft*, vol. 6 (1929)
1930,   'On the problem of the dialectic', originally in two parts in *Die*
1931   *Gesellschaft*, vols. 7 (1930) and 8 (1931), trans. Morton School-man and Duncan Smith, in *Telos*, no. 27 (Spring 1976)
1932   'The foundations of historical materialism', originally in *Die Gesellschaft*, vol. 9 (1932), trans. and republished in *Studies in Critical Philosophy* (1973)
1932   *Hegels Ontologie und die Grundlegung einer Theorie der Geschich-tlichkeit*, Frankfurt: V. Klostermann Verlag
1933   'On the philosophical foundations of the concept of labour in economics', originally published in *Archiv für Sozialwissenschaft und Sozialpolitik*, vol. 69, no. 3 (1933), trans. Douglas Kellner in *Telos*, no. 16 (Summer 1973)
1934   'The struggle against liberalism in the totalitarian view of the state', first published in *ZfS*, vol. 3 (1934), republished in *Negations* (1968)
1936   'The concept of essence', originally published in *ZfS*, vol. 5 (1936), republished in *Negations* (1968)
1937   'The affirmative character of culture', first published in *ZfS*, vol. 6 (1937), republished in *Negations* (1968)
1937   'Philosophy and critical theory', first published in *ZfS*, vol. 6 (1937), republished in *Negations* (1968)
1938   'On hedonism', first published in *ZfS*, vol. 7 (1938), republished in

Negations (1968)

1941 *Reason and Revolution: Hegel and the Rise of Social Theory*, New York: Oxford University Press; paperback edition with a new preface, 'A Note on Dialectic', Boston: Beacon Press 1960

1941 'Some social implications of modern technology', *SPSS*, vol. 9 (1941), and in A. Arato and E. Gebhardt (eds.), *The Essential Frankfurt School Reader*

1955 *Eros and Civilization: A Philosophical Inquiry Into Freud*, Boston: Beacon Press; paperback edition, New York: Vintage Books 1962. Second edition, with a new preface, 'Political preface 1966', Boston: Beacon Press 1966

1955 'The social implications of Freudian "revisionism"', *Dissent*, vol. 2, no. 3 (Summer 1955)

1956 'A reply to Erich Fromm', *Dissent*, vol. 2, no. 1 (Winter 1956)

1959 'Notes on the problem of historical laws', *Partisan Review*, 26 (Winter 1959)

1964 'Industrialization and capitalism in the work of Max Weber', first published in 1964; republished in *Negations* (1968)

1964 *Soviet Marxism: A Critical Analysis*, Boston: Beacon 1964; Harmondsworth: Penguin 1971

1965 'On science and phenomendogy', first published 1965, republished in A. Giddens (ed.), *Positivism and Sociology*

1965 'Repressive tolerance', in Robert P. Wolff, Barrington Moore Jr and Herbert Marcuse, *A Critique of Pure Tolerance*, Boston: Beacon

1967 'The obsolescence of Marxism', in N. Lobkowicz (ed.), *Marx and the Western World*, Notre Dame, Indiana: University of Notre Dame Press

1968 *Negations: Essays in Critical Theory*, Boston: Beacon Press

1969 *An Essay on Liberation*, Boston: Beacon Press

1970 *Five Lectures*, trans. Jeremy J. Shapiro and Shierry M. Weber, Boston: Beacon Press

1972 *Counterrevolution and Revolt*, Boston: Beacon Press

1973 *Studies in Critical Philosophy*, trans. Joris de Bres, Boston: Beacon Press

1978 *The Aesthetic Dimension: Toward a Critique of Marxist Aesthetics*, Boston: Beacon Press

Paul Massing

1949 *Rehearsal for Destruction*, New York: Harper

Franz Neumann

1943 with A. R. L. Gurland and O. Kirchheimer, *The Fate of Small*

Business in Nazi Germany, Washington, DC; New York: Howard Fertig (1975)

1944 *Behemoth: The Structure and Practice of National Socialism, 1933–1944*, rev. ed., London: Victor Gollancz

1953 'The social sciences', in *The Cultural Migration: The European Scholar in America*, with Henri Peyre *et al.*, Philadelphia: University of Pennsylvania

1964 *The Democratic and the Authoritarian State*, ed. with a preface by Herbert Marcuse, Glencoe, Ill.: Free Press

Frederich Pollock

1929 *Die planwirtschaftlichen Versuche in der Sowjetunion, 1917–1927*, Leipzig: C. L. Hirschfeld

1941 'Is National Socialism a new order?', *SPSS*, vol. 9, no. 3 (1941)

1941 'State capitalism: its possibilities and limitations', *SPSS*, vol. 9, no. 2 (1941)

1957 *The Economic and Social Consequences of Automation*, trans. W. O. Henderson and W. H. Chalmer, Oxford: Basil Blackwell. Originally published as *Frankfurter Beiträge zur Sozologie*, vol. 5 (1956)

1975 *Stadien des Kapitalismus*, ed. with an introduction by Helmut Dubiel, München: C. H. Beck. Pollock's key essays in political economy written between 1932 and 1941 for the *ZfS* and *SPSS* are reprinted in this volume

The writings of Jürgen Habermas

1962 *Strukturwandel der Öffentlichkeit*, Neuwied: Luchterhand

1963 *Theorie und Praxis*, Neuwied: Luchterhand

1970 'On systematically distorted communication', *Inquiry*, vol. 13 (1970); 'Towards a theory of communicative competence', *Inquiry*, vol. 13 (1970). These two articles are reprinted in Dreitzel (ed.), *Recent Sociology*, New York (1972)

1970 'Summation and response', *Continuum*, vol. 8, nos. 1 and 2 (1970)

1970 *Towards a Rational Society* (a collection of essays written in the middle and late 1960s) trans. Jeremy J. Shapiro, London: Heinemann

1970 *Zur Logik der Sozialwissenschaften*, Frankfurt: Suhrkamp

1971 *Knowledge and Human Interests*, first published in German 1968; trans. Jeremy Shapiro, London: Heinemann

1971 *Philosophisch-politische Profile*, Frankfurt: Suhrkamp

1971 with Niklas Luhmann, *Theorie der Gesellschaft oder Sozialtechnologie – Was leistet die Systemforschung?*, Frankfurt: Suhrkamp

1971 'Why more philosophy?', *Social Research*, vol. 38 (1971)
1973 *Kultur und Kritik*, Frankfurt: Suhrkamp
1973 'Wahrheitstheorien', in H. Fahrenbach (ed.), *Wirchlichkeit und Reflexion: zum sechzigsten Geburtstag für Walter Schulz*, Pfüllingen: Neske
1973 'What does a crisis mean today? Legitimation problems in late capitalism', *Social Research*, vol. 40 (1973)
1974 'Habermas talking: an interview', interviewer Boris Frankel, *Theory and Society*, vol. 1 (1974)
1974 'The public sphere', trans. Sara Lennox and Frank Lennox, *New German Critique*, vol. 3 (Fall 1974)
1974 'On social identity', *Telos*, no. 19 (1974)
1974 *Theory and Practice*, abridged ed. of the 4th German ed. of *Theorie und Praxis* (1971), trans. John Viertel, London: Heinemann
1975 'The place of philosophy in Marxism', *Insurgent Sociologist*, vol. 5 (1975)
1975 'A postscript to *Knowledge and Human Interests*', in *Philosophy of the Social Sciences*, vol. 3 (1975)
1975 'Towards a reconstruction of historical materialism', *Theory and Society*, vol. 2, no. 3 (1975)
1976 'The analytical theory of science and dialectics', in T. Adorno *et al.*, *The Positivist Dispute in German Sociology*, London: Heinemann
1976 *Legitimation Crisis* (first published in German 1973), trans. Thomas McCarthy, London: Heinemann
1976 'A positivistically bisected rationalism', in T. Adorno *et al.*, *The Positivist Dispute in German Sociology*. Previously published in A. Giddens (ed.), *Positivism and Sociology*, London: Heinemann 1974
1976 'Was heisst Universal Pragmatik?', in Karl-Otto Apel (ed.), *Sprachpragmatik und Philosophie*, Frankfurt: Suhrkamp. English translation in *Communication and the Evolution of Society* (1979)
1976 *Zur Rekonstruktion des Historischen Materialismus*, Frankfurt: Suhrkamp. Parts of this work have appeared in *Communication and the Evolution of Society* (1979)
1977 'Hannah Arendt's communications concept of power', *Social Research*, vol. 44 (1977)
1977 'A review of Gadamer's *Truth and Method*', in F. Dallmayr and T. McCarthy (eds.), *Understanding Social Inquiry*, Notre Dame, Indiana: Notre Dame Press
1979 *Communication and the Evolution of Society*, trans. Thomas McCarthy, London: Heinemann
1979 'Conservatism and capitalist crisis', *New Left Review*, no. 115 (May–June 1979)

Secondary sources directly relating to one or more of the critical theorists

Apel, Karl-Otto, 'The *a priori* of communication and the foundation of the humanities', *Man and World*, vol. 5 (February 1972)

Apel, Karl-Otto, *et al.*, *Hermeneutik und Ideologiekritik*, Frankfurt: Suhrkamp 1971

Arato, Andrew, and Gebhardt, Eike, *The Essential Frankfurt School Reader*, Oxford: Basil Blackwell 1978

Arato, Andrew, 'Lukács theory of reification', *Telos*, no. 11 (Spring 1972)

Arato, Andrew' (ed.), Special issue on Walter Benjamin, *International Journal of Sociology*, vol. 7, no. 1 (1977)

Arendt, Hannah, Introductory essay to Walter Benjamin, *Illuminations* (1969)

Bauman, Zygmunt, *Towards a Critical Sociology*, London: Routledge & Kegan Paul 1976

Benjamin, Jessica, 'The end of internalization: Adorno's social psychology', *Telos*, no. 32 (Summer 1977)

Bernstein, Richard, *The Restructuring of Social and Political Thought*, Oxford: Basil Blackwell 1976)

Bradley, James, 'Frankfurt views', *Radical Philosophy*, vol. 13 (Spring 1975)

Bramson, Leon, *The Political Context of Sociology*, Princeton 1961

Breines, Paul (ed.)' *Critical Interruptions: New Left Perspectives on Herbert Marcuse*, New York: Herder & Herder 1972

Breines, Paul, 'Praxis and its theorists: the impact of Lukács and Korsch in the 1920s', *Telos*, no. 11 (1972)

Bubner, Rüdiger, *et al.*, *Hermeneutik und Dialektik*, Tübingen: J. C. B. Mohr 1970

Buck-Morss, Susan, 'The dialectic of T. W. Adorno', *Telos*, no. 14 (Winter 1972)

Buck-Morss, Susan, *The Origin of Negative Dialectics: Theodor W. Adorno, Walter Benjamin and the Frankfurt School*, Hassocks, Sussex: Harvester 1977

Carlebach, Julius, 'Marx and the sociologists: Max Horkheimer', in his *Karl Marx and the Radical Critique of Judaism*, London: Routledge & Kegan Paul, 1978

Christie, Richard, and Jahoda, Marie, *Studies in the Scope and Method of 'The Authoritarian Personaliy'*, Glencoe, Ill.: Free Press (1954)

Cohen, Jerry, 'The philosophy of Marcuse', *New Left Review*, no. 57 (1969)

Connerton, Paul (ed.), *Critical Sociology*, Harmondsworth: Penguin 1976

Dallmayr, Fred R., 'Critical theory criticized', *Philosophy of the Social Sciences*, vol. 2, no. 3 (1973)

Dallmayr, Fred R. (ed.), *Materialien zu Habermas' 'Erkenntnis und Interesse'*, Frankfurt: Suhrkamp 1971

Dallmayr, Fred R., 'Reason and emancipation: notes on Habermas', *Man and World*, vol. 5, no. 1 (1972)

Dallmayr, Fred R., and McCarthy, Thomas (eds.), *Understanding Social Inquiry*, Notre Dame, Indiana: The University Press, 1977

Dubiel, Helmut, 'Dialektische Wissenschaftskritik und Interdisziplinäre Sozialforschung: Theorie und Organisationsstruktur des Frankfurter Instituts für Sozialforschung (1930ff)', *Kölner Zeitschrift für Soziologie und Sozial-Psychologie* (26 Jahrgang 1972), 2

Dubiel, Helmut, 'Ideologiekritik versus Wissenssoziologie', *Archiv für Rechts- und Sozialphilosophie*, vol. 61, no. 2 (1975)

Finagarette, Herbert, 'Eros and utopia', *Review of Metaphysics*, vol. 10, no. 4 (June 1957)

Fleischer, Helmut, *Marxism and History*, trans. Eric Mosbacher, New York: Harper & Row 1973

Frisby, David, 'The Popper–Adorno controversy: the methodological dispute in German sociology', *Philosophy of the Social Sciences*, vol. 2 (1972)

Giddens, Anthony, *The Class Structure of Advanced Societies*, London: Hutchinson 1973

Giddens, Anthony, 'Habermas's critique of hermeneutics', in *Studies in Social and Political Theory*, London: Hutchinson 1977

Giddens, Anthony, 'Positivism and its critics', in *Studies in Social and Political Thought*, London: Hutchinson 1977

Giddens, Anthony (ed.), *Positivism and Sociology*, London: Heinemann 1974

Habermas, Jürgen (ed.), *Antworten auf Herbert Marcuse*, Frankfurt: Suhrkamp 1968

Herf, Jeffrey, 'Science and class or philosophy and revolution: Perry Anderson on Western Marxism', *Socialist Review*, vol. 35, no. 7 (1977)

Hesse, Mary, 'Theory and value in the social sciences', in Christopher Hookway and Philip Pettit (eds.), *Action and Interpretation*, Cambridge: Cambridge University Press 1978

Howard, Dick, and Klare, Karl (eds.), *The Unknown Dimension: European Marxism since Lenin*, New York: Basic Books 1972

Jacoby, Russell, 'Marxism and the critical school', *Theory and Society*, vol. 1, no. 2 (1974)

Jacoby, Russell, 'The politics of crisis theory', *Telos*, no. 23 (Spring 1975)

Jacoby, Russell, *Social Amnesia: A Critique of Conformist Psychology from Adler to Laing*, Boston: Beacon Press 1975

Jacoby, Russell, 'Towards a critique of automatic Marxism: the politics of philosophy from Lukács to the Frankfurt school', *Telos*, no. 10 (Winter 1971)

Jameson, Frederic, *Marxism and Form*, Princeton, NJ: Princeton University Press 1971

Jay, Martin, 'The concept of totality in Lukács and Adorno', *Telos*, no. 32 (1977)

Jay, Martin, 'Crutches vs. stilts: an answer to James Schmidt on the Frank-furt school', *Telos*, no. 22 (Winter 1974–5)

Jay, Martin, *The Dialectical Imagination: A History of the Frankfurt School and the Institute of Social Research, 1923–1950*, Boston: Little Brown 1973

Jay, Martin, 'The Frankfurt school's critique of Karl Mannheim and the sociology of knowledge', *Telos*, no. 20 (Summer 1974)

Jay, Martin, 'The Frankfurt school's critique of Marxist humanism', *Social Research*, vol. 39, no. 2 (Summer 1972)

Jay, Martin, 'The Frankfurt school in exile', *Perspectives in American History*, Cambridge, Mass., vol. 6 (1972)

Keane, John, 'The legacy of political economy: thinking with and against Claus Offe', *Canadian Journal of Political and Social Theory*, vol. 2, no. 3 (1978)

Kellner, Douglas, 'The Frankfurt school revisited: a critique of Martin Jay's *The Dialectical Imagination*', *New German Critique*, no. 4 (Winter 1975)

Laplanche, Jean, 'Notes sur Marcuse et le Psychoanalyse', *La Nef*, vol. 36 (January–March 1969)

Larrain, Jorge, *The Concept of Ideology*, London: Hutchinson 1979

Leiss, William, *The Domination of Nature*, Boston: Beacon Press 1974

Lichtheim, George, *From Marx to Hegel*, New York: Seabury Press 1974

McCarthy, Thomas, *The Critical Theory of Jürgen Habermas*, Cambridge, Mass.: MIT Press 1978; London: Hutchinson 1978

McCarthy, Thomas, Introductory essays to Habermas's *Legitimation Crisis* (1976)

McCarthy, Thomas, 'A theory of communicative competence', *Philosophy of the Social Sciences*, vol. 3, no. 2 (1973)

Mitchell, Stanley, Introductory essay to Walter Benjamin's *Understanding Brecht* (1973)

Paetzold, Heinz, *Neomarxistische Aesthetik*, vols. 1 and 2 (Düsseldorf: Schwan 1974)

Piconne, Paul, and Delfini, Alexander, 'Herbert Marcuse's Heideggerian Marxism', *Telos*, no. 6 (Fall 1970)

Radnitzky, Gerard, *Contemporary Schools of Metascience*, Chicago: Henry Regneny 1973

Ringer, Fritz, *The Decline of the German Mandarins: The German Academic Community, 1890–1933*, Cambridge, Mass.: Harvard University Press 1969

Robinson, Paul, *The Sexual Radicals*, London: Temple Smith 1969

Rose, Gillian, *The Melancholy Science: An Introduction to the Thought of Theodor W. Adorno*, London: Macmillan 1978

Rovatti, Pier Aldo, 'Critical theory and phenomenology', *Telos*, no. 15 (Spring 1973)

Schmidt, Alfred, *The Concept of Nature in Marx*, trans. Ben Fowkes,

London: New Left Books 1971

Schmidt, Alfred, *Die Kritische Theorie als Geschichtsphilosophie*, München: Carl Hanser 1976

Schmidt, Alfred, *Zur Idee der Kritischen Theorie: Elemente der Philosophie Max Horkheimers*, München: Carl Hanser 1974

Schmidt, Friedrich W., 'Hegel in der Kritischen Theorie der "Frankfurt School"', in Oskar Negt (ed.), *Aktualität und Folgen der Philosophie Hegels*, Frankfurt: Suhrkamp 1971

Schmidt, James, 'Critical theory and the sociology of knowledge: a response to Martin Jay', *Telos*, no. 21 (Fall 1974)

Schmidt, James, 'Lukács' concept of proletarian Bildung', *Telos*, no. 24 (1975)

Schmidt, James, 'Offensive critical theory', *Telos*, no. 39 (Spring 1979)

Schoolman, Morton, 'Introduction to Marcuse's "On the problem of the dialectic"', *Telos*, no. 27 (1976)

Schroyer, Trent, *The Critique of Domination*, New York: George Braziller 1973

Schweppenhäuser, Hermann (ed.), *Theodor W. Adorno zum Gedächtnis*, Frankfurt: Suhrkamp 1971

Siebert, Rudolf, 'Horkheimer's sociology of religion', *Telos*, no. 30 (1976)

Snow, Benjamin, 'Introduction to Adorno's "The actuality of philosophy"', *Telos*, no. 31 (1977)

Tiedemann, Rolf, *Studien zur Philosophie Walter Benjamins*, Frankfurt: Europäische Verlagsanstalt 1965

Wellmer, Albrecht, *Critical Theory of Society*, trans. John Cumming, New York: Seabury Press 1974

Wolff, Kurt H., and Moore, Barrington, Jr (eds.), *The Critical Spirit: Essays in Honor of Herbert Marcuse*, Boston: Beacon Press 1967

Index

502   *Index*

here he has been working). Remember we have the
: in our keeping. Have you drafted the *Communist*
to?

ᴌs (*taking a manuscript from his pocket*). What do
ᴀk of this for an opening? "A specter is haunting
—the specter of Communism."

. No, Friedrich: that will never do. That's not the
ᴜt it. Make it: "A specter is haunting Europe—the
f Progressivism."

gress of the Workers' International. Lassalle and
, looking furtively about them, slip into the empty

ɪN. I've got the bomb ready and will stand right here
ᴏr. When Marx comes in, I'll throw it.
ʟᴇ. There's nothing like individual terrorism!
elegates begin to gather, Bruno Bauer and Proudhon
em.

ʙᴀᴜᴇʀ (*to Proudhon*). They say that Comrade
ᴏing to announce a change of policy.
and Engels come in, Engels with his lifelong com-
ᴌary Burns.

ʜᴏɴ (*with a lewd French leer*). And how is the
demoiselle?

ʙᴜʀɴs. Faith, Misther Proudhon, us Irish may have
bribed tools of British imperialism once, but today
the vanguard of the proletariat, an' I'll thank ye to
ᴠil tongue in yer head an' not be callin' me anny of
ᴌy French names!

ɪ. You must be careful, Comrade Marx: remember
ᴌad dogs of reaction are trailing you.

ʙᴜʀɴs. Jesus, Mary and Joseph! There's that spal-
ᴀlle again!

ɪ. How many times must I tell you, Mary, that re-
ᴌe opium of the people?

No, Friedrich: that's what I said when I was young,
· we must not exclude the possibility of a broad
ᴏnt with the Vatican.

Appendix A

Karl Marx: A Prolet-Play

(*Reported to have been written for the WPA theater by a
member of the League of American Writers.*)

*The von Westphalens' garden in Trier, Germany. Young
Karl Marx comes in, a fine manly lad of fifteen.*

ᴋᴀʀʟ ᴍᴀʀx (*calling up to a window on the second floor of
the house*). Comrade Jenny! Oh, Comrade Jenny!

ᴊᴇɴɴʏ ᴠᴏɴ ᴡᴇsᴛᴘʜᴀʟᴇɴ (*putting her head out the window*). Hello, Karl: I'm coming right down.

*Ferdinand Lassalle skulks in, a boy of about Marx's age.
He wears spectacles, a mustache and a pointed beard, and has
a mane of black hair, which stands up on his head.*

ʟᴀssᴀʟʟᴇ. One moment, Comrade Marx: let me give you
a word of warning. Your attentions to Jenny von Westphalen
are beginning to verge on class betrayal. Remember that
Fraülein von Westphalen belongs to the feudal nobility: your
solidarity is with the workers!

ᴍᴀʀx. No, Comrade Lassalle: you are mistaken. The correct line is a popular front which will take in the liberal
nobility as well as the militant working class. You have been
misled into a left deviation.

*Jenny appears from the house. Lassalle slinks away, with
a look of hate.*

ᴊᴇɴɴʏ. I don't like that Lassalle boy hanging around here.
Papa says he is a potential fascist.

ᴍᴀʀx. Oh, Ferdinand is a good comrade, I think. Let us
give him the benefit of the doubt.

ᴊᴇɴɴʏ. He tried to flirt with me at the rally last week, and

I can tell that he's peeved with me now because I showed that I wasn't interested. And now he is chasing after that reactionary Sophie Hatzfeldt.

MARX. Hm: not very consistent!—And I don't like his trying to cut me out.

JENNY. Nobody could do that, Comrade Karl!

MARX. Have you thought about what I asked you? Will you share my struggles and exile?

JENNY. I will always be your comrade, Karl.

He embraces her.

MARX. But we must not yield to romantic escapism. There is a meeting of the fraction at five, and we must not weaken the discipline by lateness.

Bonn University, Germany. Office of Professor Hegel. Marx and Engels come in arm and arm, in the costume of German students. They are fine vigorous laughing young fellows. They find Bruno Bauer, a young professor, who stands looking out the window.

MARX. Why, Bruno, old boy!—why so gloomy? You ought to be mustering all your forces to liberate Germany from the reactionary feudal government of Friedrich Wilhelm IV!

BRUNO BAUER. Old Hegel has violated my academic freedom. He hates me on account of my bold championship of the Young Hegelian League, which was named after him but which he now repudiates. He has summoned me to dismiss me from my chair; and I hear that he is going to put in my place a lackey of the interests named Sidney Cook, who teaches a mishmash of Dialectic and Pragmatism.

MARX. How shameful! We must unmask old Hegel!

Hegel enters. He wears a mask, but his identity is betrayed by his slight stooping figure, his spectacles, his white mustache, and a small tuft of hair that stands up on the back of his head.

HEGEL (*unctuously, rubbing his hands*). Well, well, young men: what a beautiful sunny morning! We must all believe in the Dialectic on a lovely sunny morning like this!

MARX. Haven't you been letting the Dialectic get a bit

rusty lately, Professor? It has been months without your even taking it

ENGELS. Everybody knows that but petty bourgeois Instrumentalism educational methods are merely disorientation!

HEGEL (*raging*). I will suppre opinion!

MARX AND ENGELS. Ha ha!

Joyously they unmask him and s

MARX (*snatching the Dialectic f* Dialectic now!—Come, Bruno: you although you have defended it s get your card today!

The three march out arm in a for we are coming!

The Revolution of 1848: just l and sounds of fighting. Enter Eng Engels has a bloody bandage arou

ENGELS. Phew! that's hot wo forces with the liberal bourgeois monarchy, we must bring pres liberalism to grant our just deman

Marx emerges from the doorwa

MARX. What, Friedrich: still f you know that we must turn the we have acquired through our bo institutions of our own class?

LASSALLE. Intellectual weapo d'état!

MARX. Always a careerist, Co counter-revolution.

PROUDHON. Why can't we j we won't have to do any more fi

MARX. That's the poverty of We must not shrink from viole Friedrich, your place is there v

house Dialect Manife

ENG you th Europe

MAR way to specter

A co Bakuni hall.

BAKU by the c

LASSA The among

BRUN Marx is

Marx panion,

PROU petite m

MARY been th we're in keep a c those fil

ENGE that the

MARY peen Las

ENGE ligion is

MARX. but toda popular

LASSALLE (*to Bakunin*). Why don't you throw the bomb?

BAKUNIN. That will always be unexplained.

ENGELS (*addressing the audience*). Our beloved leader, Comrade Marx, will announce a new directive.

Prolonged applause. Marx appears on the platform. Tumultuous applause and cheering.

MARX. Comrades, we must combat the menace of Bourbonism, which is threatening Europe today. We must support the people of France under the progressive leadership of Napoleon III in their struggle against monarchism in Italy.

ENGELS. Long live the Eighteenth Brumaire of Louis Bonaparte!

Prolonged applause and tumultuous cheering.

MARX. We must stamp out the gangsters of Bourbonism!—and for this we have our weapon ever-ready, the spearhead of the proletariat: the Marxist-Hegelist Dialectic! (*He opens the leather case and takes out the Dialectic, which is in the form of a gleaming revolver. He points it at Bruno Bauer.*) Confess, Bruno Bauer: have you been in contact with Bourbon agents?

BRUNO BAUER. I stewed in my own juice and took orders from the Duc de Guise in the Hotel Adlon in Paris.

MARX (*shoots him with the Dialectic, then points it sternly at Proudhon*). And you, M. Proudhon—confess!

PROUDHON. I conspired to give Alsace-Lorraine to the Italians in return for aid against Louis Bonaparte and our leader, Comrade Marx.

Marx shoots him.

MARX (*to Bakunin*). And you!

BAKUNIN (*reduced to abject terror*). I promised the traitor Lassalle to assassinate you.

MARX. And where is Lassalle, the Bourbonist bandit?

BAKUNIN. He has fled the country, the reptile.

MARX (*shooting Bakunin*). Good: he may live to take a treacherous part in some even more sensational conspiracy.

ENGELS (*snatching the Dialectic from Marx*). I, too, have been disloyal to Comrade Marx! I take full responsibility for everything! I did not know about the plot and failed to prevent it. (*He shoots Mary Burns and himself.*)

MARX. And now we may tear up the Gotha Program prepared by the mad wolf Lassalle and poisoned with the counter-revolutionary demand for equal pay for officials and workers. Forward to socialist inequality and democracy!

Marx takes off his beard and reveals the smiling face of Comrade STALIN.

CURTAIN

Appendix B

Marx on the Differential Calculus

Karl Marx's mathematical papers, to which Engels attached so much importance, but which he did not live to publish, were printed by the Soviet philosophical review, *Pod Znamenem Marksizma,* in the issue of January-February 1933. As I had never seen any discussion of them, I submitted them to one of the most distinguished of American mathematicians, who has kindly sent me the following report.

The three articles on mathematics by Marx appear to be the notes of an intelligent (but somewhat befuddled) beginner, who is just starting to understand the meaning of differentiation. I doubt whether they were ever intended as a serious contribution to mathematics.

Marx seems to be dealing, in the main, with the differentiation of a function,

$$(1) \qquad\qquad y = f(x)$$

in the very simple case where $f(x)$ is an ordinary polynomial. Suppose we give x an increment Δx. Then the corresponding increment of y is

$$(2) \qquad\qquad \Delta y = f(x + \Delta x) - f(x)$$

Therefore, if we divide both sides of (2) by Δx, we get

$$(3) \qquad\qquad \frac{\Delta y}{\Delta x} = \frac{f(x + \Delta x) - f(x)}{\Delta x}$$

Now, if $f(x)$ is an ordinary polynomial in x, the expression $f(x + \Delta x) - f(x)$ is an ordinary polynomial in x and Δx. Moreover, we easily verify that all terms cancel out from $f(x + \Delta x) - f(x)$ except the ones having Δx as a factor. Therefore, the expression can be written in the form

$$f(x + \Delta x) - f(x) = \Delta x . \, \varphi \, (x, \Delta x)$$

If we substitute the last expression in the right hand member of (3) and cancel Δx in numerator and denominator, we get

$$(4) \qquad \frac{\Delta y}{\Delta x} = \varphi \, (x, \Delta x)$$

Finally, if we set $\Delta x = 0$ in (4), (whence, also $\Delta y = 0$), we get an expression of the form

$$(5) \qquad \frac{0}{0} = \varphi \, (x, 0)$$

In other words, we arrive at the following "paradox." The left hand member of (5) is the meaningless expression $\frac{0}{0}$; yet, lo, and behold, the right hand member has a definite meaning, and turns out, in fact, to be the desired derivative of $f(x)$!

You can see that a paradox like the above is duck soup for a dialectical materialist and can give rise to long discussions about thesis, antithesis, the negation of the negation, etc., etc., etc. On all of this, I am incapable of expressing any opinion. To me, it is just so much metaphysical mumbo-jumbo. The straightforward mathematical explanation is elementary and requires no philosophical soaring. It is simply this:

If the expression $A = B$ is true, you can conclude that $\frac{A}{C} = \frac{B}{C}$ is also true *provided that C does not vanish*. If C vanishes, the second equation is, in general, quite meaningless.* Consequently, Equation (3) can only be expected to follow from Equation (2) for *values of Δx different from* 0, and we must not be surprised to get a meaningless result (5) when we set $\Delta x = 0$ in (3). Now, how does it happen that, in spite of all this, *the right hand member of (5) actually is the derivative of $f(x)$?* Well, simply this. The derivative of $f(x)$ is, *by definition*, the value *approached* by $\frac{\Delta y}{\Delta x}$ as Δx approaches 0. (The value *approached* has a definite meaning,

---

* "Division by zero" leads to obviously false results. Indeed, $1 \times 0 = 2 \times 0$ is a true equation, since both members vanish. But we obviously cannot strike out the factor 0 on both sides and conclude $1 = 2$.

although the value *at* $\Delta x = 0$ has none.) Moreover, the right hand member of (4) (which equals the left hand member for all values of Δx except 0) is an ordinary polynomial and, therefore (unlike the left hand member), has a definite value even for $\Delta x = 0$. Moreover, since a polynomial is continuous, the value *approached* as Δx approaches zero is identical with the value *at* $\Delta x = 0$. Therefore, φ $(x, 0)$ is the desired derivative.

In conclusion, let me say that there is nothing new that I can see, in the *mathematical* side of the three papers by Marx.

I have tried on numerous occasions to fathom the mysteries of dialectical materialism and have each time been left baffled and bewildered. Engels has a section on mathematics in his famous *Anti-Dühring* (which is supposed to echo the voice of the Master himself). Unfortunately, the mathematics itself is all cock-eyed. It is a pity to build an elaborate philosophical system on a series of gross mathematical errors.

Appendix C

Engels to Marx, February 13, 1851

Since the following letter of Engels has never, so far as I know, been translated except in fragments, it may be worth while to give it at length. It was written—February 13, 1851 —at a time when a new commercial boom was already under way, and Marx and Engels had been forced to recognize that no further wave of revolt could be expected till the next serious economic crisis. The old movements were breaking up, petering out. The first paragraph, omitted below, indicates Engels' dissatisfaction both with the leaders of the English Chartist movement, of whom the Harney mentioned was one, and with the German leaders of the Communist League in the roles which they were playing in exile. Marx had just written Engels (February 11, 1851) that he was "much pleased with the public and authentic isolation in which we find ourselves now, you and I. It perfectly corresponds with our principles and our position. The system of reciprocal concessions, of half-measures tolerated only in order to keep up appearances, and the obligation to share in public with all these asses in the general absurdity of the party—all that is done with now."

Dear Marx . . .

This idiocy and tactlessness of Harney's have annoyed me p e r s o n a l l y more than anything else whatever. *Au fond* of course it makes no difference.

We have now got a chance again at last—for the first time in a long while—to show that we need no popularity, no *support,* from any party whatever of any country whatever, and that our position is totally independent of all such shabby considerations. From now on we are responsible for ourselves alone, and when the moment comes when these gentlemen find they need us, we shall be in a situation to be able to dictate our own terms. Till that time we shall at least have peace. To tell the truth, even a certain loneliness—*mon Dieu*, I've had it already for three months here in Manchester and got accustomed to it, and with a *bachelor's* life, besides, which—here, at least—is terribly dull. And we really haven't much reason for complaining that the *petits grands hommes* are shy of us; haven't we for God knows how many years been pretending that Tom, Dick and Harry were our party, when we really haven't had a party and when the people who, at least officially, we counted as belonging to our party, *sous réserve de les appeler des bêtes incorrigibles entre nous*, didn't understand even the rudiments of what we were getting at? How can people like us, who avoid official positions like the plague, ever find ourselves at home in a "party"? We have always spat on popularity and we have always become doubtful of ourselves as soon as we began to be popular, so what should we do with a "party," that is, with a collection of asses, who swear by us because they take us for asses like themselves? Truly it is no great loss if we don't figure any more as the "correct and complete expression" of these half-witted idiots, with whom we've been thrown these last years.

A revolution is a real natural phenomenon, which is governed by physical laws rather than by the rules which determine the development of society during ordinary periods. Or rather, in revolution these rules take on a more pronouncedly physical character, the material force of necessity comes into play with greater violence. And from the moment one figures as the representative of a party, one is swept away into the whirlpool of irresistible natural necessity. Only in so far as one keeps oneself *independent* so that one is more revolutionary a c t u a l l y than the others, can one escape at least for a time becoming involved in that whirlpool—for finally, of course, one will oneself be carried down into it like the others.

This position we can and we must maintain when the next of these affairs occurs. Not only no p u b l i c office, but even as long as possible no official position in the p a r t y, no sitting on committees, etc., no responsibility for asses, pitiless criticism for all, and along with this that cheerful serenity, of which the conspiracy of all the dunces combined will be powerless to deprive us. And this we shall be able to do. Essentially, we can in this way be a great deal more revolutionary than the phrase-makers, because we have succeeded in learning something, whereas they have learned nothing, because we know what we want whereas they know nothing, and *because, after what we have seen for the last three years, we shall take it a great deal more coolly than anyone who has an interest in the business.*

The principal thing for the moment is: some way of getting our ideas into print—either by means of a quarterly, in which we can attack directly and make our position clear to d e f i n i t e   p e r s o n s, or in substantial books, in which we accomplish the same purpose without being under the necessity of even mentioning any of these spiders. Either way is satisfactory to me: in the long run and as the reaction becomes worse, it seems to me that the opportunities for the first of these courses will decrease and that the second will come more and more to be the method to which we shall have to resort. What will be the use of all the idiotic stories that the whole crew of émigrés together will ever be able to circulate against you when you answer them with your Political Economy?

I'll get after the letter to Harney tomorrow. *En attendant salut.*

Yours,

F. E.

Appendix D

Herr Vogt and His Modern Successors

The situation during the fifties of the last century of those believers in Napoleon III who considered him the continuator of the French Revolution and a great potential liberator of peoples, has been paralleled in our own day by those foreign believers in Stalin who, at the time of the Bonapartist reaction in Russia, have persisted in assigning him a similar role. Karl Vogt, on the testimony of Herzen and others, was by no means the fatuous worm depicted by Marx and Engels, but an honest and well-meaning man, of some distinction in his field of Zoölogy, who unquestionably imagined that, in propagandizing for Napoleon, he was working for human progress.

The war on Italy disillusioned these liberal Bonapartists, as the Soviet-Nazi pact and the Russian invasion of Finland have disillusioned the liberal Stalinists. It is interesting to read the passage in Herzen's memoirs in which he reports a conversation with one of the former: "I was in Paris at the time of Garibaldi's first arrest. The French did not believe in the invasion by their troops. I happened to meet with people of very different classes of society. The inveterate reactionaries and clericals desired intervention, but yet doubted. At the railway station a distinguished *savant* said, as he was taking leave of me: 'Your imagination, my dear northern Hamlet, is so constructed that you can see nothing but what is black; that's why the impossibility of war with Italy is not obvious to you. The Government knows too well that war for the Pope would set all thinking people against it; after all, you know, we are the French of 1789.'"

569

Index

506–7; appearance of, 497–8; as "aristocrat of revolution," 503; and art, 489; autobiography of, 474–76, 503–5, 508–10, 519–20; as a Babeuf, 504; carelessness with money, 484; consciousness of superiority, 504–19; conversion to cause of revolution, 475–79; in crises, 507; daughter of, 480–81, 482; described by Lunachársky, 506; and freedom, 518; and history, 501–19; humanity of, 516; impressions of London, 485–86; imprisonment and exile, 479–81, 482, 498; and Kronstadt mutiny, 518–19; and Lassalle, 489; and Lenin, 448–49, 485–86, 489–90, 491, 500, 507–8, 509, 518–19; limitations of, 501; on lying, 513; marriage of, 480; and Marxism, 476–79, 481–82, 502–5, 506–10; and moral authority, 505; as orator, 493; as "Peró," 483; persecution by Stalin, 504–5; and power of history, 510–11; reliance on theory, 527; and revolution of 1905, 493–517; and Sedóva, 489; sons of, 489; takes name "Trotsky," 483; and theory of "permanent" revolution, 498–99, 500, on trade unions, 517; trial in 1905, 496–98; writings, 482–83, 507–8

"True Socialists," 180, 182, 208

Trumbull Phalanx, 122–23

Turgénev, I. S., 311, 312, 313, 417

Ulyánov family, 411–12
Ulyánov, Alexander I. (brother of Lenin), 416, 417; arrest and execution, 419–21

Ulyánov, Dmitri I. (Mítya) brother of Lenin), 417, 419, 427, 428, 444–46, 447

Ulyánov, I. N. (father of Lenin), 410–17; death of, 418

Ulyánov, Vladímar Ilyích. See Lenin, Nikolai

Ulyánova, Anna I. (sister of Lenin), 418, 420, 421, 423, 426, 427, 429, 430, 444, 445, 486, 512, 536, 554

Ulyánova, M. A. (mother of Lenin), 411–16, 420, 421, 422, 423, 427, 429–30, 444, 512

Ulyánova, María I. (sister of Lenin), 444, 533

Ulyánova, N. K. See Krúpskaya, N. K.

Ulyánova, Olga I. (sister of Lenin), death of, 429–30

Unemployment, cause of, 110; technological, 110–11

Union of Soviet Socialist Republics, 269; New Economic Policy, 517; persecution of Trotsky, 504–5

United States, 377–81; early socialist communities, 120–30; in 1848, according to Marx and Engels, 190; ignorance of, shown by Marx, 376–77; International Working Men's Alliance in, 331

"United States of Europe," 319

"Universology," 122

Utility theories of value, 349–50

Utopianism, 119–30

Value, labor theory of. See Labor theory of value
Value, according to Michelet